P9-CLG-718

LITERATURE IN THE GREEK AND ROMAN WORLDS

Literature in the Greek and Roman Worlds

A NEW PERSPECTIVE

Edited by Oliver Taplin

OXFORD
UNIVERSITY PRESS

Great Clarendon Street, Oxford OX2 6DP

Oxford University Press is a department of the University of Oxford.
It furthers the University's objective of excellence in research, scholarship,
and education by publishing worldwide in

Oxford New York

Athens Auckland Bangkok Bogotá Buenos Aires Calcutta
Cape Town Chennai Dar es Salaam Delhi Florence Hong Kong Istanbul
Karachi Kuala Lumpur Madrid Melbourne Mexico City Mumbai
Nairobi Paris São Paulo Singapore Taipei Tokyo Toronto Warsaw

with associated companies in Berlin Ibadan

Published in the United States
by Oxford University Press Inc., New York

British Library Cataloguing in Publication Data
Data available

Library of Congress Cataloging in Publication Data
Literature in the Greek and Roman worlds: a new perspective / edited by Oliver Taplin.
Includes bibliographical references (p.) and index.
1. Classical literature–History and criticism. I. Taplin, Oliver.
PA3003.I.54 2000 880'.09—dc21 99–057693

ISBN 0–19–210020–3

1 3 5 7 9 10 8 6 4 2

Typeset by RefineCatch Limited, Bungay, Suffolk
Printed in Great Britain by
Biddles Ltd, Guildford and King's Lynn

Contents

Preface

This is not just another collection of piecemeal essays: it is an attempt at an overview of a wide expanse of literature from a fresh perspective. The contributors have between them tried to survey all the major productions of ancient Greek and Latin literature (though inevitably some works are more fully covered than others). It is all the more remarkable that without exception they have been so prompt and responsive that the book has kept to its schedule—a rare feat! I wish to thank all for their good humour, flexibility, punctuality, and for their patience with my handwriting.

The relatively smooth and rapid progress of this book also owes much to the excellent team at Oxford University Press, especially George Miller, the editor who launched the project, and Shelley Cox, who skilfully piloted it over the waves to harbour. I would also like to thank Ela Harrison, Mary Lale, and Mary Worthington for their efficient and intelligent work on various stages of the voyage. Many of the contributors are mutually indebted to each other for advice and help. One or other of us would also like to thank Ed Bispham, Jane Chaplin, Roger Crisp, Andrew Garrett, Mark Griffith, Edith Hall, Rachel Jacoff, Sandra Joshel, Bob Kaster, Tony Long, Kathleen McCarthy, Donald Mastronarde, Kathryn Morgan, Robin Osborne, Tony Woodman.

I have encouraged the contributors to quote liberally and try to give a taste of the literature they are discussing. All translations are by the author of the chapter in question, unless indicated otherwise. (Complete translations have been recommended in the section on Further Reading.)

The situation with the spelling of proper names is not so straightforward. Since this book deals with both Greeks and Romans and with their interactions, I have insisted that Greek names should be transcribed direct rather than into their more traditional Latin spelling. We have, however, kept the traditional spelling for names from both languages which are very familiar in their Englished form (such as Homer, Virgil, Athens, Rome, Oedipus (actually the Latin!), Hadrian etc, etc). The dividing line round this category is inevitably arbitrary (thus Ithake yet Attica, for example). Furthermore, when Greek names are being used in Roman or Latin contexts they are Latinized; when they are turned into adjectives they are Englished (eg callimachean, aeolic). This is an issue on which it is impossible to please everyone—indeed it is probably impossible to please anyone.

With the book as a whole we hope it will prove the reverse.

Oliver Taplin
Oxford
30 September 1999

List of illustrations

List of maps

Notes on contributors

OLIVER TAPLIN is Professor of Classical Languages and Literature at Oxford University, where he is a Tutorial Fellow at Magdalen College. He is also co-director (with Edith Hall) of the Archive of Performances of Greek and Roman Drama. His books include *Homeric Soundings* (Oxford, 1992) and *Comic Angels* (Oxford, 1993). He maintains the importance of reaching wider audiences, and has collaborated with various productions in radio, television, and the theatre.

CHRIS CAREY is part of the Liverpool diaspora. He studied at Jesus College, Cambridge and has taught at Cambridge, St Andrews, the University of Minnesota, Carleton College, and Royal Holloway, London, where he is Professor of Classics. His interests include Greek lyric poetry, drama, oratory and rhetoric, and law.

CATHERINE CONNORS is Associate Professor of Classics at the University of Washington, Seattle, and the author of *Petronius the Poet: Verse and Literary Tradition in the Satyricon* (Cambridge, 1998).

MICHAEL DEWAR studied French and classical literature at Oxford, and now teaches Classics at the University of Toronto. He has published books on Statius and Claudian, and a number of articles on Latin poets ranging from the age of Augustus to the sixth century.

PHILIP HARDIE is a University Reader in Latin Literature at Cambridge, and a Fellow of New Hall. He specializes in Latin poetry of the Augustan and early imperial periods, and his publications include *Virgil's Aeneid: Cosmos and Imperium* (Oxford, 1986) and *The Epic Successors of Virgil: A Study in the Dynamics of a Tradition* (Cambridge, 1993).

CHRISTINA S. KRAUS studied at Princeton and Harvard and taught in New York before coming to the UK. After three years at University College London she moved to Oxford, where she is Fellow and Tutor at Oriel College. She has written on Greek tragedy, Latin prose style, and Roman historiography, and is the editor of *The Limits of Historiography* (Brill, 1999).

LESLIE KURKE is Professor of Classics and Comparative Literature at the University of California, Berkeley. She is the author of *The Traffic in Praise: Pindar and the Poetics of Social Economy* (Ithaca, NY, 1991) and *Coins, Bodies, Games, and Gold: The Politics of Meaning in Archaic Greece* (Princeton, 1999). With Carol Dougherty, she co-edited the volume *Cultural Poetics in Archaic Greece: Cult, Performance, Politics* (Oxford, 1998).

MATTHEW LEIGH was formerly lecturer in Classics and Ancient History at the University of Exeter and is now Tutorial Fellow at St Anne's College, Oxford. He is the author of *Lucan: Spectacle and Engagement* (Oxford, 1997), and is currently working on the culture of Republican Rome.

JANE LIGHTFOOT has been a Fellow of All Souls College, Oxford, since 1994, and is the author of *Parthenius of Nicaea* (Oxford, 1999). She is currently working on a study of Lucian's *On the Syrian Goddess*.

LLEWELYN MORGAN is Teaching Fellow in Classics at Brasenose College, Oxford. He previously taught in the Republic of Ireland. He has published on republican and early imperial Roman literature, and is particularly interested in the diverse ways in which the Roman civil wars were discussed and validated in contemporary poetry and prose. His *Patterns of redemption in Virgil's Georgias* (Cambridge) was published in 1999.

ANDREA WILSON NIGHTINGALE studied Classics at Stanford, Oxford, and Berkeley. She is presently an Associate Professor of Classics and Comparative Literature at Stanford University. Her publications include *Genres in Dialogue: Plato and the Construct of Philosophy* (Cambridge, 1996), and numerous articles on ancient Greek philosophy and literature. She is presently working on a book entitled *The Philosophic Gaze: Revisioning Wisdom in Fourth-Century Athens.*

PETER WILSON studied Classics in Australia and Cambridge and is now a member of the Department of Classics and Ancient History of the University of Warwick. He has written on the Greek theatre, oratory, and music, and his first book is *The Athenian Institution of the 'Khoregia': The Chorus, the City and the Stage* (Cambridge, 2000).

Timeline of chapters

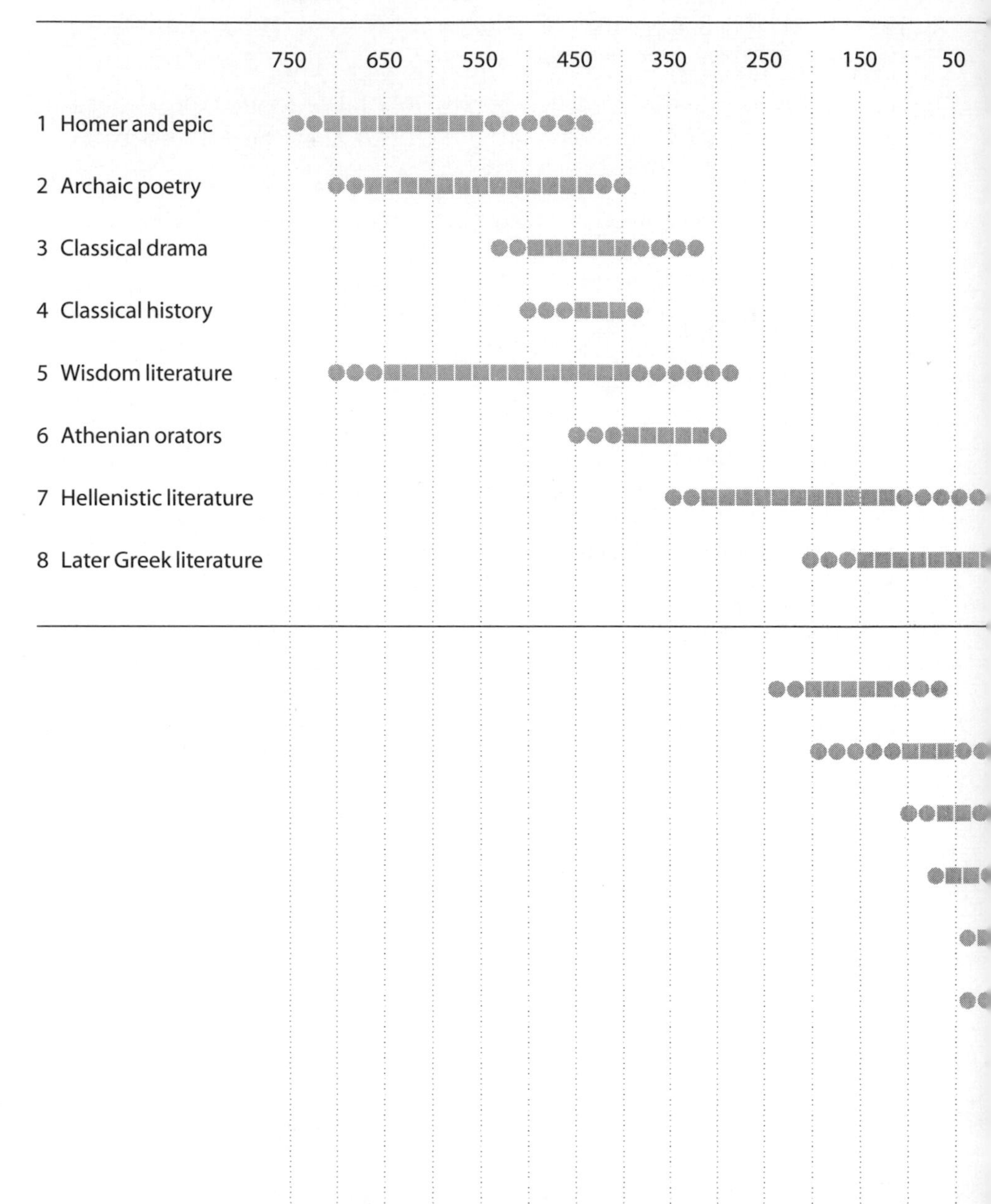

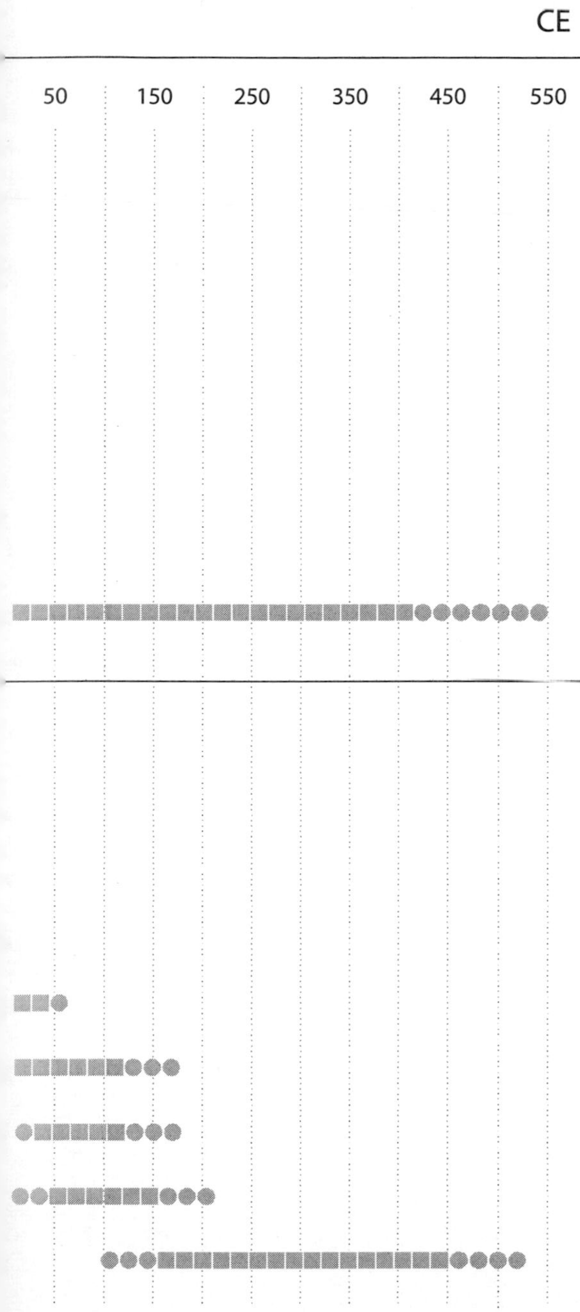

CE

50 150 250 350 450 550

9 Beginnings of Latin literature

10 Earlier prose literature

11 Poetry of late republic

12 Poetry 44–19 BCE

13 Poetry 19 BCE – Tiberius

14 Later prose literature to *c*.120

15 Imperial epic

16 Imperial leisure literature

17 Later Latin literature

Introduction

OLIVER TAPLIN

> The public is the manure round the roots of every artistic growth.
>
> (Cesare Pavese)

This book is for those who know a little and would like to know more about the literature which was written or composed in ancient Greek or Latin. It grows from a fundamental sense that these literatures still have something significant to offer at the beginning of the third millennium—indeed, that some of the works still stand among the most worthwhile achievements of human creativity from any place or time. At the same time our access to them is not simple or direct. The approach taken here is at root historical: it looks, that is, at the literature within the world that first produced it. The focus, though—and this is what makes it distinctive from most previous overviews or surveys—is on the receivers of the literature, the public, readers, spectators, and audiences. We twelve contributors are various in our specializations and methodologies, but are united in the belief that it is valuable to ask who these works of literature were for. What did those people think they were getting from their literature; why did they give it their time and attention? For all our differences, we hold that our present appreciation of Greek and Roman literature can be informed and influenced by consideration of what it was originally appreciated for. The past, for all its alienness, can affect and change the present.

There is a kind of eternal triangle of elements or parties involved in any instance of literature: these are conventionally labelled Author, Reader, and Text. *Maker* may be a preferable word to 'author' because it comes without the controversial associations of, for example, 'authority' or 'intention'. Similarly *Receiver* has advantages over 'reader' since it includes audiences, spectators, and so forth. It is obvious, once you think about it, that literature does not necessarily have to be written down, and that it can be appreciated in other ways as well as being read; and this was actually far more the case in the ancient Greek and

Roman worlds than it is in the modern era. As for the third element—the text, the words—this is clearly distinct from the other two, because, although it is conveyed through human-produced agency or technology (printed book, recitation, or whatever), it is not a sentient person. And by making the receivers our focus, it becomes obvious that there is bound to be a dynamic, an interaction, between the three elements rather than a static isolation of any one.

Claims for other parties might be made, and have been made, outside this triangle. The literature might be, for example, the creation of god or an oracle or a 'found poem'. But these are all, surely, subsidiary variations on the maker. Similarly with variant receivers such as god (again) or the universe or animals or an inanimate object. So peculiar exceptions who get wheeled out, like Orpheus, who performed for wild creatures, or Emily Dickinson, who kept her poems to herself, do not invalidate the basic claim that it takes an audience, receivers, to make literature. If Dickinson had never been discovered, her poems would not have become literature.

Most previous surveys and histories of literature have made either the authors or the texts their primary focus. It has been traditional to document the authors' biographies, the sequence of their mental lives, their interests, priorities, and beliefs, as revealed by external evidence, and as implied within their works. This kind of approach, which tends to put the fascination of creative genius in the spotlight, usually supposes that the lives of the authors somehow *explain* their literature. But is individual genius any more than a cipher as long as it is without surroundings, without circumstances of production, social context?

The approaches of some more recent literary theories, on the other hand, have tended to regard the texts as the only proper, or even possible, subject of attention. The texts have obligingly delivered meanings which 'anticipate' contemporary preoccupations with indeterminacy, the destabilization or fragmentation of conceptual monoliths, or the exposure of the operations of power through language. But these strategies should also leave room for approaches that treat the original production and communication of the texts as a valid subject for a kind of history. The fact that the history we can reconstruct is bound to be, to a greater or lesser extent, partial, speculative, and selective does not make it emptily arbitrary, merely or purely a construct. The first audiences of this literature did once live, and did once give their attention to the works.

In this interaction nearly all makers of literature want, and go out of their way to seek, an appreciative public: they desire attention and 'success'. There may be many ways of measuring that success; and it is not necessarily a matter of the numbers of the appreciative public. Artists often seek (or claim to seek, at least) the approval of only the select few—this is quite a common pose in the Greek and Roman worlds. Nor are celebrity or prosperity necessarily invariable criteria; and money is by no means the only possible reward. Sometimes success only comes posthumously, but makers prefer to have their appreciative public (and their rewards!) within their lifetimes. Correspondingly, a good proportion of those people who have the opportunity have been happy to give some of their time and resources to the benefits of literature, to become receivers, that is. The formative experience of listening to stories in childhood is undoubtedly very important here. Whatever the roots of the phenomenon, the public is generally on the look-out, perhaps surprisingly ready to be persuaded that paying attention to literature might be worth their time and trouble.

Throughout most of the history of most literatures the interaction between artist and public has, then, been by and large reciprocal, mutually beneficial. There has been a kind of *symbiosis*. The preferences and responses of the receivers have been assimilated by the makers, who have tried to meet them. And the makers, in their turn, have affected their audiences, have pleased them, and have led them to see things that were not already familiar and respectable. The maker looks to the public for attention and appreciation: the public expects some kind of benefit or gratification. Just what those hoped-for benefits were or are is elusive and shifting; and they are one of the major concerns of this book.

And yet, apparently in contradiction to this productive symbiosis, it is widely believed that most artists—or at least the great ones—suffer a flawed and difficult interaction with their contemporary public. Creative individuals are supposed to be alienated, ahead of their times, temperamental, tortured; and their potential public fails to recognize the genius in their midst. Audiences are characterized, on the other hand, as vulgar, fickle, conservative, complacent; they do not see what is good for them. This is one reason why so much emphasis has usually been put on makers and so little on receivers: the public is seen as irrelevant, and even obstructive, to genius. What is more this 'romantic' picture of the mismatch between the creative artist and the unappreciative public was familiar in the Greek (and Roman) world. The fascination with the creative misfit goes back as far as anything like literary history can be traced—though it must be pointed out that Greek and Roman literary biographies were far more overt than their modern counterparts in the invention of attractive fictions. From early days the poet was often seen as a lonely genius driven by creativity despite an unappreciative public: Euripides, and even the blind itinerant Homer, are archetypal examples. Behind this lurks a deep-seated desire for the prophet or genius to be a marginalized, tortured figure. Some great price must be paid for superhuman talent. Also, the later readers, who so love the stories of the unrecognized prodigy, can bask with hindsight in the complacent satisfaction of knowing better. We lavish on Mozart or Hopkins or Van Gogh the recognition that their contemporaries were too stupid to give. Yet how often has the creative maker really worked without *any* encouragement or appreciation, without any public? Take Euripides, who for the Greeks was the archetypal rejected and alienated genius. Year after year the Athenians welcomed him as a competitor in their highly selective tragedy competition; it is clear from the comic Aristophanes and other sources that he was the centre of much attention; he was already highly appreciated outside Athens in his own lifetime. The fact that he hardly ever won the first prize makes him more like the best-seller who does not win the Booker or the Nobel Prize than like a bohemian starving in a garret.

Hand in hand with this segregation of the individual genius from the mass of receivers goes a certain condescension and snobbishness—which can be seen already in Plato—towards the public of art, especially large popular bodies of receivers. This is another of the main reasons, I suspect, why they have been largely excluded from most accounts of literature. How could the crude people of that bygone age have appreciated the subtlety and complexity of the (our) literature? The artistry is too fine, the ambiguity too far-reaching, to be dragged down by mass appreciation. It needs the greater sophistication and insight and theoretical awareness of a later age (ours, of course) to see its true quality, to create meaning for it. There is often a taint of this superior self-promotion in recent academic writing.

It is bound to be true that we read very differently from the original receivers, but that does not necessarily mean that we read better. In fact, there is a disturbing presumptuousness about supposing that we can interpret and appreciate *better* than the audience that the literature was made for. The work was in a real sense made to their specifications—the carpenter built the house for them to live in. The literature came into existence in their world, in their language, society, and mental landscape. It might well be argued that, if we find any society in the past which has produced a particularly rich crop of creative achievements, then we should be asking what it was about the people of that time, the receivers and their symbiosis with their makers, that stimulated the productivity. We should be looking to them for ideas, not treating them with condescension.

Any work of literature that has stood the test of time has, by definition, been appreciated by many later receivers as well as the original public who had it fresh-minted from the maker. It has been the achievement of Reception Studies, especially in the last third of the twentieth century, to emphasize that all those many receptions are still of interest; and that many, if not all, of them contribute to our contemporary interpretation of the work. But the fact that a work of literature has survived across the centuries, and has been valued or devalued in various ways as time goes by, does not alter another fact: that it was once new, that before a certain time and context it did not exist, and that afterwards it did. Some theories have led to the claim that the genesis of the work in the symbiosis between maker and receivers is of no special interest (the term 'the originary fallacy' has been coined). But this volume takes the more historically minded view that the contextual genesis is bound to be particularly suggestive for our modern interpretation. To deny this is like digging up an artefact and having no curiosity about why anyone wanted to have that artefact in the first place.

So we believe that audiences and readers matter; that without them creative makers do not make. We do not believe that art is solely for art's sake: we believe that it is, and always has been, for people. And we do not believe that art is created in a vacuum, or in the isolated crucible of the unique mind. To have the potential to outlast its original public, it must have had an original public. Who were they? And what did they think that their literatures were for?

A sketch of the territory

Through this book we are talking of a span of time that extended for well over a thousand years, from roughly 750 BCE to even more roughly 500 CE. We are also talking about a geographical area greater than modern Europe, which spread, at one time or another, from Tunis to York to Budapest, from the Black Sea to the Dead Sea, from the Rhône to the Nile to the Euphrates. And the edges and limits of these times and places are quite indistinct; they are not neatly demarcated by frontiers and significant battles. It is often implied, and occasionally asserted, that the 'The Classical World' (or 'The Ancient World') has some special, stable unity: this is a myth.

On the other hand, we can, for the purposes of this volume, circumvent many difficult problems of military and administrative history, and of acculturation and ethnicity. The worlds in question are made up of the people who heard, watched, and read literature. What 'the Greek World' means here is, in effect, the primary receivers of Greek literature; and 'the Roman World' means the primary receivers of Latin literature. And that means that some people belonged to both worlds: while not a large number of Greeks learned Latin beyond what was needed for administration, many Romans took advantage of Greek.

It seems best to 'plot' the people we are talking about against the two basic axes of Time and Place. Although there are other ways of 'locating' people historically, this will still make for the clearest introduction. The points that I plot against these axes will all have the making and receiving of literature primarily in mind; and they are, of course, highly summary and selective. What follows is, then, a kind of small-scale map of the literary lands that the rest of this book will be visiting in more detail.

Greece had enjoyed a materially and culturally advanced (and literate) era back in the second millennium BCE, the so-called Mycenean Age. But, while memories of this are reflected in myth and in Homer, no literature survived. There followed a time of severe economic and demographic depression (one of the so-called 'Dark Ages'). While there can be no doubt that during this some kinds of literature were performed, it is no coincidence that the earliest literature which was to be eventually preserved in writing comes from the following era of explosive development, cultural as well as economic and geographical.

Until about 750 the potential receivers of Greek poetry lived only in the southern parts of the Greek mainland , the islands of the Aegean Sea, and the coast of what is now western Turkey (Asia Minor). During the next two hundred years they spread to strings of newly founded communities all round the northern Aegean, the Black Sea, the coasts of Sicily and southern Italy, and even to scattered foundations in southern France and Spain and in North Africa. Generally these remained coastal settlements which interacted with the local non-Greek people but did not attempt to subdue them. The first material traces of Greek literature are lines of verse scratched on pottery dating from the second half of the 700s BCE, not long after the (re-) introduction of the alphabet into Greece (from the Semitic Phoenicians). A nice indicator of this spread of the Greek world is that one of the very earliest scraps of Greek verse has been found on a cup which was made in Rhodes but was buried in a grave on the island of Ischia in the bay of Naples (see illustration on p. 32).

But early Greek literature was performed not written; and performances of the poems of Homer and Hesiod (Ch. 1) in something like the forms in which we have them probably date from around 700. While some poetry had presumably been recorded in writing by 600, it was to be a long time yet before any literature was made exclusively to be read, or even to be read rather than to be heard. This protracted, and arguably never complete, transition must have somehow gone hand in hand with the rapid growth of significant *prose* literature in the 400s, continued in the 300s.

Throughout the 400 years or so that have conventionally been given the labels 'Archaic' and 'Classical'—say from the 730s to the 330s—each Greek *polis* (city-state) did its best to maintain an independent identity, even though this

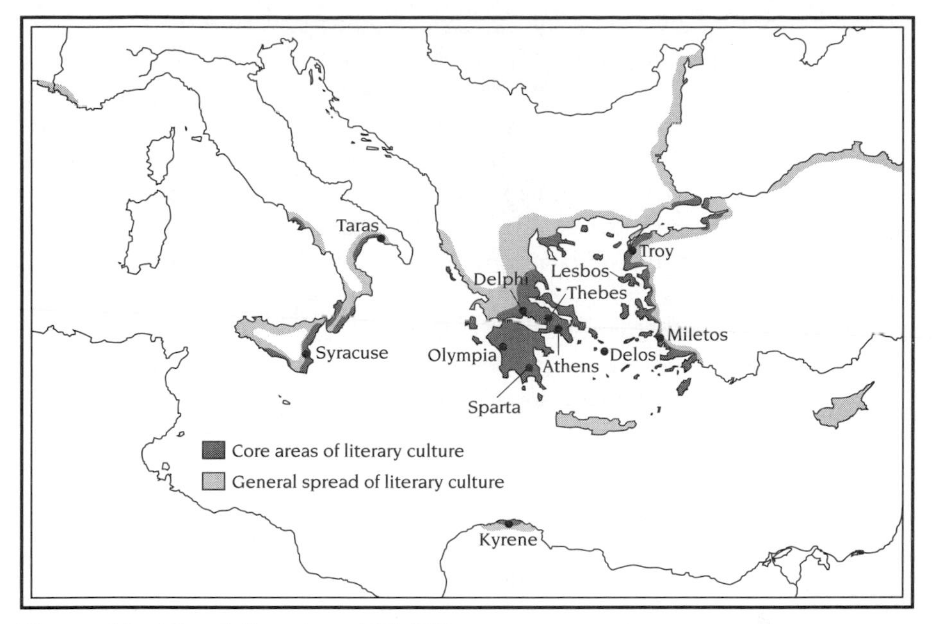

The world of Greek literature: 700–350 BCE

led to much terrible conflict between them. This independence extended to institutions, constitutions, religious cults, dialect, alphabet, coinage, measures, and even calendars. One might have expected this diversity, especially the differentiated dialects, to lead to highly localized and restricted literatures; but, if anything, the opposite is the case. There subsisted a sense of shared Hellenic culture, which was reflected in the underlying language, social values, mythology, and religious practice, and which found symbolic expression in the great shared cult-centres and athletic festivals (above all those at Olympia and Delphi). This also found practical expression in the successful co-operative resistance to territorial threats launched by the Persian empire from the East, Phoenicians from North Africa, and Etruscans and others from central and northern Italy. In keeping with this sense of shared culture—and cutting across political and military lines—there was a fair amount of freedom of movement for those who were perceived as experts, reflecting an appreciation for achievements of culture, arts, and crafts, regardless of which polis had originally produced them.

So poets and word-craftsmen—just like architects, scientists, painters, musicians, and many others—enjoyed considerable inter-polis mobility. And so did their works. The Homeric epics, above all, were evidently performed from earliest days throughout the Greek world. Other early poets (Ch. 2) quickly became known throughout the Greek world, despite their differing dialects. They came from the shores of the Aegean and from Sicily, but above all from the islands. Lesbos, for example, in the north-east Aegean, and Keos, not far from Attica, were especially productive of craftsmen of words. Simonides of Keos, the first man to make a fortune from literature, composed for commissions from Thessaly, south Italy, and Sicily, as well as for 'customers' nearer his home island. Eventually he managed to become more or less the official celebratory poet of the great victories over the Persians in 480–79. Commissions for poetry of various kinds from the Theban poet Pindar came from as far afield as Macedonia, Rhodes, Sicily, and Kyrene (in Libya), as well as places nearer home.

Tragedy and comedy (Ch. 3) were astounding innovations, yet grew from within this culture. Theatre was in effect invented at Athens in the fifth century for a predominantly Athenian public. But this central locality did not stop it from spreading rapidly and easily through the whole Greek world. During the fourth century virtually every polis of any note built an auditorium for performances. Soon the makers were coming from Asia Minor, the Black Sea, southern Italy, and many parts of the Greek mainland as well as Athens.

Down to, say, 390 BCE the turbulent, triumphant Greek world was exuberantly productive of fine poetry, and many kinds of poetry. It also inaugurated highly worked prose literature of the kinds that we now call history (Ch. 4), rhetoric, science, and philosophy. The next hundred or so even more turbulent years, although a period of great prosperity and of creativity in the arts in general, was a relatively thin time for poetry, at least poetry other than drama. But it was a highly fertile and formative period for rhetoric (Ch. 6), pedagogy, and above all for philosophy (Ch. 5). Prose cannot be transmitted by memory in the way that poetry can, and it makes sense that this great age of prose literature was also the era when literacy first reached a relatively large proportion of the population—a third or more at Athens, still the cultural centre—and also became really widespread throughout the Greek world.

The hundred years from (roughly speaking) 360 to 260 saw a crucial and irreversible re-formation of the Greek world, which meant that in most important ways the southern mainland ceased to be the centre of gravity. To the west the Greeks of Sicily and southern Italy enjoyed a time of great prosperity and cultural activity; but at the same time they came under increasing pressure from the Carthaginians (Phoenicians in what is now Tunisia), and from various Italian 'tribes'. Charismatic leaders were imported from the 'motherland', and helped to hold up the tide, but it eventually proved irresistible. And one particularly ambitious power in central Italy became ever-increasingly dominant: Rome.

But before sketching the development of the interaction and overlap between the highly advanced Greek and just beginning Roman worlds in the

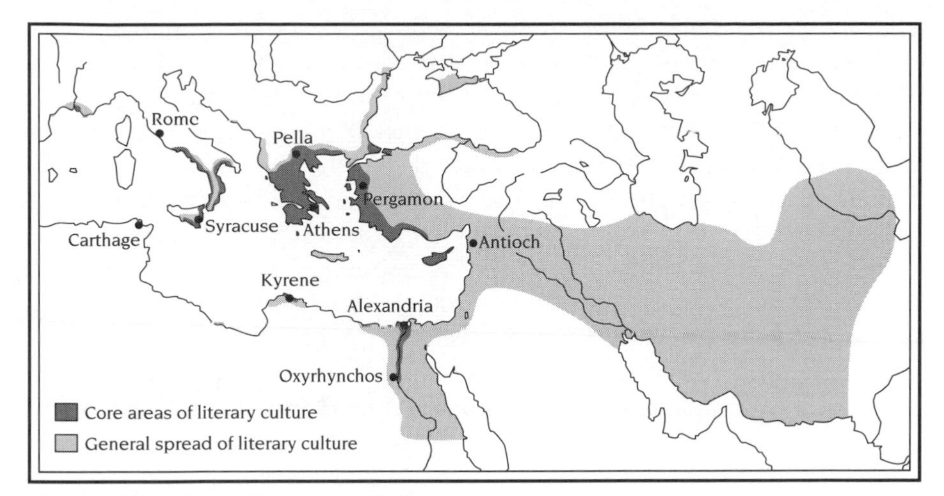

The world of Greek literature: 350–1 BCE

West, we should follow first the awesome expansion of the Greeks to the East. The Macedonians, for long ethnically marginal in the north of Greece, developed a great military machine which overran the divided mainland during the 350s and 340s, under the leadership of King Philip. His successor, the charismatic, superhuman, and all-too-human Alexander, turned the Macedonian army against the empires to the East. Between 334 and his death in 323 he conquered not only the Near East (including present-day eastern Turkey, Syria, Israel, Jordan, Iraq), but also Egypt. He then went on into what are now Iran, Uzbekistan, Afghanistan, Pakistan, and even across the Indus. This vast, sudden empire broke up, of course, and some of it, especially in the further East, never became seriously part of the Greek world. But cities run by Greek settlers, and complete with the accoutrements of Greek life, such as the agora (civic centre), gymnasium, and theatre, were planted all over a vast area. At the same time the *koine*, a dialect based on that of Athens, became accepted everywhere. It is hard to know how many, or how few, of this far-flung diaspora ever became significant receivers of Greek literature; but texts have been found not only in (for example) Syria and Jordan, but as far east as Afghanistan.

During this period, which is standardly labelled Hellenistic, old Athens remained a cultural focal point, especially for philosophy and higher education. But other new centres flourished with rival cultural ambitions, for example on the island of Rhodes, and at Pergamon in Asia Minor and at Antiocheia (Antioch) in Syria. But Alexandria towards the western edge of the Nile delta (one of the many cities named after himself by Alexander) was to eclipse them all. Here the Macedonian dynasty of the Ptolemies founded their capital, which rapidly grew into a huge cosmopolitan melting-pot of some half-million inhabitants. The kings invested lavishly to turn it into the new cultural capital of the Greek world, attracting artists, scientists, and poets. During the 200s BCE there was an efflorescence of a new kind of wholly literary, self-conscious poetry (Ch. 7). While its receivers seem to have been well spread over the Greek world, its centre, and probably its core audience, was in Alexandria. The cluster of major poets came there from, among other places, Kyrene, Syracuse, Samos, Kos, and Soloi (south-east Turkey).

The learned 'post-golden' culture established in Alexandria and the other great centres of the Hellenistic world during the 150 or so years from the 280s BCE was sustained, with various lapses and resurgences, throughout the Greek-speaking world for another 500 years or more (Ch. 8). The receivers of literature that we happen to know most about lived in a scatter of places through Egypt, where their texts, written on the standard writing-material of papyrus, happen to have been preserved in the dry sand. It is interesting to find, for example, how well read and widely read were the citizens of the middle-sized town of Oxyrhynchos in the second and third centuries CE. It is true that little of their literature was contemporary or from their immediate world; at the same time, while the great classics, above all Homer, are predominant, there is also quite a lot from this long 'post-golden' world.

This long autumn of Greek culture produced little worthwhile poetry but plenty of interesting prose of a variety of kinds, mostly reflecting the centrality of rhetoric to education and to official public life. The modern questioning of the traditional canon of 'The Classics' has led to some lively revaluation of the literature of this era. The most important authors of the productive cultural scene known as the Second Sophistic (roughly 60–230 CE) came from all over the place, but they tended to gravitate to the cultural centres of Athens, Pergamon, Smyrne, and Ephesos (all these latter three are in Asia Minor). And, of course, many of them went to Rome.

During the five 'golden' centuries of breathtaking creativity in the Greek world, there was no literature to speak of in the as yet only incipient Roman world—at least if there was we know nothing of it. It would be misleading, though, to picture Rome as a backwoods village of wild men. During the 500s BCE, when Rome was first becoming dominant over the surrounding fellow Latin towns, the city itself, as archaeology has revealed, was quite developed

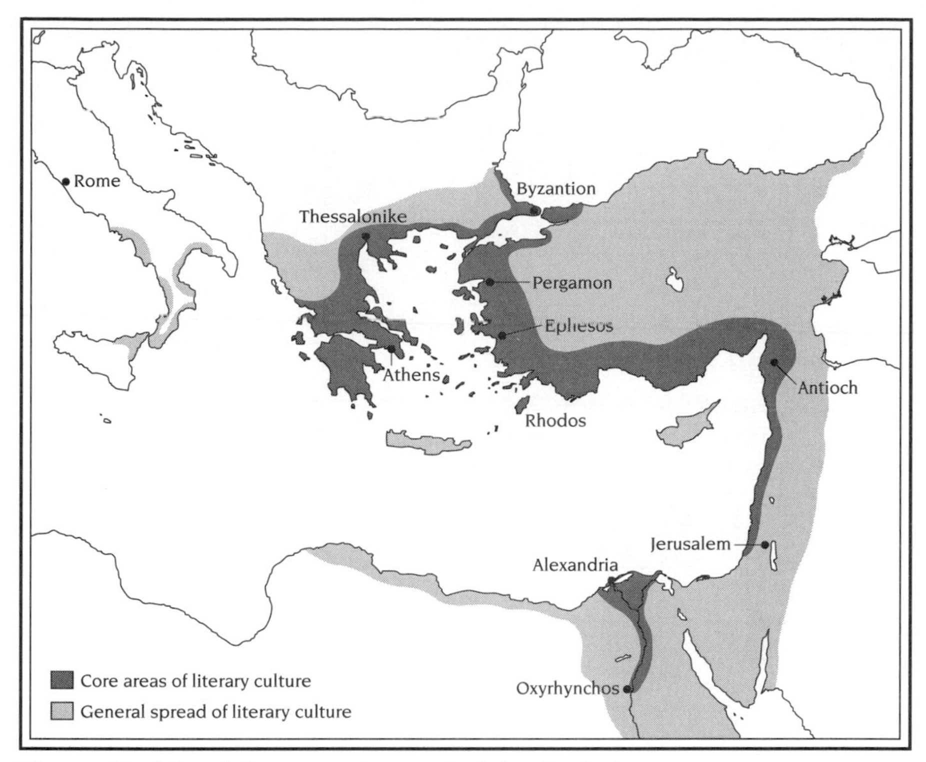

The world of Greek literature: 1 CE–end of the classical era

and cosmopolitan, and even had some literacy. But it was to be a long time before any memorable literature came onto the scene: the Romans were, it seems, too busy developing a sense of national identity, working out a powerful social system, and subduing an ever-increasing area by military conquest or by dominating treaties. By 300 Rome was the greatest power in Italy: her expansion took in not only Etruscans, Umbrians, Samnites, and a host of other Italian tribes, but also the highly developed Greek cities round the southern coasts. The last to succumb was the great artistic centre of Taras (Latin: Tarentum) in 272; Sicily, a focus of Greek civilization for nearly 500 years, was added before long.

One reason, it may be, why Rome did not nurture a Latin literature sooner was that there was such a mature concentration of awe-inspiring Greek civilization on the doorstep. The nearest substantial Greek city, Neapolis (Naples) was little over 200 kilometres away. A high-quality Roman road, the Via Appia, had reached there before 300 (and it was extended to Taras before long). So if a Roman wanted to watch or listen to a Greek performance, it was not a long journey; and it may well be that Greek touring artists visited Rome. Once a

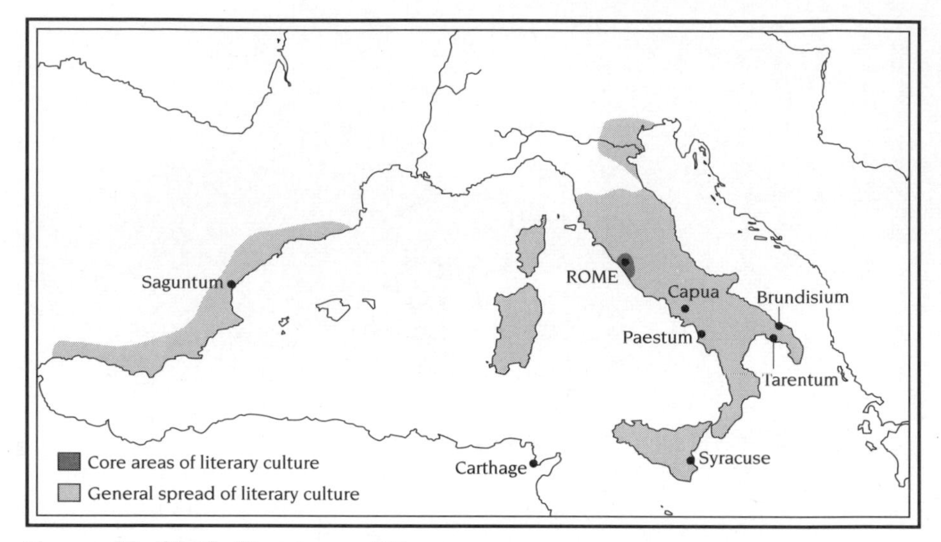

The world of Latin literature: c.*150* BCE

Roman learned Greek, the whole literary heritage was opened—and it must have seemed above emulation, inimitable, far beyond reach in simple Latin.

Once the Romans had overcome the threat of the Carthaginians under Hannibal in the late 200s, the ensuing expansion of power and wealth was stunning: northern Italy, southern Spain, mainland Greece, and central North Africa had all come under Rome by 146 BCE. As the Greek historian Polybios, who spent much of his life at Rome, observed, this one city had become the greatest power in the Mediterranean world in the space of some fifty years. It is from around this period that Roman literature emerges (Ch. 9). The early makers mostly came from the Greek parts of southern Italy, and learned Latin as a second or a third language (meanwhile a Roman wrote local history in Greek). And it was these poets who superimposed Greek metrics on the Latin language, a foreign surcharge that would persist for over 500 years. The turning of the prestige art-forms of tragedy and comedy into Latin was a crucial landmark; and the comedies of Plautus and Terence are the first complete works of Latin literature to survive. In the same era as them Ennius composed the first national epic of Rome, in the style and metre of Homer. Clearly there was a public, even if composed mainly of rich aristocrats, for these Latin transformations of Greek literature, and for crafted political rhetoric also. It is a great pity that, apart from the comedies, only a mass of tiny fragments of Latin literature survive from before about 70 BCE.

This preparation of the ground, so to speak, continued through the first half of the first century. Further territorial expansions into the Greek world in Asia Minor and the Near East continued, to culminate in the addition of the Egypt of the Ptolemies (last queen—Kleopatra) in 30. The cultural aspirations of the Roman aristocracy are reflected in the way that they brought larger and larger numbers of Greek intellectuals, especially philosophers and poets, to Rome and to their luxury villas in Italy. Some of these were slaves, others were a kind of mobile intellectual labour force. At the level of public display, grand theatres and libraries now began to be built at last: the most powerful city in the world wanted to become the centre of the cultural world also.

In the middle of the first century BCE Cicero and his contemporaries greatly developed the power of prose in Latin, rhetorical, academic, and historical (Ch. 10). New movement in poetry owes much to two remarkable and contrasted makers, who may well have been composing for the same group of receivers (though they never name each other): Lucretius and Catullus (Ch. 11). Catullus clearly sees himself as belonging to a group of fashionable, mutually admiring literary people, who agree in despising poets who are too conventional to be daring. The public for Lucretius and Catullus was evidently an élite, mainly the 'idle rich' of the metropolis. But their larger importance is that, through the symbiosis between them and their receivers, however exclusive, a new facility and subtlety in the handling of the Latin language, and in its exploitation of the Greek metrics, was developed. Latin literature had become significantly and distinctively Roman as well as Greek.

The world of Latin literature: c.*27* BCE

It is hard to say whether the horrific upheavals and civil bloodshed in the 40s, centred on the assassination of Julius Caesar, were more a kind of suppression to creativity or a stimulus. Either way, once Octavianus and his associates—and eventually Octavianus as monarch, with the title Augustus—had reimposed relative peace and security, there was an extraordinary literary flood. At least half of the top ten in any standard canon of Latin literature were active in the half-century from 40 BCE to 10 CE (Chs. 11 and 12). They and their public were aware that they were living through a great flowering, which was turning Latin into the language of a great literature in its own right, a literature which would survive as long as mighty Rome herself.

Virgil only lived to the age of 51, yet already in his lifetime he was seen as a great 'classic'. His poetry spread through the Roman world, and was, far more than any other, reflected in art-works, and even in graffiti. Augustus' agent for literature, Maecenas, made sure that Virgil and other talented poets were comfortable, and that they were given recognition. Many of the élite at Rome have an ode by Horace addressed to them. And Augustus himself commissioned a celebratory poem from Horace for his big jubilee in 17 BCE. Conversely, when Augustus decided that Ovid was a bad thing, he attempted to have his poetry totally suppressed. It tells us something about the dissemination of literature that (fortunately) he failed.

This was undoubtedly a highly élitist society; and presumably literature did not filter far down the social scale beyond the rich and powerful. But the public for literature was spreading: libraries were being built at Rome and other major cities; and there was by now a substantial book trade. The first stone theatre at Rome was built as late as 55 BCE; but over the next two centuries theatres were constructed in towns throughout the empire. Rome was, however, the unique centre of the Roman world. And no doubt this one city—an unprecedentedly vast city of over a million inhabitants—accounted for the core reception of virtually all Latin literature. This is very different from the widespread Greek scene.

Another limitation on the potential public was that Latin was never imposed on the empire, outside Italy that is, except as the language of administration and of the law. Thus, there are over fifty times as many Greek literary papyri from Egypt than there are Roman. Of the forty or so examples of Latin literature proper that have been excavated, half are of Virgil, trailed next by Cicero and by the historian Sallust. But it is worth remembering that Latin-speaking soldiers were stationed all over the empire; and that tens of thousands of Romans and Italians were settled in colonies the length and breadth of the provinces, from Merida (in remote Spain) to Cologne (Köln, Latin *Colonia*) to Beirut to Caesarea (one in Palestine, another in Algeria, and several others). A totally unpredictable reminder that we should not over-restrict the scope of the Roman literary world turned up in 1979. At a briefly held frontier fort far up the Nile excavators found a papyrus scrap written in the 20s BCE: it turned out to contain poems by Virgil's friend and contemporary Cornelius Gallus (see illustration on p. 337).

The maturing of Latin literature during the rule of Augustus was so fertile that the standard periodization of literary history has tended to cut it off from what followed, most obviously by applying the labels Golden and Silver. This is more misleading than helpful. Although the security of the lives of the makers became less stable, especially under Nero (50s and 60s CE), it can be argued that the great age of Latin literature continued for another 120 years (Chs. 14, 15, 16). At the same time, it cannot be denied that more memorable literature was produced during the insecure times of the Julio-Claudian dynasty in the first century than in the celebrated prosperity and patronage of the arts under Trajan and Hadrian in the second. In its own way the first century CE can claim to be another, related but different, 'golden age', emulating that of the first century BCE.

But from now on the slope of the terrain is intermittently downhill. One might trace the beginnings of the end of the Roman world, and of the Greek world under the Romans, right back to the death of the philosophical emperor Marcus Aurelius in 180 CE. The usual kind of imperial and military history is told in terms of endless complicated power struggles and frontier wars; but the less extended and less contested worlds of literature were not in such turmoil, as the thousands of texts from the rubbish tips of Oxyrhynchos remind us. In both the Roman and the Greek worlds various interesting, and occasionally surprising, works emerge from the highly professionalized culture of the rhetoric schools. The recent repudiation of an established canon of 'Classics' has led to some interesting revaluations of the productions of this long, less brilliant era (Ch. 17).

The Western, Latin half of the empire, based on Rome, and the Eastern Greek half, based on Byzantion (which was to become Constantinople, and then Istanbul) sporadically but inexorably grew apart. Yet the long twilight of the world of 'classical' literature was not so dissimilar throughout both. The pressure of new assertive powers, such as those of the Goths, the Vandals, and the Arabs, set up great whirlpools of insecurity. And the encroachment, and eventually triumph, of the absolute faith of Christianity, which also meant the growing importance in education of monks and clerics, was going to bring an end—as we can now see with hindsight—to the kind of pluralism that had been essential to Greek literature and to its Latin offspring (Chs. 8 and 17). One can pin-point key moments in the chronic debilitation of the 'classical' world, such

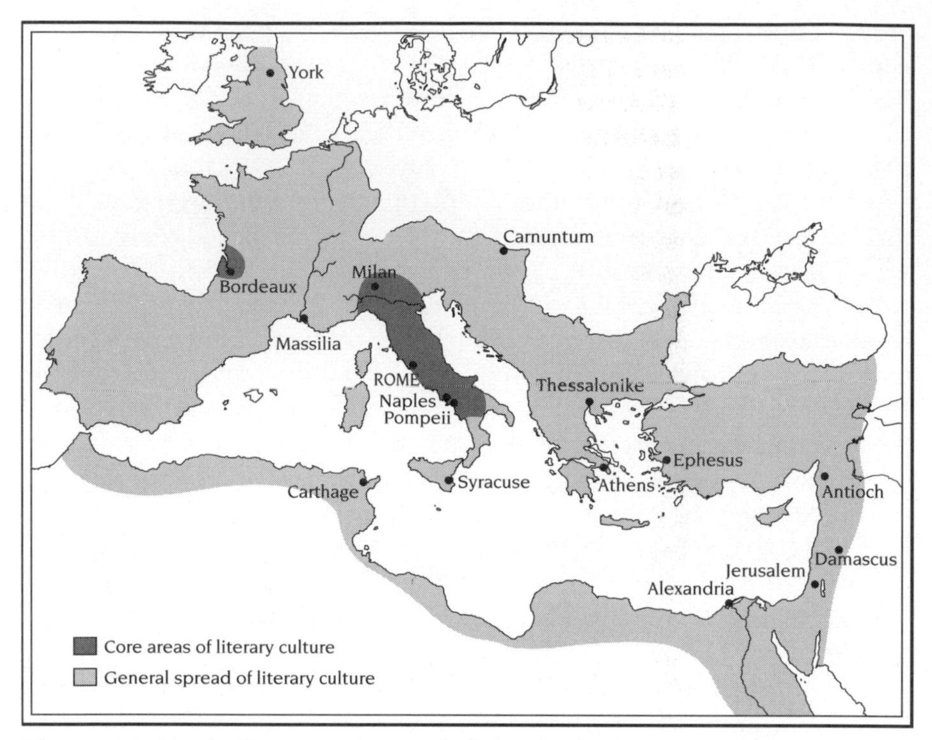

The world of Latin literature: 1 CE–end of the classical era

as the official adoption of Christianity by the Roman authorities in 312, the first sack of the city of Rome in 410, the closure of the philosophy schools in Athens in 529, but this tends to hide the long, sporadic process. The overall effect was this: in 300 CE literature was still being widely read and copied, even though not a great deal was being created; by 550 CE, in the West entirely, and in the East largely, a literary 'dark age' had closed in. No one could claim that more than minimal literature was being made any more; and the vast quantities, from the tedious to the sublime, that had been created and disseminated during the previous 1,250 years was being neither read nor copied. By the time when, two or three hundred years later, there were, in their very different ways, literary revivals—in the West under Charlemagne and in the East under the emperors of Byzantion—the great bulk of both literatures had been irrecoverably lost—rotted, discarded, or burnt.

The twin sagas of how what survived of the two literatures did survive, separately until about the 1300s, and then in the reunion of the Renaissance, is another story. Most of the literature that was recopied by 900 CE has survived until today, though not all—there were further bottlenecks and bonfires. Most of the surviving plays of Euripides and all but one of the poems of Catullus came through these hazards in only one copy, and it should not be forgotten how much failed to make it. The productions of many major makers did not survive at all except in tiny fragments quoted in other works; hardly anyone's *œuvre*, however great, has come through in its entirety. Whatever reached the era of the printed book, however, still exists today in multiple copies—and in electronic form. And the finds of papyri in the last hundred years and more have given us back a lot of lost Greek, and a little of Latin, though all too much of it is in tattered bits and pieces. The 'Literature' of this volume means inevitably the literature which has survived down to today, but it is worth remembering that this is very far short of being co-extensive with the literature which was known to its early receivers.

Greek and Latin literature have survived as texts, as the copied written records of the crafted words of their makers. They have not survived with any of their nurturing context; the dry core has been conserved without the surrounding appreciation of its receivers. It is rather like the survival of the skeleton of what was once a human who lived a life. The symbiotic creation and appreciation of the text, like the living body of the skeleton and its personal and social context, have to be painstakingly reconstructed, often (inevitably) with a fair degree of speculation. But without that original symbiosis of maker and public the literature would never have come into being in the first place. It is the mission of this book to say something about those shadowy, mostly nameless, publics of our great (though depleted) treasury of ancient Greek and Latin literature. To come alive in our far distant, far different worlds, the texts need the revivification of the audience, the readers and listeners who farmed and cultivated their growth. To develop the vivid image from the Italian poet, Cesare Pavese: although they are now rotted away, they were essential to the growth of the flowers we still pick and the fruit we still relish.

Greek Literature

The Greek World: chief places mentioned in the text

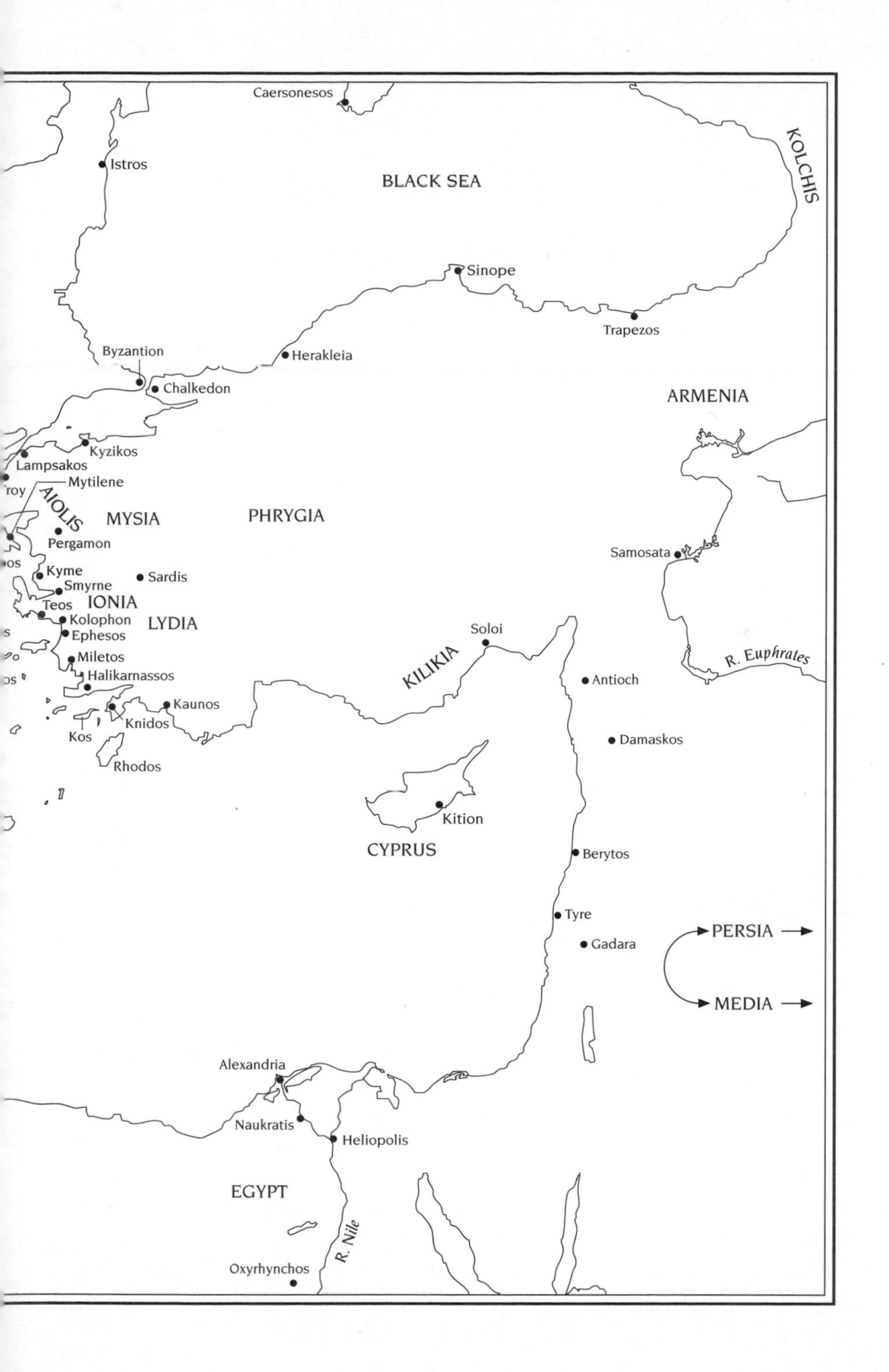
Caersonesos
Istros
BLACK SEA
KOLCHIS
Sinope
Trapezos
Byzantion
Herakleia
Chalkedon
ARMENIA
Kyzikos
Lampsakos
Mytilene
AIOLIS
MYSIA
PHRYGIA
Pergamon
Samosata
Kyme
Sardis
Smyrne
Teos
IONIA
Kolophon
LYDIA
Ephesos
Soloi
Miletos
KILIKIA
R. Euphrates
Halikarnassos
Antioch
Kaunos
Knidos
Kos
Damaskos
Rhodos
Kition
CYPRUS
Berytos
Tyre
Gadara
PERSIA
MEDIA
Alexandria
Naukratis
Heliopolis
EGYPT
R. Nile
Oxyrhynchos

1 The spring of the muses: Homer and related poetry

OLIVER TAPLIN

> Thence form your Judgement, thence your Maxims bring,
> And trace the Muses *upward* to their *Spring*.
>
> (Alexander Pope on Homer)

Archetypes and antitypes

The rosy fingers which heralded the extraordinary era we know as 'ancient Greece' first gradually spread between about 900 and 700 BCE. The sunrise is quite distinctly marked, though, by the ascent at some time within a generation either side of 700, of the two poems: *Ilias*, the poem of Ilios (Troy), and *Odysseia,* the story of Odysseus—in English the *Iliad* and the *Odyssey*. It is astonishing that we should have such early poems preserved at all, let alone that this dawn of Greek literature should bring into the light not one but two great archetypal epics. For the whole of the ancient Greek—and Roman—worlds they established the large-scale narrative poem about great men of the past as the foundational genre. And they established the long, rather complex line of the dactylic hexameter as the most venerable verse-form.

These poems would never have come into existence if there had been no public for them, if there had not been people to stimulate them, hear them and appreciate them. So who was this poetry for, our earliest 'Western' poetry? Who were the people who made the poet—or poets—who made the *Iliad* and the *Odyssey*? Richard Bentley (the great Cambridge scholar) in 1713, reckoned he knew: 'Take my word for it, poor Homer . . . wrote a sequel of songs, to be sung by himself for small earnings and good cheer, at festivals and other days of merriment; the *Ilias* he made for the men, and the *Odysseis* for the other sex.' In 1985 Joachim Latacz (a distinguished professor at Basel) is no less assertive: 'the singer could find an appreciation for such an artistry only among those from whose manner of life it originated . . . among the nobles . . . Homer could not have made clearer the natural link between nobility and heroic song, nor could he have declared more clearly his own membership in this social sphere.' As this direct contradiction indicates, the straight truth is that we can say next to nothing *for certain* about the original circumstances of production of our two poems, neither about their audience nor their author nor their context of communication. For a start, they come from a time well before any kind of firm external historical record. But this is no reason for giving up and regarding it as a waste of time to ask who Homeric poetry was for, and what it meant to them: there are still aspects of context and performance that are likely, plausible, interesting. There is still, as this chapter hopes to show, much worth saying, even though it is not 100 per cent proof definite or definitive.

The prime evidence for Homeric performance and production is bound to be the poems themselves. And there is an unavoidable circle of argument here: we interpret the poems to reach an idea of the audience, and then we feed this audience back into the interpretation of the poems. Both Bentley and Latacz have all too obviously done just that. But provided we are aware of the problem, it does not vitiate the whole project: it is still worth searching for the interactive arcs which are most suggestive, most interesting, and which fit best with external considerations. We have to be especially careful, however, with the representation of poetry as performed and appreciated within the poems themselves. This can be suggestive and illuminating, provided we keep in mind always that the poems are creating fictional worlds, set in the heroic past. The internal audiences should not be treated as direct or 'literal' evidence for the world of the external audiences—though that does not mean that there is *no* relationship between them. It is a further problem that the poet-narrator himself never ever comes out of the fictional world into the real world, or even what purports to be the real world. 'Homer' never in any way declares who he is, where he comes from, or who he is making poetry for. Even if he did, we would have to treat the declaration with care—it need not be literally true—but he has covered his own tracks so completely that this question does not arise. More than in almost any other poetry, the craftsman suppresses his own presence, and effaces his own identity.

One big question left open by this self-concealment is whether the *Iliad* and *Odyssey* are the work of the same poet. Nearly all ancient Greeks—though not all—believed that they were, and that his name was Homer, or rather *Homeros*. But modern scholarship has still not been able to settle this basic question of authorship decisively. In view of the way that the epics depend on a long poetic tradition (see pp. 30–1 below), and of the way that they may well have been preserved at first through performance, rather than as a fixed text (see p. 50

below), it is even open to question how far the modern concept of authorship is appropriate at all. While I am inclined to believe, though with no great confidence, that they *are* both fundamentally the work of one poet, the important point that seems to me beyond reasonable doubt is that they were created for very much the same audiences and occasions. While they are simultaneously highly similar in some ways and different in others, the differences are pervasively complementary. This is especially clear with the *Odyssey*, which has the Trojan War as its immediate past, even as its point of departure—when Odysseus tells of his various adventures he begins 'Leaving Ilios, the wind took me . . .' (9. 39). The other great heroes, alive or—all too many—dead, are very much the same characters as those in the *Iliad*. More than that, the experience of the war as both glorious and destructive, magnificent yet full of suffering, emerges as quintessentially similar. When Odysseus is listening to a narration of his greatest deeds at the sack of Troy, instead of glorying, he weeps:

> The tears trickled down and drenched his cheeks.
> As a woman might weep as she clasps the body of her beloved
> husband, who has fallen before the eyes of his whole people,
> trying to keep off the cruel day from his land and its children;
> she sees him in his death throes, and twining herself around him
> shrieks in keening lament. But her captors come up behind her,
> and beat her across the back and shoulders with their spears,
> as they are seizing a slave for a life full of grief and labour,
> and her face is wasted, her cheeks wracked with pitiful streaks:
> so Odysseus shed tears, drops of the water of pity.
>
> (*Odyssey* 8. 522–31)

This is very like the suffering of the Trojans in the *Iliad*, and especially of Andromache—not exactly the same, but tapping the same sensibility.

Throughout their existence most readers and audiences of one poem have seasoned their appreciation of it with their knowledge of the other. More clearly the *Odyssey* feeds on the *Iliad*, and it is generally regarded as the later poem, a kind of sequel. But there are also places where the *Iliad* appears to draw strength from the *Odyssey*. Thus it is Odysseus (who twice calls himself in a unique turn of phrase 'the father of Telemachos') who in the first sequence of the *Iliad* takes Agamemnon's special prize, Chryseis, back to her father, the one and only return-home narrated in the poem. And Odysseus already has the three epithets which are unique to him, and which capture the qualities which will see him through the *Odyssey*: 'much-subtle', 'much-enduring', and 'much-devising' (*polymetis*, *polytlas*, and *polymechanos*). These epithets belong to the antitype of the direct, 'fast-footed' Achilles. It is revealing that both of them were offered as central figures to the early Greek audiences (later Greeks had serious scruples about both, especially the deceitful Odysseus). Achilles is uncompromising, overt in his feelings, unhesitatingly ready to die in order to make good his failings: Odysseus, the great survivor, is subtle, always ready to temporize, to disguise, and to lie. Achilles speaking to Odysseus, insists:

> I detest that man as much as the doorway of Hades,
> who hides one thing inside and declares out loud another.
> (*Iliad* 9. 312–13)

But Odysseus is the great specialist at just that. On Ithake (in Latin Ithaca) Athene drops her disguise to acknowledge a man after her own heart:

> You are outstanding among men for clever and devious words,
> while I am the greatest god for cunning and for conning.
> (*Odyssey* 13. 297–9)

The archetypal antitypes go far beyond the two heroes. The *Iliad* tells directly of only a few crucial days out of the whole Trojan War; and it is almost entirely set, claustrophobically almost, at Troy. At the same time, the poem extends understanding towards a wide range of characters, and to both sides in the war. While the *Odyssey* narrates only a small number of days directly—those leading up to Odysseus' return and revenge on Ithake—it covers, by means of flashbacks, a wide spread of places, including the varied story-worlds of Odysseus' adventures. And his adventures (and those of Menelaos) are spread over some ten years. Yet, for all its range of time and place, the *Odyssey* is centred on one man and his close associates in a way quite different from the multiplicity of the *Iliad*.

The *Odyssey* is fundamentally a crime-and-punishment story: the good and the likeable triumph, and the wicked are in the end brought low. It all moves towards reunion and the establishment of a stable and peaceful society, even though that is not fully achieved by the end of the poem (the eventuality is prophesied). The *Odyssey*'s overall direction is from suffering and disruption towards restoration and the united family. The *Iliad*, on the other hand, is not evidently a story of right and wrong; it tells of a world in which all suffer, and where the suffering is not apportioned by deserving. The finest people and the finest relationships—Achilles, Patroklos, Hektor, Andromache, Priam—are destroyed. The best gets wasted; anger and conflict rule human life. The prosperous and civilized city of Troy is to go up in flames; and by no means all of the leading Achaians will get home—and even fewer will enjoy the fruits of victorious peace. Two quite different views of the human condition, then, and yet somehow a pair, like non-identical twins.

Hesiod of Helikon

Before trying to get any further with reconstructing a context for Homer, it might be a good idea to turn to another poet, one who does locate himself in a kind of scene. For the Homeric epics are not our only works from this early period, and not even the only kind of archetypal hexameter poetry. There is also Hesiod, in Greek *Hesiodos* or *Heisiodos*. And he, by contrast, *does* 'come out' of his poetry. He even names himself, something that many (perhaps most) poets do not do:

> And one day they taught to Hesiod the beauties of song,
> as he was herding his lambs below holy mount Helikon.
> And this is what the goddesses said to me first,
> those Olympian Muses, daughters of mighty Zeus:
> 'You shepherds of the fields, you disgraces, pure greed,
> we know how to tell many falsehoods just like the real thing,
> and we know, when we so wish, how to sing truly'.
>
> (*Theogony* 22–8)

In other places Hesiod says precisely where he lives below Mount Helikon (the range of mountains between the central mainland plains of Boiotia and the gulf of Corinth). He also gives details of his family history, and even tells of participating in a poetic performance. We cannot be certain how much of all this is historically true, and how much is 'falsehood just like the real thing'. But it is offered as if true, and it is still revealing for us.

We have two poems from Hesiod, traditionally known as the *Theogony* and the *Works and Days* (abbreviated as *W&D*). Our texts have both accumulated some 'unauthorized' additions over the centuries after Hesiod, especially towards the end of each poem; but, even including these, they are far shorter than the Homeric epics. Quite a few other miscellaneous hexameter poems got attached to the name of Hesiod, but we know enough about them to be confident that they date from some time later than the two which we have (see p. 56 below). The *Theogony*, in about 1,000 lines, covers the origin and genealogies of some 300 gods (many in lists of course), and it all leads up towards the establishment of Zeus as the supreme divine ruler. The shorter *Works and Days* is a kind of discursive collection of wise advice, especially about good husbandry; it tells what a man should do to fit into the natural and moral order of the world. Unlike any other early hexameter poetry, *W&D* is addressed to fellow contemporaries, mostly to Hesiod's layabout brother Perses, and partly to the local lords whom he accuses of corruption. (It is worth registering here, since it will recur, that the word for 'lord' is *basileus*, often mistranslated as 'king', which is what it meant in later Greek.)

Although so different in tone and subject from Homer, Hesiod's poems are in the same hexameter metre, and in a pretty similar style and diction. There has been much dispute over which came first, but it may well be that the two poets were contemporaries, or at least their lives may have overlapped. Homer almost certainly came, though, from the other side of the Aegean Sea, from the middle part of the Asia Minor coast known as Ionia, near its border with the more northern part known as Aiolis. Even so, it is not impossible that they both participated in the same poetic occasions sometimes. The ancient Greeks certainly liked to believe that they did, and stories about a great 'Contest' between them grew up early, probably within a few generations of their own day. This sets up a kind of contest within the whole nature of poetry: the story-teller of glamorous champions versus the font of homely wisdom.

Hesiod and Homer get cited as a pair, as the twin founders of Greek poetry, and even of the Greek mentality. Herodotos in the later fifth century wrote, 'I think that Hesiod and Homer lived no more than 400 years before my time; and they were the ones who created the gods' family trees for the Greek world, gave them their names, assigned them honours and areas of expertise, and told us what they look like. Any poets who are supposed to have lived before Hesiod and Homer actually came after them in my opinion' (2. 53). Those early thinkers who set themselves up as purveyors of new wisdom (see pp. 157–8, 162 below) denounce their primal pair of rivals. Thus Xenophanes, for example (second half of sixth century): 'Homer and Hesiod attributed to the gods all the things which among men are shameful and blameworthy.'

So what might Hesiod reveal about the audiences of his world, and possibly though less directly of Homer's also? The most revealing passage comes well on through *W&D* when, after over 200 lines devoted to the agricultural year, Hesiod turns to sea-faring as a source of livelihood, and even profit. It is built up to with circumstantial 'autobiography':

> . . . just as our father, mine and yours, you stupid Perses,
> used to go to sea in ships in his search for a good living.
> And one day he came here, making the long sea-crossing,
> quitting Kyme in Aiolis, all the way in his dark ship,
> not running away from wealth ... but from foul poverty ...
> And so he came to settle near Helikon in a miserable village
> called Askre, harsh in winter, nasty in summer, good at no time.
> (*W&D* 633–40)

There are details here that are not predictable and most unlikely to have been conventional. The migration of Hesiod's father goes against the obvious tack by leaving the relative prosperity of Asia Minor (Homer's home territory), and heading up a valley from the fertile plains of Boiotia (later Greeks planted Askre with groves and turned it into a delightful sanctuary of the Muses). There follows rather a long introduction to what will be in the end the rather short section on seafaring:

> I shall show you the measures of the reverberating sea,
> uninitiated though I am in the skills of seamanship and boats.
> For as for ships, I have never ever embarked on the broad seas,
> unless you count to Euboia from Aulis (where the Achaians
> once waited through long bad weather when they had gathered
> a mighty expedition from Greece against Troy, city of beauties).
> From there I crossed over for the funeral games
> of strong-minded Amphidamas at Chalkis
> —and many were the prizes announced and displayed
> by the sons of that great man. I declare that there
> I was victorious in poetry and won a tripod with ring-handles.
> And I dedicated it to the Helikonian Muses,
> at the place where they initially set me on the path of clear song.
> (*W&D* 648–59)

We cannot know for sure whether this is all literally true or 'falsehoods just like the real thing'. But it does sound like the real thing, and there are no clear signals that this is fiction or merely traditional tales. It is a fact that bronze tripods (vertical-legged cauldrons) were the prestige prizes and dedications of the time, as is clear from excavations at Olympia. And there is no doubting that Chalkis on the island of Euboia was very prosperous in this era; it won a famous victory over the neighbouring Eretria, which is probably reflected archaeologically by the desertion of the major site of Lefkandi in about 700 BCE. Aulis is indeed a good harbour on the opposite mainland coast, and its place in the great epic tradition is taken for granted in Homer. There is even a joke here for those who know the local topography (the first joke in Greek literature?): the distance across the straits between Aulis and the coast of Chalkis opposite is less than 100 metres ('I shall show you the measures of the reverberating sea'!)

Last but not least, it was surely Hesiod himself who established the Muses, traditionally from Mount Olympos far to the north, on his local mountain, Helikon. He even seems to have coined, in his *Theogony*, their canonical nine names, and to have put the little river Permessos and the spring of Hippokrene on the poetical map. It was there, where he was grazing his flocks, that the Muses, as Hesiod claims, once appeared to him (see above), and gave him a magic staff of laurel:

> . . . and they breathed into me a marvellous voice,
> so that I might celebrate [give *kleos* to] matters of the future
> and of the past. And they commanded me to sing poems
> of the family of blessed gods who live for ever,
> and first and last always to sing of them themselves.
>
> (*Theogony* 31–4)

(for *kleos* see further below and pp. 137–8)

Hesiod performed his poetry, then (or made out that he performed) at a big public occasion which attracted visitors and competitors. Competition can be good, he claims elsewhere (*W&D* 25–6) 'potter against potter, carpenter with carpenter . . . poet with poet'. This overlaps suggestively with a passing remark in the *Odyssey* (17. 384–5), listing certain kinds of craftsmen who are welcome anywhere: 'a seer or a healer or a carpenter in wood or an inspired poet who delights with his song.' So a picture begins to take shape of poets who travel, and whose venues include big public occasions where they can compete to win attention, prestige, and reward.

Why poetry at the funeral games of Amphidamas of Chalkis? Funeral games were meant to be a glorious memorial to the dead man; they were an occasion for his surviving relatives to be conspicuous and generous; and they were some kind of consolation for them. Mortality should not—the games declare—obliterate all delight from human life: life goes on. (The reason, I should add, why there is no poetry competition at the funeral games for Patroklos in *Iliad* 23, is because in the *Iliad* this state of mind is not fully achieved until the later scene between Priam and Achilles.)

In *W&D* Hesiod casts himself as a grim old bugger, tough, without illusions, worn down by hard labour, pessimistic:

> How I wish I didn't live in the Fifth Age of men,
> but had either died before or had been born later.
> For this is a race of iron now; and they shall not cease
> from toil and misery . . .
>
> (*W&D* 174–7)

But this does not mean that Hesiod's audience listened to him in order to get depressed. What does his poetry offer them, then? Explicitly: vivid wisdom, mythical and religious lore, and glorification of the gods, above all of Zeus. But there is an important passage in the *Theogony* which brings out a further, key reason for audiences to give time to this special form of discourse, poetry. Hesiod is talking of the behaviour and blessings of a good *basileus* (lord), and emphasizing the importance to him of the poet:

> Sweet is the speech that flows from his lips,
> for even if a man has sorrow in his breast fresh inflicted,
> and is exhausted with grief, even so the poet, attendant of the Muses,
> can sing the glorious achievements [*klea*] of the people of old,
> and can sing of the blessed gods who are on Olympos;
> and then he quickly becomes oblivious of his ills-of-heart,
> and no longer dwells on his cares. Soon the Muses' gifts divert him.
>
> (*Theogony* 97–103)

Poetry soothes, diverts, banishes angst—'Music for a while | Shall all your cares beguile'. This is why poetry is so important in a world which is as grim as Hesiod makes it out to be: it is still not *human* to dwell on our troubles and griefs the whole time. We need charms, delights, soothing salves, consolations to take our mind off them—such as poetry, music, becoming absorbed in a good story.

Aural and oral poetry

In the passage just quoted Hesiod alludes to two different kinds of poetry: poems about the gods—that is what he delivers in the rest of the *Theogony*—and poems about 'the glorious achievements of the people of old' (line 100, *klea proteron anthropon—anthropon* is not gender-specific). This is just the kind of poetry we have in the *Iliad* and *Odyssey*; and it shows that, however little travelled Hesiod was, and however godforsaken his village of Askre, he was well aware of a mainstream of epic poetry of the Homeric kind.

Hesiod refers to both kinds of poetry as conveyed live to their audience by the *aoidos* (poet-singer), who sings or recites. There is every reason to suppose that this is how early hexameter poems were composed and communicated. This is not only because Hesiod and Homer both use the same terms (*aoidos* etc.), and both speak of poets in performance, but because of the basic nature of their language and narrative techniques. It is now some seventy years since Milman Parry first demonstrated in a quasi-scientific way that both Homer's poetic diction and scene-construction, with their rich yet efficient range of formulae and repertoire of repeated sequences, are to be explained as the accumulated stock of generations of practitioners of oral poetry. Since then Parry's theory has been elaborated, strengthened, and generally accepted—and rightly so: Homer is the inheritor of a centuries-old tradition of oral storytelling. It is beyond reasonable doubt, that is to say, that Homer—and Hesiod too—learned how to be a poet by hearing and imitating performing poets, who had in their turn learned from the previous generation, and so on back through generations, even quite possibly back into the prosperous and powerful era of the so-called Mycenean Age some 500 years earlier.

No less importantly, Homer's and Hesiod's audiences will have learned to appreciate epic poetry by listening to performing poets. This is the way that they will have come to know the subject-matter and concerns of the tradition, its typically recurrent scenes, its basic strategies, and its special language. For the language of Homeric epic is far away from anything that was ever actually spoken at any one time or place. It amalgamates a mixture of dialects, incorporated over generations from different areas of the Greek world ; it also retains archaic words and grammatical forms that had gone out of spoken use long ago. Yet these are all mixed up with, and indivisible from, current words and forms, including phrases which had been coined by the particular performer, perhaps on that very occasion. If one were able to stick a little label on each half-line of Homer, coded with the time and place that that phrase had been first incorporated into poetry, it would make a thoroughly variegated and unpredictable kind of 'mosaic'. Yet this special poetic language will not have struck its hearers as artificial or outlandish, precisely because they knew it and expected it as the language of hexameter poetry. It is the language proper to the occasion that they will have assimilated from childhood. (A partial analogy might be the way that those brought up in a church where the Authorized Version of the Bible was the norm came to know its language and to regard it as special and appropriate to its context.)

It is crucial to the quality of Homer, and even of the less fluent Hesiod, that their audiences were already soaked in hexameter poetry of the traditional style. This helps to explain how what is for us the earliest Greek poetry can be of such high quality (to put it modestly). By keeping to and by departing from the expected patterns and priorities, the poetry can build on and exploit the audience's already rich experience. However 'archaic' these audiences in terms of standard chronological 'period', they were already trained in a highly developed tradition of poetry.

So far I have spoken exclusively in terms of live performances sung or recited before the audience; and Homer and Hesiod themselves allude to poetry exclusively in those terms. But what about reading and writing? There has been, and still is, a lively debate about whether the art of writing played a formative part in the composition of the *Iliad* and *Odyssey*. In fact at present (late 1990s) scholars are pretty evenly divided on the issue. The claim that Homer 'had the advantage of writing' (as it is often tendentiously put) is chronologically quite possible. The Phoenician alphabet had been adapted to Greek by the mid-eighth century, and by Homer's time (assuming somewhere between, say, 733 and 666 BCE) the skill was available and catching on. Several of our earliest specimens of Greek writing are, in fact, lines of hexameter poetry scratched on pottery. One from about 725 BCE is a beaker which refers to itself as the 'cup of Nestor'; and it has been claimed to be alluding humorously to the huge golden goblet (not the same word) which Nestor drinks from in *Iliad* book 11. But this heated scholarly discussion is all marginal to our present concerns, because, even if Homer himself learned to write, or if—as is much less unlikely—he was persuaded to let a skilled scribe transcribe his poetry (see p. 50 below) *the poetry was not made to be read.* There was no reading public. Even assuming a written version was in existence—perhaps to be studied by newly literate disciples?—it is still as good as certain that Homer conveyed his poetry to his public through performances.

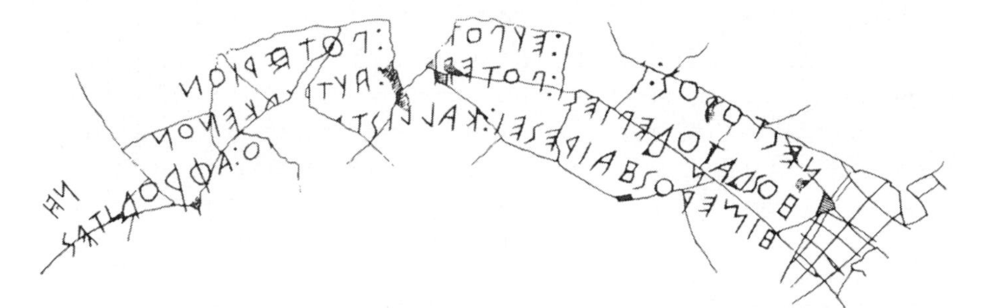

EPIC GRAFFITO? This message, partly in hexameter verse, was scratched on a beaker found at Ischia in the bay of Naples at an early Greek settlement site, dating from 700 BCE or slightly earlier. Its allusion to Nestor has led some scholars to claim that it presupposes a knowledge of the Iliad.

It is often claimed that Hesiod used writing even if Homer did not. His authoritative editor, Martin West, argues this on the grounds that Hesiod's personalized poetry—'your father and mine, Perses' etc.—could not possibly have been performed by others or transmitted orally. But there is no reason why I should not recite feelingly a highly personal lyric by Hardy or Heaney; and, more immediately to the point, later classical Greeks happily recited the first-person poems of such individualized artists as Alkaios or Anakreon (see pp. 75–9 below). In later times visitors to Askre, such as Pausanias in the second century CE, were shown a time-worn sheet of lead with the *Works and Days* (or at least some of it) scratched upon it. This is a reminder of how unwieldy writing was back in the early days before papyrus was readily available from Egypt. It is absurd to think of Hesiod reading his script from sheets of lead, let alone his public carting home literally tons of poetry. Even if they were written on prepared skins or on wooden tablets coated with wax, the texts will still have been bulky and unwieldy.

There is no allusion whatsoever to writing in Hesiod, even though *W&D* deals with his own contemporary world. There is, however, one intriguing reference in the *Iliad*. In the course of a story about the past before the Trojan War, Bellerophon is sent away to Lykia by a jealous king:

> ... he sent him off with a consignment of lethal symbols,
> inscribing deadly designs inside a sealed tablet ...
>
> (*Iliad* 6. 168–70)

The way that these inscribed signs are treated with a kind of folk-tale mystery does not necessarily mean that Homer's audience had never encountered writing, because, since the introduction of writing into Greece was pretty recent, the poet would want to avoid sounding anachronistic. (It is highly unlikely they would be aware that a different kind of writing—Linear B—had been in use back in Mycenean times.) At the same time, this passage is not conclusive evidence that the poet knew about writing himself, still less that his public read his work.

Internal audiences

It is now time to turn to the explicit mentions and accounts of the performance of poetry scattered through the Homeric epics. We have to remember the examples of Bentley and Latacz and keep on our guard against treating these simply or literally: they are set in a past heroic world, and there is no guarantee that they are self-reflecting accounts of how the actual poem was (is) being delivered. But, via a more circumspect approach, the scenes may less directly yield some significant plausibilities (not certainties) about the production of the poems and their reception.

There are passages where groups, even maybe choruses, are portrayed as performing; but interesting though these are, they are marginal to the primary search which is for solo performers telling heroic stories. What is clear, though, is that poetry and music are mostly thought of as part of the good life, especially of feasting and festivity. So it is typical that they appear in three of the pleasant scenes on the great shield that Hephaistos makes for Achilles, a kind of microcosm of human life not dominated by war (*Iliad* 18. 494–6, 569–72, 604–5—the last passage is unfortunately caught up in a serious textual problem). It is in keeping with this that the *Iliad* portrays no solo performances of poetry for entertainment, not even at any feast of the Achaians or the Trojans: a world of war does not seem to be the place for epic poetry.

With one extraordinary exception. Achilles has been taking no part in the fighting for four days, and the Achaians are in such danger of disaster the next morning that they send a small group of negotiators to try to placate him. As they approach his encampment along the shore—

> they found him pleasing his spirit by playing a melodious lyre,
> an intricate instrument, fitted with a bridge of silver,
> which he had picked from the spoils when he sacked Eetion's city.
> He was pleasing his spirits by reciting the famous feats
> of men. Patroklos alone sat facing him in silence
> waiting for whenever Achilles should close his singing.
> (*Iliad* 9. 86–91)

The phrase for 'feats of men' (*klea andron*) is used in the *Odyssey* to refer to heroic epic, and it is close to Hesiod's phrasing at *Theogony* line 100 (see p. 30 above). It would be foolhardy to jump to the inference that in Homer's own world it was common—or even known at all—for young aristocrats to strum epic poetry to themselves for their own satisfaction or that of a few close friends. Is it any more justifiable to conclude that Homer's audience 'saw its own idea of the highest form of self-realisation reflected in this combination of warrior and artist' (Latacz)? In view of the absence of epic performance elsewhere in the warrior world of the *Iliad*, there might be a better, less literal interpretation. At this stage of the poem Achilles is, in effect, *not* a warrior; he is living in a kind of capsule of peacetime activities (like his men, the Myrmidones, who indulge in athletics and wander around—2. 773–9). So the significance of Achilles' singing heroic epic may be, I suggest, that this shows his awareness that he is staying out of the war, out of the world where the 'glorious achievements of men' are enacted (though the double irony is that by doing so he is winning his special place in epic). It is, then, because of this, and because Achilles is an aristocrat and not a practising poet, that, like some archaic Hopkins, he has no performance-context and no public.

The *Odyssey* is far more poetically self-referential, or metapoetic, than the *Iliad*: poets and their audiences are a constant theme. The epic is not more than a quarter of an hour old when Phemios is introduced, the poet who has to perform after the feast for the suitors on Ithake (*Odyssey* 1. 150–5). And not long after that:

> the celebrated poet was performing a poem for them,
> as they sat in silence listening; his story was of
> the disastrous homecoming of the Achaians ...
> (*Odyssey* 1. 325–7)

Penelope rebukes him:

> 'Phemios, you can perform all sorts of other soothing songs
> about the deeds of gods and of men, such as poets celebrate [give *kleos*].
> Sing one of these for them as they sit lulled to silence
> drinking down their wine. But stop this disastrous story . . .'
> (*Odyssey* 1. 337–41)

To her surprise, her son Telemachos comes to the defence of the poet: he is bound to sing what is 'newest', meaning both with recent subject-matter and with novel touches. Already here we have some features which can be plausibly transferred—at least wishfully—to the world of the poet and his audience: the celebrity of the poet, his association with festivity, his ability to bestow fame (*kleos*), the expectation that he will provide charms or soothings. Also note how even the rowdy, over-indulgent suitors sit in silence when the poet is at work. His ability to sing 'about the deeds of gods and of men' may suggest that he should also have poetry more like the *Theogony* in his repertoire. And this may also be implied when, towards the end of the poem, Phemios pleads with Odysseus for his life, saying that he sings 'for both gods and humans' (22. 346—he is spared on the grounds that he sang for the suitors against his will).

Poetry is also important among the Phaeacians (in Greek *Phaiekes*) on their remote island of Scherie, Odysseus' last port of call before he gets home. They are intermediate between the realities of Ithake and the fantastical world of Odysseus' stories, and they lead an almost utopian existence. They have a suitably talented poet, the blind Demodokos 'held in honour by the people'—'the god had given him more than to any other the gift to please with poetry, when his spirit might move him to perform' (8. 44–5). Demodokos can play to accompany dancing, and he can sing *risqué* stories of the affairs of the gods, which also 'please' (8. 368). But his central repertoire is heroic epic, which he performs after the feast. At the midday feast in book 8 he sings

> a tale of the famous feats of men [*klea andron*],
> picking up the track at a point famed [given *kle-os*] to the skies.
> (8. 73–4)

This turns out to be the story of a dispute among the leaders at Troy, significantly similar to the opening of the *Iliad*. Then in the evening, at the special request of Odysseus, he tells of the fighting at the sack of Troy: Odysseus weeps (see p. 24 above), which prompts King Alkinoos to urge Odysseus to tell his own story. Throughout these scenes there is much praise of the poetry for its sweetness and capacity to charm.

But there is another poet in the *Odyssey*, or at least an honorary poet. The loyal farmer Eumaios tells Penelope what it was like to listen to 'the stranger':

> 'as when one stares at a poet, who is divinely inspired
> to tell delightful stories to men, and everyone
> is happy to listen to him unceasingly when he sings—
> that's how that man entranced me . . .'
>
> (17. 518–21)

Earlier Alkinoos, on Scherie, had said to Odysseus:

> 'There is such beauty in your words, and also such wisdom;
> you have told of your toils . . . so skilfully,
> you're as good as a poet yourself . . .'
>
> (11. 367–9)

It was already late evening, after the feast and after Demodokos, that Odysseus began. While telling of the underworld, over two hours into his story-telling in 'real' narrator's time, he rather abruptly stops and says it is time for bed.

> And they all sat in silence throughout
> the shadow-filled hall, enthralled under the spell.
>
> (11. 333–4)

He is persuaded to take up the thread again ('this night still stretches ahead . . . we could stay wide awake till dawn . . .', lines 373–6). And when he eventually ends, they sit in enthralled silence again (13. 1–2). Always bearing in mind that this is all fictitious, and that it is set in a distant heroic and idealized world, there are still poetic or metapoetic assumptions that it seems safe to transfer as aspirations to the world of Homer and his audience—in fact it seems unreasonable not to: the beauty of poetry, its skilled musical accompaniment, its sweet delight, the way it charms its audience, the way it reduces them to spellbound silence; and the poet as someone who is held in special esteem, someone who conveys some special kind of wisdom as well as pleasure.

The '*Odyssey* model'

If that much is 'safe', the next step might be to infer that, just as the *Odyssey* reflects the poets' aspirations for appreciation, so it reflects the actual circumstances of their performances. It is a tempting step, and one that has often been taken. Homer performed, it is claimed, for the eighth-century equivalents of Penelope's suitors and of the Phaeacian court; his public sat at the tables of lords or kings in their feasting-halls, surrounded by peers, henchmen, guests, and retainers.

There are serious objections to this, however. First, there is the scale of our two poems. On both Ithake and Scherie the performance lasts for one, two, or at most three hours. At that rate the *Iliad* or *Odyssey* would have taken a week or a fortnight of performances. This is not unthinkable—oral poets in Muslim societies observing Ramadan, for example, are known to perform evening after evening. Or maybe Homer's audiences were prepared to stay awake most of the night listening to his monumental poems—the possibility eagerly urged by Alkinoos? In that case three nights, or even two for the *Odyssey*, should have been sufficient. *But* . . . on both Ithaca and Scherie the poet is subject to interruptions and requests. He is at the beck and call of his noble patrons; at any moment he may be stopped and told to sing something quite different. For the *Iliad* or *Odyssey* to have come into existence, there must have been, I would insist to the contrary, an audience *willing to listen to the whole poem*.

Both poems add up to far more than the sum of their parts. The connections and interactions within them form such a network that any one section is seriously impoverished by being extracted or separated from the rest. Of course, it would still be possible to enjoy isolated sections; and this kind of performance of extracts may well have happened in Homer's own day. But there was no reason for the whole poems to have come into existence in the first place without occasions for performance in their entirety. So, if we are to salvage what I shall call the '*Odyssey* model' reconstruction of the primary reception, we have to suppose feasting noblemen who were a great deal more patient and persistent in their poetry-listening than the Phaeacians, let alone the suitors.

There is a way out of this problem that has been so widely advocated in the scholarship of the last fifty years, that I must, briefly, bring out its implausibility. This theory starts from the belief—a perfectly possible scenario, see p. 41 below—that the way that the poems ever got recorded was through their dictation by the poet to a transcriber. It is then claimed that this process can explain their scale and complexity: while in normal performance the poet delivered shorter bits to demanding aristocratic feasters, as in the *Odyssey* model, the process of dictation gave him the time, the thinking-space, and the opportunity to expand, and so to join separate pieces into the mighty whole that we enjoy. I cannot insist that this is impossible, but I find it very hard to believe that these hugely artful networks came into being, not for a living responsive audience, but for the sake of a material transcription, a load of scratched skins or whatever. So I do not believe that this 'dictation theory' should let the putative audience of kings and barons off the hook. If they comprised Homer's audience, they should have been not just ready, but eager, to listen for many hours without interfering in the subject-matter.

Another serious objection to them is that the poems can hardly be claimed to tell an aristocracy what they want to hear politically or ideologically. Although set in a world of great heroes, they examine and question traditional power-structures rather than ratifying or reinforcing them. Agamemnon in the *Iliad*, who is some sort of king-among-kings (or lord-among-lords) is, taken over the poem as a whole, a far from admirable role-model. It is his errors of judgement and his greed which start the troubles. The most quoted lines in favour of kingly authority (*Iliad* 2. 203–5) are spoken by Odysseus in the middle of a shambles caused by Agamemnon's mismanagement. And, once he has had his brief hour of glory in book 11, the 'king of men' has little part to play in the rest of the poem: his humiliating climbdown in book 19 is in fact the last time he speaks in the entire epic. On the other hand, Achilles is so individualistic and prepared to be so antisocial, that he cannot be claimed as an exemplar for any social group either. Hektor is admirable, but he is killed, and thus dooms his city, because he recognizes that otherwise people will say 'Hektor trusted in his own strength and destroyed his own people' (22. 107). In the *Odyssey* the local aristocracy of the Ithake area are the suitors, hardly a good advertisement. Odysseus, if only he could get home and settle down, would be, we are assured, a fine ruler, but at the end of the poem this is still only a promise, prophesied for the future. But the fact remains that during the poem he manages to lose all the men that he took to Troy with him, all twelve shipfuls. It is emphasized that this was their fault, not his; but this is hardly a story of successful leadership.

Many scholars seem to agree that the Homeric poems 'support' either traditional aristocracy or traditional monarchy. We have already met Latacz's predilection for the nobility: 'we do Homer no disservice in thinking he was encouraged and patronised by an aristocratic clientele (to whose class he himself may have belonged).' Richard Janko, for another example, writes of 'ideological support . . . to traditional images of authority'. To complete a trio of heavyweights, Ian Morris claims that the poems served 'as an ideological tool to legitimise elite domination, presenting it as natural and unchangeable . . . Throughout the poems the *basilees* are glorified, and the *demos* ignored to the point of total exclusion.' But none of this is validated by the actual poems. I have already pointed out what questionable figures the *basilees* and nobles often cut. As for the *demos*, the people as a whole, the usual word for them in Homer is *laos*, and the *laos* is constantly referred to and far from ignored. This does not (of course) make the poems 'democratic', any more than the nobles make it ideologically aristocratic, but it gives a real significance to the non-élite levels of society.

The *Odyssey* model of Homer's audience might still be defended by objecting that I am attributing an unfairly crude attitude to the eighth-century nobility. This is the poetry of suffering after all, it might be said in their defence, and we should not assume that they would be so simple-minded as to demand that all the kings and nobles are good and successful all the time. The poems are, indeed, set in an aristocratic world, and the prosperity of its societies is closely tied up with the authority and well-being of their rulers. The failings of individuals do not necessarily constitute an attack on the élite as a whole. But even accepting this, there remains a further argument against the *Odyssey* model—the most powerful and significant of all the arguments against.

In many parts of the world in modern and earlier times, heroic poetry of the great deeds of men of the past is and has been performed for audiences which are, as in the *Odyssey* model, gathered around those in power. These chiefs or potentates in the audience are normally taken to be the direct descendants of the heroes in the poems. Furthermore, this is explicitly spelled out in various ways, mainly through prophecies and genealogies. So the poets openly celebrate their living patrons by indicating that the poems are about their forebears. This kind of poetic celebration was familiar and important in ancient Greece: it is reflected, for instance, in the victory odes of Pindar (see pp. 82 ff. below). But such ancestral connections between the audience and the poem are conspicuously *absent* from Homer. There is a blank of allusions to future dynasties tracing their family-tree to Agamemnon or Odysseus or whoever, and no addresses—or references of any sort—to any particular individuals, however prestigious, in the audience. There is just one exception, the exception that accentuates the rule. In *Iliad* 20 the gods agree that they must preserve a certain mortal because he is due to have noble descendants, not an Achaian but a Trojan: Aineias. Once the family of Priam has been obliterated, says Poseidon,

> . . . mighty Aineias shall have rule over the Trojans,
> and his children's children, generations in future time.
> (*Iliad* 20. 307–8)

(No mention of Italy, of course—Rome and Aeneas (in Greek, Aineias) are still no more than a twinkle in History's eye!)

There are passing references to the future, to the era of the audience, in Homer, but they are not this kind of genealogy-related pointers to great descendants: on the contrary 'men nowadays' are dismissed as comparative weaklings. There are, however, scattered allusions to the origins of phenomena which are still to be seen in the audience's day—these are, in effect, forerunners of the aetiologies that have such a significant place in later poetry, Greek and Roman. There are references, for example, to an old tomb in the southern Troad surrounded by elm-trees (*Iliad* 6. 419–20), to the tomb of Sarpedon in Lykia (16. 671–83), or to the rock-formation on Mount Sipylos which is supposed to be Niobe turned into stone (24. 614–17—she is there 'now', says Achilles). In the

Odyssey there is an explanation of the strange rock-formations and double entrance of the Cave of the Nymphs on Ithake (13. 102–12—in classical times it housed a large dedication of ancient tripods). There are also references in both poems to tombs at Troy which will be seen by future generations. The Achaians raised one for Achilles and Patroklos,

> on a steep promontory above the level Hellespont,
> so it might be conspicuous, seen from far out at sea
> by people in the present and by generations in future time.
> (*Odyssey* 24. 82–4)

There are also a couple of interesting 'negative aetiologies'. In *Iliad* 12. 10–35 there is an elaborate explanation of how the gods eventually obliterated the Achaean camp on the shore at Troy. This alludes explicitly to times after the war is over, and strongly implies that Homer's audience would want to know why no trace survived of the camp (in contrast to the mighty walls of Troy). And in *Odyssey* 13. 125–87 it is explained how the gods turned the Phaeacians' ship into stone to make sure that they would not be seafarers any more after they had taken Odysseus home. This implicitly explains to the audience why they have never encountered them (though it did not stop the classical inhabitants of Kerkyra, Corfu, from claiming that their island was Scherie).

The important point is that these quasi-aetiologies and other forward allusions are pretty few and far between, and geographically scattered as well. We cannot highlight specific passages—with the exception of the descendants of Aineias at Troy—and claim that they are there to please particular dynasties or particular localities. A huge number of heroes and places are named, especially in the catalogues in book 2 of the *Iliad*, but none of them is given any obviously special treatment; and none seems to indicate the locality of an audience. If any specially emphasized catchments were to be claimed, they would have, I think, to be Troy and Ithake.

In later classical times all sorts of patriotic and territorial claims were made on the strength of allusions in Homer. But none of them had any explicit sanction. For example, the Athenians justified their claim to Sigeion, an important site at the mouth of the Dardanelles, on the ground that there is an Athenian contingent in the *Iliad*. But dozens of other places could make the same claim. The Athenians' rivals for control of Sigeion were from the nearby island of Lesbos, and no doubt they on their side pointed out that Achilles' beloved Briseis came from there, and that they were part of the ancient kingdom of Troy (*Iliad* 24. 544). One of the earliest external sources we have for the reception of Homeric epic involves a 'misunderstanding' of this very point about what might be called 'non-localization'. According to Herodotos (5. 67)

Kleisthenes, the monarch of Sikyon in the northern Peloponnese, during the course of a war against Argos in about 590 BCE, put a stop to the performance of Homeric epics at Sikyon because they were 'full of celebration of the Argives and Argos'. First it is not true—at least not in our poems—that Argos is given any special praise, as opposed to being frequently named; and secondly 'Argives' in epic, like 'Achaians', generally means Greeks as a whole rather than specifically men from Argos.

What is true, however, is that Sikyon is scarcely mentioned in Homer. Nor are some other places which were powerful and wealthy communities in Homer's own times, for example Corinth and Chalkis and Miletos—and indeed Athens. Homer does not even glorify his own homeland. However much the poet wandered around the place in the course of his profession, one might have expected some kind of special mention of the places of his 'home base', so to speak, and of their local dynasties. There were strong traditions in ancient times that associated him with Smyrne and with the nearby island of Chios, where there was a school of performers claiming descent from him (see p. 50 below); and there is no reason to disbelieve this tradition, which fits with the dialect-mix of the poems and with their familiarity with the Troy area. But these places, and indeed the whole area of Ionia, are given no special attention—in fact they seem to be positively disregarded in the poems. The nobility of Homer's own 'country' would, then, have found no ancestors or other boosts to their local pride in the poetry of their celebrated compatriot.

The 'Delos model'

This remarkable lack of 'favouritism', 'localism', or dynastic reinforcement in Homer is, then, a strong negative argument against the *Odyssey* model of an élite audience of indoor feasters. In fact, it might, I suggest, be turned to use as a positive pointer towards a different kind of audience and occasion altogether. It might suggest occasions where local differences were set aside, contexts of social integration rather than of local or class division. The Homeric poems are in a sense 'panhellenic'; and it has been becoming quite common to use this term of them (Greg Nagy has been especially influential here). This might not be the best word, however, since it is especially associated with later rallying of Greek unity in opposition to foreign 'barbarians'. Even in later times there were few occasions which were so fully panhellenic that there was a strict and universal truce for their duration; and even the most venerable of those, the great gathering at the sanctuary of Zeus at Olympia, was apparently local to the

Peloponnese back in the eighth century. So perhaps the term 'inter-communal', though less attractive, might be more accurate.

There were in the Greek world many gatherings which, while less all-inclusive than panhellenic, brought together a collection of communities which had some sort of geographical, traditional, or ethnic coherence. There were dozens of these inter-community festivals, mainly annual, all held in religious sanctuaries. At most (all?) there were athletic competitions—Pindar alludes to some twenty such prize-winning occasions. At some there were also competitions in poetry and/or music; and, even where there were not, artists might still take the opportunity to perform—we know that this happened at Olympia. There were enough such festivals each year for a travelling poet to give a good few performances, and to be well rewarded. Hesiod might, for example, have performed at big gatherings at Lebadeia, Thermopylai, and Delphi without travelling very far and without getting on a boat (the big local festival at Thespiai might have started because of Hesiod rather than before him). At such festivals there were often competitions for song-poems in honour of the local deity (hymns to Apollo at Delphi etc.). When there were contests for the performance of heroic epic, there is, however, no reason to think that there was any precondition that the narrative should include local allusions. Another kind of occasion where a large gathering from a considerable geographical area converged is funeral games; and we have Hesiod's explicit evidence for poetic competitions there (see p. 28 above). Another might be a big marriage—marriages are still an occasion for the performance of epic poetry in India and other parts of the world. Funeral games and weddings, being dynastic, might have encouraged elements of local praise, but not necessarily so. It is a crucial feature of all such 'pilgrimage' gatherings that they last for several days. In ancient Greece people used to travel surprising distances to them, and would camp out in tents. There were always sacrifices and feasting, as well as athletics and music. There was no need to rise early for work; and at many modern analogous occasions the performance of poetry goes on through the night. Typically it begins at dusk and goes on into the small hours.

There is no narration of any such open inter-communal gathering in the *Iliad* or *Odyssey* (though Nestor recalls a funeral games open to all-comers at *Iliad* 23. 629 ff.). There does, however, seem to be an oblique awareness of some such occasions. For example, at *Iliad* 20. 403–5 there is a simile alluding to the cult of Helikonian Poseidon: his sanctuary was at Mykale (between Ephesos and Miletos), and a gathering of all the Ionians from Asia Minor was held there. At *Iliad* 11. 698–9 Nestor tells of racing-horses sent to compete for a tripod in Elis, the place of the Olympic games. And at *Odyssey* 6. 162–5 Odysseus tells the princess Nausikaa how he once saw an astonishing palm-tree by the altar of Apollo on

SPECTATOR SPORTS. *This representation of the spectators of a chariot-race was painted in Athens c.580, but found in Thessaly. The inscriptions reveal not only that it was painted by one Sophilos, but that it is supposed to be the Funeral Games of Patroklos, the Iliadic companion of Achilles, whose name is also inscribed to the right.*

Delos. This small rocky island in the middle of the Aegean was celebrated as the birthplace of Apollo and Artemis: their mother Leto gave birth under a palm-tree that became a sacred symbol. It was here that the Ionians held a big festival for all those supposed to be of Ionian origin, including those from the islands, Euboia and Athens.

Delos is the cue for a key piece of external evidence, which, although it cannot be firmly dated, was very probably composed within a hundred years of Homer. This is a poem of over 500 hexameters which we know as the *Homeric Hymn to Apollo* (on these 'Hymns' see pp. 55–6 below). The first half celebrates Apollo's cult on Delos (and the second half, which may not be so early in date, his cult at Delphi). 'You have many temples and cults, Apollo', goes the poem,

> But you take special delight in the island of Delos,
> where the fine-robed Ionians gather themselves together
> along with their children and their decorous wives,

> when they set up contests remembering to do you honour:
> they delight with fistfights and with patterned dance and poetry.
> Anyone coming upon the Ionians gathered there
> might believe them to be unageing, undying gods;
> he would see all their grace, and feel a deep delight
> at the sight of such men and their fine-figured wives,
> and their swift ships and all their splendid goods.
>
> (ll. 146–55)

Here is the right kind of occasion, drawn from evidence outside the poems, an occasion—perhaps significantly?—unlike any within the poems. It is a delightful festive gathering which lasts several days; it brings together people from various and widespread communities. It is striking that the participants are not stratified by class; and that they include women as well as men. The rituals, athletics, and dancing took place presumably during the day; it would be in keeping with the comparative evidence from other parts of the world if the performances of epic poetry occupied the evenings and nights.

We can roughly calculate from experiments and comparisons that the *Iliad* and *Odyssey* would each take something between fifteen and twenty-five hours to perform in their entirety. The *Odyssey* falls very distinctly into two halves. The first part which has ranged across time and place and across 'levels of reality' ends at 13. 92, with Odysseus asleep on the Phaeacians' boat: from 13. 93 onwards the poem is set almost entirely on Ithake, and its events take up only six days. This could all be performed over two nights, with some intervals of course. Analogously the *Iliad* would need three nights. The first major internal division comes (according to me, at least) at the end of book 9 with the failure to mend the great quarrel of book 1. The other comes at the end of the great central day of the narrative which stretches all the way from the beginning of book 11 to midway through book 18, probably when Thetis arrives on Olympos at 18. 369.

A big occasion on the Delos model would, unlike the *Odyssey* model, have provided an audience in a tolerant communally spirited mood. This would have given some poets the opportunity and the impetus to grow their poems from shorter lays of one or two hours long into monumental epics. Of course the poets (including Homer) may well have performed shorter poems for other occasions; they may well have sung sometimes at the feasts of lords and lordlings. But that is not how the *Iliad* and *Odyssey*, with their enormous scale and scope and internal complexity, came into existence. The primary, formative audiences, those who participated in the symbiosis that produced our two great epics, were not the commissioners of extracts and episodes, but participants in longer, more open occasions.

There is a problem in this reconstruction, however, though it is not, I think, insuperable. It is clear that the events at the big inter-communal occasions were competitive. How could there be a competition between epics the length of the *Iliad*? Well, if such a festival lasted six days, there would still be time for two *Iliad*-length or three *Odyssey*-length poems. Or perhaps most poets were content with just one evening/night for their poems? Perhaps each poet would tailor the length of his poem to his assessment of the audience's capacity; and maybe only very few poems grew to such a great length as our two. We have no evidence of other Greek oral epics as long as the *Iliad* and *Odyssey*, though it is true that poems as long and even longer have been reported from various parts of the modern world.

The people who went to these festivals for several days will have tended to be the better-off in their communities: note how the *Homeric Hymn* emphasizes the Ionian pilgrims' fine life-style. So this is not really a 'peasant' audience, nor is it like the menfolk-in-the-coffee-house who are found listening to some modern oral traditions. But they are still very different from the power-élite of the *Odyssey*-model. The occasion of the Delos-model is open rather than closed, inclusive rather than exclusive, communal rather than entrenched, various rather than homogeneous. It is also the archetype for the open-air audience, as opposed to the indoor audience, a distinction which will run through later Greek literature.

We have seen how those who believe in an élite aristocratic audience claim to find suitable assumptions and values reflected within the poems. So any search for internal reflections of this wider 'Delos-type' audience needs to be aware of its methodological insecurity. Nonetheless it is interesting to find it argued recently that both the housing and the diet of the heroes in Homer show no acquaintance with the actualities of the 'upper-class' life-style in the eighth century (let alone in Mycenaean times): it is, a 'bottom-up' view of grand living. I would also draw attention to the similes, which, as is obvious, contain many scenes of 'everyday life'.

The long and unpredictable similes (four times as many in the *Iliad* as in the *Odyssey*) have always been a favourite and much-imitated feature of Homeric poetry. Two characteristic examples. The Trojans, elated by their success the previous day are camping the night out in the plain:

> As on a moonlit night the stars blaze out most brightly
> in the heaven above, when the air stands still without wind,
> and the shapes of the slopes and the mountain-tops and trees
> are silhouetted clearly, and an infinity of air is unfurled;
> each star is distinct —and a glad feeling fills the shepherd's soul.
> So many blazed the watchfires which the Trojans had lit
> outside Troy, in between the ships and the rippling Xanthos.
>
> (*Iliad* 8. 555–61)

(Imagine this delivered to an audience sitting out under the stars!) Second, in the *Odyssey*, when Odysseus has been swimming desperately for two days and nights, he glimpses land from the crest of a big wave:

> As welcome as would be the first signs of reviving life
> to a family whose father has lain suffering from fever,
> weeks wasting away, and loathed death has brushed by him,
> yet finally—welcome the gods free him from disease,
> so welcome the woods and land seemed to Odysseus.
> (*Odyssey* 5. 394–8)

(At 23. 233–40, when Penelope at last has Odysseus restored to her, it is as welcome to land to shipwrecked sailors.)

The similes, like the Delos audience are various and inclusive, and are open rather than closed. First, they are not drawn from the world of *the* audience, but of almost any audience of almost any time or place. Very few are set in a particular locality, scarcely any in a particular era; and remarkably few are specific to any particular culture. This is essential to their fresh appeal. Secondly, the subject-matter of the similes is usually in distinct contrast with the surrounding narrative: they make vivid and intensify by means of difference no less than similarity. What the similes do for the audience is to make the narrative more vivid by drawing them into it through a picture that is different from the world of the poem, while being familiar (or at least not alien) to their own world. This mirrors in miniature the way that the whole world of the poem is simultaneously very different from the audiences' world, and yet also powerfully, spellbindingly similar. A few similes draw on the gods, and a few on the world of the very rich (an ivory ornament, a team of prize-winning horses), and a very few on the world of warfare; but the great majority draw on a peacetime 'ordinary' world of crafts, seafaring, weather, animals, agriculture, herding. It is not always a happy world—it includes hard labour, dangerous natural phenomena, marauding lions—but it is also often constructive, fruitful, and intensely beautiful.

A social-historical context

I have tried to avoid arguing from external history, if only because this is still an era of prehistory: we simply do not have the kind of detail and precision that would validate such an approach. On the other hand, it should now be worth the attempt to relate the reconstruction that has been built up of Homer's primary audiences at inter-communal festivals to what can reasonably be said about the social and political history of the time. Cramming a lot of history into a small nutshell is bound to involve over-simplifications, of course, but what kind of thing was going on in the Greek world in the decades on either side of 700 BCE?

The era of Homer and Hesiod was even more a time of radical changes than most (though it is true that in many ways the Greek world was in a state of perpetual revolution from about 800 BCE for the next 500 years and more). There was at this stage, however, an exceptional widening of horizons in every political and cultural sense—in some ways, the pottery decoration of 650 set beside that of 750 makes the point at a glance. Very generally and roughly

HUMANS AS PATTERNS. This huge bowl (well over 1 m. high), made to be a tomb-marker, typifies the geometric style of painting c.750 BCE. It was found at Athens, which specialized in this kind of art-work. Mourners are grouped round the funeral of a body carried on a chariot.

NEW MOVEMENT. This band from a jug-like vessel made in Corinth c.650 BCE demonstrates the great change in techniques of representation of movement and of the human figure from the geometric style of 100 years earlier. The battle in massed ranks might suggest the new hoplite warfare, and the aulos *accompaniment is reminiscent of the war poetry of Tyrtaios (see pp. 74–5).*

speaking, Greece in 750 BCE consisted of communities which were accreted round leaders, the powerful dynasties, the *basilees* who traditionally dominated power, wealth, and the sense of local identity. This is pretty much the world of Hesiod's *Works and Days*, though he registers protests. By 650 BCE a new, larger power-base had emerged, a citizenry—far from democratic, but with a developing sense of shared power and community. This was related to (though not simply caused by) a radical change in military practice. Instead of a few aristocratic champions with a mass of retainers, there developed co-ordinated ranks of those who could afford to be heavily armed in bronze, the hoplites. Power accompanied the indispensability of each hoplite to the security of the community. At the same time communities structured themselves into conurbations with surrounding agricultural areas, the city-state or polis of classical times. Laws began to be codified for the whole area; and, thanks to the new technology of inscription, they were recorded on stone or other imperishable material, beginning the transition to a time when legislation no longer rested in the minds of the powerful few. The civic centre (the agora) conglomerated, with suitable buildings and temples. The religious dimension of the polis was also expressed in local hero-cults (the cult of the powerful dead) and in major sanctuaries with competitive festivals, often located out in the countryside.

This was also generally an era of growth in population and prosperity. Hand in hand with this went the sending out of new settlements all over the Mediterranean world (*apoikiai*, usually called 'colonies', but the word brings the wrong baggage). This important change led both to an increase in mobility, trade, and travel, and to a new awareness of what it is that binds scattered communities together. This relates to the way that certain mainland cult-centres became of the first importance. The Olympic games developed from a gathering for Peloponnesians to an occasion open to all Greeks, including those from the coasts of what are now, for example, Ukraine, Libya, and France, let alone Turkey, Cyprus, Sicily, and Italy. And the oracle at Delphi gained a special authority as an authorizer of these overseas settlements—and as the recipient of thank-offerings for display. Archaeology suggests that this was the very period of the first growth of the big inter-communal festivals (avoiding the term 'panhellenic'—see p. 41 above). Olympia explodes in activity in the mid-eighth century; Delphi and Delos two or three decades later; and many of the other main sanctuaries leave traces of substantial development around 700 BCE.

People are likely to have brought to these festivals at this period a new sense of civic polis-identity, combined with a co-operative yet competitive interaction with the other participant communities. News and ideas about politics, trade, and travel will have been exchanged. Temporarily away from the constraints and power-structures of their home communities, they will have had the opportunity to discuss and think about political, social, and cultural issues. We have here, in fact, the germ of that extraordinary combination of shared Hellenism with fierce inter-city conflict which is so characteristic of the great age of ancient Greece. The common religion and culture cut across political and military boundaries to a remarkable extent. Whatever their enmities, they share the gods, the athletics, the architecture, and the art. And they share poetry. It is here that the non-local amalgam of the 'dialect' of hexameter poetry becomes really important. And this is, I would claim, the context for the absence of 'localizations' in Homer: the poems do not give prestige and advantages to some participants over others. This may be less true of Hesiod, with his Boiotian colouring, but even his poetry is largely 'unpartisan'.

And 'ideology'? I have argued that the poems do not bolster the *basilees*: on the other hand, they do not advocate their overthrow either. The 'people' (*laos*) in Homer are important—more important than is usually recognized—but there is no message that they should have more power. The poems seem to emerge, rather, as a kind of opener of discussion, an invitation to think about and to scrutinize the structures and allocations of power and of respect. Thus, while everyone within the poems agrees that honour—the key Greek word is *time*—should be given where honour is due, they do not agree on the criteria for its allocation. So while Homer does not positively advocate any particular kind of political change, this is surely not the poetry of political conservatism or retrenchment either. It is part and parcel of an era of radically widening horizons; and it is a catalyst to change.

Setting Homer on the classical pedestal

It is a historical fact that the *Iliad* and *Odyssey* got written down. At the time of the great Alexandrian editors (see pp. 234–5 below) many cities throughout the Greek world had their own transcriptions, all slightly different. I have already argued that the poems were not created through writing, let alone for reading. It still remains a real possibility that they were dictated by the poet himself to an expert in the new craft of Phoenician-type inscribing. Another possibility is that a disciple or disciples learned the poems by heart, and that they were handed down orally until the technique of writing and the supply of papyrus were more developed. There was on the island of Chios a guild of Homer experts who called themselves the 'Descendants of Homer' (*Homeridai*). Perhaps the early Homeridai tried to act as human tape-recorders and to preserve the poems as close as they could to word perfect? It is widely objected that over the course of 100 years or more the poems would have become inevitably more and more altered, consciously or unconsciously; and it is true that most oral performers who claim that they are repeating a poem word for word are in fact making considerable changes. The 'oral transmission' theory (which I am inclined to believe myself) has to suppose either that the disciples of Homer had genuine aspirations to achieve perfect recording, or that the poems went on being developed, to a greater or lesser extent, during the first generation of their 'recording'.

Whichever of these models is right, dictation or oral transmission—and there do not seem to be any serious alternatives—it has been generally (generally, but not universally) agreed in recent times that the poems which we have are pretty close to those created by Homer, along with his audiences, in about 700 BCE. We know from the local city-transcriptions and from early papyri (third-century BCE) that there were a lot of small variations—a couple of lines added in one, a line missing in another and so on—but by before 500 BCE it is highly likely that the text was already fixed much as we have it. One reason for supposing that this version was close to Homer's version is that the poems we have are so highly crafted, and so highly integrated both on a large and a small scale—they must go back to a high point of creative symbiosis. This is admittedly an aesthetic claim, and it used to be much disputed, especially in the nineteenth century; but it is now widely agreed. The two most significant exceptions are raised in the next paragraph. The other main reason why most experts believe that the texts were not pervasively developed or changed in the 200 or so years between 700 and 500 is that there is so much in the poems which comes from the eighth century in terms of material objects, social world, and linguistic features, and so little (merely an occasional line) which betrays any sign of coming from after, say 660 BCE.

There are two major exceptions, one in each poem, to the claim that the texts which were more or less fixed by 500 BCE went back to Homer's versions. The 579-block of the *Iliad* which we know as book 10, or the *Doloneia,* is full of differences of language and tone from the rest of the poem. And, while it has been made to fit its slot in the *Iliad,* the rest of the poem makes no reference to it whatsoever. If it was added to Homer's *Iliad,* that must have been done early in the transmission and by a powerful authority; and an ancient tradition said it was added by the sixth-century ruler of Athens, Peisistratos. But this may well be only a reflection of the later cultural authority of Athens: the Homeridai are more likely to have been responsible. The other big problem, which is the ending of the *Odyssey,* is quite different. While some have traced the starting-point of their reservations and disappointments some 620 lines back from the end, as soon as Odysseus and Penelope are finally reunited in bed, there is much that is important and integral in the first half of book 24. It is in the last 200 lines, where the relatives of the dead suitors confront Odysseus, that are full of ever-increasing staggerings in both language and narrative techniques. The theory that something went wrong with the actual original recording, for example that the poet's health deteriorated, seems a real possibility. In any case, the widespread agreement among experts that these two major problems are on a different level and scale from any others is some indication of how the rest has a consistently high aesthetic quality.

Even supposing that the *Iliad* and *Odyssey* were set down in writing back in the poet's lifetime(s), somewhere not long before or after 700 BCE, there is no reason to think that they were ever appreciated by being read as opposed to being performed for at least 200 years after that. The text existed for learning from and for checking, not for 'receiving'. There seems to have been, however, an important division in the reception of Homer somewhere in between 700 and 500 BCE, as has been brought out by Walter Burkert. Before about 600 there

ILIADIC INSPIRATION. *This florid plate, painted c.600 probably in Rhodes, shows a battle scene which seems to be directly inspired by the* Iliad *(though this has been disputed). The two warriors are labelled Menelaos and Hektor and they are fighting over the corpse of Euphorbos. This particular dual is narrated in book 17 of the* Iliad.

is not one certain allusion to Homer in another poet; there are plenty of references to epic, to its values and diction as well as its stories, but not specifically to Homer. It is similar with the visual arts: while there are many seventh-century representations of heroic episodes, none points unequivocally to a telling in Homer—though there is an outcrop of vase-paintings of the blinding of the Cyclops Polyphemos in the mid-seventh century, which is arguably inspired by our *Odyssey*. In other words, our two epics do not seem to have stood out in the seventh century. The first clearly Homer-inspired visual art in my view (though disputed) is a plate, probably painted on Rhodes in *c*.600 BCE, which shows a precise moment at *Iliad* 17. 106 ff.

The Delos half of the *Homeric Hymn to Apollo* (see p. 43 above) may well date from about the same time as this, or not long after. Near the end of this the poet addresses the young women of Delos who dance a special, famous dance to Apollo, and tells them that if anyone ever asks them which performer they take to be the best of those who visit Delos,

> . . . you should all answer firmly for me:
> 'he is the blind man, his home is [*oikei*] in craggy Chios;
> and his poetry shall all stand as the finest for future times.'
> (ll. 169–73)

Either the poet is pretending to be Homer (for this poem is certainly not by the poet of the *Iliad* or *Odyssey*); or Homer still 'lives' in Chios through the skills of the Homeridai; or, as Burkert has proposed, the verb *oikei* is past and means 'his home used to be', in which case we have a performer of Homer advertising his master-poet. Whatever the right explanation, we have here the earliest trace of what became the 'Homer Myth', a collection of stories, with variations, which grew up around the 'biography' of the shadowy Poet himself. The blindness, for example, which was most likely derived from the blind Demodokos in the *Odyssey*, and the home-base on Chios, which cannot be derived from the poems, are central features of this Myth. Another, that he died on the island of Ios after failing to solve a riddle posed by some boys (the answer was 'lice'!) was already current by the time of Herakleitos in about 500 BCE.

By 500 BCE the situation is completely different from 100 years earlier. Homer is by then *the* Poet, the father-figure of Greek culture, the staple of basic education. Simonides can say

> The poet from Chios said one thing which is the most beautiful:
> 'Like the generation of leaves, such is that of men also'

and everyone knows that he is alluding to *Iliad* 6. 146. Allusions to Homer in the visual arts, as well as in poetry, have by now become common, even standard. The proto-philosophers (or 'performers of wisdom'—see pp. 156 ff., below) attack Homer in the process of setting themselves up as alternative authorities. 'From the beginning following Homer, because they have all learned . . .' began an attack by Xenophanes; Herakleitos complains: 'Homer deserves to be thrown out of the public contests and given a beating' (presumably meaning recitals of Homer at contests). By the early fifth century we begin to get proto-scholars defending Homer against such attacks, especially by allegorizing his stories ('Achilles represents the sun, Hektor the moon . . .' to give a wild but early example).

It was probably during the sixth century, then, that competitions in the recitation of Homer and other traditional epics—as opposed to competitions in performing new poems—became established at many of the festival occasions. The performers were called 'rhapsodes' (*rhapsodoi*, probably meaning 'stitchers of song'); and their art was to be practised for another 700 years or more. Some of the leading rhapsodes were Homeridai from Chios, but they had no monopoly. They never, so far as we know, performed poems of their own, only the fixed texts of the great masters of the past; and, unlike the creative oral poets, they had no musical instrument. They could become celebrated and win good prizes, although intellectuals tended to be supercilious about them and their showmanship. It is an index of Homer's growing prestige in the mid-sixth century that when Peisistratos, the ruler of Athens, put together a special new Athenian festival to be celebrated every four years, the great Panathenaia, he included a rhapsodes' competition in the official programme. We hear disproportionately much about this Athenian competition because of the Athenian domination of our sources. It is interesting to gather, though, that only Homer—and that seems to have meant the *Iliad* and *Odyssey*—was permitted at the Panathenaia.

It is, ironically enough, Homer's greatest detractor, Plato, who gives us our best external account of an audience of Homer—though this too is liable to some distortion of course. In order to build up his kind of Philosophy (see pp. 172 ff. below) as the only true access to wisdom, Plato has to discredit other traditional claimants, including poetry, and above all The Poet. In his brief dialogue, *Ion*, he does this by having Sokrates expose the rhapsode Ion (from Ephesos) as not only stupid and conceited, but also as a passive rather than active link in a kind of magnetic chain of inspiration within which even Homer is the transmitter, not the source. In the dramatic setting of the dialogue, Ion has just won the rhapsodes' competition at the festival of Asklepios at Epidauros, and is now in Athens in the hope of winning at the Panathenaia. Sokrates establishes that Ion is in a high emotional state when he performs emotional scenes (thus fudging, as Plato always does, the distinction between the emotion of a performer and that aroused in real life):

> 'Really, Ion! Can we possibly maintain that this man you describe is in his right senses? Here he is, adorned with ornate clothing and a golden garland, and yet he is weeping amid an atmosphere of sacrifices and festival, even though he has lost nothing. Or is he frightened, while standing in the presence of over 20,000 well-disposed people, although no one is trying to rob or harm him?' (535d)

And you realize, asks Sokrates, that you produce the same effect in the spectators? 'I most certainly do', replies Ion, 'I look at them from up there on the platform, and there they are weeping and staring wildly and feeling amazement in tune with the words . . .' (535e). And he adds, with the kind of commercialism that Plato despised, that if he can make audiences cry, then he will laugh all the way to the bank, while if he makes them laugh, he can cry goodbye to his money. It is Plato's aim to discredit the experience of audience, performer, and poet alike. In the process, however, he captures the ability of Homeric poetry, well performed, to grip the attention and to move a live audience, even in Athens some 300 years after it was first made.

In the wake of Hesiod and Homer

By the time of Plato, and from then onwards, epic poetry meant the *Iliad* and the *Odyssey* far above every rival. This is clear from references in our sources, from papyri discovered in Egypt, and even school exercises. But it would be quite wrong to suppose that back in the seventh century Homer already overshadowed the whole genre. There were other epics all along, and some of them must have been popular in their time. When Hesiod, going through the five ages of mankind, tells of the bronze age of heroes, he implies that two great wars dominated:

> Foul war and fearful fighting killed them off,
> some around seven-gated Thebes, in the land of Kadmos,
> as they fought over the flocks of Oedipus,
> while it drew others in ships over the great gulf
> of the sea to Troy for the sake of fair Helen.
> (*W&D* 161–5)

But, both before Homer and after, oral poetry must have told all sorts of other epic narratives as well as those of Thebes and Troy, tales about the Argonauts, for example, Herakles, Meleagros, and the rest. The visual arts in the seventh century, and to a considerable extent in the sixth and fifth as well, show that many other heroic stories besides Homer's were well known. Quite a few texts of these survived to reach the great Library at Alexandria in the third century BCE; but we now have only scraps and fragments, and all too little information about them.

Some of the epics which were recorded got attached to the name of Homer, although few were seriously considered as really his work. Aristotle comments on how inferior they are to the *Iliad* and *Odyssey* in their structure and narrative technique; and the fragments we have appear to confirm this. A large group of these epics were later set in a kind of sequence which was known as the *Kyklos* (or *Cycle*), running from the beginning of the world down to the end of the age of heroes. Some were clearly designed to fit round the *Iliad* and *Odyssey*: the *Aithiopis* even began with the last line of the *Iliad*—'So they buried Hektor; and the Amazon princess arrived . . .'. But, even if they were not brilliantly told, they provided a rich repertory of good stories for later visual arts and for literature, especially tragedy.

Yet other hexameter poems got connected with the name of Hesiod. The most interesting, usually known as *The Catalogue of Women*, was far more widely read in antiquity than the *Kyklos*, as is shown by finds on papyrus. It told of the dynasties that were founded by gods' mating with mortal women, and was known, from the recurrent transitional phrase *e hoie,* meaning 'or like the woman who . . .', as the (plural) *Ehoiai*. It purported to continue the *Theogony*, but was probably composed piecemeal as late as the sixth century. We happen to have preserved some 480 lines of martial epic which were incorporated in the *Ehoiai*, which tell of the battle between the Theban Herakles and the Thessalian Kyknos. The piece is known as the *Shield* because of its long description of Herakles' shield (like that of Achilles in *Iliad* 18). It hardly seems subjective to say that this is dreary doggerel; and, if it is at all typical of sixth-century epic, it accentuates the quality of Homer.

As well as poetry that told of the feats of great men, there was also always poetry about the gods, like the *Theogony* or like the *Battle of the Gods and Titans* in the *Kyklos*. And there was poetry which included both, like the *Ehoiai*. Some actual examples of 'gods-poetry' survive (a change from all these fragments!): we have a miscellaneous collection which is known as the *Homeric Hymns*. Quite a few are less than ten lines long, and are no more than an invocation; but the longer ones, which are attractive poetry in their own right, tell stories of the exploits of the particular god who is being honoured. Most are probably pretty late in date, some even later than the fifth century. But it is reckoned that the *Hymn to Hermes* (who steals the cattle of Apollo) and the *Hymn to Aphrodite* (who becomes the mother of Aineias by seducing the Trojan Anchises on Mount Ida) are relatively early. We have also already met the *Hymn to Apollo*, with its division between Delos and Delphi. Most interesting of all and perhaps earliest is the *Hymn to Demeter*, which tells of the goddess' sorrow on losing her daughter Persephone, and the ecological disaster it caused, leading on to the foundation of her cult at Eleusis near Athens.

Thoukydides (3. 104) refers to the *Hymn to Apollo* as a *prooimion*, a 'prologue' or 'overture', and the same word is used elsewhere of such 'hymns'. But it is hard to see how the longer examples, which would take the best part of an hour in performance, could have been only a 'warm-up' for something else. They might well have been performed, however, at the opening of festivals. While very different from large-scale epic, they share many of the same traditions of diction and narrative technique; and they are a warning against setting generic descriptions too narrowly.

After 500 BCE hexameter poetry is still to have a long history in Greek literature, and then in Latin. But from now on every poem was aware that it was, in varying ways, in the wake of Homer and Hesiod. Several early 'performers of wisdom' put forward their ideas in hexameters, sometimes in explicit rivalry (see pp. 161–2 below). In Hellenistic times the subject-matter of 'didactic epic' became less ambitious and more directly factual (see pp. 246 ff., below). But it was yet to find new life in two great and very different Latin descendants, Lucretius and Virgil's *Georgics* (see pp. 339 ff., 367 ff. below).

Returning to narrative poems that tell of great feats, there were plenty in between 500 BCE and Virgil's *Aeneid*, though the only significant one to survive intact is Apollonios' *Argonautika* (see pp. 241 ff. below). There are within this period two important changes away from the Homeric tradition and manner. One is a growth in overt self-consciousness. The epic, and the hexameter metre, are no longer the 'natural', unchallenged medium of poetry; they have to locate themselves in the literary scene. The other is a movement towards a more literal, geographical 'localization'. There had been, in fact, quite an early poem, traditionally attributed to Eumelos, which set out to put Corinth on the heroic epic map. In the mid-fifth-century Panyassis, a relation (uncle?) of Herodotos, composed an epic about Herakles, which paid special attention to his adventures over in Asia Minor. Antimachos, soon after 400 BCE, was very aware of how his native Kolophon was in the heartland of Homer country. He was a quasi-professional Homer expert who worked his scholarship into his poetry, anticipating the practices of the Alexandrian era.

To conclude with, there is a five-line fragment from the later fifth century which epitomizes the great change from the open unselfconsciousness of performed epic to a written text which is searching for metaphors to express its metaliterary self-location. This is by Choirilos of Samos, from an epic about the mythical origins of the Persians, and tracing them down to the great Persian Wars:

> Ah, happy he who in that era was expert in poetry,
> a servant of the Muses, when the meadow was still unscythed.
> But now when everything has been apportioned out,
> and the crafts all have their own spheres, we are left behind,
> like the last off the starting-grid. And though
> I glance all round, I can not light on any new chariot to harness.

2 The strangeness of 'song culture': Archaic Greek poetry

LESLIE KURKE

. . . As I know how to lead off the lovely choral strain of Lord Dionysos,
The dithyramb, when my brains are blitzed with wine.

(Archilochos)

Let the lyre sound its holy strain, and the reed pipe (*aulos*),
And let us drink, when we have gratified the gods with libations,
Saying things full of grace to each other,
And fearing not at all the war of the Medes.

(Theognis)

I breakfasted, having broken off a bit of slender honey cake,
And drained my cup of wine. And now I delicately pluck the lovely Eastern lyre,
Celebrating the festivity (*komos*) with a dear and dainty girl.

(Anakreon)

O Mistress Muse, our mother, I pray you,
In the holy month of Nemea
Come to the hospitable Dorian island of Aigina, for beside the water of
Asopos wait young men, craftsmen of honey-sounding celebrations (*komoi*),
longing for your voice. And different achievements thirst for different things,
but athletic victory most loves song . . .

(Pindar, *Nemean* 3. 1–7)

These diverse snippets of poetry (ranging from the mid-seventh to the early fifth century BCE) evoke for us the strange world of early Greek 'song culture', in

The following standard abbreviations are used in this chapter: *PLF* = E. Lobel and D. L. Page (eds.), *Poetarum Lesbiorum Fragmenta* (Oxford, 1955); *PMG* = D. L. Page (ed.), *Poetae Melici Graeci* (Oxford, 1962); *SLG* = D. L. Page (ed.), *Supplementum Lyricis Graecis* (Oxford, 1974); W, W^2 = M. L. West (ed.), *Iambi et Elegi Graeci*, 2 vols. (2nd edn. Oxford, 1989–92; W^2 = 2nd edn. specifically).

which sung and recited verse were an integral part of daily life. In this world, song was only imaginable as part of live performance in a particular context, where it forged a powerful bond between singer/speaker and listening audience. Many of the elements of this living song culture (which endured at least until the end of the fifth century) had already been lost or forgotten by the time Greek scholars of the Hellenistic Period organized definitive editions of the early poets, so that we cannot entirely rely on their categorizations and genre distinctions. Instead, we must attempt to reconstruct an older system from what we know of the social context, scattered reports about performance, and the internal evidence of the poems themselves. Modern scholars have been aided in this endeavour by the discovery and publication of substantial papyrus finds in this century: perhaps for more than any other domain of Greek literature, the understanding of early Greek poetry has undergone a revolution as a result of such papyrus finds. From the publication of substantial texts around the turn of the last century (e.g. Alkman's Partheneia and Bakchylides) to the appearance of fragments of Simonides' Elegy on the Battle of Plataia in 1992, papyri have vastly increased our corpus of lyric texts and thereby allowed us to piece together an alien system of poetry in performance. Given the scanty and fragmentary nature of the remains, any reconstruction must be tentative and hypothetical; yet it seems worth the effort of historical imagination to try to hear again the distant strains of early Greek song culture (what is conventionally—and loosely—designated 'Greek lyric poetry'). In this effort, we must avoid two misconceptions. First, that the 'age of lyric' succeeded the 'age of epic' as an organic development of the Greek spirit (to be succeeded in turn by the Hegelian 'synthesis' of tragedy). Second, a more serious misconception: we cannot expect ancient Greek lyric to conform to our modern assumptions of what lyric should be. In the modern era, lyric has become the form of poetry *par excellence*, the most private and intense expression of emotion by a speaking subject, often linked to the confessional 'I' and valued for the authenticity of feeling expressed. Because Greek lyric poets are found 'speaking' for the first time (almost) in the first person in their texts, there is a great temptation to assimilate them to modern notions of lyric subjectivity. Thus, it is often said that with archaic Greek poetry, the individual 'I' first emerges onto the stage of history, with lyric subjectivity inexorably succeeding the objective form of epic as the Greek spirit develops. Both of these claims (lyric as the invention of the self, and the organic development from epic to lyric) are romanticizing modern projections that fail to take account of the cultural specificity and difference of ancient Greek poetry.

The diachronic development from epic to lyric is, in a sense, a mirage produced by certain technological developments in ancient Greek culture. For the study of comparative metrics reveals certain lyric metres to be of immemorial antiquity (songs the Greeks were singing before they were Greeks), while the Homeric poems also provide representations of embedded lyric performances (harvest song, wedding song, paian to Apollo, *threnos* or mourning song). Thus, epic and lyric must have coexisted throughout the entire prehistory of Greek literature. What suddenly enabled the long-term survival of lyric in the period under discussion was, paradoxically, the same technological development that ultimately ended the living oral tradition of epic composition-in-performance: the invention of writing. It was, then, an accident of technology and not the necessary development of the Greek spirit that caused lyric to 'succeed' epic in the literary remains.

But if lyric poetry depended on the advent of writing to survive, it was very much an oral medium for the whole period under discussion (and this brings us to our second misconception). Greece down through the fifth century has aptly been described as a 'song culture', in which everyone sang and knew songs, and there was a highly elaborated system of songs for different occasions. In such a culture, all song-making and performance are 'embedded'—that is, intended for performance in particular public (often ritualized) contexts. Such 'embedding' makes ancient lyric radically different from our modern notion of lyric as the personal outpourings of a poet, written in private to be read in private by individual consumers. According to John Stuart Mill's familiar dictum, in the modern era eloquence is meant to be heard; poetry overheard. Greek lyric, in contrast, was always intended to be heard, not overheard.

What then was the purpose of such poetry in performance? Beyond whatever particular purpose it performed (for example, prayer to a god, celebration of marriage, mourning at a funeral), embedded song served in general as a means of socialization and cultural education in the broadest sense. In a largely oral culture, with no institutionalized schools and only minimal state structure and intervention, poetry in performance was a vital way of transmitting to each individual their store of cultural knowledge, the values to be espoused, their proper level of expectations and aspirations, and their social roles. That is to say, embedded poetry was one medium (along with, for example, family, military service, and forms of commensality) for constructing individuals as social subjects. This formative process applied to both the singers and the audience of early Greek poetry, since, throughout most of this period, the singers would have been non-professionals and members of the same community as their listeners, whether that community be the entire city or a small group of 'companions' at the symposium.

Indeed, it seems likely, given the cultural work of socialization performed by poetry in context, that the particular formation of the Greek poetic system was linked to and partly conditioned by the rise and development of the polis in this same period. The polis, or city-state, emerged as the characteristic structure of Greek community some time in the eighth or seventh centuries (cf. Ch 1, pp. 47–9). The polis was not just a built town, but the indissoluble union of city and territory (*chora*), in which the inhabitants felt themselves to be fellow 'citizens'. The constitution of the polis depended crucially on the abstraction of law and office from individuals and the notion that all citizens (however the citizen franchise might be defined) should participate in communal decision-making. In these terms, the polis is more properly understood as 'state' than 'city', and the eighth to sixth centuries as the critical period of Greek state formation.

In this same period, we find a proliferation of what appear to be new poetic genres and occasions. Thus, for example, in addition to paian, wedding song, and *threnos* (already evident in the Homeric poems), such genres as partheneion ('maiden song'), dithyramb (a cult song for Dionysos), and epinikion (a song celebrating athletic victory) developed, and all three in different ways served the interests of the civic community (as we shall see). Other genres of poetry seem to have taken their distinctive form in this period, if not *in the service of* the polis community, then *in reaction to* it. Because of this mutually informing relation of polis structure and poetic system, the remains of archaic lyric (scanty though they are) provide us with a precious view of competing values and ideologies in the period of Greek state formation (on which more below).

These two facets of early Greek poetry—its performed and performative nature within a living 'song culture'—have an important corollary: that we cannot take the 'I' of Greek lyric to be the biographical poet. There is, first, the evidence of other 'song cultures' around the world, in which the singer often adopts a persona well known to other members of the community, though he or she sings in the first person. We encounter precisely this phenomenon in Greek poetry when Aristotle mentions offhand that two first-person poems of Archilochos of which we have fragments were in fact spoken in the persona of 'Charon the carpenter' and 'a father speaking to his daughter' respectively (Archilochos, W^2 frr. 19, 122). Since we do not possess the whole of either poem, we cannot know whether the speakers were explicitly named, but without Aristotle's *obiter dicta*, we might have been tempted to take the speaker of both poems as the historical Archilochos himself. A similar situation pertains to certain first-person fragments of Alkaios and Anakreon which happen to contain words with feminine endings to characterize their speakers (Alkaios, *PLF* fr. 10B; Anakreon, *PMG* frr. 385, 432). These poems, because they cross gender lines, clearly exemplify instances of the poet speaking in the persona of another, but they should make us cautious about the rest of the poetic production from this period. How often did the poets of Greek iambic, elegy, and melic (see below for these terms) speak in a fictive persona, which, because it was gendered male, is otherwise unmarked in our texts?

The second aspect (what I have referred to briefly as the 'performative' nature of Greek poetry—its power to form singers and audience alike) provides even more compelling arguments for scepticism about the lyric 'I'. If comparative evidence shows us that the poet's 'I' *can* be a fictive persona, the consideration of the cultural work of poetry in performance suggests that in a sense it *must* be. For the poet's speaking 'I' must always have served the needs of genre and occasion, constituted so as to make the most compelling appeal to the audience while achieving the needs for which the poem was being performed.

Indeed, we should probably think of different poets or poetic names, at least in the first half of the period under discussion, not so much as authors but as traditional authorities, personae to be occupied by any composer/singer who wanted to speak from that ideological place. Thus, for example, the 'Theognidea' (a collection of brief elegiac poems running to about 1,400 lines) has traditionally been taken to contain an authentic core of poems by a historical 'Theognis', around which has accreted the detritus of generations of lesser poets imitating him. Instead of thus dissecting the corpus, we might think of 'Theognis' as the name for a particular ideological position—a disgruntled and alienated aristocrat inveighing against the evil developments in his polis to an audience of fellow symposiasts. Such a model would account for the fact that references to historical events in the Theognidean corpus seem to range from the late seventh century (the probable date of the tyrant Theagenes) to the Persian invasion of 480 BCE, as well as for the occurrence of poems otherwise attributed to Solon, Tyrtaios, and other elegists in the Theognidea. That is, we should perhaps imagine an ongoing process of composition and performance as 'Theognis', extending over two centuries and many parts of the Greek world. An even clearer example of this kind of ongoing composition in a persona is provided by the Anakreontic corpus. This light playful sympotic verse continued to be composed in the persona of Anakreon for many centuries, and it is often hard to tell where 'Anakreon' ended and the Anakreontics began.

This model of authority in place of authorship has two implications in turn. First, questions of authenticity—is this poem by the 'real' Theognis or Anakreon?—are not necessarily appropriate. Such questions are the product of a literate age, an age of books, and may well be alien to a living song culture. Second, we cannot necessarily reconstruct individual poets' biographies from their work, since they were always speaking in a persona suited to the generic occasion and calculated to make an appeal to the audience. Thus it may be that the historical Archilochos was a mercenary, that the historical Hipponax had problems with impotence, and that the historical Anakreon loved wine and boys, but we cannot safely assume these 'facts' based on their poetic production.

It should also be acknowledged that over the course of this period a shift took place from traditional authority to authorship, a shift that corresponded to a change in the conditions of production of lyric poetry. One contributing factor in this shift may have been the rise throughout the Greek world of the monarchical rulers conventionally known as tyrants. The term 'tyrant' was originally a neutral one, borrowed from Lydia to designate any sole ruler whose authority was not hereditary or constitutionally sanctioned. In the late seventh century, such tyrants appeared in Corinth, Sikyon, Megara, and Mytilene, while the sixth century saw tyrannic regimes established in Athens, Samos, and many of the Ionian cities. By the early fifth century, the 'age of tyrants' had largely passed for most of the Greek world, but the great warlords of Sicily were still founding their dynasties in the West. Historians debate the causes and effects of this wave of tyrannies, but one thing is certain: the tyrants emerged on the stage of history as the first distinctive individuals, partly because they fostered their fame and renown through the patronage of poetry. Thus, in the first 100 years of the period 650–450 BCE, poets were not professionalized, and they generally lived and worked in their own communities (for example, Archilochos, Hipponax, Kallinos, Tyrtaios, Solon, Stesichoros, Sappho, Alkaios). This began to change in the second half of the sixth century, when poets like Ibykos and Anakreon travelled abroad to join the court of Polykrates, tyrant of Samos. Ibykos and Anakreon were intermediate figures, not fully professionalized, nor yet said 'to work for pay', but affiliated with a powerful tyrant in a patronage relationship. With Simonides in the next generation, this process of poetic professionalization was completed. Simonides, we are told, was the first to accept poetic commissions from individuals 'for a fee', and he appears to have travelled all over the Greek world, wherever his various commissions took him. The lyric poets of the next generation, Pindar and Bakchylides, were fully professionalized itinerant craftsmen. Such professionalization radically altered the relation of the poet to tradition and to his audience, for it put a premium on his special, individual poetic skill (*sophia*). Because patrons were paying for the particular artistry of Simonides, Pindar, or Bakchylides, these poets emerged from the mists of tradition as the first true authors (though even in this case, Simonides remained a magnet for a whole tradition of terse and witty epigrams attributed to him throughout antiquity, so that we might say that he was both an author and an authority).

Taxonomies of song in context

In short, ancient Greek song culture was radically different from anything our modern notions about lyric poetry might lead us to expect. How, then, can we come to understand the highly elaborated system of Greek genre and performance on its own terms? Let us imagine we are anthropologists, visitors to an alien culture attempting to construct a taxonomy of native categories and performance genres.

CHART. Genres of Greek poetry and their performance contexts

	Symposium	Public Sphere
Iamboi (recited)	?	At festivals (?) Archilochos, Hipponax Semonides, Solon
Elegy (recited or sung to *aulos*) [Ionic colouring]	Brief erotic, advice poetry Mimnermos, Kallinos, Theognis, Simonides	Historical Narrative Military exhortation Tyrtaios, Solon, Simonides
Melic (sung to lyre)	Monody [local dialects] Sappho, Alkaios, Ibykos, Anakreon	Choral/Public [Doric colouring] Alkman, [Stesichoros], Simonides, Pindar, Bakchylides

Within the Greek system, genre correlated with occasion and performance context, as well as with formal features. We may think of these as two axes of differentiation (see Chart). Perhaps the most significant contexts for performance were (*a*) the small group of the symposium and (*b*) the public sphere of the city. The opposition of these two only approximately corresponds to our 'private vs. public' (since, in a sense, 'private' was an inconceivable category for the Greeks), but these terms may be helpful in conceptualizing the difference.

In the archaic period, the symposium (Greek: *symposion*) that followed the communal meal came to be the main focus of attention and ritual elaboration for the privileged élite. At the same time, early in the archaic period, the Greeks adapted from the East the custom of reclining at banquet and symposium. This shift in banqueting posture crucially limited the number of people who could participate together in a symposium at a private house. In a normal house, the

HAPPY HOUR. A typical scene of a well-advanced symposion with music decorates the outside of this mid-fifth-century Athenian wine cup. The inebriated men are by now dancing to the accompaniment of the aulos *(double reed pipe), played by a professional woman.*

andron or dining-room (so called because the symposium was an exclusively male activity, forbidden to respectable women) could accommodate no more than seven to nine couches, so that the sympotic group was limited to fourteen to twenty-seven participants (two to three to a couch). Thus, in contrast to the Homeric representation of large groups of warriors eating together, the archaic period saw the development of small, tightly knit bands of 'companions' (*hetairoi*) who drank together.

As we know from literary remains and the evidence of vase-painting, there was a whole culture of the symposium. This generally included the consumption of wine mixed with water under the direction of a symposiarch or 'master of revels'; wearing of crowns and perfumes for all the symposiasts; the ready availability of sex with boys or hired women; drinking games like *kottabos* (a kind of ancient 'beer-pong'); and the *komos* or drunken rout with which the party often ended, when the revellers would spill out of the house and careen through the streets with torches, singing and dancing. We get a clear idea of the ancient conception of the potential progress of a symposium from a fragment of a fourth-century comic poet, who puts into the mouth of Dionysos the sequence of 'kraters' or large bowls of wine and water mixed and consumed by the revellers:

> Three kraters alone do I mix
> for those who have good sense; one belonging to health,
> which they consume first; the second belonging to
> love and pleasure; the third belonging to sleep,
> which, when they have drained, wise guests
> go home. But the fourth is not still
> ours, but belongs to hybris; and the fifth to shouting;
> and the sixth to drunken revels (*komoi*); and the seventh to black eyes;
> and the eighth to the policeman and the ninth to biliousness;
> and the tenth to madness and the throwing of furniture . . .
>
> (Euboulos fr. 93, in R. Kassel and C. Austin (eds.),
> *Poetae Comici Graeci*, vol. v (Berlin, 1986))

Given the very real possibility that the symposium could degenerate into complete drunkenness and violence, the Greeks also established an elaborate code of sympotic etiquette, much of it purveyed in poetry performed in this context. This was one particular way in which song served an educative function within the symposium, but we should not limit its role to that. The élite symposium seemed to be most of all a play-space, exempt from the larger civic order, in which its participants could safely try on different identities and social roles. Through sympotic song, the revellers could momentarily mime a woman or a slave or a barbarian, even as such poetry also taught them how to be proper aristocratic *hetairoi*. The symposium as a space for role-playing and fantasy is perhaps best emblematized by the so-called 'eye-cups', ancient drinking vessels with large eyes painted on their exterior. When the drinker raised his cup to drain it, its eyes covered his own and presented to his fellow drinkers a mask. Thus Dionysos presided over the symposium not just as god of wine, but as the divinity associated with masks, altered states, and 'otherness'.

Poetry was performed either within such a small sympotic group (or *hetaireia*), which was often in competition with other small groups or with the city as a whole, or it was performed at a large public event in which the entire city (notionally) participated.

Such civic festivals were public holidays, often involving animal sacrifice and the distribution of meat; athletic and musical competitions; freedom from toil; and a general party atmosphere. Whether the performing choruses were male or female, it seems that both men and women comprised the audience, dressed in their holiday best and enjoying the elaborate spectacle of beautifully costumed chorus members singing and dancing in unison. We can get some idea of the experience of such festivals—though on a larger, 'inter-communal' scale—from a passage in the *Homeric Hymn to Apollo* describing an Ionian festival on Delos (cf. Ch. 1, pp. 41–6):

CUP AS MASK. It was a favourite conceit for the underside of Athenian drinking cups that they should reveal the representation of eyes so that the drinker would be covered by a kind of ceramic 'mask'. This particular vessel painted c.500 BCE is unusual in being in the shape of a female breast.

> But you [Apollo] take special delight in the island of Delos,
> where the fine-robed Ionians gather themselves together
> along with their children and their decorous wives,
> when they set up contests remembering to do you honour:
> they delight with fistfights and with patterned dance and poetry.
> Anyone coming upon the Ionians gathered there
> might believe them to be unageing, undying gods;
> he would see all their grace and feel a deep delight
> at the sight of such men and their fine-figured wives...
>
> (ll. 146–54)

These different performance contexts can often be correlated with different ideological positions expressed; symposium poetry often espoused élitist values, championing the supremacy of an aristocracy of birth, wealth, and status against the more egalitarian values of the civic community. Public poetry, even when it supported the claims of the élite, did so in terms of civic, egalitarian values. Thus, for example, choral poetry tended to assume that power in the city should be held in common, accessible to all citizens, and that all good citizens were moderate in wealth and needs.

In terms of formal features, our modern catch-all designation 'lyric' actually subsumes three different categories of poetry (based on metre, level of decorum, and style of performance—sung vs. recited). These are:

1. *Iamboi*: a category which included, but was not limited to iambic metre; *iamboi* were also composed in trochaic metres, and in epodes which combined iambic or trochaic verses alternating with dactylic rhythms. The defining feature of *iamboi* in this period seems to have been their coarse, 'low-class' content, sexual narratives, animal fables, and use for blame. There is dispute about their performance context, but many scholars take *iamboi* to be a kind of dramatic monologue performed at public festivals, perhaps originally associated with fertility rituals. *Iamboi* were apparently spoken, not sung.

2. Elegy: poetry composed in elegiac couplets (a dactylic hexameter followed by a shorter dactylic pentameter). All the elegy we have preserved from the archaic period shows a marked Ionic dialect colouring, suggesting that the genre of elegy developed originally in East Greece. Although in later antiquity elegy was strongly associated with funeral lament, there is no good evidence for this function in the remains of early elegy. Instead, there seem to have been two different genres of elegy: brief poems of advice and/or erotic sentiment probably performed at the symposium, and longer historical narrative elegies or poems of military exhortation probably performed at public festivals or on campaign. In style, elegy tended to be more decorous than iambic, but not as elevated as melic poetry. It appears to have been sung (though it could also be recited), perhaps to the accompaniment of the *aulos* (double reed pipes).

3. Melic: composed in lyric metres properly so called, melic is conventionally divided into monody (performed at the symposium) and choral poetry (performed in public for the civic community). Monody was sung by a solo performer, accompanying him- or herself on the lyre; choral poetry by an entire chorus singing (and dancing) in unison, to the accompaniment of a lyre (and sometimes perhaps also an *aulos*). Monody tended to be shorter and simpler in its metrical structure; choral poetry longer and more elaborate, both in diction and metre. The language of monody tended to conform to the local dialect of the composer, while choral poetry exhibited an artificial poetic dialect with a marked Doric colouring. Monody has traditionally been read as more personal, because (in our terms) it speaks to a small, 'private' group in terms of shared knowledge and shared values. Choral poetry tended to speak to and for an entire community on important ritual occasions, mapping both the unity and hierarchy of that community through the choral group.

This is, I realize, a very schematic account. In order to flesh it out, I will go through each category in turn, and briefly consider some poets whose work is characteristic of each genre.

Iamboi

The main iambic poets were Archilochos, Hipponax, and Semonides of Amorgos. Archilochos of Paros, conventionally dated to the mid-seventh century, composed in an array of iambic metres, epodic structures, and also in elegiac couplets. He is thus our first (preserved) multi-genre poet, revered in antiquity for the poetic skill which earned him frequent comparison with Homer and Hesiod. His poems range from the pensive seriousness of

> Heart, Heart . . . do not rejoice openly when you win,
> nor lament, downcast in your house when you lose,
> but rejoice at pleasant things and be annoyed at evils
> not too much, and know the rhythm that holds human beings
> (W^2 fr. 128, ll. 4–7),

to the beast fable of the fox and the eagle (W^2 frr. 172–81), to the obscene, 'Just like a Thracian or a Phrygian drinking beer through a straw, she sucked, bent over, also engaged from behind' (W^2 fr. 42).

The fragments of Hipponax of Ephesos (traditionally dated to the mid-sixth century) are more purely 'iambic', obsessed with food, sex, and excrement as they chronicle the picaresque adventures of a low buffoon in language generously mixed with Eastern loanwords. Thus in one fragment, a thievish speaker prays to Hermes,

> Hermes dog-throttler, Kandaules in Maionian,
> Companion of thieves, come to my aid here
> (W^2 fr. 3a).

Another fragment, preserved on papyrus, appears to describe a painful treatment for impotence set in a privy (W^2 fr. 92).

Greek tradition had it that Archilochos was set to wed Neoboule, but that her father Lykambes broke off the engagement. Archilochos responded with such a stream of scathing invective (apparently including the claim that he had had sex with both Neoboule and her sister in the precinct of Hera) that both the daughters of Lykambes took their own lives. We can take this story as a parable for the power of blame poetry and the social norms it enforces, for the names of the figures involved suggest that they were stock characters in an iambic 'mini-drama' performed at public festivals (the name 'Lykambes' shares a root with the genre name *iambos*, while 'Neoboule' meaning 'new plan' is apt for a fickle bride-to-be). We might imagine Archilochos in the persona of a rejected bridegroom, lampooning Lykambes and his daughters to the assembled civic community, which was united by the scapegoating of these stock characters.

We find precisely this story pattern repeated for Hipponax and his enemies, the sculptors Boupalos and Athenis. In this instance, we are told, Boupalos made an unflattering portrait of Hipponax, whereupon the poet dunned him with invective verse until he, too, committed suicide. And, indeed, the name Boupalos recurs in the scant corpus of Hipponax, for example, in the fragment, 'Hold my cloak—I'm gonna punch Boupalos in the eye' (W^2 fr. 120) and another which describes Boupalos in obscene and literal terms as a 'motherfucker' (W^2 fr. 70). The recurrence of very similar stories told about Archilochos and Hipponax suggests that the story pattern was somehow characteristic of the genre *iambos*. Indeed, some scholars have speculated that *iambos* was informed by a ritual pattern whereby a marginalized and abject persona succeeded in scapegoating others through the power of his invective.

The publication of the 'Cologne Epode' of Archilochos (W^2 fr. 196a) in 1974 has both confirmed and complicated this model of *iambos* and ritual abuse. The Cologne papyrus gives us the end of an epode describing the encounter of a young man and a girl in an isolated rural landscape. In the lost beginning section of the poem, the young man apparently expressed desire for sexual union on the spot, and, when the papyrus picks up, the girl is just ending a speech trying to dissuade him from such immediate gratification. A negotiation ensues in which the young man seems to promise that he will not 'go all the way', hints at the possibility of marriage later, and then, with a swift succession of first-person verbs, has his way with the girl in the meadow. The poem ends with his ejaculation, though it remains ambiguous (especially given the fragmentary state of the papyrus) whether this is with or without full penetration. Some modern scholars have read the poem as a charming and lighthearted erotic idyll, but such a reading does not account for a lengthy passage of scathing invective against Neoboule embedded within this encounter. The girl, at the end of her speech, apparently offers (her older sister?) Neoboule as an alternative for the speaker's desire (lines 5–8). In his speech in response, the speaker paints a blistering portrait of Neoboule in contrast to his virginal interlocutor:

> As for Neoboule—let some other man have her.
> Pah! She is over-ripe, and twice your age,
> And her maiden bloom has fallen away,
> And the grace she had before.
> For she does not . . . satiety,
> And, a maddened woman, she has revealed the limits of . . .
> Hold her off—to the crows with her!
> May the king of the gods not ordain
> That, having such a wife, I will be a source of joy to my neighbours.

I much prefer to take you;
For you are not untrustworthy, nor duplicitous,
But that one is far too keen,
And she makes many men her friends.
(W² fr. 196a, ll. 24–38)

This contrast between the 'maddened woman' the speaker reviles and the dainty, innocent girl he seduces is central to the poem, and must figure in any interpretation of it. The other fact that is often ignored in discussions of the poem is that it is not simply a sexual encounter, but a narrative thereof offered to an audience, perhaps of male *hetairoi* (cf. W² fr. 196). As such, the epode itself works to destroy the reputation of the girl by impugning her chastity. Thus paradoxically, the narrative of events collapses the distinction between Neoboule and the girl, between the virgin and the whore of the speaker's representation. (In this sense, the whole poem serves to demonstrate how brief and fragile a girl's 'maiden bloom' is.) And, since the two females involved are apparently unmarried, their sexual shame redounds to the dishonour of their male *kurios* (or guardian)—their father, if he is living. On this reading, the 'Cologne Epode' is an example of iambic abuse, though of a more insidious and subtle kind than we might have expected. By itself, furthermore, it cannot definitively answer the question whether Neoboule, her sister, and Lykambes were real persons or stock blame figures.

With Solon the Athenian lawgiver (active around the turn of the seventh to sixth centuries), we see a shift in the function to which the public performance of iambic was put. Solon used iambic to defend his political programme (and this is indeed why the fragments were preserved in the texts of later writers like Aristotle and Plutarch). Thus he justified his reforms, the 'shaking-off of debts' (Seisachtheia) and abolition of slavery for debt, in the resounding W² fr. 36:

Those things for which I drew together the demos,
which of these have I stopped before accomplishing?
She would best bear witness to these things in the court of Time,
supremely great mother of the Olympian gods,
Black Earth, from whom I once
removed the boundary stones fixed in many places,
she who was before enslaved, but now is free.
And I led back to their god-built homeland of Athens
many who had been sold, some unjustly,
others justly, and others still who had fled
under the compulsion of debt, no longer
speaking in the Attic tongue, since they had wandered far and wide.

And those who suffered shameful enslavement here,
trembling at the habits of their masters,
These I set free.

(Solon, W^2 fr. 36, ll. 1–15)

But even here, Solon simultaneously drew on the traditions of iambic in using the humble sphere of beast fable for his final image:

. . . making my defence from every side,
I turned like a wolf among many dogs.

(W^2 fr. 36, ll. 26–7)

We might thus view Solon as an intermediate figure, who adapted Ionian *iamboi* (both iambic trimeter and trochaic tetrameter) to a loftier style and content, and thereby (perhaps) made these metrical forms suitable eventually for Attic tragedy.

Elegy

Solon also composed elegies, both on public themes and in celebration of 'private' pleasures, so that his elegies seem to provide us with examples of both sympotic and civic forms. The other major elegists known from the period are Kallinos, Mimnermos, Tyrtaios (all traditionally dated to the seventh century), Theognis (seventh–fifth centuries), Xenophanes and Simonides (both late sixth–fifth centuries). Most of the extant poems of Kallinos and Mimnermos, as well as the entire corpus of the Theognidea, represent symposium poetry—short hortatory or meditative poems reflecting on the pleasures of life, love, and wine. A good example of this type is Mimnermos, W^2 fr. 1 :

What is life, what is pleasure without golden Aphrodite?
May I die when these things no longer concern me—
secret love-making and honeyed gifts and bed,
what sorts of things are the lovely blooms of youth
for men and women. But when grievous old age comes up,
which makes a man ugly and base,
always evil cares wear out his wits,
and he does not even rejoice when he looks on the beams of the sun,
but he is hateful to boys and without honour among women.
So dreadful a thing god has made old age.

(Mimnermos, W^2 fr. 1)

The lengthier collection of the Theognidea (the only archaic elegy handed down by direct manuscript transmission) allows us to see more clearly the politics that inform such symposiastic verse. Framed as advice by an older man to a boy (sometimes explicitly named Kyrnos), the corpus can be read as a kind of survival manual for an imperilled aristocracy. Thus, in addition to advice on proper sympotic behaviour, the Theognidea returns obsessively to the dangers of associating with *kakoi* or *deiloi* (social inferiors) and the paramount importance of choosing the right companions, the *agathoi* or *esthloi*. A good deal of the impact of this Theognidean refrain derives from the implicit collapse of social and ethical categories in these terms: the *kakoi* are inevitably not just socially 'base' but morally 'bad', while the aristocratic *agathoi* or *esthloi* monopolize for themselves innate 'virtue'. In addition, the speaker of the Theognidea broods about the fact that riches are bestowed indiscriminately by the gods, and that wealth has even 'mixed the race', as impoverished aristocrats marry their daughters to rich commoners (lines 182–96, cf. lines 1109–13). Through it all runs an implicit narrative of the speaker's biography: a nobleman betrayed by his friends, robbed of his property and exiled, he remains the city's true sage and lawgiver, if it could only recognize and embrace him (e.g. lines 332a–4, 341–50, 543–6, 575–6, 667–82, 1197–1202). This leitmotif ultimately constructs a kind of god-given, naturalized authority for the speaker, precisely in the period when the nature and criteria for civic authority were most contested and up for grabs. We can imagine the Theognidea—or something very like it—being sung or recited at aristocratic symposia all over Greece, as speaker and audience alike constructed and reaffirmed their legitimate authority through performance. It is perhaps evidence for the panhellenic appeal and circulation of the Theognidea that even in antiquity there was doubt about Theognis' home city: was he from mainland Megara or its Western colony in Sicily, Megara Hyblaea? This uncertainty of origin made Theognis (whose name means 'descended from god') a figure for any beleaguered aristocrat in a troubled city.

In addition to such sympotic verse, we have evidence of another genre of elegy: longer historical narrative elegy probably performed at public festivals. Thus later authors attributed to Mimnermos a book called *Smyrneis*, which may have included a narrative of the founding of Kolophon, Smyrna's mother-city (W^2 fr. 9) and an account of a battle between the inhabitants of Smyrna and Gyges, king of Lydia (W^2 fr. 13, 13a). In like manner, Tyrtaios was said to have composed a poem called *Eunomia* or *Politeia*, while we also hear that Xenophanes of Kolophon 'composed a foundation of Kolophon and the colonization of Elea in Italy in 2,000 lines' (for Xenophanes, cf. p. 162). This may well have been a poem in elegiac couplets, which included Xenophanes, W^2 fr. 3, a denunciation of the 'useless luxuries' adapted by the Kolophonian élite from their neighbours, the Lydians. A late theorist, *On Music* provides evidence for the performance of sung elegy as part of the musical competition at festivals like the Athenian Panathenaia, and that public festival context conforms to the community these fragments seem to construct for themselves. For such narratives of foundation and battle speak to (and help forge) an entire civic community, while Xenophanes' brief fr. 3 suggests that this kind of elegy could also oppose from an egalitarian position the extraordinary status markers assumed by an internal élite.

The nature of such longer narrative elegy on historical themes has been clarified recently by the publication of fragments of Simonides' Elegy on the Battle of Plataia (W^2 frr. 10–18—Plataia was the great land battle against the Persian invaders in 479 BCE). This poem began with a hymnic prooimion addressed to Achilles (through which the poet linked the glory of the Greeks at Plataia with that earned by the heroes who fought at Troy). It continued (apparently) with an account of the march of Spartan (and other) troops from the Peloponnese to Plataia, and seems to have included a description of the order of the Greek troops for battle (for example, Corinthians in the middle, W^2 fr. 15). Beyond that, the extremely tattered and lacunose papyrus fragments make it difficult to say anything with certainty, though the poem perhaps contained embedded speeches of prophecy or exhortation (W^2 fr. 14?). Scholars have speculated that the poem was commissioned shortly after the battle, to be performed at a public festival in Sparta or perhaps Plataia itself (where those who fell in battle were honoured periodically with festival and offerings).

Finally, Tyrtaios' poems of military exhortation represent a somewhat different context for public performance. The fourth-century Athenian orator Lykourgos tells us that 'the Spartans made a law, whenever they went out on campaign, to summon all the soldiers to the king's tent to hear the poems of Tyrtaios, believing that thus they would be most willing to die for their country' (*Against Leocrates* 107). It seems that in the fourth century at least (and perhaps much earlier), these elegies were performed before the entire Spartiate army assembled (though we need not imagine it occurring on the very eve of battle). Like the Spartan custom of *sussitia* (public communal dining), this performance context extended the sphere of commensality to the entire citizen population. In this context, we can imagine the profound effect of verses such as:

> This is virtue, this is the best prize among mortals
> and the most beautiful for a young man to win;
> And this is a common noble deed for the city and the entire demos,
> whatever man, planting himself firmly, stands fast in the front ranks
> unceasingly, and forgets entirely shameful flight,

setting at risk his spirit and his enduring heart,
and, standing next to his neighbour, encourages him;
This one shows himself to be a good man in war.
(Tyrtaios, W[2] fr. 12, ll. 13–20)

Melic—(*a*) Monody

Like elegy, melic can be divided into poems performed for the small group of the symposium and those performed at more public, civic occasions. As we shall see, the opposition symposium—public sphere corresponded roughly (but not exactly) to the traditional opposition of monody—choral poetry. The major surviving monodic poets are Sappho and Alkaios (both traditionally dated to the late seventh–early sixth centuries), and Ibykos and Anakreon (mid- to late sixth century). Sappho and Alkaios were both from the city of Mytilene on the island of Lesbos, and both composed in their characteristic Aeolic dialect and lyric metres.

Alkaios' poetry constructed him as a Mytilenean nobleman, heavily involved in the turbulent politics of his home city, where tyrants rose and fell; where sympotic groups of 'companions' (*hetaireiai*) plotted and went into exile; and where the poet and his group were betrayed by a former 'companion'. This was Pittakos, whom at some point, the people 'established as tyrant, acclaiming him greatly *en masse*' (Alkaios, *PLF* fr. 348). All this should sound very like the implicit biography of Theognis, for both the elegy and Alkaios' melic were poetry of the *hetaireia*, working to unite a small group of aristocratic co-conspirators and to legitimate their claims to authority within the city. Thus we find a similar range of themes in the Theognidea and Alkaian monody (though the latter dealt more in particulars): drinking songs, affirmations of the importance of noble birth, bitter laments from exile, exhortation to companions to maintain their loyalty and courage, abuse of tyrants and perceived traitors to the group. Though often denigrated in modern times as more of a political trouble-maker than a wordsmith, Alkaios was a poet of great power and precision. For example, in two lines that are almost an oxymoron in their juxtaposition of festive mood and grim reality,

Now one must get drunk, and even violently
Drink, since Myrsilos is dead.
(*PLF* fr. 332)

Sappho, Alkaios' contemporary, was the only female poet to make it into the Hellenistic canon of the 'Lyric Nine', and, indeed, one of the very few female voices preserved for us from antiquity. There is much scholarly debate about what context we should properly imagine for the composition and perform-

POETS FOR A SYMPOSIUM. This unusual vessel, a double-walled wine-cooler, was painted in Athens c.470 BCE and also has unusual subject-matter. The male and female poets represented are labelled as Alkaios and Sappho, the two great lyric poets from Lesbos.

ance of Sappho's poetry. Almost certainly, some of her poems were originally composed for choral performance; this is likely for songs such as epithalamia (wedding songs), of which unfortunately we have only exiguous fragments. But most of the poems we have (and the publication of papyrus finds in this century has greatly increased the corpus) appear to be monodic and so raise the question of the nature of Sappho's group. Some scholars propose a female sympotic group or *hetaireia* which would have been the exact analogue of Alkaios' group. Others imagine Sappho as an educator of young women, who took girls before marriage and prepared them for this life transition. This reconstruction, in turn, has several versions, which run the gamut from high secular 'finishing school' to high religious 'initiation'. According to this latter model, Sappho was the leader of a *thiasos* of young women, engaging in ritual homoeroticism to prepare them for marriage. There is almost no reliable external evidence for any of these positions, so it is perhaps best to maintain a healthy scepticism.

Yet another approach to Sappho wants to see her as definitively different from all other Greek poets, in so far as her verse seems authentically personal and intimate—much more like our modern notions of lyric. Yet here I would reiterate what was said at the outset: *no* Greek poetry was composed as private, authentic utterance to be 'overheard'. Sappho's poetry too must have been composed for performance before a group. Instead, we might read the more intimate and personal quality of Sappho's poetry as a phenomenon of the marginalization and containment to the private sphere of women *as a group* in ancient Greek culture. Thus the poet spoke intimately to other women, with whom she shared the experiences of seclusion, disempowerment, and separation. Sappho's poems often spoke openly of love and longing for other women or girls, who seem to have been separated from the speaker by forces beyond her control. Because of this pattern of separation, memory played a much greater role in the texture of Sappho's poetry than that of the other lyric poets (and conjures up for us perhaps a stronger sense of the speaker's interiority). For example, in one (fragmentary) poem, the speaker seems to comfort another woman longing for a third:

> . . . Sardis. . . . often holding her mind here . . .
> When we . . . she honoured you
> like a far-conspicuous goddess,
> and she used to rejoice most of all in your song.
> But now she is conspicuous among
> the Lydian women, as, when the sun
> has set, the rosy-fingered moon
> surpasses all the stars; and it sheds its light
> equally upon the salt sea
> and on the much-flowering fields,
> And beautiful dew is shed,
> and roses bloom and soft chervil
> and flowering melilot.
> And wandering much, remembering
> gentle Atthis, with longing
> she consumes, I suppose, her delicate heart.
> But for us to come there . . . this is not
> (Sappho, *PLF* fr. 96)

This poem is remarkable for the extended, almost epic-style simile that fills its three middle stanzas. Through the simile, the poem hollows out an imaginary space where the two women can be together in fantasy (just as they both gaze on the same moon). This reading is perhaps confirmed by the striking transfer of the epic epithet 'rosy-fingered' from Homer's dawn to the moon in the night sky. If epic represents the daylight world of men, this poem constructs a separate magical night-time realm for women.

Ibykos of Rhegion in southern Italy and his contemporary Anakreon of Teos on the coast of Asia Minor came from opposite ends of the Greek world to the court of Polykrates, tyrant of Samos. We are told that Ibykos composed long poems on mythological themes (like the earlier Western poet Stesichoros), but the few fragments we have look much more like monody. Thus Ibykos sang of love and the desirability of beautiful boys (appropriately for the pederastic context of the symposium), as in

> Eros again looking at me meltingly from under dark eyelids
> with all sorts of enchantments casts me into the boundless nets of Kypris.
> And I tremble at him as he approaches,
> like a yoke-bearing horse—a prizewinner who, come to old age,
> unwilling enters the contest of swift chariots.
>
> (*PMG* fr. 287)

or again

> O Euryalus, shoot of the grey-eyed Graces,
> and darling of the beautiful-haired Seasons, you Kypris
> and gentle-eyed Persuasion nurtured amidst blooming roses
>
> (*PMG* fr. 288)

This latter fragment seems to be an example of what Pindar and Bakchylides would later refer to as *paideioi hymnoi* ('hymns to boys'), which again probably had an important social function in context. It has been noted that the objects of such 'hymnic' praise were always young noblemen or dynasts, so that we might read the eroticism of these fragments as a conventional form of communal praise and affirmation of social pre-eminence. (Indeed, some have even read Ibykos, fr. 282, a long poem in honour of Polykrates, as an exemplar of this genre.)

Anakreon too seems to have composed for a small group of like-minded fellow symposiasts. Thus his themes are frequently the pleasures of love and wine in exquisitely turned verses, such as

> O boy of the maidenly gaze,
> I pursue you, but you do not heed me,
> unaware that you are my
> soul's charioteer.
>
> (*PMG* fr. 360)

or again,

> Bring water, bring wine, boy, and bring for us flowering
> crowns, since I go to box with Eros.
>
> (*PMG* fr. 396)

But we should not be fooled by Anakreon's light touch; there was a politics implicit in his sympotic celebrations, as his scathing attack on a social climber (*PMG* fr. 388) reveals. The language and imagery of Anakreon's attack on the low-class Artemon echo those of Theognis' lines bemoaning the fact that 'the base' (*kakoi*) have now become 'the good' (*kaloi*, Theognis, 53–60). This similarity is not accidental, for Anakreon, like Theognis, was much concerned with maintaining the purity and exclusivity of the aristocratic group, as it was threatened by the encroaching power of the city.

Melic—(*b*) Choral poetry and public poetry

Turning from monody to choral, public poetry, we immediately perceive a shift in formal features and level of style, as well as in occasion and social function. Choral poetry tended to be composed on a larger scale, with more complex metrical systems; more elevated, ornate diction; and (often) extended mythic narrative. Choral poetry was, furthermore, in some sense always religious poetry, whether performed as part of a ritual (like Alkman's partheneia) or more loosely dedicated to a particular divinity (like dithyrambs in Athens).

The earliest preserved choral poetry is that of Alkman (traditionally dated to the last quarter of the seventh century). Alkman composed 'maiden songs' (partheneia) which were performed at Sparta; papyrus finds have given us extensive fragments of one such poem and bits of another (*PMG* frr. 1, 3). Internal evidence suggests that the first Partheneion was sung by a chorus of ten or eleven girls while another girl performed ritual activities (offering a cloak or a plough to Orthia at sunrise). Such ritual conforms to the theory that in this instance, choral performance was part of an initiatory experience for the chorus members (or choreuts), perhaps marking a life-transition before their marriage. At the same time, performance of the partheneion also provided an occasion to put marriageable girls on display before the whole city, decked out in all their finery. The first half of this long poem, of which we have only fragments, narrated the story of the attempted abduction of the mythical daughters of Leukippos by a band of violent young heroes. This was offered as a paradigm of overreaching and transgressive failed marriage; thus a few gnomic lines from the myth admonished, 'Let no unwinged strength of mortals fly to heaven nor attempt to marry mistress Aphrodite.' The second half of the poem then shifted from myth to present actuality, from violent battle to girls' play and adornment, and in a sense from mythic transgression to ritual propriety. This latter half is remarkable for its carefully scripted but ostensibly spontaneous self-referentiality; the choreuts speak at length about their own ornaments and appearance and about their two leaders, Hagesichora and Agido, for whom they evince an erotic fascination. We might read this vivid erotic praise, sung by a chorus of girls before the entire civic community, as analogous to the *paideioi hymnoi* of Ibykos. Thus, the erotic interest voiced by the chorus could be said to represent the admiration of the entire community for these two (now nubile?) girls, but in a form that was safe because ventriloquized through the modest maiden chorus.

We should also note that the chorus of young girls seems to have staged in performance both the unity and the hierarchy of the community. For these ten or eleven girls represented their entire age cohort and the whole community (as their praise suggests), while they did so in clear subordination to the two leaders. Indeed, there is evidence to suggest that the name 'Agido' connects one of their two leaders with one of the two ruling houses of Sparta, the Agiad dynasty. If we are to imagine Agido as a young woman of this royal house, then the enactment and affirmation of social hierarchy through the hierarchy of the chorus would have been complete.

Stesichoros, who was active in Italy and Sicily in the first half of the sixth century, was traditionally numbered among the choral poets, but recent papyrus finds have made that categorization less definite. Stesichoros was known to have composed mythic narrative poems in lyric metres, but until the 1960s, we had only the most exiguous fragments preserved by quotation in other ancient authors. At that point, three Stesichoros papyri were published, one of which contained fragments of the *Geryoneis*. Calculations based on the size and layout of this papyrus revealed that the poem would originally have spanned 1,300 lines at least (remarkably long for a lyric poem; indeed, analogous in length to an entire tragedy). Such exceptional length (and certain odd metrical features) have caused scholars to think that Stesichoros' poems could not have been performed chorally. Even if true, this does not, however, mean that they were not *public* poetry, for one fragment of Stesichoros, at least, seems to have required a civic audience. In this case, what may have been the opening lines of Stesichoros' *Oresteia* asserted that its subject-matter was *damomata*, 'things common to the citizenry'. It was perhaps performed before an entire community by a solo singer accompanied by a miming chorus. We might then imagine Stesichoros' lyric productions as proto-dramas, which would well suit what we can deduce of his vivid narrative style and frequent use of direct quotation. For example, much of the *Geryoneis* appears to have been narrated from the point of view of Geryon, a monster killed by Herakles as one of his twelve labours. We even have a fragment which must have been spoken by Geryon's mother, begging her son to save his life (by flight?; *SLG* fr. S 13).

Another papyrus, published in 1977, has given us thirty-three virtually intact lines of a poem on the Oedipus cycle. In it, Iokaste spoke directly to her sons Eteokles and Polyneikes on the verge of war, urging them to divide their father's property by lot and thereby spare their house and city from destruction. The extended use of direct quotation (thirty out of thirty-three lines were spoken by Iokaste) would have made the poem particularly vivid in performance, while Iokaste's appeal on behalf of the 'city of Kadmos' (which did not figure in Homeric versions of the Oedipus story) may reveal something about the original civic audience to which the poem was pitched.

With Simonides, Pindar, and Bakchylides, we reach the final great period of choral lyric production (*c.*520–450 BCE). It is hard to say much about the choral poetry of Simonides, since so very little survives. For Bakchylides of Keos, however, major papyrus finds early in this century have given us substantial fragments of fourteen epinikia (poems celebrating athletic victories), as well as dithyrambs and paians. Bakchylides' dithyrambs were composed for different cities, including two for Athens. In Athens we know that dithyrambs were performed in competitions at the City Dionysia (cf. Ch. 3, pp. 102–9) and perhaps other festivals (according to the Parian Marble, the dithyrambic contests at the Dionysia were instituted in 509/8 BCE). For this competition, each of the ten Athenian tribes entered a chorus of men and a chorus of boys, each containing fifty members. They were elaborately and beautifully costumed and crowned, and danced with circular choreography as they sang to the accompaniment of an *aulos*. Such competition would have required rigorous training and would have involved 1,000 Athenian citizens and future citizens each year. As such, the dithyrambic contests played a major part in the citizens' choral education.

Like the Athenian tragic contests, instituted according to the traditional date some years earlier, the dithyramb was a song in honour of Dionysos, but like contemporary tragedy, that dedication seems not to have required Dionysiac themes as subject-matter. Thus Bakchylides' two known dithyrambs for Athens (18, 19) told the stories of Theseus' first approach to Athens as a young man, unknown to his royal father Aigeus, and of Io's wanderings after Hera transformed her into a cow. The former poem was constructed as a dialogue, with a single voice (perhaps the chorus leader) speaking in the persona of Aigeus, while the chorus responded in the role of representative citizens of Athens. The mood created was one of uncertainty and fear, as king and people alike apprehensively awaited the powerful but unknown individual who had exterminated the robbers and criminals lining the road from Epidauros to Athens (whom, of course, the audience knew to be Theseus). In its dialogic form, as well as in the asymmetry of knowledge constructed between characters and audience, this poem seems to show the influence of the contemporary genre of tragedy on more traditional choral song. It thereby told the familiar story of Theseus' youthful exploits in a novel way and allowed chorus and audience alike to unite in celebrating their national hero.

Bakchylides' exact contemporary was Pindar of Thebes (traditional dates 518–438 BCE), regarded by many as the greatest of the canonical nine Greek lyric poets. In his own time, Pindar was in great demand, receiving poetic commissions from all over the Greek world. By the Hellenistic period, his poems were collected in seventeen books (i.e. papyrus rolls of 1,000–2,000 lines each). He was thus a prolific poet who composed many different types of choral songs—hymns, paians, dithyrambs, partheneia, dirges, and epinikia among them. From papyrus finds, we possess substantial fragments of his paians and a few bits of hymns, dithyrambs, and parthenaia. All these poems exhibit Pindar's characteristic style: difficult, crabbed syntax; obscure transitions; very elevated diction; and elaborate, vivid metaphors and conceits. But all these qualities are shown to best advantage in his epinikia, of which four books survive through direct manuscript tradition.

Both Pindar and Bakchylides composed epinikia. Relatively speaking, we have a substantial corpus of this genre preserved: fourteen Bakchylidean epinikia from papyrus; forty-four Pindaric odes preserved through direct manuscript tradition. Epinikion, choral poetry composed on commission to celebrate individual athletes who had won at the panhellenic games, was a relative latecomer among the genres of Greek choral poetry (the earliest epinikion we know of was composed by Simonides in the 520s). We might understand it as an adaptation to the needs of a panhellenic élite (those with the money and leisure time to train and compete at the games), when their authority within their individual cities was no longer unquestioned. Athletic victory itself was one means of acquiring enormous prestige within the city and the aristocracy in general, but, as we know from Tyrtaios (W^2 fr. 12) and Xenophanes (W^2 fr. 2), the civic value of athletic victory could be challenged from an egalitarian perspective. Thus Xenophanes could contend in elegiac verse:

> For even if there should be a good boxer among the people,
> or one who is good at the pentathlon or wrestling,
> or in the swiftness of his feet—the very thing which is most honoured,
> of all the works of strength in the contest of men—
> the city would not on that account be more orderly.

But there would be little joy to the city in this,
if someone should win in competition beside the banks of Pisa [at Olympia];
for these things do not fatten the city's coffers.

(Xenophanes, W² fr. 2, ll. 15–22)

Against such challenges, epinikion affirmed the common value of athletic achievement. At the same time, it worked to reintegrate the victor who had so distinguished himself into his various communities. Thus epinikion praised the victor by representing him as an ideal member of his aristocratic class *and* of his civic community. Emblematic of this reintegrative function was the performance context of most epinikia: composed by a professional poet, the victory ode was sung in unison by a chorus of the victor's fellow citizens in his home town. Often the poem voiced by this representative chorus contained a myth which linked the victor's achievement with those of local cult heroes (as Pindar, for example, tended to use myths of the Aiakidai in odes for Aiginetan victors). Thus also much of the familiar rhetoric of epinikion, warning about human limitations and admonishing the victor 'not to seek to become Zeus' should perhaps be read in a political context. Such rhetoric served to reassure the victor's fellow citizens that he did not aim to use the extraordinary prestige acquired from athletic victory to wield undue political influence within the city. For example, Pindar could say, speaking in the 'generic first person' which voiced the sentiments proper to victor and poet alike:

I would desire beautiful things from god,
Striving for things that are possible within my age-class.
For finding the middle ranks blooming with more enduring prosperity throughout the city,
I blame the lot of tyrannies;
And I am strained over common achievements. And the envious are fended off,
if a man, having taken the peak of achievement, plies it in peace and avoids dread hybris . . .

(Pindar, *Pythian* 11. 50–8)

Epinikion seems also to have served a panhellenic function, as we can deduce from the large number of commissions Pindar and Bakchylides received from Greek colonies, and especially from colonial rulers like the kings of Kyrene in Libya or the Greek tyrants in Sicily. Nearly a third of Bakchylides' extant epinikia were composed for colonial victors (including three for Hieron, tyrant of Syracuse), while twenty of Pindar's forty-four surviving epinikia celebrated victors from Greek cities in Italy, Sicily, and North Africa (of these, ten were commissioned by colonial dynasts or members of their immediate families). Just as Greek colonial citizens and dynasts competed avidly at the panhellenic games and made lavish dedications at Olympia and Delphi, so also they commissioned numerous epinikia from the most famous poets of mainland Greece. All three activities derived from the same impulse—the desire of colonials to assert their Greekness and to maintain a visible presence on the Greek mainland. For dynasts on the margins of the Greek world the aspiration extended further; they wanted to affirm the legitimacy of their rule as well as their rightful membership in a panhellenic élite. This participation on the larger stage of Greek history and culture was the real substance behind epinikion's promise, frequently proclaimed, to spread the victor's fame to the very limits of the earth.

In all these different contexts in epinikion, the poet's 'I' figured prominently, but it was a flexible persona, suited in each poem to serve the needs of the victor's reintegration and glorification (again we should not deduce anything about the historical Pindar or Bakchylides from their poetic self-references). Thus in the passage from *Pythian* 11 quoted above, the poet's 'I' voiced the sentiments of an ideal middling citizen, as he did again in *Nemean* 8 (composed for a private citizen of Aigina):

> Some pray for gold, others for a boundless expanse of land,
> But I pray to cover my limbs with earth when I have pleased the citizens,
> Praising the one who is praiseworthy, and showering blame on wrongdoers.
>
> (Pindar, *Nemean* 8. 37–9)

In contrast to this middling stance, the poet's 'I' espoused a very different position in odes composed for tyrants; thus both Pindar and Bakchylides ended major odes for Hieron by asserting the absolute pre-eminence of his 'kingship' and affiliating their own poetic skill and reputation with the dynast's status:

> The furthest height caps itself
> for kings. No longer look further.
> May it be for you [Hieron] to tread aloft for this time,
> As for me to the same extent to keep company with victors, being pre-eminent in poetic skill throughout all Greece.
>
> (Pindar, *Olympian* 1. 113–115b)

> O Hieron, you have displayed
> the most beautiful blooms of blessedness to mortals.
> But for one who has been successful, silence bears no ornament;
> Together with the truth of noble deeds, someone will hymn also
> the grace of the Kean nightingale.
>
> (Bakchylides, Ode 3, ll. 92–8)

The 'new music' and the end of the 'lyric age'

Pindar's latest datable epinikion was composed in 446 BCE. In a sense, this ode marks the end of the great age of Greek lyric poetry. After the middle of the fifth century, there was no single iambic, elegiac, or melic poet deemed worthy of canonization by the later Hellenistic scholars (though poetic composition and performance continued in all three forms). What then was the cause of the abrupt silencing of Greek song culture in our sources? I insisted at the outset that we should not impose an organic, developmental model on the diachronic sequence epic–lyric–tragedy, taking these genres to correspond to different phases of the Greek 'spirit'. And yet, the end of the 'lyric age' of Greece seems to correspond with the mature phase of Attic tragedy; should we not interpret this as an organic development?

As in the case of the apparent shift from epic to lyric, the processes involved were probably more complex and more historically specific than such an organic model allows. The appearance and popularity of Attic tragedy and comedy played a part, to be sure, for both genres appropriated lyric forms that had earlier been independent (including iambic, choral song, and monody; cf. Ch. 3, pp. 88–90). The domination of tragedy and comedy may have meant that gifted poets were drawn to these forms rather than to traditional lyric composition. In what may have been partly an attempt to compete more effectively with these synthetic genres, practitioners of other lyric forms (especially dithyramb) seem to have led a musical revolution in the last third of the fifth century in Athens. This was the period of the so-called 'New Music', characterized by an abandonment of strict strophic responsion in favour of looser, astrophic forms, a much freer mixing of different rhythms and musical modes (or scales) within a single composition, and the proliferation of notes at smaller intervals.

One prominent practitioner of the New Music was Timotheos of Miletos, active in the last third of the fifth century and beginning of the fourth. Timotheos added four strings to the traditional seven-stringed lyre, thereby allowing the performer to modulate between modes (or scales) within a single composition without having to adjust the strings. Timotheos composed dithyrambs and also lyric kitharodic nomes (in which a solo singer accompanied himself on the lyre). An extraordinary example of Timotheos' work in this latter genre came to light on papyrus in 1903; our oldest literary papyrus (dated to the fourth century BCE) preserves over 200 lines of Timotheos' *Persians*. This poem, probably performed at a Panathenaic kitharodic competition some time in the years before 408 BCE, vividly narrated the Battle of Salamis (480 BCE), and ended with a series of four quoted speeches by defeated Persians, ranging from the fractured Greek of a common Phrygian soldier to the solemn lament of the Great King. Just as the rhythm shifted from the dactylic hexameter of the opening line to iambic and Aeolic measures, so also the style of the poem fluctuated from baroque dithyrambic, full of compound adjectives and elaborate metaphorical conceits, to the restrained dignity of Xerxes' lament:

> But when the King looked upon
> his all-mixed force rushing to backturning flight,
> he fell to his knees and defiled his body,
> and spoke, swelling with misfortunes,
> 'Alas the destruction of houses
> and the scorching Greek ships, which
> have destroyed the ships'
> youthful strength of many men.
> But the ships will not convey
> them on their way back, but
> the smoky strength of fire
> will flare with savage body, and groaning griefs
> will come to the Persian land.
> (Timotheos, PMG fr. 791, ll. 173–86)

Timotheos' *Persians* was a *tour de force*, a kind of compendium of the whole tradition of lyric rhythms, styles, and generic forms. As such, it helps us understand the ways in which the New Music contributed to the end of a living performance culture. This was not because (as Plato and Aristotle would have it), this New Music was morally decadent and corrupting; it was rather that, in its very virtuosity, it required performance by *professional* musicians. It was nearly impossible for amateur singers and lyre players to re-create the rhythmic and musical complexity of Timotheos' compositions (or those of the other practitioners of the New Music). But in a world with only the most rudimentary musical notation, continued reperformance was the sole route to survival and eventual canonization. Thus paradoxically, the New Music, by radically pushing the envelope of traditional musical styles, permanently altered the conditions for musical performance within Greek culture.

Another factor in the demise of the 'lyric age' was a more general shift in the techniques and style of education in classical Greece (cf. Ch. 5, pp. 167–72). With the rise of the Sophists in the last third of the fifth century, education became increasingly privatized and professionalized. For the Sophists (along with their Athenian counterpart Sokrates) insisted that education required special knowledge and expertise on the part of the educators. By systematizing different fields of knowledge (like rhetoric, mathematics, astronomy, and grammar), the Sophists worked to disembed education from its traditional cultural context, a large part of which was the choral and musical education received in a living song culture. Instead, they offered training in special skills for a fee, so that education became more of a private matter dependent on an individual's resources. It is then no accident that in the debate over the 'New Education' staged between a father and a son in Aristophanes' *Clouds*, the event that precipitates the final quarrel is the father's request that the son sing him a song by Simonides (which the son rejects as too 'old-fashioned'). With the rise of the New Education, the traditional modes of lyric performance fell out of favour and into disuse. Along with these developments, the medium of writing began to make much more of an impact in the later fifth century. In this period, new prose genres such as medical treatises, history, and philosophy were composed to be read rather than performed, and so contributed to the specialization and privatization of knowledge.

We might understand all these processes as part of a shift in the nature of performance in the polis. Public poetry of all kinds seemed to play a much less important role in the city and the education of its citizens in the fourth century. It is well to remember that Attic tragedy and comedy, which in a sense displaced other lyric production, did not maintain their unquestioned pre-eminence for long. In fact, it appears that much of the energy and prominence traditionally accorded to poetry had shifted to another domain of performance—the rhetorical displays of the lawcourts and assembly (cf. Ch. 6, pp. 196–216). Political and forensic oratory became the sites for the negotiation of speaker and audience, for the collaborative construction of ideal community that had been the function of choral poetry in performance. With this development came also the split between public oratory and private literary production, which for the first time constituted a category of the 'literary' closer to our own. Thus lyric poetry lost its crucial involvement in public ideology and was relegated to the private sphere.

Paradoxically, this meant that what had been a minority voice in the 'lyric age'—the elegy and monody performed at symposia—came to be the bulk of the lyric poetry that was reperformed and preserved. For symposia and their entertainments endured, as the sphere of public poetry did not. Historical narrative elegy was replaced by prose history, and Solon, had he lived in the fourth century, would certainly have composed speeches instead of poems. It is no accident that many of the lyric fragments we have derive from the second- or third-century CE antiquarian Athenaios of Naukratis, who wrote the *Deipnosophistai* (*Scholars at Dinner*), of which an interminable fifteen books survive (cf. Ch. 8, p. 261). Conversely, with the exception of Pindar's epinikia, all the major fragments of choral lyric we currently possess came to light from papyrus finds in this century. This happy accident of preservation has thus restored to us a domain of public poetry in performance that was profoundly different from all that came after it in the Western tradition.

3 Powers of horror and laughter: The great age of drama

PETER WILSON

The growth of tragedy from song culture

> tragedy blossomed forth and won great acclaim, becoming a wondrous event for the ears and eyes of the men of that age . . .
>
> (Plutarch, *Moralia*)

When the tragic flower first blossomed in Attic soil late in the sixth century it represented a major innovation on the horizon of Greek poetry and society. For the first time the familiar figures of myth—the men, women, and gods sung of by the Homeric bard and his successors—had miraculously come to life. They moved and interacted as real physical presences before the eyes; they spoke and sung directly to the ear of the audience; the new technology of the theatrical mask and costume introduced the possibility of total impersonation. A unique set of circumstances had produced a radically new kind of performance, and with it the first fully theatrical audience.

The origins of Greek drama remain obscure. But it is much more helpful to speak of a coalescence of different forces—historical, poetical, religious, social—whose combination was amazingly productive, and generated the phenomenon we know from its classical form. Among these, we should include the ancient tradition of 'poetry of occasion'. In the oral society of early Greece poetry was produced for specific and significant social and religious occasions—a song for the gods, or to praise a man's athletic achievements, to celebrate the founding of a new city, a wedding, a funeral, to inspire soldiers to battle. For this kind of poetry, the words were only one part of a complex performance involving singers, musicians, and, crucially, a group gathered for a social and religious event (see Ch. 2, esp. pp. 58–9, 60 on 'song culture'). It was only much later in the day of drama's life that the very idea of a 'reading public' was born. Even then (around the end of the fifth century), reading drama was still very much a minority activity. Drama was essentially a performance—a 'doing' (as the Greek word *drama* itself signifies), and a performance for the masses, for a huge public audience.

Another important ingredient in the early mix that led to drama is the specific promotion of poetic performance by the tyrants of sixth-century Athens (for the term 'tyrant', see p. 63), Peisistratos and his sons Hippias and Hipparchos (Hipparchos, though remembered for his promotion of the arts, was never himself the sole ruler of Athens.) Before their time Athens was something of a poetic backwater: by the early fifth century, it was well on its way to becoming the poetic magnetic pole of all Greece. Some of the greatest poets of the age were invited to Athens (among them the versatile Simonides of Keos and Lasos from Hermione), to practice their crafts and, no doubt, to foster local talent. As part of their aim to promote Athens as a cultural centre to vie with the other great states of Greece, the Peisistratids expended much energy on enhancing the city's programme of major festivals, especially the Panathenaia, Athena's great 'birthday party', and—crucially for the future of drama—the Dionysia, the wine god Dionysos' major city festival. Both of these came to have grand public cultural contests as a distinctive characteristic: competitions in the recitation of Homer and in instrumental playing and accompanied singing at the Panathenaia; and competitions of the new art-form of tragedy, and later of comedy as well as of dithyramb, Dionysos' special choral song, at the Dionysia.

Since classical tragedy and comedy are bound up intimately with the political forms of democratic Athens, it would be fascinating to know whether and in what ways drama served the city while still under the control of a tyrant. The shadowy, alluringly half-mythic figure of the Athenian Thespis (whence ultimately our 'Thespians') was regarded by later writers as in some sense the father of tragedy and inventor of the art of acting, and they placed his activities in the last third of the sixth century, in the period of Peisistratid rule. Thespis may well have presented his startling innovation to his fellow villagers in his birthplace, the region of Ikarion in northern Attica (in Greek, Attike), a place with which the god Dionysos had special associations (see p. 97 below). Likewise with comedy: there were certainly sixth-century predecessors to the riotous 'other face' of Dionysian drama, which tended to slink—but scarcely quietly—behind its more 'elevated' sibling of tragedy in terms of the official recognition and prestige it gained.

If Homeric epic was in some sense 'shared' by all Greece, a precious element in a broad cultural patrimony rather than the special possession of a particular place or people (see Ch. 1, pp. 40–1), the situation was very different with drama. There were other claimants to the title of the 'inventor' of drama. Dorian communities of the Peloponnese put forward claims to tragedy; Megara (a city between Athens and Corinth) and a number of Sicilian Greek cities had flourishing comic performances, perhaps as early as the mid-sixth century. But whatever the substance of these claims (and the whole idea of looking for a single 'inventor' is in any case probably misguided), they were soon overshadowed by the inordinate success of the Athenian experiment. Drama rapidly became a characteristically Athenian phenomenon. In the long-term perspective of literary history, tragedy and comedy were the two great contributions of Athens.

That drama grew up in intimate connection with the worship of Dionysos is another of the early shaping forces behind it. The qualities of this ambiguous and elusive god, and specific elements of his worship, played vital roles in the developing art-form. The mask had long played an important part in his worship. However, its transformation from an object of cult veneration representing the god to a malleable instrument of identity-change on the head of actors and chorus was decisive.

The situation with music is comparable. Music was always central to the worship of Dionysos, as of many gods. The forms of religious music for Dionysos included especially 'orgiastic' tunes and instruments, the kind of thing he was imagined as bringing with him to Greece from his journeying in the east, in Lydia and Phrygia. These were played enthusiastically by his followers, be they ordinary mortal worshippers at his various feasts and festivals, or his special possessed female followers known as maenads, or his anarchic male entourage of satyrs—see pp. 107–8 below. This ecstatic, Dionysiac music plays an important role in tragedy: Euripides' *Bakchai* is particularly full of it, as we should expect in a play with a chorus of maenads devoted to their god, who is himself its protagonist.

> —And he cries, as they cry, *Evohé!*—
> On, Bakchai!
> On, Bakchai!
> Follow, glory of golden Tmolos,
> hymning god
> with a rumble of drums,
> with a cry *Evohé!* to the Evian god,
> with a cry of Phrygian cries,
> when the holy pipe like honey plays
> the sacred song of those who go
> to the mountain!
> to the mountain!

ACTOR COMMUNING WITH MASK. This very interesting tombstone was only recently discovered on the island of Salamis near Athens. It may date from as early as 420 BCE. It evidently showed a youthful idealization of the dead man holding up the mask of a female role from tragedy. It is revealing for the importance of the mask as a symbol of acting and for the kind of 'communication' that was set up between actor and mask.

> —then, in ecstasy, like a colt by its grazing mother,
> the Bakchant runs with flying feet, she leaps!
>
> (ll. 152–69)

Ancient scholars from at least Aristotle's time believed that drama developed out of the form of the singing, dancing chorus for Dionysos, as a lead figure stood apart from the group and began to engage in dialogue with it. But the chorus stayed with drama even when its stories no longer centred on Dionysos, and it remained a strictly musical core at its centre. The basic format of all classical drama, tragic and comic, is an interlacing of the stream of *song* (and dance) from the chorus with the *speech* of the actors, in the form of iambic verse. (See pp. 72–3 on the Athenian tradition of iambic poetry.) The fact that the chorus can draw on, and imaginatively mingle together, a wide range of musical forms that existed outside drama is one of tragedy's (and comedy's) great resources. The many funerary songs and laments of tragedy, for instance, will have drawn real intensity from their relation to forms of ritual song known to the audience. The choral lament or dirge (*threnos*) sung by the slave women of the household in honour of the dead King Agamemnon in the *Libation Bearers*, the second play of Aischylos' trilogy of 458 the *Oresteia*, offers a good example. Its language, and doubtless the music that once accompanied it, shows many features characteristic of the traditional lament, including repetition of words or sounds in the same place in the various metrical units of the song:

> We have come from the house, sent here
> to bring libations. Sharp blows rained on us.
> Look at these gashes on my cheek—
> they're new; but for a long time now
> my heart has fed itself on misery.
> We've rent the fabric of our clothes in grief,
> we've torn and crushed the veils around our breasts.
> These are disasters which bring no one joy.
> (*Libation Bearers* 22–31)

This musical dimension is almost entirely lost to us, but would have been a major component of drama's ancient impact. It was here perhaps more than anywhere else that a poet could exert a direct emotional influence on his audience. The Greeks (like most modern musical theorists) regarded music's power as working directly on the emotions, as largely non-rational in its effects. And the *aulos*, the set of double pipes whose piercing sound was the usual accompaniment of tragedy, was above all instruments the one believed to seize hold of the soul in a powerfully direct manner.

We can catch a glimpse of the power of the lost musical dimension of drama, and of the ways in which it could be flexibly used to hint at or underscore developments in mood and plot, from passages where the chorus describe their own song and emotional condition as they perform. In the first part of Sophokles' *Women of Trachis*, for example, the young women of the chorus are exhilarated at the prospect that Herakles is about to return from his long exile, and hence that their mistress and friend Deianeira, Herakles' wife, will be released from her unhappiness and anxiety. They strike up what is essentially a traditional wedding-song to greet the return of Herakles, so long absent that the idea of a 'remarriage' is not out of place (lines 205–15). In poetry and (we can safely assume) musical forms that draw on elements of Dionysiac worship, they then go on to modulate their song:

> I am raised up and I shall not
> reject the *aulos*, O tyrant of my mind!
> See how it excites me—
> Euoi!—
> the ivy now whirls me round in Backhic contest.
> (*Women of Trachis* 216–20)

Particularly striking here is the description of the Dionysian *aulos* as 'tyrant of my mind'. This imagined Dionysian music—which would surely have found an echo in the music heard by the audience from the stage musician—evokes the excitement that has taken over the chorus' minds. But as so often in tragedy, the excitement and joy summoned up at such times soon show a grim, dark side, the destructive side of the ambivalent god Dionysos. For at this very moment, it is not Herakles who appears, but his beautiful object of war-booty, Iole, the young woman who threatens to usurp Deianeira's position. Her arrival throws a darkly ironic shadow back on their opening 'wedding' song, which now takes on a very different meaning. As if realizing this radical change of perspective, the last few lines of the chorus' brief song 'change their tune' once more—this time to a hymn for the healing god, Paian (lines 221–3).

Passages like this hint at the enormous expressiveness of the music that is lost to us, but which for its audience was a fundamental part of the experience of drama. Whatever the original meanings of the terms, the second part of the words *komoidia* and *tragoidia* reminds us of the central importance of song and music (*oide* is a basic Greek word for 'song').

A special form of free speech

Whatever the relative importance of these and other ingredients in the early matrix of drama, by the time of our first texts (and even in earlier fragmentary remains) a quantum leap has taken place. In a short period the pioneers had developed the immensely sophisticated poetic performance with its many formal conventions that we find in Aischylos, whose *Persians* of 472 BCE is our first surviving tragedy, though he had been producing dramas for more than two decades by then. Among the pioneers we need to include in a sense the avid early audiences too: drama of this sort could only have succeeded and progressed so vigorously with the enthusiastic support and involvement of the audience itself.

Our first substantial evidence for comedy starts much later: the earliest example to survive in full is Aristophanes' *Acharnians* of 425. At the other end of the chronological scale, our last tragedy is Sophokles' *Oedipus at Kolonos*, produced five years after the poet's death in 406, although some scholars believe that the play ascribed to Euripides called the *Rhesos* is not by him but an early fourth-century successor. For comedy the situation is rather different, since we have examples of fourth-century Aristophanic comedy (the *Women in Assembly* of 393/2 and *Wealth* of 388) which show signs of incipient change in form and function. And in Menander's (in Greek, Menandros) plays from much later in the fourth century, we can perceive that a more radical change has taken place in comedy, away from the topical and political concerns of the fifth century. Our lack of anything but small fragments of tragedy of the later period prevents us from investigating the development of the genre, although we know that new works continued to be composed for production as vigorously as ever each year for more than two centuries. (See pp. 218–26 for subsequent developments in both comedy and tragedy.)

These dates are significant: they highlight the important fact that both tragedy and political comedy (what is often called 'Old' comedy) roughly coincide in time with the most energetic and turbulent period of Athenian history—and of Athenian democracy. Absolutely crucial to the growth and to the character of drama were the massive social, political, and historical developments that swept through Athenian society from the end of the sixth century. After the expulsion of the tyrants, Athens famously adopted a new form of political organization which placed an unprecedentedly large control of affairs in the hands of the *demos*, the 'people', as opposed to the well-born aristocrats who wielded power in most other Greek cities. With the reforms of Kleisthenes (about 508 BCE) that ushered in a significantly more democratic constitution, and subsequent increasingly 'radical' developments in the democracy at various points in the fifth century, old social and political relations were profoundly changed. The new institutions of the democracy made the adult male citizen population responsible for the running of the largest and most powerful city in Greece. All the major decisions touching the lives of the citizens, their families and dependants, were now technically in the hands of the mass citizen Assembly (*ekklesia*), while the new Council of five hundred (*boule*) prepared its agenda and executed its decisions. The third major institution of the democracy, and one for which the Athenians became famous (or notorious), was the system of people's courts (*dikasteria*), which met on around two hundred days every year. They were manned by large panels of citizen-judges (up to

2,001 in important trials), and they considered not only private legal quarrels but, more importantly, all major political trials (and there were many), as well as exercising extensive powers of control over the Assembly, Council, other magistrates, and political leaders. (For orators, see Ch. 6.)

The democratic citizenry in fifth-century Athens was thus loaded with unparalleled power; and with unparalleled responsibility. It was constantly called upon to make judgements of the utmost importance—who to make alliances and war with, who to elect to high office, whose advice to follow in the leadership of the city. And with the passing decades of the fifth century the responsibilities of the citizens increased on an exponential scale, as the city became the most prosperous and powerful in the Aegean. The successful repulse of the two major Persian invasions of Greece, in which Athens played a leading role, gave the newly democratic city a powerful psychological boost of collective confidence, and confirmed it in its adherence to the ideal of fierce independence and freedom that underpinned its notion of citizenship.

The defeat of Persia was influential at more than a psychological level, however. It allowed the Athenians to assume a position at the head of a defensive league of Greek states which was designed to repel further threats from the east. This league of allies initially had its centre on the sacred island of Delos at the heart of the Aegean; but, over the course of the four decades following the Persian Wars, it turned into the 'empire' or 'domination', a federation of subservient subjects under Athens' very firm control, its treasury of collected gold tribute now the temple of Athena on the Akropolis. Athenian citizens were now masters of an extensive and immensely powerful maritime league; and one which turned to increasingly repressive means of administration and control over its 'allies'—a term which became a hollow euphemism for 'subjects'. The city's expansionism gradually drew it into conflict with the other major power in Greece, Sparta and her allies, and the last thirty years of the century saw the protracted and exhausting war (which we call the Peloponnesian War) between these two states and former allies which ended in the defeat of Athens. The pressures of the war had exacerbated social tensions within Athens, especially between rich and poor, and between city-dwellers and farmers whose lands had been left to be ravaged by the invading Spartan army. As so often happens in long wars, conventional morality and accepted values tended to be abused in practice and questioned in theory.

Throughout this seismic period of immense political, social, and historical change, the Athenians made of their theatre, not a place of escapist entertainment, but a vast sounding-board: a place in which to expose, explore, and scrutinize the ramifications of this constant upheaval and change. With tragedy, this usually operated at a level of powerful generality: though the stories told in tragedy have a very concrete particularity about them, the medium of heroic myth also provides a notable sense of distance from the here and now.

Comedy's approach was much more 'full frontal': the burning social and political issues of the day could be opened up directly on the comic stage. Comedy set itself up as a watchdog of political safety, relentlessly questioning the wisdom of the leaders and the led alike—of prominent politicians, other poetic 'advisers' (especially tragedians) and thinkers, as well as of the *demos* itself, whose gullibility and waywardness were not beyond comedy's criticism. Comedy became a special form of political criticism, a striking instance of the democratic ideal of *parrhesia* or 'free speech'. This is made clear by an anonymous writer on political matters who lived in the age of old comedy, and whose views are so radically opposed to the democratic form of politics as to have earned him the name (from modern scholars) of 'the Old Oligarch':

> the democrats do not allow ridicule and abuse of the *demos*, to avoid being criticized themselves, but in the case of individuals they encourage anyone who wishes, in the sure knowledge that the individual is not as a rule one of the *demos* or the masses but someone rich, well-born or powerful. (*The Constitution of the Athenians* 2. 18)

Although his own political views have caused the author to ignore the ways in which comedy can also criticize the *demos*, this is a precious piece of contemporary evidence for its important function as a democratic institution of criticism and ridicule. Generally this comic representation of the city's preoccupations came with a sufficiently large dose of the ridiculous, the inverted, and the fantastic to ensure that its engagement with 'live' issues did not overstep the boundaries (including laws of slander) which marked out the proper place of criticism in the democratic city. Nonetheless we should remember that in his speech of self-defence before an Athenian court when on trial for his life in 399, Sokrates supposedly spoke of the many slanderers who had created the utterly false reputation for which he was now being condemned: 'the most unreasonable thing of all is that it's impossible to discover and reveal their names—except in the case of a comic poet' (Plato, *Apology* 18d).

A range of theatrical occasions

> Genuine Athenians are shrewd students of the arts and untiring theatre-goers
> (Herakleides (third-century travel writer), *On the Greek Cities* 1. 4)

Before looking further at the ways drama engaged with the concerns of its audience, it is worth while to talk in more concrete terms about just where and how they experienced their theatre. The principal audience in any discussion will be the one that gathered in spring each year on the south-east slope of the Akropolis in Athens in the open-air theatre in the sanctuary of Dionysos, in celebration of his 'Great', or 'City' festival. It is worth pointing first, however, to a couple of other places where, by around the middle of the fifth century, the theatre-hungry Athenians produced and consumed their drama.

One of these is the so-called 'Rural' Dionysia, the name 'Rural' contrasting explicitly with the 'City' of the major event in Athens. Rural Dionysia were held by the smaller units of which the entire region of Attica, town and country, was composed—the 'demes' or 'municipalities', of which there were some 139 in all. The demes were mini-communities with their own religious traditions and political institutions at a local level, and among the gods worshipped with enthusiasm in the demes, Dionysos had an especially favoured position. Given that most of these demes were in fact 'rural' in the sense that they were located in the countryside outside the urban centre, the prominence of Dionysos, a god who was more at home beyond the city walls and identified intimately with the vine grown there, should not come as a surprise. The farmer-protagonist of Aristophanes' *Peace* called Trygaios—'Vintager'—gives a position of prominence to Dionysia in a list of the pleasures brought back to the countryside by the return of peace:

> she has the smell of harvest, hospitality and Dionysia;
> of *auloi*, tragedies, the songs of Sophokles; of thrushes, and Euripidean verselets.
> (*Peace* 530–2)

There is also a strong tradition that puts the very earliest performances of both comedy and tragedy in a rural setting before moving to the city. I mentioned the possible activities of Thespis in Ikarion (a deme), which claimed to be the first home of tragic performances. This may have some basis to it: there was a myth which associated Dionysos' first appearance in Attica with Ikarion, whose inhabitants he taught the art of turning grapes into wine. In the fifth century they held a well-organized Dionysia of their own at which, unsurprisingly, tragedy was the premier event.

Other scraps of evidence, mainly archaeological, give us tantalizing glimpses of the kinds of performance staged at these local Dionysia, and so illuminate the bigger picture of the formation of a sophisticated theatrical audience in Attica. For instance, we know that in a number of demes the community's central meeting-place, its agora, also served as its theatre—a fact that underscores the inherently 'political' character of drama in the broadest sense. These performances will not have had the grandeur of the urban event, but that will have been counterbalanced by the pride that obviously went with staging a

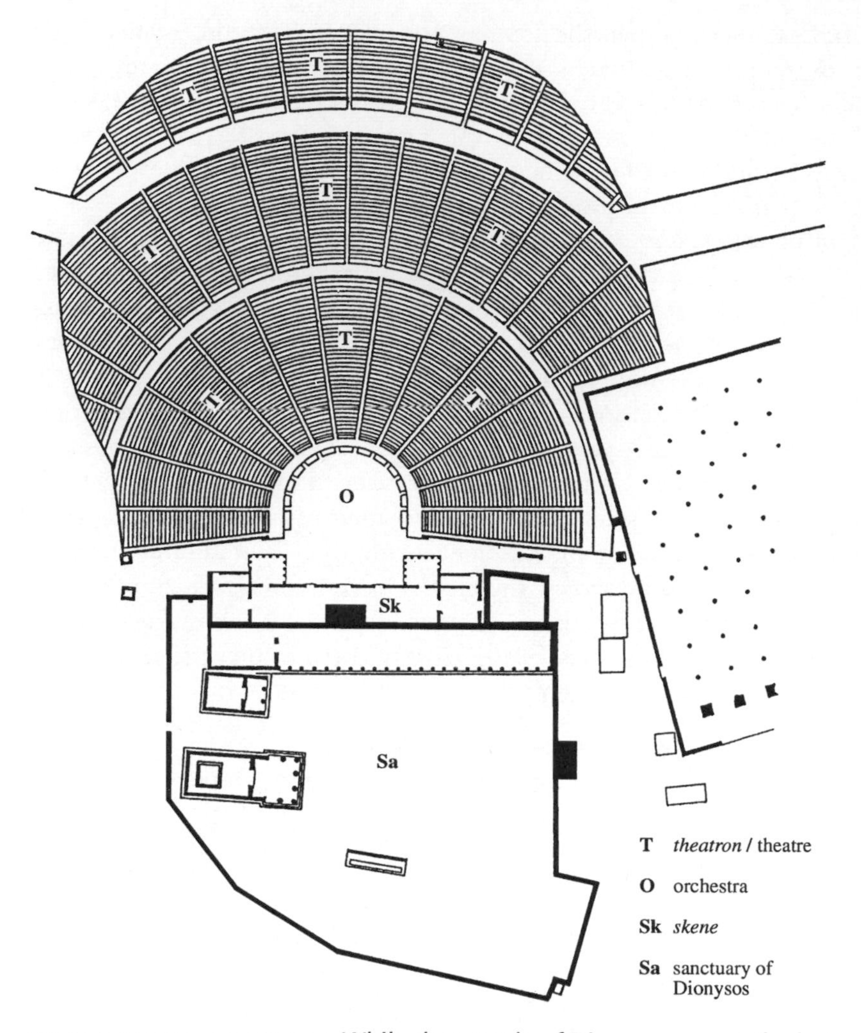

THE SACRED SPACE FOR THEATRE. While the temple of Dionysos was at the bottom of the slope at the south-east corner of the Akropolis, the entire slope above was part of his sacred precinct, and became the area for the spectators of drama. Nearly all, if not all, of the great dramas of fifth-century Athens were first performed in this space.

dramatic festival and we should not assume that they were third-rate events. Some lucky inscriptional finds have made it clear that some of the really 'big names'—Sophokles, Euripides, and Aristophanes among them—produced their works in the demes, possibly (but not necessarily) as 'repeats' after an urban performance. If they *were* repeats, this is precious evidence for the formation of the very first 'repertory' theatre of sorts. The general principle of Athenian theatre was that every play was created for a single, non-repeatable occasion, for a fixed 'slot' at a particular festival in a particular year, so that the idea of reperformance was foreign to this culture of the occasion. We are told that after the death of Aischylos the Athenians passed a law permitting the reproduction of his works: a recognition (if true) of his unique status not just as a 'literary classic' but also as an 'educator' of the city. It was only later, in the 380s, that performances of 'old' tragedy and comedy became a regular feature of the City festival. So the Rural festivals may have played an important role in fostering what was clearly a high degree of familiarity among the audience with their drama.

By the late fifth century there was also a large-scale Dionysia in the Peiraieus, technically a deme but scarcely 'rural', since this was Athens' massive and cosmopolitan port-town. Sokrates made a special effort to leave his usual urban haunts when Euripides was competing at the Peiraieus, and for once he was not isolated in his enthusiasm. We hear from Plato of those 'spectacle-lovers' who 'run around to all the Dionysia, never missing one either in the towns or in the country-villages' (*Republic* 5. 475d). Some at least of these 'local' events clearly anticipated an audience made up of more than just their own community. The Peiraieus theatre probably held over 5,000 spectators, and there are some indications that demes co-ordinated their timetabling so as not to have their Dionysia clash, no doubt so that people (and performers) could move from one to another.

Another Dionysiac festival, called the Lenaia, was held in late January, roughly two months before the City Dionysia, which took place in early spring. (The name 'Lenaia' comes from the Greek word for a wine-press, an essential piece of technology in the worship of Dionysos.) This too was a festival of the city as a whole, but a less grand occasion than *the* City Dionysia. It too was probably held in the theatre under the Akropolis (although this, like just about everything else to do with the festival, is a matter of controversy). This would make sense for our understanding of a comedy like Aristophanes' *Lysistrate*, which was a Lenaian comedy. A central plank of Lysistrate's plan in this play to force the men of Athens to end the war is the seizure of the Akropolis by the women of Athens; and this ancient, natural fortress, charged with political, religious, economic, and historical significance, almost becomes a member of the comic cast. The effect would have been that much greater if the actual Akropolis formed a natural backdrop to the performance, looming at the backs of the audience.

From an audience perspective, a number of features of the Lenaia were revealingly different from the City Dionysia. While tragedy was clearly the 'senior' performance at the City Dionysia, comedy seems to have had the upper hand at the Lenaia. Of the eleven surviving comedies of Aristophanes, five were certainly or probably performed at the Lenaia. This is in keeping with the less grand character of the festival. January was no time for travel in Greece, so the large numbers of foreign visitors who attended the City Dionysia will not have been present then. Without these 'outsiders', and at a time of year when people were starting to give some thought to what was to come in the militarily and politically more active half of the year in spring and summer, the Lenaian audience had a more domestic focus. As much is clear from a passage of Aristophanes' *Acharnians*, which also throws important light on the claims of comedy—in competition, as often, with tragedy—to a role as a mouthpiece of serious advice for the city.

Acharnians was produced after more than five hard years of war with Sparta which had seen much of the countryside destroyed, including the ancient farmlands of Acharnai, a deme whose angry, bellicose old men form the chorus of the play. The comic hero, Dikaiopolis—'Mr Just City'—is forced to defend himself before these men, his head, quite literally, on the chopping-block, for having dared to negotiate a private peace for himself and, what's more, for suggesting that the Spartans 'are not entirely responsible for our troubles' (line 310). This is the kind of remark that may well have been historically and politically true, but could only ever be uttered on the comic stage.

> Do not be indignant with me, members of the audience,
> if, though a beggar, I speak before the Athenians
> about the city in a comedy.
> For even comedy is acquainted with justice.
> (ll. 497–500)

(*'trugedy'*, the word Aristophanes uses for 'comedy' here, is a punning formation based on the word for 'grape-pressings' and is clearly meant to make a proud stand beside its more elevated rival, 'tragedy'.)

Dikaiopolis goes on to preface his 'shocking but just' advice for the city with the remark that

> This time Kleon won't allege that I'm
> slandering the city in the presence of foreigners,

for we are just ourselves and it's the Lenaian competition
and there are no foreigners here yet;
neither tribute money nor troops have come from the allied cities
[as they would two months later on the occasion of the City Dionysia].
This time we are alone, ready-hulled;
for I reckon the metics as the civic bran.

(ll. 502–8)

Kleon was the leading politician of the day, and Aristophanes had already crossed him because of an attack in an earlier comedy, perhaps stinging him to launch a counter-attack in the courts. This sort of comedy was, then, no harmless entertainment cut off from consequences in the 'real' world. Kleon's complaint seems to have taken the form of a claim that the poet had been excessively critical of the city and its leaders (i.e. himself) before an 'international' audience (the City Dionysia is implied) at a time of war when 'solidarity' before outsiders was paramount. So in this play for the Lenaia, where there were no foreigners present (on the metics or 'resident foreigners' see below), the comic character Dikaiopolis puts forward his author's rejoinder at the same time as he makes his own self-defence before the Acharnians. Audiences shape the way drama can speak.

One last (and somewhat neglected) context in which the Athenians consumed their drama: this is the very different, much more 'private' world of the (largely) upper-class drinking party known as the symposion. Here wine, conversation, pleasurable indulgences, and solo performances of various kinds circulated freely (see pp. 64–5). It had for centuries been part of the rules of the symposiastic game to be able to show off one's culture by singing a poem of some recognized master, and it is clear that some parts of tragic plays found their way into this intimate world of small-scale 'reperformance'. Given that every tragedy had a chorus of fifteen men, who had spent some months in rigorous physical and mnemonic training to learn its complex dance-songs, we should probably imagine those with such experience as important in this kind of (partial) reperformance. It is clear that an upbringing in the ways of *choreia*, the dance-and-song-culture of choral performance, was to some extent the reserve of those with the time and leisure to devote to it; and this group overlapped significantly with the kind of people who attended symposia. A story told about the defeated Athenian army in Sicily at the disastrous close of the expedition there in 413 BCE throws a fascinating ray of light on this different means of disseminating knowledge of tragedy. Some of the Athenian soldiers who were being held prisoner in the quarries outside Syracuse are said to have won their freedom by singing Euripidean songs to their Euripides-mad Sicilian captors.

The programme of the great Dionysia

The time, wealth, and level of administrative sophistication the Athenians devoted to their premier festival of Dionysos speak volumes for the importance they attached to their drama. For the best part of a week in spring the city effectively suspended all other official business. The democratic Assembly, the Council, and courts did not meet during the festival. By means of a major civic institution known as the *choregia* (literally 'leadership of a chorus') Athens required a minority of its rich élite to fund the organizational and performative 'heart' of drama, its chorus, as a form of highly honorific obligation. These *choregoi*, a kind of ancient version of the film producer—and with all the arrogance and self-interest shown by some of their modern counterparts—lavished vast sums of their wealth on drama. We hear of costumes with gold thread, gold crowns for their chorus members, specialized dietary regimes for the months of training, upkeep, and pay during this period, the hiring of various experts and of training-grounds. Individual *choregoi*, who were themselves competing for the prize, spent genuine fortunes on an evanescent event lasting only for part of a single day. And to these sums the city itself added more for the large numbers of beasts for sacrifice (over 200 bulls in one year), for the pay of the actors, prizes for poets, actors, and *choregoi*, and for the upkeep of the theatre itself, including, for most of the classical period until a stone theatre was built during the fourth century, the construction of temporary wooden benches for the bulk of the audience.

Certainly by the fourth century there were extensive regulations covering every aspect of the festival's organization, the conduct of its participants, the award of prizes, even to some extent, the behaviour of its audience. This was an occasion of truly mass participation, the largest annual gathering in Athens, and more than twice the size of a full Assembly. At somewhere between 15,000 and 20,000 strong, the comic hyperbole that describes the theatre audience as 'countless myriads' (*Wasps* 1010), 'the great crowd of people, thousands of discerning spectators' (*Frogs* 676), becomes perfectly intelligible. It is clear that it was never difficult to fill the theatre to its capacity, and this close-packed environment will have helped generate a shared, collective character of response to the emotional horrors of tragedy and the humour of comedy. Under such conditions strong emotions are infectious and readily and rapidly transmitted through a large crowd—and so too is laughter. The excitement and tensions created in such a gathering were high, and only increased by consumption of Dionysos' special gift, wine. We know of a law that prevented people taking advantage of these circumstances by, for instance, making attacks on their personal enemies. A man called Ktesikles was actually put to

COMIC SPONSORS. *This extremely interesting and well-painted vase, produced in Taras in southern Italy in c.380 BCE, was first published in 1991. It shows a scene from a comedy with stage doors, costumes, masks, etc., but includes a figure on the left (labelled Aigisthos) in full tragic outfit. On either side of the slave posturing on a wool basket are two men with the label* 'choregos', *evidently representing the wealthy citizens who put up the money for dramatic performances.*

death by a democratic court for striking an enemy with a whip as he took part in the procession. Questions of social order and status were a significant issue in the overall structure and conduct of this great festival, just as they also lay at the heart of the drama that was its most remarkable feature.

Although much of the elaborate programme of events is obscure to us, we know enough to form an idea of the grandeur and sense of display that permeated the occasion. Formal proceedings began, on the first of some five days, with a huge procession, made up of representatives of various segments of Athenian society, including of course adult (male) citizens; metics (both men and women); deputations of the states of the empire, during the period of Athenian hegemony; young Athenian men on the point of manhood and citizenship known as ephebes; the city's officials; the *choregoi*, and probably their competing teams. Opinion divides as to the involvement in the procession of Athenian women of full status. Some believe that the figure of the *kanephoros* or 'basket-carrier' who led the whole procession carrying the sacrificial knife hidden in the ritual basket, was the sole representative of the female half of the Attic population, while there is on the other hand some evidence (see Menander, fr. 55) to suggest that at least by the later fourth century women took part, if only in the capacity of spectators of the passing procession.

This procession performed a number of important functions. It not only conducted the effigy of Dionysos to a position of honour in the theatre or sanctuary. It also conveyed to the sacred altar of the god the animals to be slaughtered and consumed. The blood of hundreds of beasts was made to flow each year, and as Paul Cartledge has recently put it, 'the prospect of state-subsidised entertainment (and instruction) coupled with a beef supper liberally lubricated by Dionysos' special juice might have been a very attractive proposition indeed'. But the procession also had the important effect of dramatizing a sense of the community's identity, of producing a kind of social map on which each of the various groups represented had their 'proper' place and role, symbolized in part by what they carried and wore in the procession. The metics, for instance, were marked out by a special crimson robe, and they seem to have carried various utensils that symbolized their secondary and perhaps their 'productive' role in the community (bowls, water-pitchers). We hear of citizens simply dressing as they chose and carrying a wineskin, in honour of Dionysos no doubt, but such a show of piety would also have allowed these citizens, for whom the festival was principally designed, to refresh themselves on the way.

That the representatives of the allied states were granted a prominent place in the procession adds a significant dimension to the whole event, and distinguishes it sharply from the Lenaia. These non-Athenian Greeks, many of whom will have travelled long distances to reach the festival, were also required to deposit the tribute they paid to the imperial project led by Athens. This took place during another, special preliminary to the tragic competition, and it may be they even had to deliver it, ingot by ingot, in the orchestra of the theatre, before the assembled audience. Such an affirmation by Athens—perhaps 'dramatization' is the right word—of her position of power and control stands as a striking prelude to the tragic dramas that followed. For in the world of tragedy, the immense confidence that feeds such grand military and imperial projects is so often open to doubt, or shown to lead precisely to tragedy.

The disastrous ambitions of the Persian King Xerxes are the clearest case. At the start of the *Persians* the chorus of Persian elders sings of the military success and confidence of the great king and his people:

For divine fate has prevailed since
it enjoined the Persians to wage wars,
which destroy towers, ramparts,
and the glad tumult of horsemen,
and cities overthrown—
When the vast ocean was foaming,
by the winds boisterous whitened,
then they learned, trusting to cables
and to pontoons which convey men,
to scan the sacred sea.

(ll. 93–106)

But they immediately go on to think of the 'cunning deception of god' that leads men astray—a lesson they and their king will learn to their cost. Later in the play, the ghost of Xerxes' dead father, Dareios, draws a general moral from the Persian loss that could also have powerful resonance for the one-time victors over Persia, the Athenians themselves, on their way to becoming empire-builders: '. . . and let no one, scorning his present fortune, in lust for more, ruin his great prosperity' (ll. 824–6).

It is not only 'barbarians' in tragedy who demonstrate such behaviour. Aischylos' Agamemnon shows signs of a similar mentality and action. In the *Agamemnon*, he is very much a 'leader of ships' (*Agamemnon* 1227, cf. 114–16, 184–5), just as Athens was in 458 very much a 'leader of ships' in the Aegean. The king's maritime enterprise against Troy is depicted not as a simple pious exaction of justice, but as an act of terrible violence to the city itself, its crops, cattle, property, and religious places, bringing destruction to his own army, and of course to his own family. In its unforgiving focus on the suffering inflicted by war, particularly on the innocent and weak, Euripides' *Trojan Women* of the other end of the fifth century (415 BCE) obliterates any residual glamour that such warfare and imperialism may have had.

The competitions that formed the climax of the Dionysia occupied a full three or four days, and brought the city to the theatre from dawn till dusk. Simply being a diligent and attentive member of this audience will have been physically exacting, to say nothing of its emotional and psychological demands. Remember also the immense athleticism needed on the part of citizens for participation in one of the choruses—tragic, comic or dithyrambic—at the centre of these contests. That actors and chorus-members trained so hard and long, in particular to produce an ample volume of sound, clear articulation, and (in the case of the chorus) accurate delivery in unison, shows how important it was felt to be that everyone in this massive audience should be able to pick up the finest details of each performance. And that the Athenian audience was a sensitive (and exacting) critic is shown, for example, by the harsh treatment (especially the comic ridicule) the tragic actor Hegelochos received when he slipped up in enunciating a line of Euripides' *Orestes* (line 279), so that 'once more I see the calm after the tempest' came out as 'once more I see the weasel from the tempest'.

A comic chorus of birds imagines the useful fantasy of spectators having wings with which they could flit off when bored by tragedy (a bias we expect from comedy) and come back in the afternoon (Aristophanes, *Birds* 786–9). Weariness and hunger were doubtless part of the theatrical experience, the latter staved off by provision of snacks in the theatre—when the acting was particularly bad, as Aristotle tells us, suggesting that absorbed involvement was the norm. Theophrastos' caricature of 'The Man lacking perceptivity' (or simply 'The Dolt') demonstrates this quality by being the sole person asleep all throughout the performance, and being left behind when everyone else has gone.

We should not pass too quickly over the very fact that for the Athenians drama was an essentially, and intensely, *competitive* event. It was judged by a carefully selected panel of citizen judges whose actions could later be legally scrutinized for their propriety. And it is clear that the audience as a whole felt the panel of judges should take notice of its own collective view, as expressed (so Plato and others inform us), by whistling, shouts, hissing, and kicking against the wooden benches. The same idea is reflected in comedy through the god Dionysos' response to Euripides' indignant question, when he has been overlooked by Dionysos in favour of Aischylos in his judgement of the 'battle of the poets' in Hades:

> EURIPIDES: And do you dare look in my face, after that shameful deed?
> DIONYSOS: What's 'shameful', if the audience think it not so?
>
> (*Frogs* 1474–5)

Built into the whole experience was the sense that every individual tragic treatment of the mythic heritage, and every fantastic comic vision, was pressing its claims, giving its 'advice' and its pleasure directly alongside other, competing visions. This tendency to invite multiple and competitive views of the city in its drama is perhaps one of its most democratic qualities. It is also a sobering thought, from our historical perspective, that the competitive structure of Athenian drama consigned many works to oblivion after an unsuccessful appearance. Euripides' *Medeia* was lucky to survive its placement *third* in the contest of 431. This should make us wary of forgetting the many other poets who were involved in the fierce competitive culture of the Athenian dramatic festivals, but whose work did not survive the perilous path of transmission through antiquity and beyond, except in the most fragmentary form. Successful contenders from the fifth century include Ion of Chios, Sophokles' son Iophon and the Agathon immortalized in Plato's *Symposion*. While the fourth century—long regarded as a period of rapid decline—produced poets like Astydamas and Theodektes who were much admired and long reread. The situation is even more extreme with comedy, given the survival in substantial form of only a single fifth-century poet. But Aristophanes' direct predecessors and rivals, Eupolis and Kratinos in particular, were giants in the field (the latter won six first prizes at the City Dionysia, three at the Lenaia), doing much to forge the very shape and content of Athenian political comedy.

Dithyramb was the first event on the programme (see Ch. 2, p. 81). Dithyramb had for decades contained elaborate narratives of stories largely or entirely unrelated to its recipient god, Dionysos, and was in this parallel to tragedy, which to some ancient observers already seemed to have 'nothing to do with Dionysos'. And there was a fair degree of productive influence between genres at the Dionysia from an early date. One dithyramb by the great Kean poet Bakchylides—his *Theseus* (poem 18) of as early as *c.*490 BCE—is a dialogue, in song, between a chorus of Athenian citizens and their leader, the mythical King Aigeus, father of Theseus. This generic mixing has its counterpart in an aspect of the audience's perspective that it is difficult, if not impossible, for us to re-create imaginatively: the experience of witnessing a set of performances in four very different but related styles over a number of days—dithyramb, comedy, tragedy, and satyr play.

Thus, even before their drama had begun, the Athenians had been inundated with twenty sung narratives of divine and heroic mythology in these dithyrambs. Moreover, the emotional and psychological temperature had been further raised by the keen competition between the tribes for the prize in these two events—and it has been argued that the audience in the theatre was actually arranged into wedges of seats belonging to each of the ten tribes. The next day was (probably—again, most details are open to debate) entirely comedy's: five individual plays by different poets. The next, and climactic, three full days were for tragedy. Or rather, for tragedy and satyr play. For most of the classical period, each of the three tragedians chosen to compete (a decision resting in the hands of a leading city official, the Arkhon Eponymos) presented their audience with three tragedies followed by a single satyr play. In Aischylos' day, the three tragedies often formed a trilogy in the strong sense that they presented a continuous, connected narrative sequence, as in the case of our sole surviving example, the *Oresteia* (made up of *Agamemnon*, the *Libation Bearers*, the *Eumenides*). Even the satyr play, the *Proteus*, may have had some connection to the tragic story—though a somewhat oblique one, since it seems to have dealt with an episode in the return home from Troy of Agamemnon's brother, Menelaos.

It is important to recall the arrival of the satyrs at the end of every grand and gruelling tragic production. Satyr play—'playful tragedy' as one ancient critic dubbed it—shared with tragedy its heroic cast, as well as much of its language and conventions; and the actors may well have used the same costumes they wore in the immediately preceding dramas. But to these were added, in every case, a chorus of satyrs, those mythical ithyphallic creatures of the wild, half-man and half-beast (equine or caprine) who frequently attended Dionysos. Hedonists and masters of misrule, obsessed with wine and the pursuit of all physical pleasures, the satyrs also show a surprising intellectual curiosity—they are experimenters and explorers. A common motif of their drama was the 'discovery' of important items of culture: musical instruments, products of metal-work, fire, perhaps even woman herself (Pandora). They were also instrumental in conveying the great gift of Dionysos—wine—and the means of its production to mortals. As Richard Seaford has put it, 'The satyr is an ambiguous creature, cruder than a man and yet somehow wiser, combining mischief with wisdom and animality with divinity.'

It is very difficult for us to gauge the impact on the audience of this satyric finale, but the sudden change of gear, the injection of riotous Dionysiac satyrdom into the elevated world of heroic tragedy, must have served an important psychological function. Emotional 'release' from the intensity of long hours of tragedy is too simplistic an explanation by itself, though surely one factor behind this arrangement. The satyrs' energetic and grotesque explorations of the machinery of Greek culture will have been another important attraction of this fourth Dionysian performance. And another, the way in which it brought performers and audience alike into an intimate relation, at the end of each day, with a more joyous, boisterous, masculine, and rather less threatening side of the worship of their god.

The City Dionysia alone thus needed five new comedies, nine new tragedies plus three new satyr plays every year (not to mention the twenty, much shorter, dithyrambs)—most if not all of which, it was normally expected, would never be performed again. This demand for so many entirely new large-scale performances was something unusual in the context of ancient Greek poetic production. By the start of the fifth century epic was predominantly a genre of the reperformance of a limited number of canonical classics (see pp. 53–4). There was to be sure a vast range of poetic composition taking place in connection with all manner of social and religious occasions, but the 'literary' culture of classical Athens represents a quite new direction and scale of production. Unusual too is its propensity for innovation and diversity. We have already seen the radical nature of tragic form as *drama*, as myth 'made live'. In fact, all of its distinctive features are innovatory: its deployment of many formal elements which, though found in separate usage previously, were never combined as they are in the complex manner of drama (choral song, including a range of formal hymns and other songs from specific contexts, like victory songs, wedding songs; iambic verse; the mask and so on).

Also innovative was the technology of the stage itself, a completely new space which encouraged experiment. By about 460 the major step had been taken to introduce at the back of the open acting and dancing area a stage building, or screen (*skene*), with all the possibilities it offered as a device to represent the face of any manner of buildings (royal palaces, caves, military encampments, the homes of 'ordinary' citizens). This introduced a powerful dynamic between closed and open spaces, between the visible and the invisible. Soon a device to reveal the secrets of this interior space was developed (the *ekkyklema*); another (the *mechane*) to exploit the upper register usually reserved for gods over the top of the stage building. The stage-front itself probably saw the development of illusionistic scene-painting on movable and 'disposable' panels. All of these innovations may seem tame to a modern audience brought up on the hyper-technological entertainment culture of films or musicals, but they must have been radical, even shocking innovations in their time. From the comic side, the demand from the audience for constant originality and innovation is formulated by the chorus in Aristophanes' *Women in Assembly*:

> Make sure your plans
> are quite original in word and deed.
> (This audience hates to see old stuff served up again!)
> (ll. 578–80)

The drive to innovation and experiment evident in the Athenian theatre parallels the restless energies of Athenian society as a whole in this period. The stereotype of the Athenian character put in the mouth of a Corinthian by the historian Thoukydides surely has some core of truth: 'given to innovation and quick to form plans and to put their decisions into action . . . bold beyond their strength, risk-taking beyond their better judgement . . . ' (1. 70).

The spectators, the chorus, and the drama

When they referred to themselves as an audience the Athenians tended to use the term *theatai* or the related *theomenoi*—'spectators' or 'watchers'; their theatre, the *theatron*, was literally 'the place for watching'. This emphasis on the 'spectatorial' is crucial. Much of drama's power lay in its emphatically visual quality, on the shared experience of its *theatai* in witnessing what went on on stage. And drama was, in an important sense, also a communal act of 'self-regard'.

In its shape and size, the *theatron* focused and intensified the attention of an unprecedentedly large group. Plato writes of 'more than thirty thousand Greeks' in the theatre, and even when modern scholars have deflated this exaggeration by as much as half (see above pp. 102–3), we are left with a gathering on a vast scale by ancient standards. The audience sat in a slightly more than semicircular space that fanned out, probably in wedge-shaped blocks, from the level area where chorus and actors performed. The rows of seats were fairly steeply raked up the natural hillside, so that the considerable distance separating those seated towards the back and the acting area did not adversely affect their line of vision. This spatial arrangement also meant, significantly, that the audience 'looked at itself' to a large extent. In the bright open-air theatre in the early Athenian spring the *theatai* could very easily see their fellows all around and opposite them. This physical reality of 'self-observation' was matched by the nature of the performances: the business of 'self-scrutiny' was at the heart of classical dramatic experience.

As I have already stressed, the technology of the stage encouraged visual experiment. Although we depend on the meagrest sources to conjure up the visual dimension of drama, it is abundantly clear that a good deal of the impact of both tragedy and comedy was visual. Dramatic costume was an object of special fascination and, particularly in the case of comedy, sometimes of stunningly ingenious construction (one can only wonder at the dress that brought to life comic choruses of cities, frogs, birds, waspish judges, islands . . .). The costumes of tragedy may have presented the Athenians with a degree of lavishness and exotic luxury they did not often see, given their supposedly austere habits of normal dress. The luxury of Persian and other 'barbarian' ways was paraded before them, the majesty of the gods themselves evoked, the wealth and splendour of heroic kings, queens, and tyrants. 'Silver vessels and rich purple fabric are suitable for tragedies, not for life,' as a fourth-century comic poet puts it (Philemon, fr. 105).

But the visual dimension of drama and dramatic costume in particular were much more than a matter of dazzling the eye. Costume was a crucial resource for evoking the other peoples and other places where dramas were set, and as the genre developed, the very business of taking on a costume and playing a role itself became an increasingly fruitful thematic device. Euripides notoriously dressed some of his heroes in rags, and used this 'shock tactic' to pursue dramatic reflection on issues such as the gulf between appearance and reality, between innate character and socially constructed status and identity, on the nature of fiction itself. His *Helen* is the most breathtaking example, with its 'two' Helens, one phantom, one real, its royal Menelaos in rags, its escape plot involving disguise and deception. Drama here used its own conventions to reflect on and, at least by Euripides' day, to question the conventional in society.

In many comedies on-stage role-playing and costume change are central to the plot. Athenian women elaborately disguise themselves as men, even take a comic lesson in how to speak and 'act' like men in order to infiltrate the Assembly and so take power in the city (*Women in Assembly*). Their leader, Praxagora—'Mrs Public Action'—has called them together in the opening scene, with all the 'props' of male attire, filched from their husbands—men's shoes, walking-sticks, cloaks; one has even let her under-arm hair grow and tanned her skin to look more masculine. But women have no experience in public speech:

> But that's precisely why we've gathered here,
> to rehearse our lines before the meeting starts.
> So get your beard attached without delay,
> And likewise anyone else's who's practised speaking.
> (ll. 116–21)

Dionysos himself in the *Frogs* dresses up as Herakles (if not very convincingly) to descend, as Herakles had, to Hades. In a spectacularly self-consciously (meta-)theatrical manner, Dikaiopolis in the *Acharnians* rifles through Euripides' entire theatrical wardrobe and comes away as the tragic hero Telephos so that he can speak with added pathos as a wronged beggar-king before the angry Acharnians. In tragedy, Orestes regularly uses disguise in order to pull off his planned murder of his mother and her lover and restore himself to power in Argos—dressing up, in Aischylos' *Libation Bearers*, as a visiting stranger 'with all the equipment' and even talking of putting on an accent, 'imitating the speech of Phokian language' (lines 560, 564). In Sophokles' *Philoktetes*, under Odysseus' direction a sailor stages an elaborate 'mini-drama' to try to deceive the wretched Philoktetes into leaving Lemnos with them. The manipulative and deceptive potential of role-playing is explored here, and it is, significantly, rejected by the outcome of events. Although tricked by this 'plot' into leaving, Philoktetes' departure is prevented by an attack of his painful illness at the last minute, and the experience of witnessing this at close quarters profoundly troubles the young Neoptolemos:

> NEOPTOLEMOS: It's not just now a powerful kind of pity for this man
> has come upon me; it started long ago.

PHILOKTETES: Take pity on me, boy: don't make yourself the object of men's abuse for tricking me.

(965–8)

Neoptolemos is so moved by this spectacle of suffering that he confesses the deception and promises to stand by the old hero against all the demands of his superiors and the needs of the Greek army.

Role-playing (appropriately) permeates that most Dionysiac of dramas, Euripides' *Bakchai*. The god of the mask himself masterminds the whole drama as its 'stage manager' from the first words of the prologue when he announces he will himself be disguised as a 'Lydian stranger' (lines 1–5). Under the influence of the 'new' god the old former king Kadmos and blind seer Teiresias dress as bacchants. And, at the critical question of the 'stranger'—'Are you not eager to be a spectator of maenads?' (line 829)—the young king Pentheus, enemy of the god, submits himself to an elaborate 'cross-dressing' as a woman on stage, under the god's direction. In fact his disguise will prove worthless, and he himself, perched in a pine-tree, will become the object of the attention of all, and the centre of a horrific and 'real' drama, not its distant spectator (see esp. line 1075).

Complete inundation by the visual image, especially the moving image of film and television, is so much part of the modern Western cultural experience that it requires a great effort to imagine the profound psychological impact of seeing the 'theatricalization of myth' for the first time, to see those familiar but distant figures of myth and religion live and breathe before the eye. This radical shift into a form of performance that Plato would later call 'full *mimesis*'—('imitation')—see p. 184—escalated to an altogether new level the intensity of the emotional charge of Greek poetry. And conservative critics like Plato regarded this as a seriously invasive psychological and moral threat for its audience, at best allowing them to indulge in 'shameless emotions'. We hear of audiences spellbound, or weeping at the performances of epic (see p. 54), where the only visual impact was that conjured up in the imagination of the listeners. But drama took the further, enormous step of enacting and *showing* the actions of its heroes. The accounts we hear of the audience's response are correspondingly more intense. *Theatai* are 'stunned' or 'struck'. Aristophanes' comic Euripides accuses Aischylos of 'blasting them out of their wits and astounding them' (*Frogs* 962). One of the most famous tragic actors of the late fifth century, Kallipides, supposedly prided himself on being able to fill the seats with weeping multitudes (Xenophon, *Symposion* 3. 11) An apocryphal story even tells of women miscarrying in fear at the sight of the Erinyes in Aischlyos' *Eumenides*. Even though apocryphal, stories of this sort suggest the remembered or imagined impact of such spectacles on their original audience.

There were of course limits on what was shown. Physical violence on stage was slight, though not unknown. Aias in Sophokles' *Aias* delivers his last, immensely moving speech to an empty stage (the chorus having, ironically, gone off in search of him), and at its end he throws himself on the sword he has planted upright in the earth.

> The slayer stands so it will be its sharpest, –
> if I've the time for such a calculation:
> a gift of Hektor, the most hated man of all
> I ever met, most loathsome to look upon.
> So it stands fixed in the enemy soil of Troy,
> freshly sharpened by the iron-devouring whetstone.
> I fixed it there, and carefully set it out
> to bring this man the comfort of quick death.
> So, I am well equipped.
>
> (ll. 815–23)

Whatever was actually shown to the audience, this is certainly an on-stage suicide, and the great body of the dead hero remains there for much of the rest of the play, to be fought over by his brother Teukros and his enemy Agamemnon.

The acts of most extreme violence, especially those of death (as in the case of the women who go inside to end their lives) or mutilation (as in the case of Oedipus' self-blinding) are nearly always concealed from the audience's gaze by taking place behind the stage-front. But such concealment at the critical moment has the effect of intensifying their impact; and what is not shown on stage is described after the fact by messengers, often at great length and in vivid detail. 'How? Tell us, how?' is an often-repeated request of the chorus on hearing the report of a death, and it triggers a verbal cavalcade. The messenger from inside the palace where Oedipus has blinded himself frames his account with these words:

> What deeds am I to tell of, you to see! . . .
> He shouts for someone to unbar the gates
> and to display to Thebes the parricide. . . .
> . . . these wounds are greater
> than he can bear—as you shall see; for look!
> They draw the bolts. A sight you will behold
> to move the pity even of an enemy.
>
> (*Oedipus Tyrannos* 1224, 1287–8, 1293–6)

A complex interplay between the visual and the verbal is crucial to drama and its power.

At their tragic performances the Athenians gathered together to witness 'grand' but terrible actions: violence and suffering of all kinds; the trampling underfoot of accepted values; the abuse of social relations, especially troubling when, as so often, they are those especially strong ties that should bind *philoi* or one's 'close circle' of family and friends together. Rather, brothers fight and kill one another, parents kill children, and children parents, wives deceive and kill their husbands. And yet there was benefit to be derived from such things: the power of horror, and of fear, could be beneficial. A sense of order, of the proper boundaries to be observed in relations with one's fellow man and with the gods, could be built, in part, from a controlled contemplation of their disruption. The general point is made by the Erinyes (Furies) in the concluding play of Aischylos' great *Oresteia*. Turned at last from their fury at their defeat in the trial of Orestes by Athena's persuasion and her offer of an honoured role in the city of Athens as promoters of fertility and civil order, the Erinyes are given the right to exercise for the good of the city of Athens the principal of 'beneficial fear'. They sing of 'a place where the terrible is good and needs to stand as silent guardian on watch over the mind' (*Eumenides* 517–19); and, when Athena remarks at the very close of the trilogy on 'the great advantage for my citizens from these terrifying faces' (lines 991–2), we might think too of the advantages being gained by the citizens of Athens in their theatre from these 'terrible faces' of tragedy.

As the earliest critics of drama pointed out, and as Athenian audiences knew from the start, this beneficial spectacle of suffering and disorder was also *pleasurable*. There is a pleasure to be derived from confronting disaster, terror, and crises personal and public that are without any real comfort or practical solution, from having extreme, dangerous emotions aroused, temporarily and artificially, in a 'safe' environment, the context of the special time of the Dionysiac festival; and from experiencing all this in a highly wrought artistic form of language, of crafted speech and song, that was full of poetic beauty and power.

In this connection, one of the important roles of the chorus is to act as a kind of 'internal audience'. They are always close, physically and emotionally, to the horrors of each drama. Often they are tied to the suffering protagonists by powerful bonds of loyalty, dependence, and friendship. And yet, like the audience, however much they are affected by the fate of the individual heroes, they themselves are immune from serious danger. Though they often have good cause for fear during the course of a play—the women of Aischylos' *Suppliant Women* are the best example, pursued as they are by their violent and threatening cousins—choruses never die and are seldom in direct physical danger. They spend much of the time watching, commenting, responding, both emotionally and rationally, to what they see and hear. And in this they offer the audience a set of possible models for their own responses. The views of the chorus are only ever partial, as they have no special access to some greater knowledge or higher truth: it is wrong to see them, as was once fashionable, as 'ideal' spectators, or even as the 'voice of the community'. They do sometimes represent a generalized response of a wider collective, a kind of normative or expected reaction, but more often than not they are made up of groups who could have no real say in the formation of 'community opinion'. They are very often women, sometimes slave women, or foreigners, or frail old men well beyond their physical prime and perhaps even marginal politically, or even, rarely, divine or semi-divine creatures (such as the Okeanids of Aischylos' *Prometheus*). It is only very rarely that they are the kind of adult male members of a citizenry that we might expect to serve as the mouthpieces of an authoritative, communal view.

Important unwritten 'rules' govern just how much distance there needed to be between the world of the contemporary audience's immediate experience and the world of tragedy. The worst horrors of tragedy were not allowed to come too close to Athens: tragedy, on the whole, happens elsewhere. Early in the century, the tragic poet Phrynichos produced his *Destruction of Miletos*, a 'historical' tragedy which dealt with the capture and annihilation of the Ionian city of Miletos by the Persians only a year or two earlier. Miletos was a city with which Athens had close ties of kinship and culture, and its destruction was a matter of collective grief and, since they had given little assistance in the hour of need, probably of guilt. This subject proved quite literally 'too close to home' to be turned into tragedy for the Athenians. Herodotos tells us that the entire audience in the theatre burst into tears, the work was banned and the poet heavily fined 'for reminding the Athenians of troubles close to home [*oikeia kaka*]' (6. 21. 2).

The scenario of Phrynichos' play was perfectly 'tragic'. At its centre was the destruction of a city, with the intense pathos that evoked for the city-centred Greeks, the obliteration not only of lives, but of ancient traditions, its famous temples and oracular site, noble public buildings, roads and ancestral lands; the horror of enslavement for women and children, and of death for men. In later tragedy the city of Troy would return time and again to the stage as the iconic example of the sacked city. But unlike Troy of the heroic age, Miletos was a Greek city firmly within the contemporary orbit of Athens, and the spectacle of its destruction on stage lacked the necessary 'safety gap' that could make the intense emotion pleasurable and valuable for its audience.

Herodotos' account of an audience response to a specific drama very early in the fifth century is precious indeed. Its stress on a shared, basically undifferentiated emotional reaction is striking, and is confirmed in general terms by one of the (highly parodic and exaggerated) 'character types' sketched by Theophrastos over a century and a half later. This 'Disgusting Man' (11) is described as the type who when 'at the theatre will applaud when others cease, hiss actors whom the rest of the audience appreciate, and raise his head and belch when the theatre is silent so that he may make the spectators look around.' What makes this so effective an example of 'disgusting' behaviour is the way that it so ostentatiously and systematically runs against the grain of the group theatrical mood and response. This was a collective and communal experience.

Such other evidence as we have suggests the Athenian theatre audience as a whole could also have a generally active, noisy, demanding, even unruly character, so much so as to have needed a special kind of 'theatre police' (*rhabdouchoi* or 'rod-bearers') to maintain order. 'Audience participation' was especially important for comedy, and in more than the form of the punctuating rhythm of laughter at the right moments. Applause is actively solicited, for instance, for their poet by the chorus of *Knights*:

> raise a great tumult for him and send him
> a good hearty Lenaian clamour,
> so that our poet can depart rejoicing and successful,
> radiant with gleaming . . . forehead.
>
> (ll. 546–50)

At other times, however, the instruction is to pay attention or not to interrupt, 'to restrain yourselves and not hiss' (Timokles, fr. 19) as a character tries to explain something. The audience as a whole—and its representative panel of judges in particular—is regularly cajoled, bribed, flattered, or threatened into voting for a comedy:

> I'd like to make a little suggestion to the judges:
> let the wise, mindful of our wisdom, vote for me;
> let those who enjoy a good laugh, vote for me for my jokes;
> so it's basically all of you I'm telling openly to vote for me.
>
> . . . .
>
> Don't perjure yourselves, but always judge the choruses fairly.
> Don't behave like bad whores who can only ever remember their last customers!
>
> (*Women in Assembly* 1154–7, 1160–2)

'Cued' responses were sometimes vital to the progress of the play, as when at the start of the *Wasps* a slave has the audience guess who it is who is suffering from the 'strange disease' inside the house (lines 67–73). The fact that these 'guesses' are preserved in our texts of the play, and that they are prompts for jokes at the expense of the (well-known) figures who make them, shows that the scene was not really one of impromptu interaction between stage and audience; but it also suggests that more and less formal levels of this interaction were invited rather than avoided in comedy.

A theatre for political issues

Nietzsche wrote that 'the Athenians went to the theatre in order to hear beautiful speeches', and although not the whole story, this captures an important truth which needs to be set alongside the visual impact of drama: most of its serious work was done with words. The use of crafted speech in public contexts of debate and performance was central to all Greek society, from at least Homeric times on (see Ch. 6). And classical Athenian society gave an especially privileged place to the spoken word, for the institutions at the heart of its democracy were run by words. Crafted speech was so vital to the operation of the democracy that it has been aptly dubbed 'the political tool *par excellence*' (Vernant). In the Assembly, the Council, and the elaborate court system, all the major decisions affecting the most powerful city in Greece, as well as the lives of many beyond it, were taken by citizen 'audiences' after weighing up the arguments put before them by speakers. As the democracy developed there developed with it an increasingly sophisticated culture of speech makers and consumers, of arguers and assessors of argument. This is a vital part of the context in which we need to place drama's relentlessly argumentative character, its obsession with words.

This is no dry, intellectual or purely rhetorical concern. Rather, drama itself was for the Athenians a political institution (in the broad sense of 'political') which could focus attention on the meaning of complex key terms in the city's political language, and scrutinize the power of language in operation, either in the serious key of tragic debate or through the absurdist debunking of comedy. Drama became a forum where the huge, unwieldy, and often unanswerable questions generated by the rapid changes in society in the fifth century could be raised. Those changes set the Athenians on a psychological course that veered between euphoric confidence and deep-seated self-doubt, and it was above all in their drama that they found a place to confront and explore these tidal shifts.

Tragedies often centre around a key social concept, or set of concepts: 'justice' in the *Oresteia*, 'power' in the *Prometheus*, 'law' or 'custom' in the *Antigone*, 'desire' and 'self-restraint' in the *Hippolytos*. And all the resources of tragic language, with its immense powers of allusion and compression of meaning, set up a kind of 'debate' through each drama around these key concepts and show a fight taking place over the meaning of the words characters use. For instance, the radical conflict of the *Antigone* is explored through language which, ironically, shows that the opposition between Antigone and Kreon is not in fact absolute, that neither of the two opposed attitudes can by itself be right until it grants to the other its due place. Throughout the play, Antigone appeals to a concept of religious custom to justify her burying the brother who had died leading an army against his own city. Hers is a notion of religious custom attached principally to the family, and centred around the private, domestic hearth and the cult of the dead (lines 452–60, 519, 908). At the same time, the leader of the city, Kreon, justifies his edict requiring the death of anyone who attempted to bury the 'traitor' by appeal to the law—the law of the city and its gods. However, even as they stand against one another in irreconcilable opposition, Antigone and Kreon use the very same language to describe the principles they support. For Antigone, the term *nomos* means the 'custom' of burial and respect due to the family's dead: to Kreon the very same word is the 'law' of the city. The two use the same terms to describe sharply opposed ideals. Yet the very fact that they do so suggests to the audience that their positions in fact converge—or must converge—at a certain point. It is characteristic of tragedy that this full recognition of the multiplicity and complexity of meaning and values is only achieved by the audience, not by the protagonists themselves (hence much 'tragic irony'). Sometimes the clash of meanings and values that is played out in this way is also a clash of the past with the present, of an older principle with a more 'modern' one. This to some extent is the case with the *Antigone*. For the 'law' which Kreon endorses is very much a civic law, a law of a polis (Thebes) which also has magistrates and generals and is at least to some extent reminiscent of the contemporary city of Athens. By setting up a drama of language in this way between past and present tragedy will have been a very productive means for its audience to reflect on the nature of concepts central to their lives in a world of great change. One could not easily institute a debate in the busy practical democratic Assembly on the changing nature of justice, or on the conflicts developing between the claims of the family and those of the city.

At the most basic level of form drama shows its attachment to a culture of speech-making and debate: from the rapid-fire exchange of single lines of continuous dialogue (known as *stichomythia*), to the scenes where characters deliver long, rhetorically complex speeches to explain their position and justify their actions, often answering one another point for point like opponents in an Athenian court (see below, p. 196). The most famous example is one of the earliest and most influential of all tragedies, the fully-fledged 'court-room scene' in the third play of the *Oresteia* of Aischylos. Here the very creation by the goddess Athene of one of Athens' courts, the Areopagos, is depicted in mythic time, its first case the trial of Orestes for the murder of his mother. Athena selects 'the best of my townsmen . . . to decide this issue in accordance with the truth' (lines 487–8), and they listen in silence to the arguments of Apollo for and of the Erinyes against Orestes before casting their votes. The debate as to whether killing a husband, father, and king is worse than killing a mother, is made to turn on the nature of 'parentage', with Apollo claiming that the father is in fact the 'true' parent of the child ('the parent is the man, who mounts'), the mother little more than 'a stranger who preserves a stranger's offspring'. However we are to imagine the impact of such arguments on a fifth-century Athenian audience (and there are good reasons to believe they may have found them more credible than we can easily imagine), it is clear that the dramatization of the process of decision-making serves an immensely important function for the city of Athens. This tragic myth of origins serves to exalt the majesty of an important institution and its power to resolve conflict, a conflict that threatens to engulf all Athens in violence. And this it does at a time (458 BCE) when the real city of Athens was still shaken by threats of internal discord following on recent further democratic reforms of its institutions, including the very court of the Areopagos. The mythic story thus served to stress the vital importance to the citizens of taking their democratic responsibilities as assessors of arguments seriously indeed. And it also serves to warn that the operation of such institutions was always perilously fragile, that persuasion was never far from violence, and that clear decisions acceptable to all parties were never easily won.

Nearly half a century later tragedy still continues to show its concern with the power and problems of language. In Euripides' *Trojan Women* of 415 there is, however, little or no sign of the cautious optimism or pride of the *Oresteia*, and the audience is, as often in Euripides, left with an overwhelming sense of the failure of argument and debate to achieve justice. In the central scene of the play Menelaos judges the case for and against his errant wife Helen. Helen speaks first, defending herself before her husband, the captive queen of Troy Hekabe, and the women of the city about to be carried off to slavery. In a rhetorical *tour de force* Helen blames Hekabe herself for the misery about them for having given birth to Paris, her seducer; and supports this with an assertion that the goddess Aphrodite is to blame, and none can fight a god. Hekabe answers these arguments with a rationalizing attack on the story of the judgement of Paris: 'Why should the goddess Hera have such a desire for the prize of beauty? . . . or was Athena hunting for a marriage among the gods—who sought from her father the gift of virginity, and fled the marriage-bed? Don't make the goddesses out as fools to give your crime a fine appearance' (lines

976–82). Deploying a word-play (impossible to capture in translation) based on the similarity in sound between the name of the Greek goddess of desire, Aphrodite, and a word for folly, *aphrosyne*, the queen shows herself just as adept as Helen in all the modern techniques of rhetorical argumentation:

> You looked at him, and sense went Cyprian at the sight,
> since Aphrodite is nothing but the human lust
> named rightly, since the word of lust begins the god's name.
> (ll. 988–90)

Eastern wealth and men, she adds, were what Helen wanted, not a return to her Spartan husband (lines 991–1022). These speeches reflect the interest in the specialized and controversial techniques of argument refined by experts in late fifth-century Athens, masters of rhetoric known (mainly by their detractors) as Sophists, who claimed to be able to argue any case, to defend seemingly indefensible and controversial positions (see pp. 145–6 and 167–70). They show the medium of public debate infected by a cleverness and rhetorical skill whose logic is perversely divorced from the real moral issues at stake. Menelaos at first concurs with the chorus' judgement that his wife must die, only to retract his decision to stone her at once with the promise to put her to death when back in Argos. Yet, as the audience knew from their *Odyssey* and, like the internal audience of this scene, from the behaviour of Menelaos when faced with his beautiful and persuasive wife, Helen will live on unpunished. In the end all the sophistications of rhetorical language fail to secure the least punishment for the woman who is held to have caused the extreme suffering seen all through the play.

Comedy also made extensive use of the forms of public debate to press its own claims as a voice to be heard in the public realm. We looked earlier at the scene of the *Acharnians* in which the comic hero Dikaiopolis defends himself before a 'jury' of angry old farmers, drawing on all the reserves of poetic technique—comic and tragic—to put advice before the audience concerning the contemporary political scene that was in its way fundamentally as serious as the lessons of tragedy. The *Wasps* on the other hand is entirely centred on the political institutions of Athens, in particular the system of popular courts. The chorus is made up of old men who fill their panels, taking their daily pay of 3 obols and lording it over anyone who comes before them:

> If you thoroughly inspect us, you will find in all respects
> That in way of life and habits we are very much like wasps.
> In the first place, there's no creature, once provoked,
> More sharp-spirited than we, none more cantankerous.
> . . . .

> And to make a living we are very well equipped,
> For we sting everybody and procure a livelihood!
>
> (ll. 1102–5, 1112–13)

For all the mileage that is made from parodying the foibles of the Athenian court system, and especially of its judges as obsessive, power-hungry vindictive men in it for money rather than from a sense of civic duty, the most potent critical fire in this comedy is directed at misguided citizens like Philokleon ('Kleon-lover') and the politicians (Kleon above all) who misguide them with their flattering rhetoric. Far from being the mighty Zeus-like (line 619) man of power that Philokleon fondly imagines he is as he sits in court, in reality, his son argues, he is a slave, receiving a pittance while the politicians who hoodwink him put away massive bribes (see esp. lines 665–72, 682–5, 703–11). At the core of comedy's powerful and complex political criticism are the concerns of speech and persuasion: 'You're bamboozled by that kind of speaking, and so you choose that kind of speaker to rule you' (line 668).

One of the most important formal features of old comedy that permitted its poet to address his audience more directly, often on matters of contemporary political and poetical concern, was known as the *parabasis*—literally the 'coming forward'. This occurred after the main conflict of the play had been established. The actors have left the stage and the chorus, probably through its leader, adopts the stance of its poet, and often his very voice. Although to modern eyes this can seem a rather odd interruption of the dramatic flow, it has the effect of powerfully linking the world of the drama with that of the external world of political and social reality. In the *parabasis* of the *Acharnians*, for instance, we find in addition to further abuse of Kleon—

> never shall I be found
> to be, like that man, a wretch and a bugger
> in matters of state
>
> (ll. 663–4)

—a claim for the poet's powers in a more 'choral' voice:

> Fame concerning his daring has already reached so far that,
> When the Great King tested the Spartan embassy,
> He first asked them which side prevails with ships,
> And then which side this poet rebukes;
> For he said that these men have become much better,
> And would triumph in war, possessing this counsellor.
>
> (ll. 646–51)

Comedy established for itself a place in the city from which it could exercise the twin ideals of *isegoria* and *parrhesia*. Basically, these are respectively the equal right of any citizen to speak and give advice; and an ideal of 'open speech', a willingness to bring any matter, however sensitive, before the people. It is no coincidence that comedy was given a formal institutional place in the competition of the City Dionysia in 486, a year known for important democratic reforms in the city, including the introduction of ostracism, a means for removing a political 'tall poppy' by a mass vote of the citizenry.

Who was there?

All that we have seen thus far of drama's context and content shows us a poetry aimed at the citizens (the *politai*) of Athens, at those for whom the weighty matters of responsibility, of leadership and judgement were intensely live issues, and for whom the control of language was crucial because they alone in the community exercised the power of using language 'politically'. Much else supports this idea that the citizens were the 'target' audience of drama, that it was their own special form of education, self-scrutiny, and entertaining reflection. In comedy, for instance, speakers often address the audience as 'Men of Athens', the same expression employed in the Assembly and courts where none other than fully fledged citizens were allowed. And the fact that citizens (only) could receive a small cash distribution from their local deme administration to assist their attendance in the *theatron* also very strongly suggests that this was perceived as a kind of civic duty directly analogous to sitting as a judge in a court or attending the Assembly.

Of course the audience could never literally constitute the citizenry of Athens. Although the theatre was very much larger than the space where the Assembly met, it did not have the capacity to admit the entire citizen body. Also, we have seen that foreigners attended in some numbers; and we know that men sometimes took their sons with them (an early inculcation in some of the 'big issues' of adult life). On the other hand, it is also clear that some Athenians were unable to attend. We should remember that some Attic farms were more than thirty miles from the city. In this connection, the long Peloponnesian War (431–404) made a powerful impact on the theatre audience and hence on the nature of theatre itself and the drama it left behind. The official Athenian policy, to abandon the countryside each spring to the enemy and depend largely on imported grain and the power of the navy, saw thousands of country-dwellers move inside the city walls. The most obvious theatrical response to this change is Aristophanes' *Acharnians*, which takes this calamity as the starting-point for its pro-peace fantasy, and this helps explain its idealization of the rustic life.

Nor was the theatre audience an entirely undifferentiated mass of democratic equals. There were front-row seats reserved for important officials, military and civic, for priests, foreign dignitiaries, and men honoured by the city for special services. There also seems to have been a special zone marked out for the fifty presiding members of the Council; and possibly for the year's 'ephebes', the Athenian adolescents on military service just prior to becoming full members of the adult, citizen community. The special place physically accorded the ephebes in the theatre has generated interesting speculation about the orientation of tragedy in particular around 'ephebic' concerns. It is certainly true that many tragedies seem to speak of the problems and perils facing a young man on the point of adulthood. One thinks of the depiction of Neoptolemos in Sophokles' *Philoktetes*, the young 'cadet' faced with his first serious 'campaign'; or of the numerous tellings of Orestes' ordeals, ever returning to the stage to claim his proper place at the head of his household and city, but having to do so through the extreme and deeply problematic path of matricide, a crime whose justification seems less and less sound as its tellings proceed across the generations of tragic poets. Another 'difficult ephebe' is Hippolytos, the companion of Artemis and eternal hunter (a very ephebic activity), whose refusal to recognize Aphrodite and take on the responsibility of adult sexuality (that is, to cease to be an ephebe) is an important element in his tragedy. At the very least a strong case can be made for the impact on tragic drama of this special segment of its audience.

Despite this clear civic focus of drama, it is one of the extraordinary characteristics of the tragic stage that its plays were regularly set in places other than Athens and populated by non-Athenians. This means by non-Athenian Greeks—Thebans and Argives figure most prominently in our surviving plays—and by barbarians, whether from the very edges of the Greek world, like Thrace, or well beyond it, as with the many Persians, Phrygians, and Egyptians who appear. It also means by non-Athenian women; and in general by figures whose social status put them above (kings, tyrants, even gods) or below (slaves) the level of the Athenian citizen. Some of these groups, we have already seen, were sometimes part of actual dramatic audiences in Athens. It remains to see how far this inclusion of 'others' in the audience and drama of Athens may have extended.

Part of the explanation for the fact that most tragedies are not set in Athens is the 'safety-gap' argument (see p. 115 above). Not only did this arrangement give Athens the satisfaction of seeing tragedy happen off their soil: a more rigorous, even relentless examination of social and moral problems was possible if they were not seen to form part of the city's own mythic past. The other side of this coin is the way that when Athens or Athenians do appear in tragedy, it is generally in a highly positive light. The end of the *Eumenides* is the classic example, as the polis of Athena emerges as the place where the disastrous history of self-destruction of the royal house of Argos can at last be resolved. A less subtle case is the way the venerable epic story of the 'Seven against Thebes', the campaign of Oedipus' son Polyneikes and his followers to recover power in his ancestral home, acquires in Euripides' *Suppliant Women* an entirely new sequel in which the Athenians now take centre stage, in the capacity of protectors of the weak and defenders of the sacred rights of burial. But as ever with tragedy, things are not quite so straightforward. We need think only of the way that, after the terrible murder of her own children, Medeia flies off from Corinth, entirely free from punishment, to a safe haven prepared by her earlier in the drama—in Athens!

We can safely rule out the presence of non-Greeks in the theatre audience. As Edith Hall demonstrated in her classic study, 'the barbarian' in tragedy was a figure of the imagination created for the tragic stage, a negative embodiment of Athenian civic ideals. 'Barbarians' as a group perpetrated all the social and political crimes like incest, polygamy, sacrilege, despotism ,and having women in power in strict opposition to which 'the Athenian' defined his own ethical and political position. Once again, the Athenian remains the proper recipient of the dramatic message.

The case of metics is significantly different, as is that of slaves. Metics were almost certainly in the audience, perhaps in some numbers, given that many were city-dwellers. Metics were non-Athenians, immigrants usually from other Greek cities who had certain rights of residency in Athens, but no political rights, and various obligations to the city, including a special poll-tax. By the middle of the fifth century the metic population was large, and it played the leading role in conducting Athens' burgeoning trade and commerce. 'Metic issues' are central to a number of tragedies. In Aischylos' *Suppliant Women*, for instance, the Greek city of Argos, which despite being ruled by a king is depicted in markedly democratic colours, is faced with the weighty problem of whether to extend help to a group of outsiders. The Danaids, the daughters of Danaos who have some hereditary claim to the support of Argos through their Argive ancestor Io, have fled there from Egypt to escape the violent courting of their cousins. It is clear that to help them will involve the community in war, but the Argive assembly is shown as accepting this possibility and granting the young women a kind of metic status (line 609, cf. lines 994–5). This decision is presented as morally upright, but the fact that these 'metics' will indeed prove such a source of trouble for the city makes of the tragic treatment a complex rumination on the values and dangers of dealing with such outsiders.

The Erinyes of the *Eumenides* offer perhaps the best example of the issue as to how to incorporate potentially troublesome, and beneficial, outsiders. Athena's solution to their continuing anger after the acquittal of Orestes is to find a place of honour for these ancient goddesses within the city that will see their powers turned to the benefit of the city:

> I foresee—the flowing course
> of time will bring greater honours
> to these my citizens, and if you have a place
> of honour by the palace of Erechtheus
> an endless line of men and women will present to you
> gifts you would never get from any other race
> (ll. 852–7)

In Athena's own language this offer transforms the Erinyes into 'metics':

> Now you,
> descendants of Kranaos, keepers of this city,
> you must lead these honoured immigrants [*metoikoi*];
> the citizens must learn to understand
> their riches
> (ll. 1010–13, cf. l. 1018)

And as a visual marker of this new condition whose significance would not escape the audience, when the Erinyes participate in the great procession with which the entire trilogy closes, they put on crimson robes and march off stage, just as 'real' metics did when they joined in the most important procession of Athenian religious life, that of the Panathenaia. What metics in the audience made of this we can only speculate. Were they honoured at the analogy that saw their status-group depicted as a source of prosperity and security for the glorious future of Athens? Or, rather, offended by the reminder of the manipulation and degree of control exercised over them, at the extent to which for all the benefits they brought the city, they were firmly placed as 'second-class' citizens? This seems to be another case where the presence of this significant group within society, and within the theatre audience, has affected the concerns of some dramas, but where the 'message' is still principally for those with the power to make real-life decisions, with responsibility for managing the city and all its inhabitants.

Much the same point could be made for that even more silent and powerless group in Athenian society, slaves—we know some to have been in the theatre, but only in the capacity as attendants of their masters. In real life, slaves had virtually no agency. They were the legal possessions of their owners, and regarded by some at least in dehumanizing terms as little more than mechanically useful items of property, 'by nature' incapable of the power of judgement that was central to the identity of the free citizen. Yet they have an extraordinary prominence in drama, tragic and comic, where they can take on active roles of great consequence. It is easy not to notice how challenging a figure the slave Xanthias is in Aristophanes' *Frogs*. His prominent and active role appears to be an innovation in the comic tradition, where slaves' principal functions had hitherto been to set the scene in expository prologues, and to serve as objects of 'amusing' physical and verbal abuse. Xanthias, however, dominates his own master, Dionysos, makes a fool of him, and ends up having him beaten by the doorkeeper in Hades. This innovation in the comic slave may in part be a response to the fact that in the previous year a large number of slaves had been freed because of their contribution as rowers to the desperate Athenian war-effort in the battle of Arginousai. The Athenians may have been forced to reassess the possibilities of this largely silent group, even to question the 'naturalness' and permanency of that sharp and deep divide between free citizen and slave.

The prominence of slaves in tragedy suggests that here too drama was a means for 'thinking through' issues that found little scope for expression elsewhere. And, although from the mouth of a comic caricature and not the real poet, the Euripides of Aristophanes' *Frogs* claims he was 'doing the democratic thing' (line 952) by letting the slave talk as much as mistress, master, young woman, and old. The shepherd-slave of Sophokles' *Oedipus Tyrannos* is revealing here. For this man is a crucial link in the drama of Oedipus' life, and vital to his knowledge of it. Only he knows the secret of Oedipus' birth, because against all the normal expectations of the proper behaviour of the slave, he had taken the momentous decision, entirely on his own account, to ignore the order to expose the baby Oedipus. Similarly with the Nurse of the *Hippolytos*, a slave with dangerous rhetorical proficiency (see esp. lines 433–81) who takes the initiative, explicitly prohibited by her mistress, of revealing Phaidra's passion to Hippolytos, with all the tragic consequences that follow.

A few contemporary voices claimed that Athenian democratic conditions had obliterated or at least blurred the distinction between free citizen and slave. We should take such claims with much more than a grain of salt, but the important point, as far as drama is concerned, is this: the new, more open conditions of Athenian democratic society had shaken social expectations and accepted norms to such an extent that claims of this sort could at least be made—and that there was less complacency about the (supposedly) 'natural' order of social status.

Women at the theatre?

I have left the most intriguing and difficult case till last. Were women part of the theatrical audience in Athens? And if they were, what impact did their presence have on the works produced there? Were they close to the model of the male viewer, active participants in a moral, emotional, and intellectual event that was central to their lives as Athenian citizens? Or was their involvement more akin to that of the metic or slave, in that their 'presence' as a hugely significant sector of society at large had a major influence on the images shown in the 'mirror' of drama, while those images were still intended for an audience of citizen viewers?

We can begin from one point of certainty. Women made no contribution to the theatre in an active, creative capacity. There were no female tragic or comic poets in the classical period, no female actors. Medeia, Klytaimestra, Phaidra, the hundreds of 'young women' chorus members, goddesses, and slaves who crossed the stage were all acted by men, an extraordinary case of cross-dressing (fitting for Dionysos) on a grand scale. Nor so far as we know did women play any other part in the organization of the contests, as producers, musicians, trainers, or the like. In this most basic sense drama was 'men's work', and the words of every impassioned female in drama were the words of men, from a male mouth.

We simply are unable to answer the 'hard', factual question as to whether women were present in the audience. For decades scholars have squeezed the same few pieces of evidence for all they might offer, but the result has only been a lack of consensus; and a genuinely ambivalent picture emerges. At a minimum it is possible to say that, if women did attend the theatre, our sources are surprisingly unclear on the fact (whereas they are not on the matter of foreigners, for instance). And this is significant in itself. For it is consistent with a general policy of silence with respect to 'good' Athenian women, a policy most famously formulated by the Thucydidean Perikles in his address to the war widows: 'Great is your glory if you do not fall below the standard which nature has set for your sex, and great also is hers of whom there is least talk among men whether for praise or in blame' (2. 45).

A glance at a couple of the more important pieces of 'evidence' will show just how elusive an answer to this question is. The relevant texts are from comedy and Platonic dialogue, and are thus both very slippery and far from straightforward as evidence for what actually went on in the theatre. Comedy is in the habit of totally reshaping reality for its own ends, while Plato is notoriously biased against theatre, indeed against nearly all poetry, on broadly moral grounds. In a scene of Aristophanes' *Peace*, Trygaios' slave is throwing barley-groats to the audience at his master's instructions, in part because a sacrifice is about to take place, and grain was thrown as a preliminary ritual act at sacrifices, but in part also in keeping with the comic practice of getting the audience on side by distributing 'refreshments', usually fruit and nuts. The slave informs his master that 'there isn't a man in the audience who doesn't have barley' (and, crucially, the Greek word for 'barley' is also slang for 'penis').

> TRYGAIOS: But the women didn't get any.
> SLAVE: The men will give it to them tonight!
>
> (ll. 966–7)

From this some deduce that women were there in the theatre, but perhaps out of reach of the ballistic barley, at the back or far edges. Equally energetic are those who argue it proves they were *not* there, and that it shows rather that they were at home (where their husbands would return to 'give them their barley' after the performances were over). Supporters of this last line cite a passage from the *Women at the Thesmophoria* where a woman complains about Euripides' 'misogyny':

> Where has he not yet slandered us women, wherever
> there are audiences, tragedies and choruses,
> calling us adulteresses and man-crazy,
> wine-tipplers, traitoresses, chatterboxes,
> good-for-nothings, the scourge of husbands.
> Now as soon as they come home from the benches
> they give us suspicious looks and immediately start searching
> the house for a hidden lover.
>
> (ll. 390–7)

Firm foundations cannot be built on such shifting comic ground. And the 'strongest' passage of Plato is hardly more secure. It is from a dialogue largely devoted to an attack on rhetoric, the *Gorgias*. Sokrates argues that poets are rhetoricians, and he dismisses what they do as 'a kind of rhetoric directed at a public composed of children together with women and men, slave and free' (502d). Even this seemingly clear reference to an audience that includes women turns out to be elusive, for Sokrates does not connect it specifically to Athens, nor specifically to dramatic audiences. More importantly, it is clear that Sokrates' overarching desire to tarnish poetry and the performing arts in general has determined the kind of audience he alleges or imagines it to have—a hotch-potch which mixes men up with the less than fully human (slave) and the irrational (child, woman).

Apart from passages like this, we depend largely on the more general images that can be formed of the character of Athenian society and of the festival. These tend to be divided between two schools. There are those who stress, as I have, the largely 'political' character of the occasion, and the general tendency of Athenian society to limit the occasions on which women, especially unmarried girls, appeared in public. And on the other hand, those who stress the 'sacral' nature of the occasion, and the fact that it was precisely in the area of religion that women participated and could even play prominent public roles. Although we cannot answer the factual question, framing it encourages us to make valuable reassessments of our assumptions concerning the nature of ancient theatre and society.

We are left with a powerful sense of paradox. For while Athenian society did maintain a high degree of silence about its women, and liked to think of them remaining in the shadows of their 'proper' place inside the household, it filled its stage every year with women, including many young women, speaking in public, taking all manner of decisions on their own account, and putting their decisions into action—and not infrequently, actions of the most transgressive kind, like the murder of their own husbands and children. Our 'safety gap' argument comes into operation here too. Women on the tragic stage are very rarely 'Athenian' women. They are distanced by mythic time, by place of birth, by their excessively high (divine, royal) or low (slave) status. Apart from Kreousa, the daughter of the mythic King Erechtheus, and the crucial link in transmitting the line of male Athenian kings and proto-citizens (see Euripides' *Ion*), the only example of Athenian tragic women that we know about falls into the special category of 'sacrificial virgins'. They are Kreousa's sisters, the so-called 'Erechtheids' who died, apparently willingly, to save their city from destruction (their story was told in the *Erechtheus* of Euripides, of which important fragments survive). Far from being transgressive females they are thus highly conformist in their devotion to the future of their political community.

Comic Athenian women are a slightly different matter. We have perhaps one or two examples of 'real' Athenian women named in comedy (where hundreds of real Athenian males are regularly named, and regularly for abuse). But the most promising exception proves the rule, since it is Lysistrate, and her 'real life' equivalent was a priestess of Athena, an entirely honourable and public function. Comedy does however present generic Athenian women with all the stereotyped vices ascribed by men to their sex—addiction to drink, adulterous sex, and deceit. And while the goals of the schemes they devise, like the peace plans of the *Lysistrate*, often seem to 'make sense' and strike a sympathetic note with their audience, it is the very impossibility and fantasy of the means they use to promote them—sex-strikes, women taking over power, and the like—which make them possible in comedy.

However, just as non-Athenian men in tragedy offered useful models for the Athenian viewer through which to pose questions to himself, so with these 'other' women. Tragic women provide an immensely rich array of types and scenarios for Athenian men to think through, to worry at, or to wish away some major problems. A recurrent concern of Greek literature, and an obsession of Greek society in general, is the continuity and purity of the male line of each free man's household (*oikos*). The anxiety is at least as old as Homer, with Telemachos' reply to the disguised Athena's question as to whether he is the son of Odysseus:

> My mother says that I am his child, but I
> do not know. Never yet did any man himself know his own parentage.
> (*Odyssey* 1. 215–16)

This concern certainly did not disappear in fifth-century Athens. Far from it, for now the prize of citizenship, which depended on legitimacy of birth, was so much the greater. This is an important background to the prevalence on the Athenian stage of so many tales of threatened childlessness and the end of family lines (*Ion*, *Antigone*, *Seven against Thebes*), of dysfunctional marriages and the dangers of adultery (*Oresteia*, *Hippolytos*).

Women in tragedy also act out to the full the male belief that womankind was excessively given over to the passions, much more prone to being overwhelmed by them than men, whose control of their passions was an important cultural ideal. Thus figures like Phaidra and Stheneboia are shown as victims of excessive desire (*eros*) in a way men on the tragic stage never are. Comparable are the many scenes where women give full rein to the expression of the intense pain and suffering that is peculiarly theirs as women—as victims of male violence in war (*Trojan Women*, *Hekabe*), as wives and child-bearers (*Medeia*, Klytaimestra in *Agamemnon*), as grieving mothers and lamenters for the dead (Euripides' *Suppliant Women*). These passions were attended in real life by fear and in some cases (public lamentation, for instance) they were subject to legal control. In drama they were given full expression, and the disasters that followed from them (particularly in the case of female desire) may have served to confirm the audience in their belief in the need to maintain a vigilant control over their real-life expression. But they perhaps also permitted men to experience, vicariously, the force of such passions that in the ordinary course of their lives they resolutely suppressed. This more complex response to the 'female' in tragedy suits a performance for a god of ambiguous gender.

Another important set of issues whose dramatization is made possible by tragic women are those concerned with conflict between the public and private dimensions of life; where the political, military world of the city at large comes into conflict with the family, with its own partly independent needs and traditions. The city and family, polis and *oikos*, were certainly not a sharply opposed pair of entities in Athenian life. The city was in an important sense made up of the many separate households, and to be a citizen required a man to be the head of a household. However, as Athens grew as a force in the wider Greek world and devoted more and more of its energies (including the lives and land of its citizens) to grand military and civic enterprises (above pp. 94–5), areas of sharp tension between the public and private realm did emerge. In tragedy when women act 'out of place', beyond their 'proper' domain of the household, they often do so because they perceive some threat to it. And so they come forth from the stage building which so often represents the household (*oikos*), into the space before it which is a kind of no man's land between the private and public realms. Antigone explicitly signals her entry into this area for the purpose of discussing her seditious plan with her sister Ismene; both of them, as unmarried young women, are transgressing the moment they enter this place:

> I summoned you here outside the gates of the courtyard
> because I wished you to hear this alone.
>
> (*Antigone* 18–19)

Antigone remains out of place by venturing even beyond the city walls to tend to her dead brother's body (while the 'good' sister Ismene returns indoors). Yet in the outcome this transgression by the young woman against the order of the city in defence of the family is shown to have been to the good of the city itself, since it protected it from the pollution of an unburied corpse. (And, in a further irony, it turns out to have been detrimental to the continuity of her own family, since her actions led her knowingly to her death, in the face of pleas to desist from her sister and promised husband.)

This curious combination of benefit and danger in the tragic woman is not confined to Antigone. Even a figure like Klytaimestra, who must in many ways have seemed a nightmarish creation to the husbands and campaigning soldiers in the audience, is not without her complexity and even her claims for sympathy. She is of course the adulteress, the murderer—wielding a sword, like a man—of her own husband, the king; and she shows an 'unnatural' craving for the male prerogatives of power, and an equally 'unnatural' ability to acquire them through her intelligence and rhetorical skill. All of this makes her a clear 'negative paradigm', a model of the transgressive woman that plays on some of the most deep-seated male fears. And yet she is, for all that, allowed to make an eloquent defence of her actions, a crucial part of which is the claim that she was acting in response to the attack on 'the glory of our household' (*Agamemnon* 208) by Agamemnon who,

> not caring a thing about it, just as if an animal was dead
> from his abundant flocks of fleecy sheep,
> killed his own daughter, dearest fruit sprung from
> my labour-pangs, to charm away the winds from Thrace.
> (ll. 1415–18)

Even though an Athenian male in the audience would hardly have seen this as a justification for the queen's actions, the play does allow the argument to be heard, and it supports her general claim in the way it shows Agamemnon's great public, civic enterprise at Troy as a brutal and impious act of wanton destruction (see above p. 105). So too it allows Klytaimestra to voice her resentment of the sexual inequality that allows the husband to have his concubines while the wife must remain faithful (cf. esp. lines 1437–43), a situation that was the norm in Athenian society.

Tragedy is full of such apparently unacceptable behaviour and arguments from the mouths of 'women'. Even if real women were not there to hear them, these perhaps more than anything else left their audience with the most challenging of all their dramatic lessons.

4 Charting the poles of history: Herodotos and Thoukydides

LESLIE KURKE

History before prose/Prose before history

Herodotos and Thoukydides, the two fifth-century practitioners of history whose works survive, together defined the parameters of history for the Western tradition. Thus, though the books they wrote are in many ways very different, they need to be read and considered in tandem. In the modern world, the relative respect and attention the two have received tend to correlate directly with contemporary notions of what history is or should be. When 'scientific history' was in vogue (mid-nineteenth to mid-twentieth centuries), Thoukydides was a hero of objectivity and accuracy, while Herodotos was denigrated and pitied for his *naïveté* and childlike story-telling. In more recent years, in the wake of the postmodernist contention that all truth is constructed, multiple, and unstable (as well as with the rise of social and cultural history and anthropology), Herodotos has come into his own as a model for cultural relativism and 'thick description', while we have become more and more uncomfortable with Thoukydides' pose of sublime objectivity. In the event, none of these modern stereotypes does justice to Herodotos and Thoukydides; we must instead, as far as we can, try to reconstruct the historical, intellectual, and cultural climate in which the two produced their remarkable texts.

Herodotos came from the Dorian city of Halikarnassos (modern Bodrum, in south-west Turkey). We are told that he was born around 484 BCE. He probably came from a prominent family and, to judge from the name of his uncle Panyassis, one that had intermarried with the native Carian population. We are told that he was exiled from Halikarnassos for his opposition to the tyrant Lygdamis, and then spent some time on the island of Samos. He also seems to

The fragments of the Greek historians are cited from F. Jacoby, *Fragmente der griechishen Historiker* (Leiden, 1954–69), conventionally abbreviated *FGrH*.

have spent time in Athens, and eventually participated in the panhellenic foundation of Thourioi in southern Italy in 443 BCE. This settlement ultimately failed because of civil strife between those of Dorian and Ionian ethnic affiliation within the city, a process which Herodotos could well have witnessed first hand. It is also usually assumed, based on the text of the *Histories,* that Herodotos travelled widely in Egypt and the Near East, though other scholars deny that he travelled at all, pointing to the mistakes and inaccuracies in his descriptions of foreign lands and peoples. I would contend that this is a sterile debate, in which both sides apply to Herodotos an anachronistic standard of accuracy or truth. We must accept the fact that we simply cannot reconstruct in detail exactly where Herodotos travelled from his text.

This is about all we can say about Herodotos the man (much of it already ancient conjecture). As for the *Histories* itself, the date of its composition is still very much an open question. All we can do is establish rough parameters. An odd speech in Sophokles' *Antigone* (lines 904–15) seems to be an imitation of a story Herodotos tells about the Persian wife of Intaphrenes (3. 119). If this speech is genuine and based on a Herodotean model, parts at least of Herodotos' narrative would have been known in Athens around 442/1 (the probable date of *Antigone*). We cannot, however, assume that the story was already fixed in written form at this time. As for the date of completion, the latest events referred to in the *Histories* fall in the first few years of the Peloponnesian War, so that scholars have traditionally assumed the completion of the *Histories* (and even Herodotos' death) by approximately 425 BCE. This span of at least fifteen years suggests a long process of composition, perhaps in oral form, over an extended period of time.

With the recent discovery of fragments of Simonides' Elegy on the Battle of Plataia, we confront the fact that historical narrative very likely existed in Greece before 'history'. Indeed, it has been suggested that one of the proper generic forms for elegy in the seventh–sixth centuries was extended narrative of the foundation, mythic traditions, and recent history of individual cities, performed at public festivals for a local civic audience (see Ch. 2, pp. 73–4 above). Such narrative elegy may account for some of the poetic production of Mimnermos, Kallinos, Tyrtaios, and Xenophanes, though almost all the texts of this genre of elegy have disappeared, overshadowed by the rise of prose history. Another practitioner of this genre may have been Panyassis, the uncle or cousin of Herodotos, who, we are told, composed 'a history of Ionia, in pentameters, dealing with Kodros, Neleus, and the Ionian colonies in 7,000 lines'. In the literary development from Panyassis to Herodotos, we see a shift from poetry to prose, which entailed simultaneously a shift in audience addressed.

Yet the fact that archaic poetry comprehended historical narrative publicly performed should make us wonder all the more about the development of prose history. Contrary to our assumptions, history does not require prose, nor is it self-evident that prose is the 'natural' medium for genres such as history or philosophy. We must therefore ask why prose genres first developed in Greece, and what the models were for Herodotos' remarkable undertaking. For Herodotos, the 'father of History' (as Cicero called him), conceptualized and wrote his work before 'history' existed. What, then, did Herodotos think he was doing? And why in prose?

Before Herodotos, we know that Herakleitos, Anaximander, and other Ionian *physiologoi* or 'writers on nature' wrote prose treatises (see Ch. 5, pp. 161–4). There were in addition (according to the first-century BCE critic Dionysios of Halikarnassos) a large number of prose writers who were earlier or contemporary with Herodotos, including Hekataios of Miletos, Akousilaos of Argos, Charon of Lampsakos, Hellanikos of Lesbos, and Xanthos the Lydian. They are shadowy figures to us, for whom only fragments and sometimes book titles are preserved. Yet even this is enough to give some sense of their themes and topics: these writers composed prose accounts of mythology (in all probability rationalized), genealogies, local histories, histories of individual peoples (entitled, for example, 'Persian Things', 'Lydian Things', 'Greek Things' (*Persika, Lydiaka, Hellanika*)), Annals or *Horoi*, and geographical treatises (the *Periegesis* or *Periodos Ges*). In his topics, Hekataios (the only one from Dionysios' list of earlier writers Herodotos mentions by name) is representative of the whole group: he wrote two books, a *Genealogiai* and a *Periodos Ges* (in two volumes, 'Europe' and 'Asia'). The first sentence of Hekataios' *Genealogiai* sounds the same self-confident critique of earlier traditions that occurs later in Herodotos and Thoukydides: 'Hekataios of Miletos narrates (*mutheitai*) thus; I write these things as they seem to me to be true. For the stories (*logoi*) of the Greeks are many and ridiculous, as they appear to me' (*FGrH* 1 F 1a). Wherever we have fragments of these authors, their dialect is Ionic, whether they derive from Ionian, Aeolian, or Dorian cities, suggesting that Ionic rapidly became the proper dialect for the early *logopoioi* ('prose writers' but also 'narrators of *logoi*, stories'). The fact that Herodotos (from Dorian Halikarnassos) composed his *Histories* in Ionic affiliates him with this group of writers, as also his use of the term *historie*, 'research, enquiry', does. It is to this word that we owe the term 'history'.

It is worth quoting the assessment of Dionysios of Halikarnassos on what distinguishes Herodotos' work from that of his predecessors and contemporaries among the early Ionian historians:

> All of these showed a like bent in their choice of subjects. . . . Some wrote treatises dealing with Greek history, the others dealt with non-Greek history. And they did not blend together these histories ⟨into one work⟩, but subdivided them by nations and cities and gave a separate account of each, keeping in view one single and unvarying object, that of bringing to the common knowledge of all whatever records or traditions were to be found among the natives of the individual nationalities or states, whether recorded in places sacred or profane, and to deliver these just as they received them without adding thereto or subtracting therefrom, rejecting not even the legends which had been believed for many generations nor dramatic tales which seem to men of the present time to have a large measure of silliness . . . . In contrast to these men, Herodotos of Halikarnassos . . . expanded and rendered more splendid the scope of his subject matter. Not deigning to write the history of a single city or a single nation, but forming the design of comprising within a single treatise many varying deeds of people of Europe and Asia, he started with the Lydian empire and brought his history down to the Persian Wars and narrated in a single work the history of the intervening period . . . (Dionysios, *On Thoukydides,* ch. 5, trans. W. K. Pritchett)

Dionysios' remarks suggest that Herodotos shared the methods and interests of his predecessors and contemporaries, but conceived his work on a much more global scale, synthesizing different strands of local and ethnic history into a complex whole.

Between orality and literacy

Like the other Ionian *logopoioi,* Herodotos' work took shape on the cusp between oral tradition and written record. Throughout the period of the Ionian historians (approximately down to the time of the Peloponnesian War), Greece was still largely an oral culture, reliant on traditional oral means of preserving and transmitting knowledge and social norms. Thus, when the *logopoioi* researched the distant past—in the form of founding stories, genealogies, or the ultimate causes of Greek–Barbarian conflict, which Herodotos traced back to Kroisos—they were almost entirely dependent on oral traditions, story, and anecdote. Herodotos might, of course, have had at his disposal the written texts of all the *logopoioi* who preceded him, but significantly, he maintains a fiction of pure orality. He never cites earlier written 'researches' as such, although we know from several later authors that on many occasions (especially in his account of Egypt) he borrows from Hekataios (according to one source, even

Herodotos' striking formulation 'Egypt is the gift of the Nile' comes from Hekataios).

And just as the *logopoioi* depended to a great extent on oral sources, they probably presented their work in oral form, even while they also committed it to writing. Such a model of combined oral and written dissemination is implied in Hekataios' opening sentence, which uses first the solemn Homeric verb *mutheitai* ('Hekataios speaks thus authoritatively . . . '), then immediately shifts to *grapho* ('I write'). Late sources (Plutarch and Lucian) preserve accounts of Herodotos' oral performances at Olympia or Athens. Their portrayal of Herodotos' activities is heavily influenced by the slightly later practices of the Sophists (Hippias, for example, famously gave oratorical displays at the panhellenic festival at Olympia; cf. Ch. 5, p. 168), and yet, given what we can reconstruct about Herodotos' sources, period of composition, and milieu, the idea of some kind of public performance is not implausible. Especially if we envision Herodotos' text taking shape over a period of decades, it is easy to imagine him honing and polishing different parts of his narrative through oral performance. At some point, though, Herodotos committed the entire narrative to writing, thereby producing a mammoth, comprehensive text that was itself far too long for public performance (modern estimates of the time required to read the *Histories* aloud range from twenty-four to fifty hours). It needs to be emphasized that, at the time it was composed, Herodotos' text was uniquely and prodigiously long (about twice as long as the *Iliad* or *Odyssey*). The comparison with the Homeric poems may well be relevant, for in their case we possess oral compositions that had over time become too long to be contained in the performance context of a bardic recitation accompanying a feast (see Ch. 1, pp. 36–45). It may be that Herodotos was partly inspired by the scale of Homeric epic.

In Herodotos' first sentence we find evidence both for his Homeric conception of his project and for the convergence of oral and written methods that shaped his text. Herodotos begins, 'This is the display of the research *(historie)* of Herodotos of Halikarnassos, in order that the things done by men not become faded in time (*exitela*), nor the great and marvellous deeds, some displayed by Greeks, others by barbarians, come to be without fame (*aklea*), both the rest and why they came into conflict with each other.' Herodotos' choice of the adjective *aklea* ('without fame') links his work with the tradition of epic poetry, which characterizes itself as *klea andron*, 'the fames of men'. *Kleos*, 'fame' (derived from the verb *kluein*, 'to hear') is essentially *oral* remembrance preserved through time, the highest aspiration of the Homeric heroes (see Ch. 1, pp. 34–5 above). In addition, Herodotos' formulation 'this is the display of the research' (*histories apodexis hede*) puts the emphasis on the public oral performance of his findings; indeed, the verb from which the noun *apodexis* is derived itself occurs in the same sentence, to characterize 'the great and marvellous deeds *displayed*' by Greek and barbarian alike. This verbal repetition implies that Herodotos' work is a significant public performance, on a par with the great deeds it chronicles.

But if these terms affiliate the *Histories* with heroic epic and oral forms of commemoration through performance, other elements of the preface align Herodotos' text instead with written monuments. Thus the adjective 'faded' (*exitela*), which is co-ordinated with *aklea* in a parallel clause, is a metaphor apparently derived from the Greek practice of highlighting the letters of inscriptions with bright-coloured pigment to make them more visible. *Exitelos* describes the fading of the pigment, so that from a distance the inscribed letters seem to disappear. Along with this term, we should note the slightly odd syntax of the first clause of the sentence: Herodotos does not say, 'Herodotos of Halikarnassos displays (or displayed) these researches.' Unlike Hekataios before him or Thoukydides after him, Herodotos is not himself the subject of his first sentence; instead his name figures in the genitive, with the presentifying deictic *hede* ('this here present') attached to the noun *apodexis*. This construction resembles nothing so much as the form of early inscriptions, which 'speak' from the position of the object inscribed, while they characterize their absent owners in the genitive and the third-person ('this is the cup—or the tomb—of so-and-so'). That is to say, the syntax of Herodotos' first clause is predicated on the connection made between reader and text in the absence of the author.

The echo of epic *kleos* in Herodotos' first sentence is significant, and points us towards many other affiliations and influences on his project besides Ionian *historie*. We can see Herodotos' epic aspirations in his monumental narrative of a great war between East and West, as in particular moments like his catalogue of the invading Persian forces (7. 61–99), and his characterization of the twenty Athenian ships sent to assist the Ionian Revolt as the 'beginning of evils' (5. 97. 3, echoing the characterization of Paris' ship that carried off Helen in the *Iliad*). In addition, it is worth noting that while Herodotos only ever mentions two Ionian *logopoioi* by name (Hekataios and Skylax of Karyanda), archaic poets and sages figure prominently in his text. Thus Herodotos mentions five of the canonical nine lyric poets (Alkaios, Sappho, Anakreon, Pindar, and Simonides; cf. Ch. 2, pp. 75–84), as well as Archilochos, and Arion who, he reports, first composed and taught dithyrambs in Corinth. Even more striking, Herodotos' first book contains extensive anecdotes about six of the traditional Seven Sages (Bias of Priene, Pittakos of Mytilene, Thales of Miletos, Chilon of Sparta, Periandros of Corinth, Solon of Athens, while the seventh, Anacharsis the Scythian, figures prominently in bk. 4). Most famously, the encounter of Solon and Kroisos early in book 1 is widely agreed to be programmatic for the work as a whole, even while significant echoes of Solon's own poetry have been detected in the speeches Herodotos puts in his mouth. If Solon is to be read as a mouthpiece for Herodotos (as many have argued), perhaps we should see that ventriloquism as part of Herodotos' own competition with the Sages as 'performers of wisdom' (cf. Ch. 5, pp. 158–61). Herodotos' text vies with these figures even as it appropriates their authority.

The *Histories* furthermore includes a great deal of material that might have circulated for a long time in purely oral form, purveyed by traditional storytellers and oral remembrancers (*logioi* and *mnemones* in Greek). Such normally ephemeral 'speech genres' for oral performance would comprehend miracle stories (for example, of mysterious superhuman figures who assist in battle, 6. 117); dedication stories (for example, how a particular object came to be dedicated, 1. 50–1); oracular narratives (for example, how a riddling oracle came to be fulfilled, 1. 47–9); and travellers' tales. Such stories are often fantastic and usually partisan (in that they serve and aggrandize the interests of the original local audiences). Because his narrative includes such tales, Herodotos has long been accused of excessive credulity, but as he himself characterizes his method at one point, 'I'm obliged to say the things that are said (*legein ta legomena*), but I'm certainly not obliged to believe them all, and let this formulation hold for the entire account' (7. 152. 3).

Even without this explicit articulation of principle, a careful reading of Herodotos frequently reveals the calculated subversion of one partisan story by its juxtaposition with others that contradict or undermine it. To take just one example, the sequence of stories about the extremely rich, aristocratic Athenian family of the Alkmeonidai in book 6 (121–31) starts from the denial that they could have attempted to betray Athens to the Persians after the Battle of Marathon, insisting that they had always been great 'tyrant-haters' (6. 121. 2). And yet, several of the stories that follow immediately undermine this claim, tracing the sources of the family's fantastic wealth back to the favour of an Asiatic despot (Kroisos, 6. 125) and a Greek tyrant (Kleisthenes of Sikyon, 6. 126–30; for the term 'tyrant', cf. Ch. 2, p. 63).

Another form of oral tale that seems occasionally to impinge on the text of Herodotos is the 'Life of Aesop' tradition. According to late versions of the 'Life' which survive, Aesop (in Greek, Aisopos) was a Thracian, hideously ugly, enslaved to a philosopher on the island of Samos in the sixth century BCE. It is pointless to ask whether there was a 'historical' Aesop: already by the fifth century a whole set of popular stories had grown up around him, describing his cleverness, his constant outwitting of his philosopher master, and especially his use of animal fables for didactic purposes. These tales probably circulated for centuries in oral form before being committed to writing. Herodotos clearly knew the Aesop tradition, since he mentions Aesop himself as the slave of the Samian Iadmon (2. 134), and since, on occasion, he puts Aesopic fables into the mouths of his historical characters (e.g. 1. 141). The inclusion of Aesop's fables and other 'Aesopika' represented a bold generic mixture on Herodotos' part, since prose beast fable occupied the very bottom of the hierarchy of 'literary' genres that culminated in heroic epic. Herodotos' text in fact incorporates the whole gamut of genres, often employed in ironic juxtaposition to one another.

Herodotos is thus a collector of the *logoi* of others who aspires to a comprehensive account, but always maintains a critical distance between himself and the stories he transmits. As Dionysios of Halikarnassos observes, Herodotos' great achievement is his ability to synthesize into a single encyclopaedic whole all the disparate strands that make up his work—disparate strands not only of local histories (Dionysios' focus) but also of the many different genres and traditions, high and low, oral and written, that inform his narrative. Ultimately, it seems that what allows Herodotos his ironic distance on his material is the fact that, first as prose, and then as written record, his narrative is disembedded from a specific ritual or religious performance context. At the same time (and related to this difference in context), Herodotos is free from the pressure to produce simply a celebratory narrative that serves the interests of any single community—in contrast to historical elegy or the tales of *logioi* and oral remembrancers. Instead, Herodotos aims at a comprehensive panhellenic—or even global—account, producing thereby a uniquely capacious and complex text that seems to include the entire world as Herodotos knew it.

It is easy for us to miss the anomalousness of Herodotos' account, which inheres precisely in his generic mixing, ironic detachment, and incorporation of many different, conflicting traditions. In order to appreciate how startling these qualities may have been to ancient readers, we need only consult Plutarch's treatise *On the Malice of Herodotos*. Writing five centuries after Herodotos' composition, Plutarch complains bitterly that Herodotos was a 'barbarian-lover' whose account is filled with 'malice' against the Greeks, since he does not produce a purely celebratory history of the great achievements of the Persian Wars. The first charge (of being a 'barbarian-lover') speaks to Herodotos' even-handed treatment of all concerned—recall that even in his opening sentence, Herodotos promises to memorialize the 'great and marvellous deeds' of Greeks and barbarians *alike*. Plutarch clearly also feels that Herodotos has betrayed the Greeks and sullied their greatest achievements by his inclusion of the many conflicting claims and counter-claims of different Greek states in the Persian Wars proper.

Structure and purpose

What is the structure of the work and what can we infer from this structure about Herodotos' purpose in writing? In the most schematic terms, Herodotos' structure is dictated by the progressive expansion of Eastern empires, first Lydia (1. 5–92), then Persia. As the Persian empire expands, coming into conflict with ever new peoples, Herodotos takes the opportunity to fold into his narrative the histories and ethnographies of various peoples conquered or threatened by Persian expansion. Thus the Lydian ethnography of 1. 93–4 forms the pivot between Lydian and Persian domination of Asia Minor, while book 1 also incorporates the early history of the Medes and the history and ethnography of Babylon and the Massagetai, as the Persian King Kyros encroaches against them. Book 2 is dedicated to the history and ethnography of Egypt, on the occasion of its conquest by Kyros' son Kambyses; book 3 narrates the succession crisis in the Persian monarchy after the death of Kambyses and the eventual establishment of Dareios as Great King; book 4 chronicles Dareios' failed expedition against Scythia, incorporating its history and ethnography along the way; book 5 narrates the events that led up to and precipitated the Ionian Revolt, bringing Greeks and Persians into direct conflict. Books 6–9 then chronicle two successive Persian invasions of mainland Greece, the first of 490 BCE, repulsed at Marathon (book 6), the second, much larger, invasion by Xerxes in 480–479 BCE, in which Greek and Persian forces clashed at Thermopylai and Artemisium (books 7, 8), at Salamis (book 8), and finally at Plataia (book 9). The remainder of the last book narrates the Greeks' taking the initiative and driving east against the Persians, and the combined land and sea battles at Mykale in Ionia. Herodotos' structure thus makes his work a kind of antithesis of the Near Eastern Royal Chronicle, which traditionally records as an unbroken sequence the effortless and divinely sanctioned conquests of the reigning king. Herodotos, by contrast, although he allows imperial expansion to structure his narrative, tends to write from the perspective of those who are threatened or conquered, and shows a particular interest in those peoples who successfully resist royal aggression.

An old theory of Herodotean composition posited that Herodotos began, like Hekataios, as a geographer and ethnographer and only slowly came to realize that his true subject was the great conflict of East and West. According to this theory, much of the first half of the *Histories* represents the relics of Herodotos' original geographic project, awkwardly shoehorned into a frame-narrative of developing East–West conflict (thus, for example, all of book 2, the history and ethnography of Egypt, would be a largely irrelevant digression). More recently, however, a unitarian school of reading Herodotos has marshalled

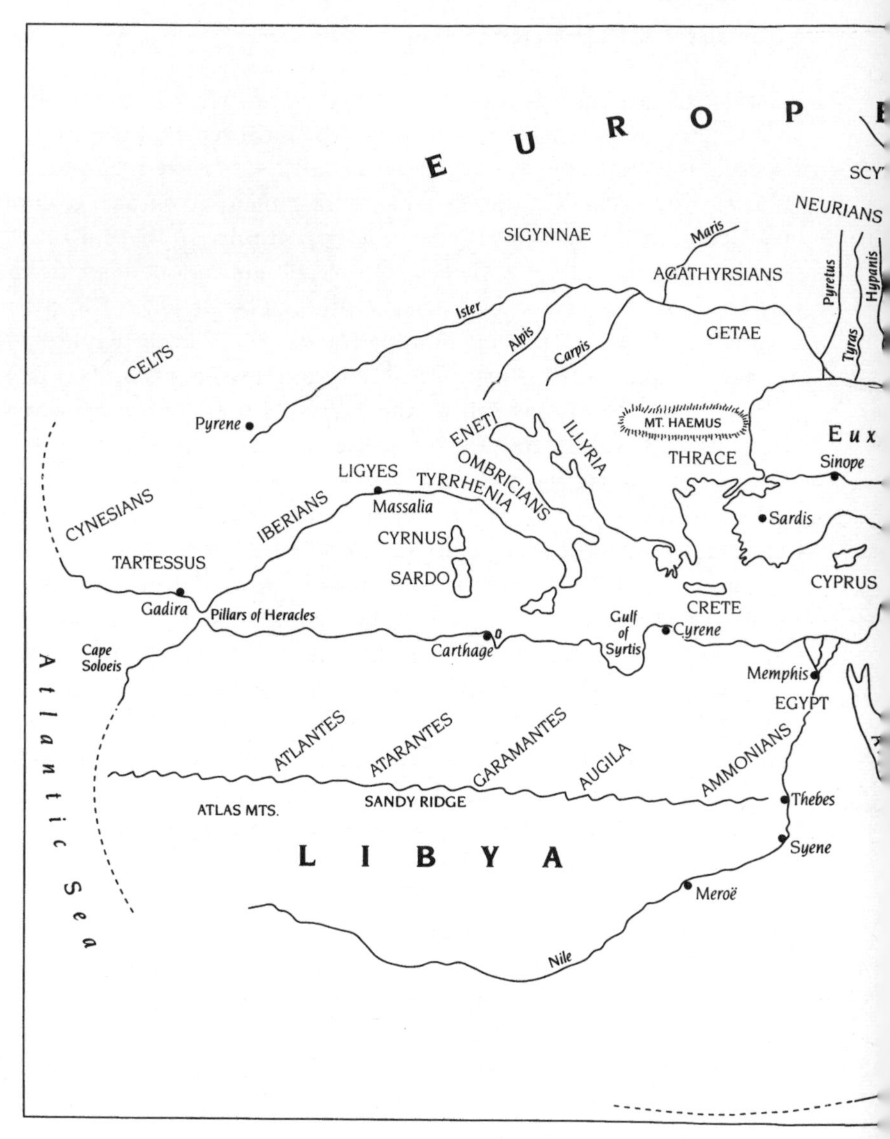

A HERODOTOS-EYE VIEW OF THE WORLD. *This modern 'map' attempts to give some idea of the world as represented in the work of Herodotos in the form of the kind of map-making which was rapidly developing during the fifth century BC*

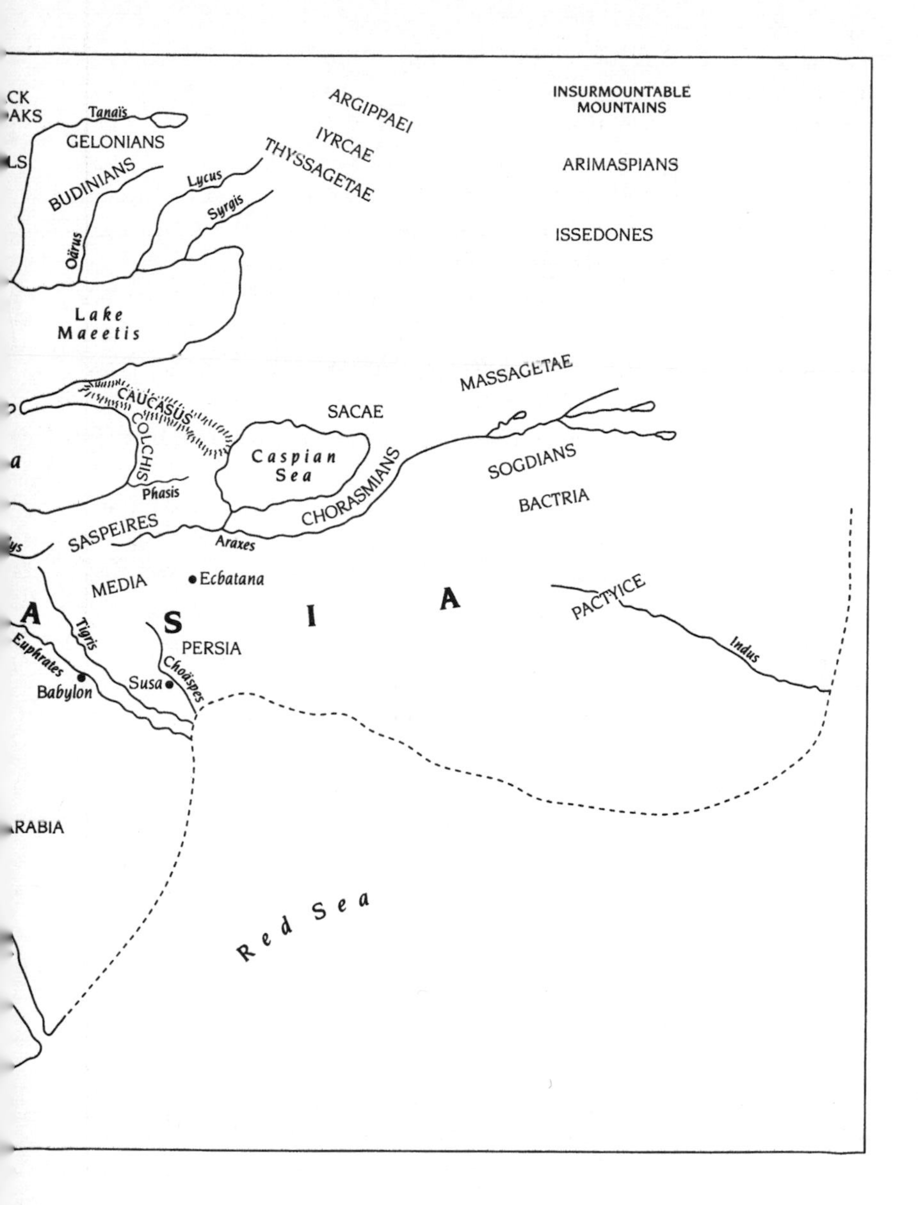
INSURMOUNTABLE MOUNTAINS
ARGIPPAEI
IYRCAE
THYSSAGETAE
ARIMASPIANS
ISSEDONES
Tanaïs
GELONIANS
BUDINIANS
Lycus
Syrgis
Oärus
Lake Maeetis
MASSAGETAE
CAUCASUS
SACAE
COLCHIS
Caspian Sea
CHORASMIANS
SOGDIANS
Phasis
BACTRIA
SASPEIRES
Araxes
MEDIA
Ecbatana
A S I A
PACTYICE
Tigris
PERSIA
Indus
Euphrates
Choäspes
Babylon
Susa
RABIA
Red Sea

strong arguments against this theory, demonstrating the integral interconnections between the more ethnographic, wide-ranging first half of Herodotos' *Histories* and the more narrowly focused, historical second half.

Thus one pervasive pattern throughout the *Histories* is the contrast between what we might call 'hard' and 'soft' cultures. Hard cultures tend to inhabit rough countries with a shortage of wealth and means of livelihood; they are under-civilized and usually politically decentralized. Soft cultures enjoy luxurious living, specialization of arts and skills, they are hyper-civilized and are usually ruled by strong centralized monarchies. Paradigmatic hard cultures are the Massagetai (end of book 1) and the Scythians (book 4); paradigmatic soft cultures are the Lydians, the Babylonians (book 1), and the Egyptians (book 2). In war, hard cultures always conquer soft cultures (as the Persians conquer the Lydians and Egyptians), but often themselves become enervated once they are exposed to the cultures they have conquered. Thus the Persians start out as a hard people under Kyros, but become soft from enjoying the fruits of their vast empire, so that a generation later they are no match for the rugged Scythians. Through this pattern, Herodotos elaborates an ethnographic theory of different peoples which also has a historical dimension. For 'hardness' and 'softness' are not dictated simply by geography and climate (as they are in the contemporary Hippokratic medical treatise *Airs, Waters, Places;* cf. p. 147 below), but also by the interaction of peoples and by individual peoples' own deliberate choice through custom and legislation (*nomos*). In the end, this pattern helps account for the 'astonishing' fact that Greek armies could successfully resist much larger invading forces led by Persians in 490 and 480–479. As in the case of the Persian invasion of Scythia (book 4, which reads in many ways like a preview of the Persian War narrative of books 6–9), the Greeks are a 'hard' people who can therefore resist the depredations of the now soft Persians. Thus the expansive sweep of the *Histories'* first half establishes patterns that help us understand the historical events of its second half.

Yet the fact that the Persians in Herodotos' conception could go within two generations from hard to soft suggests that Herodotos' purpose is not merely to explain the past. Many elements in his work (especially in the later books) imply also a didactic purpose that looks to the future: Herodotos' narrative offers a warning to the conquering Greeks not to be seduced in their turn by the lures of luxury and empire. We should remember that Herodotos himself lived through the débâcle of Thourioi (where the panhellenic colony ran into difficulties because of infighting between Dorian and Ionian settlers) and through the great years of the Athenian domination or 'empire' (478–430, Thoukydides' Pentekontaetia or 'fifty years'). Indeed, it is clear that he lived into the first years of the Peloponnesian War at least. Given this context, we can see the didactic element implicit in several vignettes that Herodotos offers in the closing books. There is first the story of the Spartan King Pausanias, the victorious commander at the Battle of Plataia, amazed by the opulence and luxury of the tent of Xerxes captured in the battle. On a whim, he has the Persian king's servants prepare their normal royal meal, which he juxtaposes to the plain fare of the Spartan *sussitia*. He then calls together the other Greek commanders, as he says 'to show them the folly of the Persian, who, when he had such a life-style, came against us to take away our miserable fare' (9. 82). In context, Herodotos' narrative can only be heavily ironic, since, as he tells us discreetly elsewhere, Pausanias would, within a couple of years, be accused of plotting with the Persian king, dazzled by the wealth and luxury he here disdains (Herodotus, 5. 32, 8. 3. 2).

Herodotos' closing vignette of the Athenians is no better. The very last event he narrates in the *Histories* is the Siege of Sestos, commanded by the Athenian Xanthippos (father of Perikles). Xanthippos allows the vengeful Greek populace to crucify the Persian commander Artauktes and to stone his son to death before his eyes (9. 120). These are acts of 'barbarian' savagery comparable to the mutilation of the corpse of Mardonios, which Pausanias had nobly abjured after the Battle of Plataia (9. 78–9). And significantly, this assimilation of Greek behaviour to barbarian norms takes place 'on the shore where Xerxes yoked the Hellespont'. Thus the crucified body of Artauktes marks the crossing-point between Europe and Asia, and ominously foreshadows the ways in which the Athenian empire will come to imitate more and more closely the violent Persian regime it was first formed to oppose. Through these anecdotes, Herodotos shows us implicitly how the Greeks could be corrupted by their success, and how greed and ambition for empire would eventually break down their fragile alliance and lead to the terrible internecine conflicts of the later fifth century.

Between science and rhetoric: Thoukydides

As with Herodotos, we know very little about Thoukydides' life and background beyond what he tells us himself in his *History*. One important bit of information is that his father's name was Oloros; this is a very unusual name, which we know belonged to a late sixth-century Thracian king who gave his daughter in marriage to Miltiades, son of Kimon (who would later be the Athenian commander at the Battle of Marathon). This name strongly suggests that the historian was himself a member of the family of Miltiades and Kimon, one of the wealthiest and most prestigious families in Athens. Thoukydides' wealth and noble birth, as well as his Thracian connections, tend to be confirmed by what he tells us himself: he was elected Commander (*strategos)* in 424/3 (a position that still almost invariably went to prominent aristocrats at this time), and he was in 424 'in possession of the working of the goldmines on the Thracian mainland' opposite the island of Thasos (which implies the acquisition of prodigious wealth from slave-worked mines; Thoukydides, 4. 105. 1). Probably because of his Thracian connections, Thoukydides was dispatched as leader of a campaign force to this area, charged with preventing the defection of Athenian allied cities to the Spartan commander Brasidas. Thoukydides (possibly on his first mission as Commander) miscalculated and arrived just hours too late to prevent the defection of the strategically important city of Amphipolis to Brasidas (Thoukydides, 4. 104–6). Rather than face the wrath of the Athenian people for this crucial military failure, Thoukydides chose voluntary exile for the next twenty years (as he tells us himself, 5. 26. 5). He wrote the history of the Peloponnesian War, starting, as he tells us, when the conflict first began and proceeding by summers and winters down to the twenty-first year of the war (411 BCE), when his account stops abruptly at a semicolon in the middle of a paragraph. We do not know why Thoukydides left his account unfinished; it is usually assumed that his death intervened, but this is not necessarily the case. Calculating back from his stint as Commander, scholars assume that Thoukydides was born in the early 450s; and he certainly survived the end of the War in 404 BCE (again as he tells us himself, 5. 26. 5), perhaps dying in the early 390s. Thoukydides' text reveals to us that he was profoundly influenced by the intellectual developments of his day, especially the Sophistic movement and Hippokratic developments in medicine. The so-called Sophists were performers, writers, and teachers who claimed to be able to impart to students the arts of rhetoric and political governance. Many of them came to Athens in the latter half of the fifth century, drawn by the city's imperial wealth and by the growing need for political and rhetorical training as its system of government came to depend more heavily on public debate and persuasion. The first great generation, including Protagoras of Abdera, Hippias of Elis, Prodikos of Keos, and Gorgias of Leontinoi, were polymaths who systematized many different fields of knowledge (e.g., astronomy, medicine, mathematics, etymology and grammar, ethics), but they seem to have had their most profound impact in the domain of political rhetoric (see Ch. 5, pp. 167–9).

They were the first to teach rhetoric in a systematic way, claiming that there were two opposing arguments (and only two) to be devised on any issue (Protagoras' *dissoi logoi*), while they purveyed distinctive styles of argument, such as the argument from likelihood (*eikos*). Aristotle, in the *Rhetoric*, offers a vivid example of how the argument from likelihood could be used in the lawcourt. Imagine, he says, that a small man beats up a larger man, who brings him up on charges. In court, the accused argues, 'Is it *likely* that I, a small man, would attempt to assault a much bigger man?' The accuser, in turn, argues, 'Is it *likely* that I, a bigger man, would face the shame of this accusation if it were not true?' Thus (notice), the argument from likelihood can be used in the service of the construction of opposing arguments on the same theme (see Ch. 6, pp. 192–3). In like manner, the Sophists popularized a set of conceptual oppositions which could form the basis of opposing arguments: convention vs. nature (*nomos* vs. *phusis*), and the advantageous vs. the just (as Aristotle advises, if your opponent argues from nature, you shift the ground and argue from convention; if, contrariwise, he argues from convention, you argue from nature). The Sophists' rhetorical teaching as well as their other writings reveal them to be pragmatists and relativists, who expressed agnosticism about divine causes but displayed unlimited faith in the power of human reason, ingenuity, and perception. Hence Protagoras' famous dictum, 'Of all things the measure is mankind, of the things that are, that they are; of the things that are not, that they are not'.

Allied with the Sophists in their optimistic faith in progress through the exercise of reason and technique were the Greek medical writers, many of whose treatises have come down to us under the name of the famous fifth-century physician Hippokrates of Kos. The medical writers of the late fifth century had come to reject supernatural causes for illness; instead, they established medicine as a *techne*, a specialized skill and field of knowledge based on close observation and the compilation of many case studies. Thus the Hippokratics engaged in very accurate recording of the empirical facts and symptoms of disease, as a basis for *diagnosis* (distinguishing each illness from every other) and *prognosis* (accurate prediction of the future course of illness). One basic contention of this new medical *techne* was that the combination of past experience and careful observation enabled the practitioner to deduce unseen causes from perceptible symptoms.

Thoukydides' text reveals over and over again the profound influence of these two intellectual movements. The influence of the medical writers is perhaps most obvious in the clinical description of the plague in Athens (2. 47–55), but it informs many other passages of description and analysis as well. For example, in his succinct formulation of the causes of the war: 'I consider the truest cause (*alethestaten prophasin*), though the most invisible in discussion, to be that the Athenians, as they became powerful and provoked fear in the Lakedaimonians, compelled them to fight. But the openly acknowledged grievances on either side were these, which caused them to dissolve the treaties and go to war' (1. 23. 6; Thoukydides then proceeds to narrate the immediate conflicts over Potidaia and Kerkyra). Notice that like the medical writers, Thoukydides rejects any divine cause behind the war, but instead perceives an invisible, underlying motive in Spartan fear of Athenian expansion (*prophasis*, Thoukydides' word for this invisible, underlying cause, was in fact a technical term in Greek medical writing for the visible symptoms of the onset of disease). The form and diction of such passages suggest that Thoukydides regarded the war as a disease that infected the whole of Greece, and took it as his own task to describe its onset and progress.

The Sophistic influence on Thoukydides is even more pervasive, detectable at every level of the text, from his penchant for antithetical expression, to the frequent pairing of opposed speeches in debate, to the speakers' repeated invocation of the argument from advantage and the claim that 'might makes right' (which we can read as a strong form of the nature vs. convention argument). Sophistic models also lie behind many elements of Thoukydides' methodology. For example, immediately after the proem, Thoukydides embarks on a brief survey of early Greek history (1. 1. 3–1. 20). This survey (traditionally called the 'Archaeology') presents a relentlessly materialist analysis, eschewing divine motivation, of human progress through the gradual acquisition of surplus money, defensive walls, and ships. In this account, Thoukydides not only introduces several of his key themes, but also offers a *tour de force* demonstration of his method: deduction from visible evidence (*tekmeria*) and argument from likelihood (*eikos*; see e.g. 1. 9. 4).

In like manner, Thoukydides' well-known statement of his policy with regard to speeches must be understood against a Sophistic background. The historian explains: 'And however many things each of them said in speech before or during the war, it was hard to recall in detail the accuracy of the things said, both for me, of the speeches I myself heard, and for those reporting them back to me from somewhere else, but as it seemed to me that each party would most say the necessary things (*ta deonta*) concerning the things present on every occasion, while I held as nearly as possible to the general idea of the things that truly were said, thus it has been said' (1. 22. 1). A huge amount of ink has been spilled on this statement, debating whether or not Thoukydides gives us an accurate transcription of speeches actually delivered, and what his statement of policy here means. But it is comprehensible as a statement of the Sophistic principle that for each argumentative position (for example, for or against war), there is only one set of things that could or should be said (*ta deonta*).

Given these marked intellectual influences, we must finally ask: did Thoukydides share the Sophistic views articulated by his speakers—making him, as many have thought, the first great advocate of *Realpolitik* and *Machtpolitik*—or was he critical of them? And did he share the optimism, the faith in rationality, of Sophists and medical writers alike? I will return to these questions, but first we need to consider Thoukydides' relation to his written medium.

Writing and textuality: making readers

There was an age gap of at least twenty to twenty-five years between Herodotos and Thoukydides, a gap that perhaps partly accounts for Thoukydides' profoundly different relation to the technology of writing and the constitution of his text. Herodotos, as we saw, on the cusp between orality and literacy, produced a uniquely capacious text, collecting and preserving oral traditions from many different sources. Thoukydides' work, by contrast, is more narrowly focused, both in terms of time and range of subject-matter. In contrast to Herodotos' 220-year sweep, Thoukydides concentrates almost exclusively on contemporary history (the Peloponnesian War, which he himself lived through). More significantly, Thoukydides severely restricts his range of topics to politics and war—men talking and men fighting. He hardly anywhere mentions women or families, social or cultural practices, religion, temples, or sacred space. As such, he is the inventor of political history narrowly construed, a form which seems quite 'natural' to us, but which was at the time (especially in the wake of Herodotos) hardly a self-evident choice.

Thoukydides' self-imposed restrictions are conditioned partly by his methodological assumptions (thus, for example, he seems to think that accuracy can only be attained in the reconstruction of relatively recent events), partly by an uncompromising rationalism—hence his downplaying of religious elements—but also by a greater adaptation to the possibilities and limitations of the written medium than his precursors attained. Thus many passages of Herodotos, in their concreteness and proliferation of contextual detail (for example, descriptions of dedications at Delphi or the layout of battlefields) seem almost to mime the experience of an oral performance in which the audience is itself already well acquainted with (say) Delphi or Plataia. Thoukydides' *History*, by contrast, offers a much sparer, decontextualized account and therefore achieves much greater autonomy as a written text. At the same time, Thoukydides tends to present issues and events in the most general and abstract form possible (as has been noticed, this is a striking feature of the speeches especially). This tendency toward generalization and abstraction further exploits the peculiar strengths of the written medium. Finally, in contrast to Herodotos' constant, multiple citation of sources, Thoukydides almost never cites sources, offering us instead the finished and apparently seamless results of the historian's own laborious enquiries and analysis. Where Herodotos' account attempts to capture in written form the complexities of multiple oral traditions, Thoukydides' text maintains an awesome and severe autonomy, constituting itself as the definitive account of the period.

This contrast in the two historians' deployment of the written medium is clear already in their first sentences: while Herodotos designates his account *histories apodexis hede* ('this display/performance of enquiry'), Thoukydides says simply, 'Thoukydides the Athenian wrote up (*xunegrapse*) the war of the Peloponnesians and the Athenians, how they warred against each other, having begun straightway when the war started and anticipating that it would be great and more worthy of report than all previous events, judging from the fact that both sides were at the peak of their power in all preparation at the time, and seeing that the rest of Greece had aligned itself on either side, part straightaway, the rest also contemplating it.' In contrast to Herodotos' emphasis on performance, Thoukydides chooses the modest verb *xunegrapse*, commonly used of writing up a report or a technical treatise. And yet, the implication of this verb is not so modest after all, since it suggests that the 'facts' to be written up are clear and unambiguous, in need only of recording. It is noteworthy also that, in contrast to both Hekataios and Herodotos, Thoukydides uses no deictic pronoun that might attach his text to a present of performance (not, for example, 'Thoukydides wrote up *this* war', or '*Thus* Thoukydides wrote up the war'). The language of the text makes it completely autonomous. Indeed, when Thoukydides returns to the topic of the greatness of the war at the end of the 'Archaeology', even his authorship has been effaced by the self-evident autonomy of the written text (now fused in perfect adequation with the events it describes): 'And this war . . . will make clear to those considering from the events themselves that it was greater than all others' (1. 21. 2).

We must finally ask why Thoukydides chose the medium of writing and why he wrote the way he did, constituting an austere text that comes to be coextensive with—even to replace—the war itself. One answer has been that Thoukydides so completely removes himself from his written text in order to achieve perfect objectivity. But perhaps we have been too quick to construct Thoukydides in the pattern of a modern scientific historian, for the ancient answer was very different. Ancient readers knew Thoukydides as an acknowledged master of *enargeia* ('vividness'), who used that technique (and others) to engage readers' emotions at a visceral level. As Plutarch observed, 'Thoukydides always strives for this vividness in his narrative, and all but makes the reader an actual spectator and listener present at the astounding and dreadful events he describes.' Part of this effect of immediate emotional engagement is achieved by the absence of explicit authorial intervention and commentary, so that events seem to be conjured up directly before the reader without any mediation.

It is, furthermore, telling that Plutarch refers explicitly to 'astounding and *dreadful* events', because at one point Thoukydides himself reveals the centrality of suffering to his historiographic project. In his first sentence, he asserts that the Peloponnesian War was 'greater than all former events and most worthy of recording'; when he returns to the topic of the greatness of the war after the 'Archaeology', he elaborates: 'Of former deeds, the Persian War was the greatest thing accomplished, and this still had a swift resolution through a pair of naval battles and a pair of land battles. But the great length of this war surpassed it, and sufferings (*pathemata*) occurred for Greece during the war such as had no equal in a comparable length of time' (1. 23. 1). Here the measure of the Peloponnesian War's greatness, which inspired Thoukydides to make his historical record, is the unparalleled suffering it caused. This is Thoukydides' real theme, and his seeming authorial objectivity is not the goal, but the means by which he conveys to the reader as immediately and vividly as possible the experience of war. In order to experience the tragic effects of Thoukydides' narrative techniques, the reader need only peruse his description of the first and second ships dispatched to Mytilene (3. 49), the final attempt of the Athenian ships to break out of the Harbour of Syracuse (7. 70–1), or the devastation of Mykalessos by a band of renegade Thracian mercenaries (7. 29).

But these same written techniques have more than just an emotional impact on the attentive reader. Notice, for example, how the deeper meaning of the 'magnitude' of the war only emerges gradually, through the sequential reading of Thoukydides' text. This (small) example offers us a paradigm of how the text works upon the reader, guiding him or her to a richer understanding by subtle shifts and modulations. This pattern is repeated—writ large—for almost every important issue and theme in the *History*, for example, the original causes of the war, or what Thoukydides thought went wrong with the Sicilian Expedition. Traditionally, scholars used to attempt to account for these complex shifts in perspective by positing different layers of composition; after all, if we take Thoukydides at his word in the first sentence, he began writing when the war began and continued for twenty-seven years at least. Surely in that time his thinking changed? And yet, decades of such separatist analysis have produced no consensus on the order of composition or on what Thoukydides' views 'really were', and most scholars have now abandoned this 'Thoukydidean question' as an unproductive line of enquiry. If, however, we shift our focus from production to reception (from the author to the reader), the many minute inconsistencies detected by separatist scholars become evidence for the exact processes by which Thoukydides' text progressively educates its readers. From this perspective it is clear that the text resists easy answers and assumptions at every level and does so in ways that *only* a written text can achieve. Thus, at the level of style, the text consistently fractures conventional antitheses and makes them asymmetrical, while its generalizations are often so deeply embedded in particular situations that they are not extractable. In like manner, juxtaposed speeches and narrative elucidate each other, but in complex and uneven ways that compel the reader constantly to revise his or her understanding.

Thus the text's resistances offer an ongoing intellectual, as well as emotional, challenge to the reader. And here we return to the question of Thoukydides' relation to the Sophists. As we saw, Thoukydides' text is permeated with Sophistic rhetorical techniques and methodology, and the 'Archaeology' (for example) seems to display a characteristically Sophistic confidence in the progressive development of human resources and technology. The first two books also show us on several occasions (especially in the speeches of Perikles) an ideal balance between public deliberation and action. Thus, as Perikles puts it in the Funeral Oration (a model public speech for the Athenian war dead of each campaign, which Thoukydides incorporates into the narrative of book 2), 'In contrast to others, we have also this characteristic: that the same people most of all take risks and also deliberate concerning the things we will attempt, while for others ignorance produces boldness and calculation delay' (2. 40. 3). And yet, as the text continues, we see rhetoric turned more and more to the service not of rationality and reasoned deliberation, but of violence and unrestrained ambition. Thus we can chart a progression from the Mytilenean Debate in book 3—in which the destruction of the rebellious city of Mytilene is narrowly averted—to the Melian Dialogue in book 5 (in which representatives of the neutral state of Melos fail in their argument from honour and traditional values and their entire city is condemned), to the debate on the Sicilian Expedition in book 6—in which Alkibiades inflames the Athenian people with desire for conquest, based on ignorance, misrepresentation, and uncontrollable imperial ambition. Indeed, at one point, Thoukydides even puts into the mouth of Kleon a critique of the damaging effects of competitive rhetorical displays on the Athenian people: 'You yourselves are to blame for stupidly instituting contests of speeches, you who are accustomed to be regular spectators of speeches, but of actions you only hear about them—judging that future actions are possible from those who praise them, but as for the things already done, you do not consider the events you yourselves have witnessed more persuasive than what you hear from those who skilfully reproach you in speech' (3. 38. 4). The fact that Thoukydides consistently portrays Kleon himself as a violent and manipulative demagogue—he is, after all, arguing here for the execution of the entire adult male population of Mytilene (cf. Ch. 6, pp. 194–5)—does not entirely vitiate his denunciation of the Athenians' addiction to rhetorical displays. Here we may have yet another reason for Thoukydides' choice of the written medium and for his peculiar style. His text is defiantly literary; it is deliberately written to be difficult to comprehend when heard, in order to short-circuit the exchange of specious persuasion and public enjoyment that Sophistic rhetoric promotes. Instead, Thoukydides' text forces its audience into isolated—and effortful—private reading.

We have still not yet quite exhausted Thoukydides' critique of Sophistic rhetoric. For it is not just that rhetoric misleads, replacing reasoned deliberation with specious persuasion, but that, in the course of the war, language itself becomes a form of violence. This is perhaps clearest in Thoukydides' devastating description of civil war in Kerkyra, where 'even words were forced to change their meaning in adequation to events', the new terms justifying the most ruthless slaughter (3. 82. 4–5). As *logos* collapses into irrationality and *peitho* (persuasion) into *bie* (force), the *History* offers a scathing indictment of the Sophistic movement and the idiom that forms the text's very fabric.

In like manner, Thoukydides seems simultaneously steeped in the methods of Hippokratic medicine yet ultimately sceptical about their efficacy to change or effect a cure. Thus, at the end of the 'Archaeology' (1. 22. 4), he seems to sound a fairly optimistic note that, human nature being what it is, his careful historical account will serve as a means of diagnosis and prognosis for human upheavals in the future; and, indeed, the statesmen Thoukydides seems most to admire, Themistokles and Perikles, display in his account precisely this extraordinary skill in prognosis (cf. Ch. 5, p. 160). And yet, as his *History* proceeds, it becomes less and less clear that the accurate detailing of symptoms can, in fact, lead to any kind of diagnosis of causes or cure. In the case of the plague at Athens, for example, Thoukydides promises, 'I will discuss what the process was like, and I will clarify those factors from which, if the affliction ever again occurs, one might, by having some advance knowledge, not fail to recognize it' (2. 48. 3), but at the same time, he studiously maintains agnosticism about the cause and acknowledges that there was no successful treatment of the disease: 'Some died in neglect, others died though they were extremely well cared for. As for a remedy, there was nothing—no, not one—that those applying must benefit the sick; for what helped one harmed another' (2. 51. 2).

Analogous to the physical destruction of the plague in Thoukydides' account is the moral and social disintegration of civil war, captured in all its horror by the historian in his 'case study' of Kerkyra (3. 82–5). Here, accurate knowledge of the past and the characteristic trajectory of civil war offers no hope for treatment or improvement, only a clear recognition of the viciousness of human nature:

> And many difficulties fell upon the cities in civil war, the kind that occur and always will occur as long as human nature is the same, but sometimes more mildly and varying in forms, as each set of changes of circumstances arise. For in peace and prosperity, both cities and individuals use higher standards on account of not falling into compulsions against their will; but

> war, by taking away the easy satisfaction of day-to-day needs, is a violent teacher and assimilates the passions of most people to their present circumstances. (3. 82. 2)

Thus, in his deeply ambivalent engagement with the optimistic, rationalizing movements of his time, Thoukydides produces a profound critique of 'human nature' under the pressures of war and imperialism. His written text never offers the reader easy answers, but instead guides him or her to probe ever deeper in the process of an exacting private reading.

Postscript: Xenophon and the 'disembodied' reader

It is a truism that all the major historians of the classical period—Herodotos, Thoukydides, and Xenophon—were exiles, and that the status of exile, with its disengagement from embedded political action, was the pre-condition for the writing of history. It is worth acknowledging, though, how exile produced very different effects on the first great practitioners of *historie*. For Herodotos, it was perhaps what inspired the 'global vision' that informs his work, while for Thoukydides, it seems to have enabled the carving-out of a private space for meticulous writing and effortful reading.

The third great classical historian, Xenophon, was also an exile from his native Athens, first by choice and then by necessity, for most of his adult life. A generation younger than Thoukydides, he picked up the narrative of the Peloponnesian War where Thoukydides had left off and completed it, ultimately carrying his *Hellenika* (or 'Greek Things') down to the Battle of Mantinea in 362 BCE. As a young man in 401 BCE, Xenophon had joined an expedition of Greek mercenary soldiers to support the rebellion of Kyros, younger brother of the reigning Persian king. Kyros' army marched from Sardis to Babylon, where Kyros was killed in battle and the Greek commanders were treacherously done away with. Xenophon, who had been largely an observer, helped lead the stranded force of ten thousand Greek mercenaries back to Greek-occupied territory, an expedition he himself recounts in the *Anabasis*, or 'March Up Country'. In 395, Xenophon joined the expedition of the Spartan King Agesilaos to liberate the Greeks in Asia Minor from the Persians. Because of his assistance to Sparta, Athens' enemy, he was at that time officially exiled, though the Spartans rewarded him with an estate near Olympia in the Peloponnese. Late in his life, Xenophon's exile was repealed but we do not know if he ever returned to Athens.

Xenophon's career trajectory looks very different from that of Herodotos or Thoukydides because it was much more shaped and governed by the para-political system of aristocratic guest-friendship: it was guest-friendship (or *xenia*) that motivated his joining the Ten Thousand, and again, joining the expedition of Agesilaos. In this sense, it was not so much that Xenophon chose or was forced to abandon the political engagement of the citizen, but that he spent much of his life participating in an alternative order of networking élites and dynasts, spread over the entire Greek world, Persia, and Thrace. He was thus a throwback to an older kind of aristocratic ideal, as he was in some ways in his writing. For Xenophon was an extremely prolific writer in many genres: in addition to the *Anabasis* and *Hellenika*, he composed treatises on horsemanship, hunting, and estate-management (all traditional aristocratic pursuits). And since he had been a friend and follower of Sokrates in Athens in his youth, he composed a Defence (*Apology*) of Sokrates, a *Symposium* as a Sokratic Dialogue (perhaps in part his response to Plato's *Symposium*), and *Memorabilia*, his recollections of Sokrates framed as a defence of his civic 'usefulness'. In these Sokratic treatises Xenophon engages most directly with Athenian politics and civic order, unsurprisingly perhaps given their agenda of defending Sokrates posthumously against the charges on which he was executed by the Athenian state.

But the single topic that engaged Xenophon most in his writings was the leadership of men, and the qualities of the ideal leader. This issue informs his short dialogue *Hieron*, his biographical sketch *Agesilaos*, and his lengthy 'historical novel' *The Education of Kyros*, an idealizing portrait of the education and conquests of Kyros the Great, the founder of the Persian empire. Projected onto the sixth-century struggles for Persian hegemony, Xenophon constructs Kyros as the perfect prince, a canny strategist in war and generous leader in peace, who binds his subjects to him with ties of love and admiration.

In another sense, however, Xenophon diverged markedly from the archaic aristocratic ideal, in that he composed for a disembodied readership. In this respect, we can see Xenophon's writing as the confluence of the developing traditions of history and philosophy. Together, these two traditions bequeathed to the eclectic Xenophon their didactic impulses, their use of exemplarity, their ethnographic fascinations, and perhaps most importantly—by the time of the mid-fourth century, their audience of readers.

5 Sages, sophists, and philosophers: Greek wisdom literature

ANDREA WILSON NIGHTINGALE

Wise men and the performance of wisdom

The Greek thinkers in the archaic and classical periods performed their wisdom in different ways and in front of different audiences. As a modern audience that encounters these 'philosophers' only in written works, we tend to disconnect their doctrines from their historical and cultural contexts. By focusing on philosophic 'performances' of wisdom—both oral and written—and by examining the audiences addressed by these thinkers, we can better appreciate their lives and activities and, indeed, their different conceptions of the nature of wisdom.

The discipline of Philosophy came properly into existence in the fourth century BCE, when intellectuals laid claim to a distinct mode of wisdom which called for a novel title and an honorary place in Greek society. Philosophy was first defined and legitimized as a specialized discipline by Plato, who appropriated the term *philosophia*—which had previously designated intellectual cultivation in the broadest sense—for his own activities and ideas. How, then, did philosophy evolve as a cultural practice, and what are the links between the fourth-century philosophers and the intellectuals and wise men of the previous centuries? How did these thinkers present their ideas to their fellow Greeks, and what forms of discourse did they use? To attempt an answer to these questions, I will discuss the 'performance' of philosophic wisdom—in speech, in writing, and in action—from the sixth to the fourth centuries BCE; and in particular, the audiences that these thinkers addressed and the contexts in which their ideas were communicated and exchanged.

It is customary to say that Thales of Miletos, who lived in the early sixth century, was the first philosopher. This attribution is due to Aristotle, who (over two hundred years later) was the first to give 'philosophy' a history and a pedigree. Although Aristotle provides precious evidence for the shadowy figures who are counted as early philosophers, we must remember that he was not a historian but himself a philosopher searching for thinkers who adumbrated his own theory of causality. Aristotle's 'history' of philosophy in the first book of his *Metaphysics* is, in fact, a narrative in which philosophy begins as a babbling infant and grows into the mature work of Aristotle. As he says there, 'although all the causes have been spoken of before in one sense, in another they have not been stated at all; for the earliest philosophy spoke about everything in baby-talk, inasmuch as it was new and in its infancy'. Clearly, these early thinkers were not saying exactly what Aristotle wanted them to say. It is for this reason that he accuses them of speaking 'muddily', 'metaphorically', and 'vaguely'. When viewed from Aristotle's perspective, the early Greek thinkers often sound a bit obtuse; thus in chapter 4 Aristotle compares them to 'untrained soldiers who rush around in battle, often striking good blows, but not acting with knowledge; these thinkers do not understand their own statements'.

Resisting Aristotle's revisionary history, I want to examine the early Greek thinkers in their own terms. These men were mature thinkers in their own right, and were not simply paving the way for Aristotle. Rather than locate each individual in his social and political context—there are far too many and they hail from all over the Mediterranean—I will look in more general terms at the activities of these men, both practical and intellectual, and at their intended audiences. By focusing on these issues, we can better understand the kind of wisdom that these 'philosophers' professed.

But let me say right off that I do not believe that we should call the thinkers of the sixth and fifth centuries BCE 'philosophers'. They did not use this term for themselves, nor did others refer to them in this way. The words 'philosophy' and 'philosophize' were very rarely used until the fourth century BCE and, when they were, did not pick out a special and distinct group of thinkers. Rather, the words *sophos* and *sophistes* were the coveted titles: the early thinkers wanted to be ranked among 'the wise'. In this period, wise men came in many forms: poets, prophets, doctors, statesmen, astronomers, and various kinds of inventors and artisans were identified and honoured as '*sophoi*'. Although these different kinds of wise men were clearly seen to be practising distinct activities, there was nonetheless a generalized competition among the different groups for the title of 'wise man'.

To be called wise was to receive a certain kind of 'symbolic capital', a payment in the form of power, status, and honour rather than money or goods. This kind of capital was, of course, a scarce commodity, and had to be won against stiff competition. Thus early historical and 'philosophical' thinkers found it necessary to compete with Homer, Hesiod, and other wise men in order to put themselves on the map as intellectual authorities or 'masters of truth'. We must remember that this was not a culture in which one went to school to get credentials: each thinker had to demonstrate his own authority and expertise to his fellow citizens and Greeks. Since Homer and Hesiod were considered the wisest and most important voices in the tradition, the early Greek thinkers were compelled to work in their wake. In the tenth book of his *Republic*, Plato refers to the 'ancient quarrel between poetry and philosophy'. In fact, the early thinkers did not attack poetry *per se* but rather entered into a competition with a few great poets. In fact, some thinkers such as Xenophanes, Parmenides, and Empedokles rivalled Homer and Hesiod by writing hexameter poetry of their own: they, too, were poets, but with a different theme and message.

The archaic sages

I begin with a brief look, then, at Thales, who is in the peculiar position of being ranked by posterity as both a Sage (one of the élite Seven) and a Philosopher. The fifth-century historian Herodotos offers several short accounts of him in the *Histories*. In book 1, he tells us that Thales predicted an eclipse and that he diverted the river Halys for the benefit of Kroisos and his army (when they were attempting to invade Persian territory); Herodotos also reports that, when the Ionians in Asia Minor were being subdued by the Persians, Thales advised the Ionians to set up a deliberative council on the island of Teos, and to make this the capital of a confederation of city-states. Diogenes Laertius (third century CE), whose *Lives of the Philosophers* is a key source of information about Greek philosophy, relates another story about Thales' 'cunning intelligence': in order to demonstrate how easy it was to get rich, Thales, foreseeing that it would be a good season for olives, rented all the oil-presses and obtained a monopoly on the proceeds (Diogenes Laertius, hereafter DL, 1. 26). These stories about Thales portray a man of many skills. Alongside his astronomical expertise, he demonstrates a great deal of practical wisdom: engineering the diversion of a river, acting as a leader in the political affairs of the day, and exhibiting a keen understanding of agriculture and business.

It comes as a great surprise, then, when fourth-century philosophers such as Plato, Aristotle, and Herakleides of Pontos represent Thales as the prototypical contemplative. In the *Theaetetus*, for example, Plato tell us that Thales fell into a well when he was contemplating the stars; a maidservant mocked him for being so eager to know what was going on in the sky that he did not see what lay at his feet. As Plato goes on to say, this is the lot of all philosophers, who are by definition ignorant of the world of society and politics, having given themselves over to the contemplation of higher truths. In a similar vein, Herakleides of Pontos (a member of Plato's Academy), wrote a dialogue in which Thales claims that he always lived in solitude as a private individual and kept aloof from state affairs (DL 1. 25–6). And Aristotle tells us in his *Nicomachean Ethics* (6. 7. 5) that Thales was 'wise' but not 'prudent' since he did not look to his own interests; Thales possessed a wisdom that was 'rare, marvellous, difficult, and superhuman'—the kind of wisdom that is, Aristotle says, 'useless' (*achreston*) in the practical sphere, since it does not deal with things 'that are good for human beings'. According to Aristotle, Thales is the first known philosopher in so far as he claimed that the world originated from water; his other skills and activities are simply irrelevant. How, then, do we get from the practical, political, polymathic Thales to an other-worldly contemplative—from a performer of wisdom in the social and political arena to a detached spectator of truth?

In order to understand this development, we need to look briefly at the archaic sage and the culture in which he lived. What sort of wisdom made the Seven Sages wise? Although these sages were by no means the only wise men of their day, they were clearly among the most famous and exceptional. To be sure, our evidence for them is scanty and late, and often bears the mark of fictionalized representations; but these at least tell us what counted as wisdom in the archaic period, and this is sufficient for our present task. The extant accounts suggest that the seven sages were a disparate and, to some extent, changeable group of individuals. The most commonly recognized members of the group are Solon of Athens, Thales of Miletos, Pittakos of Mytilene, Bias of Priene (near Miletos), Chilon of Sparta, Kleoboulos of Lindos (on Rhodes), and Periander of Corinth. Many scholars have claimed that what characterized these sages was their poetic and/or political activities. In fact, five of the seven sages were reported to have written poetry, and five to have been involved in politics. But many men of this age were fine poets and politicians, and only a few made it to the ranks of the seven sages. As Richard Martin has recently shown, what distinguished these individuals was their extraordinary 'performances' of wisdom.

The sages could 'perform' their wisdom in different ways. First, by non-verbal actions, as when Thales made a fortune by monopolizing the olive harvest: here, the sage enacted a clever idea and the outcome proved that he had special knowledge. Second, the sage could demonstrate his wisdom by a combination of action and utterance. For example, when Solon wanted to convince his countrymen to renew the war with Megara over Salamis (a proposal that had been declared illegal in Athens), he feigned madness, rushed into the Agora with a garland on his head, and recited a poem that he had written on Salamis which called for war; the Athenians were duly roused to anger, and proceeded to recapture Salamis (DL 1. 46). Here, Solon pretends to madness in order to evince his wisdom and sanity; in addition, his poem is performed in the space of the agora (the civic centre), where discourse is traditionally converted into political praxis.

Both of these examples evince a kind of wisdom that often eludes the modern scholar: what the ancient Greeks called *metis*. *Metis* is a fundamentally practical form of wisdom which is often associated with cunning and clever behaviour. This kind of wisdom does not focus on abstract truths, but rather on the complexities of practical life with all its chancy and changing forces and exigencies. The person who possesses *metis* has a keen eye for the main chance, for what the Greeks called *kairos*—the right thing at the right time. Thus Thales must seize the moment when he perceives that the olive crop will be abundant; Solon must find the right time and the right place to perform his poem (not to mention the demeanour and dress which enables him to get a hearing while breaking a law). An excellent example of an individual with *metis* is Themistokles, who saved the Athenians when they were being attacked by the Persians by convincing them to take refuge in their ships rather than their city. As the historian Thoukydides tells us, Themistokles 'was able to arrive at the most correct idea concerning the future, taking the widest point of view and foreseeing, as far as possible, the hidden advantages and disadvantages in what cannot be seen' (1. 138. 3). Here, *metis* includes an understanding of the larger context of a situation, an intuition of what is hidden in the future, and an unerring sense of what is advantageous at the present moment. *Metis* works with what is at hand, connives with the present: its exquisite sense of timing—of *kairos*—befuddles opponents and brings surprising successes. This kind of wise person does not gaze upon a truth which is detached from the human world; on the contrary, he immerses himself in the tide of events and acts in response to the particularities of the situation. *Metis* is thus a clever form of practical wisdom, and is displayed by men as different as Odysseus and Sokrates.

This notion of the 'performance of wisdom' sheds light on the context if not the content of the wisdom of the archaic and early classical periods. The content of wisdom, in fact, could come in many and various forms: but the contexts of its dissemination were finite. In the most general terms, the wise man operated in a social and political arena in which knowledge was demonstrated by a performer to an audience in a public or a private gathering. When one considers that the technology of writing was only beginning to take hold in the sixth and fifth centuries, it should come as no surprise that wisdom had to be orally or physically enacted; although some individuals did make use of writing, they could have reached only a tiny audience in this period by the circulation of written texts. In the absence of a literate public, a person could be declared wise solely on the basis of the exhibition of exceptional actions or exceptional discourse (be it poetic, political, religious, or intellectual).

Masters of truth

The early sages who later came to be called 'philosophers' formed a small subset of the large group of *sophoi* that populated the culture of this period. Take, first of all, Thales, Anaximines, and Anaximandros, sixth-century thinkers who all lived in Miletos, an Ionian city on the west coast of Asia Minor. Each of these men offered (among other things) a cosmology that explained the operation of the universe by recourse to 'natural' forces rather than individualized divinities struggling for power. These early thinkers initiated a tradition of recording their research (*historie,* cf. p. 135) in prose treatises (some fifth-century representatives of this tradition are Zeno, Anaxagoras, and Demokritos). The use of prose looks like a deliberate rejection of poetic discourse and its popular audiences, since poetry was designed for group pleasure rather than intellectual enquiry. In fact, scholars often ascribe to the early Ionian thinkers the heroic feat of liberating philosophic discourse from the shadowy realms of '*mythos*' (since their 'naturalistic' accounts of the cosmos rejected the poetic accounts that attributed causality to the weddings and wars of the gods). But the many scholarly attempts to trace the movement from poetry to philosophy—'from *mythos* to *logos*'—have foundered on the problem of defining the intrinsic qualities of 'myth' and of 'rational argumentation', and of identifying texts that are either purely mythic or purely analytic. Since the Greek poets were quite capable of constructing arguments, and the 'philosophers' were unable to avoid metaphor and myth, it is difficult to draw a clear distinction between *mythos* and *logos*. To be sure, we see in the Ionians a new way of thinking about the world; but we cannot say that their accounts are devoid of any mythical notions. What we can say is that these thinkers adopted a critical attitude towards received wisdom and were prized for their original speculations.

A very different kind of wisdom was cultivated by Pythagoras, who emigrated from the island of Samos to southern Italy in the second half of the sixth century. Because Pythagoras himself almost certainly did not publish any writings and his society observed a strict code of silence, the sources dealing with early Pythagoreanism offer little reliable evidence about this sage. We do know that he founded a religious society in the city of Kroton. The members of this society, which included women as well as men, lived a life of austerity and discipline, which included a vegetarian diet, the practice of self-examination, obedience to precepts known as *akousmata,* and a vow of silence about Pythagorean doctrine and practice. Pythagoras and his followers, then, were performing an entire way of life; their ideas and doctrines translated directly into daily *praxis* (for example, their belief in the immortality of the soul and its transmigration into animals led them to abstain from meat). In so far as Pythagoreanism offered its members hidden knowledge that could not be divulged, it resembled the mystery religions, which promised to benefit initiates by the revelation of secret wisdom. It is important to emphasize, however, that Pythagoras was fully involved in political life; in fact, he and his followers are said to have taken over the government of Kroton. Like other early sages, Pythagoras' wisdom was practical and political; his access to secret wisdom did not cut him off from the life of the city.

The sixth-century Ionians did not offer their research to large audiences, but rather to small groups of like-minded pupils and associates. And Pythagoras positively prohibited the dissemination of his doctrines to non-initiates. Many early thinkers, however, packaged their ideas so as to reach a broader public. Xenophanes (570–475 BCE) wrote elegiac and hexameter poems; Herakleitos (*fl.* 500 BCE) constructed riddling aphorisms that emulate the discourse of the Delphic oracle; and Parmenides (515—?440) and Empedokles (492–432) opted to rival Homer and Hesiod by writing hexameter poetry. These thinkers set out to compose literary art-works (albeit in different genres) rather than merely to document their ideas in writing. It is worth noting that Xenophanes attacks Homer explicitly, and Herakleitos inveighs not only against the poets Homer, Hesiod, and Archilochos, but also against Hekataios (a proto-historian, cf. p. 135), Xenophanes, and Pythagoras. Such attacks remind us that these thinkers conceived of themselves as rivalling 'wise men' in general rather than the specialized group of intellectuals who were later called philosophers. The fact that Herakleitos' opponents include poets and prose writers, as well as a religious/political guru such as Pythagoras, gives us a good idea of the breadth of 'wisdom' that he himself recognized as authoritative.

What can we say about the dissemination of the works of these thinkers? Unfortunately, the evidence is scanty and, for the most part, derives from the texts themselves. Diogenes Laertius tells us that Xenophanes 'rhapsodised' his own poems (DL 1. 18). This is a bit puzzling, since rhapsodizing generally referred to the performance of Homeric poems (cf. Ch. 1, p. 54). It is nonetheless possible that Xenophanes offered a rhapsodic performance of his hexameter poetry, fragments of which reveal a radical theology attacking the traditional anthropomorphic gods as they are portrayed in Homer and Hesiod. If so, he would have been addressing the same audiences as the Homeric singers. In the case of his elegaic poems, we can infer that these were performed at aristocratic symposia, which were the traditional venue for this kind of verse (cf. Ch. 2, pp. 66–7).

As Diogenes Laertius reports, Herakleitos wrote a book 'On Nature' which he dedicated and placed in the temple of Artemis, deliberately making it more obscure so that only the select few would have access to it (DL 9. 5). Did Herakleitos really opt for the written word as a way of avoiding mass audiences? The mere fact of the survival of his works in ancient times (substantial fragments are still extant) must indicate that this thinker achieved a degree of fame comparable to (at least minor) poets. Many scholars have questioned whether Herakleitos did in fact use writing as a medium for communication, pointing out that the surviving fragments take the form of oral pronouncements put into a pithy, striking, and therefore easily memorizable form. Certainly the fragments resemble oral apophthegms, though this does not mean that Herakleitos did not also commit them to writing. It seems unlikely, however, that the dedication of the book in the temple was designed to keep it hidden from the masses; on the contrary, dedications at temples were generally a form of display. This would have given Herakleitos' book an extraordinary status (hence the legend) and ensured that a fixed text would remain for posterity.

Herakleitos did not simply document his research: he was 'doing things' with his words. Using an oracular form and voice, Herakleitos makes paradoxical and enigmatic pronouncements. He says in fragment 93 that 'the lord whose oracle is in Delphi neither speaks nor conceals, but offers a sign'. Since Herakleitos himself uses language in precisely this way, we may infer that he was deliberately adopting Delphic discourse. He did this, no doubt, because the riddling discourse of the oracle was well suited to conveying his central claim: that unity consists of coexisting opposites. Consider, for example, fragment 10: 'Things taken together are wholes and not wholes, something brought together and brought apart, something in tune and out of tune; from all things one, and from one all things.' Here, the riddling form fits the riddling content.

In adopting this style, Herakleitos also adopts the voice of divine authority that is associated with oracular discourse. Herakleitos speaks from on high to confused mortals:

> Although this account holds forever, men prove to be uncomprehending, both before they have heard it and when once they have heard it. For although all things happen according to this account, men are like those who lack experience, even when they experience such words and deeds as I set forth, distinguishing each thing according to its nature and declaring how it is; but other men fail to notice what they do when awake just as they forget what they do when asleep. (fr. 1)

When encountering such a statement, one may well imagine that Herakleitos is addressing only a few intelligent initiates—after all, the mass of men are far too stupid to get the point. But, at the same time, he claims that the masses have indeed heard the *logos* and experienced his account of the truth. This indicates that his audience is not confined to a few élite associates. Indeed, one could argue that this is a clever piece of rhetoric which invites the ordinary man to remove himself from the common herd by using his reason and tapping into the *logos*. More specifically, it places its audience in the role of the interpreter of an oracle (a not unfamiliar role for ancient Greeks): it exhorts its audience to aspire to wisdom by solving some difficult enigmas. A contradiction arises, then, in that the discourse divulges to the public a knowledge that it proclaims to be unavailable to the majority.

This same paradox is found in Parmenides, whose poem wavers between the discourse of mystery religion and argumentation that is subject to reason and its rules. For Parmenides presents his views about the world in a series of formal arguments using logic that is open for inspection. Yet his poem takes the form of a mystic journey in which wise steeds carry the poet on a chariot escorted by the daughters of the sun. After passing through the gates of the paths of Night and Day, a goddess greets the poet and promises to unveil the truth. 'Come now, and I will tell you—and you shall hearken and carry my word away,' begins the goddess (fr. 2). Parmenides must learn the truth and then convey—'carry'—it to others. This opening recalls the scene in the *Theogony* where the Muses meet Hesiod on Mount Helikon and tell him what to sing (cf. p. 26). But, unlike Hesiod, Parmenides meets his muse in a 'place' that transcends the physical world. The goddess states that there are only two 'routes' of enquiry: the first is the 'path of persuasion' (the 'Way of Truth'), and the second is a track completely closed to enquiry. After expounding the truth of the first track, the goddess turns to a discussion of mortal opinions; here, she gives an account of the very phenomena whose existence is disproved in the first part. Scholars have puzzled over the relation of this (poorly preserved) part of the poem, the 'Way of Seeming', to the first part, the 'Way of Truth'. But its denigration of opinion and 'seeming' is not in doubt: mortals on the path of opinion

> . . . wander, two-headed,
> knowing nothing; for helplessness
> guides the wandering thoughts in their breasts;
> they are carried, deaf and blind at once,
> altogether dazed—hordes devoid of judgement,
> persuaded that to be and not to be are the same yet not the same;
> so the path they all take is backward turning.
>
> (fr. 6).

Like Herakleitos, Parmenides suggests that the 'hordes' of men are ignorant fools. But the audience is nonetheless invited to follow the poet off the beaten track and to enter the realm of Truth. We, too, can be the religious initiates receiving the words of the goddess rather than the blind and deaf hordes who persist in poor reasoning.

As I have suggested, both Herakleitos and Parmenides designed their work for an audience wider than their immediate associates and followers. Each developed a mode of discourse that was poetic and protreptic (from the Greek word *protrepein*, meaning to 'urge on' or 'exhort'). Each used a rhetoric of legitimation that claimed for its author a near-divine authority and conferred on all nay-sayers the status of fools. These thinkers were not only preaching to their converted students but also seeking to make converts (and attract followers) in the wider world. This does not, of course, tell us anything about the size and constituency of their audiences, nor can we be sure of the venues in which these texts were performed.

We know a bit more about Empedokles of Akragas (in Sicily), whose poem the *Purifications* is said to have been performed by a rhapsode at the Olympic games (DL 8. 63). If this is true, then we can say that his work was broadly disseminated by way of oral recitation. Aristotle offers the tantalizing observation that men could recite the verses of Empedokles when drunk, though they are speaking without understanding. This suggests that the work of Empedokles was part of the discursive fare of drinking parties or symposia—a common context for reciting poetry, posing riddles, and performing other intellectual feats. It is worth noting that Aristotle, in a lost dialogue called the *Sophist*, says that Empedokles was himself an accomplished orator who deserves the title of the inventor of rhetoric. Finally, Empedokles' claim that he is a great doctor (which evinces his practical wisdom) is proven by the many references to him in later medical writings. This evidence suggests that Empedokles' poems were widely disseminated, and should warn us against the notion that philosophical ideas were confined to tiny audiences of intellectual élites.

The fragments of Empedokles were originally ascribed to two different works: *On Nature*, a 'naturalist' poem, and *Purifications*, a supernatural story of reincarnation. But some scholars have claimed that the fragments belong to a single poem (a view which is now given strong support by the recent and very exciting discovery of new fragments of Empedokles); as they argue, the separation of the naturalist from the mythical poem is based on the false assumption that true philosophy has no room for the supernatural. The poem begins in the first person, with an address to a man named Pausanias—a gesture that recalls Hesiod's address to his brother in the *Works and Days*. The poet calls on a muse who is a 'much-remembering white armed maiden' to assist him in his narrative, which offers an account of the basic principles of the universe. He claims that two divinities, Love and Strife, act to combine and separate the four 'roots' (earth, air, fire, water), thus bringing the cosmos into different phases or cycles. In this poem, Empedokles responds directly (but not explicitly) to Parmenides, who had deduced that being is changeless, timeless, homogeneous, and unitary. According to Empedokles, the world consists of four distinct elements which everlastingly oscillate between unity (their combination) and plurality (their separation). Here we find a philosophical debate designed for intellectual specialists couched in a poem that reaches out to a wider audience.

Like his predecessors, Empedokles makes use of the topos of the foolish dissenters: 'Fools—for they have no far-reaching thoughts, | who fancy that that which formerly was not can come into being | or that anything can perish and be utterly destroyed' (fr. 11). The audience is encouraged to side with the wise poet rather than join the mass of the ignorant. The poem also contains a pronouncement to the people of Akragas:

> Friends who dwell in the great city of tawny Akragas
> . . . I greet you.
> An immortal god, mortal no more, I go about honoured by all,
> as is fitting, crowned with ribbons and fresh wreaths.
> Whenever I enter the prosperous townships, I am revered by all,
> both men and women; they follow me in countless numbers,
> enquiring where the path to gain lies, some seeking prophecies,
> while others, long pierced by grievous pains, ask to hear
> the word of healing for illnesses of all kinds.
>
> (fr. 112)

In this passage, Empedokles imagines himself adulated as a god and a healer by countless throngs: here is a man who clearly longed for a huge audience! This part of the poem is a visionary account of the story of the soul's exile from happiness, its wandering through many different lives, and its eventual restoration to divine purity. In a number of intriguing fragments, Empedokles describes his own reincarnations, which range from the lowly life of a bush to the lofty heights of godhead. The poem as a whole is unveiled from the divine perspective (how things looked from the point of view of the bush is never, alas, revealed). Even more blatantly than his predecessors, Empedokles lays claim to divine authority.

The work of these remarkable thinkers reveals their need to compete against the most influential 'masters of truth', Homer and Hesiod. Since these were the great educators of Hellas, any wise man offering an intellectual (rather than a practical or technical) product had to match himself against this kind of sage. I am not suggesting that these philosophical poets achieved the kind of popularity enjoyed by more traditional poets: the point is that they exploited traditional forms of poetry in an effort to put themselves on the map. Of course, even as they made use of poetic discourse to gain a hearing, they engaged in a specialized discussion of the nature of the universe, of change, and of reality. Although, at times, the early 'philosophical' thinkers were content to ignore the public and talk primarily to one another, the need to attract followers and to gain authority and (at least local) fame was a basic feature of the life of an intellectual. This can be seen especially clearly in the mid-fifth century, when certain intellectuals decided to make a business out of imparting their ideas and skills.

The variety of professional 'sophists'

The intellectuals in question are those that came to be called the 'sophists'. Although, in the fifth century, the word *sophistes* did not pick out a specific group of intellectuals (until the fourth century, it was often used as a synonym for *sophos*), the term came to designate those men who travelled around the Greek world advertising and selling the products of their wisdom. The most famous 'sophists' of the fifth century are Protagoras of Abdera, Gorgias of Leontinoi, Prodikos of Keos, and Hippias of Elis. The very category 'sophist' has the effect of placing all these individuals in a group, when in fact they did not work in association with one another and did not even purvey the same kind of wisdom. Although they are often bunched together as 'teachers of rhetoric', this categorization conceals the wonderful variety of these thinkers. These men did not form a movement or school; rather, each was a lone ranger, offering a unique product to the growing market.

This is not to deny that many sophists did offer teaching in the 'art' (*techne*) of effective speech and action; certainly there was a wide market for training in the skills that were required for success in the public world. One of the most able masters of rhetorical art was Gorgias, who developed a unique and highly poetic prose style. As he himself claims, poetry is simply 'speech with metre' (fr. B11. 9). In his famous *Encomium of Helen*, he not only demonstrates the power of rhetoric but also offers an explicit analysis of the nature of persuasive speech. The following passage gives a good idea of Gorgianic discourse and ideas:

> Speech is a great lord, which by means of the smallest and most invisible body brings about the most divine deeds: it can stop fear and destroy pain and produce joy and augment pity. . . . What cause prevents the assertion that Helen, similarly, came under the influence of speech against her will,

> as if ravished by the force of the mighty? . . . For speech persuading the soul that it persuaded, compelled it both to believe what was said and to approve what was done. . . . For just as different drugs drive out different secretions from the body, and some bring an end to sickness and others to life, so also in the case of speeches, some create pain, others pleasure, some cause fear, others make listeners confident, and some drug and enchant the soul with a certain evil persuasion. (fr. B11. 8–14)

Here, Gorgias persuades us with his musical style even as he discusses the slippery nature of persuasive speech.

As I have suggested, training in rhetoric was only one of many areas of expertise cultivated by the sophists. Consider Hippias, whose expertise included astronomy, geometry, arithmetic, musical theory, orthography, and an astonishing mnemonic art. As Plato reports in the *Lesser Hippias*, when he came to perform at an Olympic festival, Hippias claimed to have made everything he was wearing and carrying himself: a ring, a seal, a strigel, an oil flask, shoes, a cloak, a short tunic, and a woven girdle circling the tunic. This reminds us that Hippias did not confine himself to the higher or 'liberal' arts, but professed a wide variety of manual and technical skills that made him a true polymath.

In what venues did the sophists perform and teach? We know that Gorgias and Hippias reached large audiences by performing their work at the Olympic and Pythian games; these venues offered the sophists a panhellenic platform. Another popular spot was the Athenian agora, the political and economic centre of the city. Since, by the middle of the fifth century BCE, Athens was the bastion of intellectual life in the Greek world, this city was on the itinerary of every major sophist. Although the sophists were held in suspicion by many Athenians, it is clear that they were hugely successful there. Thus we see a large crowd gathering at the Lyceum for two rather minor sophists in Plato's *Euthydemus*, cheering each round of the argument; in Thoukydides, moreover, the politician Kleon chides the men at the Athenian assembly for acting like an audience attending a performance of sophists, seeking diversion rather than serious activity (cf. p. 152). Of course the sophists also performed at private gatherings, where they addressed their hosts and prospective students. In Plato's *Protagoras*, for example, we find the sophists Protagoras, Hippias, and Prodikos living as guests at the house of Kallias, a wealthy Athenian. Here, the sophists are shown addressing smaller groups, though it is noteworthy that Protagoras has brought a flock of foreign followers and a prize pupil along as an entourage (a sort of ready-made audience). Let me add, finally, that the sophists also took advantage of the technology of writing, which was slowly taking hold in the fifth century BCE. Although there are only scanty remains of sophistic texts, we must remember that the sophists were writers and theorists as well as performers, mixing these media to suit their professional needs. Sophistic writings served as performance texts, as exemplary models of rhetorical techniques and, ultimately, as lasting advertisements of the author's wisdom.

The distinction between the sophists and the sages is not hard and fast. Perhaps the most important point of difference is that the sophists were paid professionals: these men were after material as well as symbolic capital. Protagoras is said to have been the first to have taken money for his teaching. We know little about the actual fees, although they seem to have ranged from Hippias' 50 drachma lecture on grammar and language to Protagoras' 10,000 drachma course of study, which was no doubt quite lengthy (a drachma was a qualified worker's daily wage). The fact that Hippias also offered a 1 drachma lecture as an alternative to the 50 drachma lecture suggests that sophists readily adapted themselves to audiences of different sizes and constituencies. Plato compares their activities to that of merchants and salesmen. Like merchants, sophists travelled all around the Greek world, offering their wares to complete strangers. This kind of business transaction was different from those carried out by citizens in their own cities, where exchanges were embedded in a network of social and political relationships. Indeed, the reason why the sophists were held in suspicion in Athens was because they were foreign men who presumed to be telling Athenians how to run their public and personal affairs. They were, then, cosmopolitan intellectuals rather than local sages; not surprisingly, some were strong advocates of panhellenism, urging the Greek cities to put aside their differences and unite against foreign foes.

The medical practitioners of the fifth and fourth centuries resembled the sophists in a number of ways. In addition to treating the sick, Greek physicians offered live performances of their wisdom and expertise. Both Plato and Xenophon provide evidence that doctors performed in public spaces as well as at the bedside; they indicate that physicians addressed the Athenian assembly as experts, and even competed with one another for the office of Public Physician of Athens. Further evidence of the performance of medical wisdom is found in the treatise *On the Nature of Man*, which ridicules those doctors who engage in competitive debates with one another in front of crowded audiences:

> Clearly [these physicians] do not know anything. One can see this especially by attending the debates of these men. For when these men debate with one another in front of the same listeners, the same man never wins three times in a row, but now this man wins, now that one, and then again the man whose tongue is the most fluent in front of the crowd.

The treatise entitled *Precepts*, finally, claims that some doctors wore fancy headgear and exotic perfumes to attract attention, though the author discourages this kind of showy behaviour.

Many medical practitioners also wrote treatises on their own theories and practices. These 'Hippocratic' texts range from technical discussions of medical treatments to more general pieces aimed at a wider public. In these texts, many of which are extant, we can clearly see a group of professionals varying their discourses to suit both specialized and lay audiences. Indeed, many treatises explicitly address the question of how to speak persuasively to the lay public. Like the sophists, the medical practitioners claimed to have an art or skill—a *techne*—which could be taught and put into practice. This kind of wisdom could be systematized and placed in a written package; it was therefore less reliant on *metis*, which was spontaneous and intuitive knowledge that could not be reduced to systems and rules.

Sokrates among the sages

The fifth century also featured the most famous of all Greek wise men: Sokrates the Athenian (469–399 BCE). Although Sokrates did not write anything down and therefore did not contribute directly to the corpus of Greek literature, he has the peculiar distinction of having spawned an entirely new literary genre, the *Sokratikos Logos*, a representation in prose of Sokrates' philosophic conversations. Although there were numerous authors of Sokratic dialogues, all that remains of this vital genre is some few fragments of Aischines and the fourth-century writings of Plato (Greek: Platon) and Xenophon. Unfortunately, Plato and Xenophon offer very different portraits of this elusive figure, and this has led to the problem of identifying the 'true' Sokrates. Already in the fifth century, the comic poet Aristophanes had written a play that featured Sokrates as the protagonist (the *Clouds*). That Sokrates could command this kind of attention suggests that he was very well known in Athens. Interestingly, Aristophanes offers an extremely negative portrayal of Sokrates: he is part scientific quack and part purveyor of shady rhetorical practices. Of course, Aristophanes is trying to raise a laugh, and he can hardly be aiming at verisimilitude. Plato and Xenophon, by contrast, adulate Sokrates, though Xenophon's hero is a pious do-gooder while Plato's is a cagey, complex, and charismatic figure. We must remember that neither of these men was attempting to write a biography of Sokrates; both offered a blend of fact and fiction. If we favour Plato's version, it is because he alone portrays a character who is provocative enough to be put to death at the hands of the Athenians.

Sokrates was put on trial in 399 BCE for corrupting the youth and worshipping deities not recognized by the city. This may not have been the first time that the Athenians put an intellectual on trial; there is some (questionable) evidence that Protagoras and Anaxagoras were indicted for meddling in Athenian affairs. Even if these legends are false, their existence indicates that intellectuals occupied a somewhat dangerous position in democratic Athens. In the case of Sokrates, it appears that the underlying problem was political. Since Sokrates was known to have associated with aristocrats like Alkibiades and Kritias (who had done enormous harm to their city during the Peloponnesian War), he was identified as an enemy of the democracy. He was therefore dragged into court and made to defend himself before a jury of 500. In Plato's *Apology*, Sokrates is represented as delivering a stunning speech challenging the Athenians to take justice and virtue seriously. He claims that he has never been in a lawcourt before, and is unfamiliar with the language of the place. But Sokrates' discourse is a brilliant piece of rhetoric—rhetoric which cries out for an audience of good men. Sokrates' jury voted 280 : 220 against him; his fiery provocations were no doubt insulting to many. Where Sokrates failed, however, Plato succeeded: by writing the *Apology* and other dialogues, Plato ensured that Sokrates found his true audience, albeit after his death.

As a rule, Sokrates did not perform in the political fora of Athens (i.e. the assembly and courts). Instead, he journeyed around the city and its environs striking up conversations wherever he went: in the gymnasia and wrestling schools, in the groves of the Academy and Lyceum (before the famous schools were instituted there), in the agora, at symposia, in the workshops of artisans, and at private houses. He claims in the *Apology* that he deliberately sought out poets, politicians, and craftsmen, since he thought that they might have some wisdom to impart. He is also seen regularly with adolescent boys and young men. Finally, he is portrayed as sparring with many different sophists, sometimes in front of a good-sized crowd.

Although some scholars have argued that his avoidance of political gatherings makes him a 'performer in exile', there is in fact no more embedded and embodied philosopher than Sokrates. Embedded, because he rarely left Athens, and even chose death rather than exile at his trial. To be sure, Sokrates played by his own rules, rejecting traditional social, political, and economic exchanges; but his in-your-face approach to philosophy kept him intimately tied to his fellow Athenians. As he says in the *Apology*, 'I went like a father or an older brother to each of the Athenians' (31b). Sokrates' wisdom was also embodied, for he enacted his wisdom in deeds as well as words: crucial to his performance of wisdom were his extraordinary powers of physical endurance and self-control. He could drink all night without getting drunk, go barefoot in the snow in freezing weather, and had complete control over his sexual appetites (even resisting the beautiful Alkibiades when he stole under the covers with him in a vain attempt at seduction). Sokrates' death, too, is a powerful performance, as he bathes his soon-to-be corpse and drinks up the hemlock in perfect serenity.

Although Sokrates is taken to represent a new turn in Greek philosophy (hence the modern term 'Presocratic Philosophy'), in many ways he is *sui generis*. Here was a thinker who claimed that he did not have knowledge and was not acting as a teacher. Yet he did have some basic principles. For example, his belief that wisdom is necessary and sufficient for virtue (to know the good is to do the good) forms the basis of his philosophy, which centres on the search for knowledge of the essence of the virtues—courage, piety, self-control, justice, etc. In conducting this search, Sokrates adopts a question-and-answer format (now called the 'Socratic method'). He generally plays the role of questioner, though he always insists that he does not himself have the answers. If one focuses on Sokrates' rhetoric and irony as well as his arguments, one can see that he is a master of *metis* (see p. 160); responding to the vagaries of every argument and to the particularities of the characters he interrogates, he always manages to outfox his opponents. Sokrates, in fact, is a consummate performer of wisdom, cut from the same cloth as the early sages. Although some Athenians (like Aristophanes) may have identified him as a sophist, we must remember that Sokrates did not take money, did not travel around Greece as a teacher, did not claim to possess knowledge or any other intellectual product, and in fact never wrote anything down. His performances were very different from those of the sophists: whereas the latter, on many occasions, delivered set pieces that had been composed in writing, Sokrates' discourse was purely oral, formally dialogical, and always *ad hominem*. Moreover, Sokrates' wisdom was not simply intellectual: his practical and physical enactment of the traditional virtues mark him as a sage rather than a sophist.

The 'first philosophers' and their schools

If Sokrates performed his wisdom for all the citizens of Athens ('young and old, rich and poor'), the philosophers of the fourth century focused primarily on writing and private teaching, creating the first official schools of higher education. I say 'philosophers' because Plato and Isokrates were the first intellectuals to appropriate for themselves (and their models) the term 'philosopher' (*philosophos*), a rather rare word which had previously been used to identify anyone pursuing intellectual cultivation. Both Plato and Isokrates offered explicit (and very different) definitions of 'philosophy'; each went to great lengths to defend and legitimize his own brand of wisdom and to debunk that of his rivals. Although we now consider Isokrates a master of rhetoric rather than philosophy, he himself laid claim to the title of 'philosopher'. Given that Philosophy was first constructed as a specialized discipline in the fourth century, we need to pay careful attention to the rhetoric that these intellectuals used in defence of this new cultural practice. These thinkers used the powerful discourse of philosophical protreptic to stake a claim to wisdom, negotiate space, rebuke rivals, and advertise their different styles of pedagogy.

Although Isokrates and Plato were greatly indebted to previous intellectual enterprises, they created brand new fora and forms for promulgating wisdom. Isokrates was the first to found his own school, which was located near the Lyceum (*c.*393 BCE). By creating an educational institution which was permanently settled in one place, Isokrates could offer a lengthy and systematic course of study. Like the sophists, he charged a fee for his teaching (1,000 drachmas for a three- to four-year course of study), but he was neither a traveller nor a performer. In fact, he claimed in a number of speeches that he had a poor voice and lacked the confidence for public speaking. Soon after Isokrates, Plato founded his own school, which was located in the Academy (Greek: *Akademia*), a park just outside north-west Athens dedicated to the hero Hekademos. Plato turned to Pythagoras as a model, creating a *thiasos* or religious brotherhood that was devoted to the cult of the Muses. Plato's school was a legal entity defined by its tutelary deities; the master did not charge fees for his teaching. People from all over the Greek world came to study with Isokrates and Plato, many of whom would have been attracted by the written works of these philosophers. An Arcadian woman named Axiothea, for example, is said to have come to Athens after reading Plato's *Republic* (unlike Isokrates, Plato had female students in his school), and a farmer from Corinth is reported to have joined Plato's school after reading the *Gorgias*.

These institutions of learning conferred on their heads an established position and great prestige in the Greek world. The need for public performances of wisdom was thus reduced if not eliminated. Isokrates' education focused exclusively on rhetoric and its implementation in public and political life, whereas Plato offered a wide array of subjects, including mathematics, astronomy, geometry, logic, metaphysics, epistemology, ethics, and political theory. It is important to emphasize that Plato's school, like that of Isokrates, attracted many influential and powerful students and colleagues (Plutarch lists twelve famous politicians who associated with Plato, and other sources suggest that there were more). Plato's involvement in the political affairs of Sicily, particularly his association with the tyrant Dionysios of Syracuse, is a reminder that he

THE THINKERS. This mosaic of a group of seven philosophers was made in the first century CE to decorate a villa near Pompeii on the bay of Naples. There has been much discussion whether the figures can be identified with individual philosophers. One theory claims that the figure pointing to the globe with a staff is Plato and the figure on the extreme left is Aristotle. In the background possibly the Akropolis at Athens.

did not repudiate politics or public life, though he had little involvement in the democratic government of Athens.

Isokrates and Plato, as Athenian intellectuals who belonged to the wealthy élite, would have been expected to participate in the democratic government of Athens. Both opted out, Isokrates because he was unfit for public speaking, and

Plato because he did not approve of Athenian government. By avoiding the political fora of the assembly and lawcourts, they were effectively rejecting the mass audience and its values. Plato was of course far more critical of the democracy than Isokrates was, but both chose to address an audience of élites by way of private teaching and the circulation of written texts. Although literacy was more widespread in the fourth century than in the fifth, only wealthy and educated individuals had the leisure and the money required to buy books and to study them.

Isokrates gives us a good idea of the process of writing and publishing a work in the *Panathenaic Oration* (200–72). He tells us how, after writing the first version of this speech, he 'revised' it in the company of three or four pupils. Upon reviewing the speech, the entire group pronounced it excellent, though it lacked an ending. Isokrates then decided to call upon a former pupil, an admirer of Sparta who himself lived in an oligarchic state, to find out whether anything he said about the Spartans was amiss. This man came and 'read' the speech, and he found fault with Isokrates' critical treatment of the Spartans. Isokrates tells us that he proceeded to deliver a short speech censuring this pupil for his ignorance, a speech which was applauded by the other pupils who were present. A little while later, he 'dictated' this latter speech to his slave, who added it on at the end of the former speech. Several days later, however, as he was 'reading and going over' the speech, Isokrates grew troubled about his handling of the Spartans. He came to the brink of 'blotting out or burning' his text, but opted instead to call in those of his former pupils who lived in Athens and to ask whether the speech should be destroyed or published. When this group comes, the speech is 'read aloud' and (not surprisingly) given a huge applause. Eventually, of course, the students persuade him to publish the speech, 'if he wishes to gratify the worthiest of the Greeks—those who are truly philosophical and not pretenders'.

Both Isokrates and Plato aimed their written work first and foremost at élite and educated men who could read (or listen to another person read) long pieces of prose. But neither was fully confident that his books would find the right readers or evoke the correct response. Isokrates expresses his ambivalence about the written word in *To Philip* 25–7:

> I do not fail to recognize the extent to which spoken speeches are more effective at persuasion than written ones, nor that all assume the former are uttered on important and urgent matters while the latter are written for display and profit. . . . When a speech is deprived of the speaker's reputation, his voice, the variations which are made in the delivery, and of the advantages of timeliness and seriousness about the matter at hand . . . and when someone reads it unpersuasively, without depicting any character, as

> though he were reading a list, it is not surprising that it seems to the listeners to be a poor speech.

Here, Isokrates acknowledges that written texts lack the force of embodied discourse, since they must circulate in the absence of the author and his voice. But he argues elsewhere that writing has the advantage over speech in that it offers a fixed document of exactly what one thinks, and does not toady to its audience in the way that oral performers generally do (e.g. *Epistle 1*). In fact, as he claims in the *Antidosis* (*On the Exchange of Property*), a written text can create an 'image' of its author for all time to come; the text is thus 'a monument, after his death, finer than statues of bronze' (7). Indeed, in the *Antidosis* Isokrates goes so far as to include lengthy passages from four of his other speeches. Here, for the first time in literature, we find a writer creating an anthology of his own work—a 'Portable Isokrates' which can 'lay bare the truth' about the life and ideas of its author (140–1).

Plato's view of writing is very different. In a famous passage in the *Phaedrus*, Socrates suggests that

> [writing] will introduce forgetfulness into the souls of its learners because they will neglect to exercise their memory; indeed, on account of the faith they place in the written word, they will recall things by way of alien marks external to them, and not from within, on their own. (274e—275a)

As Sokrates explains, written texts are neither 'clear' nor 'reliable', since they need the presence of the author to defend them when they are under attack. The disembodied written word can only say the same thing again and again, and it 'doesn't know how to address the right people and to keep silent before the wrong people' (275d—e). Finally, since writing is, as it were, an 'illegitimate brother' of the spoken word, it should not be taken seriously or treated as though it contained real truth. This passage has received a great deal of scholarly attention, since it appears to undermine Plato's own writings. As I see it, Plato is suggesting here that philosophical truth cannot be finalized and placed in a written package, since it demands ongoing argument and enquiry and is simply not suitable for the fixity of writing. Plato demonstrates this principle in most of his texts, refusing to offer final conclusions and pointing towards truths which are beyond the scope of the dialogue. What, then, did Plato intend to accomplish by writing dialogues? First, he wanted to issue an invitation to the philosophical life (and, indirectly, to his own school), offering a sample of the issues and methods involved. And, second, he wanted to entice and perplex the readers, thus pressing them to investigate the issues for themselves. Although Plato placed a much higher value on oral discussions of philosophic issues (which were no doubt the main activity in the Academy), he did not completely reject writing; rather, he tried to create texts that acknowledged their own provisionality.

What can we say about the circulation and reception of these texts in fourth-century Athens? Clearly, a written text could travel the Greek world far more easily than its author. The disembodied word had the advantage of communicating across great distances, and of creating a community of readers that transcended the boundaries of the city-states and their politics. Both Isokrates and Plato attracted pupils from all over the Greek world; this would suggest that their writings were widely disseminated. Although Havelock went too far in claiming that the technology of writing was the cause of a conceptual shift that made philosophic thinking possible, it is clear that writing facilitates the presentation of long and technical arguments and gives readers a chance to study and respond to difficult ideas. By reaching beyond the boundaries of Athens, thinkers like Isokrates and Plato could communicate with like-minded, educated Greeks, thus forming an élite community of cultured intellectuals. In fourth-century Athens, wealth and power were no longer markers of aristocratic superiority, for many members of the 'lower classes' were able to acquire money and political power. The 'liberal' or 'philosophical' education thus emerged as a new marker of élite status. In short, many aristocrats opted for culture and learning rather than power. In theory, of course, the liberal education claimed to prepare young men to be good leaders; but this claim did not always pan out in practice.

Isokrates' philosophic discourse

According to Isokrates, philosophy is a form of practical wisdom. As he says in the *Antidosis*,

> It is not in the nature of man to attain a scientific knowledge (*episteme*) which, once we possess it, enables us to know what to do or to say. I therefore consider those men wise who are able by means of conjecture to hit upon the best course of action; and I give the title of 'philosopher' to men who are engaged in the studies which make them achieve this kind of wisdom most expeditiously. (271)

Here, Isokrates suggests that ethical and political action cannot be turned into a science; because philosophic wisdom must respond to the shifting events of human life, it must be based on conjecture and experience. Isokrates goes on to attack his rivals (including Plato) for cultivating the wrong kind of wisdom:

> They say that the people who pay no heed to things that are necessary but enjoy the outlandish discourses of the ancient sophists are philosophers, but that the people who are learning and practising the things which enable them to manage wisely both their private households and the commonwealth of the city are not philosophers. (285)

Isokrates claimed, then, to teach men how to live and govern well. But his actual teaching focused primarily on *logos*, since the mastery of the right kind of rhetoric, he believed, would lead to the proper *praxis*.

Isokrates was an ambitious man: he wanted to influence Athenian politics without speaking in the democratic assembly; he wanted to be seen as an Athenian insider but also to participate in the affairs of other states (including oligarchic and tyrannical regimes). He walked a fine line between these disparate audiences, sometimes incorporating different ideologies into the same speech. The *Areopagitikos* and *On the Peace*, for example, take the form of speeches delivered to the Athenian assembly, and the *Antidosis* takes the form of a court speech in a public trial. In these texts, Isokrates portrays himself as a good democrat and a benefactor to his city, using many of the commonplaces found in Athenian rhetoric. The democratic rhetoric in this and other speeches was not, of course, aimed at the Athenian demos, but rather at an educated readership consisting of orators, politicians, and other influential democrats. Isokrates offers them strong arguments for their own position even as he exhorts them to live up to the early glories of Athens. In the same speeches, however, he inveighs against the ignorance and gullibility of 'the many', and criticizes the sycophants who are infecting the political process. Here, he shows his anti-democratic readers that he is not just a party hack. By skilfully tapping into different ideologies, Isokrates appeals to a disparate audience of literate and leisured Greeks, some of whom favoured democracy, others oligarchy, and yet others monarchy.

Although Isokrates made an impact on Greek politics by educating various princes and leaders, he also wanted to wield power by means of his writings, many of which discuss political issues and urge specific courses of action. In short, he wanted his speeches to be speech-acts: words that make or remake the world. In several of his late speeches, Isokrates openly admits that his written texts had little effect on political decision-making. He says more than once that his *Panegyric Oration* created an enormous stir and brought him great fame, yet he bitterly complains that no one took the advice he gave there. His texts, as it seems, were admired but not obeyed. Because he refused to declaim his discourses, he was unable to convert his *logos* into praxis; in this period, a written text simply could not compete with oral performances. In addition, Isokrates' musical and verbose rhetoric produces a smooth elegance that does not have the power demanded of political speeches. Even when his writings take the form of forensic and political speeches, he uses an artful style associated more with display and entertainment than with power politics.

In the *Antidosis*, Isokrates expresses his astonishment that the Athenian people voted against him at a trial concerning the payment of a liturgy (an expensive civic service that was compulsory for the richest Athenians). Here, he portrays himself as a great benefactor to the city of Athens: he admits that he has not participated in the public discourse of the assembly and courts, but claims that his wisdom has brought immense glory to the city. His speeches and his school, he asserts, have done an extraordinary service to Athens, and should be seen as a new kind of liturgy. In addition, since Athenians are known to be 'the best educated in thought and speech' of all the Greeks (294), Isokrates' intellectual activities render him the quintessential Athenian. Thus he suggests that his disembodied voice (i.e. the written speeches) can and should be embedded in Athenian social and political discourse. This is a novel and fascinating endeavour, even if it did not produce the desired results.

Plato and philosophic performance

Plato developed a quite different relation to the city and culture of Athens, one that evolved and changed as he matured. Plato's works are generally divided into three periods: the early, which include the *Apology, Crito, Euthyphro, Protagoras*, and *Gorgias*; the middle, which include the *Symposium, Phaedo, Republic*, and *Phaedrus*; and the late, including the *Sophist, Statesman, Timaeus*, and *Laws*. In his early dialogues, Plato focuses on Socratic discussions of ethical and political concepts. Sokrates, of course, was no aristocrat, and his language reflects the class of artisans from which he came; indeed, he is 'always speaking about pack asses, or blacksmiths, or cobblers, or tanners' (*Symposium* 221e), exploring the difference between the technical knowledge of the craftsman and the ethical wisdom of the sage. This kind of language clearly annoyed Athenian aristocrats; in the *Gorgias*, for example, Sokrates positively revels in this low language in his encounter with Kallikles (an aristocratic snob):

> SOCKRATES: What about cloaks? Perhaps the best weaver should have the biggest cloak, and the most cloaks, and go around in the prettiest cloaks.
>
> KALLIKLES: Cloaks indeed!
>
> SOCKRATES: Well, clearly shoes then. He who is the best and wisest expert in shoes should have the lion's share of them. The cobbler, I suppose,

should have the biggest shoes and the most numerous shoes in which to walk around. . . .

KALLIKLES: By god, you never stop talking about cobblers and fullers and cooks and doctors, as though our argument were about them.

SOCKRATES: Then please say what things the stronger and wiser man should get more of, when he justly overreaches and takes more than his share.

(*Gorgias* 490d—491a)

Plato's use of common and lowbrow discourse in a prose text is a bold new venture in Greek literature; since his readership consisted of wealthy and educated men, this serio-comic uncrowning of 'high art' is even more remarkable.

Although Sokrates' dialogues take place in the presence of relatively small groups of people, the political context and ramifications of these conversations are often underscored. In many texts, Plato creates a historical or political frame for the discussion that is to come. At the opening of the *Charmides*, for example, Sokrates explains that he has just returned from a battle in Potidaia—an event that illuminates the dialogue's discussion of virtue and self-control. In the *Euthyphro*, the protagonist encounters Sokrates just before he goes to trial on a charge of impiety; their dialogue, not surprisingly, focuses on the nature of piety. The *Apology* re-enacts Sokrates' trial and indictment, an event that occurred five years after the disastrous end of the Peloponnesian War. In this speech, Sokrates turns the tables and puts Athens on trial for impiety and injustice; he openly criticizes the democracy and claims that he would have been put to death long ago if he had engaged in Athenian politics. In these and other early dialogues, Plato portrays Sokrates as a sage whose intellectual and physical activities are performed in a specific cultural context. This context serves as a reminder that an individual's ideas and values have momentous consequences: true knowledge, as Sokrates conceives it, necessarily produces good and virtuous action (and, correlatively, ignorance produces vicious action). In Plato's early 'dramas', then, we see how *logos* affects *praxis*, how ideas affect deeds. He thus encourages his readers to pursue a brand of wisdom which is fundamentally practical and civic in orientation.

In the middle dialogues, Plato introduces a new kind of philosopher, a sage who is not at home in Athens or any other Greek city, and is not even really at home in his own body. In the *Symposium*, for example, we are told that, as he was walking to the drinking party, Sokrates wandered off to a nearby porch to enjoy a period of silent contemplation (174d—175a). Later in the dialogue, Alkibiades tells a story about Sokrates when they were on a campaign together:

One day, at dawn, he started thinking about some problem or other, and stood there lost in thought, and when the answer didn't come he still

> stood there thinking, refusing to give up. By midday, many soldiers had seen him and, quite surprised, they told each other that Sokrates had been standing there thinking ever since dawn. He was still there when evening came, and after dinner some Ionians brought their bedding outside (this was in the summer) partly because it was cooler and more comfortable and partly to see whether he was going to stay out there all night. Well, he stood on that very spot until dawn, and then he said his prayers to the sun and went away. (220c—d)

Here, Sokrates plays a novel role—that of a contemplative philosopher, lost to the world as he labours in thought. We find no trace of this kind of activity in the early dialogues. Plato offers here a new conception of the 'true' philosopher: this new sage is most at home when he is engaging in *theoria* (contemplation). In the *Republic*, Plato will insist that the philosopher who has found a happy contemplative life outside the cave must journey back into the darkness to educate and—ideally—rule over the ignorant masses (514a—518b). He has certainly not given up on politics or *praxis* (his two most monumental works, after all, are the *Republic* and *Laws*), but he has created a philosopher who, by nature, belongs in a higher world.

Plato's new philosopher is not embedded in the (non-ideal) city and its affairs, and is only tenuously attached to his own body. As he says in the *Theaetetus*, the true philosopher does not know the way to the market-place or lawcourts or council chamber; does not know whether people are upper or lower class; and never takes part in popular entertainment. Indeed,

> he is not even aware that he is ignorant, for he holds aloof not for reputation's sake, but because it is really only his body that resides and is at home in the city, while his thought, considering all such things petty and worthless, disdains them and takes wing . . . studying the plains by means of geometry and investigating the heavens though astronomy, seeking the true nature of all that exists . . . and never lowering itself to what lies close at hand. (173d—e).

To be sure, this portrait is somewhat exaggerated; Plato himself would not have met these criteria. But since, for him, human souls are immortal and can dwell outside the body, it is the task of the philosopher to 'practise death' by separating his soul and mind from his body as much as possible during this present incarnate life (see esp. *Phaedo*). In the middle dialogues, Plato erects a new metaphysical system which calls for a new kind of philosopher. It also calls for a new kind of literature—a mode of discourse which can investigate and reveal an incorporeal world that exists beyond the borders of earthly life. To communicate this new vision, Plato availed himself of a huge variety of styles, often mixing high language with low, and austere philosophic analysis with myths, allegories, and ornate rhetorical speeches. This unique style is designed to engage readers both intellectually and emotionally—to make them understand that their very lives are on the line.

Most of Plato's middle and late dialogues are devoted to the analysis and defence of the many facets of this new metaphysical system. Whereas in the early dialogues he dealt exclusively with ethical and political issues, in the middle and late dialogues he tackles a wide range of topics, including epistemology, ontology, psychology, logic, and cosmology as well as ethics and political theory. Although some of the middle and late texts are more conclusive than the open-ended dialogues of the first period, he never abandoned the dialogue form. In addition, by refusing to speak in his own person in any dialogue, Plato avoids setting himself up as an authority. Rather, he invites his readers to enter into a dialogue with the text—to investigate the philosophical issues for themselves rather than accepting the author's own views. For Plato, dialogue is the only way to 'do' philosophy; his choice of the dialogue form thus directly reflects his philosophical methodology.

In addition to developing the vocabulary and argumentation to suit his metaphysical system, Plato also creates a new kind of rhetoric—a rhetoric of conversion—which spirits the reader into the 'real world' existing above and beyond the material realm. The famous 'allegory of the cave' at the opening of book 7 of the *Republic* offers an excellent example of this kind of rhetoric: we humans are shackled in a cave (Sokrates tells us) watching the shadow-play reflected on its back wall; but if we are released from these bonds by a philosophic guide, we can journey into the real and radiant world existing outside the cavern. Consider, too, this passage from the eschatology at the end of the *Phaedo*:

> Next, said Sokrates, I believe that the earth is vast in size, and that we who dwell between the river Phasis and the Pillars of Herakles inhabit only a tiny portion of it—we live around the sea like ants or frogs around a pond—and there are many other peoples inhabiting similar regions. There are many hollow places everywhere in the earth, places of every shape and size, in which water and mist and air have collected. . . . We do not perceive that we are dwelling in its hollows, but think that we are living on the earth's surface. . . . But if someone could reach the summit, or take wing and fly aloft, when he put up his head he would see the world above . . . and he would know that this is the true heaven and the true light and the true earth. (*Phaedo* 109a—e)

This kind of rhetoric says to the reader: you know not where you are. It exhorts

THOUGHT IN WRITING. This fragment from Plato's dialogue Gorgias, *written in the second century CE, is typical of the pieces of papyrus excavated from the sands of Egypt in the last 100 years in that the writing is very well preserved but the papyrus survives only in small pieces. A classical Greek text was normally written in columns (without word divisions) along the length of one side of a long roll of papyrus. The lettering of a literary text was usually as here neat and easy to read.*

the audience to make a heroic journey beyond the body and outside the city and its puny affairs.

Plato's decision to write dramatic dialogues—complete with heroes and villains—reminds us of the debt he owes to Attic tragedy and comedy: he deliberately borrows from both these genres. It is easy to see the comic spectacle in a dialogue like the *Protagoras* (which makes fun of the sophists) and the tragic undercurrent in texts like the *Gorgias* and *Phaedo* (which deal with the death of Sokrates). Plato also exploits the device of dramatic irony, where the readers know more than the characters in the drama. Whereas Sokrates' irony centred on his disavowals of knowledge, Plato's irony is more wide-ranging, sometimes affecting the entire structure of a dialogue. In the *Menexenos*, for example, Sokrates demonstrates to Menexenos how easy it is to give a successful funeral oration; but Plato indicates to his readers that this kind of discourse is hollow and, indeed, harmful. Consider also the passage in the *Phaedrus* which discusses the technology of writing: here we find Sokrates, who did not write anything down, offering a critique of writing in a dialogue written by Plato.

In spite of his borrowings from tragedy and comedy, Plato announces in *Republic* that there is an 'ancient quarrel' between philosophy and poetry, especially tragic poetry. In books 2 and 3, he offers a lengthy critique of the treatment of gods and heroes in epic and tragic texts. Here, he draws a formal distinction between tragedy and epic: the former consists entirely of 'imitation' or dramatic impersonation, whereas the latter includes long narrative portions and is therefore less reliant on impersonation. Plato makes it clear that he prefers the form of epic, yet he himself is writing in the dramatic or 'imitative' mode. In book 10, he takes his critique even further by banishing all poetry from the ideal city (except for hymns to gods and encomia of good men). In particular, he claims that the poets do not possess knowledge and thus end up infecting the viewers' minds and 'feeding' their appetites and emotions.

As Plato says in the *Laws*, Athens has shifted from a 'rule by the best' to 'rule by the audience' (a 'theatrocracy'). This is, in part, the fault of poetry, which has fostered the irrational and unruly elements in the souls of the spectators. Once again, however, Plato's own writings are implicated: for his dialogues do not simply appeal to reason, but also play on our emotions and desires. The dialogues, after all, contain a good deal of myth and rhetoric; this kind of discourse is designed to evoke a passion for truth, shame for living in ignorance, and fear of its painful consequences. Plato uses this discourse because he wants to convert his audience—to turn his readers into lovers of truth. Like many of his predecessors, he incites his readers by claiming that only a few élite individuals can achieve wisdom. By making the ordinary world look dark and strange, and offering his readers a home in the 'real' world, Plato attempts to make a new kind of man.

I have suggested that Plato in his middle dialogues portrays the philosopher as a man who revels in *theoria*, even though the truth that he contemplates contains an injunction to virtuous deeds and actions. But note that, even as Plato privileges *theoria* over *praxis*, he conceives of contemplation as something that is performed: Sokrates stands contemplating for all to see on a stranger's porch, or he gets lost in a trance in front of the entire Greek army. The contemplative philosopher described in *Republic* 5–6 and the *Theaetetus* is said, moreover, to appear foolish and ridiculous to the common man. This philosopher is on view, performing a new kind of wisdom that consists in contemplation; *theoria* becomes a sort of heroic feat in the eyes of intelligent people. So Plato's dramas manifest an interesting tension. On the one hand, they create a philosopher who is neither fully embodied nor embedded, since his mind dwells elsewhere and his activities are detached from civic life. At the same time, however, he enacts a bodily performance of *theoria* for the benefit of his fellow citizens (though most men will see him as useless rather than beneficial). In spite of the move towards detached contemplation, then, Plato's philosopher is still a performer of wisdom. As Sokrates says in *Republic* 5, the philosopher is the most useful man in the city, but people do not know how to put him to use. The contemplative philosopher performs a new kind of wisdom, and thus appears to the many as a comic fool. It is perhaps for this reason that Plato prefers oral or 'living' discourse to the disembodied voice of the written text: unlike Isokrates, he believes that wisdom must be performed by an active soul in a human body.

From performer to spectator: Aristotle

Aristotle (Greek: Aristoteles) came from Macedonia to Athens in 367 BCE and spent twenty years in Athens as a pupil of Plato. After Plato's death in 348, he left Athens for twelve years, during which time he travelled in Asia Minor and Macedonia, and served as the teacher of Alexander of Macedon (then in his teens). In the 330s, Aristotle returned to Athens and established his own philosophical circle in the Lyceum (Greek: Lykeion), a grove sacred to Apollo located just outside of Athens. Initially the Lyceum, as this school was called, was housed in public buildings, but Theophrastos (Aristotle's successor as the head of the Lyceum) bought property near the grove and created a permanent place for the school. A very wide variety of subjects was studied in the Lyceum (also known as the Peripatos), including biology, zoology, cosmology, logic, ethics, politics, metaphysics, history, and literature.

As a metic or resident alien in Athens, Aristotle was barred from political life. His orientation to the civic affairs of Athens was therefore very different from that of Isokrates and Plato. During his residency in Athens Aristotle could not participate in political *praxis*, so it is perhaps in keeping with this that he completely separated practical and theoretical reasoning, privileging the latter over the former. As he argues, the man who leads a contemplative life will not spend much time on practical or political affairs, since his gaze is fixed on the 'eternal and unchanging' rather than on the vagaries of human life. Although the philosopher will need to engage in some kinds of *praxis* in order to sustain a contemplative life, he will keep these to a minimum, since they can 'obstruct' philosophic activity (*Nicomachean Ethics* 1178b). Correlatively, the man who perfects his practical reasoning and chooses a life of politics will not have the leisure to engage in contemplation. Aristotle makes it clear that the contemplative life is superior to the political life, though both are considered good lives.

Aristotle composed two kinds of written works: those he called '*logoi exoterikoi*', which were aimed at intellectuals outside of his school, and those called '*logoi kata philosophian*', which were technical treatises designed for his philosophical colleagues and pupils. Unfortunately, the 'exoteric' works are no longer extant; only the technical treatises have survived. These latter texts, often referred to as 'lecture notes', are written in a terse, economical style, and are not works of literature in the full sense. Although they have been edited by later writers, they give us a good idea of Aristotle's style as a lecturer and teacher. His 'exoteric' works, which survive only in fragments, were literary treatises and dialogues comparable to Plato's written works. As the fragments attest, these texts contained a good deal of protreptic discourse; they were clearly designed to reach the educated élite in the Greek world. Unlike Plato, however, Aristotle chose to cast himself as a character in these dialogues, thus creating a very different effect. For these texts tell us exactly where Aristotle stands, offering the fixed conclusions that Plato took such pains to avoid.

One of Aristotle's technical treatises must be mentioned in a discussion of literature, since it deals explicitly with literary discourse: the *Poetics*, one of the most influential works of literary criticism ever written. In the *Poetics*, Aristotle rescues tragedy from the clutches of Plato: 'the standard of what is correct in the art of poetry is not the same as in the art of politics or any other art' (1460b). Contrary to Plato, who focuses on the effects that the performance of poetry has on the polis, Aristotle claims that the performed 'spectacle' (*opsis*) of tragedy can be ignored, since the 'art' inheres in the structure of the drama. Aristotle offers a formalist interpretation of tragedy, paying no attention to the socio-political context in which the plays were performed. He does, however, discuss the effect that a good tragedy has on the soul of the reader or viewer: by arousing 'pity and fear', tragedy brings about a '*katharsis* of these emotions' (1449b). There are many different interpretations of the concept of *katharsis*; all of them agree, however, that it somehow involves a purgation of the soul that is beneficial and pleasurable. The *Poetics*, then, uses an analytical discussion to defend the art of poetry. For Aristotle, there is no 'quarrel' between tragic poetry and philosophy, since the two modes of discourse are completely distinct and offer different kinds of instruction and pleasure.

A brief look at Aristotle's *Protrepticus* (now fragmentary) exemplifies the rhetoric and discourse he used in his 'exoteric' works. Like Plato, he wants to make philosophers out of his readers. The following passage sketches out his conception of the true philosopher:

> It is not surprising, then, if wisdom is not useful or advantageous; for we say that it is not advantageous but good, and it should be chosen not for the sake of any other thing, but for itself. For just as we travel to Olympia for the sake of the spectacle, even if we got nothing more out of it (for the spectacle is more valuable than a large sum of money), and just as we are spectators at the Festival of Dionysus not so that we will gain anything from the actors (in fact we spend money on them), and just as there are many other spectacles that we would choose over a large sum of money, so too the contemplation of the spectacle of the universe must be honoured above all things that are considered to be useful. For it is not right that we should take such pains to go and see men imitating women and slaves, or to see men battling and running, but not think it right to contemplate the nature of reality and truth without any reward or payment (fr. B44)

Here, Aristotle suggests that true wisdom consists in viewing the spectacle (*theoria*) of reality, which produces nothing beyond itself but is chosen entirely for its own sake. This conception of wisdom as 'useless' and non-productive is quite new. For the Greeks had always expected their sages to be useful; even Plato insists that philosophers are beneficial to society. For Aristotle, the wisest man is a spectator rather than a performer, casting his gaze on that which is eternal and unchanging.

We find this same notion outlined in the last book of the *Nicomachean Ethics* (one of his technical treatises, given the title *Nicomachean* to distinguish it from another work on Ethics, known as *Eudemian*). Although Aristotle spends most of the first nine books analysing practical wisdom, he turns in book 10 to a form of wisdom which is far superior—the divine activity of contemplation (*theoria*). This book is considered by some scholars to contradict the arguments in the rest of the treatise, since it celebrates a quite different kind of life: the impractical life of the contemplative. Consider the following passage from book 10:

> The generous man will need wealth in order to perform generous actions, and the just man will need it in order to pay his debts (since mere intentions are invisible and even unjust men pretend that they wish to act justly). And the courageous man will need strength if he is to perform any brave actions, and the temperate man will need opportunities for intemperance. For how can he or any other man be visibly virtuous? . . . But the contemplator (*theoron*) needs none of these externals to engage in his activity; in fact, these things are generally a hindrance to contemplation. (1178a–b)

Here, Aristotle elevates the life of *theoria* over that of ethical *praxis*. Interestingly, the practical life is identified by its 'visible' performance, whereas *theoria* is the activity of the invisible power of the mind (*nous*). As Aristotle indicates at 1178a22, *nous* may exist 'separately' from the body, whereas practical virtue is performed by the 'composite' of body and soul. The contemplative man, in short, is not a performer but a disembodied spectator; he does not perform *theoria* (as Plato's philosophers do) but rather engages in the divine activity of 'thought thinking itself'.

I have emphasized the emergence of an ideology that privileges contemplation over practical reasoning because this both reflects and legitimizes the detachment of the philosopher from the political life of his city. It should be emphasized that the ideology of detachment was not always put into practice. Indeed, the fourth-century philosophers I have discussed all engaged in politics at some point in their lives (not to mention their ventures into political science). But these philosophers did not take part in the political gatherings of democratic Athens, and thus avoided the demotic audience. Opting instead for written discourses, these philosophers invited their readers to adopt a new cultural practice designed only for the select few. Rousing their readers with complex arguments and powerful protreptics, the great philosophers of the fourth century created new forms of literature.

Epilogue: The Hellenistic period

From the reign of Alexander the Great onwards, the Greek city-states were no longer politically autonomous. Beginning in this period, the Greek world was divided into larger political units whose rulers lived at great distances from most of their subjects. This political shift diminished the local loyalties of the city-states and encouraged a more cosmopolitan culture. After Alexander died

(323 BCE), there followed a period of wars and dynastic struggles throughout the Mediterranean. A new bastion of Greek culture was established in the city of Alexandria; although Alexandria replaced Athens as the centre of arts and sciences, Athens remained pre-eminent in philosophy.

In a world of rapidly changing cultural and ethnic boundaries, traditional notions of personal and political identity were being called into question. Responding to the breakdown of social, political, and cultural cohesion, the philosophers developed new systems of thought and specific styles of life that were grounded in these systems. In fact, many of the philosophers of this period were consummate performers, since each set out to model a unique 'art of living'. Though their philosophies differed in many crucial ways, both Epikouros (familiar Latin spelling Epicurus) and the Stoics advertised and enacted a life of supreme tranquillity, free from anxiety and psychic turmoil.

It is a great misfortune that so few philosophical texts from this period survive. There is no complete text from the early Stoics (Zeno, Kleanthes, and Chrysippos), little early evidence of either Pyrrhonian or Academic scepticism, and only scanty remains of Epikouros' voluminous writings. We do know that these schools attempted to attract followers from a wider social group than did Plato or Aristotle, and a brief look at the Stoics and Epicureans will give some sense of the audiences addressed by the Hellenistic philosophers. Both 'Schools' set out to popularize their teaching, attempting to gain followers from all walks of life. In his *Letter to Herodotos*, Epikouros says that he has prepared an epitome of his philosophy for those unable to study his technical writings. He also compiled a set of simple ethical maxims, explicitly designed to be learned by heart. The Stoics, on their part, composed pieces they called 'suasions and dissuasions'; these offered moral advice that was easily accessible to the ordinary reader.

Epikouros came to Athens from the island of Samos, establishing his school there in *c.*307/6 BCE. Diogenes Laertius says that Epikouros' writings ran to 300 rolls. Among his most important works were *On Nature* (thirty-seven books), *On the Criterion*, and a collection of ethical texts including *On Lives*, *On the Goal*, *On Choice and Avoidance*. His school—known as 'The Garden'—was a closed community, located just outside the city; its members were allowed to bring women and children into the group, and they had few reasons to be in contact with their former associates in their native countries. In his will, Epikouros speaks of the membership in the community as a commitment 'to spend one's time there continuously, in accordance with philosophy' (DL 10. 17); pupils were explicitly instructed not to engage in political life. Epicureanism, in short, offered personal salvation and group solidarity.

Epikouros' ethical philosophy focused on the proper approach to pain and pleasure and the avoidance of anxiety and fear (especially the fear of death); its ultimate goal was tranquillity (*ataraxia*). His natural philosophy, based on the thesis that the universe is composed of atoms and void, offered a scientific grounding for his ethics. As he says in the *Principal Doctrines*: 'If we were not troubled by alarms at celestial phenomena, nor by the worry that death somehow affects us, nor by a failure to understand the limits of pains and desires, we would have no need to study the science of nature' (11). The Epicurean, then, engages in *theoria* for the purpose of *praxis*. Thus, Epicurean wisdom is fully embodied, since its adherents must perform an entire way of living. This philosophy is not, however, embedded, for the full Epicurean must be detached from his or her city of origin and of all its social and political affairs. Indeed, it is precisely this detachment that enables the Epicurean to achieve happiness and tranquillity. Not surprisingly, Epikouros communicated his philosophy to the Greek world by way of the written word. He confined his personal performances to the (relatively) small and select audience of men and women who left their cities to come and live in the Garden.

In 301/300 BCE, Zeno of Kition (in Cyprus) began to philosophize in the Painted Colonnade (Stoa) in Athens, thus founding the Stoic school (DL 7. 5). The Stoa was located alongside the agora, in the very centre of town. Zeno takes his place in a succession of philosophers moving from Sokrates and his follower Antisthenes to the Cynics Diogenes and Krates (who was Zeno's teacher). Like these predecessors, Zeno performed his philosophy in the public eye. To be sure, Zeno was not as extreme as his Cynic forerunners; Diogenes, after all, was wont to masturbate, urinate, and fart in public—'to use any place for any purpose' (DL 6. 22). More in keeping with Sokrates, Zeno was austere and frugal, and apparently impervious to cold, rain, heat, and disease; when he did take part in parties and festivities, he was completely unaffected (DL 7. 26–7). Zeno made a point of performing a life of poverty, even begging for money from bystanders in the Stoa (DL 7. 13–14). Since Stoicism was a way of life as much as a system of thought, the masters of this school had to enact what they taught. It is noteworthy that Zeno's public performances commanded the attention of a man as powerful as Antigonos Gonatas (a king of Macedon), who frequented his lectures and even invited him to attend a party. Having elicited this royal invitation, Zeno proceeded to steal away from the festivities, thus exhibiting a Stoic indifference to the trappings of power (DL 13). Zeno played to a public audience that ranged from the ordinary person to rich potentates. At the same time, his written works reached a huge audience of readers all over the Greek world.

Zeno is reported to have written treatises such as *Life According to Nature, Emotions, That which is appropriate, Universals, Disputatious Arguments*, and *Homeric Problems* (DL 7. 4). Of his immediate successors, the most important are

Kleanthes (300–232 BCE) and Chrysippos (281–201 BCE). Of the writings of the early Stoics, only fragments survive. Later sources indicate that the Stoics constructed a philosophy in which ethics, physics, and logic formed a completely coherent and systematic whole. The Stoics represented this system by portraying philosophy as a fertile field in which logic corresponds to the surrounding wall, ethics to the fruit and harvest, and physics to the soil or vegetation. According to this philosophy, the universe is fully accessible to human reason, since it is itself a rationally organized structure; reason (*logos*), which enables humans to think and speak, is embodied in the physical universe. In contrast to dualistic philosophies that denigrated nature and the body, the Stoics developed a monistic theory that identified rationality with the physical universe. Thus when the Stoics encouraged their followers to live a 'life in accordance with nature', they were referring to a natural world that was providentially guided by a rational cosmic principle. Since humans are akin to the universe in so far as they possess reason, all men are therefore citizens of the world. Only the wise man, however, can offer the perfect embodiment of Stoic philosophy, since he alone understands the universal *logos*.

Stoicism was a philosophy that addressed, at least in principle, the entire human race; this forced the Stoics to develop many different kinds of teaching and writing. Take, for example, Kleanthes' *Hymn to Zeus*, a hexameter poem that dealt explicitly with Stoic principles:

> Nothing occurs on the earth apart from you, god,
> nor in the divine vault of heaven nor on the sea,
> except what bad men do in their foolishness.
> But you know how to make the odd even,
> and to order things that are disorderly;
> to you the things that are alien are akin.
> And so you have blended all things into one, the good with the bad,
> so that there arises a single everlasting *logos* of all things,
> which all bad men shun and neglect,
> unhappy wretches, always longing for the possession of good things
> they neither see nor hear the universal law of god,
> obeying which they would have a good life accompanied by reason.
> (ll. 15–25)

Like the Epicureans, the Stoics offered their followers a happy and tranquil life; but this was not to be achieved by abandoning one's city or community. On the contrary, the Stoics claimed that the wise man should take part in politics and attempt, so far as possible, to create a just and humane society. The serious Stoic was therefore embedded in his own society at the same time as he took his place in the cosmic community.

6 Observers of speeches and hearers of action: The Athenian orators

CHRIS CAREY

From art to science

Oratory was always part of Greek public or semi-public expression. It already plays a major role in the fictive society of Homeric epic. The education of the Homeric hero (exemplified in the case of Achilles) was designed to make him 'a speaker of words and a doer of deeds' (*Iliad* 9. 443). When Odysseus and Menelaos visited Troy to argue for the return of Helen, they found an audience which could appreciate their oratory (*Iliad* 3. 204–24). The three envoys sent to Achilles in the ninth book of the *Iliad* each deliver a speech to him in turn, to receive a speech in reply. If we jump three and a half centuries from Homer's Greece to the fourth century BCE, we find ourselves struck more by the continuity than by any radical change. When Athens began peace negotiations with Philip of Macedon in 346, they sent ten ambassadors to open negotiations. We have an account of the meeting with Philip from one of the participants, the Athenian politician Aischines (Aischines, 2. 25–38). Like those sent to Achilles, each of the ambassadors in turn delivered a speech (some evidently long) to Philip and his circle. After a brief recess, Philip gave an extended response, dealing in turn with each Athenian speaker's arguments. For Greeks of all periods past and present alike were characterized by extended spoken discourse as a means of persuasion.

It would be a mistake, however, to suppose that nothing had changed in the interval between Homer and the age of Demosthenes. The sixth and fifth centuries saw a remarkable effervescence of intellectual activity, in physical science, medicine, geography, and ethnography, historiography (see Chs. 3 and 4). This is an age when the world is subjected to a set of rules. The fifth century in particular sees the rise of the *techne*, the technical manual. Within this intellectual trend it is not surprising that oratory too was gradually systematized. The basic structures of the speech were mapped out and lines of argumentation developed. Particularly important for the future of oratory was the identification of argument from probability as a staple tool for the process of persuasion. Argument from probability gave a speaker the means to capitalize on any facts which might support his own case and undermine his opponent's case by arguing from general patterns of human conduct to particular instances, instead of relying entirely on traditional sources of proof such as witnesses, oaths, and laws. To illuminate the new-found awareness of the susceptibility of fact to manipulation by argument from probability, I have taken an illustration from two speeches in the first of the *Tetralogies* (a collection of speeches offering matching prosecution and defence in a series of fictitious trials) of the late fifth-century politician and speech-writer Antiphon. The fictive situation is that a man has been murdered. The accused, an enemy of the dead man and therefore an obvious suspect, needs to offer alternative scenarios for the killing, while the prosecution needs to anticipate and counter the defence arguments:

> [PROSECUTION] ⟨It is unlikely that the murder was committed by robbers.⟩ Nobody would have exposed his life to the most extreme danger and then abandoned the profit which had been acquired and achieved; for the victims were found with their clothing.
> [DEFENCE] It is not improbable (as my opponents maintain) but probable that he was killed for his clothes while wandering late at night. The fact that he was not stripped is no indication. If they didn't have time to strip him but left him on being frightened off by some people approaching, they showed good sense and were not crazy in valuing safety over profit.
> (Antiphon, *Tetralogy* 1)

The development of argument from probability is very much of a piece with the other rationalizing advances of the period, since it is based on the underlying assumption (found also in Thoukydides' history) that human nature too is subject to rules and that a given set of circumstances will in general prompt a predictable mode of behaviour. The genesis of rhetorical theory thus belongs as much in the realm of behavioural psychology as in that of verbal artistry. The same (tacit) element of behavioural psychology is also present in the underlying assumption that audience response too is predictable and that a knowledge of modes of argumentation enables a speaker to steer the audience towards a favourable decision.

Tradition (and there is no obvious reason to doubt our sources) associates the beginning of this process with Sicily, specifically with the democracy which followed the overthrow of the ruling house of Syracuse in the 460s. It is no coincidence that decades later the new skills found a favourable climate in one of the other great democratic cities of the period, Athens. Although we have ample evidence that oratorical skill could be deployed to good effect in non-democratic states, the connection between oratory and democracy is made repeatedly by our ancient sources when they explore the ethical problems raised either by rhetoric or by democracy. It is made for instance by the Argive herald who engages in political debate with the Athenian king Theseus in Euripides' *Suppliants*. Though he is clearly an unsympathetic character, his speech illustrates the connection between unscrupulous oratory and democracy in one strand of fifth-century political debate:

> The city from which I come
> Is controlled by one man, not by the mass.
> Nor is there anyone who deluding it with words (*logois*)
> Turns it this way and that for private gain,
> And by ingratiating and giving much pleasure for the moment
> Harms it later, and then with fresh slanders
> Conceals his former failures and escapes justice.
>
> (Euripides, *Suppliants* 410–16)

Democracy offered more occasions and larger audiences to be manipulated by effective public speaking. The political context, combined with the cultural prominence of Athens in the fifth century, attracted visits from the sophists, whose course offerings included the art of speaking, for which they found a ready market in Athens (cf. pp. 167–8). The pupils of the sophists were able to exploit their technical expertise in the political arena or to earn substantial sums by hiring their services to write speeches for the lawsuits heard by the jury panels of classical Athens.

Though many of the broad effects, and some specific devices, of classical oratory are prefigured in earlier poetry, and must have played a role in pre-rhetorical oratory, the new focus on rhetoric as technique gave the art of speaking the impact of a new medium of communication for Greeks of the fifth century; like all new media, it raised prospects which were simultaneously exciting and disturbing. The excitement generated by the new perception of the power of the word is vividly captured by the fifth-century sophist Gorgias, a native of Leontinoi in Sicily, in his *Helen*, a fictitious defence speech for Helen of Troy which simultaneously advertises (through its argument and opulent style) and celebrates the power of speech, *logos*. In the extract quoted on pp. 67–8, Gorgias attributes to persuasive speech an almost magical power over the mind of the hearer, an idea in earlier generations associated with the poet.

Both the notion of words as magic and the use of the language of power (*logos* is a *dynastes*, 'master', 'ruler' it has *dynamis*, 'power') present speech as a means of control, with the skilled speaker as the manipulator and the audience as passive objects. Though one has to view with caution the professional rhetorician's claims for the product of his training, Gorgias' own career is itself testimony to the intoxicating effect of verbal skill in the fifth century, for according to our ancient sources the Athenians were captivated by his oratory when he came to Athens on a diplomatic mission in the 420s. Not only did this win pupils for his lectures on rhetoric, his highly artificial style had a profound effect on subsequent prose writers. It is important for the modern reader, in an age of entrenched divisions between high and low culture, to bear in mind that, although the customers of Gorgias and the other sophists were drawn from the propertied classes, the admiration for rhetorical skill was not confined to the wealthy. The audience which was captivated by Gorgias was not an élite group but the popular assembly. The historian Thoukydides puts into the mouth of the fifth-century Athenian politician Kleon a diatribe against the Athenian fondness for bravura oratory:

> You're the ones to blame for this with your mismanagement of these contests. Your habit is to be observers of speeches and hearers of action, assessing the possibility of future events from good speakers. But as for things which have already happened, you don't take what's been done as more plausible because you've seen it than what you've heard, under the influence of people who produce a clever verbal critique. . . . Each of you wants ideally to be the most able speaker, and failing that you compete with such speakers by seeming not to be slow-witted in following them . . .
> (Thoukydides, 3. 38. 4)

As always with oratory, nothing here is straightforward. The criticism is disingenuous, since the style in which it is expressed is itself highly artificial, and the speaker is deliberately adopting the posture of a blunt and simple man. More than this, we cannot be certain how far the wording and even the content of Kleon's speech (as with all speeches in Thoukydides) is the invention of the historian. But the overall picture the speech gives of a popular audience which took genuine pleasure in carefully crafted oratory is confirmed by the pronounced influence of formal oratory on Athenian tragedy, another art-form performed for a mass audience.

The response to the growth of rhetoric was not unambiguously positive. Passages in both comedy and tragedy indicate that the appreciation of skilled oratory coexisted with a profound suspicion of an art which threatened to substitute illusion for truth. This anxiety has its roots in the same conception of the audience as under the control of the speaker which we find in Gorgias. This suspicion persisted and is manifested most clearly in courtroom contexts where speakers either directly or indirectly lay claim to lack of experience in public speaking. The following is one of many examples: 'I could have wished, gentlemen, that my powers of speaking and experience of affairs were equal to my misfortune and the evils which have befallen me. As it is I have more experience of the latter than is fair, while in the former I am more deficient than is safe.' (Antiphon, 5. 1)

Unfortunately we have little oratory from the late fifth century BCE. Apart from the surviving pieces of Gorgias, our earliest texts, from the politician and speech-writer Antiphon, date to the period between 420 and his death after the short-lived political coup of 411 which briefly replaced the democracy with a narrow oligarchy. Some of these were written for the courts; others (the *Tetralogies* cited above) were composed for fictitious legal cases, as a means both of exemplifying and advertising the rhetorician's art. We also have the speech composed by the politician Andokides some time after 410 (*On his Return*) pleading for permission to return to Athens from exile. Otherwise our most important source for fifth-century Athenian oratory are the speeches which Thoukydides puts into the mouths of the characters in his history.

Oratory in context(s)

In his *Rhetoric* the fourth-century philosopher Aristotle divides oratory into three categories, symbouleutic, dikanic, and epideictic. The primary basis for the definitions (as for almost all archaic and classical literature) is the performative occasion. The first kind (symbouleutic) is aimed towards deliberative bodies and is the ancient equivalent to the parliamentary speech. In the Athenian context this means primarily speeches delivered before the Assembly (*ekklesia*). Athenian democracy, unlike most systems known to us, was a direct democracy; policy was decided not by a small cohesive group ('the government') with an advertised political programme but by the popular Assembly. Although attendance figures for the Assembly are controversial, and there must always have been a preponderance of city-dwellers and those living near the city at Assembly meetings, there was evidently little difficulty in enticing several thousand Athenian citizens, and at least for some occasions as many as six thousand, to attend public meetings which devoured a substantial portion of the day and to listen to extended speeches on major policy issues. The Athenian populace was by any standards an unusually politicized group. Though all adult male citizens were entitled to participate in the decision-making, in reality policy was driven by individuals, often organized into loose and shifting groups, who had the private means to devote their time to politics. And they achieved and maintained influence through the spoken word. The Assembly met regularly and its business ranged from major issues of peace and war and legislation (though from the fourth century the actual drafting of law was devolved to legislative panels) through to honorary decrees for public benefactors. It also included control of the magistrates. There were regular opportunities for the Assembly to vote its officials out of office if their conduct was perceived as unsatisfactory. We know from a number of sources that addressing the Assembly was no easy task. A passage in Plato gives some flavour of an Assembly meeting:

> 'Why, when,' I said, 'a large crowd are seated together in assemblies or in court-rooms or theatres or camps or any other mass public gathering, and with loud uproar express disapproval of some of the things that are said and done and approve others, both in excess, with loud clamour and clapping of hands, and beyond this the rocks and the region round about re-echoing redouble the din of the criticism and the praise.' (Plato, *Republic* 492b—c)

Although Plato, no lover of Athenian democracy, presents us with a scene of indiscipline, what it really demonstrates to the unjaundiced reader is the lively engagement of ordinary assembly-goers with the issues addressed, and the absence of a culture of automatic deference to influence and authority.

The second type of oratory is directed towards the lawcourt. Though the legal system was based on a principle of trial by a panel of ordinary citizens, Athenian lawcourts were quite unlike anything experienced in the modern world. The jury panels themselves were massive by our standards. For the least significant private cases the minimum panel size was 200, while for public cases (which for the Athenians meant not only overtly political cases but also trials for offences which were felt to affect society at large) the panels would begin at 500 and increase in size by multiples of 500, on occasion reaching a scale in the thousands. The distinction between the juries and the Assembly must not be pressed too hard: the lawcourts were an accepted arena for fighting political feuds. In this respect the courts were an extension of the Assembly and the audiences must have overlapped to some (unquantifiable) degree. Addressing the jury panels required no small measure of nerve. Athenian juries did not comport themselves with the sober silence expected of modern juries. The testimony of Plato about the behaviour of the juries (quoted above) is amply confirmed by many places in the orators where the speaker tries to anticipate a hostile (and vocal) response from the jurors. This passage from a fourth-century speech may exaggerate, but presumably it is

*SPACE FOR DEMOCRACY. The Assembly (*ekklesia*) in classical Athens was open to all citizens and was held on the hill of the Pnyx to the west of the Akropolis and the agora. This view of the space where the Assembly listened to their orators looks towards the south.*

based on a shared perception of just how difficult an audience an Athenian jury might be:

> He read out this and told all the other lies he thought useful, and he put the jurors in such a frame of mind that they refused to hear a single utterance from us. (Demosthenes, 45. 6)

In a memorable debate in *Wasps*, produced in 422, a play devoted to the legal system (cf. pp. 120–1), the comic playwright Aristophanes presents the jurors as vindictive, self-indulgent old men who like to be flattered and feared and who revel in the irresponsible and capricious exercise of power. On the basis of this and other evidence it is sometimes supposed that the courts are no more than another area of élite competition in which the rights and wrongs are ultimately of secondary importance. But with comedy, as with oratory, caution is needed in interpreting the evidence. Although our perception is distorted by the fact

VOTING BEFORE ATHENA. The myth narrated how the leaders of the Greeks at Troy voted after a debate between Odysseus and Ajax for the award of the great armour of Achilles. On this cup painted in Athens (c.470s BCE) the votes can be seen accumulating on the low plinth, under the supervision of Athena.

that surviving lawcourt speeches are the work either of politicians or of professional speech-writers writing for moneyed clients, with the result that we lack any direct evidence for smaller cases involving more humble characters, it is an inescapable fact that the courts were in fact an arena for competition among men of property. And the susceptibility of the jurors to flattery is amply demonstrated in surviving oratory. Furthermore, the feeling of power over the wealthy which Aristophanes describes must have been a real psychological bonus for the jurors, as well as confirming on a daily basis the principle of equality which underpinned the ideology of democracy. At the same time, a cursory reading of the orators reveals the pains taken by speakers to argue the case on its merits, however much (like litigants at all periods) they may digress, distort, and obfuscate. The jurors were considerably more shrewd, and a more intellectually demanding audience, than their critics suppose. It is important to bear in mind that Aristophanes in *Wasps* is particularly concerned with the political role of the courts. It was much easier to engage in systematic evasion in political trials, where the specific issues came wrapped in larger questions of public policy, than in private cases.

But one important point which does emerge from Aristophanes' lampoon of the legal system is the entertainment value of the courts. We should not imagine that the jurors were motivated solely by a desire to do their civic duty or even to collect the pay for service (about half the labourer's daily wage in the late fifth century, about a third in the fourth century when inflation had lowered the purchasing power of the drachma). Other people's lives are endlessly fascinating and the courts offered a spectacle comparable in certain ways with the grander dramas played out on the tragic stage.

The third kind (epideictic) is intended for public occasions where no formal outcome is sought. In essence it is oratory of display, *epideixis*, though the English word trivializes what for the Greeks was a serious activity. The term also ignores the overlap between *epideixis* and civic ideology, the importance of the speaker's status, and the tendency of epideictic speakers to take an explicitly competitive stance towards their predecessors and to utilize devices which identify them as in some sense the advocate of those they praise or exculpate. Epideictic oratory is exemplified especially (though not exclusively) by the speeches composed for delivery at the mass civic funerals which Athens held at the end of each year in times of war to honour the war dead. The historian Thucydides tells us that it was the custom for a distinguished public figure to speak in praise of the dead. These funerals offered an opportunity for the assembled citizen body to celebrate the achievements of the dead and the greatness of the city and constitution in whose name they fought and died. Like all ritual, they are as much about the shared identity of the audience as about the overt religious activity.

This tripartite division is not rigid. The boundaries are permeable. Even a cursory reading of lawcourt oratory reveals that in public cases at least there is room for a pronounced epideictic element. Politicians involved in trials not infrequently draw on the motifs (praise of ancestors, references to the great events of the past) which are the raw material of the public funeral orations. Deliberative oratory often has a pronounced adversarial element to it, inevitably given the nature of political competition in democratic Athens. It may be useful simply to draw attention to a single example. In 330 the politician Aischines brought to trial a minor political figure, Ktesiphon, for his proposal to give a crown of honour to Aischines' political enemy Demosthenes for conspicuous merit in the service of the city. A decade earlier Aischines had been a major player in Athenian politics and had been influential in negotiating peace between Athens and Philip of Macedon. By the date of Ktesiphon's trial, however, the peace had failed and Aischines was a spent force in Athenian politics. His sense of himself as an outsider is reflected in the way he presents the dominant political group (3. 250–1):

> Or don't you think it monstrous that the Council chamber and the Assembly are ignored, while the letters and embassies come to private

houses, not from people of no consequence but from the leading men of Asia and Europe? . . . And the people are discouraged by their experiences, like someone senile or out of his mind; they preserve only the name of democracy, while they have surrendered the real thing to others. Then when you go home from Assembly meetings you have not decided policy but like men coming from a picnic you have been given a share of the scraps.

The politicians get the benefits, the people get the leftovers. There is, however, nothing new in all this. The themes are encountered for the first time in surviving literature almost 100 years earlier in Aristophanes' *Wasps*, where the character Bdelykleon argues his father out of his passion for jury service by showing that the jurors are the dupes of the politicians:

> PHILOKLEON: So where does the rest of the money go?
> BDELYKLEON: To these 'I-shall-not betray-the-Athenian-rabble
> but-will-fight-for-the-masses-forever' types.
>
> . . . .
>
> BDELYKLEON: Just look how, when you and everyone else could be rich,
> you've been circled about without realizing by the perpetual 'people' people,
> you who rule the most cities from the Black Sea to Sardis
> and get no benefit but this small wage. And this they always drip
> into you with wool like oil by drops to keep you alive.
> They want to keep you poor, and I'll tell you why:
> so you'll know your keeper, and then when with a whistle
> this man urges you on against an enemy, you leap on them savagely.
> (Aristophanes, *Wasps* 665–7, 698–705)

More significantly for our purposes, this presentation has a marked affinity to a description of the leading group by Demosthenes in 349/8 in his *Third Olynthiac*, almost twenty years before Aischines' speech, when Demosthenes had yet to become a major political force:

> Now the reverse is the case; the politicians control the benefits and everything is done through their agency, while you the people, hamstrung and stripped of money, allies, have been reduced to the position of servant and appendage, content if these men give you a share of the theoric money or hold the Boedromia, and—the most manly thing of all!—you're even grateful to get what belongs to you. (Demosthenes, 3. 31)

Demosthenes' account occurs in a deliberative speech, Aischines' in a lawcourt speech, but the theme and stance are the same. On occasion epideictic oratory adopts the stance of other forms. But for all the dangers of restrictive application, Aristotle's categories are not to be dismissed. Each category is directed towards a different context and that context has a profound impact on its form and content. Although there is a constant transmigration of motifs, the motifs are often deployed to different ends. When the great deeds of the past are used in epideictic contexts, the aim is straightforward praise of the dead and, through the pride and shared origin enacted in the narrative, a ritualized celebration of group identity which unites speaker and audience. When they appear in forensic oratory the pride engendered by the epideictic motifs serves an ulterior purpose.

Often, it is utilized as a means of isolating the opponent; pride is a means to stimulate other emotions, as when the late fifth-/early fourth-century speech-writer Lysias briefly slips into epideictic mode during the prosecution of Nikomachos early in the fourth century for alleged misconduct in his office as drafter of the revised lawcode. Nikomachos (himself probably a man of servile extraction) is placed on one side of the balance, the ancestors who built the fifth-century empire on the other, and the audience is invited to express a preference:

> I gather he claims that I am guilty of impiety in putting an end to the sacrifices. Personally, I would think that Nikomachos could make this sort of statement about me if I were making laws. As it is, I am asking him to obey the shared and established laws. I am surprised that he does not reflect that, when he alleges that I am behaving impiously in saying that we must sacrifice according to the *kyrbeis* [the early lawcode] and the columns according to the drafts, he is also accusing the city. For this is what you decreed. And if you think this is intolerable, you must surely suppose that those men did wrong, who only carried out the sacrifices on the *kyrbeis*. And yet, judges, one should not learn piety from Nikomachos but reflect on the basis of past events. Our ancestors while carrying out the sacrifices on the *kyrbeis* handed on the city as the greatest and most successful in Greece, and so it is right that you make the same sacrifices as those men because of the good fortune which resulted from those offerings, if for no other reason. (Lysias, 30. 17–18)

For Aristotle (*Rhetoric* I. 3. 5) the particular goal of deliberative oratory is the expedient; that is the speaker must persuade his audience that a policy or course of action is to their advantage or disadvantage. In fact, appeals to the interests of the judges play a significant role in lawcourt oratory, though as a means to an end (it is to the advantage of the judges or the city to convict/acquit) not as an end, as for instance in the following passage from a speech written by Demosthenes for the prosecution of a man named Konon for an alleged assault:

> But Konon will beg and weep. Now consider: who deserves more pity, the man who suffers what I have suffered at his hands, if I leave the court as a victim of further outrage, deprived of justice, or Konon, if he is punished? Is it more advantageous for each of you that people should be free to commit assault and outrage or not? I think not. Now if you acquit, there will be more of these people, but if you convict, there will be less. (Demosthenes, 54. 43)

The goals of each oratorical category are not exclusive to that category; they are merely the final goals to which all other considerations are subordinated.

The means of persuasion

Aristotle in the *Rhetoric* recognizes two kinds of means of persuasion, the *entechnos pistis*, that is the means which derives from *techne*, art, technique, and the *atechnos pistis*, 'artless/inartificial means of persuasion. I shall return to inartificial means of persuasion later. For now I shall concentrate on 'technical' proof. Aristotle lists three kinds of technical proof. The first, character (*ethos*), is not personality but moral character, that is the impression created through the speech that the speaker possesses qualities which invite trust and belief. The second, emotion (*pathos*), is the emotional effect created in the audience by the speech. The third, argumentation (*logos*), is the most obvious for us. It is for Aristotle also the most important of the proofs; but because the rhetorician must operate in the real, not an ideal, world, Aristotle accepts the importance of the other two types.

Character (in the sense of the character of the speaker) is equally at home in all oratory. To induce the audience to share his view of the political situation and support his political stance, the speaker in the Assembly must establish his authority; so too must the litigant in court or the speaker over the war dead or at the panhellenic festival. There is however a difference. The speaker in the Assembly comes with a past, since he is located in a particular set of affiliations and brings with him an implied context; the audience brings with it both its knowledge of this larger context and a set of (often conflicting) prejudices. The speaker of declamatory oratory is likewise a man with a past, particularly in the case of the funeral oration, where he owes his selection to his public credentials. This would of course also apply to politicians in court. But in the case of the ordinary Athenian in court, plaintiff or defendant, character is indeterminate until he begins to speak. This is sometimes forgotten in discussions of *ethopoiia* (character delineation) in the orators; some modern writers suppose that the speech-writer fits the speech to the (real) character of the speaker. But in the case of obscure individuals only a minority of judges (if any) would know anything of them in advance. Rather, the character of the speaker in such cases is generated by rhetorical need. All self-presentation is to some degree fictive; that is, it involves the adoption of roles dictated by the expectations of the audience as much as by any desire for self-revelation. What distinguishes law-court oratory is the thoroughness of the fiction, or at the least the clear space free for fiction, which is not delimited by any previous experience of the hearer. The speaker's character is a blank page to be filled in by the speech-writer according to his needs. There is another way in which lawcourt oratory has more room in character portrayal: the character of the opponent. It is not true that speakers in the Assembly do not resort to character assassination, but it is obviously more difficult to disguise this as relevant to the subject at issue. In contrast, in the courts theoretically any personal information can be offered as relevant. The loose Athenian conception of relevance in legal contexts means that there are few slanders which cannot be uttered against one's opponent. The absence of firm rules on relevance in most Athenian courts makes such considerations germane to the discussion. The following example, taken from a relatively insignificant speech written for an inheritance case by Isaios (who specialized in such cases), shows how readily the Athenians resorted to quite serious allegations:

> For my opponent, when he was living here, was first of all arrested in the act as a thief and taken to prison. Then after being released by the Eleven along with some others, all of whom you publicly condemned to death, he was later denounced to the Council as a felon; he slipped away and failed to appear, and from that time he did not return to Athens for seventeen years, until the death of Nikostratos. He has never in your service served in the army or paid any levy, except since he laid claim to Nikostratos' property, nor performed any other public service. (Isaios, 4. 28–9)

Emotion too is at home in every kind of oratory. Long before the age of technical rhetoric Greek speakers realized that the emotional response of the hearer is as much a part of the decision-making process (and therefore as much a part of the speaker's task) as the intellectual engagement with ideas and arguments. The use of emotion differs according to oratorical type. In general, the range of emotions generated by the most common form of epideictic oratory, the funeral oration, is quite narrow. A sense of loss may be created, though emotion of this kind is limited; more common is the feeling of awe at and pride in achievement, as for instance:

> But indeed I do not know what need there is to lament this way. For we were well aware that we are mortal. So what need is there to complain now

> over a fate we long since were expecting to suffer, or to grieve so heavily at natural misfortunes? For we know that death is the common lot both for the basest and for the best. He does not spurn the wicked or admire the good but offers himself equally to all. If it were possible for those who escape death in war to be immortal for the rest of time, it would be proper for the living to lament the dead for all time. As it is, our nature is subject to disease and age, and the power that has control of our destiny is inexorable. So it is right to consider those men most happy who ended their lives by facing danger for the greatest and most honourable of causes, who did not trust their fate to the arbitration of chance or wait for that death which comes in its normal course but chose the most noble one. (Lysias, 2. 77–9)

The range of emotions in deliberative and forensic oratory is much wider, as the situations arising are more varied. It is, however, in forensic oratory in particular that emotions tangential to the case (in particular gratitude for service to the state) are utilized as a means of persuasion. Though, as the passage from Demosthenes' *Third Olynthiac* quoted above demonstrates, speakers addressing the Assembly try to generate hostility against their rivals, the Assembly is not asked explicitly to vote out of goodwill for the politician or hostility or distrust for his rivals. Though arguably that is a significant part of the whole deliberative process, it is implicit at most. In court the audience is invited explicitly to show its gratitude to the speaker. It is also asked explicitly to hate the opponent and to register this hatred when casting the vote. This, taken from Ariston's prosecution of Konon for assault, is not untypical:

> So I urge you, judges, now that I proved my case in full justice, and have given you a pledge in addition, that just as each of you would personally hate the perpetrator if he had suffered this, he should feel the same anger against Konon here on my behalf, and not regard as a private matter any such thing which might perhaps befall anyone. Whoever it befalls, you should give aid and grant justice, and hate people who in the face of their crimes are bold and impetuous and when put on trial are shameless and wicked and care nothing for custom or anything else in their efforts to escape punishment. (Demosthenes, 54. 42)

The third of the rhetorical means of persuasion, *logos*, is more difficult to accommodate, simply because it would require a book-length discussion to determine the differences between different rhetorical modes. Here we are largely confined to forensic and deliberative contexts, since the largely descriptive thrust of the funeral oration leaves little scope (or need) for logical argument. It would be interesting to examine logic in forensic and deliberative contexts to see whether there is any significant difference. In general, however, a cursory survey suggests that there is no difference between the two categories so far as the quality of the argument is concerned. Just as the logical means (essentially argument from probability) are the same, so the logical strength is not a function of genre but of situation and writer. But equally my impression is that forensic oratory differs from deliberative oratory in that in many cases its approach to argument is accretive, that is, there is often a tendency in the courts to pile up arguments in order to hit the target from as many directions as possible, to survey arguments in rapid succession where deliberative oratory tends to maintain its themes for longer. There is greater diversity and less sustained argument in the courts. This is not necessarily a strength, since in some writers (particularly Lysias and Aischines) the result can be a rather loose concatenation of arguments. In the following passage an anonymous client of Lysias, charged with destroying the stump of one of the sacred olives scattered about Athenian territory, moves rapidly from argument to argument, as he presents his case before the Council of the Areopagus, which had jurisdiction in many religious matters:

> And was it more in my interest, Council, to break the law under the democracy or in the time of the Thirty? [the ruthless junta which ruled Athens briefly at the end of the fifth century] I say this not because I had influence then or because I'm suspected now but because it was much more open for anyone to do wrong then than now. You will find that I committed no crime of this sort nor any other in that period. How, unless I was my own worst enemy, when you take such care, could I have attempted to eradicate a sacred olive from my farm, when there is not a single tree in it but a single olive stump (so my opponent says), and the road surrounds it on all sides and neighbours live on both sides, and the farm is unfenced and visible from every direction. (Lysias, 7. 27–8)

Shaping the speech

The function and context of oratory also impacts on structure. The most significant difference is in the role of narrative. For Aristotle narrative is an essential part *only* of the courtroom speech, but the case is overstated (in fact his language indicates that the reality is rather more complex); one has only to think of the pronounced narrative element in the Athenian funeral oration to realize this. But the narrative in the funeral oration is itself merely a variant on narratives shared by the city. That is, the speaker praising the war dead may reshape collective history or city myth but the raw material remains broadly familiar and indeed the same themes often recur. Marathon, one of the defining moments of Athenian history, is a regular theme in praises of the city, as in this extract from a funeral speech ascribed to Lysias:

> Ashamed that the barbarians were in their country, they did not wait for their allies to hear of it or aid them, and they did not feel that they should be grateful to others for their rescue but that the other Greeks should be grateful to themselves. With this shared resolve they met them, few against many. They thought that to die was a fate they shared with all mankind to die but to show courage was a fate they shared with few . . . No wonder then that though these deeds were performed long since their courage is admired now still by all mankind as though the deeds were fresh. (Lysias, 2. 23–6)

Within the sphere of political oratory, indirect evidence suggests that there was more room for narrative in ambassadorial oratory than within purely internal political debate. But even ordinary political debate allows room for narrative, as can be seen from Andokides' speech *On the Peace*, composed in the late 390s. Andokides had served as one of the Athenian delegates at a peace congress held at Sparta, and the speech was delivered on his return. In an attempt to persuade the Athenians to conclude peace with Sparta he surveys Athenian history and demonstrates (by a rather cavalier use of the evidence) that peace has always been beneficial, while war has been ruinous. But again this is a variation (however distorted) on shared narrative, while the narrative in court is not shared but individual. The juror looks to the litigants for basic information as well as opinion and argument to a degree found in no other context. When the speaker of Lysias 1, a man on trial for homicide who defends himself on the ground that he found the dead man in adultery with his wife, presents his case, he is our sole authority for the events he narrates and his case to a large extent stands or falls on his ability to impose his version on the jurors. This passage presents his account of his wife's duplicity after she was seduced:

> After a time, gentlemen, I came home unexpectedly from the country. After dinner the baby cried and howled; he was being tormented by the maid on purpose to make him, because the man was in the house—afterwards I discovered all of this. And I told my wife to go off and give the baby the breast to stop him crying. To start with she refused, as if she were pleased to see me back after a long absence. When I grew angry and told her to go she said: "Oh yes, so that you can have a go at the serving girl here! You've groped her before too when you were drunk!" I for my part laughed, while she stood up, went out and closed the door, pretending she was joking, and then turned the key. And I thought nothing of all this and suspected nothing, but went to sleep gladly, having come from the

country. When it was almost daylight, she came and opened the door. When I asked why the doors banged in the night, she said that the lamp by the baby had gone out and so she had got a light from the neighbours. I said nothing, and believed that this was true. But I thought, gentlemen, that she was wearing make-up, though her brother was not yet dead thirty days. Still, even so I said nothing about the matter but went off without a word. (Lysias, 1. 11–14)

The pronounced narrative component in courtroom speeches brings more to the text than diverse material. There is a difference of manner. The narrative voice is usually distinct to some degree from the voice of argument. The narrative section provides ostensible fact either alone or interspersed with judgement. The argument section usually brings a marked change of presentational mode, from 'fact' to overt argument and opinion, generally a series of arguments from probability. This difference can best be appreciated if we compare the narrative in Lysias 1 with the speaker's arguments later in the speech. These two passages deal with events leading up to the killing of the wife's lover:

But first of all I want to give you an account of what took place on the last day. I had a close friend, Sostratos, whom I met on his way from the country after sunset. I knew that having arrived so late he would find nothing he needed at home, and so I invited him to dinner. We reached my house and went upstairs and dined. When he had eaten his fill, he went off while I went to sleep. Eratosthenes, gentlemen, came in, and the serving girl woke me at once and told me that he was in the house. Telling her to watch the door, I went downstairs in silence and left the house. I called on one man after another; some I didn't catch at home, while others, I found, were not even in town. (Lysias, 1. 22–3)

As I said before, gentlemen, my close friend Sostratos met me on his way from the country around sunset and dined with me, and when he had eaten his fill he went off. Yet consider first of all, gentlemen, whether, if I was plotting against Eratosthenes that night it was better for me to dine elsewhere myself or to bring a dinner guest home. For in the latter case Eratosthenes would have been less likely to venture into the house. Then again, do you think I would have let my dinner guest go and leave me alone and unsupported, or ask him to stay, so that he could join me in taking revenge on the seducer? Furthermore, gentlemen, don't you think I would have sent word to my associates during the day and instructed them to gather in the nearest of my friends' houses, instead of running around during the night as soon as I found out, without knowing whom I would find at home and who would be out? (Lysias, 1. 39–41)

In this case the difference of manner is so great that the modern reader, with time to reread and interrogate the text at leisure, is struck by the marked difference between the innocent transparency of the character presented by the narrative and the sharp and skilful arguments built on the foundation of the earlier 'factual' narrative. It is almost as though there were two speakers. But the formal difference within the speech is an illusion. The role of the narrative is to induce the hearer to accept a particular version of events as reliable, not to provide the audience with transparent fact. A good narrator deploys a whole variety of narrative devices to shape the audience's response without explicit comment.

Controlling the agenda

A related difference between the three categories of oratory is the question of agenda. The audience of the epideictic speech have come to listen to a declamation on a set theme. There are no competing voices and the only surprises in content consist in variations on set themes. The deliberative speech starts with an agenda which is essentially predetermined. Again the audience brings with it a shared knowledge and a shared set of expectations. There is always scope in debate to spring surprises; but the terms of the debate have been significantly delimited in advance, since the context of discussion is shared by all participants. Peace or war, alliance or not, military intervention or not, the broad issues are a given, and the broad issues bring with them both in general and in the individual context a set of arguments which the audience can predict to some degree.

The same is true, though to a lesser extent, of those forensic debates which arise from political rivalry. The prosecution of Ktesiphon by Aischines in 330 for his proposal to honour Aischines' enemy Demosthenes was clearly intended by Aischines as the final showdown in a political feud which had raged for a decade and a half. When the jurors sat down to enjoy this magnificent grudge match, they could predict the broad tenor of the opposing cases with reasonable confidence. But the element of predictability dwindles in direct proportion to the public visibility of the participants. It has been maintained that all trials in classical Athens are potentially political, since the litigants are almost always drawn from the moneyed classes and this is the sector of Athenian society which engaged in politics at the crucial level of initiative (as distinct from attendance at the Assembly). The socio-economic point is correct: as was observed above, financial litigation, often on a substantial scale, is prominent in surviving oratory, while the cases that bulk large in our system, what we would call 'criminal' cases, are conspicuously few. But the conclusion is suspect. Most surviving speeches which are not directed towards political issues are apolitical in the further sense that they avoid reference to questions of policy or influence. Where the case turns on non-political issues (or involves people who are not prominent in public life) the agenda is not a given. By agenda I mean the facts of the case, the identity, personality, and general conduct of the litigants. The agenda is a vacuum, and it becomes the duty of the speech-writer to fill this vacuum for the audience with a sustainable version of the events and participants. There is far more room for manœuvre in court.

The need to control the agenda is increased by the nature of the judicial process. The politician facing Assembly or Council is usually operating within a set of broader goals. The individual moment is important, but there is always the possibility that defeat can be reversed either in later meetings of the Assembly or through the medium of political trials, as for instance the eventual reversal in the power ratio between the proponents and opponents of peace with Macedonia, which was both advanced and signalled by the political prosecutions of the late 340s. Defeat in court is not entirely irreversible—for one thing there is always the prospect of attacking the opposition witnesses for perjury. But there is no appeal on the main action and, even where collateral actions are possible, the loser starts at a disadvantage, since a previous jury had found for his opponent. This means that everything must be subordinated to a single goal, immediate victory.

Despite all this, there is one respect in which lawcourt oratory is more circumscribed than other forms. In Aristotle's discussion of the means of persuasion, it is noteworthy that, although the artificial means of persuasion (character, emotion, argument) are applicable to all modes of oratory, the artless proofs (*atechnoi pisteis*)—that is the proofs which do not depend on the rhetorician's art—are all peculiar to forensic oratory. Aristotle lists (*Rhetoric* I. 15) laws, witnesses, contracts, tortures, oaths. This means that unlike other oratorical forms, forensic rhetoric must engage directly with external material. Epideictic oratory is free to select as it chooses from the topics available. Deliberative oratory, though it cannot escape its external context, is free to reshape that context through argument. Forensic oratory has a problem in that in order to command belief it must include external proof to substantiate the speaker's statements. We do on occasion find courtroom speeches which make no use of documentary evidence; and although some of these are supporting speeches (in which case the leading speaker may well have provided a substantial body of evidence), some certainly represent the only speech delivered for this side in court. But the rarity of such speeches indicates that this is a strategy avoided by litigants wherever possible. Which in turn means that the audience were reluctant to trust a litigant who could not bring some element of independent evidence to bear. So the speaker has to include a body of alien material. These external voices must be mastered and brought under the control of the speaker. In fact Athenian litigants make use wherever possible of friendly witnesses. But even so the witness is outside the speaker's control to the extent that he does not simply say whatever the litigant wants him to say, unless of course he is unusually obliging, foolhardy, or unscrupulous; there was always the possibility of prosecution for false evidence and our texts indicate that the Athenians were ready to use this tool against their opponent's witnesses. From about 380 BCE written testimony was used; this was read out by the clerk and the witness simply confirmed the text he heard. The text itself, where we have evidence for the drafting, was the work of the litigant, but the witness still had to verify the statement and so the litigant cannot simply invent. It becomes the litigant's task to shape the deposition in such a way as to obtain maximum support from the witness.

Another important voice in oratory is the law. Not only do speakers speak about law, they also cite laws (that is, the law itself is read out in court in the clerk's voice). And again the law needs on occasion to be massaged. An example from Aischines' speech for the prosecution of a rival politician, Timarchos, for (alleged) homosexual prostitution in 346/5 may clarify. The clerk is about to quote the law dealing with the law banning prostitution by citizens. But Aischines himself quotes it, mixes it up with pejorative details relating to Timarchos (here presented in italics), and so at one and the same time associates the law with Timarchos, puts a negative complexion on Timarchos' public life, and wraps the law in an emotional haze:

> But once he is entered in the deme register and knows the city's laws and is now able to determine right and wrong, the legislator from now on addresses nobody else but at this point the individual himself, Timarchos. And what does he say? If any Athenian (he says) prostitutes himself, he is not to have the right to serve as one of the nine archons (*the reason being, I think, that these officials wear a sacred wreath*), nor to undertake any priesthood, *since his body is quite unclean*; and let him not serve (he says) as advocate for the state or hold any office ever, whether at home or abroad, whether selected by lot or elected by a vote; let him not serve as herald, nor as envoy (*nor let him bring to trial people that have served as envoys, nor let him bring malicious prosecutions for pay*), nor let him voice any opinion in the Council or the Assembly (*not even if he is the cleverest speaker in Athens*). If anyone acts against these provisions, he has allowed for indictments for prostitution and imposed the most severe penalties. Read this law out to them as well, to make you aware of the noble and decent character of the established laws, against which Timarchos has dared to address the Assembly, a man whose way of life is known to you all. (Aischines, 1. 18–20)

I have so far presented this external material as somehow threatening, though it can also be an enormous help for the speaker in need of support. The law is not always relevant to the case. Sometimes it represents a rather desperate attempt to establish a case by analogy, as in Hypereides 3, where the speaker tries to fill what looks like a gap in the law of sale by building up a set of tendentious parallels. His opponent has sold him a perfumery run by a slave who has run up some massive debts for which the speaker now finds himself liable. It looks as though Athenian law made no specific provision for this and so the speaker has to argue at length from comparable legislation. In [Demosthenes] 46 the speaker quotes law after law irrespective of its immediate relevance, evidently as a means of browbeating the jurors into seeing things the speaker's way. It would be easy to see this as evidence for a cavalier attitude to law in Athenian society. But the reverse is true. The law speaks with authority and the litigant is exploiting the voice of the law (as authoritative text) to strengthen his case.

It remains a distinguishing feature of forensic oratory that the speaker must absorb alien material in its raw form within the speech, neutralize it where necessary, enhance its support where possible. And while making this material subservient to his will, the speaker must maintain the authority which comes from the seeming independence of the support he cites. Unlike the other forms of oratory, forensic oratory presents a seeming multiplicity of voices, with its move between argument and narrative and its need to draw in external support. The multiplicity is however illusion, impersonation, for ultimately the voices are reducible to one, the speaker's, and that voice is devoted to the single task of persuasion.

Style and context

Aristotle notes that the three categories of oratory differ in style. A detailed account of the style of Athenian oratory is beyond the scope of this discussion; but the different occasions do create different audience expectations and these in turn determine stylistic tendencies. The most cautious branch of oratory in this respect is courtroom oratory. Even here, however, some speeches were written for delivery in court by active politicians while others were delivered by ordinary citizens, and as was noted, the writers for the courts tend to fit their speeches as far as possible to the person of the speaker. This extends to style as well as statements explicitly or implicitly characterizing the litigant. So speeches for private citizens tend to be less grand in language, with a general avoidance of extended simile or metaphor. This is not true of the earliest period of professional speech-writing; the disclaimer of experience in speaking made by the young man who delivered Antiphon 5 (quoted above p. 196) uses an elaborate style which is at odds with the claim made, and it is difficult to believe that the audience would fail to detect the professional speech-writer behind the litigant. Any stylistic effect which creates a rift between the avowed personality and the mode of expression risks creating a simultaneous rift between speaker and audience; the audience must feel that the speaker can be trusted. Accordingly Antiphon's successors as forensic speech-writers were more cautious. Lawcourt speeches delivered by politicians are not subject to the same restraint. The jurors expect politicians to sound like experienced speakers and so such speeches are closer in style to deliberative oratory, which more readily admits grand effects.

The following two passages from Demosthenes' *Third Olynthiac* (a deliberative speech of 348 in which Demosthenes argues for the redeployment of state hand-outs to fund Athenian intervention to protect the city of Olynthos from the expansionist ambitions of Philip of Macedonia) and his speech *On the Crown* (written for the trial of Ktesiphon in 330, when Demosthenes acted as supporting speaker for Ktesiphon) show the convergence between political speeches in court and in the Assembly:

> If even now at last you were to abandon these habits and agree to serve as soldiers and behave in a manner worthy of yourselves and use this surplus domestic revenue as a basis to achieve external benefit, perhaps, just perhaps, men of Athens, you could gain some complete advantage and be rid of hand-outs of this sort, which are like the food given by doctors to the sick. For the latter neither provide strength nor allow the patient to die. Likewise, what you receive now is not sufficient to provide any substantial assistance nor does it allow you to give it up and do something else; no, this is what increases the sluggishness of each one of you. (Demosthenes, 3 [*Third Olynthiac*]. 33)

> [To Aischines] You talk to us now about the past? You are like a doctor who when he visits his patients while they are sick gives not a word or an indication about the means by which they will escape their illness, but once one of them dies and his funeral rites are being performed goes with the procession to the tomb and holds forth: 'if this man had done this or that, he would not have died'. (Demosthenes, 18 [*On the Crown*]. 243).

During the mid- to late fourth century at least, the grand manner becomes even more overt, as politicians make free use of passages from classic poetry and drama to achieve emotional effects and to enhance their authority, as for instance with this passage from the speech written by Aischines for the prosecution of Ktesiphon of 330:

> The poet Hesiod expresses himself well on situations like this. He says at one point, as he seeks to educate the masses and advise the cities, that they should not tolerate corrupt demagogues. I shall pronounce the verses; the reason I think we learn by heart the poets' thoughts as children is to make use of them when we are men.
>
> Often enough the whole city has paid for an evil man
> who does wrong and devises deeds of wickedness.
> Upon them from heaven Cronus' son brings great woe,
> famine and plague together, and the people perish.
> He may destroy their vast army or their walls
> or take vengeance on their ships at sea, far-seeing Zeus.
>
> If you remove the rhythm and examine the poet's sentiments, I think you will see that they are not Hesiod's poetry but an oracle directed at Demosthenes' political career. For indeed army and fleet and whole cities have been obliterated as a result of his policies. (Aischines, 3. 134–6, quoting Hesiod, *Works and Days* 240–5)

Similar effects are achieved in the political-forensic speeches of his enemy Demosthenes and the one complete surviving speech (*Against Leokrates*) by their contemporary, the distinguished politician Lykourgos.

Lawcourt speeches for politicians and deliberative oratory form an intermediate stylistic class between forensic speeches for private citizens at the more sober end of the scale and epideictic speeches at the grandiose end of the scale. The audience for oratory of display has come to participate in a great public occasion, with the full expectation that the speech will be appropriate to that occasion, both as sentiment and as performance. The speech written for declamation wears its verbal craftsmanship with pride, indulging in musical and rhythmical effects which would be avoided, or used less flamboyantly or liberally, in other oratorical types, as this passage from the funeral oration attributed to Lysias illustrates the point:

> It is not easy for one man to narrate the dangers faced by many nor to declare in a single day deeds performed through all time. For what speech or time or speaker could be sufficient to tell the courage of the men who lie here? With the greatest toils and the most illustrious trials and the noblest dangers they set Greece free . . . (Lysias, 2. 54–5)

From audience to reader

We encounter the Athenian orators as written text. But in most cases their status as literary texts is either accidental or secondary. These speeches were first and foremost performed works. It is important to bear in mind when reading the orators that what we have no more reflects the full experience of the work for its first audience than do the texts of tragic and comic plays. We have ample evidence that some of the more controversial political orators in the late fifth century adopted a flamboyant mode of delivery; and although both contemporary comic playwrights and later sources tend to present this as a striking departure from tradition, probably we are dealing with a difference of degree rather than of kind.

In the fourth century we know that the politician Aischines, who had worked as an actor, had a very impressive speaking voice, which must have more than compensated for features of his speeches which are often perceived as flaws by students of rhetoric. In the fifth and early fourth century it was by no means inevitable that a speech would ever reach the status of text. Early in the fourth century we still find Gorgias' pupil Alkidamas (in his essay *On the Authors of Written Speeches*) praising the flexibility of the unwritten, extemporized, speech over the rigidity of the written speech. But the practice not only of writing down but also of publishing speeches had already begun in the fifth century. There was a book trade in Athens in the late fifth century and the fictitious speeches of teachers like Gorgias, even if they began their lives as performed exemplars designed to illustrate the potential of specific effects, were clearly also available in book form. The same is presumably true of the *Tetralogies* of Antiphon.

The practice of publishing lawcourt speeches had also begun by the end of the fifth century. The speeches of Antiphon written for real trials show a degree of polish which suggests that they were at least prepared for publication during the author's lifetime. Although the market for such speeches probably consisted largely of people interested in acquiring speaking skills, the embedded Greek appreciation of good oratory—attested in particular by the frequency in tragedy of speeches displaying the influence of formal rhetoric—suggests that even at this stage there must have been an aesthetic as well as a practical interest in the speeches. In political oratory the practice of publishing speeches did not begin until the fourth century. Apart from the aesthetic and practical appeal of such texts in a society dependent on speech-making in most public contexts, the publication of political speeches allowed them to achieve a second life as pamphlets in continuing political debate both before a contemporary audience and ultimately before the audience of future generations. In the case of the speeches written by Demosthenes and Aischines for their showcase political contests in the lawcourts we have ample evidence that changes were made to the speech during the process of revision for publication. As a result we can never be entirely sure how far our written text deviates from the oral-aural text of the first performance. During the fourth century, as we can see from the sheer volume of surviving speeches, there was a substantial market for published oratory of all kinds and this market continued into the Hellenistic period and beyond. The scholars of the Ptolemaic library at Alexandria edited and commented on the Athenian orators, and the texts continued to play a major role in the education of both Greeks and Romans.

7 Sophisticates and solecisms: Greek literature after the classical period

JANE L. LIGHTFOOT

Hellenistic, post-classical—the old world's spiral into decline? The mainland Greek states continued their old squabbles for supremacy after the Peloponnesian War; but a new power was rising, and within a couple of generations it produced a figure who, in thirty-two years of life, would change the whole political geography of the world for good. The power was Macedon, and the figure was Alexander, soon known as the Great. He swept across Greece, Asia Minor, and Persia, obliterating the last Persian king; and, that done, stampeded over the central Asian steppe, only to be brought up short in the Punjab by a mutiny. But he had shown them regions no Greek had ever seen, and monarchy on a scale yet undreamed of; and when he died, in Babylon in 323 BCE, he had also irrevocably altered the Greeks' cultural horizons.

Inevitably, the successors of this neo-Homeric hero were lesser men, who immediately started wrangling over his legacy. They carved out domains for themselves and hacked away at each other for years before any sort of steady state emerged; but by the time the dust cleared, there were immigrant Greeks resident in new, royal foundations in kingdoms in Egypt, Asia Minor, Syria, Mesopotamia, Central Asia—all the way to modern Afghanistan and India. It is against this background that we have to measure the literature of the Hellenistic period, many of its producers and consumers no longer the classical city-states of mainland Greece, but residents of the new world, further east.

The new foundations had constitutions that looked like those back home; but they were under the thumb of the king; and the looming presence of the Hellenistic monarchs is vital when we come to consider what became in our period of the literary genres of archaic and classical Greece. So is the newness of the terrain: Greeks were now resident where no Greek had ever lived before. The old view, now rather threadbare, would portray them in their new communities as restless, uprooted, trying to defend their Greekness against the natives of threatening, unfamiliar territory. But it is an exciting period, precisely because of this newness of terrain, because of the possibility of testing responses to conditions the Greeks had never before encountered, because of the new sorts of literature which resulted from their dislocation from their old homes and ways.

It is also probably the first period of Greek literature in which we have a substantial body of direct information about audiences and readers as well as authors, about the consumers of literature as well as its producers. It was in the Hellenistic period that there first developed a para-literary industry: scholars and interpreters for the first time gathered and edited and commented on literary texts. We even know something of the sorts of scrutiny to which they subjected them and ways in which they read them. We owe much to the sands of Egypt, where numerous sites have yielded a wealth of texts on papyri which, though mostly documentary in character, also include a substantial body of literary material. Information from these sources can tell us what was being read, in what form (for example, it can indicate the state of a particular author's text at any one time), and occasionally even *how* and *by whom*. Find-contexts can—though all too rarely—tell us a little about the owners, while marginal annotations may tell us a little about the concerns of readers and of the sorts of questions asked of texts. Meanwhile a different sort of evidence for readers and audiences in the Hellenistic period comes from epigraphy—inscriptions mainly from mainland Greece, the Aegean islands, and Anatolia. Being for the most part public inscriptions these record different sorts of activity, and form a necessary and important counterbalance to the Egyptian papyri with their evidence for mostly private reading. The inscriptions concern festivals and recitations, performances and displays which took place in theatres and concert-halls in Greek cities, and remind us that in a world of increasing textuality the traditional enunciative, performative aspect of Greek culture was not on the wane.

Players and plays

To begin with drama, the great public genres which the Greek world inherited from classical, democratic Athens, is to emphasize the continuity of this aspect of Greek culture—and, indeed, its massive success and influence in the Hellenistic period. Drama was Athens' most enduring literary legacy, for it came to be seen as a necessary constituent of urban life: to have a theatre was to be Greek. We are only now coming to understand the pace at which theatres were established all over the Greek world, right from the end of the fifth century onwards—in mainland Greece, in southern Italy in the Hellenized area known (in Latin) as Magna Graecia, and then, after Alexander's conquests, in the new foundations where Greek immigrants settled. Particularly famous is the site of Ai Khanum on the northern limit of modern Afghanistan: a theatre, a gymnasium, and a library were three indispensable elements of Greek culture that not even so remote a colony could do without.

There was a rash of new festivals, founded for a myriad of reasons: to honour a king (or 'liberator'); to commemorate an accession, or a victory, or the repulse of an enemy (the Soteria are famous, marking the defeat of the Gauls who had descended on Delphi in 279); or because someone, invariably with some ulterior motive, had declared that the local deity had appeared and ordained it so (a famous example is the Leukophryena, founded at the end of the third century in Magnesia on the Maeander following an epiphany of the local equivalent of Artemis). Or there were Dionysia in the time-honoured way—but not quite like the classical festivals, for the god's range of powers was now extended to include all the performing arts, music and singing as well as theatre. Athletic events too had a place in these great occasions. Dionysos was also the special god of the new Macedonian rulers of Egypt, the Ptolemies (named after their founder, the general Ptolemaios), who also loved pageantry. So it is not surprising to find them as assiduous patrons of festivals, an interest reflected in many epigrams and other works by contemporary poets. Theokritos (of whom more anon), praising King Ptolemy II, claimed that 'No man who knows how to sing a clear melody has come to the sacred contests of Dionysos without receiving a gift worthy of his skill'.

Yet, transplanted from the city in which it grew, Hellenistic drama has often been supposed to have been in a parlous state. Allegedly, the Hellenistic monarchies rode roughshod over the cities' freedom, leaving their political institutions worn out and exiguous: there was no longer any forum for what is seen as drama's main function in the classical polis—the assertion and/or interrogation of civic culture and values (cf. pp. 117–22). Allied to this is the loss of most Hellenistic drama: isn't it obvious that it didn't survive because it was no good? On the other hand, evidence for the widespread revival of classical plays begins in the Hellenistic period. This is all of a piece with the crystallization in this period of notions of 'the classics'; but has also been held to point to the drying-up of creativity. It is difficult to redress this situation, since virtually all Hellenistic tragedy and satyr drama is sadly lost, and much the same is true of comedy, although here at least we have Menander at the very beginnings of our period (see below). But we do have much valuable evidence of other kinds—including the excavations of theatres—and a great deal of documentation about the performance of drama. Using what we have will enable us to make some interesting and useful observations about what concerns us most here—the public.

It is true that the performance of drama slipped from the hands of ordinary citizens, but specialization in the obviously skilled business of the theatre is detectable from very early in its history. Already in the middle of the fifth century in Athens we hear of prizes awarded to principal actors; by the middle of the fourth, Aristotle in his *Rhetoric* could pronounce that actors had become more important than the poets themselves. The fourth century saw the rise of the star—men like Aristodemos and Neoptolemos, Theodoros and Polos, whose boast was that they could have whole audiences in tears. Theodoros, apparently, succeeded in so moving the hard-hearted tyrant Alexander of Pherai that he had to leave the theatre lest he be seen to weep. Despite the elaborate gear they had to wear—masks and increasingly high-soled boots—their acting is praised in terms of emotional realism, as when Polos is supposed to have made uniquely affecting his portrayal of Elektra's grief for the dead Orestes, by carrying in his hands the urn containing the ashes of his own dead son.

By Aristotle's day there were probably also professional or semi-professional members of choruses; and we hear also of troupes of actors touring the countryside. They prided themselves on their *techne*, or artistry (or better still, craftsmanship); and it is hardly surprising to find that by the 280s they are orchestrated into large professional bodies calling themselves 'Artists' or, better, 'Artisans' or 'Craftsmen', of Dionysos. They comprised not only actors but others associated with the theatre—chorus-trainers and costumiers; and they admitted not only those musicians who supplied the accompaniment for drama, but instrumentalists and singers of all kinds.

Inscriptions tell us a lot about these groups. The big three in the Hellenistic period were those at Athens, at Isthmia and Nemea, and in the Ionia and Hellespont region. There was another in Alexandria, and groups and leagues of poets were present in Rome by the early second century BCE. There was strength in numbers: it was a little like belonging to an actors' union able to secure for its members contracts, privileges, and often extremely good wages; and able, furthermore, to ensure safe conduct over the long journeys which participants in the festival circuit then had to travel. Internal organization was elaborate, as the guildsmen constituted themselves into miniature cities-within-cities, conducting negotiations on equal terms with the cities who contracted for their services. They were often associated with the royal house (as at Pergamon), and contributed to royal shows and pageants; and they had a liking for ceremony, presenting themselves and their activities with a distinctly religious cast. According to their ideology, the performance of drama was the discharge of a sort of civic piety—a religious duty, even at this late stage in drama's evolution.

Hellenistic performing artists were a highly skilled, articulate, vain, noisy, self-protecting group—and at the higher end of the profession extremely well-off. They were perhaps a little like the star operatic singers of the eighteenth century.

Hand-in-hand with the growing specialization of performing artists went changes both in theatre staging and in the internal structure of plays. From the early third century onwards, theatres began to be built with a high raised stage. This consisted of a portico whose 'roof', raised two or three metres above ground level, was in fact a place for reciting or declaiming. The clearest consequence was that chorus and actors could no longer interact as they had done in classical drama. Indeed, the chorus dwindled and was relegated to musical interludes, transferable from one play to another: Aristotle associates this change with a tragic poet, Agathon, active at the end of the fifth century. Delphic inscriptions record choruses of no more than fifteen for a lyric genre, dithyramb, where fifty had been the classical norm; and seven or eight for comedy. Tragedy probably had a similar number, though inscriptions do not make this explicit. On the other hand, the actors themselves started to sing lyrical set-pieces of exhibitionist emotionality called 'monodies': again, the beginnings are discoverable already in Euripides. A group of progressives at the end of the fifth century had started employing music very much more elaborate than the traditional 'modes' associated with tragedy, with different sorts of scales, virtuosic ornamentation, and 'bends' (cf. pp. 85–6): it all sounded very strange and degenerate to traditionalists when first introduced, but by the Hellenistic period had won the day. The case of the traditionalists has hijacked our attention because it is stated on the formidable authority of Plato and Aristotle; but what the Hellenistic public wanted to hear were the sophisticated new works of the modern virtuosi. When drama was reperformed, it was not always in its original form: actors made their own additions, deletions, and 'improvements' (which have sometimes found their way into the preserved texts of drama, creating headaches for modern editors); and its original music was replaced by something more modish. Often reperformance took the form of the recital of highlights: to illustrate this we have a third-century BCE papyrus which contains lyrical excerpts from Euripides' *Iphigeneia in Aulis*, equipped with music. These trends continued so that, by the imperial centuries, even the iambic passages of dialogue were set to music—which no classical dramatist would ever have dreamed of doing. The recognition that these were the 'classics' did not stop their being drastically revamped: most unlike the modern fashion for authenticity.

Less is known of audiences. Material evidence allows us to say that theatres were often built to accommodate a very large proportion of a town's population; the theatre of the Egyptian provincial capital, Oxyrhynchos, could hold 11,000 of a total population probably of around 30,000. But further details are more elusive. Since so much information about Hellenistic drama derives from public inscriptions, it uses honorific language which tells us much about group ideology but little about the composition of the audience—let alone public response. We depend for that on anecdotal evidence, which presents (as we might expect) colourful, dramatic episodes, on whose reliability there is little check. If an audience disliked an actor, we hear, they might throw things at him, or hiss, or physically eject the object of their displeasure from the stage. On the other hand, supporters might mobilize claques to orchestrate applause—it all sounds quite familiar. What we read of the emotionality of audiences ties in with the reports of performance style: stories of tearfulness abound. Flattery of the audience's taste and discrimination are counterbalanced by reports of actors and poets lowering themselves to suit the tastes of a base, depraved public: every statement has to be scrutinized in its context. We should dearly like to know what expectations, indeed what knowledge the various sections of the public brought with them when they went to the theatre. Aristotle in his *Poetics* famously states that even the best-known stories are only known to a few. But knowledge of plots would increase as circulation of texts increased; the Hellenistic period saw many educators, and even one or two quite well-known scholars, turn their hands to writing plot-summaries and mythographical handbooks and comparative studies of the myths in tragedy. The greater the availability of texts, perhaps, the more likely the audience was to have a base-line from which to scrutinize the play—old or new, traditional or adapted—on stage before its eyes.

The new kind of comedy

Of the surviving literature, we are served best by the remains of comedy. By the end of the fourth century, Old, Aristophanic, comedy had given way to New. And we return, once more, to Athens, where the genre's main practitioners were residents or natives. It was at the traditional Attic drama festivals of the Dionysia and Lenaia (cf. pp. 96–101) that these playwrights first staged their works, but the style was so popular that it was quickly exported all over the Greek world, wherever theatre companies took it. It was carried to Egypt, where papyri have allowed the rediscovery of very sizeable portions; to the Greek-speaking areas of southern Italy, and thence to Rome. And it is Rome that provides our other major source of evidence for New Comedy, since the Greek New Comedy, adapted to Italian dress—the so-called *comoedia palliata*—

flourished there between about 240 and 160 BCE (see pp. 297–9, 301–4). Indeed, the fates of New Comedy in the two halves of the Mediterranean world are in curious contrast. Our papyri of its most celebrated Greek practitioner, Menander, fail after 500 or so, and apart from transmitting quotations from him in anthologies, the Byzantines had no interest in him. Plautus and Terence, on the other hand, never fell from favour, and Terence, in particular, remained the second most widely read Latin poet after Virgil throughout the Middle Ages; his influence on the Western tradition of comic drama has been profound.

The most famous poet of New Comedy was Menander (in Greek, *Menandros*), *c.*342–290 BCE. His career was much shorter than that of Alexis, whom an ancient source claims as his uncle, and both shorter and less successful in terms of recorded victories than that of another contemporary, Philemon. But Menander it was whom later antiquity remembered as the classic exponent of the genre. Of his hundred known plays we have one virtually complete—the *Dyskolos*, or *Misanthrope*—and substantial portions of another six. In them we encounter a world very different from the one we left with Aristophanes (see pp. 99–101, 120–2). Anarchic fantasy has been replaced by something more rule-governed: stock character-types have crystallized, many of them drawn from Old Comedy, but now constrained in a bourgeois world revolving round a limited number of themes. The political awareness of Old Comedy (cf. pp. 6, 121) has all but vanished; up-to-dateness and topicality have been replaced by a homogenized sort of universalism, of which the most obvious sign is the disappearance of the episode where the chorus would come forward to harangue the audience on matters of contemporary concern, the *parabasis*. In fact the chorus has almost entirely disappeared: the papyri divide the plays into five acts separated by a direction to the chorus to perform its song, but this was a separable adjunct and bore no relation to the matter in hand. Another salient formal feature is the drastic reduction and simplification of metre: Menander uses only two, the basic iambic trimeter which came closest to everyday speech, and a livelier, racier metre, the trochaic tetrameter. But contrasts of other kinds—of pace and intensity and individual speech-styles—can still be used to vary the dramatic texture.

The plays are mostly set in Attica, but local detail is of little importance (and ironed out still further in Latin adaptations). The absence of interest in politics seems eloquent about the level of contemporary political consciousness in Athens—or at least about the fora in which politics could be discussed. Part of what may have happened is a change in the demographics of the audience: in the classical theatre a *theoric* (or viewers') fund subsidized theatre attendance for the less well-off, and by some point in the fourth century this fund had ceased to operate. Scholars have pointed to 322/1 as a plausible date, since lower limits were then placed on the property-holdings of those eligible to take part in political life. The plays can be seen, amongst other things, as entertainment for this relatively moneyed, urban constituency. Interestingly, satyr drama in the Hellenistic period seems to have taken a parallel path: an epigram praises a poet, Sositheus, for restoring it to its rightful, traditional context—away from the city, and back in the wilds; this implies that in most other playwrights, satyr play had become a fundamentally civil affair, shorn (perhaps) of its wilder Dionysiac excesses.

In the third quarter of the fourth century in Athens, the theatre was rebuilt with a permanent stone auditorium and stage building. This represented a set of dwellings and their entrances: a city street is the most usual (but by no means the only) setting for New Comedy, which is peopled with bourgeois types and their concerns. The marital affairs of well-born Athenians are its stock-in-trade. An amorous young man is thwarted by a father who controls the purse-strings; a greedy uncle plots to marry his niece, an heiress; a slave-girl prostitute schemes to restore an exposed child to its rightful parents; doubts raised by an impossibly early pregnancy are dispelled when it transpires that the husband himself raped his wife before their marriage. The basic unit is neither the polis, nor the individual, but the family. The plays seem deeply conservative in this respect: they are preoccupied with socially appropriate and procedurally correct unions 'for the harvesting of lawful children', as the traditional Athenian formula of betrothal had it. Indeed, they seem to speak of an audience so preoccupied with the legitimacy of their offspring that even a violent rape can be a plot-device to bring about the desired happy ending. Often a mass of detail about the characters' circumstances is presented at great speed, suggesting an audience both alert and with a taste for the complicated intricacies of family relationships. With due allowance made for the fictionality of drama, the plays provide good evidence about Athenian marriage law and the status of women. The reluctance to show unmarried free women on stage reflects Athenian unwillingness for them to appear in public in all but ritual or ceremonial contexts. With further allowance made for fictionality, and for the dramatic context in which each statement is made, the plays also provide evidence for male attitudes towards women. All the dramatists, and most if not all audiences, were male, and if there were any women present in his audience, Menander could afford to overlook them when, at the end of the *Misanthrope*, he appealed for applause to 'youths, boys, and men'. On the whole it is not a very cheering picture: demands for women's liberation are made by those so disenfranchised as to make them sound absurd. Yet when a male character is over-hasty in

COMIC MUSIC. *This fine mosaic was made for a villa at Pompeii in about 100* BCE. *The stage and the masks show clearly that it is a scene from New Comedy. The plays of Menander provided favourite subject-matter for paintings and mosaics; and it is likely that this scene of musicians playing outside a door is drawn from his play* Theophoroumene *(The Possessed).*

misjudging or condemning a woman, the plot will sometimes gratifyingly prove him wrong.

Menander is extremely inventive in devising complex domestic imbroglios from which his characters have to extricate themselves. Although the gallery of characters is not unlimited, it can be enriched by variations on familiar types. It is some of the minor figures who are most familiar—the parasite, or hanger-on, who boards with the well-to-do in return for services rendered; the boastful soldier; the complaining chef, forever feuding with the waiter; the put-upon slave. The plays have a certain rhetoric of *noblesse oblige,* but these are platitudes addressed to the well-off, not serious calls for reform, and take their place among other bland pietism and moralizing. As Gorgias says to the hero in the *Misanthrope*:

> You've approached this business without disguising your character,
> Straightforwardly, and you've been prepared to do anything for the sake
> Of this marriage. Though loving luxury, you took a mattock, and dug and
> Were ready to sweat. A man of your class shows himself best when he's prepared,
> Though rich, to level himself with the pauper. This kind of man will bear up best
> To changing Fortune.
>
> (ll. 764–70)

Fortune, or Tyche, is one of the most important deities, reflecting the more general rise to power of this personified abstraction in the Hellenistic period. She could stand for Fortune in a good or bad sense, but the 'theology' of New Comedy is less one of shifting, capricious chance than one of confidence that ultimately all will get their due. She wears her more capricious aspect with regard to wealth, for wealth is easily lost; but the more important message is that virtue, finally, will prevail.

New kinds of tragedy?

In the case of tragedy, very much less survives. What we do have, and in its entirety, is a work which is, if not a tragedy, at least in the form of a tragic messenger's speech; but it is so untypical, so monstrous, and so rebarbative, that it is difficult to use it to say very much at all about the wider context of Hellenistic drama. It was written in Alexandria by the early third-century poet Lykophron of Chalkis in Euboia, who had come to Egypt's new capital to work on the texts of drama. The *Alexandra,* his only surviving work, has the distinction of being quite the most repellent poem to survive from antiquity (some claim this distinction for Nonnos, but I do not believe them: cf. pp. 282–4). It purports to be a prophecy some 1,500 lines long by Kassandra (the Alexandra of the title), spelling out in lugubrious tones the doom of the Greeks returning from Troy. Lykophron's hyper-riddling verse goes on like this for pages:

> Alas, poor nurse, who formerly was burned
> By trouble-breeding warships built of pine—

THE POWER OF FORTUNE. The goddess Tyche or Fortune was a favourite figure for Hellenistic sculptors. This marble statuette dating from the second century CE was first published in 1994. It represents her, as often, wearing a crown of towers, symbolizing her power over a city (or cities) as well as individuals.

—The lion of three evening's, who was once
Devoured by Triton's hound with jagged teeth.
(ll. 31–4)

(Who would have guessed the reference is to Herakles' sack of Troy?) The poem also has something to say about the rosy future of the Roman descendants of the Trojans—the theme of Virgil's *Aeneid*. Indeed, certain sections on the rise of the Romans look as if they were written much later than Lykophron, and one recent hypothesis is that the problem passages are later interpolations with an Italian audience in mind, made when the play was adapted for performance by travelling groups of actors. The Craftsmen of Dionysos often performed excerpts, so that similarly styled additions may have been made to Lykophron's poem for performance in a southern Italian programme in (probably) the late second century BCE. If this is right, then there were sections of the public with a very high tolerance of learned mythological poetry and with very strong stomachs. Perhaps the reciter made frequent pauses and waited until his audience guessed the riddles.

More interesting, and untypical of Hellenistic drama in quite a different way, is a sizeable fragment by an Alexandrian Jew called Ezekiel, dramatizing at length the first fifteen chapters of the Septuagint version of *Exodus*. It is important evidence for the way Hellenized élites borrowed the clothes of Greek literary high culture to represent themselves to each other, and also to Greeks. As an illustration of the translation of the Jewish mode into the Greek one, consider first, the biblical version of the episode in which God transforms Moses' rod into a snake and back again:

> And the Lord said unto him, What is that in thine hand?' And he said, A rod. And he said, Cast it on the ground. And he cast it on the ground, and it became a serpent; and Moses fled from before it. And the Lord said unto Moses, Put forth thine hand, and take it by the tail. And he put forth his hand, and caught it, and it became a rod in his hand. (Exodus 4: 2–4)

And now Ezekiel:

> GOD: What is this in your hand? Say now!
> MOSES: A rod, to punish four-foot beasts and men.
> GOD: Now hurl it to the floor and rush away.
> A frightful snake, a marvel, shall appear.
> MOSES: Lo, I have cast it down. Be gracious, Lord.
> Oh, frightful, monstrous: mercy on me, Lord!
> I shudder at the sight, my limbs all quake.
> GOD: Fear not, stretch out your hand and take its tail,
> And, as before, it will become a rod.
>
> (ll. 120–8)

Here Ezekiel hits off tragic stichomythia with stop-gap sentence-fillers, and its explicit enactment of emotional and physical responses which are only implicit in the Hebrew. Other features of Greek tragic idiom—the narrative prologue, the messenger-speech—are present elsewhere. Unfortunately we know nothing about the performance context of this fascinating hybrid but—if indeed it was written with performance in mind—it would interestingly imply that, whatever later rabbis may have had to say on the subject, at least some Jews in Alexandria at this time went to the theatre.

Other great classical public genres lived on—adapted to new circumstances, and formally much simpler, but still important vehicles for public display and sentiment. The dithyramb, for example, sung by massed forces in honour of Dionysos (cf. pp. 81–2, 107), continued to be performed—though with reduced, professional choirs—in festivals on Delos, and in Athens until the second century CE. Very little of these is left; but we do possess two Hymns to Apollo performed by the Athenian guild of the Craftsmen of Dionysos during one of the Athenians' periodic mass pilgrimages to Delphi (127 BCE). Propaganda, pageantry, and piety combine in these great display pieces. These are fascinating and unique texts, since we know, not only the occasion on which they were performed, but also something of what they sounded like, for they are accompanied by musical notation.

Another important type of hymn is the Paean in honour of a human ruler or military leader. These could be performed both in festivals and on other occasions. They have been taken to demonstrate the servility that set in with that notorious new departure in Hellenistic religion, ruler-cult, and simultaneously to testify to the decline of traditional religious feeling. The one that usually gets quoted was performed by the Athenians with choirs and dancers in honour of Demetrios Poliorketes in 291, and includes the lines: 'For other gods are a long way away, or have no ears, or do not exist, or pay not a jot of attention to us: but we see you before us, not in wood or stone, but in the flesh.' To the ancient author who quotes it, no less than to us, this sounded like flattery, but before we start announcing the twilight of the gods, we have to set this statement in a wider context. It is an extreme specimen of the hyperbole used as cities struggled to come to terms with the new phenomenon of their super-powerful foreign leaders. And its language is henotheistic rather than monotheistic: this means that it pays special homage to one god, without denying the existence of others.

Mime: Mini-sketches

Closely related to comedy from the beginnings of its history was the 'mime'. This, in its origins, was a sub-literary form, in which punchy, robust sketches, often from low life, were performed by a single actor or a troupe. Narrative was less important than the vigorous evocation of personality and scene. Mime exploited situations and character-types which it shared with comedy, both because of direct borrowings (and parodies), but also because of common origins and parallel development. Comedy's ancient relations lived on healthily in the Hellenistic period. A second- or third-century CE text preserves vivid and tantalizing details about the many sorts of popular entertainer familiar to the Hellenistic public. We hear, for example, of *hilarodoi,* 'joyful singers', who dressed in white robes, boots, and a golden crown to parody tragedy to the accompaniment of a harpist: one or two papyrus fragments, including a free-wheeling farce based on Euripides' *Iphigenia among the Taurians* show the sort of thing they may have got up to. The *magodoi* or *lysiodoi*, meanwhile, took their parts from comedy, cross-dressed, and noisily took the parts of whores, pimps, and drunkards. The *Ionikistes*, also known as a 'shameful singer', specialized in lavatorial humour and abuse. Yet this genre had some surprisingly distinguished exponents, including Sotades, who worked in Alexandria and was known to Kallimachos. On one occasion he addressed a notorious remark to the king, Ptolemy II, about his incestuous marriage to his sister Arsinoe, claiming that the king was 'thrusting his prick into an unholy hole'. His indiscretions finally sank him—quite literally—for he was shut in a lead container and dropped in the sea.

Surviving mime from the Hellenistic period is represented mainly by two poets—and in true Hellenistic fashion, it has been made complex, fused with other forms. The mimes of Herodas are known as 'Mimiambi', a cross between the subject-matter of mime, usually in prose, and the metrical form of iambus, used by the archaic poets for realistic subjects—sex, food, vituperation (cf. pp. 68, 69–72). They are vignettes of about a hundred lines each: characters from New Comedy people them, along with other urban grotesqueries—an old procuress, a brothel-keeper, a delinquent schoolboy, women having affairs with their slaves, or enthusiastically discussing dildoes purchased from a man who purports to be a shoe-maker:

> He works at home and sells in secret—
> Every door now trembles at the tax-man.
> But his work—what work it is! You'd think
> You were looking at Athene's handiwork,
> Not Kedron's. When I saw them—you see, Metro,
> He came with two—my eyes popped out at the sight.
> Men don't make phalloi (we're on our own) so straight.
> And not just this: they're soft as sleep, and their little straps
> Are wool, not straps.
>
> (*Mimiamboi* 6. 63–73)

Recent work on these texts emphasizes the sophistication of their form, rather than the crudity of their subject, which is mimesis of urban low life. This makes it all the more desirable to know something of their public, a matter on which the texts themselves are silent. Probably they were performed, but whether by a single actor or whole troupe is unclear. Their content may look undemanding, but their language, which imitates the Ionic of the sixth-century Hipponax, is incompatible with the idea that they were intended for an unlettered public.

The other author is Theokritos of Syracuse. What he is best known for is a collection of thirty poems (a few spurious), most of which are in hexameters. The shortest is effectively an epigram, the longest over two hundred lines long. Antiquity called them *Eidyllia*, 'Idylls', which just means 'Poems in different styles'. They are indeed very different, but the largest group among them consists of mimes, understood in the same sense as poems which present a piquant or evocative mini-drama. They also include other species: a few short mythological narratives; poems in which the speaker addresses, or admonishes, a young (male) beloved; poems which praise a monarch, appeal for patronage, or accompany a gift. The praise-poetry and the appeals for patronage are important documents for the literary history of the period and the contexts in which poets operated; but it is the mimetic poems for which Theokritos is best known.

The majority of these are set in a fictive and idealized countryside that is peopled with herdsmen and shepherdesses. They show off, quarrel, compete in song, exchange gifts—and above all lament unrequited love, all in a curious high-flown poetic version of the Doric dialect, mainly of Theokritos' own devising. Yet there are also echoes, however distant, of traditional rural songs, refrains, and amoebean (antiphonal) singing, all refracted through the extreme refinement of the epic hexameter. The effect is perfectly calculated, and derives not least from a three-way incongruity between the speakers and subject-matter, linguistic register, and literary form:

> I go to serenade Amaryllis, while my goats graze
> On the mountainside, and Tityrus drives them on.
> Tityrus, my well-loved friend, please graze my goats,
> And drive them to the spring. The billy-goat—
> The yellow Libyan—watch out for him, in case he butts.
> —O lovely Amaryllis, why no more
> Do you peep from yonder cave and call me in,
> Your sweetheart? Do you hate me? Do you think
> Me snub-nosed, nymph, and bearded, when close by?
> You'll drive me to the rope. But see, I bring
> Ten apples, from the place you told me, and
> Tomorrow I'll bring you another ten!
>
> (Theokritos, *Idylls* 3. 1–11)

This is obviously sophisticated urban entertainment, and no one for a minute would have been misled by these underemployed languishing rustics. The very fact that they could be represented like this is eloquent testimony to the distance that the poet and his readers had moved away from the reality of the countryside and its traditions. Theokritos is not the first poet to have written about the countryside, but he is the first known to have cultivated this bizarre, nostalgic, anti-realist form, and antiquity remembered him principally as its first pastoral poet.

The other two who wrote in Greek were Bion and Moschos. The following extract (falsely attributed to Moschos) illustrates another aspect of bucolic poetry—not its frivolous or mannerist side, but a capacity for poignant reflection on human mortality that is reflected in the tradition of the bucolic lament:

> Alas, for the mallows, which die in the garden,
> Or the green parsley, or thick bushy dill,
> Again come to life and another year flourish;
> Yet we men, so tall and so strong and so wise,
> When once we die, then in hollow earth heedless
> We sleep the long sleep with no end and no dawn
>
> ([Moschos], *Lament for Bion* 99–104)

But Theokritos' non-bucolic *œuvre* is equally interesting, and until recently comparatively neglected. The fourteenth *Idyll* exploits the tension between country and town, between unreality and contemporary life, when the main speaker announces his intention of giving up rustic frivolities and going to enlist as a mercenary under Ptolemy. Virgil's *Eclogues* would take this disjunction much further (cf. pp. 359–66). And with the very celebrated fifteenth poem we enter the world of contemporary Alexandria itself. Two Syracusan housewives, Gorgo and Praxinoa, are on their way to the palace to see a display put on by Queen Arsinoe as part of the annual festival of Adonis. The poem begins with a domestic scene showing their gossip; it accompanies them as they push through the streets to the palace; and then it describes what they see when they get there—a magnificent tableau with tapestries and figures of the goddess and youth disposed on a couch. It concludes with a hymn sung by a professional female reciter, in an elevated and quite different style from the rest of the poem. What makes the poem particularly interesting, for our purposes, is that it dramatizes a public response to a work of art. Firstly, the women marvel at the embroidered tapestries in the tableau: their only criterion of excellence is realism. 'The figures stand and turn so naturally they're alive, not woven.' Then they marvel at the singer's knowledge: 'Praxinoa, the woman is cleverness itself. Happy to know so much, happy above all to have so sweet a voice.' And then the mundane and bathetic: 'Still, it's time to go home. Diokleidas hasn't had his dinner.'

The women have often been considered 'vulgar'—not just because their critical vocabulary is so limited, but because of their very obvious characterization throughout the poem as prattling urban housewives incapable of thinking an original thought. But how are *we* supposed to respond to the hymn, in the light of their response to it? Their terms of praise seem misplaced: the singer has not really displayed out-of-the-way mythological erudition. Equally, though, it is not at all clear that we are supposed to take the composition merely as a tawdry crowd-pleaser. Is it that Gorgo and Praxinoa can still appreciate a display of virtuosity that they don't fully understand? To move away from Arsinoe's palace altogether, might a broadly common value-system allow quite large sections of the public to appreciate fairly demanding material—not to understand it in every single detail and nuance, but to be familiar enough with its background and conventions to be able to enjoy it? Might the enormous popularity of (say) tragedy also be framed in this way? While we should not split the public into the lettered few and the unlettered many, it remains the problem to try to define more precisely the constituency of each literary genre and each type of performance.

The Mouseion and Alexandria

And so to the literature of Alexandria itself. This dominates the high Hellenistic period, and raises some of the most important and controversial questions about literature and the public in this chapter of literary history. 'Alexandrian literature' is a phrase often used as if it is synonymous with 'Hellenistic literature', the geographical term coterminous with the chronological one. This is, strictly, incorrect; but it is easy to see how the usage came about.

In Alexandria, at the mouth of the Nile—originally Alexander's foundation—the first Ptolemies established a sort of research centre, following in the footsteps of Aristotle, some of whose pupils and followers oversaw its founding. This centre comprised the famous Library and Museum, which lay within the palace quarter. The Museum derived its name from the older Greek *Mouseion*, originally a sanctuary of the Muses, but now with primarily literary and cultural connotations. These were places that supported philosophy and the arts. Literary studies, then, were but one of the many specialisms in Alexandria, which acted as an international magnet to scholars attracted by the promise of a well-paid collegiate life with magnificent resources at hand, all of which of course redounded to the glory of the Ptolemies. Alexandria and later similar institutions, for example at Antioch, and, later, Pergamon on the west coast of Asia Minor, were among the most concentrated centres of literary activity in the Hellenistic period, as they were of intellectual excellence in general. But before coming to the creative literary activity that went on in them, we need to consider their treatment of the literature of the past, which they carefully husbanded and reappraised, and to which they devoted scholarly attention on a scale hitherto unknown in Greece. Some of the best-known and most characteristic poets of the Hellenistic period are the so-called scholar poets, whose philology informed their creative activity.

The Ptolemies were egregious book collectors, and formed the astonishingly completist ambition to secure for their library a copy of every book in existence (their holdings have been estimated at about 500,000 rolls of papyrus). In this they were probably inspired by the ideals of Aristotle and his school, the Peripatetics, who collected information with the ultimate aim of explaining all things. The Ptolemies impounded books which arrived on ships in the harbour, and acquired others in the famous book-markets of Rhodes and Athens. They did not restrict their ambitions to works written in Greek, for the ancient Zoroastrian scriptures were also translated and filed away in their new library, while a priest from the holy city of Heliopolis, Manetho, wrote a Greek reinterpretation of ancient Egyptian history. The Greek translation of the Jewish scriptures known as the Septuagint has been attributed to royal impetus, but it is more likely to be due to private initiative, and to the need to render the scriptures comprehensible to Greek-speaking Jews within the synagogues themselves. The scholars who came to work on this huge body of assembled material ordered and classified it, and set about its textual criticism and elucidation. The works which attracted their attention were, in the first place, the classic works of epic and drama: only later was scholarly attention given to prose (beginning with Herodotos' *Histories*) and works by contemporary writers. These early scholars established the basic genres of literary scholarship still practised today—editions, commentaries, specialist studies, and monographs. One should not expect their work to have had much impact beyond the walls of their academies, yet in at least one famous instance it did: the Alexandrian scholars succeeded, within a very short space of time, in standardizing the very divergent texts of Homer in public circulation. This is the more remarkable when one considers the ancient method of producing and distributing books: with each text copied out by hand, and with no possibilities for mass production, there was no way for an author to impose a standard text or format on the market.

Scholarly sifting led in turn to the grouping of texts into literary genres—in the case of poetry mostly by metre and/or setting, in the case of prose mostly by purpose of composition or occasion of delivery. But this was done in a pragmatic and untheorized way. Thence came the drawing-up of canons of the approved authors (classics, not moderns) in each genre, a set of choices sanctioned by time and tradition and in part by popular taste: Homer and Hesiod inevitably topped the list of epic poets, while the contention for pre-eminence in tragedy, satirized in Aristophanes' *Frogs*, was settled by the Hellenistic canons which grouped the top three dramatists in each genre. This process of sifting has been considered symptomatic of an age which now acknowledged its discontinuity with, and inferiority to, the past; only now, it is claimed, had the Greeks acquired a sufficient sense of distance from classical literature, work on which had now become a labour of imaginative reconstruction no longer linked by living participation. But it is very doubtful how far we can go down this path: a sense of 'belatedness', of coming at the end of a tradition, had already been expressed in some famous lines by Choirilos of Samos at the end of the fifth century (quoted above p. 57).

The elements of Alexandrian philological method emerged well before the Alexandrians; so too, in certain genres, did the notion of a classic. The scholars' lists were not in themselves prescriptive. Our papyri do not indicate that they inhibited the reading of non-canonical authors in the world at large; but they formalized tastes and preferences which were probably not so very different from those among the educated public. When classical tragedy was revived, it was usually Sophokles or Euripides, while with dithyramb it was Timotheos, whose statue was also one of those that adorned the library at Pergamon.

So too with the alleged 'two publics' of the Hellenistic period, the lettered and the unlettered. A central theme of this chapter is that even the most learned members of Hellenistic society can nonetheless be seen as representing the extreme end of a very wide spectrum whose members shared a broadly common value-system held in place by the very conservative nature of Greek literary education. The scope for learnedness was very much increased, at least in well-off areas: beside the royal libraries we hear of a growing number of public libraries, mostly in the old, wealthy cities of mainland Greece, Asia Minor, and southern Italy and Sicily. In a few tantalizing cases we even have hand-lists of some of their books. There was also a change in the pattern of the education of young men, which came to embrace at least a smattering of literary culture in addition to athletic training: beauty of body *and* mind was now the ideal, the cultivatedness or *paideia* which the Greeks prized so highly. Yet the state never made much provision for primary education, which was left to the generosity of private benefactors and probably cost money which many people could ill afford. In many rural areas there is likely to have been little or no education available at all, except at home. When we talk about the 'public' or even the 'publics' of Hellenistic literature, we have to bear in mind that although resources improved in many areas in the Hellenistic period, the numbers of those who could read and had access to education, books, and libraries were probably still relatively small. In this respect, therefore, distinguishing between an 'élite' and a 'popular' readership is not very helpful.

As for the ancient scholars, what is most interesting about them are their methods, wherever discoverable, and their ways of reading. To deal with a work of literature was to set its text in order, to understand it on a lexical level—whence the compilation of lists of rare or dialectal words or *glossai*—and to elicit information about topics arising from it. The plot of a drama could be summarized and compared with other forms of the myth, genealogies could be given, antiquarian information of all kinds could be accumulated to shed light on the matter in hand. Aesthetic or literary-critical judgements could be formulated too, as we know from Homeric commentaries—which, while often banal, are still capable of insight or sophistication which is impressive even by modern standards. There are also papyri containing commentaries that seem to emanate from the private study or the schoolroom. Here, too, the text is subjected to paraphrase, gloss, and factual scrutiny. In general, we would do well to remember the ways in which ancient readers approached their texts, and the concerns they brought to bear on them—above all, that Homer should be elevated and edifying; the growing sophistication of their analytical technical vocabulary; the very fact-based, antiquarian drive to amass supporting detail. It is salutary to recall the apparent gulf between what texts seem to *us* to be saying and what ancient readers seem to have made of them, though we should also acknowledge that the bald and barely adequate marginal annotations can hardly be expected to tell the full story of ancient readers' responses to texts in all their complexity and richness.

Alexandrian poets: Kallimachos

The most creative century of the Hellenistic period, in literary terms, was the third, especially its first half; and many (but by no means all) of its most famous names were associated with the new royal capitals. Those associated specifically with the royal libraries—Alexandria, principally, but also Pella in Macedon, and Antioch in Syria—are the representatives of that notorious Hellenistic hybrid, the 'scholar poet'. He is variously regarded as a perfect blend of poetry and scholarship that prefigured the best aspects of Renaissance humanism, or, less romantically, as a token of the degeneracy of the Hellenistic age, which could produce only learned, trivial footnotes to the golden-age classics. Actually we should keep in mind the great mass of Hellenistic poets whose *œuvre* is all but lost, who are barely names to us, and who never set foot in the royal capitals in their lives. But the most famous poets of the age are undoubtedly those who worked in Alexandria. In the first generation there was the elegiac master Philitas of Kos, who came as tutor to the young Ptolemy II, then after him Kallimachos and Eratosthenes, both, in their different ways, polymaths; there was also Apollonios, born in Alexandria but with a Rhodian connection. The tragedians Lykophron of Chalkis (see above, pp. 226–8) and Alexandros of Aitolia worked in both Alexandria and Pella, while Aratos, who came from Soloi in Kilikia, divided his time between the Syrian and Macedonian capitals but has no known connection with Alexandria. Theokritos was certainly resident at some point in Alexandria, but we do not know that he had any connection with the Library.

The most famous of all was Kallimachos. A Cyrenean by birth, he was in Alexandria at the latest by the time the second Ptolemy came to the throne, in 283, and perhaps before that. Kallimachos was never Librarian, but he was the library's tireless bibliographer, and he devised a cataloguing system for it on tablets called *Pinakes*; he also wrote copious treatises on antiquarian, literary-historical, and literary-critical subjects. But his main fame is for his poetry, whose versatility and multiformity owed much to the diversity of the material at his command. Of his huge output, only six Hymns have come down to us through the manuscript tradition, as well as those epigrams of his preserved in the big Hellenistic and post-Hellenistic anthologies. The hymns are all in hexameters, except the fifth, and divide into three which purport to re-create the occasion of performance (2, 5, 6) and three which do not (1, 3, 4). Orthodoxy, never quite unassailable, is that the first group seeks no more than to create the illusion of performance:

> How Apollo's laurel branch is shaking,
> How the whole shrine moves! All sinners, flee!
> Apollo's handsome foot already beats
> The doorway: don't you see? The Delian palm
> Has given a sudden pleasing nod, and in the sky
> The swan sings sweetly. Bolts, be now drawn back;
> Be now withdrawn, you bars: the god is near.
> Young men, strike up the song, prepare to dance
> (*Hymn* 2. 1–8)

They are extremely subtle compositions, traditional in so far as they invoke the god through his or her epithets, enumerate powers, and lay special emphasis on the birth or the coming-to-power of the deity; untraditional in their occasional political agenda (1 hails king Ptolemy), their mixing-up of dialects and metres never mixed before, and their wry self-consciousness and wit.

What else we have derives from papyri and citations in other works, and neither sort of source is very conducive to the fluent reading or easy comprehension of this accomplished but formidably difficult poet. Papyri may be badly copied, scrappy, or incomplete, while excerpts are chosen for citation precisely on account of their difficulty. Kallimachos' other major works of poetry are his four-book elegiac poem *Causes* (in Greek, *Aitia*), which ferrets out the origins of festivals and rituals, statues and cities; and the *Hekale*, a new and conspicuously unheroic sort of epic poem on a much-reduced scale, which told the story of an elderly lady who once entertained Theseus on his way to slay the Marathonian bull. His thirteen *Iambi* are as thematically varied as they are (in fact) metrically diverse; now purveying wisdom through fables, now vituperating, now on the defensive, now recounting yet more stories of origins, Kallimachos ranges much wider than the sixth-century Hipponax (cf. pp. 69–70) whom he claims as his model. He also wrote a large number of occasional poems: victory poems to celebrate success in competitions, for example, or a marriage-poem for the queen, Arsinoe.

Kallimachos' is the most individualistic voice among all the Hellenistic poets. He is staggeringly erudite, and does not wear his learning lightly; and there are times in his *Causes* when self-advertisement carries over into self-parody. There is a banquet and heavy drinking going on all around, but Kallimachos, not one to waste an opportunity to add to his store of recherché knowledge, is busily quizzing his neighbour, who hails from Ikos: 'Do answer my question: why *is* it your ancestral custom to worship Peleus the king of the Myrmidons?' He rounds off the famous narrative of the love of Akontios and Kydippe by versifying the names of his historical sources, as if a love-story needs footnoting; elsewhere he proclaims, 'I sing nothing that is unattested'. He loves attitudinizing, and finds especially congenial the pose of the aloof and fastidious aristocrat which he took especially from Pindar, poet of aristocrats (cf. pp. 82–4). 'Tread the paths that carriages do not follow,' Apollo is supposed to have told him: 'do not drive your chariot in the common tracks of others.' 'Let another man bray like the long-eared beast,' he continues in his own voice a little later on in the same passage; '*I* am the refined one, the winged one.' Returning to the authoritative Apollo, at the end of the *Hymn* to this god, he makes him contrast the large and filthy river Euphrates with a small, pristine freshwater spring—metaphors for undiscriminatingly copious poetry and his own choice verse. He loves to portray himself as embattled, bedevilled by ignorant critics: he knows they mutter malice against him, carping because his poems are too short, or unheroic, or too generically miscellaneous. Yet his songs are 'more powerful than malignity', mightier than Envy, whom Apollo, his spokesman, spurns with his foot.

Until very recently, Kallimachos was (rather oddly) taken at his word. He has been seen as the hypersensitive aesthete in whom he would have us believe, favouring a sort of small-scale, exquisite poetry, a highly wrought artefact that would stand minute scrutiny and was the product of profound erudition. He affects a psychotic aversion to the vulgar mob: 'I detest everything public' is one of his more notorious *dicta*. And the tastes of these vulgarians have been reconstructed in minute detail on the basis of the way he himself characterizes them. His enemies complained that he did not churn out 'continuous poems' in 'thousands of lines', while they themselves wrote about 'kings and heroes'—from which it is inferred that they continued to write epic pastiche in the old style. Popular taste, therefore, was for tired, dead literary forms. But if it is mistaken to infer biographical details from an author's work in any over-simple way, it can be no less so to try to reconstruct his milieu from his own heavily loaded account of it. Recent work has sought to modify the traditional account of the literary wars Kallimachos portrays himself as waging, to redraw the battle-lines. Each of his polemical statements has a particular literary context and background: they should not all be bundled up together and turned into a manifesto or dogma. For example, there is no evidence that he laid down a ban on imitating Homer; and little indeed that he was surrounded by a horde of semi-literate third-rate epic pastichists. The portrayal of his opponents should be recognized for what it is, tendentious caricature.

Kallimachos can teach us the dangers of making *a priori* assumptions about the public. Since his own verse is so difficult, it has been inferred that it *must* have been written for coteries of intellectuals: he is viewed as the archetypal ivory-tower poet, and his *Causes* are the quintessence of this aesthetic. His polemic is read as academic in-fighting, and squabbles have been reconstructed (such as a notorious feud with Apollonios of Rhodes) for which good evidence is seriously lacking. Perhaps a more serious error still is to oppose his poetry to what lay outside the ivory tower, as if there were murky areas of popular culture out there to which the Kallimachean spirit was deeply alien. Because he is lexically difficult, allusive, recondite in his subject-matter, it is presumed that only scholars could read and appreciate him. But papyri are coming to light which indicate that he was popular outside the élite circles of Alexandria.

Here perhaps we should introduce a distinction between the envisaged and actual readership, for an ancient author had no control over the circulation of his works once they were in the public domain. Ancient poets would make their works public in the first place through recitals, only afterwards circulating them in book form—presumably primarily among friends. But whatever circles Kallimachos originally wrote his poetry for, it appears that they soon reached readers elsewhere who were able to identify with the devious sinuosities of Egypt's most accomplished poet. Our prize exhibit is the Lille papyrus, recovered from the bandages of a mummy of the late third century BC—only a generation or so after the poet's death—which came from the Fayûm, a large oasis area on the west bank of the Nile which was a favoured site for Greco-Macedonian colonization. The very substantial fragments of Kallimachos it preserves come from the beginning of the third book of the *Causes*, and tell the story of the origin of the Nemean games, at which the Egyptian Queen Berenike had won a chariot-race. They are interspersed with a commentary that is obviously not pitched at a very high level: it might, for example, be the work of a local schoolmaster. The notorious 'I detest everything public' apparently did not prevent his being enjoyed by the sort of public who had to have their mythological allusions spelled out to them, and even the relations of their royal family underscored.

At first sight it seems easier to find a 'how' than a 'why' to Kallimachos' popularity: Greek education was so conservative, and so privileged 'the classics', that it might seem strange to have a modern author canonized so quickly. Yet traditional hermeneutic methods could easily be applied to him. If he was lexically demanding, so was Homer himself; and he could be glossed and paraphrased and his adaptations of (for example) the vocabulary of epic or Attic drama could be noted by diligent schoolboys. If he was allusive, then the classical texts to which he made allusion could be identified. Above all, if he sought out innumerable recondite myths and dwelt lovingly on the minutiae of local tradition, it was quite within the competence of ancient readers to deal with them. They had been taught to ask about sources, variants, the mythographical and historiographical backgrounds to their texts. We have papyri of Kallimachos—albeit from the second century CE and later—which well exemplify the way ancient readers approached a text: they explain difficult words and provide background for allusions; they summarize the story, and cite ancient authorities. The total number of papyri of his work which contain marginal annotations is higher than that of any other Hellenistic author, showing that ancient readers rose to the challenge of interpreting this interesting and complex poet.

In respect at least of its concern with foundation legends and aetiologies (the search for origins), Kallimachos' *Causes* was typical of its age. In his very individual way, and as a poet rather than as an antiquarian, he was treating the same sorts of themes with which the Greeks habitually constructed their political identities, wrote their histories, and talked about their religion. The Greeks' extraordinary taste for heroic genealogies in the archaic period is seen as a way of structuring their own history, and of viewing and manipulating the relationships between different ethnic groups. We should perhaps understand the interest in local traditions in a similar way: not, or not only, as antiquarianism, but as a sort of universally understood currency. Local antiquities—foundation myths, details of ritual and cult practice—were the topic of many recitals at local festivals (including at Alexandria). They were an expression of local patriotism and pride. They were also a way to bring cities geographically or culturally on the margins within the pale of Greek civilization: the inhabitants of Kanobos on the Nile delta could relate to other Greeks, and vice versa, if they claimed it was founded in memory of Menelaos' steersman (for example). Traditions might also be used as diplomatic counters and had international bargaining power, as when ambassadors arrived in a foreign city and prefaced their requests to that city with claims to kinship extending back into the heroic period. They might even use poetry to support their case, as when a couple of diplomats sent out from Teos in about 170 BCE to several cities in Crete in order to secure a grant of immunity for a local temple. They presented their request before several cities, but for some reason the citizens of Knossos and Priansos got special treatment—a diatribe about those cities' origins, including a cithara recital of excerpts from the dithyrambic poets Timotheos and Polyidos and others, and a whole cycle of myth synthesized from poets and historiographers on Crete and its native gods and heroes.

The varieties of epic: Apollonios

There is some evidence for epic poems written about particular races or regions, but for the most part we know little more about them than their names: thus, we hear of the works on Aitolia, Oita, Thebes, and perhaps Boiotia by one of the Nicanders, and an epic in sixteen or more books by Rhianos, who also wrote an epic on one of the wars fought by archaic Sparta with her Peloponnesian neighbours. There is, however, surprisingly little evidence for the sort of epic which has long been postulated as the most popular and characteristic of the Hellenistic period—multi-book historical epic, of the kind certainly written by Roman writers for encomiastic purposes. The one full-length epic which we possess from the Hellenistic period is in fact on a mythological theme—the *Argonautika* of Kallimachos' contemporary, Apollonios of Rhodes. And few texts reflect the age's abiding interest in aetiology, in charter-myths of cults and cities, and in religious topography, more clearly than this one. Apollonios also wrote a number of foundation poems about cities of Egypt, Asia Minor, and the Aegean—Alexandria and Naukratis, Kaunos, Rhodes, and Knidos—which evidently had a similar bent, but only fragments of them survive. But it is the four-book *Argonautika* which best illustrates his concern to ground contemporary practices, especially religious practices, in heroic antiquity. Formally it might seem to be heir to a hundred earlier poems on the same theme. In fact it is a curious mixture of the traditional and the (very) modern—though it is hard to say how experimental it is, because of the loss of other material with which to contextualize it.

Jason leaves Thessaly for Kolchis to fetch back the golden fleece from the Kolchian tyrant, Aietes. Once there, he is helped in the superhuman trial of strength imposed as a condition of the fleece's recovery by Aietes' daughter, who has fallen in love with him. Medeia is a sorceress, and enables Jason both to overcome fire-breathing bulls and sow a field with dragon's teeth, and to rescue the fleece from the formidable serpent which keeps guard over the tree where the fleece is kept. She then escapes her father's fury by fleeing back to Greece with Jason. The story is familiar, the tale-type (that of the youth who leaves home to prove his manhood) traditional. The literary form is conservative, and the narrator's obviously intimate knowledge of the Homeric poems—which inform the poem on every level, from set-piece episodes to similes, characterization, and divine machinery—might even suggest that this was some sort of throw-back to cyclic epic. But nothing would be further from the truth. Here are literary textures, narrative complexity, and authorial self-consciousness like nothing ever seen in Homer.

First is Jason himself: by turns lacking in initiative, despondent, bungling, and very much less than competent in battle, he is anything but heroic. Here, for example, is his reaction to Aietes' challenge:

> Thus spoke Aietes; Jason fixed his eyes
> Down on the ground in silence, and sat nonplussed
> By this disaster. Long he turned the matter
> This way and that, but found no brave device
> To undertake a task that seemed so huge.
>
> (*Argonautika* 3. 422–5)

Yet his advocacy of speech and strategy is as double-edged as was Odysseus', and his duplicity is shown to far worse effect in the shocking scene of the murder of Medeia's brother, Apsyrtos (4. 464–81). Jason is at the centre of a love-intrigue with the Kolchian king's daughter, and the romantic interest is a large part of the poem's attraction for modern readers. Consider the sensitivity of the following simile and observation:

> . . . And her whole soul grew warm inside
> And melted, as when dew on roses melts
> When warmed by light of dawn. Now shyly both
> Fixed eyes upon the ground, and now again
> Upon each other they would cast their gaze,
> With tender smiles beneath their radiant brows.
>
> (*Argonautika* 3. 1019–24)

Yet the relationship shows severe signs of fraying already in the course of the poem, and anyone who has read Euripides knows its calamitous sequel: it is therefore extremely hard to see Jason as a romantic hero either. The love-theme looks very new in epic, but has to be set beside a certain amount of earlier mythographic evidence about the Argonautic legend, and above all beside the great escalation in erotic themes across the field of Hellenistic poetry. The prominence of the female domain in general, the close interest in the psychopathology of female passion look back to Euripides (of course); so, uncomfortably, does the story of Medeia in particular, whose characterization as the archetypal Greek 'other', woman and barbarian, becomes increasingly menacing as the poem progresses.

The *Argonautika* is laden with aetiology. In the first and second books we have an account of the outward journey of the Argonauts; and in the fourth, of their return. We read of the various stops made by the Argo's crew, a journey made in mythological time but in real space, and of customs, rites, and landmarks instituted by them, which the poet claims are 'still in existence to this very day'. A good example is the story of Kleite, a young queen of Kyzikos on the Black Sea coast who kills herself for grief on the death of her husband. This story becomes in typically Hellenistic fashion the origin of both a local spring and a custom at a modern festival, as the private and pathetic story broadens out to encompass timeless features of the landscape and the contemporary festival calendar:

> The woodland nymphs themselves bewailed her death;
> And from the tears which rolled down from their eyes,
> The goddesses wrought a spring called Kleite still,
> The famous name of that unhappy girl.
> Most grievous dawned that day for all the folk,
> Women and men, of the Doliones; for none
> Could bear to eat, and long throughout their grief
> They took no thought for grinding meal, but lived
> Just as they were, eating the uncooked food. And even now,
> When Kyzicene Ionians year by year
> Pour offerings to the dead, the common mill
> Is where they grind the corn to make their meal
>
> (*Argonautika* 1. 1065–77)

The attitude to past, present, and future is profoundly different from Homer's. In the *Iliad*, the only explicit and detailed forward-reference to an event outside the framework of the poem is to the obliteration of the Greek wall in a deluge, that is, to an act of destruction; the Hellenistic writer, on the other hand, characteristically binds mythological past and present together in a continuum in which real-life detail is constantly explained by its reference to the past. The tragic vision which keeps the heroic world at an insurmountable remove is completely absent.

Apollonios studs his poem with other sorts of detail that point to the present: recent discoveries in Alexandrian science spill over into it, as when, famously, Medeia's overwrought state is described in terms of the nervous system which doctors had recently discovered, or as when Eros, the Hellenistic putto, is cajoled into action with the lure of a sphere representing state-of-the-art astronomy. The poem dramatizes the confrontation of Hellenes with barbarians, exhibiting some of the cultural over-confidence typical of the Greeks in their encounters with non-Greek culture, though Apollonios' heroes emerge by no means uniformly well. Interestingly, the Kolchians were believed to be descended from the Egyptians, but Apollonios has chosen not to highlight this, let alone reflect ethnic confrontation in the Egypt of his day. The ultimate superiority assumed for Greek culture and the elevated epic genre have flattened out the contours of any serious attempt to individualize the portrayal of the Greek–barbarian opposition.

Who read the *Argonautika*? As with Kallimachos, there are papyri of the poem—about half as many as there are of Kallimachos, but still enough to bear ample witness to its popularity; they date from about the first century BCE to the fifth CE. Some note textual variants, gloss the more difficult words, and explain other points of interest in marginal scholia. Internal evidence from the poem itself can tell us little enough about the contexts in which it was read. Obviously it no longer belonged even distantly to any oral tradition (cf. pp. 30–3); nor would its length be amenable to its complete performance viva voce at festivals. Yet the ancient biography of Apollonios which tells the story (myth?) of the failure of the poem's first edition speaks of Apollonios 'reciting' the poem, as if this is at least plausible, whether or not it actually took place. Neither the work's inherent complexity, nor the fact that its literary language was both archaic and extremely artificial, are themselves factors that would prevent the public recitation of at least selections from the poem.

Our information about the poem's readers, however, comes mainly from its adaptation by other poets. There is certainly contact between the *Argonautika* and Kallimachos' *Causes*, but if it is the case, as seems likely from the placement and content of the passages at issue, that it is Apollonios who is the borrower, then we are deprived of evidence for Kallimachos' treatment of this epic. The same may be true of the two episodes Apollonios has in common with Theokritos, the story of Hylas and the fight of Amykos and Polydeukes. The *Argonautika* was enjoyed in late Republican Rome, where a translation was made by Varro of Atax, and his poem provides framework and context for Catullus' celebrated sixty-fourth poem (cf. pp. 349–50). Here Catullus tells how Peleus and Thetis met during the *Argo*'s outward voyage, an event absent from Apollonios, who speaks only of their separation towards the end of his poem; both poets give different sorts of intimation about the couple's terrifying offspring, Achilles, and create different sorts of foreboding about the story's aftermath. But Apollonios' most sensitive ancient reader by far was Virgil in the fourth book of the *Aeneid* (see pp. 395–7).

The other famous mythological epic from the Hellenistic period was *Hekale*, by Kallimachos himself—but modern terminology often refers to it by the diminutive term 'epyllion'. Since it is only known from fragments, we do not know exactly how long it was, but it has been put at at least a thousand lines—perhaps, therefore, approaching the length of one of Apollonios' shorter books. The term 'epyllion' was invented by early modern scholars to embrace a category including various narrative hexameter poems shorter than a traditional epic. But their dissimilarity with one another—their lengths varying from under a hundred to perhaps sixteen hundred lines, their style and manner varying just as much—should make us think twice before using the term to imply anything like a cohesive set. *Hekale* was one of Kallimachos' most popular poems—every bit as popular as the *Causes*. Its subject-matter resembles that of the *Argonautika* in being the story of a young man's coming to manhood; but its treatment is also similar to the extent that the centre of interest is elsewhere than on the hero's prowess. It is named after an old woman who had fallen on hard times and was living in poverty in Attica, and who gave shelter to Theseus when he was coming from Troizen, place of his upbringing, to rid Attica of the menace of the Marathonian bull. After Theseus has killed the bull, there is a sizeable digression presenting a conversation between two birds: the crow seems to be reciting stories whose moral is that bringers of bad news are unpopular. And indeed, when Theseus returns in triumph to Hekale's hut he finds her lying on her funeral pyre. In her honour he sets up a precinct to Zeus Hekaleios, and institutes the Attic deme named after her. So it is yet another Hellenistic foundation myth.

The basic elements of this story are epic—the hero on a quest, his kindly host who lives in noble poverty; the story counts as a single, discrete action with beginning, middle, and end, so corresponds to Aristotle's requirements for an epic. What is non-traditional is the emphasis: it is as if a short epic were to be written in which Odysseus and Eumaeus, or Odysseus and Eurykleia, featured as the two main characters. The poet's use of local colour lets him show off his erudition: there is loving detail about Attic myth and topography, and among the great wealth of glosses that enrich Kallimachos' vocabulary are many from Attic Old Comedy. The poem was particularly admired for its use of the hospitality theme: the imitations, both Greek and Roman, tend to linger over the details of the humble meal that seems obligatory fare on such occasions, just as Kallimachos had dwelt with loving botanical accuracy and lexicographical precision on the species of Attic olive which a kind old lady had served up to her guest:

> Olives which grew ripe on the tree, and wild olives, and the autumn ones
> Which she had set aside to soak in brine while still light green.
>
> (fr. 36, Hollis)

Ethical pleasure in the old lady's nobility is matched by the aesthetic piquancy of describing her humble surroundings in high literary vein. The famous and fantastic episode of the garrulous crow was also influential. Unexpected twists like this are characteristic of Hellenistic narrative, as if poets shunned linear sequence; another way of doing it was to include a set-piece descriptive passage or *ekphrasis* which could also be a literary and rhetorical *tour de force*. An example is a poem by the second-century Moschos about the rape of Europa, an important document, for it is one of the very few surviving poems from the second century which is not epigram. This includes a description of the mythological scenes on Europa's basket—in fact pointedly relevant to her own situation. Of Catullus' sixty-fourth poem, over half is formally a descriptive digression, the *Lamento di Arianna* (cf. pp. 349–50). Ekphrases occur throughout Hellenistic and imperial literature, based ultimately on epic sequences such as the shield of Achilles in *Iliad* 18; and we have already met an important Hellenistic example, Theokritos' *Adoniazousai*, which also dramatizes the response of the viewer to the art-work.

Impractical didactic

The other major sort of epic written in the Hellenistic period was didactic, and followed the precedent, not of Homer, but of Hesiod (cf. pp. 26–30). Of these works unquestionably the most immediately and enduringly popular was the *Phainomena* of Aratos. Kallimachos knew how to praise it when he wrote that

> The song and manner are Hesiod's. Not the poet
> To the very hilt, but, one might say, the sweetest
> Of his verses has the man of Soloi creamed off. Hail, subtle verses,
> Product of Aratos' wakefulness
>
> (*Palatine Anthology* 9. 507)

The man of Soloi here is Aratos: Soloi was a city of Kilikia, and Aratos exemplifies a common pattern for Hellenistic intellectuals in that he gravitated to a major centre of culture from obscure origins, in his case in a city that was not even fully Greek. (Even its Greek speakers spoke Greek so badly that the term 'solecism' (*soloikismos*) was coined after them.) In adult life he spent time in the courts of Macedonia and Syria, and was not employed in Alexandria even though Kallimachos knew his work. The *Phainomena* is a hexameter work in 1,150 lines on the subject of the night sky and weather lore. Its conception is piously Stoic (cf. pp. 190–1): Zeus is the Providence that presides over all aspects of the world, and ordained that the stars should order times and seasons and that the sky should also furnish weather-signs for humans to interpret.

In fact the larger part of the text versifies a treatise about the heavenly bodies by the astronomer Eudoxos of Knidos. In the event, it was not very accurate. No matter: its popularity was guaranteed long before anyone ever bothered to point out its mistakes. It describes the placement of the constellations, its content much more neutrally descriptive than mythological or aetiological, though there is a famous description of the embodiment of Justice, Astraia, leaving the earth in disgust at humanity's growing wickedness to become the constellation Virgo:

> But when her people thronged the hilly heights,
> She warned them and chastised their evil ways,
> Refusing to attend them in their plight:
> 'How inferior was the race your fathers left
> After the Golden Age! Yet worse shall be
> Your own. For wars, and unrelenting strife
> Await mankind, and bitter sorrow's load.'
> And with these words she sought the hills, and left
> The folk behind, gazing towards her still.
> Yet when they too were dead, and in their place
> The Bronze Age came, and men more vicious yet—
> The first to forge the highwayman's dark blade,
> And first to taste the ploughing oxen's flesh—
> Then did Justice hate that race, and fly
> Up to the heavens. And she made her home
> There, where the Maiden still appears by night
> To mankind, near to Bootes the far-seen
>
> (*Phainomena* 120–36)

The career of this poem in Rome is well known: Cicero translated it as did Varro of Atax, Germanicus, and Avienus, and Virgil was influenced by the section on weather lore in his *Georgics*. The story told less often is that of the poem's career in Greece itself—apart from its ringing endorsement by Kallimachos. Its reception outside learned circles is both informative and neglected. Astronomy was taught in gymnasia and formed one of the subjects lectured on by itinerant sophists and rhetors who, not unlike their classical forebears (see pp. 167–70), travelled the centres of Greek culture and gave talks to paying audiences. The text of Aratos was at the centre of their curriculum. It offered an ideal field for grammatical, mythological, and technical scholarship: among decrees and epigrams that commemorate educators of astronomy is one mentioning a man who was both Homeric commentator, astronomer, and geometer. This combination of expertise—polite learning, the modest polymathy offered by Hellenistic education—evokes an important context in which Aratos' work could be read and enjoyed. Perhaps the subject-matter appealed to an age increasingly interested in astrology; but astrology is absent from the text itself, and the section on weather-signs is different again, imparting rural lore whose juxtaposition with the modern treatise is actually very representative of ancient science in general. Virgil's adaptation emphasizes still further the dislocation between sophisticated form and quaint, archaizing content; this was not a manual that anyone would seriously think of using. But readers could enjoy the narrator's pious traditionalism and Stoic stance, his conception of a Zeus who had ordained the universe for mankind's benefit. And they could appreciate Aratos' use of the didactic form, used neither with Hesiodic rambling nor Virgilian complexity, but to impart information with quiet authority and the characteristic Kallimachos had diagnosed in it all along, 'refinement'.

There are two other didactic epics which survive from the Hellenistic period, the *Theriaka* and *Alexipharmaka*, both by Nikandros of Kolophon on the improbable subject of poisonous animals and the remedies for their bites. The extant poems and fragments make reference to the cult of Apollo in Klaros just outside Kolophon, where the author is said to have been hereditary priest. This is an important datum. Kolophon was one of the ancient Ionian cities of Asia Minor, and had strong poetic traditions that reached back to the archaic period. Not only did it lay claim to Homer (along with dozens of other cities) and Mimnermos, but was also home in successive centuries to the rationalist Xenophanes; the scholarly Antimachos, sometimes seen as a Hellenistic poet *avant la lettre*, whose best-known work *Lyde* was the topic of lively debate in Kallimachos' Alexandria; and the elegist Hermesianax. We also have the funerary epigram of one Gorgos, another priest of Klarian Apollo, dating from the late Hellenistic period. It describes him as a priest, a poet, and a polymath—a bibliophile, a lover of *sophia* (poetic wisdom), an 'elder' among bards who culled the fruits of the written page (a semi-coherent but telling mixture of poetic terminology, ancient and modern). Gorgos' poems are entirely lost, but he very probably wrote hymns (and oracles) for the shrine of Klarian Apollo. He suddenly brings into focus for us the numbers of Hellenistic poets no longer known even by name, but who continued to thrive outside Alexandria and the grand new royal courts in the traditional centres of Hellenic culture. It is most suggestive that his mourners praised his poetry in terms of the very same aesthetic—erudition—usually seen as the hallmark of the poets of the Library.

No one could say that Nikandros is not erudite. He is—obsessively, wearisomely so. Like Aratos, he borrows his erudition from a prose treatise; but both subject and manner of presentation are far more esoteric, and though Nikandros claims that his work will be useful to the ploughman, herdsman, or woodcutter who finds himself in need of a remedy, this is impossibly unlikely. No one suffering from a snake- or scorpion-bite would dream of consulting an epic poem which describes its menagerie of poisonous animals in heroic terms, the wounds they inflict in gory but unscientific detail, and their herbal remedies either in impenetrably specialist vocabulary—or often not at all:

> . . . As for the sufferer,
> Sometimes his throat is parched with a dry thirst,
> Often he freezes to his fingers ends
> And surging wintry blight invades his limbs.
> Often he vomits up a load of bile,
> All jaundiced, and a clammy sweat more chill
> Than falling snow pervades his limbs. Sometimes
> Like gloomy lead his complexion will seem,
> Or murky, or like metal particles
>
> (*Theriaka* 249–57)

(The poem might, on the other hand, be of interest to those interested in ancient taxonomies of animal species, though this is poetry not science.) It belongs to a mini-genre of baroque snake-bite descriptions, attested also in Apollonios' *Argonautika*, and later and most famously by Lucan (cf. pp. 472–7). Nikandros exemplifies the virtuosic handling of poetically intractable material, and whether it ever found a wider readership than some of the Latin poets of the late Republic is difficult to judge.

The golden age of epigram

Hexameters have dominated our survey of Hellenistic poetry because they dominate the surviving material. But what needs emphasis is the great success in this period of the elegiac metre as well. In the long term what had happened was that the diverse lyric metres of the archaic and classical periods had died out, or lived on in a few etiolated and radically simplified forms, and elegiacs moved in to colonize much of the ground they had forsaken. (An example of a lyricist still active in the Hellenistic period is Korinna, a Boiotian poetess who specialized in lyric narratives, at least one apparently performed by a choir of local women: her style is plain-spoken and direct, her metres simple, her interests patriotic and mythological.) But there was also a loosening of the general categories of applicability of metre to subject-matter. This means that Kallimachos (for example) could write victory odes in elegiacs, that hymns were beginning to appear in elegiacs, that Nikandros could turn even his uniquely baneful didactic genius to elegiacs. That elegiacs could be used for longer narratives was already the case in the archaic period (cf. pp. 73–4), and was even more clearly asserted by the *Lyde* of Antimachos (*c.*400 BCE), which perhaps used the death of the poet's wife or mistress to frame long sections of mythology and stretched to at least two books. The controversy surrounding this 'thick and unclear' poem in Alexandria should highlight rather than obscure its great influence on the Hellenistic elegists. Philitas of Kos, long famous as an elegiac master, is mostly an unknown quantity because only scraps of his work survive—a particularly cruel loss. Kallimachos, of course, was a grand master; and the great Eratosthenes in the next generation wrote an admired elegy on the Attic heroine Erigone (perhaps an opportunity for an excursus on the origins of Attic tragedy). But the lesser figures who accompany these men should also be allowed to enter the picture—Hermesianax of Kolophon, Phanokles, Alexandros of Aitolia, all of whom survive only in fragments, though in a few cases quite long ones. What they delighted in was catalogues of various kinds; their frequent predilection for erotic subject-matter was not necessarily incompatible with, let us say, a robust sense of irony:

> And even the bard, by divine fate ordained
> Of all Muses' servants sweetest soul—
> Godlike Homer himself—for wise Penelope
> Set lowly Ithaka to verse, for love.
> For her he suffered much, and left his broad
> Country behind for a mean island home.
> Ikarios' race, Amyklos' folk, he famed;
> And Sparta, all in keeping with his woes
>
> (Hermesianax, fr. 7. 27–34, trans. Powell)

Who read them? Hard to say, but at least the numbers of authors writing in this mode show that it was modish. And with the elegiac metre there was at least the theoretical possibility of performance. But it is interesting and perhaps surprising that, whereas the inscriptions which mention events in musical and poetic festivals refer to prizes for 'epic' (i.e. hexameter) poets, they do not do the same for elegists.

It is another curious fact that elegy of any length disappears after the end of the third century. What continues is epigram, which indeed dominates the field until a renaissance of third-century genres came about in late Republican Rome with Parthenios of Nikaia (cf. p. 338). An epigram is literally an 'inscription', a poem written on something, and as such it had already been practised in Greece for centuries—in epitaphs, dedications on objects, sometimes inscribed on victory monuments to record success in a competition. It was mainly, but not exclusively, written in elegiacs (the very earliest were in hexameters), and its characteristics were directness and simplicity.

It was early in the third century that it was expanded from its original context and raised into a literary form. Of its early practitioners, Leonidas of Taras and Anyte of Tegea represented a Doric tradition, further developing the epigram in its existing contexts of grave-inscriptions and dedications. Anyte wrote dignified epitaphs, among them several for animals, while Leonidas developed a distinctively convoluted, dithyrambic style and had a keen eye for the working lives of those who lived off the land. The following example is by Nossis, a poetess from South Italy, and is an epitaph for a writer of farces or *phlyakes* in the southern Italian and Sicilian tradition:

> Pass by with a loud laugh and a kindly word
> For me: Rhinthon of Syracuse am I,
> The Muses' little nightingale; and yet
> For tragic farce I plucked an ivy wreath
>
> (*Anthologia Palatina* 7. 414)

On the other hand, epigrams increasingly came to borrow from the traditional subject-matter of archaic and classical elegy, as performed at symposia—love, wine, and song (cf. pp. 72–3). For such subjects we look, not to the Doric tradition, but to Asklepiades of Samos, who moved in the same circles as Kallimachos (and is supposed to have been one of his literary enemies) and Theokritos, whose seventh *Idyll* refers to him as a master poet. He handled the epitaph genre as well, but it was Asklepiades who first turned his hand to writing of mistresses and revels, bittersweet love and sorrows drowned in wine, in the form of epigram:

> Imbibe, Asclepiades. Why woe and tears?
> Not you alone has Kypris victimised,
> Not you alone have felt the smart of Love's
> Arrows and bow. Why, living, lie in dust?
> Let's drink Bakchos' pure drink. The day's a thread.

Shall we await the lamp that bids us sleep?
Let's drink, sad lover. The time is not far away,
Sad wretch, when we must sleep the long-drawn night
(*Anthologia Palatina* 12. 50)

Kallimachos, Aratos, Theokritos, and Poseidippos took the genre still further. Kallimachos whimsically reflects on all the subjects in epigram's domain—love, death, and dedications—and many more besides: Aratos' newly published *Phainomena*; the pitfalls and exigencies of producing drama; family history, and anecdote. It was certainly the Hellenistic period's growth genre, and its first practitioners were also great metrical experimenters. It could be turned to political lampoons, to the description of natural marvels, and apparently even to metamorphosis stories. But we sometimes have to reckon with looseness of terminology and borderline cases, and situations in which it can be hard to distinguish between short elegy and long epigram. What is most characteristic of Hellenistic literary epigram is not innovation, but elegant or witty or otherwise pointed retractation. One poet caps another, surpassing him in wit. Or it can remain true to its archaic character and the traditions of monumental epigraphy, which required ideas to be expressed in the simplest and most straightforward way—which was often the most poignant, too.

Poseidippos' is an interesting case, because in addition to the twenty epigrams assigned him by our main source for the genre, a huge Byzantine compilation known as the Palatine Anthology, we are also awaiting publication of a papyrus roll, now in Milan, containing another hundred of his epigrams, subdivided into broad classes. This roll dates from the second half of the third century, and is much our largest ancient collection of epigrams on papyrus, though it is not alone. Poets do seem to have published collections of poems which they wrote, presumably, as occasional pieces, and anthologies of different authors were also compiled from quite an early date.

The first anthology to have had a big impact is Meleagros' *Garland*, published in about 100 BCE. Meleagros was a Syrian from Gadara—home not only of Gadarene swine, but also of Philodemos, a philosopher whose controversial view that we should not pretend that poetry is of any ethical benefit whatsoever is presumably reflected in his own extant raunchy epigrams. Meleagros claims to be trilingual in Greek, Phoenician, and Syrian, and inhabits a world in which Greek erotic epigram can be written about a love-triangle involving a Jew for whom 'love burns hot even on cold Sabbaths' (*Anthologia Palatina* 5. 160). This infiltration of Greek literary idiom into Semitic territory is as fascinating as the case of Ezekiel (above, p. 228). Prefacing his collection with an introduction assigning every named poet a flower (whence the collective name

Anthology, or Garland), Meleagros arranged his poems by alternations of author and thematic links. It made an immediate impact in Rome when it was published there: aristocratic poetasters turned their hand to imitating Greek conceits. At the same time, however, and across the Greek world, we have to bear in mind the continuing production of epigrams for their traditional purpose—on tombs, and on votive objects. The impact on these of their more literary cousins is an untold story. Once or twice, in relatively out-of-the-way places, we find that a local stone-carver has inscribed a poem in bombastic vocabulary, or in a curious or pretentious metre, and we wonder what gave him the impetus to do it.

Hellenistic prose

Why so little mention of prose, in all of this? Principally because so little of it survives. After the fourth century there is very little Greek prose substantially extant until Polybios in the middle of the second century (cf. pp. 254–5, 263), and after him a number of historiographers whose date brings them within the scope of the next chapter. Yet we have enough fragments, and testimonia, and references, to have some idea of the size of the wreck, and of the character and range of what is lost. More material was committed to writing than ever before, a lot of it of a specialist nature; yet the age's wealth of historiographical, rhetorical, philosophical, scholarly, scientific, technical and non-technical writings, compendious and brief, educative and diverting, are mostly just names to us, their loss due to accident, or to their ephemeral nature, or to the fact that they were later superseded and forgotten. In a survey like this, we must skim over writings which barely classify as literature—the mathematical treatises of Archimedes and Apollonios of Perge, the work of the mathematical astronomers (all but vanished because superseded by Ptolemaios), the fragments of medical writers, great though their discoveries were.

The works of the philosophers also survive, where they survive at all, mostly in paraphrases in later commentators, critics, and excerptors. Just about the only treatises to survive in their original wording are the letters of Epikouros (familiar Latin spelling, Epicurus), of which the longest fascinatingly expound the master's physical and ethical system in atrocious prose (Epikouros didn't care for style), and the treatises of his later disciple Philodemos, preserved in a charred and crumpled state in the library of a villa in Herculaneum. Their interest is even greater but their style is, if anything, worse still. Yet the availability of written treatises may be just one factor in the unprecedented popularity and influence of the philosophical schools in the Hellenistic period.

When the Roman rhetorician Quintilian came to survey the historiographical achievement of the Greeks, his list jumped from the historians of Alexander the Great to the Augustan Timagenes (*Institutiones* 10. 1. 73–5). This reflects the belief that history had hit a low point in the Hellenistic period, which in turn is at least partly a reflection of the fact that it was not on the curriculum of schools (unlike its close cousin, rhetoric). The papyri show the popularity of Herodotos, Thoukydides, and Xenophon, but Hellenistic historiography does not seem to have been subject to canon-formation and judgements about what constituted a classic.

Yet the period did produce several very influential figures. Ephoros of Kyme and Theopompos of Chios are both reputedly connected with Isokrates (cf. pp. 172–7), and are the two main Hellenistic exponents of rhetorical historiography. This means that their work employs rhetorical figures, speeches, character-assessments, and moralizing in accordance with history's perceived ethical purpose. Theopompos (mid-fourth century) had in fact worked as an orator. He continued Thoukydides' history down to the year 394, but his main work was a history of Philip of Macedon in fifty-eight books, in fact a history in the Herodotean tradition of the 'deeds of Greeks and barbarians' with Philip's career as its organizing principle. When he produced a prose epitome of Herodotos, he became the first known exponent of a genre with a great future—the boiled-down, user-friendly, easy-to-take-in summary. Ephoros wrote thirty books of *Histories*, known above all from the substantially extant history of Diodoros of Sicily, who uses him (not always straightforwardly). They covered the post-mythological era from the return of the Heraclids until the year 340. With a wide scope, lively interests, and an organization in which individual books seem to have been concerned with particular areas, Ephoros was considered by Polybios to have been the first universal historian. At the same time, the local histories continued to flourish, both within works of a larger compass (Ephoros was particularly interested in city foundations), and in more specialist, independent chronicles: the Atthidographers who specialized in the history of Attica are the outstanding examples here.

Our longest extant text of any Hellenistic historian is Polybios, who was concerned with the rise to power of Rome—a subject no historian after 200 BCE could ignore, and therefore really a topic for the next chapter (cf. p. 263). His informative discussions of method distinguish histories dealing with city foundations and kinship, genealogies, and political history. He would have us believe that he was one of the select few to opt to write the last kind, but of course his self-advertising suggestion that he stands magnificently alone is over-simple. He also attacks the writers of so-called 'tragic history', purveyors of sensationalism and purple prose, whose ringleader is Phylarchos. This might seem in tune with the emotionality in vogue in other genres, but his polemic may well distort or mislead, because it obscures the prevalence of emotive writing throughout the genre—even in the Master, Thoukydides.

The sophistication of Hellenistic literature, its allusiveness and awareness of place in a tradition, the burgeoning literature in prose, and the greater availability than ever before of written material all tend to give the impression that the public were now above all readers. Despite the fact that much ancient reading was done aloud, the tendency for written matter to create a sort of private mental world for its reader has somehow fed into a much broader myth that the Hellenistic period was characterized by 'alienation', the distancing of people from the traditional social structures and supports of the classical city. The individual was now, it is claimed, alone. But as far as concerns reading versus performance, the traditional performative element in Greek culture was still demonstrably alive and well, and still adaptable. We have encountered festivals, competitions, and recitals of new poetry—tragedy, comedy, and dithyramb, hexameter verse and lyric; and revivals of the literary classics. The Homeric epics were still performed, though in excerpts. Athenaios speaks of rhapsodes and 'Homeristai', and their introduction into theatres first in the Hellenistic period; he talks, too, of the 'chanting' of Homer, Hesiod, Archilochos, Mimnermos, and Phocylides, implying that they were set to new music, and he also mentions the comic 'acting' of Semonides of Amorgos, Homer and Hesiod, as if these poets were mauled about for popular entertainment.

But it would be wrong to identify popular culture solely with performance, and élite culture solely with books. Virtually any sort of composition could be performed and has plausible contexts for performance. Many scholars suspect that certain poems in the Theokritean corpus (for example 16, 24) were written for particular competitions, though in the absence of independent evidence it is difficult to be sure. While we cannot rule out the possibility that poets sometimes fictionalize performance-contexts in their poetry rather than evoke real ones, we know also that histories were read aloud. In fact, most of our evidence for the recital of history comes from the Hellenistic period; and we even hear from time to time of the performance of learned, scholarly, or antiquarian material. One man even seems to have recited historical notes or *hypomnemata* at Delphi.

Many of the questions we most want to ask about the Hellenistic public are unanswerable (as indeed they are about any period). Nevertheless, we must ask them. Who *was* the public for Hellenistic literature, in all its variety? To what audience would each literary genre have appealed, and with what overlap?

Would any of the audience who enjoyed the antics of the magodes also have enjoyed Menander—and if Menander, then also Euripides? How many were literate, and to what level? How many went to school, or beyond school to the gymnasium? A recent book has suggested that the high point of Greek literacy occurred in certain Hellenistic cities, but even then reached only 20–30 per cent. But that figure seems a little arbitrary. In any case how does literacy or illiteracy affect the appreciation of literature in performance? And to what extent was there regional variation?

We are in the best position to assess élite culture, which leaves behind most traces; what we can see of it gives the impression of homogeneity. The educational system was conservative, and pressed the same texts into service wherever it spread. Canonical pieces of wisdom were disseminated—for example the maxims of the Seven Delphic Sages written on a wall at Ai Khanum, or epigrams and inscriptions which purvey standardized, prepackaged information: names of islands, rivers, poetesses, the Seven Wonders of the World. The Greek dialects gradually died out during the Hellenistic period, to be replaced by a species of international Greek known as *koine*, the common tongue. Did those who had been through a Greek education therefore come out knowing, speaking, thinking the same? Against the homogeneity thesis stands the wealth of local customs and traditions in each and every area that came within the orbit of Greek civilization, which could affect those of Greek descent as well as Hellenized non-Greeks; against it, too, the different forms Hellenism took when cross-bred with the pre-Greek civilizations of Egypt, Anatolia, Syria, Iran, or further still. Even with so much material before us, there is still so much that we do not and cannot know about this fascinating period.

8 Romanized Greeks and Hellenized Romans: Later Greek literature

JANE L. LIGHTFOOT

The fact of Roman rule

Kallimachos knew a story about Gaius the Roman, which he included in his *Causes*. Gaius was the hero of a battle against the Peucetii, who were besieging the city of Rome. But he was wounded in the battle, and the wound gave him a limp. His mother was as unsympathetic as Roman matrons of the old school always were. She just told him to stop complaining (fr. 107 Pfeiffer).

Not very informative perhaps, but typical. Like a Greek, Kallimachos only names Gaius by his praenomen, and we have hardly any idea who he was. The main point, though, is that Kallimachos has already reproduced a Roman story exactly in accordance with the ideology that created it. The Greeks had had long experience of this insistently militaristic nation through their dealings with southern Italy and Sicily. It was in 229 BCE that Roman military might first obtruded itself on the Greek mainland—a petty enough action against Illyrian pirates, but within not many decades a succession of military campaigns took advantage of the irresolution of the Hellenistic monarchies to bring what the historian Polybios called 'the whole inhabited world' under Roman sway. Mainland Greece became the Roman province of Macedonia when Lucius Mummius defeated Corinth and razed it to the ground in 146 BCE. (The Roman historian Tacitus thought that this was when theatrical performances were first imported into Rome: in fact they had existed long before, but the causal connection is quite a revealing mistake.) Imposts, taxes, and racketeering by officials led to the reduction of Greece to a state of miserable poverty and depopulation, so that by the first century one of Cicero's correspondents could point to the desolation of some of its most famous sites and cities—Aigina, Megara, Peiraieus, Corinth—to draw philosophical solace about the mutability of human affairs (*Ad familiares* 4. 5. 4).

But this was not the end of the matter: the fortunes of Greece and the Greek

East were to improve. The senatorial historians may have hated the Emperor Nero, but Nero was also one of the more extreme manifestations of Roman love of Greek culture; and he even briefly gave the Greeks their freedom. Under successive regimes Greek provincial aristocrats were admitted to the Roman senate, while philhellene emperors, especially Hadrian, bestowed benefactions which in the earlier Empire, no matter how well disposed their rulers had been to the Greeks, had somehow failed to materialize. In the second and third centuries CE Greek culture reached such heights of prestige, and educated Greeks had been so successful at brokering it to the Romans, that the Greek East actually enjoyed a prosperity such as it had never enjoyed before. These centuries have left some of antiquity's most splendid monuments. In mainland Greece, think of Herodes of Attica's beautification of Athens; and in Asia Minor, think of Ephesos. And there were no costly wars to dissipate the wealth gained by imperial patronage, nor to destroy the public monuments erected by rich benefactors eager to flaunt their goodwill. The age was no less abundant in its production of works of literature. This state of felicity was disrupted in the middle of the third century, with several decades of misrule; the period thereafter is conventionally labelled the Low or Late Empire, Christianized under Constantine (d. 337 CE). Yet many areas still enjoyed prosperity; barbarian invasions were more successfully repelled by the East than the West, while Christianity countered pagan religion and culture more successfully by borrowing its vocabulary than by warring against it. As the Roman Empire fell apart, literary education nevertheless managed to hold its own for quite a while in the eastern empire, though one by one the schools eventually closed. A symbolic date sometimes chosen for the final collapse of pagan culture is 529 CE, when Justinian closed the philosophical schools at Athens—though even then it was not altogether final.

Within a chronological and geographical framework as broad as this, generalizations are the best we can do. It is clear, though, just as with the Hellenistic period, that literary culture—high culture—was only available to relatively few. The state still did not bother with provision for elementary schools, for the assumption was that elementary education was to be had privately. Typically, though, the state *was* concerned to provide the prestigious high-profile resources enjoyed by the élite, as emperors founded 'professorships' of rhetoric and grammar in the big cities, and towns provided funding for middle- and high-level teachers. Libraries are more widely attested: the remains of the magnificent library of Celsus in Ephesos, for example, are among our most glamorous witnesses to the privately funded building projects in the second-century renaissance of the Greek East. But Ephesos was one of the chief centres of literary culture in Asia Minor: such privileged resources are still hardly

SHOWPIECE LIBRARY. *When Celsus, the distinguished citizen of Ephesos in Asia Minor who had become a Roman consul, died c.120 CE, his heirs built a magnificent monument over his mausoleum. This was a library which hoped to rival (in architecture at least) those of Pergamon and Alexandria.*

common. Oxyrhynchos in Egypt, whose life we now know so intimately from the contents of its ancient rubbish-dumps, must serve to illuminate the sorts of literature that might be available in a middle-ranking town (though we have no check on how typical it was). It is pleasing to find here, not only the inevitable Homer and Euripides and Menander, but also a good deal of exotica. Book-production, as ever, was subject to chance and circumstance, as scriptoria in which books could be produced and distributed *en masse* were still lacking. The normal method for a poet to publicize his works was still to give a reading and then distribute a copy among friends afterwards.

Greek literary culture is still strongly stamped with its traditional performative character. The performing arts, tragedy and comedy, are still attested (though nothing composed in this period survives), at least until local festivals peter out in the third and fourth centuries. So is dithyramb, the art of singing to the cithara, and other sorts of virtuoso recitals that took place in theatres. A genre which had a tremendous vogue was the art of the mime or pantomime—mimetic dancers who assumed roles from tragedy, myth, and romance, and acted them out to musical accompaniment. A series of inscriptions from the Greek East refers to these 'actors of rhythmic tragic movement', in honorific language as courteous as that employed for any performing artist, and show us that they were eventually allowed to take part in competitions in the traditional Greek festivals. We even possess a treatise enumerating their various roles, claiming they share their subject-matter with tragedy (Lucian, *On the Dance* 31). Its detractors might sneer at it, as at mere 'popular entertainment' (a typical piece of cultural snobbery), while its admirers rallied to its defence by alleging its kinship with tragedy, and (less plausibly) its educative and morally uplifting nature.

A great deal of Greek literature—in fact the bulk of what we possess—survives from the imperial period, but it does not come from such circles. Most was written by well-educated Greeks from the cities of old Greece or Asia Minor, which regained their old primacy in literary culture against the cities founded by the Hellenistic princes: even Alexandria was no longer the leading light. To well-educated Greeks careers were now open in the imperial administration, and much of our literature is written by those at, or with access to, the centres of political power. They, or their offspring, could become senators, or hold lucrative administrative posts, or, at the very highest level, provincial governorships and consulates. Those who achieved such heights tended to come from families which had held, and continued to hold, provincial dignities—priesthoods, magistracies, and important local offices. They and the philhellene Romans could understand each other because they aspired to a similar cultural ideal, that of polite learning or *paideia*. It was achieved by progressing through the stages of an élite education which the Greeks called *enkuklios paideia* and the Romans the *liberales artes*, conventional in subject-matter and predominantly rhetorical in approach, which was supposed to equip its beneficiaries for a laudable and suitably ill-defined goal—to receive 'virtue'. Our imperial Greek literature is mostly a literature of privilege, produced and received by the possessors of this polite culture.

The ideals of *paideia* and its largely homogenizing effects on those who possessed or sought it are illustrated on page after page. One of the most characteristic products of the age is the *Deipnosophistai*, or *Sophists at Table*, of Athenaios, a learned writer from Naukratis in Egypt who was active at the end of the second century CE. It documents, as do several other imperial treatises including Plutarch's *Questions of the Banqueters*, the longevity of the symposium in élite circles. Originally in thirty books but now in fifteen, it describes the course of a banquet, extending over several days, at which the learned guests include professors of literature, orators, jurists, philosophers, doctors, and a musician. Greeks and Romans all (it is hard to tell them apart when Greeks might carry Roman names through their acquisition of citizenship, and provincial Greeks might be descendants of Italian settlers), they are gathered in the house of a wealthy Roman bibliophile who is praised for his antiquarian learning in legal and religious history. He has been impelled to make his researches independently 'because of the decay of popular taste' (the ostentatious separatism is characteristic). The topics of the diners are as wide-ranging as their professions: law, music, literature, medicine, philosophy, food, and above all the conventions of the symposium itself. None is presented with any degree of originality, and indeed to require originality would be to miss the point. These learned gentlemen show off their knowledge using literary tags, and their refinement is demonstrated by their degree of intimacy with Greece's literary and cultural past. The epiphany of each new dish on the table is accompanied by quotations from a whole encyclopaedia of Greek authors (the work is far more often treated as a treasure-trove of excerpts from lost works than for its own sake), and it is characteristic of the age that knowledge itself is treated as a delicacy to be enjoyed by connoisseurs: 'the plan of the discourse reflects the rich bounty of a feast, and the arrangement of the book the courses of the dinner' (1b). 'Polymathy' is a term of the highest praise, and it is clear that it connotes genteel amateurism in a wide variety of pursuits. The first thing we hear of the great jurist Ulpian himself is his insistence on correct linguistic usage as attested in works of literature, an obsession he carries with him in public streets, avenues, bookshops, and baths.

Here is another important point: usage. From the middle of the first century BCE onwards, a literary movement had been gathering momentum, whose goal was the restoration of the linguistic usages—syntax and vocabulary—of fourth-century BCE Athens, which had now been canonized as the golden age of Greek prose. This Atticist movement obviously had different realizations and goals as times changed and the living language moved ever further away from the original Attic; different authors also exhibited very different degrees of commitment to the ideal. Nevertheless it was in principle an archaizing, purist movement whose adherents demonstrated their level of culture by classicism. At the end of the first century BCE the orator Dionysios of Halikarnassos recommended a range of ancient authors whose style might profitably be imitated; by the second century CE prescriptive lexica were in existence (the *Onomastikon* of Pollux, the *Ekloge* of Phrynichos) which labelled words 'Attic' or 'Hellenic' (that is, contemporary), or, worse still, 'common', to be avoided.

They had less to say about the contexts in which Atticism was to be put into practice, and the situation is complex because the living language itself had an educated form which might be preferred in some contexts for the sake of precision of meaning or conciseness of expression. Nonetheless the significant point is that now the issue had been raised, the language of literary prose could be as artificial as the literary language of poetry. Furthermore, the pursuit of Atticism was a mark of status, since no attempt was ever made to prescribe the linguistic usages of the non-élite. Galen (see p. 272), no lover of Atticism, makes this absolutely explicit by associating it with professional people and the well-to-do, or the merely ambitious; this was something to which the mob could not aspire.

What underlay such backward-looking classicism? According to some, it had come about precisely because the Greeks were now, effectively, politically impotent: it was a form of nostalgia for the days of the city-state. This needs nuancing: Greeks could rise to the highest positions of state albeit within the *Roman* administration, and the passion for classicism affected their political masters, the Romans, as well. In certain moods the Romans, no less than the Greeks, missed—or affected to miss—the cut and thrust of political rhetoric in the turbulent days when things were really happening, and expressed anxiety about their present state of well-fed inertia. Nevertheless the basic point remains: for the Greeks the question underlying this whole, huge, period, a key theme in the present chapter is, how does one respond to the realities of Roman rule?

The historiography of Empire

The genre that best illustrates the shifting responses to this question, and the changing contexts in which it was posed, is historiography. The first to consider is Polybios, born around 200 BCE in Achaia, but taken to Rome in 167 as one of a thousand political detainees who were held there, indefinitely, without charge. His *Histories* were originally intended to cover the period from 220 to 167, but he explains in a preface that he extended his former design by a further ten books, so as to cover the years up to the destructions of Carthage and Corinth in the year 146. Of the forty books of the entire work, the first five are intact, and most of the remainder survives in abridgements and excerpts. For Polybios, the sudden irruption of Roman power needed explanation, and though he refers several times to a Roman readership (and an élite readership at that), it is more likely that the majority of his readers would be Greeks, as bemused by Rome's sudden ascendancy as he. Not that Polybios' brand of hard-headed *Realpolitik*—'pragmatic history' is what he calls it—tells his readers what to think. In dispassionate Thucydidean tones he tells them that, while it would be reasonable to expect Greeks to help other Greeks out in time of trial, 'by defending them, masking their errors, or deprecating the wrath of the ruling power', nevertheless history's sole aim should be to tell the truth (38. 4. 7–8), and it will help them avoid similar mistakes in the future. Polybios is more specific than Thucydides about history's value as prophylaxis.

Writing a century after Polybios, Poseidonios of Apamea no longer needed to come to terms with the upstart newcomer: Roman rule was a fact of life. His work began where Polybios' left off and took the story up to the 80s, or perhaps the 60s, BCE. Although it was an extensive work, in fifty-two books, history was not by any means the speciality of its author, a Stoic philosopher and leading intellectual. But since it survives only in fragments, the reconstruction of its attitudes is fraught with difficulty.

In the Augustan period a trio of writers emerges—Diodoros of Sicily, Nikolaos of Damaskos, and Dionysios of Halikarnassos. Two are writers of 'universal history'—in theory, the history of all peoples in the known inhabited world: it is no accident that this efflorescence of universal writings coincides with Roman universal dominion (the universal geographer Strabon, discussed on pp. 272–3 below, was also in the same circles of patronage as Dionysios). Nikolaos (born *c.*64 BCE) was court historian of Herod the Great, and wrote on wonders and marvels in the genre of 'paradoxography', also an autobiography, and a panegyric of Augustus. But of his 144-book universal history, the only surviving excerpts come from books 1–7, dealing with early history up to the time of the Achaemenids, and 123–4, on the reign of Herod the Great. The situation is very different with Diodoros, of whose forty-book universal history to the year 60 BCE, books 1–5 and 11–20 survive in their entirety, the rest in excerpts. This is a substantial amount of text. Diodoros' primary interest is in Greece and his native Sicily until his sources for Roman history begin to fill out at the start of the First Punic War. And then there is Dionysios, whose *Roman Antiquities* in twenty books cover the entire period from Rome's foundation to the end of the First Punic War. We still have the first eleven books, and excerpts of the rest. Diodoros and Dionysios were both immigrants to Rome, a move typical of the demographics of first-century BCE intellectual life. But their responses to the ruling culture are in great contrast. While Diodoros' relations to the Romans seem to have been somewhere between distant and hostile—we hear of no links with Romans of influence—the well-connected Dionysios threw himself energetically into the task of elaborating the old Greek myth of the Romans' Trojan descent—a story Diodoros actually denied. It was a traditional Greek mechanism for dealing with a non-Greek people to make them their kinsmen by mythical descent; Dionysios goes further by emphasizing connections with Greece throughout every stage of Rome's cultural infancy.

He explains his procedure in his preface. Many Greeks labour under a misapprehension about the Romans, considering them vagabonds whom Fortune has unjustly brought to power: he, therefore, will demonstrate the truth of the matter (1. 4. 2–3). He will instil his message into minds willing to hear the truth about the Romans, so that they cease to feel indignant at Fortune: the superior inevitably rule the inferior (1. 5. 2). Early Roman history, moreover, abounds in virtuous deeds and doings which hitherto have lacked their historian, so that the Greeks have been unaware of them: and he, Dionysios, will step into the breach. This apparently targets Greeks as the audience. Yet things are not quite so simple. Whereas one suspects that a Greek readership may in fact underlie Polybios' references to Roman readers, in Dionysios it is evident that his references to Greeks in fact imply Roman addressees. For a little later, he adds his hope that the descendants of these early Roman heroes will be fired by ambition on hearing the tales of their ancestors (1. 6. 4). He means to map their conduct onto that of modern-day Romans, so it is they who are targeted by his encomia. He thus presents the Romans with an idealized model, of which the subject nation naturally hopes its rulers will be worthy. His cleverly devised work is worthy of his profession as an orator, and his other special claim on our interest is that we possess several of his works of literary criticism—studies of Thoukydides and of individual orators, and works on imitation and prose style, where he unsurprisingly emerges in the van of the Atticist movement. He associates the triumph of Atticism with the triumph of Roman civilization and rationality, a happy union of the stylistic and the political. With Dionysios we see principles put into practice in rhetorical historiography.

After the Augustans no Greek historian seems to have cared to write a synoptic history of Rome until the middle of the second century, with the twenty-four-book *Roman History* of Appian of Alexandria. Appian enjoyed imperial patronage, at a modest level. He chose a novel format for his work—not the annalistic one covering events year by year, but treating each people separately in order as they fell under Roman domination. This means he was able to present Rome's rise to power from the provincial viewpoint, and he makes no attempt to whitewash the Romans. Of his great work, the portions that survive deal with Rome's civil wars, and wars with the Celts, Spain, Hannibal, Carthage, Illyria, Syria, and Mithridates. Lost are the books on the regal period, Egypt (a particularly unfortunate loss), Dacia, and Arabia, and on the conquest of Greece. He is entirely dependent on his sources, though he has good taste in choosing them.

Appian's contemporary Arrian (born 85–90 CE) was the first known Greek senator from Bithynia. His contemporaries knew him best as a philosopher, and he published a record of the teachings of the Stoic Epiktetos whom he had heard in Nikopolis in north-western Greece in the 120s. But he was also, like many others, exercised by Greece's famous past. His *Anabasis* told of a journey which easily rivalled Xenophon's in his work of the same title (cf. p. 154)—the history of Alexander the Great. Other works are adjuncts to this: a virtuoso piece of Indian ethnography in the Ionic dialect, and a lost continuation of the Alexander history. Persistent loyalty to a native land he had left behind can be seen in his *Bithynian History*, while devotion to the Trajanic regime can be surmised in the *Parthian History* and its Roman set-up. These twin focuses of loyalty are typical of Greek intellectuals of his age. Most imperial historiography, whether in Greek or in Latin, was written by senatorial historians, following a principle first exemplified by Thoukydides, whereby the historian was also a man of affairs. This remained true even in times whose political uneventfulness led to complaints that historiography, real historiography, had lost its bite. By the time the last full history of Rome was written by the reactionary senator Cassius Dio in the first half of the third century, the author had identified so completely with Rome that he did not feel the need to eulogize or even to discuss her at all.

The second era of 'Sophists'

Rhetorical historiography, with its speechifying, *exempla*, floridity, and high moral tone, was a typical product of its age. For all types of formal and public language had now become rhetoricized. The Attic orators (cf. Ch. 6) were the objects of greatest admiration. Indeed, the contexts in which public speeches had been made in classical times were still occasions for rhetoric, but a great many more now joined to them. One would make formal speeches on deputations to an emperor, or provincial governor, or to welcome a dignitary into one's own city. There were speeches of praise, invitation, thanks, pleading, and condolence; speeches to mark arrivals and departures; epideictic or display-rhetoric on public occasions, and private speeches at weddings and funerals.

Not the most distinguished, but among the most characteristic, works of the period are the two treatises which date from the third or fourth centuries and go under the name of Menander Rhetor—a *rhetor* is an exponent of the art of public speaking, which became a distinctive profession in these days of display and showmanship. They codify the typical motifs, tropes, or *topoi*, of the various genres of speeches as we see them exemplified in literature—not, of course, as mechanically as this, but still creatively deployed within a very conventionalized framework. The first treatise begins with the general theory of epideictic oratory, and concentrates mainly on encomia of countries and cities. The second work gives detailed rules about speeches on miscellaneous public and private occasions, and even lays down a framework for a type of talk whose purpose is to give a semblance of spontaneity, the *lalia*. They both point out appropriate classical, and some 'modern', stylistic models for use in particular contexts—Plato for a rapt, visionary tone, Xenophon for graceful language, Isokrates and Demosthenes for their handling of particular genres of forensic or epideictic rhetoric. Stilted, platitudinous, even laughable they may be (witness the *kateunastikos logos* or 'bedroom speech', an earnest sermon delivered to the bridegroom outside the bridal chamber); nevertheless they are eloquent about the sorts of rhetoric which public and private occasions required and expected. Displays requiring bravura handling of conventional material were ways in which the age demonstrated its *politesse* and its continuity with the past.

There was a period from the end of the first century to the middle of the third when the declamation was the most highly regarded of all literary activities, and the most celebrated professional orators enjoyed unparalleled influence and privilege. This age was called the 'Second Sophistic' by the man who wrote it up and gathered *Lives* of its foremost exponents, Philostratos, writing at the beginning of the third century. Philostratos distinguished the Second Sophistic, which took historical themes or personality-types as its subject-matter, from the 'First Sophistic', spearheaded by the classical sophist Gorgias (cf. pp. 167–8). Oddly, Philostratos specified that Aischines was founder of the Second Sophistic movement, though he was unable to name more than a very few continuators of his alleged school before the imperial centuries. But in so far as the imperial rhetors did not spring from nowhere, he was right. They were the descendants of the Hellenistic orators who acted as international diplomats, of the prize speakers in inscriptions documenting performances at festivals, and of the literary gentlemen of the Greek East who came on embassies to Rome from their beleaguered homelands at the end of the Republic and beginning of the Empire. It had always been their literary culture that had given them the right to speak and be heard by their political overlords, and in our period they attained a prestige which peace, prosperity, and the possibilities of advancement available to Greeks could translate into real political and economic power.

Some of the biggest names among this new type of sophist include Herodes of Attica, Adrianos of Tyre, and Favorinus the anomaly from Gaul (who, to make matters worse, was supposed to be a eunuch). Most of their works are lost: Herodes' gorgeous embellishments to the city of Athens have survived, while his literary monuments, save one extant in Arabic translation, have not. Of the authors mentioned in Philostratos' *Lives*, the only ones whose work survives in bulk are Dion of Prousa (eighty treatises attributed to him) and Aelius Aristeides (over forty surviving works). Yet both men's status as sophists is questionable. Dion is part-rhetor, part-philosopher (the two professions are in theory distinct and not infrequently hostile, yet have a wide overlap), while Aristeides called himself a 'rhetor' yet never 'sophist', would not declaim extemporaneously, and spent much energy trying to extricate himself from the expensive public duties or 'liturgies' which a prominent public figure would be expected to undertake.

Sophists sometimes declaimed on forensic themes, taking improbable scenarios whose rights and wrongs they elaborated with gusto. But more often they preferred the historical topics mentioned by Philostratos as characteristic of their repertoire. Invariably these pertained to the golden age of classical Greece, the orators, or Alexander's conquests. Innumerable episodes are on record as declamation topics from the Peloponnesian War, the career of Demosthenes, or the meeting of Dareios and Alexander (cf. e.g. Aristeides, 5, *On Sending Reinforcements to those in Sicily*, and 6, *The Opposite Argument*). Aristeides shadow-boxed with Plato on the worth of rhetoric. Philostratos also understands elegant trifles—unserious encomia, such as Dion's *Encomium of a Parrot*, or Lucian's *Encomium of a Fly*—as fit matter for sophistic rhetoric. But his definition barely allows for the political speeches made by sophists—encomia of cities (for example, praises of Rome, Athens, Kyzikos, all by Aristeides, and sounding suspiciously alike), speeches of advice to cities and emperors (Dion's four *Discourses on Kingship*, all probably addressed to Trajan), tonics for civic discord (Aristeides, 24, *To The Rhodians: Concerning Concord*), praise of gods (Aristeides' prose hymns to Athene, Asklepios, Dionysos, Herakles, Zeus), fundraising appeals for cities (e.g. Aristeides, 17–21, the series of orations concerning Smyrna, which had been devastated by an earthquake and sought imperial funds to restore it). The ceremonial function of these speeches was far more important than the pragmatic value of what was said. One of Dion's most famous and constantly imitated speeches or *Orations* was the Euboian discourse, in fact a misty-eyed evocation of the life of virtuous Euboian peasants, followed by a profoundly unrealistic programme of urban social reform (*Orations* 7). By far his longest speech, the Rhodian Discourse (*Orations* 31), fears for the Rhodians' international reputation as a result of their practice of rededicating statues; *Orations* 33 lengthily rebukes the Tarsians for an obscure national vice usually translated as 'snorting'. Matters of great international moment these were not; they were the pastimes and amusements of the affluent in well-off cities.

It was more than this, of course. It was power and prestige for its practitioners, wealth for the cities who hosted the events, and above all, advertisements by all who took part that they possessed Hellenic *paideia*. In his twelfth Oration, held at the still-great panhellenic centre of Olympia, Dion evoked the crowd's pleasure in the 'formidable rhetors, delightful writers of verse and prose, sophists with their followers, lifted up as if on the wings of their reputation like peacocks'. It was, for him and for them, a great pageant. The great sophists performed with such theatricality that their techniques were sometimes referred to as a *skene*, the word for the backdrop of a theatre. Philostratos describes the performances of Polemon thus:

> He would come forward to declaim with a relaxed and confident face ... He would consider the proposed subject, not in public, but withdrawing briefly from the crowd. His voice was clear and true, and there was a marvellous ringing quality in his delivery. Herodes says that he even leapt from his chair at high-points in his argument, so great had his impetus become, and when he rounded off a period he would pronounce the final phrase with a smile on his face as if to demonstrate the ease with which he said it; at certain points in his arguments he would stamp his feet just like the horse in Homer. (*Vitae Sophistarum* 537)

No matter that the content of the sophists' speeches was mostly trite and commonplace: it was sheer artistry. Audiences would cheer to hear the masters round off their beautifully turned, effortless periods.

Sophists tended to come from mainland Greece—Athens, to be more precise—and the old cities of Asia Minor, especially Ephesos and Smyrna. And they usually came from wealthy backgrounds, since their training and professional activities entailed the outlay of large amounts of money, for fees, travelling expenses, and above all for the benefactions expected of prominent individuals and office-holders. When Lucian (Greek Loukianos) was a young man, as he later told the story, he was first apprenticed to a stonemason, deterred from the further pursuit of *paideia* by its expense. He returned to education as a result of his unhappy experiences as an apprentice and after a dream in which Paideia herself made him grandiose promises—fame and illustrious friends—and showed him a vision of all the lands where he could reap eloquence's rewards.

Lucian was a native of Samosata, a former provincial capital of Roman Syria. He refers several times to himself as a Syrian, wearing Syrian costume in his youth and speaking, not Greek, but Aramaic. His Greek culture was a secondary acquisition, a fact which may explain his touchiness about his Greek, and he never became a star sophist; Lucian himself distinguishes his 'popular rhetoric' (*rhetorike demosia*) from that of the sophists (*Apology* 15). He describes his own activity in several passages: he travelled the cities giving lectures (*epideixeis* and *akroaseis*), not always in the most prestigious locations (Philippopolis, modern Plovdiv, was not the big time for a sophist), in some places more than once, and at least once returning to his home town. The talks, prepared in advance, were sometimes preceded by a prologue or *prolalia*, some of which are extant. He says more than once that the crowd found his talks strange and novel; but he professes to *want* to be praised, not for novelty, which matters nothing in itself, but for the virtues the age admires most: good, Atticist vocabulary; conformity to the ancient canon; keenness of mind; and good construction.

But what was the novelty? About eighty works by Lucian survive, and include a few sophistic pieces of the types noted above. Many are harangues or essays delivered in the first person, but his main novelty lay in the genre perhaps most characteristic of him, the dialogue. Not the Aristotelian dialogue, given over as it was to lengthy exposés in essay form, but a racy version of the Platonic dialogue dedicated to Lucian's favourite subject, the relentless exposure of pretension, folly, and vice in all its species. As he himself views the matter, his dialogues have married the philosophic dialogue, comedy, the sort of popular harangue or diatribe associated with the Cynic school, and a type of social satire combining prose and verse and known as 'Menippean' after Menippos of Gadara. Here, for example, is Lucian's take on the rhetorical circuit in which he lived and the crowds which it drew, in the form of pseudo-advice to a would-be rhetor:

> So they admire the copiousness of your speeches, begin with the *Iliad* or the wedding of Deukalion and Pyrrha, or whatever takes your fancy, and take the story as far as the present day. There'll be few who will understand you, and they'll mostly keep silent out of courtesy anyway. And even if they do say anything they'll be thought to do it out of envy. Most people will marvel at your get-up, voice, gait, bearing, sing-song delivery, high-heeled shoes and affected diction; and when they see you sweat and pant

> they won't be able to stop themselves believing you a formidable opponent in debates. Anyway, your extempore skill will make up for a lot and will make the crowd admire you. Be sure never to write anything down or come forward prepared, as that is sure to show you up. (*Rhetorum Praeceptor* 20)

This does not make for comfortable reading, but beyond what he tells us we hardly know how people reacted to him. His great subsequent popularity as a hard-hitting and witty cynic tells us nothing about ancient responses. Only one contemporary, Galen, mentions him, and that is to tell a story about how he forged a treatise in the style of Herakleitos: a philosopher wrote a learned commentary on the work, and Lucian enjoyed his discomfiture when he revealed the work as a fake. It would be typical, if true. It takes a Lucian to show us the counter-side of all those refined gentlemen discussing sympotic culture in Rome—an ignorant Syrian book-collector who amasses books out of the proceeds of a legacy merely in order to show off. Instead of the internationally famous sophists, he shows us meretricious attention-seekers, with nothing to recommend them but loud voices and lubricious manners. And instead of professors of philology, pedants.

The varieties of learning

The connections between rhetoric and philosophy are illuminated by many other authors besides Lucian. They might lie at the level of literary form: Lucian borrowed the clothes of the dialogue and diatribe. Or they might consist in the use of rhetorical techniques of delivery. What qualified representatives of very different professions to be dubbed 'sophists' by Athenaios was skill at expounding their various subjects (they include a lawyer, a musician, and a doctor). But the connection subsisted especially at the level of content. Dion's treatises are replete with commonplaces from the dominant philosophical sect of imperial times, Stoicism. Philosophy and rhetoric reached their happiest union, however, in Plutarch (Greek Ploutarchos) of Chaironeia (born before 50 CE, died after 120). 'Philosopher', if anything, is what he should be called. But he was also a scholar, either with access to an extremely well-stocked library of his own, or gifted with a prodigious memory—and probably both. And for the last thirty years of his life he was a priest at Delphi, combining faith in traditional religion and expertise on cultic antiquities with a more intellectualized, philosophic piety. The following passage is taken from Plutarch's account of the Egyptian deities Isis and Osiris. Far from trying to anathematize them as tainted 'oriental' monstrosities, he claims that they stand for things common to all mankind. It is typical of Plutarch, presupposing readers who share his sort of benign universalism, and a framework in which potential tensions between competing races and religions can be smoothed out by calm rationality:

> Nor do we think that different people have different gods, barbarian and Greek, south and north. But just as the sun and moon, ocean and land and sea, are common to all, though called by different names among different peoples, in the same way for the one Reason that ordains all and for the one Providence that governs them, and for the assistant powers appointed over all things, there are different conventional names and prerogatives among different peoples. They sanction the use of symbols, some of which are obscure and others clear, which direct the intellect towards the divine. (*Isis and Osiris* 67)

The seventy-eight surviving treatises which together constitute his so-called 'Moral Essays', or *Moralia*, represent about a third of his original output in this field: Plutarch was fluent, relaxed, and discursive. As a philosopher he has little claim to originality, nor is it easy to trace much development in his thought. He too uses the dialogue form, but this time in the Aristotelian rather than Platonic mould, with long speeches of exegesis—not, however, entirely at the expense of characterization. He writes mainly on themes of popular moral philosophy, emphasizing ties of private affection, devotion to the gods, and acquiescence in Roman rule. He seems to have been only on the fringes of sophistic culture: no true sophist would have stayed in a backwater like Chaironeia, and Plutarch claims his residence was in order to stop the place becoming smaller still. It is the dedications of his treatises that give us the clearest idea of his audience (not that they need imply any degree of intimacy with their dedicatees): they include Greek notables, literary men (Dion among them), but also those involved in imperial administration. His biographies—to which we shall return—are dedicated to Q. Sosius Senecio, twice consul (99 and 107 CE). Yet the treatises are also peopled by locals and by those Plutarch had known in his student days in Athens: doctors, philosophers, literary men. 'Plutarch's aim was to convey the essence of Hellenistic *paideia* to his pupils, to his powerful contemporaries, and to posterity', in the words of his most distinguished recent commentator.

Medicine, at this period, is also closely allied with philosophy. Rhetoric could do little more than influence the style of its presentation; yet medicine might lend itself to display and *epideixis*. Dion scathingly describes public displays put on by doctors, who 'sit themselves down in our midst and run through all the linkages of joints and articulations of bones and their juxtapositions and that sort of thing, pores and respirations and filtrations. And the crowd are all agog and more spellbound than children.' But it was doubtless a course of lectures of a very different kind that helped bring Galen, Greek Galenos (born 129 CE), recognition in Rome; Galen is not to be connected with the sophists. Perhaps the most prolific writer of the entire imperial period, and certainly its most formidable polymath, his writings fill over twenty volumes in the standard nineteenth-century edition. Here I cannot even begin to sketch his achievements in anatomy and physiology, pathology and psychology, his scholarly labours on the writings of the Hippocratic school, nor his influence on contemporaries and posterity. Yet we cannot overlook a man who exercised his talents in so many fields—including grammar and philology and the philosophy of language. Born in Pergamon to wealthy parents, Galen had pursued the normal school curriculum for a boy of his class, and though he had little time for either literary connoisseurship among Greeks or for philhellenic posturing among Romans, he never lost his concern for language as a tool for precise self-expression, nor his flair for rhetorical self-promotion.

Another subject allied to philosophy was geography. There are two important imperial treatises on geography: the *Geography* of Strabon and the *Periegesis* of Pausanias. Strabon, writing in the reigns of Augustus and Tiberius, was the author of the first universal geography in seventeen books. An essentially descriptive and mostly practical account, it works slowly from west to east, stretching from Spain to Iran, Arabia and Egypt; Strabon himself is located in Rome, the political centre. He is a priceless source for ancient geography, topography, ethnography, social and political history, and for Augustan intellectual culture in general. The broad sweep of the first two books, which discuss theoretical matters, the philosophy of geography, his predecessors, and the geographer's proper attitude towards Homer (an unavoidable question), is complemented by the rich, empiricist detail of the remaining fifteen. He emphasizes the need for wide learning, *polymatheia*, in order to write geography. But his addressees are men of affairs, not theoreticians, and can be relied on to have a basic level of technical competence, beyond which they need only the general attainments of *paideia* in order to be able to follow the book. He stresses his subject's practical utility, especially for rulers, statesmen, and generals, those 'who bring together cities and peoples into a single empire and political management', and he claims that its uses are in the domains of politics and the public weal; his work is explicitly intended for 'those in high office' (1. 1. 23). Yet his true critics, those most fit to judge his work are those acquainted with 'virtue and reflection and the studies that pertain to them' (1. 1. 22): in other words, his addressees, the ruling élite, are the gentlemen amateurs. He writes from Rome, addresses Romans, and is an apologist for Roman rule. Yet he shows his greatest degree of personal involvement when discussing Greek intellectual culture of Asia Minor, his political and cultural horizons somewhat out of focus in a way which also emerges in the writings of Galen and other Greek intellectuals. Greeks could also read his work, and there is some limited evidence that they did; and Strabon's representation of Greeks and Romans to each other looks both backwards and forwards to other historians and orators.

Pausanias' work is very different in character. Written in the middle of the second century CE, it is essentially a study of the monuments of old, mainland Greece; Pausanias takes little note of anything later than Hellenistic. 'Periegesis' is literally a 'leading around', and the work, in ten books, conducts its reader through an ambitiously large, but still delimited space, concentrating on cults and temples, votive monuments and other works of art, myth, history, and the grey area in between. He appears to have witnessed most of them for himself, and he is a demonstrably accurate guide. There is no programmatic introduction, no theoretical preface: Pausanias launches straight in with 'On the Greek mainland opposite the Kyklades islands and the Aegean sea, the promontory of Sounion projects from the Attic land', beginning, as only appropriate, with Attica.

He himself seems to have come from Magnesia-on-Sipylos in Lydia, and his references to persons are, yet again, predominantly to the Greek intellectuals of Asia Minor. We are left to infer his readership from the work itself. The itineraries are planned so that real travellers could follow them, but there is also matter for the armchair tourist. The combination is perhaps not very practical in either context, but Pausanias' envisaged audience is anyone who wanted to know about Greek antiquities. In theory it could be Greeks or Romans, in practice it was perhaps slightly likelier to be Greeks, but in actuality there is no evidence about any ancient readership until he came to be excerpted by the late imperial grammarian Stephanos of Byzantion, who rather missed the point, being interested only in geographical names and their ethnic adjectives.

Perhaps the most famous episode from Pausanias is an anecdote eloquent about the international culture of its day and the intellectual *koine* shared by Greek-speakers from all over the Empire (7. 23. 7–8). He recalls meeting a Phoenician from Sidon in an Achaian sanctuary of Asklepios. The Phoenician, strikingly silent about the traditional Sidonian identification of their patron deity as Asklepios, instead launches into a philosophic discourse in which he asserts that Phoenician notions are superior to the Greek: Asklepios is really the fresh, healthy air. Nonsense, interjects Pausanias: this is a Greek idea just as much as a Phoenician one. To such an extent had these banal rationalizations become common currency that both cultures, Greek and Phoenician, could wrangle over them and claim them as their own.

Fiction

Greek fictional writing seems to answer many of our own requirements: to revalue the canon, to engage with what could be seen as antiquity's most postmodern genre, to elicit evidence about evolving ancient attitudes to the relation of the sexes, in which the novels are so rich. But the novel in antiquity is an amorphous category embracing different types of narrative under a single umbrella, defined, of course, in modern terms. We need to distinguish several types of narrative. 'Ideal' romances are concerned with the trials of a boy and a girl who, in the standard plot, fall in love at the outset, are then separated and suffer such slings and arrows as abduction by pirates, slavery, mock-sacrifice, and, worst of all, the predatory advances of would-be seducers, but who are eventually reunited with their fidelity more or less intact to consummate their love-match. This category extends from relatively simple narratives, such as the anonymous romances of Ninos and of Parthenope and Metiochos, to fully fledged novels. Of these Chariton and Xenophon of Ephesos are relatively plain, while at the other end of the scale are the three 'sophistic' novels by Heliodoros, Achilles Tatius, and Longus, so-called because they exhibit the literary, linguistic, and rhetorical sophistications of the age of the sophists. Goethe liked Longus' novel about the loves of the innocent rustics Daphnis and Chloe so much that he recommended yearly rereading. It dramatizes their loss of innocence against the background of the changing seasons. Here is the moment when Chloe first falls in love with Daphnis, which illustrates the *faux-naïf* tone which is sustained throughout the whole:

> She persuaded him to have another bath, and watched him bathe, and as she watched, touched him, and went away praising him, and her praise was the beginning of love. The young country-bred girl had no idea what had happened to her, never having even heard the name of love. Her soul was in distress; she was not mistress of where her eyes wandered; and she kept babbling Daphnis' name. She forgot to eat, stayed awake at night, ignored her flock. Now she would smile, now cry; now she slept, now started up. Her complexion was pallid, but suddenly burned with a flaming blush. Never was cow more tormented by a gadfly.

Such tender and—mostly—chaste loves are very different from the salacious romps we find in another class of narrative—the tales of innocence lost in squalor and knockabout bawdry in works such as Petronius' *Satyricon* in Latin (cf. pp. 502–3), and, in Greek Lollianus' *Phoenician Tales* or the Iolaos story (both preserved on papyrus). Then there are novels of travel and wanderings: Antonius Diogenes' *Wonders Beyond Thule*, or Philostratos' own *Life* of Apollonios of Tyana, or the send-up of such writings in Lucian's *True Story*, a Swiftian broadside against travellers' humbug, and indeed a great influence on *Gulliver's Travels*. And there are also novelistic elaborations of the deeds of historical kings: most influentially, the Alexander Romance, but also tales of the Pharaoh Sesonchosis (Herodotos' Sesostris) which may go back to narratives with which the Egyptians trumped their arrogant Persian overlords. A classical prefiguration of this genre is Xenophon's pious romanticization of the childhood of Cyrus, the *Cyropaedia*. Pseudo-historical backgrounds confer a patina of historiographical authenticity on other works, too: the court of Polykrates of Samos is the setting for the romance of Parthenope and Metiochos, while the heroine of Xenophon of Ephesos was supposedly the daughter of the statesmen who led Syracusan opposition to imperialist classical Athens. Another sort of narrative is the Troy romance, with surviving specimens in both Latin and Greek. Characteristically, these are apocryphal chronicles purportedly written by participants in the conflict, and set out to elaborate on the accounts of the Trojan War in the epic cycle. Finally, via embroideries on the lives of national heroes, romantic motifs find their way into apocryphal religious literature: such are the novellas of Joseph and Asenath, or of St Paul and Thecla.

Our earliest specimen of narrative fiction is a papyrus romance about the Assyrian king Ninos, the handwriting datable to some time between 50 BCE and 50 CE. The latest may be the *Ethiopian Story* of Heliodoros, conventionally of the late fourth century, though an influential new view would place it towards the middle of the third century, also the date of Philostratos' *Life* of Apollonios (cf. p. 279). As for place, it seems that a, or the, major area from which the novel's influence radiated was the west coast of Asia Minor. For this is a focus of interest for several novels, and the purported homeland of many novelists. It is also the notional setting of a species of seedy narrative called 'Milesian Tales' which influenced episodes in some of the extant novels. On the face of it, some of our works of fiction could be products of the long-established Greek communities of the eastern Aegean and Anatolia, where high levels of culture were available for élites in the cities. Chariton, author of one of the less complex ideal romances, claims to come from Aphrodisias in Caria.

The question of the origins of the novel is now seen as something of a dead-end. We cannot hope to separate out the ingredients of so complex a confection, nor assign clear-cut genealogies to so inveterate a hybrid. The novel is grand panjandrum appropriating, as it needs them, elements of historiography, epic, tragedy, comedy (especially New Comedy), plot-devices lifted from myths and folk-stories, facts and fantasies from travel literature, and topoi scavenged from suitable earlier material. On the other hand, it is well worth debating the question of readership. It is true that we have very little evidence indeed outside the texts themselves, so that we are as unlikely to reach a definitive answer. Nevertheless, the questions are real, and need to be asked.

One view of the matter is based on anachronistic assumptions. Like modern pulp fiction, the novels were written for mass consumption, and since their subject-matter—love, in the case of the ideal romances—is trivial, the readership was mainly female, or juvenile. The alternative would be to believe that adult males in the senescence of Greek civilization had sunk to reading such rubbish. The women-and-children thesis is now quite out of favour, recognized as a mostly modern projection, unsupported by probability that very many women or juveniles had the requisite literacy levels, and uncorroborated by the fragments discovered on papyrus. On the one hand, the physical form of these is not different from that of other literary fragments; on the other, they are conspicuously few in number, far fewer than those of the favoured prose authors. And both sophistic novels and the more 'popular' works are represented. So this was no mass-produced plebeian genre: antiquity had no such thing as pulp fiction. Papyri inform us that some inhabitants of the middle-ranking towns of Roman Egypt read fiction ranging from Lollianus to Achilles Tatius, but other data is harder to find. Mosaics of Ninos and Metiochos in a second-century villa in Antioch were not necessarily inspired by novels rather than mimes. And while we can certainly find scattered allusions to various novels in imperial literature, literary sources almost by definition are records of élites. So we cannot conclude either that the novels in question were *meant* primarily for a readership of that level, or that they even *reached* mainly those readers.

Deductions drawn from the novels themselves are no less slippery. The narrative technique of the earlier ones tends to be simpler—but need this imply a 'simpler' audience? And if, on the other hand, the narrative technique of the sophistic novels is more complex, need this imply a more sophisticated readership? The sophistic novels use Atticizing Greek, while others are linguistically much less polished (Lollianus, for example). But would it really be fair to conclude either that a classically educated gentleman had little time for Lollianus, or that *none* but the classically educated gentleman can have enjoyed Achilles Tatius? Yet allusiveness is, in many novelists, at such a premium that an advanced education must have been an advantage, if not a requirement. Chariton (not even among the sophistic novelists) draws on a formidable array of archaic, classic, and Hellenistic works from the canonical authors in many genres. It seems reasonably likely that the educated who knew and relished the domestic complications of Menander, the emotionality of a Euripidean tirade, and the courtroom rhetoric of Demosthenes, would be the novel's optimal readers. A further point to note is the novel's intertextuality, not only with other genres, but with itself. The sophistic novels seem to presuppose the readers' familiarity with the conventions of the genre, while even the most *outré* of the novels, exhibiting the bawdries of Lollianus, Diogenes, or the Greek original of Apuleius' *Golden Ass*, gain in richness if they are seen as pointed travesties of the 'ideal' romance. The genre is self-referential and potentially self-parodic even in its early manifestations.

There are also richer veins to be tapped on the subject of their milieux. One view has been that novels play out the spiritual isolation of rootless Hellenistic and post-Hellenistic man; the other side of this coin, equally suspect, is that the novels are in fact designed to guide initiates by means of coded messages to personal salvation in mystery religions. The novel has become the playground for social, even intellectual, historians, seeking to recover reflections and refractions of society's changing attitudes to love, sex, marriage, the city, the gods. Their emphasis on highly eroticized chastity *for males* as a prelude to marriage seems unlike anything in the classical period. Does this new emphasis (which Christians could exploit in novellae about the virgin brides of Christ) reflect a change in sexual morality, or is it not quite so simple?

Above all, the ideal novels bring married love to the fore and endow mutual passion with a positive value not hitherto seen. Women could perhaps identify with this, though it is still far from proving that they *did* read these works—and it is further still from genuine sexual equality.

And so to a genre which, in certain incarnations, can be a species of prose fiction, biography. Yet it is important to stress that with biography, we are not speaking of a single category at all, but rather, of a body of writing loosely defined in modern terms by its subject-matter, which in ancient texts can manifest itself in writings of enormously different types. And in the imperial period there was a huge effloresence of many types of biography, some in the old style—lives of generals and statesmen and philosophers—and many more in new forms, such as the life of the holy man or saint or Christian martyr. The reasons lie in complex political, social, intellectual, and spiritual developments whose momentum effected other types of change throughout society. There are two things to keep in mind. First, through all the complex ramifications involved in a discussion of the ancient concept of 'character', it is to be remembered that throughout antiquity there remained a basic notion that man was an objectifiable unit in a rational, fundamentally knowable universe. Secondly, biography reflects just as much on its writer as on its subject.

The culmination of the classical tradition of biography is Plutarch. In total we possess forty-eight of his biographies, of which forty-four belong to a series of *Comparative Lives* of Greeks and Romans. The scheme was not his invention, but he wrought it to its most elaborate form. The life of a Greek is juxtaposed with that of a Roman who pursued a similar career, and the two are followed by a comparison or *synkrisis* which follows the method of the rhetorical schools (and does not show Plutarch at his best). The best lies in the ambitiousness of the overall design and its amassing of rich and evocative and sympathetic detail. Essentially what he gives are vignettes bridged by link-passages, rather than continuous narrative, each of which is underpinned by the question, 'What sort of a man was he?' These heroes are all knowable and fundamentally static.

The design is thought-provoking: is it an assertion of cultural parity? Did Plutarch intend it as a demonstration to both Greeks and Romans of each other's capacities? Did he even, as has sometimes been suggested, intend to show Romans that Greeks were generals as good as they, and Greeks that Romans were just as civilized? There may be something in this, for one of Plutarch's other treatises, *The Glory of Athens*, presents a similar argument about the Greeks, which may have been topical at a time when Greeks were being newly admitted to the Senate. Yet in the *Lives* themselves, Plutarch only ever speaks of an ethical purpose. He tells us in the preface to the *Timoleon* that he began the work 'for the sake of others', to teach and improve them. Hearing of virtue and nobility immediately generates an imitative zeal in the listener. Plutarch is the culmination of a tradition of biographical writing which holds its subject up for judgement, and presents him as a potential model for action.

It was not the only way to go about it, of course. Biography could be there to monumentalize a subject wholly unreachable by emulation, like the Alexander of the countless Alexander histories. Alternatively, monumentalizing and holding up for emulation could go together, as they did in those most curious productions of all antiquity, the Christian Gospels, which certainly have a place in *a* biographical tradition, even if it is not necessarily a Greek one (Jewish historiography surely has a bigger role in their genesis). One of the most important functions of the great body of ancient biography is to present models or anti-models of behaviour according to which its audience should regulate its own—that is, it is normative. This is a powerful motive in the lives of Christian martyrs, monks, and other holy men which are produced towards the end of our period in vast numbers. Some of them are explicitly written for emulation.

Pagans and Christians

Another bizarre production of late paganism which may well have been written under the influence of these Christian lives of holy men and quite transmutes its pagan inheritance is a *Life* of Apollonios of Tyana, a holy man from Cappadocia in the second half of the first century CE. His biographer, Philostratos, is the same man as the author of the *Lives* of the sophists, but here shows himself in very different guise, narrating an eight-book story of an ascetic pagan saint who 'wooed wisdom and soared above tyrants', discoursed with mages and Brahmins and Egyptian divines, foresaw the future, raised the dead, and quite confuted everyone with his esoteric wisdom culled from the traditions of Pythagoras. Paganism appears in this text as defiant, perhaps embattled, asserting itself against the upstart Christians. At one point, Apollonios is brought to trial before the Emperor Domitian, suspicious of a man who claims to be a god. Apollonios takes an option apparently unavailable to Christ in a similar position before Pontius Pilate: confounding his captors he simply vanishes into thin air. Pagan biography has here become fantastic wish-fulfilment—an assertion of unanswerable superiority before tyrannical Rome on the one hand, and the galloping blight of Christianity on the other.

So what was it about this strange Jewish heresy which meant that it eventually won out, not just over poor Apollonios, but over all of classical paganism? How did it, within just three centuries, become the religion of Constantine, and thence of the Roman Empire? Adaptability, opportunism, cunning, argumentativeness, infuriating persistence, and sheer good fortune all had a part. But above all, Christians proved extremely articulate communicators, with a whole armoury of rhetorical techniques and literary genres at their disposal. They used letters and homilies, biographies and dialogues to get their message across. And since the appeal of their religion was universal from the outset, their literature potentially addressed itself to everyone. This is in total contrast to the situation which prevailed with all the pagan literature considered hitherto, produced by and for an élite.

One of the most important of the early churches was at Corinth, established by St Paul in about 50 CE. Some of the converts were Jews, but more still were Gentiles; many belonged to the poorer classes, among them slaves (which is not necessarily incompatible with their being well educated). In addressing himself to them, Paul uses a language which is apparently classless and universal:

> Unto the church of God which is at Corinth, to them that are sanctified in Christ Jesus, called to be saints, with all that in every place call upon the name of Jesus Christ our Lord, both theirs and ours. (I Corinthians 1: 2)

A little later his words, while hinting at the low social status of some of the community, exalt this lack of status in a new and subversive Christian value-system:

> For ye see your calling, brethren, how that not many wise men after the flesh, not many mighty, not many noble, are called: But God hath chosen the foolish things of the world to confound the wise; and God hath chosen the weak things of the world to confound the things which are mighty; And base things of the world, and things which are despised, hath God chosen, yea, and things which are not, to bring to nought things that are. (I Corinthians 1: 26–8)

Women were also an important part of the community, and Christianity and its literature makes them visible in a way that pagan literature does not—albeit sometimes by accident. They are recipients of letters (some of the letters of the New Testament address them), or dedicatees of treatises and meditations. They are the subject of saints' lives which hold them up for emulation. Sometimes they can do better and leave behind writings of their own—a letter, the record of a pilgrimage, occasionally something more; in one exceptional case, a *cento*, or patchwork, made up of lines rearranged from Homer to spell out a Christian message. Is the situation really this rosy? Hardly. It is still relatively unusual for women to be addressed, especially in genres—like the letter—whose main aim is to get something practical done (for which women were of less use than men), and it is all too clear, when they are addressed at all, that the space Christianity has made available for them is one that maps onto them simple faith and unprovocative chastity, denying them the wider cultural references available to their male counterparts.

As it spread and came into conflict with paganism, one of Christianity's initial strategies was to insert itself within an existing literature of opposition, protest, and defiance. Thus a small body of Alexandrian nationalist literature dating from the second and third centuries CE documents various showdowns between city-leaders and the emperor. The consequences for the former are predictably fatal—but the unassailable moral high ground gained by martyrdom is the whole point, as it was also for those Roman Stoics who stood out against the emperor's tyranny and left behind accounts of their suicides in the Roman historiographers. It was the Christians, though, who best understood this genre. They knew how to die, and how to write about it, to maximum effect, and their martyrologies were as much acts of self-advertisement as testimonies to bitter or ingrained antagonism with the Roman state.

The next extract is from one of the most famous texts, narrating the martyrdom of Polycarp, bishop of Smyrna. It uses unembellished, occasionally colloquial, prose, and is very concerned to authenticate itself as an accurate transcript of what went on. The immediate addressees are the members of a neighbouring Church, but they are asked to pass on the testimony 'to our more distant brothers', so that its outreach is potentially to 'all the communities of the holy Catholic Church everywhere'. Despite, or rather because of, its harrowing content, the reader is constantly spurred on to emulative zeal, for this is an example which 'everyone desires to imitate':

> When he had said his Amen and rounded off his prayer, the men in charge of the pyre kindled it. As a great flame blazed out, those of us privileged to see it beheld a great miracle, which we have preserved so as to relate the events to others. The flame made the shape of an arch like the sail of a ship bellying out in the wind, and encircled the martyr's body as if by a wall. And in the middle it was not like burning flesh, but baking bread, or gold and silver being smelted in a furnace. And we perceived such fragrance as if from gales of incense or some other costly perfume. (*The Martyrdom of St. Polycarp*, § 15)

For all their high profile, however, persecutions of Christians were not all that frequent: most of the time pagans could afford to let Christians be. But while the pagan world-view could usually, with certain constraints, tolerate monotheism, the converse was not the case. Literary evidence takes us beyond competing ideologies and shows how the oriental newcomer borrowed and was parasitic on the classical culture made available to it. For in the long term, the appropriation of pagan genres and methods of argumentation was more effective than head-on collision. Indeed, it was inevitable that Christians should use the language and literature of the society in which they lived, the culture in which they had been educated—what else was there? The twist, though, was the appropriation of the arguments of classical philosophy to attack classical philosophy, rhetoric against rhetoric, meaning against meaning. The techniques are already in place in Paul himself. If (for example) we return to his first letter to the Corinthians, we find him protesting that when he came to visit them,

> My speech and my preaching was not with enticing words of man's wisdom, but in demonstration of the Spirit and of power. (2: 4)

He opposes persuasive words of wisdom to practical demonstration. 'The Greeks seek after wisdom', he has said, but his own 'demonstration' is definitive and final: it is of the power of God. Yet the terms of both halves of the antithesis—persuasion and demonstration—are already familiar from classical analyses of rhetorical technique. So in a way, Paul has trumped pagan rhetoric too.

As Christianity took hold of the upper classes, we encounter such figures as the dazzlingly well-educated Gregory of Nazianzus (in Cappadocia), a fourth-century bishop whose speeches and letters are steeped in classical rhetoric, whose verse is studded with allusions to the authors on the school curriculum (and a good many others encountered in Gregory's wider reading). The audience is no longer the urban poor of Corinth, but, potentially, those who have received the most privileged of educations. Conversely, we also encounter a pagan culture transformed by its encounter with the newcomer and coming increasingly to have to stand its ground against it. Above all the pagan offensive was led by the Emperor Julian (d. 363), himself an apostate from Christianity, so knowing well how to turn Christian polemic back on the Christians—which he did, venomously. And it is perhaps in this context that we ought to introduce one of antiquity's most extraordinary productions.

The imperial period is not a great one for Greek poetry, so it is all the more notable that it has produced the longest surviving poem to survive from all antiquity, the forty-eight-book *Dionysiaka* of Nonnos of Panopolis in Egypt (*fl.* mid-fifth century CE). Often this epic about the career of the late-antique Dionysos is written off as unpalatable, turgid, monotonous, for Nonnos uses very strict metrical principles with predictable patterns of stress, a uniformly lush, many would say overwrought, style, and strives after effects of blood-and-thunder Baroque monstrosity. Yet I must put in a defence of this wonderful, misunderstood—and significant—poem. Nonnos is formidably learned, and one way of approaching him is as a cross between an archaeological site and a treasury whence relics of antiquity's lost poetry can often be recovered. His use of his predecessors is sometimes heavy-handed but often intelligent. But he is also a priceless document about the tastes and spirit of his age. His account of Dionysos' entire earthly career, and his construction of its chronology, involves the melding of traditions drawn from epic and mythography and Alexander histories with the extraordinary imperial literature of phoney Dionysiac mysticism attributed to Orpheus, all overlaid with the age's abiding passion for astrology.

The poem traces the birth of three successive incarnations of Dionysos, each as a result of a divine rape. This extract comes from Zeus' rape of Semele, and illustrates some important aspects of Nonnos' poetry—Dionysiac excess, grotesqueness, and an unflinching and uninhibited range of voyeuristic detail:

A writhing snake crept over her, and licked
The rosy neck of that affrighted bride
With gentle lips, then mounting on her chest
Encircled her firm breasts' circumference,
Hissing a wedding-song, and pouring forth
A swarming bee's sweet honey, not the gall
Of deadly vipers. Zeus prolonged the match,

DIONYSOS IN A CHRISTIAN WORLD. These fragments of a huge linen and wool tapestry were woven in Egypt in the fourth century CE. Although made in the Christian Coptic culture it represented (as often in Coptic art) figures from pagan antiquity. This panel represents Dionysos. Note the halo!

And as beside a wine-press, cried 'Euhoi'
Engendering the son who'd love that cry.
And love-mad mouth to mouth he pressed, and gushed
Intoxicating nectar for his bride,
So that her son would be the harvest's prince

(*Dionysiaka* 7. 328–38)

The result is a Dionysos who is now the Euripidean god of brute irruptive force, now a new Alexander, conqueror of India, now a prancing insouciant adolescent—and yet also a great saviour divinity who undergoes a passion out of love for humankind for all the world like a pagan riposte (yet another one) to Christ. 'Lord Bakchos wept tears, that he might allay mankind's sorrows.' Some said that Nonnos became a Christian bishop. The fact that he appears to have written a paraphrase of St John's gospel in exactly the same overblown style as the *Dionysiaka* is immensely eloquent about the relationship between paganism and Christianity in Nonnos' Egypt. However limited our data about the *Dionysiaka*'s immediate readership—for papyri do not serve us well, and the 'Nonnian style' in fact seems to have got underway rather before Nonnos himself—the insights to be gleaned from Nonnos about the spiritual culture of late antiquity are priceless. He reflects, not only an intensely lettered yet still adaptable paganism, but also a Christianity which seems to have been happy to dress up in paganism's gaudiest clothes. For the sting in the tail is that it looks increasingly as if the *Dionysiaka* was written *after* the paraphrase, that is, after Nonnos became a Christian. What does that tell us about the relationship of Christian and pagan culture?

Imperial Greek literature, like most classical literature, is mainly the record of the winners. We possess little not written by the élites. One of the few non-prestige genres of which anything survives is that of the fable, traditional parables of homespun wisdom. But even this could please refined palates with its arch simplicity and traditionalist morality, and indeed parables were often used in high literary genres. If imperial literature is the story of the winners, it is set against a complex background in which the Greek élites were increasingly Romanized into the political culture of their overlords, yet Romans were increasingly Hellenized into the more prestigious intellectual culture of Greeks.

The ideal Roman, from the Greeks' point of view, was Larensis, the Roman host of Athenaios' Greek sophists who makes them feel that 'Rome is their native land', and does this by being bilingual and having antiquarian interests, learning, well-stocked conversation—in short, gallons of *paideia*. How many Romans lived up to Greek fantasy is another matter altogether. Imperial Greek literature shows us various stages in this process of accommodation: first, assigning the Romans a place in a still Hellenocentric universe (some even claimed Latin as a dialect of Greek); then with various uneasy assertions of parity, or admissions of weakness which could be tempered by harking back to a glorious past. Yet, on the part of many, there was a publicly unproblematic identification with Rome, for Strabon already uses 'we' of Rome. And eventually Greeks, enfranchised as Roman citizens along with the rest of the Empire in 212 CE, became Romans, *Romaioi*.

Latin Literature

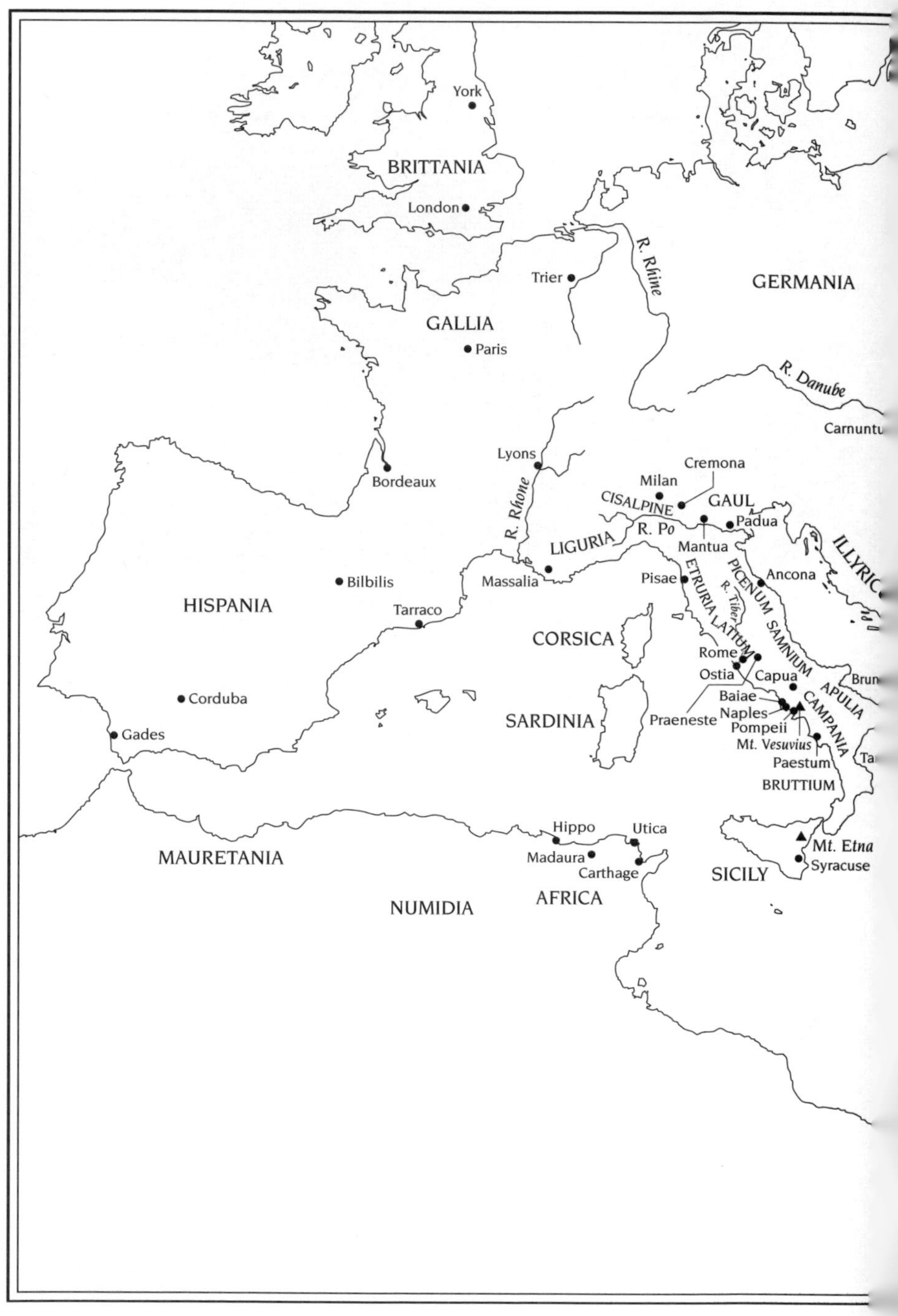

The Roman World: chief places mentioned in the text

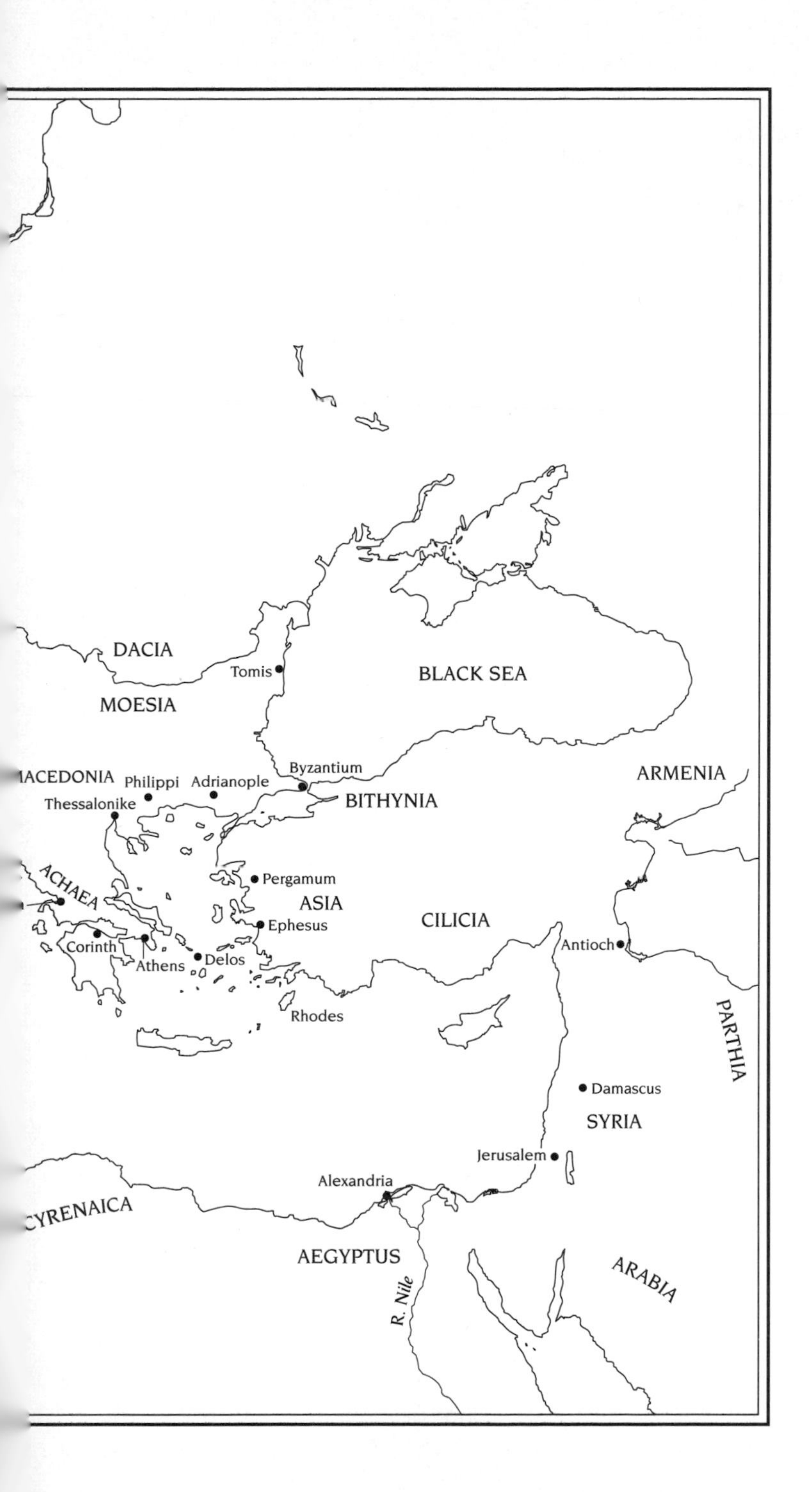
DACIA
MOESIA
Tomis
BLACK SEA
Byzantium
ACEDONIA
Philippi
Adrianople
Thessalonike
BITHYNIA
ARMENIA
Pergamum
ACHAEA
ASIA
CILICIA
Ephesus
Corinth
Athens
Delos
Antioch
Rhodes
PARTHIA
Damascus
SYRIA
Jerusalem
Alexandria
CYRENAICA
AEGYPTUS
R. Nile
ARABIA

9 Primitivism and power: The beginnings of Latin literature

MATTHEW LEIGH

To later Latin critics the very earliness of the earliest phase of Latin literature is bound up with the perception of its primitivism and the image which they have of their predecessors is strikingly visual in form. The dominant metaphor is that of the barbershop: to Cicero and Quintilian, the prose-style of Cato the Elder is rough or hairy, to Gellius it is unkempt; to Ovid and Propertius, the verse of Ennius is shaggy or hirsute. A proper modern style is therefore neat, restrained, and tasteful. An excessive pursuit of innovation prompts talk of perfumes, ringlets, and curling-tongs.

Consider the implications of the tonsorial metaphor. When the satirist Juvenal, writing in the late first and early second century CE, evokes the life of man in the golden age, he houses him in caves, makes him sleep on skins and straw and gives him a wife hairier than her acorn-belching husband. To Juvenal, therefore, hairiness can be a marker of absolute primitivism. To Marcus Terentius Varro (cf. p. 321), a century and a half before him, the picture is more complex. He adduces that there were no barbers in early Rome from the fact that all the statues of the men of this time have long hair and beards and adds that the first barbers were brought to Rome from Sicily at the start of the third century by one T. Ticinius Mena. Ancient Sicily was a profoundly Greek culture and it is clear that Varro understands the introduction of shaving as a stage in the Hellenization of Roman culture. Pliny the Elder implies much the same when he states that the great general and statesman Scipio Aemilianus was the first Roman to adopt the practice of daily shaving. As will be seen, he too had a major role in the cultural development of Rome in the late second century.

There is a significant paradox to be drawn from this pattern. Both Cato and Ennius will play a major part in accounts of Roman culture in this period. Neither, it may safely be assumed, lived in a cave—they are not Juvenal's absolute primitives. Yet their response to accusations of shagginess or unshavenness of style might well have been very different. When Horace talks of 'unshaven

Cato' the idea which he seeks to encode is that of the rigorous morality and austere life-style to which he devoted himself. Ostentatiously to have worn a long beard would have been entirely in tune with Cato's public stance of strident political and cultural Hellenophobia. The archaizing tendency in all that Cato did would have had little trouble accommodating imputations of artistic shagginess were that seen as proof of his freedom from all Greek corruption. To Ennius, however, the very implication would have provoked horror. For all that he becomes the epic voice of Roman success in arms, Ennius is only too aware of the Greek culture in which he was raised, of his profound debt to Greek literary forms and models. He takes intense pride in his own artistic modernism, parades the Greekness of this modernism, and mocks his own 'primitive' predecessors for their dependence on native Italian forms (cf. pp. 294–7).

Another author who is perceived as unrefined is the great comic writer Titus Maccius Plautus (*c.*254–184 BCE). In the twenty-one extant comedies of Plautus we have the first complete Latin works of all and the most extensive of any writer in this early period. The judgement of Horace on his work is also a judgement on his audience—no concern for artistic coherence as long as the play is a commercial success:

> Comedy is thought to be no sweat, its subject
> drawn from every day, but it's all the tougher
> the less it is indulged. Look at Plautus
> and how he sustains the role of the young Romeo,
> the watchful pa, the tricky pimp,
> see what an antiquated hick he is among his tricky parasites,
> with how loose a slipper he races round the stage,
> he's striving just to bank his fee, no matter
> whether the play should stand or fall after that.
>
> (Horace, *Epistles* 2. 1. 168–76)

The audience which gives him his success without worrying about the defects of his artistry is clearly not as sophisticated as it might be. The insinuation has stuck and Plautus is often dismissed as slipshod, his public as 'groundlings'. On closer inspection, however, it will be found that he remains well ahead of his critics and that his audience are a little more knowing than might be inferred.

Plautus frequently parades the fact that his drama is adapted from an original in Greek New Comedy (cf. Ch. 7, pp. 220–6). In doing so he positively embraces the implication that he has debased his model by stating that he has translated it into barbarian. The criticisms of the Greek-speaking snob are not deflected, they are made part of the comic experience. If anyone had called

Plautus shaggy to his face, he would have bought the biggest possible wig and made a joke out of it. As for his audience, the best thing that we can do is to be ready to divest ourselves of any prejudices, and be as prepared to be surprised by them as they were by him.

The prologue of the *Poenulus* or *Little Carthaginian* is the best antidote to any complacent assumptions about Plautus or his audience. Two factors must particularly be emphasized. The first is the level of literary sophistication which we must assume in author and audience. This is an issue from the very opening lines of the play:

> I am inclined to translate the *Achilles* of Aristarchus;
> I'll take my beginning from that tragedy.
> Pray silence and be quiet and pay heed,
> the general . . . manager bids you listen.
> (Plautus, *The Little Carthaginian* 1–4)

The audience have flocked to hear a comedy by Plautus but they will require rather more theatrical knowledge than one might expect. Aristarchos wrote his *Achilles* around 450 BCE and wrote it, of course, in Greek. At some point in the early second century BCE, Ennius adapted it for the Roman stage and Plautus is plainly parodying the speech of a herald not from Aristarchos but Ennius. Yet he does not mention Ennius at all. For this joke to work, therefore, his audience must both identify the parody of a noted scene from Ennius and know enough of the literary filiation of his work to explain the attribution to Aristarchos.

Parody, meanwhile, requires an ear familiar with the resonances of the work parodied. How far this process continues in the prologue remains uncertain but there is a clear interruption at the end of the fourth line: 'Pray silence be quiet and pay heed, the general . . . manager bids you listen.' The general could be one of the Greek commanders at Troy and the words those of his herald—of a Talthybius to his Agamemnon—but Plautus coins his own adjective (*histricus*) and the general of tragedy suddenly becomes the general manager of a company of actors. The audience laughs because it knows the high tone of the tragic genre, can recognize its imitation and engage with the bathetic return to professional theatrical reality which subverts it.

The evidence of this passage would suggest that Plautus plays to a surprisingly sophisticated and dexterous audience. Other considerations might also lead us to believe that they are also rather more tolerant than might have been imagined. The prologue-speaker reveals the details of the plot. The action is set in Kalydon in Aitolia but the family whose vicissitudes it recounts are Carthaginian: two daughters stolen away with their nurse when 4 and 5 and sold into prostitution, their cousin who was kidnapped at 7, and their father, Hanno, who roams the Mediterranean in the hope of finding them. When the speaker comes to describe the father, it is noteworthy that he does so in such a way as to suggest that there are some things which his audience just must know about Carthaginians:

> But the Carthaginian father of the girls, ever since he lost them,
> has been hunting for them high and low over land and sea.
> Every time he gets into a town, straightaway
> he looks up all the tarts wherever each one lives;
> he pays his cash, books a night, then asks where
> the girl is from, which land, whether she was captured or kidnapped,
> in what rank she was born, who her parents were.
> So cleverly and cunningly does he hunt his daughters.
> And he knows every language and knowingly pretends
> he doesn't know: a perfect Carthaginian. What more need I say?
> (Plautus, *The Little Carthaginian* 104–13)

Yet what is it that this audience knows about Carthaginians and how is this to aid interpretation of the play?

At some point in the middle or end of the 300s, the Greek comedians Alexis and Menander both wrote comedies called *Karchedonios* or *The Carthaginian*. In the mixed-up world of Mediterranean trade and travel this title was perhaps no more significant than *The Girl from Perinthos* or any number of other equivalent forms. Yet for a Roman audience of the late third or early second century the very word Carthaginian could scarcely fail to conjure up the most painful of associations. How many had witnessed Hannibal and his army at the walls of Rome? How many had seen service in the Second Punic War? The trauma of Hannibal, the hateful memory of the faithless, treaty-breaking, Rome-hating enemy was kept alive for generations afterwards. To allude to 'the perfect Carthaginian' would seem therefore to play on just such a collective understanding. These very lines have even been cited as part of a litany of anti-Carthaginian prejudices which any Roman reader would have to carry with her and impose on the complex and suffering figure of Virgil's Dido. Yet Plautus' Hanno is not at all what he might be assumed to be. The very title under which this play is transmitted, *The Little Carthaginian*, is itself reassuring: the feared enemy is now far enough in the past to be patronized, his wounded dignity a source of gentle humour, his rediscovery of his daughters the happy ending of the tale. This gentleman's skill with languages, moreover, is not quite of the sort for which the bogeyman was loathed. It is likely that, in the contested areas of Sicily and Greek southern Italy, the Carthaginians were found to be much more adept in the local Greek language than their Roman enemies; but they are damned in some of our sources as *bilingues*, not because they were bilingual but because of their faithlessness, because they ever spoke with forked tongue.

Plautus calls on his audience's knowledge of what makes a 'perfect Carthaginian' but then treats them to something very different. When Hanno does use his skill in languages it is only in order to rescue his daughters. There is a truly faithless villain in this drama but it is the Greek pimp Lycus. Hanno's linguistic dexterity is as much as anything a mirror for that of Plautus himself, who translates from Greek into Latin and, for good measure, throws in an extended passage of what may well be genuine Punic but is no less comical for all that.

The audience flock to laugh at Plautus' plays and to celebrate the reunification of a dispersed family, even a Carthaginian one. The prologue reminds them of their prejudices about Carthaginians, the drama subverts them. They still cheer. We will do well to assume as little as possible in advance about the literary sophistication and the political preconceptions of those people who took Plautus to their hearts.

What was a proper Roman of the middle Republic like? Marcus Porcius Cato the Elder (234–149 BCE) could have told you. A proper Roman was not of the city at all, but a child of the land, hardy and thrifty, a man of few words, a stout soldier, religiously devout, well fed on indigenous Italian fare and kept healthy by traditional local medicine. Cato made his own contribution to the development of Roman literature, propounding his cranky vision in anything from farming manuals to published speeches, and on to the earliest work of Latin prose history, the *Origines*. His baleful charisma endures, his campaign to refashion Rome in his own image as successful today as ever. Nowhere is he more successful than in his hijack of the debate surrounding the famous *Lex Oppia* and its ban on female ornament. Discussions often go no further than recording the opinions offered by Cato in its defence as proof of the austerity of Roman morality in the period. That this was only ever a wartime emergency measure, that Cato's opposition to its repeal was intended to make such conditions permanent, that Livy offers a version of the speech of the senior magistrate for the year urbanely refuting his claims, that Cato was defeated and the law repealed all seems to get lost along the way.

When Cato took to writing history, he invented Rome's original identity: that which ever had been ever should be. The self-servingly antiquated perspective of this farmer-soldier-politician was suddenly bolstered by an array of myth-historical predecessors, his vision of what was truly Roman authenticated by the discovery that he was not a freak but the last representative of a long and noble tradition. Yet it must be emphasized that this was a fundamentally reactionary vision. By this I mean not just that it was stridently old-fashioned, but rather that it was a conception of Romanity whose genesis lay in reaction to and distress at the inevitable changes overtaking a city-state already controlling the Italian peninsula and gradually advancing to a much wider empire. The pernicious fictions purveyed by Cato were perforce opposed. That part of Roman society which could see no harm in acquiring a Greek literary education or filling its houses with the statuary of a plundered world was reassured by rival inventions which asserted that their city was a Greek foundation, and that many of their cults were the creation of the greatest of Greek heroes, Hercules. If the uncouth and warlike Romulus was to be the first king of Rome, then no less importance should be attached to his successor Numa, who taught the people law and religious observance, who conversed with the Greek mage Pythagoras and effectively refounded the city in his own distinctly Hellenic image.

Nowhere was the new cosmopolitanism of Roman culture more apparent than in the world of the arts. The one factor, indeed, which links all the great creators of Roman literary culture is the fact that they do not come from the city itself. In comedy, for instance, the two authors whose plays have been transmitted in complete form to us are those of Plautus, a native of Sarsina in Umbria, and of Terence, a former Carthaginian slave freed by his noble patron Terentius Lucanus.

In this same period, three further writers distinguished themselves by their ability to compose works in epic poetry, tragedy, and comedy all at once. Of these, the oldest, Livius Andronikos, was a Greek slave freed by a member of the Roman *gens Livia* (hence his name, half-Greek, half-Roman); Naevius a Roman citizen from Capua near Naples; Ennius a native of Rudiae (a small town between Brindisium and Tarentum) which Strabo calls Greek but where he also learned Oscan. Like Plautus and Hanno he was noted for his trilingualism. Of these authors only Naevius is likely to have been born into the citizenship, and even his Campanian upbringing can hardly have failed to expose him to cultural influences very different from what a Catonian could have taken for authentically Roman. Likewise, anyone reading the first epic, the *Odyssia* of Livius Andronikos, could not help but be struck by its cultural hybridity: the poem is composed in the indigenous Latin metre, the Saturnian, the hero of the poem is given the Latin name Ulixes, but the work preserves the Greek title of the Homeric epic which it translates. The mixture of Greek and Roman elements even extends to the name of the author himself. By contrast, the readers of the *Bellum Poenicum* of Naevius and the *Annales* of Ennius will have been confronted with a literary form which has now been adapted to narrate the myths of their nation's origins and to describe the specifically Roman historical experiences of the First and Second Punic Wars. Yet even here the cultural standard is Greek. Ennius mocks Naevius for composing in the Saturnian and implicitly prides himself on fitting the Homeric hexameter to the Latin tongue. He no longer seeks his inspiration from the Latin Camenae but rather from the Greek Muses; and from the Greek he coins the terms *poemata* to describe his verses and *poeta* for himself. Pride in native military achievement and embarrassment at indigenous cultural forms are inextricably intertwined.

Ennius in the schoolroom

How is the audience for early Roman epic to be imagined? An important element here is the tendency of aristocratic generals and politicians to keep authors in their personal retinue. Quintus Ennius (239–169 BCE) is said to have been brought to Rome by none other than Cato the Elder in 204 BCE. He later followed the consul M. Fulvius Nobilior on campaign in Aitolia in 189 BCE and composed the celebratory drama, the *Ambracia*, in his honour. The vengeful Cato delivered an oration damning Fulvius for taking poets with him to his province. Though Ennius marks the closure of the fifteenth book of his *Annales* and its account of the very same Aitolian campaign as the end of his narrative, he was later induced to add three further books and to take the story up to the Istrian and Macedonian Wars and around the year 171 BCE. Pliny the Elder attributes the addition of the sixteenth book to Ennius' admiration for one T. Aelius Teucer but it is hard to imagine that he would have felt such overwhelming esteem for one who could offer no further inducement.

If early Latin epic is made in a culture of patronage and perhaps finds a first audience at recitations in the household of the patron, it still remains to explain how it attains to a much wider audience. Here again, an important role seems to have been played by M. Fulvius Nobilior, who brought back from his Ambracian campaign the statue group which formed the centre-piece of the Temple of Hercules of the Muses dedicated in 179 BCE. While the first evidence for the association of this temple with the College of Poets concerns an event towards the very end of the life of the tragedian Accius (*c.*170–88 BCE) around the year 90 BCE, it is very possible that this guild met here to listen to recitations from the beginning. Evidence in Livy and Festus for a College of Scribes and Actors meeting in the Temple of Minerva on the Aventine in the late third century BCE would support such an inference.

Yet it is as a published text that the epic of Ennius must finally have reached its widest public. So it is important to consider the implications of the claim that Ennius established himself on the Aventine and pursued the profession of *grammaticus* or teacher. For the canonical status of the *Annales* in all Roman culture up to the time of Catullus and Lucretius must reflect the practices of the schoolroom, the rote learning and recitation of generations of pupils. There remains extant not one serious epic poem between Ennius and the *De rerum natura* of Lucretius in the 50s BCE (cf. Ch. 11, pp. 339–49). Such poems were composed, but none even threatened to displace the *Annales*. Where fragments and brief quotations of works such as the *Bellum Istricum* of Hostius are found, they show no significant advance in style or content from the work of Ennius and suggest only a reverent reproduction of the master they have been taught to admire. To Marcus Tullius Cicero, Ennius was 'the second Homer'. To Roman schoolboys he must have dominated the literary curriculum in the manner of Shakespeare in England or Manzoni in Italy.

Yet what was the vision of their nation's history which the *Annales* presented to the youth of Rome? When all that is left of a seventeen-book epic is something short of six hundred lines of verse, and none of these fragments lasts longer than twenty lines, it is rash to make any too confident pronouncements. Yet a clear indication of the ennobling character of some of Ennius' verse may be drawn from episodes such as the description of the solitary resistance of a stalwart subaltern in the Istrian War:

> From all sides like rain the spears fell on the tribune;
> they pierce his shield, the boss rings with the tips,
> the helmet with a brazen din; yet no man can
> tear his body with the steel, press from all sides though they may.
> At every moment he breaks and brandishes the spears abundant.
> Sweat covers all his body and he labours much,
> nor is there time for him to breathe: with winged steel
> the Istrians were pressing him, casting spears from their hands.
> (Ennius, *Annals* 391–8, trans. Skutsch)

The solitary warrior holding off the foe has a powerful appeal at Rome; for this we need think only of the myth of Horatius Cocles on the bridge. Cato himself had found another heroic military tribune in his contemporary Q. Caedicius, and in the *Origines* he celebrates his resistance as the equal of that of Leonidas and the 300 holding the pass at Thermopylai. Ennius is doing much the same. He too chooses a middle-ranking officer—the military tribune and the centurion are specifically charged with the task of holding the line, of organizing and sustaining the resistance of their legion—and he too colours this action with an unmistakable heroic tint. For we possess these lines only thanks to the late Latin author Macrobius, who notes explicitly the lines of Homer which inspire Ennius' verse. From books 13 to 16 of the *Iliad* there is scarcely a moment when Hektor and the Trojans are not just about to set fire to the ships of the Greeks and drive the invader back into the sea, scarcely a moment when the massive, immobile Aias (Latin 'Ajax'), the 'rampart of the Greeks', does not stand firm with his giant shield of seven ox-hides and hold them at bay. Ennius adapts the lines which mark the very culmination of Aias' resistance but he transfers them not to one of the great generals of Rome but to a figure of far lower rank and lesser name, to one who lives and fights in a very different world but who can, by his example, turn his indomitable legion into an Aias for the modern world.

Other passages are more complex. In one which is recorded by Cicero, gold is refused as a ransom and the enemy challenged to the test of *virtus*, of martial courage. Yet those bearing gold are the Romans, and the speaker who twice invokes the quality which the martial nation held most dear is none other than the great Greek general and self-proclaimed descendant of Achilles, King Pyrrhos. A further passage, 'Blunted back were spears that clashed against oncoming spears', is quoted by an ancient commentator as the inspiration for the opening lines of Lucan's despairing poem of civil war, the *Pharsalia*. Does Lucan take a stirring line from Ennius' account of war in Spain and turn it to negative effect? Both Romans and Spaniards are said to have used the particular type of spear described, so this is quite possible. Alternatively, we may look to Livy and his account of the Latin wars where Rome fought a foe so like her in military equipment and organization as to make the combat feel like a form of civil war. Perhaps Lucan finds a first expression of his pained consciousness in a darker section of Ennius' poem.

Latin literary scholars are well used to searching for difficult and potentially troubling messages in the national poetry of Virgil. To do so in the works of 'shaggy Ennius', the primitive epic forefather affectionately constructed by the self-consciously refined Augustans, may seem captious. Yet Ennius himself is determined to project an image of modernity and sophistication, and to purvey a vision of the *Annales* as without nuance or reflection is to risk falsifying the importance of the poem for the generations of readers raised on it. Perhaps the most famous line of the entire work is one recorded by Cicero in his *De re publica* (On the State): 'On manners and on men of good old time stands firm the Roman state.' It has been noted that the initial letters of the first four words of this verse (*moribus antiquis res stat Romana virisque*) spell out Mars, at times the god of war and at times its metonym. The ancient customs and men are thus the ways of war and the warriors who sustain them. Which martial culture could not adopt this line for itself? How many young warriors from Pydna to Passchendaele have not had it drilled into them? Yet this tells us nothing of how it was actually understood by the readers of the *Annales*. A precious clue is, however, preserved in the eighth book of the histories of Livy. Here, a father chastises his son with the complaint that 'as far as in you lay, you have broken the military discipline by which the Roman state has stood unshaken until this day' (*quantum in te fuit, disciplinam militarem, qua stetit ad hanc diem Romana res, solvisti*). That father is T. Manlius Torquatus. Livy tells us that he was the son of L. Manlius Imperiosus, and that the father obtained his name from his imperious treatment of others, most notably his close relations. The young Manlius Torquatus is kept from the family home, the city, and the forum and consigned to a gaol or workhouse by his father, and all for the simple reason that a defect in his speech and his perceived stupidity render him an embarrassment. He endeavours to win back his father's affection by heroic endeavour when the latter is arraigned by the tribunes but only finally achieves glory when accepting the challenge of single combat against a giant Gaul, slaying him and stripping him of the chain or torque from which he gains his name. Now, a generation later, his own son has sought to impress his father by an act of heroic bravery. Yet the son has done so in violation of the order that no soldier may engage the enemy without the strict instructions of the general: to make an example of this violation of discipline, Manlius Torquatus executes his own son. The severity of his deed does much to restore discipline and is not without benefit to the cause, but it is also repulsive to the Romans who witness it; and 'Manlian commands' become proverbial in Rome for excessive severity in the exercise of power. If our one-line fragment of Ennius is spoken by T. Manlius Torqautus and comes from the same speech as Livy records, then the message it conveys to the schoolboy readers of the *Annales* is far more complex than the decontextualized tag might imply. To learn about the nature of fatherhood and the proper exercise of authority may be just as valuable as to be taught to hold the line.

Theatre and festival

If it is hard to imagine a mass audience for epic outside the classroom, the opposite is true for tragedy, historical drama, and comedy. In the Athens of the fifth and fourth century, the great dramatists composed primarily for contests held at two civic festivals lasting a total of only six days a year (cf. Chs. 3, 7). It is therefore a phenomenon of central importance that the Rome of the late third and early second century saw a veritable explosion of such annual festivals, from the Ludi Romani in 240 BCE to the Ludi Plebeii around 220, the Ludi Ceriales some time before 201, the Ludi Apollinares from 212, the Ludi Megalenses in 204, and the Ludi Florales perhaps first held in 240 and an annual festival from 173 onwards. Each of these festivals seems to have begun in fulfilment of a vow or in celebration of a specific occasion, and each appears to have followed the pattern of a day or days set aside for theatrical games or *ludi*

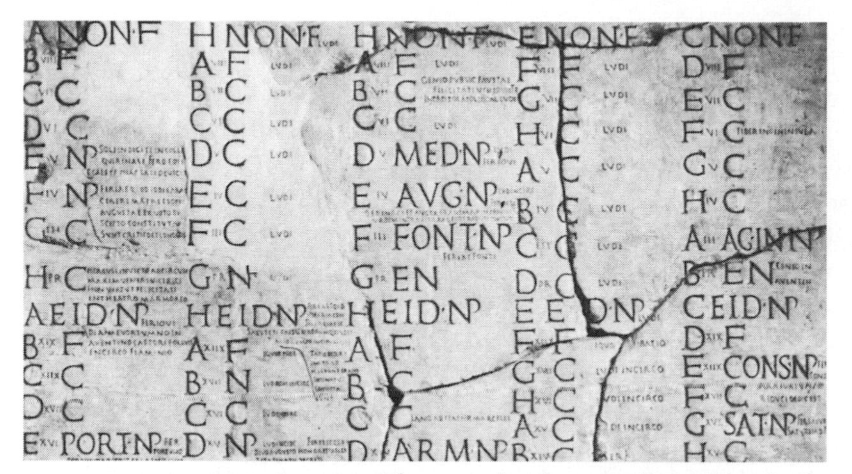

FESTIVALS AND HOLIDAYS. An extract from a calendar compiled c.25 CE. In the Roman world there was no regular pattern of rest days, and religious festivals, which included the celebration of athletics and theatre, provided opportunities for holidays. On this calendar they are marked LUDI.

scaenici followed by a shorter period of circus games or *ludi circenses*. By the time of the Augustan calendar, no fewer than forty-three days a year were devoted specifically to theatrical games at Rome. Even if this constituted a considerable advance on the mid-Republican period and even if certain events, in particular the Ludi Florales, were devoted to erotic mime and sub-literary indecency, this still represents a thriving theatrical culture. When one adds in the frequency with which these festivals might be subject to the religious obligation of reperformance or *instauratio,* and notes the propensity of Roman aristocrats intermittently to put on theatrical shows at the dedication of temples, at funerals, at triumphs or in payment of a vow for victory in battle, it is possible to wonder whether the phenomenon of the 'resting' actor was ever seen at all in the Rome of this period. No surprise perhaps that the great writers for the Roman stage from Livius to Accius were almost all active in the third and second centuries.

Where there is evidence for the first performance of a Roman drama of this period, the context is always a festival of one sort or another. For serious drama the best documentation is that provided for the *praetexta* or Roman historical drama (named after the *toga praetexta,* worn by senators). Many of the examples recorded celebrated recent events and were composed for one of the special non-recurring festivals in payment of a vow, at a triumph or a funeral. The whole enterprise reeks of self-promotion. As for *tragoedia,* the adaptation into Latin of Greek mythological tragedy, an interesting example is the *Thyestes* of Ennius which was performed at the Ludi Apollinares of 169. Unlike most plays with this title, this is not about the Thyestean feast but its aftermath, the exile of Thyestes in Thesprotia and his return to Argos to overthrow his brother Atreus. A notable element in Latin accounts of this part of the myth is the advice of the oracle of Apollo to Thyestes, and such an episode would have involved a felicitous harmony between festive context and dramatic content.

It would be satisfying to detect such a relationship between the *Eunuch* of Terence and its performance at the Ludi Megalenses of 161, for the cult of the Great Mother was the preserve of her eunuch priests, the Galli; but the *Girl from Andros*, the *Self-Tormentor*, and the *Mother-in-law* were also put on at the same festival in 166, 165, and 163 and none of these overtly thematizes the problem of castration. It is also worth thinking about the interaction between the themes of the *Brothers* and the traditions surrounding the life of L. Aemilius Paullus Macedonicus, at whose funeral games it was performed in 160. This drama which infuses discussion of whether to raise children strictly or with indulgence with the language of forgiveness (*clementia*) and of the power of the ruler (*imperium*) is peculiarly appropriate for a man who achieved almost as much fame for his humanity to his defeated enemy as he did for finally conquering the homeland of Philip and Alexander. For Plautus the evidence is more sketchy but it is relevant that his masterpiece, the *Pseudolus*, was performed at the Ludi Megalenses of 191, a particularly auspicious occasion since that year also saw the dedication of the Temple to Flora and the Great Mother. The only other drama for which we have a date is the *Stichus*, which was put on at the Ludi Plebeii of 200, games which were reperformed in their entirety three times in just one year. It has been suggested that this *instauratio* was induced by public zeal for Plautus' comedy. There is no ancient evidence to support this hunch but, were it correct, it would tell us a good deal about the power of audiences in this period.

It is not easy to account for the popularity of Greek mythological tragedy in the early years of the Roman theatre. In comedy, it is possible to analyse the process of adaptation involved in the presentation of Greek New Comedy at Rome. It is clear, for instance, that nobody attempted to Romanize the exuberant fantasies or contemporary political humour of Aristophanes, and the other masters of fifth-century Old Comedy. Rather, the pieces which won such favour with Roman audiences were those which adapted the domestic, bourgeois New Comedy of late fourth- and early third-century authors such as Menander, Diphilos, and Philemon. Some ancient critics praised Menander in particular for his naturalism, for the mirror which he held up to life. When he presented an Athenian youth on the stage he wore clothes which had been subject to some degree of stylization but which were not dissimilar to those typical of his class in the world outside the theatre. In a Roman palliate comedy (named after the *pallium*—Greek-style cloak, to designate the Greek origins of the genre, contrasted with partly Roman 'togate' comedy), every time a character refers to 'my *pallium*' he is also drawing attention to his theatrical costume, to the marker of the burlesque national identity which he has embraced. Plautus veritably proclaims the Greekness of his comic world, even to the extent of having his characters make comments about Romans as barbarians. Yet for tragedy there is no obvious reason to want to create the same ironic distance from the form in which the author has chosen to compose. When Livius wrote his *Achilles* and his *Tereus*, Naevius his *Lycurgus* or Ennius *Medea*, their efforts at Greek high culture in Latin must have been free of all the self-conscious ethnic play which characterizes Plautine comedy. In a later period it is evident that the audiences of Accius in particular were accustomed to treat the theatre as a political forum, to respond to significant intonations from the actors, to identify contemporary politicians behind the masks of the tragic heroes, and to boo Caesar as a Tereus or weep for the exiled Eurysaces as a Cicero, but there is no record of anything of the sort in the very early years.

The fact which remains is that tragedy was a continuing success at Rome for at least two centuries. Even when no great creative talent emerged to replace the aged Accius after his death around 88 BCE, his plays continued to be revived throughout the period of the late Republic. If Cicero is anything to go by, then the tragedies of Accius, Pacuvius, and even Ennius provided a powerful armoury of allusions and quotations for dialogues, works of philosophy, and speeches. Nor would it be appropriate to think of Roman tragedy as a high-brow pursuit which attracted only the limited audiences who frequented the tragic recitations of the imperial salons. If so, it is hard to imagine quite why popular comedy, particularly that of Plautus, should be so full of parodies of the tone and content of the tragic drama. We have already seen an extreme example of this in the prologue of the *Little Carthaginian* (pp. 290–2 above), but the practice is widespread.

Imagine the impact of attending the first performance of Plautus' *Amphitryon*. Gone are the two bourgeois houses and the city street of New Comic tradition, in its place the palace and courtyard of the royal family of Thebes. Mercury comes forth—and there must still be some recognizable part of Mercury in him—but this time the messenger of the gods is dressed in the guise of a comic slave. The conflicting visual signals which setting and costume send out are then embraced in a crucial section of Mercury's speech:

> Now, first of all, I'll tell you what it is I have come to ask of you,
> then I'll let you know the plot of this tragedy.
> What? You frown, because I said this
> would be a tragedy? I'm a god, I'll change it.

This same play, if you wish, I'll turn from
tragedy to comedy and never change a single verse.
Do you want me to, or not? But that was a bit thick of me,
I who am a god pretending not to know you want it.
I quite appreciate your feelings on this matter:
I'll mix it up; it can be a tragicomedy.
After all, I don't think it would be right to
make it 100 per cent; comedy, with kings and gods on stage.
What then? Since there's a slave involved as well,
I'll do just as I said and make it a tragicomedy.
(Plautus, *Amphitryon* 50–63)

The drama which follows teeters constantly on the verge of madness, loss of identity, violence towards kin and the other staples of Attic tragedy. Appropriately for a drama set in the palace of Thebes, it engages repeatedly with the central themes of two other works describing the destruction of the royal family of that city: *Bakchai* and *Hercules Mad* of Euripides. It appeals, in other words, to a public with a highly developed theatrical consciousness. Later writers like Molière and Dryden have refashioned the *Amphitryon* by emphasizing its comedy; others, most importantly Kleist, respond to the potential darkness of its vision. It is a marker of the low esteem under which Plautus labours that a critic of a recent London production of Kleist's *Amphitryon* credited the German playwright with taking Plautus' frothy comedy and turning it into a tragicomedy. Yet it was Plautus who coined the term 'tragicomedy', and it was surely the pleasure which his audience took in tragedy and the sophisticated understanding of the form which they possessed which made it possible for the *Amphitryon* to be.

A mirror to the audience

There is no doubt a danger in identifying the most sophisticated manifestations of Plautine comic technique and drawing from these generalizing inferences about the cultural awareness of the audience as a whole. The value of certain jokes to those who get them is only heightened by the consciousness that there are others watching who are left entirely bemused. Yet it is surely better to discover the audience of Roman drama through what the evidence of the text suggests that the writers thought it possible to convey than to cling to a dogmatic assumption of primitivism and then hack away at the text in order to make it banal enough to conform to this assumption (though this has not been an uncommon practice among experts). Another phenomenon, which underlies all the modern editions of the comedies is the excision of great swathes of text which are condemned for their repetition and reduplication of previous information. What emerges is decidedly neater than what is contained in the manuscripts but it is uncertain whether it is actually any closer to an authentic Plautine script. What may seem like tedious repetition to the modern reader of a text (or even to the modern audience in an indoor theatre with near-perfect acoustics) may have been a vital resource to the second-century actor struggling to make himself heard to a potentially restless festive crowd from a temporary wooden stage with only the sky as a roof.

The audience of Plautus should be sought in the plays of Plautus, not imposed from outside: and that audience is a constant presence in the dramas themselves. The poets and chorus of Greek Old Comedy frequently step out of their roles and address the theatrical audience directly on issues of dramatic technique, rivalry between authors, and the competition between the plays on show, but they do so in the formal section of the drama known as the parabasis (cf. Ch. 3, pp. 121–2). Menandrean New Comedy features a range of divine prologue-speakers who address the audience directly and sketch out the plot of the drama to follow; characters in Menander occasionally recount some off-stage incident to the audience and address them as 'Gentlemen'. Terence in turn will adopt the prologues of Menander, but eliminate all expository content in favour of literary criticism and polemic against competitors. None of these writers, however, comes close to the intense interaction between actor and audience which typifies Plautine comedy.

The tendency of characters to speak 'outside the comedy' is condemned as a particular failing of Plautus by the late grammarian Evanthius, and Terence is praised for his avoidance of this mode. Yet Evanthius is a textualist by profession and his knowledge of Plautus is acquired in the library, not the stalls. This is not to say that the far greater naturalism of Terence and Menander is not theatrically effective in its own way, just that the particular mode which Plautus represents loses far more of its impact without an audience, without a theatre. For the Plautine actor, the stage on which he takes his stand is both an Athenian street and the space in which a theatrical performance takes place. When that actor enters a house or departs for the country or the port, he revels in the fact that he is also leaving the stage for the changing-room; what the actor wears is always costume before it is dress; the edge of the stage is not an invisible boundary over which the actor must never step but a garden wall across which the actor gossips and flirts with the public as if they were neighbours; conversations between two characters pullulate with knowing asides to the audience.

Naturalistic theatre seeks to submerge the identity of the actor in that of the character played and the theatrical space in the world represented; Plautus does not dispense with this illusion, but its function in Plautus is as an idea, a possibility, and as a reflection of what the characters on stage are doing. The idea of acting is often expressed in Latin through verbs of simulation (*simulare, dissimulare*). In Plautus, the theatrical event is therefore reproduced in microcosm as characters use the same verbs to express the intention to present themselves to an unwitting third party as that which they are not: the slave-hero of the *Pseudolus* deludes Harpax the representative of the boastful soldier by taking on the part of the pimp's doorkeeper; the courtesan Acroteleutium in the *Boastful Soldier* snares the infinitely vain warrior with the pretence that she is the lustful young wife of the venerable Periplectomenus.

The inevitable accompaniment of the adoption by characters of a separate identity in order to effect a deceit is the employment of a disguise. Again, this allows Plautus to offer another microcosm of the theatrical experience. For the disguise worn by the characters is never clothing (*vestis*), always costume (*ornamenta*). In the *Three-Bob-Day* (*Trinummus*), the disguised swindler makes it clear that he has obtained his costume from none other than the *choragus*, that is to say the props manager commissioned by the magistrates to supply costumes for the play. The slave hero of the *Persian Girl*, Toxilus, instructs Saturio to bring the girl in outlandish, foreign costume and advises him to secure it from the *choragus*; when she returns, we are told that she has learned her lines better than any tragic or comic actors are wont to do. The constant changes of costume and identity undertaken by the hero of the *Curculio* prompt the *choragus* actually to come on stage and express his despair at ever recovering what has been borrowed.

Compare all this with the *Eunuch* of Terence. Here the disguise adopted by Chaerea has a double function. Within a play which generally eschews the self-conscious theatricalization of the Plautine stage, the clothes put on by Chaerea are the proper garb of one character, the eunuch Dorus, before they ever become the disguise of the youthful deceiver. And the paradox is that they fit Chaerea much the better. It is Chaerea who really looks like a high-class present for a high-class courtesan; Dorus is only mangy and unattractive, scarcely fit to put his own outfit on. I cannot think of a single Plautine disguise which starts the play as the dress proper to another character. This distinction between the method of the two playwrights is subtle, but telling.

Procedures of this sort give a central position to the experience of the audience. If it is the actor who supplies the experience of having perpetrated a deceit, it is the audience, who believed him to be the character he represented, who know what it is to have been taken in. Similarly, the play often appeals to the immediate experience of the audience by establishing a festive context for the events which are taking place on stage. In the *Pseudolus* of Plautus and the *Self-Tormentor* of Terence, the characters find themselves on the evening of or before the festival of Dionysos, and both plays involve a party inside one of the private houses on the stage. In the *Persa* and the *Stichus*, Plautus has his slaves freed long enough from the authority of their masters to celebrate an informal Eleutheria or festival of freedom. In the *Casina*, the prologue speaker proclaims that the games (*ludi*) are on and that an Alcedonia is being celebrated in the forum. The name of this particular fictive festival refers to the time of the year when the sea is so calm that the halcyon makes its nest upon the waves, expressing the abandonment of workaday concerns in favour of the spirit of play. No surprise perhaps that some of the most common terms for the playing of a trick by one character on another turn on the same key-word *ludus* and invoke the idea of making a game out of one's victim (*illudere, ludos facere, ludificari*). More troubling to consider the location of so many of the acts of sexual violence, on which numerous comedies turn, in the drunken, nocturnal licence of the Cerealia or Adonia. Is this part of what the audience associate with their experience of festival? If so, do their misadventures always resolve themselves into the happy endings which comedy is generically obliged to supply?

Terence: The invitation to join the coterie

Terence (in full: Publius Terentius Afer) knows how to make his audience think through these problems. The world of his dramas (185–159 BCE) is undoubtedly more naturalistic and less theatricalized than that of Plautus, but those moments where his works reflect the dramatic and comic process which has created them can often have a significant impact. In the *Eunuch*, Chaerea commits a rape by daylight, when sober, and without any festival as a cover for his deeds. He is 16 years old and not even out of the period of military service after which a Terentian hero might well turn to the high life. His arrival on stage entirely smitten with his future victim prompts the slave Parmeno to muse that the madness of a passionate Chaerea will make the activities of his elder brother look like a game and a joke (*ludum iocumque*). Yet Parmeno takes the girl for a prostitute and decides to educate Chaerea in the ways of this class by sneaking him into the house of the courtesan Thais and urging him to 'take your food with her, be near her, touch her, play with her, sleep by her'. Parmeno never means Chaerea to do anything like what he actually does. What then is to be made of the emergence of the distressed maid Pythias? She recounts the rape to the audience and complains that Chaerea has made a mockery of the girl, that the women of the house have been laughed at in unworthy ways. When Chaerea returns, she assumes that he must mean to laugh at them all over again. Is this then funny, a fit subject for laughter? Were Chaerea to think of his rape as getting the laugh over his victim, what would that mean to the audience?

Terence uses the language proper to the experience of the comic audience in order to frame the questions implied. Even more striking is the way that the same terms recur at the close of the drama. Is the question answered or the problem put forward again? Pythias has blamed Parmeno for suggesting the plan to Chaerea and complains again of being mocked. Yet she will not go unavenged. Rather, she in turn performs a trick on Parmeno by pretending that Chaerea is receiving an adulterer's punishment, causing the slave to warn the boy's aged father Laches, who therefore bursts into the house of Thais. The result is a joke which, as she puts it, she alone got. Pythias therefore celebrates and assures Parmeno that she cannot tell him what *games* he provided indoors. Now it is Parmeno's turn to complain that he is being laughed at. There is something deeply uncomfortable about this process. The reciprocity whereby I laugh at you and then you at me and we both go off hand in hand is too neat and schematic. It makes us think that it is all over, that one level of conflict has been resolved. But it does so by inviting us to imagine that a foolish jape with an old man and a slave is in some sense commensurable with a rape, when any rational judgement would tell us that they belong to entirely separate scales. The process which began by helping us frame the question 'Is Rape Funny?' closes by telling us that rape can somehow be accommodated within a process of comic exchange. But can it? The audience of the *Eunuch* have come to be entertained and to laugh, but it is not obvious that they find in the laughter of Pythias the perfect reflection of their aspirations.

Much of the appeal of Terence's comedy is cerebral. Yet it is worth bearing in mind that this same *Eunuch* earned Terence the unprecedented fee of 8,000 sesterces, and that its first performance was received with such acclaim that it was reprised that very day. Terence the success, the crowd-pleaser does not feature very prominently in literary histories and he has only himself to blame for it. The fault lies with the two prologues which accompany another of Terence's works, the *Hecyra* or *Mother-in-law*, both of which tell of calamitous events at the first two attempts to put on the play. No more famous tale of artistic disaster has come down from antiquity. According to the first prologue, the première could not be seen or heard because the people became captivated by the counter-attraction of a rope-dancer. The second prologue is rather more elaborate. The speaker now is the great actor-manager L. Ambivius Turpio and his stated resolution is to show the same persistence in backing Terence as once he did with the great Caecilius Statius (*c.*225–168 BCE). This is how he tells the tale of the initial failure of the play:

> Now as for what I seek for my own sake, your benevolent attention please.
> I bring you the *Mother-in-law*, a play I have never been allowed
> to perform in silence; so cruelly has disaster dogged it.
> Your understanding will ease that disaster,
> if it will give assistance to my zeal.
> The first time I started to perform it, the boasting of boxers,
> (and the eager expectation of a rope-walker to boot)
> the gathering of fans, the din, the shouting of women,
> drove me off the stage ahead of time.
> I decided to follow my old method of
> experiment with a new play: I put it on again.
> For the first act they loved me; when the story went around
> that gladiators were next on, the crowd rushed in,
> rioted, shouted, fought for a place.
> Now there is no disturbance: peace and quiet reign:
> I am granted the time to act; you are given
> the chance to add some splendour to the theatrical games.
> As much as you can, let not the art of the muses
> fall into the hands of the few; make your authority
> favour and aid my authority.
>
> (Terence, *The Mother-in-law* 28–48)

Much has been made of this story. Some dismiss it as a charming fiction; others assume that the other less elevated attractions deprived Terence of the attention of his audience and that they rushed off to wherever they were being held. Others rightly point out that the real trouble only starts when word gets round that boxers and gladiators are due to *follow* the performance of the *Mother-in-law* and on the same stage. In other words, what actually goes wrong is that the refined entertainment on offer is drowned out by the fight for seats as grapple-fans and aesthetes come to blows. Even when aesthetes are foolish enough to involve themselves in such disputes, it tends to be the grapple-fans who win.

A later source assures us that the third performance of the *Mother-in-law* was a hit. Its popularity may not have matched that of the *Eunuch*, perhaps, but a success it was for all that. How then are we to reconcile these protestations of failure on the part of the author with what seem to be the facts of his actual good fortune? The answer surely is that Terence has constructed a comic personality for himself. His comedies display a genuine subtlety and intellectual refinement and they eschew the most physical and farcical elements of Plautus.

There are not the burping, drunken slaves of *Pseudolus* and *Stichus* or the piggy-back riding with which the *Asinaria* concludes. The best way then to see off the inevitable accusations of élitism is to embrace them and make a joke out of them. The audience which stays with the *Mother-in-law* until the very end can identify itself with the culturally refined and against the boorish mob.

The same procedure is apparent in other Terentian prologues. In the *Phormio*, for instance, a 'malevolent old poet' is said to complain that Terence's previous plays are slender in language and lightweight in composition (*tenui . . . oratione et scriptura levi*). A century later, Cicero will characterize the stylistically ultra-refined speeches of the orator C. Licinius Calvus as too attenuated (*attenuata*) to appeal to any other than the most attentive of audiences. Calvus was also one of the most prominent of the neoterics (cf. Ch. 11, pp. 349–52) who set out to bring a new stylistic refinement to Latin poetry and who paraded their rejection of a mass audience in favour of the select few who could appreciate their work. The protestation of slenderness becomes a watchword amongst their heirs, the elegists. The audience of the *Phormio* is lured with the chance to be part of the coterie, to belong to that refined grouping who truly appreciate the new literature.

A comparable principle underlies Terence's refusal in the *Brothers* to grow indignant at the accusation of the same 'malevolent old poet' that he has had a hand in writing his comedies from unnamed aristocratic friends. Terence just notes that he considers it a mark of distinction to please those who 'please the people and all of you'. If the poet embraces the implication that he is a friend of the most powerful his language reminds the audience that they share his esteem for the people who esteem him. They are not so detached from the circle which sustains the poet; they can choose to be part of the group.

The advantages of noble friends

There is a wonderful paradox in the idea that Terence, a 25-year-old Carthaginian former slave, was able to produce Latin of such purity and excellence that it became a school text for the rest of antiquity and the Renaissance. He is even claimed to have met his early death in a storm at sea as he sailed back to Italy from Athens with fresh texts of Menander to adapt for the Roman stage, a martyr to the cultural transformation of his adopted land. Perhaps the very strangeness of his achievement provoked the gossip and calumny to which he offers his insouciant response. For a certainty that gossip was not wholly unwelcome. The claim that Terence did not work alone inevitably rebounds on the detractors because it is a mark of his distinction that men so great should be willing to risk association with his work. Terence, meanwhile, enjoys the reflected glory of collaboration with the best public men that Rome could produce.

It will be noted that Terence does not identify his noble friends. Ancient writers are not slow to supply us with names. Around the end of the second or start of the first centuries BCE, the scurrilous poet Porcius Licinus identifies these men as the great P. Scipio Aemilianus, C. Laelius, and Furius Philus; he also alleges that the relationship was as sexual as it was literary, and implies that poor Terence was taken advantage of, tricked, and abandoned. Fifty or so years later, Cicero and Nepos also report the claim that Terence associated with Scipio and Laelius though they add none of the venomous allegations. Other authorities contest the association with Scipio, Laelius, and Philus on the grounds that they were too young at the time that the comedies were composed, and propose a rather older generation of friends. It is more than likely that none of our sources does more than offer a plausible supplement to Terence's deliberately unspecific references and that the identity of the noble friends will never be known. Yet the significance of the issue is not exhausted in this.

Half a century before Terence, the poet Naevius was put in prison. His offence was to have insulted the leading men of the day in his comedies. One line of verse attributed to him assaults a family closely allied with the Scipios, the Metelli, while another takes as its target the great victor of the Second Punic War, Scipio Africanus himself. A law of the archaic Twelve Tables banning malicious incantation was twisted to fit the offence and the first known libel trial at Rome begun. Plautus in the *Boastful Soldier* alludes darkly to the fate of his fellow poet. About a generation after Terence, two further libel trials took place. Both resulted from things said from the public stage in comic mimes. Accius the tragedian launched a successful suit for defamation, Lucilius the father of Roman satire failed. It is worth considering the implications of this pattern.

All six of the 'noble friends' who are alleged to have given Terence a hand in the composition of his comedies had held or were destined to hold the consulship, the highest magistracy at Rome. This is not accidental. What it represents correlates perfectly with the peculiar fact that the only libels recorded as having led to prosecution were those delivered in the theatre. The senatorial rhetoric of the late Republic is often magnificently free with its insults and abuse—the *Against Piso* of Cicero is the most obvious case—and it is unlikely that the orators of the second century were much different. Yet a slander delivered in the Senate, by one of equal status and before one's peers, can be absorbed and poses no threat to class solidarity. A slander from the stage and before the massed ranks of the festival audience is a far more threatening matter. It is evident that the senatorial class were only too aware of the threat to public order posed by the theatre. It is probably for this reason that no permanent stone theatre was permitted in Rome until 55 BCE. Many proposals were made for its construction, one was even set up in 154 BCE and then taken down stone by stone. The principle of the annual erection and then removal of a wooden structure is underscored by the sense that the theatre must be policed and cannot expect unconditional indulgence.

The account of the suits launched by Accius and Lucilius specifies their objection to being mocked by name; when Aulus Gellius states that the jokes against the great of Naevius followed the Greek manner he refers to the tendency of the comedian Aristophanes to make fun of named contemporaries. The link between the prosecutions is evident. Strange therefore to read in Horace and others that the true heir of Aristophanic comedy and Archilochean iambus at Rome was none other than one of our plaintiffs: Lucilius (148–103 BCE). There is indeed scarcely a description of the poetry of Lucilius in antiquity which does not emphasize the pile of insults under which he buried the likes of L. Cornelius Lentulus Lupus, the venomous mockery which he directed at the hapless Q. Caecilius Metellus Macedonicus. To anyone who feels that a satirist should be able to take what he himself dishes out, it will surely come as a relief to note that Lucilius failed in his own prosecution. Yet what truly requires investigation here is not why Lucilius was frustrated in his attempt to protect his own name, but rather how he was able for so long to get away with besmirching that of others.

The origins of satire are obscure. Livy and Valerius Maximus refer to the performance of dramatic *satura* on the stage but it is entirely unclear what form this took. Ennius composed literary *Satires* but only thirty-one lines of these remain. The different fragments touch on food and parasitism, wine-drinking, and a figure very like the comic running-slave; they also display some virtuoso word-play and deploy an Aesopic fable. The affinities to comedy in terms of content and style are therefore apparent, but it is hard to conceive how a complete Ennian satire might have looked. For later Roman satirists the true father is, in any case, Lucilius. For it is Lucilius who, after much experiment, fixes on the dactylic hexameter as the metre for satire and it is he who associates the form with the laceration of contemporary mores and of representative debased individuals. Even when Horace, Persius, and Juvenal confess the impossible hazards of emulating the outspokenness of Lucilius, he is still acknowledged as the authentic model for the satiric mode.

How then did Lucilius achieve the freedom to speak out as he did? In part, the answer must lie in his social status, which was considerably closer to the senatorial class than to that of a Naevius: a member of the equestrian order, a landowner of some significance, the uncle of the future Pompey the Great.

When Horace sizes himself up against Lucilius, he confesses that he is below him in rank as well as innate gifts. Even more significant perhaps is the emphasis of later writers on his close friendship with the very same men whom Porcius accuses of writing the comedies of Terence: Scipio Aemilianus and C. Laelius. The only difference is that Lucilius enjoyed their friendship, not in their early youth, but in their days of power, when they were truly the leading men of the state. There is a famous anecdote which tells of Laelius stumbling on Lucilius as he chases Scipio around the couches with a knotted napkin; it reveals a great deal about the position of safety from which Lucilius could fire off his attacks. Most important of all, however, must be the evidence supplied by Lucilius in what became confusingly listed as book 26 of his *Satires* but was in fact the very first which he published. In a significant passage, Lucilius disavows the desire to appeal to a very high-brow audience and chooses instead men of the middling sort like Decumus Laelius and Iunius Congus who are neither highly educated nor unlettered and untaught. What must be noted here is the phrase 'I care not that Persius should *read* me'. The works of Lucilius are book literature, not for performance from the public stage. They may insult the powerful but they are in no danger of reaching so wide an audience as to threaten the stability of the senatorial class.

The earliest writers of Latin literature engage with an ever-changing audience. The same work may pass through the hands of aristocratic admirers, satisfy both the watchful magistrate who buys it and the mass audience of the festival, then end up canonized for the purity of its diction and learned by heart in all the city's classrooms. In the examination of the *Little Carthaginian* and the *Annales* with which this chapter began, it was my aim to demonstrate that we can learn (or rather unlearn) a huge amount about the nature of the audience simply by remaining alert to the peculiarities of the work. If the *Little Carthaginian* remains an extremely eccentric cultural production for the years straight after the Second Punic War, then we should reconsider our assumptions about the Roman audience with which it was presumably such a success. With the closing investigation of the law of libel, the importance of powerful friends and the difference between festive performance and limited edition publication, I have endeavoured to show how the political, economic, and social conditions of reception can fundamentally alter the significance of a literary work. Naevius and Lucilius both bring the traditions of Aristophanes and Archilochos to Rome; but the same insult thrown out on the public stage can mean far more than when it is written down in a book by one who can always summon a Scipio to his aid.

10 Forging a national identity: Prose literature down to the time of Augustus

CHRISTINA S. KRAUS

Greece and the beginnings of Latin prose

> Cato was an old man when Karneades the Academic and Diogenes the Stoic philosopher came to Rome. . . . Karneades was highly charismatic, no less impressive in reality than in reputation, and it was he in particular who won large and sympathetic audiences. Like a wind, his presence filled the city with noise, as the word spread about a Greek with an extraordinary ability to amaze his audiences. People said that he had instilled in the young men of the city a fierce passion which caused them to banish all their other pleasures and pastimes, and succumb to love of knowledge. . . . Right from the start Cato . . . worried that the young men of the city might find a reputation for eloquence more desirable than one gained for practical and military achievements. . . . In the course of trying to turn his son against Greek ways, he predicts, in an almost oracular fashion, that Rome will be destroyed when it has become affected by Greek learning. But now we can see that this slander of his is hollow, since we live at a time when Rome is at a pinnacle of political success and has appropriated Greek learning and culture. (Plutarch, *Life of Cato the Elder* 22–3, trans. R. Waterfield)

Writing about the influential political and literary figure Marcus Porcius Cato (234–149 BCE), the first century CE biographer Plutarch here shows clearly how from an early point in its development Rome wrestled with the twin problems of foreign influence and imperial expansion (see pp. 292–3). The city's foundation myths, codified in the first century BCE but existing long before that, described a mingling of cultures: Trojan and native Italian; Etruscan, Sabine, and Roman; Greek and Roman. In the middle of Romulus' new city, founded, according to one ancient calculation, in 753 BCE, was a place called the 'asylum', designed to attract new citizens: 'some free, some slaves, and all of them wanting nothing but a fresh start', in the words of the Augustan historian Livy.

As the city grew by virtue of its exceptional military skill and boundless appetite for territory, it assimilated lands and peoples at first immediately adjacent—the Sabines and the Etruscans—and then further and further afield, until by the time of the birth of Christ Rome dominated the Mediterranean, Europe as far as the Rhine, Turkey, the Middle East, North Africa, and more. Each act of conquest was also an act of negotiation. The roads that the Roman armies marched down from the capital into the provinces carried Roman customs, laws, demands for taxes, and other instruments of imperialism. They also, however, famously led back to Rome: and on them, from the beginning, travelled foreigners bringing with them their own customs, ideas, and literature. Strikingly, almost no important Latin literary figure whose work has survived from the Republic and the Empire was born in Rome (see pp. 293–4): Ennius came from the heel of Italy, Cato the Elder from Tusculum, Cicero from Arpinum, Sallust from Amiternum, Livy from Padua (all small Italian municipalities); Catullus, Virgil, Horace, and Ovid from similar Italian towns; Tacitus and Frontinus from southern France, the Plinys from northern Italy; the Senecas, Martial, Quintilian, and Columella from Spain; Terence and Aulus Gellius (probably) from North Africa.

The process of assimilation, adaptation, and incorporation of Greek, native Italian, and other foreign ideas into Roman literature is one that is hard to document before the third century BCE, largely owing to our lack of evidence—and for all periods our best evidence is for the assimilation of Greek culture. We know that Greek cults were accepted into Roman religious practice beginning back in the fifth century; that Roman aristocrats took Greek nicknames in the late fourth and early third centuries; and that in 282 BCE a Roman ambassador to Taras, in southern Italy, tried to conduct his negotiations in Greek. His Greek was so flawed, so the story goes, and the Tarentines' insulting reaction was so humiliating, that the Romans ended up at war with Taras. True or not, the story is revealing. The Romans would eventually settle on Latin as the language of state, diplomacy, and formal occasions; but Greek increasingly became the cultural language of the literate élite, whose teachers and companions were Greek, and whose education often took place partly in Greece. These Romans, members of the governing aristocracy, wanted to show that, as they had mastered Greek territory, so they could master the language of Homer and Plato; but they also wanted to acquire some of that ancient intellectual and cultural heritage. Their intellectual project was fuelled by geopolitical reality: in the early second century Rome won distinguished victories over the royal successors to Alexander the Great. After each war, booty flowed back to the city: hundreds of statues, paintings, *objets d'art*, and at least one royal library. In 133 the last king of Pergamon, one of the two premier centres for scholarship and literature in the Hellenistic world, bequeathed to Rome his kingdom—including his library. And in 86, as the crowning touch, Sulla sacked Athens and brought Aristotle's library to Rome.

Along with the physical objects, during these years there also came to Rome Greek intellectuals, either as hostages (like the historian Polybios, who arrived in 167—see p. 263), as slaves or as voluntary exiles (the Stoic philosopher Panaetios, in the 140s), or as ambassadors, like Krates of Mallos in the 160s or Karneades the Sceptic, head of the Platonic Academy in Athens, in 155. The quotation from Plutarch's life of Cato the Elder which formed the epigraph above shows some of the excitement, and some of the ambivalence, that these Greeks aroused in Roman audiences. Karneades' speeches were show-piece orations, delivered on successive days, arguing for and against the idea of justice (see pp. 145–7, 192–4). These 'eristic' declamations, which demonstrated the priority of argument over substance, may have pleased the Roman youth, but they profoundly shocked the more conservative senators. Yet however much these men inclined towards Cato the Elder's (perhaps apocryphal) advice, 'grasp the content and the words will follow', they also recognized that governing a growing Empire increasingly demanded competence not only in military but also in political skills, first and foremost among them the ability to argue persuasively in favour of one's policies, both at home and abroad.

Political oratory—persuasive speeches delivered to a senatorial or a (primarily) citizen audience—existed at Rome before Karneades. When Lucius Postumius Megellus spoke at Taras, he spoke in prose, perhaps delivering a full-scale oration. Oratory is imagined as going back to the very beginnings of the Roman Republic: Livy has Brutus, one of the men who drove the kings from Rome, address the people in 509 BCE, and Cicero attributes a speech of popular appeal to Valerius Poplicola, consul in the first year of the Republic. The earliest speech for which there is more reliable historical evidence is one given by the patrician senator Appius Claudius the Blind in 280, advising the Senate against making a treaty with King Pyrrhos of Epeiros, who was leading the Tarentines against Rome. From that point until the first speech of the great orator Cicero (*For Quinctius,* 81 BCE), we have only fragments of Roman oratory. The largest number come from Cato the Elder, whose senatorial career, stemming from humble, non-aristocratic beginnings, spanned the period of geopolitical expansion mentioned above, and whose more than 100 published speeches marked the beginning of Roman oratory as a literary genre. He is a key example of someone whose ambivalent reaction to the Hellenization of Rome demonstrates both the appeal and the threat of Greek literature to its new, Roman audience. The considerable, though fragmentary, remains of his speeches show the unmistakable influence of Greek rhetorical training, and yet are throughout concerned with moulding his Roman audiences ethically and morally in ways consistent with Roman tradition. In one of the longest extracts, he persuades the senate not to take extreme vengeance on the island of Rhodes, which had failed to oppose Rome's enemy King Perseus of Macedon:

> As for me, I think that the Rhodians did not want us to win as complete a victory as we did. . . . They were frightened that, if we had no one to fear and could do what we liked, they might fall under our sole sway and be subservient to us. It is their concern for their liberty, in my view, that prompted them to follow this policy. Yet the Rhodians never aided Perseus officially. Consider how much more cautiously we behave between ourselves in private. For each one of us, if he thinks that his interests are threatened, strives his utmost to prevent this—and this is what has happened to them. . . . Shall we today abandon in one fell swoop such an exchange of services on both sides, so great a friendship? Are we going to be the first to set about doing what we accuse them of wanting to do? . . . If it is not right to receive a badge of honour if one has said that one wished to do good but has not done so, shall the Rhodians suffer prejudice not because they have done wrong but because they are said to have wanted to do so? (Cato, *Origins* fr. 5. 3, trans. M. R. Comber)

Cato here appeals to the traditional building-blocks of Roman self-image and imperial values: liberty, self-interest, advantageous alliances, and the importance of deeds over words. Speaking to an audience of equals, in power if not in prestige (this speech dates from the height of Cato's long and distinguished career as a senior senator), he also insists that they put themselves in the Rhodians' shoes. He interweaves his own opinion with that of the Romans, speaking for his audience, encouraging them to see things through his eyes. And yet he asks them to imagine that they are someone else as well, Greeks who have nothing in common with Roman traditions. Cato's audience can thus feel both superior to, and empathetic with, the people of Rhodes. This bold, persuasive strategy at once associates the Romans with their enemy and invites the Senate to practice mercy, in effect to treat the Rhodians as the Romans would like to be treated if the circumstances were reversed. It is a small but important example of the power of political oratory, specifically of its ability to manipulate audiences in more than one direction at once, and subtly to question, while at the same time to reinforce, cultural stereotypes.

Cato, followed in short order by Tiberius Gracchus and Gaius Gracchus, famous popular leaders of the 130s and 120s, used Greek technical virtuosity to make political oratory into an effective weapon. The ability to control persuasive discourse is the first step towards controlling opinion: hence Rome, as a growing imperial power, prized rhetorical skills. In the years between Cato's death in 149 BCE and the start of the careers of the conservative statesman Cicero and the radical aristocrat Julius Caesar, around 80 BCE, Greek learning and literature steadily established itself as both a model and a challenge for Roman writers. And as the City (*urbs*) gradually overlapped with the world (*orbis*), so the Romans added a literary/cultural empire to their political one, developing the prose genres of oratory, history, philosophy, and technical prose with characteristic speed.

'The light of day, the Forum, the faces of my fellow citizens'

When Marcus Tullius Cicero returned to Rome in 74 BCE after a year as assistant governor of Sicily, he learned a valuable lesson:

> I thought at the time that no one at Rome was talking about anything but my quaestorship. . . . The Sicilians had dreamed up unprecedented honours for me. So I left Sicily expecting that the Roman people would rush to lay everything before me. But by chance on my trip I happened to call in at Puteoli [a sea-side resort near Naples] when it was crowded (as usual) with all the best people. Gentlemen, I nearly fell over with surprise when someone asked me what day I had left Rome and if there was any news. . . . That incident, judges, may have done me more good than if everyone had come up and congratulated me. Once I realized that the Roman people have slightly deaf ears, but that their eyes are keen and sharp, I stopped thinking about what people might hear about me and saw to it that they should see me in the flesh every day. I lived in their sight, I besieged the Forum. (Cicero, *For Plancius* 64–6)

The only place that mattered was Rome, and specifically the Forum, where trials, open-air speeches in the *comitium* (public gathering-place), and other business took place. During the last years of the Roman Republic, the three decades or so preceding the assassination of Julius Caesar in 44 BCE, Cicero and other advocates developed political oratory into what was later regarded as its finest, freest form. Cicero's are the only speeches which survive in their entirety; for that reason, as well as for the high quality of his work, he has long been known as 'eloquence personified', as the scholar Quintilian called him 150 years later. Though he spent a year in exile in Greece and another year as governor of the eastern province of Cilicia, and though he regularly travelled to his country villas in Italy, for most of his life he followed his own advice, making Rome his base of operations, building and then securing his reputation as the wittiest, the most patriotic, and (at times) the most respected, statesman in town.

Such a reputation depends on an audience. Cicero spoke both in the Senate House, to his peers, and outside, to juries and—in addresses to the people (*contiones*)—to anyone who wanted to listen. Despite the deep-seated Roman suspicion of any kind of intellectual activity for its own sake, the urban populace, both aristocratic and plebeian, was eager to listen to oratory. And Cicero—who himself, like Cato the Elder, was the first member of his provincial family to rise to the Roman Senate—knew how to manipulate a variety of audiences. He begins one of his most successful speeches with an apology for taking up a festal day with business:

> If, members of the jury, there should happen to be present among us here today anyone who is unfamiliar with our laws, courts and way of doing things, I am sure he would wonder what terrible enormity this case involves, since on a day of festivities and public days, when all other legal business is suspended, this court alone remains in session—and he would have no doubt at all that the defendant must be guilty of a crime so terrible that, unless action were taken, the state could not possibly survive!

Having raised his audience's expectations that they will be trying a spectacularly vicious crime, well worth missing the games, Cicero suddenly changes tack and as good as promises that his case will be just as entertaining as those missed theatrical shows (which themselves might well have featured young men at the mercy of prostitutes):

> If he were then to be told that no crime, no enormity, and no act of violence had been brought before the court, but that a brilliantly able, hardworking, and popular young man is being accused by the son of someone he has prosecuted . . . and that this attack on him is being financed by a prostitute, he would find no fault with the prosecutor's sense of filial duty, he would consider that a woman's passions should be kept under control, and he would conclude that you yourselves are overworked, since even on a public holiday you are not allowed the day off! (Cicero, *For Caelius* 1, trans. D. H. Berry)

Throughout the speech Cicero exploits the closeness of oratorical to theatrical performance, delivering a *tour de force* of comic argument that must have provided more than adequate compensation for the jurors' forgone holiday. The analogy between the two kinds of performance is an essential one. Roman literature had always been performative, both in the technical sense of the dramas of Plautus, Terence, and others (see pp. 298–307), and in the more general sense that it was more often heard than read silently. By the end of the 30s BCE, public recitations of literature were being given on a regular basis to small groups, usually friends of the author. But it is oratory which had always had particular affinities with stage performance. The three aims of a speaker, says Cicero—who wrote handbooks of rhetorical instruction as well as practical examples of speeches—are 'to charm, to teach, and to move'. All are focused on the audience; the success of each depends on the orator's creation of a successful bond between himself and his listeners, be that a group of his peers, a preselected jury, or a randomly assembled crowd in the Forum. And each audience required a slightly different technique: different levels of intimacy, different means of arousing sympathy or indignation, different applications of humour.

But acting was also dangerous, not least because it was the province of the lower classes and of Greek professionals. Aristocratic horror at the Emperor Nero's public performances in the first century CE arose primarily from his violation of class boundaries: aristocrats didn't act. But there was more to this fear of theatrical technique than class prejudice. Just as Karneades had demonstrated that words can be manipulated to argue both sides of any question, so acting exposed the inherent slip between appearance and reality. Cicero's most successful speeches are those in which he exploits his relationship with his audience, creating a persuasive persona which can carry his listeners along with him: the outraged, deeply traditional consul in the *Against Piso*; the sophisticated man-about-town and gentle but firm father-figure in the speech for Caelius; the ideal Roman politician, friend of the people and upholder of tradition in the *For Sestius*; the philhellenic Roman devotee of literature in the *For Archias*. But in every case he had to make sure that the mask was not perceptible as a mask, that the dramatic illusion was not broken—or, if it was, as in the *Caelius*, whose humour depends partly on the audience's complicity with Cicero's fun, that it was broken with the listeners' full awareness and acceptance. Nor were these easy audiences to fool, being both connoisseurs and experienced hecklers:

> I laughed at someone in court lately
> Who, when my Calvus gave a splendid
> Account of all Vatinius' crimes,
> With hands raised in surprise announced
> 'Great Gods, the squirt's articulate!'
>
> (Catullus 53, trans. G. Lee)

The crowd, or *corona*, was as important to an orator as any judge or jury, and Cicero was an expert at playing to it. So in his third speech against the revolutionary Catiline, for instance, Cicero uses the topography of the Capitoline hill and the Forum, and particularly a freshly erected statue of Jupiter Optimus Maximus (the Best and Greatest, the city's presiding deity), to sway the crowd:

> Certainly you remember that when Cotta and Torquatus were consuls many things on the Capitol were struck by lightning: the images of the immortal gods were moved, statues of many ancient men were thrown down, and the bronze tablets of the laws melted. Even the statue of Romulus, who founded this city, was struck. . . . And the soothsayers said that murder, fire, the end of the law, civil war, and the fall of the entire city and empire were at hand unless we appeased the immortal gods. . . . They ordered us to make a large statue of Jupiter, and to fix it in a high location . . . saying that if that statue which you now see looked on the rising of the sun and the Forum and the Senate House, those secret conspiracies directed against the safety of the city and of the empire would be brought to light so as to be clearly visible to the Senate and the Roman people. And the consuls ordered the statue to be so placed; but it was not set up . . . before this very day. (Cicero, *Against Catiline* 3. 19–20)

Here the orator mixes appeals to fear, hope, and the power of the state persuasively to reassure the audience: at last the danger threatening Rome from the rebel Catiline is under control, and Cicero lets us know that it is *his* control.

But what happens when the crowd is not friendly? In 52 Cicero spoke in defence of his friend Annius Milo, who was tried on the charge of having murdered a popular, and violent, fellow politician. The court was ringed with the soldiers of the powerful general Pompey the Great, then sole consul, whose rule was law. Cicero lost the case. Later, however, he published a new version of the *For Milo*, a version which was never delivered orally but which shows how he would have manipulated the audience if he had not been intimidated by the fierce *corona* of soldiers:

> I realize, members of the jury, that it is disgraceful, when beginning a speech in defence of a man of great courage, to show fear oneself, and that it is highly unbecoming, when Titus Annius is less concerned for his own survival than for that of his country, not to show equal strength of character in pleading his case. But even so, the unfamiliar look of this unfamiliar court alarms my very eyes. . . . You the jury are not hemmed in by a ring of spectators as you used to be, nor are we surrounded by the usual packed crowd. Those guards which you can see in front of all the temples cannot fail to cause a speaker a twinge of alarm. . . . As for the rest of the crowd gathered here, it is, inasmuch as it consists of Roman citizens, entirely on our side. You can see the people looking on from every direction, from wherever any part of the Forum happens to be visible. They are eagerly awaiting the outcome of this trial; and there is not a man among them who does not support Milo's courage and believe that himself, his children, his country, and his fortunes are this very day at stake. (Cicero, *For Milo* 1–3, trans. D. H. Berry)

As in the *Caelius*, Cicero asks his audience to identify with him, alarming them with the importance and novelty of their position. Also as in the earlier speech, he then lets them off the hook: the new situation is not as alarming as it seems; we are in fact being protected by these soldiers. He then turns to emotional appeal: it is not only the defendant whose life and family and country is at stake, but every one present. And as in the speech for Plancius (above), Cicero appeals not to sound but to sight: the spectacle of this trial, the sight of the Forum, is all-important. The emotional argument expands, therefore, to take in not only the speaker but also the man on trial, as the audience is moved to identify both with the orator guiding them and with the defendant whose fate they are to decide. It is a brilliant introduction to a brilliant speech. Milo, in exile in southern France (partly owing to the failure of Cicero's original effort), is said to have replied that he was glad Cicero had not delivered the rewritten version: otherwise, he would never have had the chance to taste the excellent Marseilles fish. The failure of the first speech did not stop Cicero from rewriting, and publishing, his second version. Though Roman oratory was a public phenomenon, fully integrated into the experience of citizens, who in turn had an important role in regulating the political and social prestige of the speakers, there was more than one venue for the distribution of political speeches—and, indeed, for the publication of other kinds of prose literature.

Select audiences

It is not certain what proportion of Romans could read. Though the city was covered with inscriptions recording the texts of laws, treaties, dedications to the gods, epitaphs, and the achievements of statesmen and generals, it seems clear that a high proportion, at least, of this ubiquitous writing functioned simply as display, as reinforcement of status, a declaration and affirmation of Romanness. The market for books (as opposed to performances of drama or oratory) was restricted to a small, educated, and therefore largely affluent group, mostly comprising men who were also involved in government or in high-level business of some kind, such as Cicero's friend Atticus. The circumstances of book production had a great deal to do with keeping the market small: books had to be copied one by one, and the ancient format of a papyrus roll was easy neither to read nor to store. There may have been something of a more general market for technical manuals such as Vitruvius' *On Architecture* (from the Augustan period) or Columella's Neronian treatise on farming, and we know that in the late first century CE the professor Quintilian complained that notes from his lectures on oratory were being circulated without his

SCHOOLWORK. *On this sarcophagus from the second century* CE *a father (or teacher) is shown instructing a boy as is symbolized by the papyrus rolls they hold in their hands. Rhetoric would have been the fundamental element of all such education at this period.*

approval. But the tendency of Roman society to encourage a highly competitive governing élite, which judged its leisure (*otium*) as much as its work (*negotium*) by how it was perceived from the outside, reinforced the tendency even for literature to remain within a small, select circle (see pp. 336–8, 492–518). This élite took up new developments in so far as they reinforced traditional ways: hence the popularity of rhetoric, which could enhance traditional values via persuasive oratory. In other disciplines, too, the areas in which Roman intellectual growth is most marked in the late Republic are those which match aristocratic vested interests: agriculture, history, ethical philosophy, practical science such as engineering, grammar (a branch of rhetoric), law, and the history of religion, whose practice was also in the control of the political élite.

The producers of much of this prose literature as well as its consumers were members of the governing class. It is not until the Ciceronian period, or perhaps just slightly before, that any professional writers of history appear on the scene, and they are only isolated cases; other fields, especially mathematics, astronomy, music, and medicine were reserved for Greeks. But the period is rich in prose written by and circulated among the educated classes: political tracts such as the *For Milo* (and, indeed, Cicero's first major court success, the

Against Verres of 70); farming manuals (including an influential early one by Cato the Elder); grammatical treatises; histories of Rome and its conquests; and collections of 'antiquarian' information on ancient customs, religious ritual, and the like. The Sabine Marcus Terentius Varro (116–27 BCE) had a writing career which was itself a microcosm of this intellectual activity by and for the élite: a senator and general, he wrote over 600 books, including 150 of satirical verse; the core, however, was a series of wide-ranging studies in almost every branch of scholarly activity, the most influential concerned with Roman customs, language, and religious tradition.

The setting of many of these works brings their select audience home, as for instance the beginning of Varro's treatise in dialogue form on farming (37 BCE):

> On the festival of the Sementivae ['Sowing'] I had gone to the temple of Earth . . . where I found my father-in-law Gaius Fundanius, Gaius Agrius, a Roman knight and a Socratic philosopher, and the tax collector Publius Agrasius, all looking at a map of Italy painted on the wall. . . . When we had sat down, Agrasius said: 'You have travelled through many lands—have you seen one more cultivated than Italy?' (Varro, *On Rural Matters* 1. 2. 1, 3)

The inner circle here is not only close and familial, but each of the men with whom Varro will converse about farming has a name derived either from *fundus* ('estate') or *ager* ('field'): an inside joke for the educated reader. Varro's contemporary Cicero likewise begins several of his philosophical and political treatises with a group of close friends: so the *On Friendship, On the Laws, On the Nature of the Gods,* the *Brutus* (a history of oratory), etc. The ultimate models for these conversations are Greek dialogues, but the Roman writers cast them into distinctly Roman form, by devices such as Varro's punning names. What is more, these treatises are regularly dedicated to a single person—Varro's, for instance, to his wife *Fund*ania—enhancing the impression of a personal communication. The relationship between writer and dedicatee is often envisaged as that between one who requests and one who grants that request, as at the beginning of Cicero's *Orator* (46 BCE):

> I have long been in great doubt, Brutus, whether it is worse to refuse you . . . or to do what you have often asked. On the one hand, it seems very hard to refuse someone of whom I am particularly fond and who I feel returns my affection, especially since his request is reasonable and he longs for something ennobling; but I thought that to undertake so great a task . . . was scarcely appropriate for one who fears the criticism of learned and judicious men.

For what has Brutus (allegedly) asked? Only that Cicero, the fount of authority on the subject, write a treatise on the best kind of orator and the best method of public speaking. Cicero's introduction tellingly interweaves his own (underplayed) qualifications, the importance and closeness of his addressee, and the larger, but select, audience of readers whose judgement he fears.

The enormous number of letters written by and to Cicero during the middle decades of the last century BCE provides both a glimpse into and an example of this close coterie of aristocrats. Several collections survive: sixteen books of letters to Titus Pomponius Atticus, Cicero's closest friend and a lifelong sounding-board for the orator's political ideas, personal feelings, and academic interests; letters to his brother Quintus, a smaller set which show the orator's familial, often protective persona, but which also give us an insight into the troubles of a family on its way up the social ladder; those to Marcus Brutus, one of Julius Caesar's assassins; and the letters to his 'circle', or *familiares* (often translated 'friends'), which range from personal communications to mini-essays on the good life and other topics, to official state missives. This last group in particular lets us hear the voice not only of Cicero but of his peers, as he kept copies of many of the letters he received as well as those he sent. Even the most personal of these missives shows a concern with self-image, as Cicero and his contemporaries strive to create personas that will show them to their best, or most persuasive, advantage. One example, from a famous letter consoling Cicero on his adult daughter's death, makes this clear:

> As I was on my way back from Asia . . . I began to gaze at the landscape around me. There behind me was Aegina, in front of me Megara, to the right Piraeus, to the left Corinth; once flourishing towns, now lying low in ruins before one's eyes. I began to think to myself: 'Ah! how can we mannikins wax indignant if one of us dies . . . when the corpses of so many towns lie abandoned in a single spot?' . . . You too must dwell instead on recollections worthy of the character you are. Tell yourself that Tullia lived as long as was well for her to live and that she and freedom existed together. She saw you, her father, Praetor, Consul, and Augur. . . . Almost all that life can give, she enjoyed; and she left life when freedom died. . . . And then do not forget that you are Cicero. . . . We have seen more than once how nobly you sustain prosperity, and how great the glory you gain thereby. Let us recognize at last that you are no less able to bear adversity. (Cicero, *To his Friends* 4. 5, trans. D. R. Shackleton Bailey)

The writer, Servius Sulpicius Rufus, a prominent solicitor, shows a concern both for his own image and—especially—for Cicero's: even in the most personal grief, he exhorts the orator not to let his private feelings destroy his public image, and above all, to consider the impact of his actions on the state, and on posterity. The cosmopolitan setting, the Roman values, and the intimate yet formal communication are all typical of one strand of Cicero's correspondence.

The Roman model of intimate, mingled political and intellectual discussion fits well with the story which the Romans themselves told about the beginnings of scholarship in Rome. According to this story, Krates of Mallos, an eminent Homeric scholar and the head of the school of rhetoric at Pergamon, came to Rome (probably in 168 BCE) on a political embassy. While there he fell and broke his leg in the *cloaca maxima*, Rome's greatest sewer and a source of tremendous local pride (in engineering); during his recovery he gave lectures on rhetoric and grammar to aristocrats and intellectuals. The combination of the inner circle, the Greek teacher, and the concentration on the power of rhetorical knowledge would permeate all subsequent Roman philosophy, rhetoric, and political thought.

The craze for rhetoric is understandable, given the Romans' desire for power and for controlling the knowledge that brings power. The question remains, however: what do farming, religious rites, dialectical logic, legal history, or technical grammatical questions (such as the proper way to spell words) have to do with social prestige, or indeed with politics? And why would men like Julius Caesar, who was busy conquering first Gaul, then Rome itself, interrupt his French campaign (in the mid-50s BCE) to compose a work *On Grammatical Analogy*? The answer lies at least partly in the political pressures of the late Republic and in the capacity of literature to generate and respond to the values shared by a community of readers.

During the last century BCE Rome was under extraordinary pressure from without and, particularly, from within. The Empire was now large enough to be difficult to control, and even the sensible Roman practice of letting the provinces run themselves (providing they paid taxes) was putting a strain on central administration. Military commanders were given increasing autonomy in the field, with correspondingly large and loyal armies; fierce competition between them meant that a few strong men—the most famous being Pompey the Great and his adversary Julius Caesar—eventually grew powerful enough to threaten the stability of the state and its traditional republican organization. Rome was on the brink of returning to the form, if not the name, of a monarchy. From the outside, pressures came in the form of foreigners and freed slaves thronging to Rome; as the provinces were gradually allowed more and more political rights, and as classes that were traditionally excluded from government became wealthy and powerful enough to participate in the administration of Empire, familiar systems broke down, some of them irreparably. Much of the technical prose literature of the last years of the Republic reflects an attempt, in various ways, to stabilize this decline.

So in his political and philosophical treatises, for example, especially his

Republic, Cicero attempts to forge a stable language to bolster an increasingly unstable reality. Here he re-creates the nostalgic world of Scipio Aemilianus, the great general and statesman who died in 129 BCE just as popular political agitation was changing Roman politics for good. It is a world in which ancestral values and respect for authority hold sway, in which novelty is distrusted, and in which language follows orderly rules and mirrors a calm, predictable world. Cato the Elder provides the anchor of stability, as shown here in Scipio's introduction to his brief history of Rome:

> As you know, I was especially fond of old Cato and admired him greatly. . . . I devoted myself to him, heart and soul, from my early days. I could never hear enough of his talk—so rich was the man's political experience, which he had acquired during his long and distinguished career in peace and war. Equally impressive were his temperate way of speaking, his combination of seriousness and humour, his tremendous zest for obtaining and providing information, and the closest correspondence between his preaching and his practice. (Cicero, *Republic* 2. 1, trans. N. Rudd)

The key here is the harmony between Cato's life and his words: no gap between appearance and reality, between rhetoric and fact. This nostalgic picture was, by the time Cicero was writing the *Republic* (*c*.51 BCE), already lost; but this and other such treatises were powerful appeals against the inevitable changes that were in progress.

Similarly, works like Marcus Terentius Varro's on the Latin language or on Roman religious history—or even on the history of Roman theatre and the plays of Plautus—strove to reinforce a traditional way of life and an idealized morality. The collection of facts about the past and the establishment (as by Varro and Atticus) of a firm historical chronology offered one defence against frightening political and social change. Biographies of famous men, written by Varro and by Cornelius Nepos (the dedicatee of Catullus' poetry), provided a portrait gallery of exemplary lives to imitate and to avoid; Varro's was accompanied by a volume of 700 pictures with verse epigrams (the *Images*).

In philosophy too, an area up till now dominated by the Greeks, the writers of the late Republic successfully created a distinctively Roman genre, moulding Greek theories and ideas with Roman sensibilities and Roman ideology. Cicero, who is again our chief surviving example, was a leading figure, tackling topics not only of political philosophy (in works such as *The Republic* and *The Laws*, modelled primarily on the Platonic dialogues of the same name), but also of ethics (especially in *On the Limits of Good and Evil, On Duties,* and the *Tusculan Disputations,* on what makes the happy life), epistemology (the *Academica*), and theology (*On the Nature of the Gods, On Fate*). Cicero had been trained both in

Greece and in Rome by eminent philosophers, while his rhetorical training allowed him to argue more than one side of any question. Though he was himself a moderate adherent of Scepticism, he shows special skill in putting arguments from different philosophical schools into the mouths of his characters—for many of his works are in dialogue form, imagined conversations among the learned, aristocratic Romans of the days, set during their leisure time. Writing with incredible speed (many of his philosophical works were produced between February 45 and November 44 BCE) and while pursuing his political career, Cicero created nothing less than a whole language and literature of Latin philosophy, from the most technical academic treatises (the *Paradoxes of the Stoics)* to the most relaxed and elegant of essays (such as *On Old Age,* centring on the character of Cato the Elder, and *On Friendship*).

Finally, to return to the opening of Varro's *On Agriculture*, the scene is set by the participants looking at a map (literally, a 'painted Italy') on the temple wall. Obviously appropriate to the subject of their conversation, this may have been a sort of agricultural survey map—or something more sophisticated. For a growing interest in maps, geography, and ethnography (the study of nations), present already in the Hellenistic scholars in Rome but fuelled by new Roman conquests, led writers like Julius Caesar, Nepos, and others to investigate and record the nature of the lands and peoples whom the Roman armies were conquering. In the midst of all this sat Rome, at the ideal centre of its geographical universe:

> How then could Romulus have achieved with more inspired success the advantages of a coastal city, while avoiding its faults, than by founding Rome on the bank of a river which flowed with its broad stream, smooth and unfailing into the sea? Thus the city could import whatever it needed, and export its surplus; and thanks to the same river it could . . . draw in by sea the commodities most necessary to its life and culture. . . . And so Romulus, in my view, already foresaw that this city would eventually form the site and centre of a world empire. (Cicero, *Republic* 2. 10, trans. N. Rudd)

Rome's position, as these writers made clear to their public, both justified and was justified by its Empire. Foreign tribes became not only a fascinating object of contemplation, but also a means of reinforcing national identity, as they demonstrated what Rome was not. The readers of Nepos' (now lost) *Geography*, for example, must have felt as proud about Rome as they were intrigued by the descriptions of the peoples on its frontiers (see pp. 272–3).

Against this backdrop of imperial expansion and cultural anxiety, one can perhaps begin to see how scholarship itself became a political weapon. How

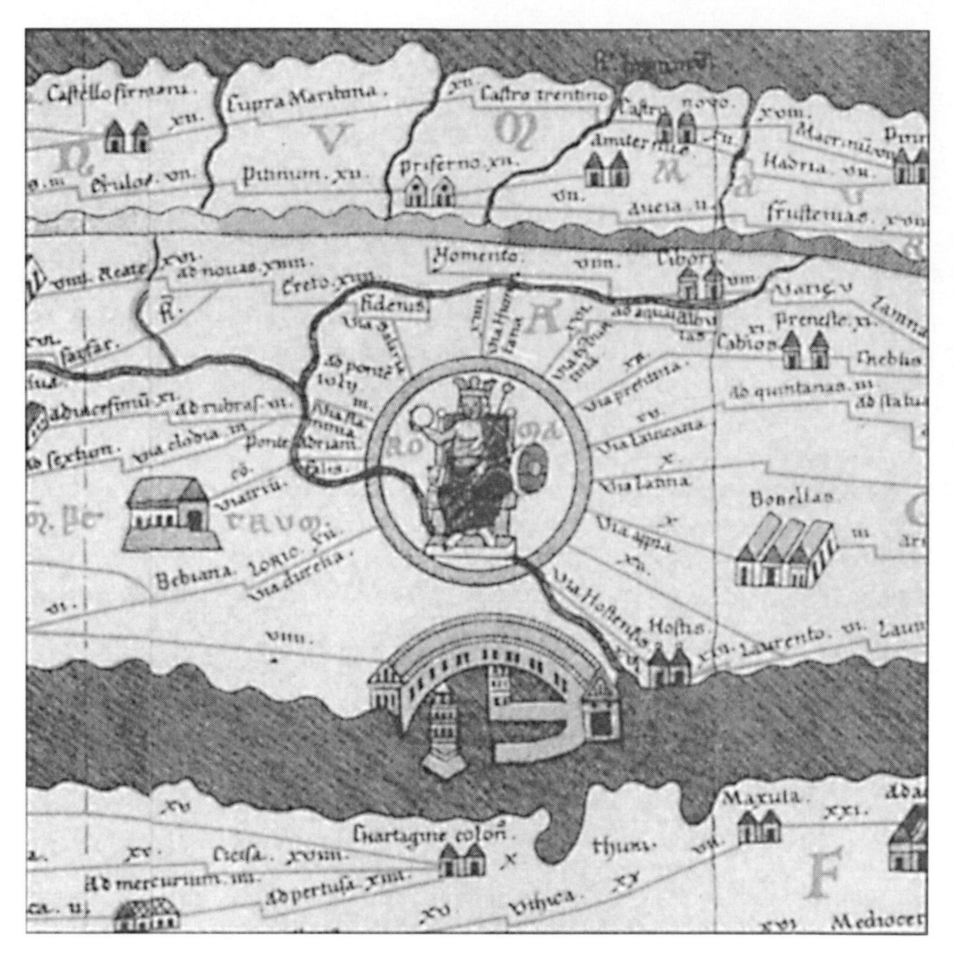

A PAINTED ROMAN WORLD. *The map known as the Peutinger Table was made in c.1200 CE, but based on an itinerary map from the Roman imperial period. Some 7 m. long but only 34 cm. high, it gives a highly distorted version of the Mediterranean world and beyond. This segment is dominated by the city of Rome and its harbour Ostia.*

people spoke, even what words they used and what style they favoured, was seen as a reflection of character, illustrating the doctrine that 'the style is the man' (or, in Latin, *qualis oratio, talis homo*). Correct Latinity, and especially *appropriate* Latinity, was a mark of breeding, judgement, and status (see pp. 266–7). Anthropologists today speak of how a dialect or a local accent functions as cultural currency; Romans like Cicero spoke of those who were 'best' (the *Optimates*) and 'good' (the *boni*), setting up a scale of moral/ethical goodness matching a scale of intellectual and physical decorum. The equation of physical grace with mental dexterity and ethical fitness goes back to the *Iliad*, to the low character Thersites (who had neither); it is alive and well in the late Roman Republic. *Urbanitas*, a word which can mean everything from 'city-smarts' to 'elegance', meant at heart the quality of being Roman: properly Roman, that is, deeply and seriously committed to the city's traditions and to preserving them, as well as being able, in season, to be lighthearted and sophisticated.

What side one took in the debates on proper speech and spelling, what style of oratory one chose to use, what style of physical delivery one affected—all of these declared one's allegiance on the sliding scale of Romanness. Caesar scratched his head with one finger, and was immediately suspect (an effeminate gesture, it also suggested an unhealthy degree of self-absorption—did he perhaps also shave his body?); to wave one's arm too vigorously while orating might indicate a louche character; a toga worn unbelted signified loose morals. So, too, a fondness for Greek epigram or raunchy mimes could indicate an immoral disposition; and over-flowery oratory (tellingly called 'Asiatic'), which revelled in figures of speech, simile, metaphor, and extravagant verbal combinations, might be considered beneath proper Roman dignity. Clarity of expression, however, had to be matched with dignity of style: ordinary language could not become too ordinary, or its distinctively noble character would be lost. The language of comedy, for instance, so appropriate for public performance, was out of the question in a speech on political matters, or in a learned treatise addressed to educated readers. The grammatical, philological, and stylistic debates that occupied the attention of Caesar, Cicero, Brutus, Varro, and others were far from trivial: in them, these men were negotiating their own future and the future of the Republic.

Negotiating the past

> They say that when someone asked the great Themistokles, the greatest man in Athens . . . whose voice he took the greatest delight in hearing, he answered that it was the voice of him who best celebrated his own merit. . . . And so the famous Marius particularly esteemed Lucius Plotius, whose talent, he thought, could best celebrate his achievements. . . . And the poets whose genius celebrates our generals' deeds celebrate at the same time the glory of the Roman people. . . . So we ought to wish that our glory and our fame extend as far as our weapons have reached. . . . How many historians of his deeds is Alexander the Great said to have had with him! And yet, when he stood at the grave of Achilles on Cape Sigeion, he said, 'What a lucky young man you are, to have had Homer as the herald of your

glory!' He spoke the truth: for if the *Iliad* had not existed, the same tomb which covered Achilles' body would have also buried his renown. (Cicero, *For Archias* 20–4)

History. The word can denote many different kinds of writing: full-scale history, which in ancient Rome meant for the most part the history of the Roman Empire under the command of its successful and charismatic generals; biography, which can in some ways be seen as a slice of military history, concentrating on the deeds of single leaders; and *commentarii*, or 'commentaries', relatively unelaborated accounts of a period. Full-scale history could take one of three forms: (1) history 'from Remus and Romulus', as it was known, i.e. beginning with the founding of the city and continuing on, sometimes to the writer's own day; (2) monographs focusing on a particular slice of that long time period (usually a war); (3) 'universal' history, which covered the known world, including but not restricted to Rome. Examples of each type survive, though from the period before 35 BCE the monographs of Sallust on the *Conspiracy of Catiline* and the *War with Jugurtha* (both written in the 40s) and the *Commentaries* of Julius Caesar (and others) on the *Gallic*, *Civil*, and related *Wars* (from the late 50s and 40s), are all that have come down to us in their entirety.

Roman history was written in Greek before it was written in Latin; history in Latin, like oratory, began with Cato the Elder. He adopted a Greek genre, *ktisis* or 'foundation' literature, to his own purposes, producing seven books of *Origins* on the founding and early history of Rome and various Italian towns, a work which modulated (we are not sure how) into a chronological account of the growth of Rome to Cato's own time. At the end it became semi-autobiographical, as the writer included some of his own deeds and speeches (including the one on behalf of the Rhodians, quoted above). Even in the fragmentary remains, we can see that Cato's history testified to the greatness of Rome and Roman leaders—though, curiously, it is said not to have named the generals, but to have depicted them simply as representatives of the Roman people.

It also bore witness, as does the extract from Cicero just quoted, to the power of the written word. Here is Cato's story of a military tribune who during the first Punic War (mid-third century BCE) allowed the bulk of the army to escape by drawing enemy fire on his own small band. He fell together with the 400 men whom he commanded, but:

> The immortal gods accorded the military tribune good fortune to match his courage. This is what happened: although he was wounded many times, his head remained unharmed . . . they picked him up and he recovered. Often thereafter he gave brave and energetic service to the state;

> and by his act of leading off those soldiers, he saved the rest of the army. Yet the same service is considered very differently according to the way in which it is viewed. The Spartan Leonidas did the same thing at Thermopylai and the whole of Greece adorned the glory and extraordinary popularity that his virtues had deserved by the most conspicuously magnificent monuments: portraits, statues, inscriptions, stories among other things showed the very high value placed upon his exploit. But the military tribune received only scant praise for his deeds, although he had done the same thing and saved the state. (Cato the Elder, *Origins* fr. 83, trans. M. R. Comber)

There is a determined rivalry here with Greek memorialization: Cato's history will do for the tribune what all of Greece did for Leonidas—and yet he will do it in a Roman way, without extravagance, in a Latin which avoids excessive ornamentation, in a simple, memorable style. The same tendency towards giving a moral lesson that we saw in Cato's oratory is visible here as well: it is not just the tribune's courage that earns his immortality in this text, but the fact that he saved, and continued to save, the state. He thus becomes an *exemplum*, a model for readers to imitate.

The political and military bias of most Roman history is hardly accidental. Cato's tribune would have been imitable not only in theory but in practice by many of his readers, as history was, above all, written by and for the governing class. Not until over half a century after Cato began writing were there any historians who were not also senators (i.e. politicians or commanders); and then only a handful of professional Roman historians came to any prominence. Of their works only that of the Augustan writer Livy has survived in any quantity.

As texts written by and for the men who ran the state, history at Rome occupied a peculiarly privileged position. It was a means of creating and preserving memory. What happened? When? What will be forgotten, what preserved? Which actors of the past will be remembered, and how? It is remarkable, for example, that as far as we know only one overtly pro-plebeian history existed—written by Licinius Macer, who held the office of tribune of the plebs in 73 BCE. The techniques of rhetoric, in which all educated Romans were steeped, offered a powerful tool for rewriting the past: for ancient history, even more than contemporary history, reflected the ideological aims and desires of its authors and its audiences. Being primarily moral and didactic, designed to teach while informing, history was envisaged as a communal effort, in which readers and writers alike participate.

It is easy to see how the writer could influence the reader; but it worked the other way as well, since the history that lasted would be the history that created an image of the Roman past that the Roman present wanted to use. This need not be purely panegyrical, like the military histories that Cicero praises in his *Archias*: Gaius Sallustius Crispus (Sallust), a politician and writer active in the 40s BCE, sees history and the memory of the past both as an inspiration and as a means of social critique:

> I have often heard that Quintus Maximus, Publius Scipio, and other eminent men of our country used to say that when they looked at the portrait masks of their ancestors, their spirits were enthusiastically fired with a desire for virtue. Obviously, the wax of the masks does not itself have such power in it, but because of the memory of their deeds this flame grows in the breasts of outstanding men, and does not die down until their virtue has equalled the reputation and glory of their ancestors. (Sallust, *War with Jugurtha* 4)

> One may become famous either in peace or in war. Both actors and those who describe actions are often praised. And though the narrator earns much less renown than the doer of deeds, the writing of history is, in my opinion, a peculiarly difficult task. . . . My inclinations led me, like many other young men, to throw myself into politics. There many things were against me. Instead of self-restraint, integrity, and virtue, unscrupulous conduct, bribery, and profiteering held sway. . . . So, after suffering many troubles . . . I decided that I must spend the rest of my life away from politics . . . and write the history of the Roman people, choosing portions that seemed particularly worth recording. (Sallust, *Conspiracy of Catiline* 3–4)

There is a close connection in the second extract between Sallust's own political career, which was derailed after he was tempted into 'unscrupulous conduct' (he does not tell us, but he was in fact expelled from the Senate), and the history he chooses to write about. For he does not, like Cato, go back to the beginnings of Rome, except in brief flashbacks; instead he picks relatively recent history, topics chosen to illustrate the decline of Roman society and to reveal the origins of the corruption in which he himself was caught.

Sallust has a preference for villainous heroes, flawed men like the rebel aristocrat Catiline or the African guerrilla fighter Jugurtha, figures whom he can use partly to mirror, and partly to contrast with, decent Romans. Catiline is a particularly apt illustration of the dangers of aristocratic competitiveness overwhelmed by luxury and greed. His conspiracy is especially close to Sallust's own times, coming as it did in 63 BCE, the year of Cicero's consulate, four years before Julius Caesar took command in Gaul, and the year of the future Emperor Augustus' birth. In Sallust's hands Catiline becomes a model for and reflection of an entire civilization, an object lesson in what Rome should avoid:

> Lucius Catiline, a man of noble birth, had great power both of mind and of body but an evil and twisted nature. From his youth he had revelled in civil war, slaughter, robbery, and political strife, and among these he spent his early manhood. His body could endure incredible degrees of hunger, cold, and sleeplessness; his mind was reckless, crafty, and versatile, capable of any pretence or concealment. . . . His monstrous spirit constantly craved things extravagant, incredible, out of reach. . . . He was spurred on by a corrupt society plagued by two opposite and disastrous vices: extravagance and avarice. (Sallust, *Conspiracy of Catiline* 5)

In counterpoint to this figure, who incarnates the grim backdrop of contemporary corruption, Sallust places an impossibly rosy picture of what Rome was once like:

> Good morals were cultivated in peace and in war. The closest harmony prevailed, and avarice was almost unknown. Justice and goodness were strong not so much by law as by nature. Quarrels, strife, and enmity they directed towards their enemies; between themselves they contended only for virtue. In their offerings to the gods they were lavish; at home they lived frugally; to their friends they were loyal. With these two arts, boldness in war and justice when peace came, they took care of themselves and the state. (Sallust, *Conspiracy of Catiline* 9)

Sallust also wrote an extended *History*, covering the period from 78 BCE to (at least) 67, but its fragmentary state does not allow us to see much of its original effect. His monographs, however, show a fairly conventional thinker formulating ideas of the good old days and contemporary moral decline. He does so, however, in startlingly modern language. Though he may not really have been as stylistically innovative as he now seems (the lost history of Cornelius Sisenna, in particular, who wrote in the generation before Sallust, seems to have been similarly experimental), in our current state of knowledge his Latin stands out as a remarkable illustration of how language can reflect thought. Sallust's world is corrupt, broken, deceptive, unexpected: men act contrary to tradition, contrary to Roman values, pursuing only their own self-interest. So too Sallust's Latin. In the words of the later critic Seneca, his sentences are 'amputated, his words end before you expect it, and he considers an obscure brevity to be refinement'. His unbalanced syntax uses connectives where they are not wanted and omits them where they are, links non-parallel expressions by means of parallel structures, upsetting our expectations, and reverses the order of common expressions, especially those familiar from political or state language ('peace and war' rather than 'war and peace', for example). In choice of words as well, he defeats his audience's expectations, selecting diction now from the archaic language of Cato the Elder, now from the repertoire of high poetry such as epic; he invents new words and extends Latin's syntactical range; and he shows up the clichés of contemporary oratorical and political rhetoric by putting them in a new context which reveals their essential emptiness. He thus created (or codified) a new language for history, distinctly different from the academic prose that Cicero was inventing for philosophy, and from Varro's clear but unadorned technical prose, and above all from the smooth, punchy, followable, aurally attractive style of the orators. It is a style that depends on its readers' surprise and hard-won understanding for its effects, thus demonstrating particularly well the close, almost collaborative relationship between history and its audience.

With the emergence of the powerful military leaders whose rivalry led to the bloody civil wars that ended the Republic, the history of Rome became the history of individuals—individuals whose often illegal actions needed justification, even fictionalization. The importance of the audience to history can be seen further in the development of the genre of autobiography and memoir, 'histories' designed even more than most to persuade their readers of the rightness of the author's position. The two Sallustian monographs fit, to some extent, into this pattern, but they lack the partisan slant: despite his service under Caesar, Sallust writes as the 'unbiased' historian, partisan only to a lost, moral Rome. In choosing to write short works based on the lives of individuals he is, in fact, drawing on an already existing trend. Starting in the second century BCE leaders such as Rutilius Rufus, Aemilius Scaurus, and the charismatic and dangerous patrician general Cornelius Sulla all wrote apologetic military memoirs. None of these survives; but from the very late Republic we have what must have been the most successful of all, the *Gallic War* and the *Civil War* of Gaius Julius Caesar, written during his French campaigns (59–49 BCE) and in the first years of his final war against the armies of his fellow senator Gaius Pompeius Magnus (Pompey the Great).

As commentaries, these are ostensibly 'camp notes', designed to be 'written up' by a later historian. But as Cicero remarked of these *Commentaries*, 'I think they are much to be commended. For they are naked, upright, and charming, stripped of all stylistic ornament. . . . Caesar aimed to give others a source from which those who wanted to could write history, and in this he may have done a favour to incompetents: men with sense, however, he has deterred from writing. For there is nothing sweeter in history than pure, shining brevity' (Cicero, *Brutus* 262). This, the reaction of a contemporary reader—albeit carefully and flatteringly worded—is telling. Caesar's Latin was famous for its purity—one word for one thing, nothing fancy, nothing out of the ordinary—following his own well-known advice, to 'avoid an unfamiliar word as you would a submerged rock'. The point, presumably, is to avoid jolting your reader—none of

ROMAN SOLDIERS. The Column of Trajan was dedicated over Trajan's tomb in 113 CE. In a spiral of 155 scenes stretching more than 200 m. it narrates Trajan's successful campaigns against the Dacians (modern Romania). As well as battles it shows all the background to a campaign such as marches, constructing forts, sacrifices, diplomatic activities, etc.

Sallust's amputated thoughts here. But an unjolted reader can also be an unthinking reader. Caesar's prose is designed to produce exactly that: readers who trust; who are moved and thrilled and disgusted by the things Caesar shows them, and in the way Caesar wants them to be; and above all readers who accept Caesar's version of the motivations and the ethical stance of his characters.

He achieves all this partly through the deployment of a simple, clear, exciting military style; and partly through the brilliant choice of narrative voice. The man who speaks to us from his pages has no name; only on rare occasions is he 'I' or 'we', and then almost exclusively when speaking as the scholar-author, in discussing the habits of the Gauls, for example, or in posing as a commander evaluating strategy from a theoretical point of view. The actor 'Caesar' is always referred to in the third person. The effect is that of letting the story tell itself; the impression that of a competent historian, one with access to vivid first-person accounts (though, as often in ancient history, such vividness can be wholly an imaginary creation), and yet one detached from the action. Here is an example:

> The enemy formed up in battle order within the woods . . . then suddenly rushed out in full force and launched an attack on our cavalry. . . . They then ran at astonishing speed down to the river, and so seemed—almost at one and the same moment—to be near the woods, then in the river, and now already upon us. With similar speed they made their way up the hill to our camp and attacked the men who were working on the fortifications. Caesar had to see to everything at once. The flag had to be unfurled . . . the trumpet sounded, the soldiers recalled from working on the defences. . . . He must draw up his battle line, encourage the men, give the signal. There was too little time, the enemy pressed on so fast, to complete these arrangements.
>
> Two factors counterbalanced these difficulties. The first was the knowledge and experience of Caesar's men. . . . Secondly, Caesar had forbidden any of his officers to abandon either the defence-works or their individual legions before the fortification was complete. . . . Once he had given all the appropriate orders Caesar ran down where luck would take him to encourage the men—and ended up among the Tenth legion. His speech was long enough only to urge them to remember their long-established record for bravery, and not to lose their nerve but to resist the enemy assault courageously. . . . Then he gave the signal for battle. (Caesar, *Gallic War* 2. 19–21, trans. C. Hammond)

Classical scholars debate whether these *Commentaries* on the Gallic Wars were directed towards the Roman people as a whole—a possible, though difficult, audience to reach, given the way books were distributed, copy by copy—or towards the Senate, Caesar's peers. In either case, the prose is carefully tailored to produce a simultaneous impression of excitement and order. The enemy's attack is not trivial, the result turns on a knife-edge (and Caesar *did* lose engagements against these tribes): but the combination of the general's forethought and his troops' experience makes victory here inevitable. Caesar matches the enemy's speed with his own, and is carried along by luck as well as skill; the reader is drawn in not only by the hyperbolic prose ('astonishing speed', 'too little time', 'so fast') but also by words like 'our cavalry' (appealing to patriotism), and by the unexplained significance of the Tenth legion (Caesar's favourites and his best soldiers), designed to speak to an audience that already knows the players in this tense scene. All reinforce the sense of 'our brave lads' versus the frightening, but doomed, barbarian hordes.

Caesar's famous authorial detachment shows still more clearly in accounts of political action. Here, he presides over some elections: 'In his capacity as dictator [i.e. sole head of State, traditionally a position created only during a dire emergency] Caesar held the elections, at which Gaius Julius [i.e. Caesar] and Publius Servilius were elected consuls' (Caesar, *Civil War* 3. 1. 1). How many Caesars are there? Three, from all appearances: the dictator, the consul, and the author. And in explaining his position *vis-à-vis* his great rival Pompey, he stresses his own adherence to constitutional procedure:

> By means of legislation brought before the people by praetors and tribunes Caesar restored their property in full to some people who had been condemned under Pompey's law on electoral corruption . . . at a time when Pompey had legionary forces in the city [during the trial of Milo, 52 BCE]. . . . He acted like this because he had decided that these persons ought to receive restitution by decision of the Roman people before being seen as restored by his own favour, so that he would not seem to be either churlish in repaying a kindness or arrogant in pre-empting the right of the people to confer a favour. (Caesar, *Civil War* 3. 1. 4–5, trans. J. Carter)

'Legislation', 'the Roman people', 'repaying a kindness': Caesar, who in fact holds an irregular office of dictator, who is fighting a civil war against his fellow citizens, and who has himself held the city by force in the not too distant past, seduces his audience into seeing him as the upholder of law and fairness. Interestingly, he borrows a trick from the orators, widening the perspective at the end of this extract to include a hypothetical audience looking at him ('being seen', 'seen to be': one can compare Cicero's use of the foreign onlooker in the *Caelius* or the anonymous patriotic Roman in the *Milo*): reputation is what matters, and Caesar plays here both to an imagined crowd within the text and to the reader.

Both Caesar and Sallust look backward in many ways: Sallust from the vantage point of an irremediably corrupt present to a bygone ideal Rome; Caesar to the immediate past which has put him where he is today. In the next generation, a history will emerge that takes up the challenge of making the Roman past into something useful for the future. Livy's *From the Founding of the City* (see pp. 461–3) will confront the problem of change by engaging its audience in a process of comparison and imitation.

11 Escapes from orthodoxy: Poetry of the late Republic

LLEWELYN MORGAN

Captivated Roman élite

In late 46 BCE Julius Caesar made a journey from Rome to southern Spain. To while away the time on the road he composed a poem entitled *Iter* ('Journey'), describing the trek as he made it. The upshot of this rather civilized-sounding journey was the final, most brutal act of the civil wars which had raged between Caesar and the supporters of Pompey the Great since early 49. In March 45 Caesar won a crushing victory at Munda, leaving 30,000 Pompeians dead on the battlefield.

Twenty years later, a Roman officer on active service at Primis in the very south of Egypt (ancient Egyptian Nubia) left behind the book he was reading, love poems by Gaius Cornelius Gallus (70/69–27/6 BCE). That officer's carelessness provided us with the only sizeable chunk of Gallus' poetry we possess, but it also, along with Caesar's *Iter*, provides a vivid illustration of how central a place literature occupied in Roman culture. Here we see two Romans doing a characteristically Roman thing—fighting—and writing and reading poetry at the same time. It is a little paradoxical to picture that soldier, in a military encampment beyond the furthest reaches of the Empire, cumbersomely unwinding his 'book' (a long roll of papyrus), and reading out loud (as Roman poetry was designed to be) Gallus' trials and tribulations with his girlfriend in Rome.

Rome was ruled by a small aristocratic and militaristic élite. A Roman aristocrat was first and foremost a soldier, trained from childhood to pursue success in the military and political arenas (for Romans these were two sides of the same coin), and it was this martial ethos which had won for Rome its enormous Empire. By the time of Caesar, however, this remarkable military entity had added to its accomplishments. The Roman aristocrat was now highly educated, sophisticated, and artistic. For example, Caesar was a brilliant and ruthless

EARLIEST ROMAN MANUSCRIPT. The frontier post of Primis far up the River Nile was occupied by the Romans only briefly in the 20s BCE. This scrap of papyrus excavated there in 1978 proved to contain some lines in elegiac couplets by the poet C. Cornelius Gallus. Gallus had been left as governor of Egypt by Augustus after the defeat of Kleopatra, but had been forced to commit suicide in 26 BCE. The name of Gallus' mistress Lycoris can be read in the first line.

general; but he was also the second-best orator in Rome (after Cicero), and wrote the *Iter* on the road and in only twenty-four days. Gallus, too, besides being a love poet, also enjoyed a very successful military career, before ambition got the better of him and he found himself on the wrong side of the Emperor Augustus.

This (to us) peculiar state of affairs was in fact a direct consequence of Rome's military success. In the course of the previous 250 years Rome had gradually conquered the sophisticated Greek communities first of southern Italy, and then of the eastern Mediterranean, and this contact with the Greek world had profoundly altered Roman culture, turning warriors into aesthetes. The Romans recognized the irony: a race they had conquered had come to dominate them culturally. As the poet Horace put it, 'captive Greece made a captive of her rough invader, and brought the arts to rustic Latium' (Latium is the area around Rome, modern Lazio). Rome's attitude to Greece was in consequence complex. A strong vein of anti-Greek prejudice persisted even amongst the most educated Roman aristocrats. Respect for their artistic achievements vied with contempt for their (perceived) lack of the 'Roman' qualities of military ability and administrative efficiency. So we shall find Lucretius bemoaning 'the poverty of our native language', as compared with Greek, but also Catullus managing to outrage Roman sensibilities by the ostentatious 'Greekness' of some aspects of his way of life.

One more anecdote will encapsulate this contradictory attitude. In the 70s and 60s BCE Rome was involved in a long-running series of campaigns against the Greek King Mithridates of Pontos. In the course of them the Greek poet Parthenios was taken prisoner, enslaved, and brought to Rome. The man who brought him to Rome may well have been the poet Cinna, most famous now for being lynched in Shakespeare's *Julius Caesar* (cf. Ch. 12, p. 359), but before his death a leading light of the so-called New Poets who dominated the Roman literary scene in the mid-first century BCE. Parthenios arrived in Rome as a slave, but was subsequently released in recognition of his learning, and went on to exercise a profound influence over two generations of some of the leading exponents of Roman poetry, including Cinna, Gallus, and Virgil. Rome was captive to a captive Greek.

Caesar and Gallus were thus writing for, and at the same time members of, a sophisticated audience of literature, but also a fairly small one. Familiarity with Greek culture did not filter very far down the rigidly stratified society of Rome. The readership of poetry was limited to the upper-class élite, and in the main (we have to assume) to the male members of that élite. The small scale of the audience, and the high level of education it possessed, explain the remarkable complexity and sophistication of the poetry composed at this time, but also the preoccupation with Roman public life which all the poets to some degree display. Poetry was rarely so immediately politically relevant as oratory or historiography—Caesar's *Iter* may have had no political rationale beyond wanting to give the impression that Caesar was an aesthete, not a butcher. But nevertheless the writers and readers of Roman poetry were still to a considerable degree coextensive with the men who wielded political power in Rome, and Rome in the first century BCE was a country in political crisis. Centuries of rapid expansion, fuelled by the aristocratic ethos, had given way to violent internal competition for power and status. A series of civil wars, punctuated by periods of serious civil unrest, eventually brought a bloody end to the aristocratic system of government, and ushered in a monarchical system of government under a single, all-powerful emperor. The terrible events of this period led some Roman aristocrats to question those cherished values which had underpinned their rise to power in the Mediterranean world. Both of the two main poets we shall meet in this section, Lucretius and Catullus, are directing their work at an audience traumatized by recent events and susceptible, potentially at least, to some very radical reassessments of how a Roman aristocrat should lead his life. The culture they were addressing had lost its centre, and the alternative ways of life promoted in contemporary literature are correspondingly diverse. What the authors share, however, is a profound disenchantment with orthodox Roman culture, given expression—paradoxically—in ambitious literary forms which bespeak considerable confidence about the potential of literature in Latin.

Revolution through familiarization

The poem *De rerum natura*, 'On the Nature of the Universe', of Titus Lucretius Carus (?97–?55 BCE) is sometimes claimed as the greatest poem ever written in the Latin language. It is certainly one of the most ambitious. Its aim, simply put, was to convert whoever read it to the philosophical school of which Lucretius was a passionate devotee, Epicureanism. We can gain something of a sense of the enormity of the task Lucretius set himself if we consider the main points of Epicurean doctrine, and ask ourselves how attractive it was likely to appear to the kind of aristocratic reader of Roman literature sketched in the previous section.

Epicureanism was named after Epicurus (Greek: Epikouros), its founder (341–270 BCE). Epicurus was a Greek thinker who formulated a startling solution to what he saw as the evils bedevilling human existence (cf. Ch. 5, pp. 189–90). Epicurus' *ethical* theory (i.e. his view of how humans should live their lives) was built upon an elaborate *scientific* theory about the structure of the universe. Lucretius follows Epicurus' theory very closely, and this explains why a poem with the stated aim of teaching its reader a new and better way of living spends most of its time in abstruse scientific arguments. It also explains the title of Lucretius' poem, which owes something to the title of Epicurus' most important philosophical work, 'On Nature', as well as to another 'On Nature' written by the Greek poet-scientist Empedokles (cf. Ch. 5, pp. 165–6). In addition, it accounts for the scale of the poem. The *De rerum natura* is written in the epic metre, dactylic hexameters, and on an epic scale (about 7,400 lines). This vehicle is appropriate to the poet's lofty aspirations: not only to convert his readership to a totally new pattern of life, but also in the process to present an account of nothing less than the entire universe.

Epicurus believed that human life was miserable, needlessly so. What made it

PORTRAIT OF FREEDOM FROM PAIN. Portrait busts of philosophers were a favourite art-form in the Greek and Roman worlds. The portrait of Epicurus based on a third-century BCE original is known in over thirty copies. Its severity and concentration suggest Epicurus' philosophy of freedom from pain rather than a philosophy of hedonism.

miserable were irrational anxieties, the most serious of which, in his view, were the fear of the gods and the fear of death. These anxieties caused pain to those who experienced them, and a central tenet of Epicurus' philosophy was that happiness was only possible if such pain was removed. Pleasure, the absence of pain, was the ultimate object of Epicureanism. This doctrine has often been misinterpreted. Epicureanism, we should appreciate (though many contemporaries did not), was an extremely rigorous and difficult creed, and the 'pleasure' which Epicurus had in mind was more of the nature of an unruffled psychological serenity than abandonment to sensual excess. In fact the *ataraxia* (Greek), *securitas* (Latin), or 'freedom from anxiety' to which Epicureans aspired often involved avoiding precisely such sensual abandonment. Epicureans were *not* hedonists.

To secure *securitas*, Epicureans believed, the first and most important step was to develop a rational, clear-sighted understanding of the way the physical world worked. In particular, Epicurus adopted a scientific theory developed by the fifth-century BCE Greek thinker Demokritos, Atomism, the theory that everything in the universe is ultimately constructed of tiny, indestructible particles. Epicurus made this theory the basis of his own radically materialistic account of the universe. If absolutely everything consists of atoms moving in a void, and nothing else; and if everything in the universe is created when these atoms, falling through the void, happen to combine, and destroyed when the atoms that compose it disperse and go on to form other things, then some important consequences follow. First, there is no room for the gods, not at any rate in their traditional role as powers which created the world and interfered in it at will. The gods did exist, according to Epicurus, but were utterly irrelevant to human life: they lived far away in a state of Epicurean *securitas*. Terrifying events commonly attributed to the action of the gods, like earthquakes or thunderbolts, had a perfectly rational explanation, and the gods were thus nothing to be afraid of.

The second consequence of the Atomic Theory was that death was nothing more dramatic than a dispersal of atoms, just as birth was simply a combination of them. In fact death was a prerequisite of life: only through death could the atoms become available which were necessary to create something new. Death and life were thus interdependent. As Lucretius beautifully expresses it,

> With the sound of funerals mingles the howl
> that children raise when first they see the shores of light.
> And no night has ever followed day, or dawn night,
> which has not heard, mingled with these feeble howls,
> the wailing that attends death and black funerals.
>
> (2. 576–80)

Human souls are made up of atoms in the same way as anything else, and there is consequently nothing that can survive after death to suffer punishment in the underworld, a major cause, according to Epicureans, of the fear of death. Hence the *ethical* implications of Epicurus' *scientific* theory: a proper understanding of the physics of the universe proves the irrationality of the anxieties which on his view prevent us from attaining to happiness.

Lucretius stuck very closely to Epicurus' theories, but he also invested the doctrine with a strong contemporary relevance for Romans of the first century

BCE: his poem was probably completed in the late 50s BCE. We know next to nothing about his life, but he gives the impression of being himself a member of the Roman upper classes, attempting to convert men who are his equals to the liberating truth of Epicureanism. But a lot stood in his way. The Epicurean credo conflicted point after point with some of the most cherished values of the aristocratic society at which the poem was directed.

All anxiety, according to Epicurus, is inimical to true pleasure. Lucretius gives particular emphasis to two sources of anxiety (besides the fear of death and the gods), love affairs (4. 1037–287) and political ambition. Lucretius actually sees these 'subsidiary' anxieties as direct consequences of the underlying fear of death. Desperate to affirm their existence in the face of annihilation humans hunt out tangible symbols of life :

> Moreover the greed and blind lust for distinctions
> which drive unhappy men to overstep the bounds
> of law and at times make them accomplices and instruments of crime,
> straining night and day with extreme effort
> to rise to the top in power—these wounds of life
> are fed in no small part by the fear of death.
> For shameful ignominy and bitter poverty
> seem far removed from sweet and secure life,
> and like lingering already before the gates of death.
> From there, driven by groundless terror,
> men wish to escape and remove themselves far, far away,
> and amass a fortune in civil bloodshed, double
> their riches in their greed, piling slaughter on slaughter.
> Heartlessly they rejoice at the tragic death of their brother;
> and they hate and fear the hospitality of their own kin.
>
> (3. 59–73)

The Epicurean will withdraw from all the tensions and distractions of public life and nurture a serene philosophical calm in private. But for a traditionally minded Roman aristocrat this was a revolutionary doctrine. The Roman male was trained from the cradle to value, and struggle for, military and political success and the status that went with them. Status meant being *recognized* for one's achievements: success without visibility was worthless. But Epicurus' central ethical tenet was *lathe biôsas*, 'Live unnoticed' or 'Pass unremarked'. How could Lucretius possibly persuade his readership to abandon what was arguably the very essence of their culture?

For these reasons in particular Epicureanism did not exert a natural attraction for Romans. They tended to find Stoicism (cf. Ch. 5, pp. 166–7), a philosophy which encouraged participation in public life, much more agreeable. But as we have seen, the upheavals which Rome experienced in the first century BCE had created a fertile environment for the questioning of traditional values, and Lucretius' poem is explicitly a response to these upheavals. This is clear from the passage I have just quoted, with its reference to civil warfare, and clear, in fact, from the very beginning of his poem, where Lucretius prays to the goddess Venus and begs her to put a stop to the violence in which Rome is involved. In the very first words of the poem Lucretius identifies Venus as 'mother of the race of Aeneas', 'mother of Rome' in other words.

In addition, Lucretius addresses his poem to 'Memmius'. This was Gaius Memmius, a senior politician of the period. Lucretius thus takes pains to adapt the doctrine he is expounding to his Roman readership in the mid-first century BCE—we shall return to the question of whether a Memmius could possibly have felt sympathy for statements like the following on the political career to which he, as a typical Roman aristocrat, had devoted himself. The ambitious Roman politician is compared to Sisyphus, an over-ingenious mortal punished for eternity in the underworld, according to myth, by having to roll a boulder to the top of a hill, only for it to roll back down again :

> Sisyphus also is here in this life before our eyes,
> thirsty to win power from the people,
> and always retiring defeated and depressed.
> For to seek power, a vacuous thing which is never given,
> and always to endure hard toil in pursuit of it—
> this is to push a boulder laboriously up a steep mountain,
> only to see it, once the top is reached,
> roll back down in a rush to the flat levels of the plain.
> (3. 995–1002)

'The plain' here is a loaded term. The *Campus* or 'plain' in Rome was where political elections took place.

The *De rerum natura* is a 'didactic' poem, that is, it teaches a lesson, and the stance that Lucretius adopts is very much that of a teacher, albeit a rather strict, 'Victorian' teacher, dunning knowledge into wayward children. One of the greatest strengths of the poem is Lucretius' mastery of teaching technique. For example, a good teacher will explain the unfamiliar by analogy with the familiar: if the earth is a grain of sand, and the sun a cherry stone three feet away, the nearest other star in 140 miles away, and so on. 'Familiarization' of this kind is one of Lucretius' basic strategies. He has an astonishing gift for evoking the everyday, and using it to clarify the often very difficult scientific theories he is attempting to explain. Since his illustrations have to be familiar to his reader-pupil it is natural that he selects images from contemporary Roman life. At

4. 973–83 he is explaining why we tend to dream about events we have recently witnessed, and he chooses for his illustration the games, which might include exotic theatrical performances, at which his male readers enjoyed relaxation from their busy lives :

> And whenever men have given their unremitting attention
> to the games for many days on end, we usually see that,
> when they have now ceased to perceive them with their senses,
> nevertheless there are paths in the mind left open
> where the same images of things can enter.
> And so for many days those same things hover
> before their eyes, so that even while awake they seem
> to perceive figures dancing and swaying supple limbs,
> and to hear in their ears the fluid tune of the lyre and its speaking strings,
> and to perceive the same crowd and along with it
> the brilliant, multicoloured decorations of the stage.
>
> (4. 973–83)

Elsewhere Lucretius brings vividly before our eyes the ceaseless movement of atoms in the void, the cause (according to his theory) of all phenomena in the world :

> Of this phenomenon there is, now I think of it, an illustration and image
> constantly hovering and present before our eyes.
> Do but pay attention whenever the beams of the sun
> are admitted into a house and pour their light through its dark places:
> you will see many tiny particles mingling in many ways
> throughout the void in the light of the beams,
> and, as if in everlasting conflict, battling, fighting,
> struggling in hosts without a pause,
> agitated in constant meetings and partings.
> From this you may picture what it is for the first elements of things
> to be tossed about perpetually in the great void.
>
> (2. 112–22)

This is a particularly significant sight, Lucretius goes on to say, because the movements of the particles in the sunbeam are actually a *consequence* of the unending movements of the atoms which are hidden from our sight. It is the motion of the atoms which sets off the movements of the visible particles. Here Lucretius renders abstruse science immediately familiar: the poet shows us the atoms, mainspring of the entire universe, in our own front rooms.

As I have suggested, this is good teaching technique. But that doesn't convey what great poetry it also makes. At the same time as Lucretius 'familiarizes' these mysterious elemental processes, he also invests everyday phenomena like motes of dust with all the momentousness and grandeur of the universe: that dust exemplifies the nature of the entire cosmos. This is an important point, since many readers have been put off the *De rerum natura* by what they see as its unpoetic material. And it has to be admitted that Lucretius' poem is an acquired taste. Its often austere scientific content makes it 'difficult', as the later author Quintilian called it (and as the poet himself admits more than once). John Ruskin, the influential Victorian art critic and reformer, asserted that he 'held it the most hopeless sign of a man's mind being made of flint-shingle if he liked Lucretius', but many others have appreciated the power of his vision. Some of these have been atheists and materialists like Karl Marx, who regarded Epicurus as a forerunner of many of his own beliefs, and in the conclusion of his doctoral dissertation, *The Difference between the Democritean and Epicurean philosophy of Nature* (1841), quoted Lucretius' praise of Epicurus as the conqueror of religion at 1. 62–79. But the twentieth-century philosopher George Santayana recognized that the philosophical vision of the totality of things which Lucretius presents to the reader makes for a powerful poetic experience: 'But the vision of philosophy is sublime. The order it reveals in the world is something beautiful, tragic, sympathetic to the mind, and just what every poet, on a small or on a large scale, is always trying to catch.' There is a tremendous intellectual excitement in the idea that dust in the sunlight reflects the fundamental creative principle of the universe.

Redirecting the reader's mind

Lucretius' core strategy of *making familiar* pervades every level of the poem. Epicureanism was a revolutionary doctrine, and it is a truism that the most successful revolutions are those that bear as close a resemblance as possible to the state of affairs that preceded them. In this way they are less unsettling, more acceptable, and more likely to succeed. Lucretius' appreciation of this fact explains many aspects of his poem, but in particular the striking way he introduces it.

A contemporary, non-Epicurean reader of the *De rerum natura* would feel quite at home in the first few lines of the poem. It begins in a very conventional way with a hymn to a god, Venus, requesting her help with the composition of his poem: a standard poetic approach. But this opening has bothered critics greatly, for the simple reason that a central tenet of Epicureanism, and a central argument of the *De rerum natura*, was that gods did not interfere in the world: they did not do things like cause earthquakes, hurl thunderbolts—or inspire poets. The only conclusion seemed to be that Lucretius was being plain inconsistent. But this is to misunderstand the purpose of the poem, by interpreting the *De rerum natura* as a testament of Lucretius' beliefs rather than what it really is: a course of teaching. Like the good teacher that he was Lucretius meets his pupils on their own ground, starts with what is familiar to them, and leads them gently from this starting-point to the (very different) truth. This is precisely how the hymn to Venus works. In the course of the poem the powers attributed to the goddess Venus in the hymn are piece by piece reattributed to the rationalistic Epicurean guiding principle of *natura*, 'the laws of nature'. Gradually, imperceptibly, the non-Epicurean belief in the gods with which we started is replaced by orthodox Epicureanism. As we read the poem, in other words, we are being delicately *converted*.

As will be clear, Lucretius, though a hard taskmaster, tried very hard not to startle his readers. He wants the truth (as he sees it) to seem obvious to us. Consequently, he does not simply reject out of hand the beliefs his readers started with, but redefines them. He even does this with the notions of the gods and the afterlife which he regards as the great bane of human existence. In one passage (partially quoted on p. 343) he dismisses a set of myths concerned with the underworld. There is no such thing as life after death, no Sisyphus suffering eternal punishment in the underworld. Or at any rate there are no such figures *in the underworld*, because the underworld does not exist. There *are* such figures, but they are here, in the real world: they are the poor benighted creatures who have not heard, and acted upon, the wisdom of Epicurus. Their lives are truly a 'Hell on earth' (line 1023). The same applies with the gods. The gods have no involvement in human affairs, and as far as human life is concerned they might as well not exist. But there *are* people here, on earth, who fulfil the role of the traditional gods, Epicurus above all, of whom Lucretius declares, 'he was a god, a god, noble Memmius' (5. 8); but also anyone who internalizes the precepts of Epicureanism and lives a life of unruffled calm: 'He therefore who has vanquished all these anxieties and banished them from his mind, by words not by weapons, will he not surely be worthy of a place among the gods?' (5. 49–51).

Again, this is a subtle revolution. Our cherished beliefs are, as far as possible, adapted rather than abandoned. We shall 'worship' Epicurus, not Venus, 'fear' the fear of death, not death. The conversion is made as easy as it can be, although the revelation of the Epicurean 'truth' of the nature of the universe is none the less compelling for that. Another way of describing Lucretius' overall strategy is as *demystification*. His world-view, like Epicurus', is a thoroughgoing form of materialism. Everything that matters is here, now, and tangible. Repeatedly Lucretius insists that we should never give way to *wonder*. Everything (no matter how bizarre) has a rational explanation: there is nothing mysterious, or disturbing, about death, for example—it is merely a dispersal of atoms, and those figures from myth like Sisyphus are here, now, visible all around us. As for the gods, *you* can be a god. Just read this poem . . .

But as with the hymn to Venus at the start of the poem, the religious emotions Lucretius criticizes are not so much to be rejected as *redirected*. Lucretius *does* feel wonder, but this is wonder before the marvellous doctrines which will heal his readers' lives; and for a philosopher committed to a strictly rationalistic approach to life he is perhaps strangely passionate. The following passage, from his argument to prove that 'Death is nothing to us' (3. 830), nothing worth concerning ourselves with, is representative. Lucretius demands his reader to think why he should be anxious about death when so many great men have undergone the same experience in the past :

> Epicurus himself died when his life's light had run its course,
> he whose intellect surpassed humanity and made them all
> look dim, as the rising of the heavenly sun does the stars.
> And will *you* hesitate and complain about dying?
> You whose life is almost death while you still live and have sight,
> who waste the greater part of your life in sleep,
> and snore while awake and never stop dreaming,
> and bear a mind harried by empty fears . . .
>
> (3. 1042–52)

The criticism of the non-Epicurean life is aggressive and passionate, but the result of a characteristic empathy on Lucretius' part for his fellow humans. The poet fully recognizes the power for ill of the human fear of death, and consequently reserves some of his most powerful arguments and rhetoric to counter it. There is also a remarkable intimacy and humanity about the relationship Lucretius maintains with his readers, even at his most hectoring. Addressing his arguments in the first instance to Memmius, for example, makes a critical difference to the effect of the poem. Reading is an essentially solitary activity, and Epicureanism a doctrine which is all about withdrawing in on oneself and abandoning wider society. Consequently a poem on Epicureanism could easily become quite a bleak and lonely experience. Memmius is one of the strategies Lucretius employs to create the illusion that we are engaging in a form of social interaction, when in fact we are reading to ourselves. As the poem goes on, in fact, the references to Memmius become fewer and fewer, to be replaced by the intimate *tu*, 'you' (in the singular). Vitruvius, a writer on architecture, aptly described the experience of reading the poem as 'like arguing face to face with Lucretius about the nature of the universe'. So Lucretius is capable of powerful and passionate rhetoric, but it always takes as its starting-point an acute understanding of the state of mind of the readership he is trying to convert, and of how best to mould it.

The psychological sophistication of passages like this makes our only contemporary response to Lucretius' poem all the more disappointing. In a letter to his younger brother in 54 BCE (our best evidence for the date of the poem) Cicero writes that 'Lucretius' poetry is as you say, sparkling with natural talent, but with plenty of technical skill. But we'll discuss it when you come.' It would certainly have disappointed a poet who stated that his poetry was merely an attractive vehicle for a life-changing revelation (cf. 1. 926–50, 4. 1–25) to see his poem assessed in such formal, literary-critical terms. Cicero and his brother enjoyed the poem as a poem, but were they converted? No. When Cicero's Epicurean friend Atticus tried to persuade him to withdraw from the perilous political scene after the assassination of Julius Caesar in 44 BCE he received a blunt response: 'You mention Epicurus and *dare* to say "keep out of politics"?' For most Roman aristocrats politics was in the blood.

It is the same story with Memmius, the addressee of the poem, but in his case dramatically so. In two letters Cicero refers to a dispute in the city of Athens in 51 BCE between a leading Epicurean named Patron, and Memmius. Memmius had had an unfortunate few years. A candidate for the consulship in 54 BCE, he had lost the election, been convicted of electoral bribery, and gone into exile. The dispute centred around the ruins of Epicurus' house. Memmius seems to have intended to build on the site, a plan to which Patron (naturally) objected. The situation suggests in Memmius a man far from sympathetic to Epicureanism, in fact violently antagonistic towards it. Certainly his no-holds-barred pursuit of the consulship was, in Lucretius' terms, the behaviour of a classic Sisyphus. Even after decades of violent political upheaval there were few Roman aristocrats ready to retire from the fray.

Lucretius' poem attempts to persuade and control his reader to an unusually intense degree. As we have seen, it even maps, in its course, the psychological development of its ideal reader. But for all his pedagogical genius there was no guarantee he would have any more success than teachers generally do. Ovid, a generation later, warmly praises the *De rerum natura*: 'The poems of lofty Lucretius will perish only when one day gives over the world to ruin.' The *De rerum natura* had become a literary classic. But for Lucretius the work of art was just a means to an end, to be left behind when that end—enlightenment—was attained. Lucretius insistently tells us to *visualize* the universe he describes, to understand his philosophy in our own minds, internalize it, and leave the text behind. The *De rerum natura* will have served its purpose when we have learnt to live the good life. But the prevailing literary climate tended to value art for its own sake, not for its message. Then again, Lucretius, who died in the late 50s, would not (on his own principles) have been in a position to worry :

> When we no longer exist, when the parting has happened
> of body and soul, from which we are made a single being,
> then (have no doubt about it) nothing at all will be able to happen to us,
> who will then no longer exist, or to stir our feelings,
> not if earth be mingled with sea and sea with sky.
>
> (3. 838–42)

We do not find in Lucretius the kind of aspiration to poetic immortality so common in other poets. The dead Lucretius is blissfully unconcerned about his audience.

The erudition of the 'new poets'

Lucretius and Gaius Valerius Catullus were contemporaries. Catullus' dates (perhaps 84–54 BCE) are no less uncertain, but his poetic output seems to date, like Lucretius's, from the 50s BCE. Nevertheless, at least at first sight, they could hardly seem more dissimilar. Where Lucretius warns against the dangers of involvement in day-to-day life, Catullus engages passionately with the urban culture of contemporary Rome. And whereas Lucretius reserved his special disapproval for men who abandoned themselves to the pursuit of love, Catullus is above all a love poet: a large proportion of his poems concern an ill-starred love-affair with a married woman he calls 'Lesbia'. But these sharp dissimilarities between the two poets are themselves symptomatic of the splintering of Roman culture at this juncture. Despite their differences, the poets have at least one thing in common: each offers an aggressive critique of traditional Roman values; and each offers alternative, and (as they see it) more satisfactory, ways of life.

Lucretius' revolution was as much literary as cultural. He took the format of the hexameter epic, conventionally the vehicle for panegyric of Rome, or of successful Roman generals, and used it instead to promote a man (Greek, at that), and a way of life, which constituted an outright rejection of Roman military and public values. Catullus' poetry also constitutes a literary rebellion which entails simultaneously a rebellion against the whole traditional Roman way of life. Catullus prides himself on being part of a literary movement which rejects Roman models of poetry in favour of Greek, and one Greek poet in particular, Kallimachos (cf. Ch. 7). Poem 66, Catullus' version of a poem in honour of an Egyptian queen from Kallimachos' most influential work, the *Causes*, emphatically advertises the Roman poet's literary affiliations. These poets claimed to be breaking with the past, to be modernizers: Cicero calls them 'new poets', probably reflecting the way they talked about themselves.

There was in fact nothing especially new about a lot of what the New Poets were doing: Roman poets had been imitating Kallimachos for quite some time. But as the manufacturers of washing powder, and political spindoctors, know so well, claiming one's formula to be new, whether it is or not, is always an effective marketing device. The literary ideals which *these* New Poets found and admired in Kallimachos were careful craftsmanship, intellectualism (the ethos of the 'scholar poet'), and above all *brevity*: Catullus, like Lucretius, rejects the option of writing the traditional, long epic in praise of Roman national achievement. He dismisses an example of that kind of poetry, the *Annals* of Volusius, as 'paper crap' (poem 36). Poem 64 is written in the epic metre, dactylic hexameters, but deliberately avoids both the kind of material and the predictable narrative style a reader would normally expect in that metre. The exotic and erotic material of poem 64—Peleus' marriage to Thetis and the abandonment of Ariadne by Theseus—could not be further removed from the nationalistic themes of poems like Volusius' *Annals*. A major model for this poem was Kallimachos' *Hekale*, another hexameter poem which sets out to defeat the expectations which readers had of that metre (cf. Ch. 7, pp. 245–6). Crucially, too, poem 64 is highly polished, learned, and (comparatively) *short*: only 400 lines long.

C. Helvius Cinna was a friend of Catullus and a fellow New Poet. What ancient poetry did or did not survive through the Middle Ages to the Renaissance was always largely a matter of chance; though it does seem true that contemporaries of the two late-Republican poets who did survive, Catullus and Lucretius, regarded them as the best of their time. Nevertheless, Catullus only just made it, rediscovered on a single, very corrupt manuscript in the fourteenth century. The other New Poets (including the poet-orator Gaius Licinius Calvus) were not so lucky, and very little survives of their work, but we do have an epigram which Cinna wrote about a copy he had brought to Rome of Aratos' *Phainomena* (cf. pp. 246–7), a poem which enjoyed great popularity in first-century BCE Rome:

> This poem, which informs us of the fires of the sky,
> the product of long vigil by the lamps of Aratos,
> written on the dry bark of the smooth mallow plant,
> I have brought to you as a gift, in a little Prusiac ship.

This poem was evidently typical of Cinna's style of poetry. It was deliberately recondite, or, put another way, 'allusive': whereas Lucretius aimed at clarity—he dismisses Herakleitos (cf. Ch. 5) as 'renowned for his opaque sayings | among the more empty-headed of the Greeks' (1. 639–40)—with a view to persuading the reader of his argument, Cinna offered hints to his audience which only the very well-informed reader was in a position to follow up. As compared with Lucretius, then, the reader is given much more work to do. In this little poem, for example, Cinna expects his readers firstly to understand that he is talking about Aratos' *Phainomena*, then to pick up an allusion to a poem by Kallimachos in praise of Aratos (which has the effect of associating Cinna with Callimachean literary ideals), recognize that the ship comes from Bithynia, a country which had once had a king called Prusias, and also recognize a pun in the word which I have translated 'on the . . . bark': it can also mean 'in a little book'—the odd material that the book is written on, not paper but bark, is designed to match the recondite nature of the poetry written on it. The enjoyment of the wit and brilliance—the *exquisiteness*—of the poetry is what Cinna is trying to encourage in his readership, and also the intellectual pleasure the readers derive from their involvement in the interpretation of the poem: reading Cinna is a bit like doing a cryptic crossword. Only a generation later readers needed a commentary to interpret Cinna's most important poem, *Zmyrna*. The author of the commentary, Crassicius Pansa, was praised in a humorous poem:

> The lady Zmyrna has agreed to give herself to one man—Crassicius:
> leave off trying to win her in marriage, you ignorant men.
> She has said that she is only willing to marry Crassicius,
> since only he knows her intimate secrets.

In Cinna's poem Zmyrna was a young woman who had an incestuous relationship with her father Cinyras. This poem amusingly suggests that Crassicius, her interpreter, has replaced Cinyras in her affections. It is an interesting insight into the intellectual complexity of this poetry that readers soon needed commentaries, but also an indication of the type of reader it was written for—and created—that Crassicius' commentary on Cinna's brilliant poem elicited a witty and allusive poem in response. The New Poets made poets of their readers.

Perhaps the major difference from Lucretius here is that the artistry of the poet, rather than information he is conveying, is the primary focus of interest. This was the case with Aratos too. Like the *De rerum natura*, the *Phainomena* was also, theoretically, a 'didactic' poem, an explanation of celestial phenomena. But it did not *really* aim to teach anybody anything. The greater part of the *Phainomena* was a versification of a scientific treatise by the astronomer

Eudoxos, and if you wanted to learn something about astronomy *that* was the only sensible place to look, not in Aratos' poem. What readers like Cinna enjoyed in Aratos was the skilful and witty way he converted prosaic or scientific material like astronomy or the croaking of frogs when it is about to rain (lines 947–8) into poetry, rather than the intrinsic interest of the material itself. Again, this was a very *formal* achievement, art for art's sake, and this, we recall, was pretty much how Cicero responded to Lucretius' poem. Cicero liked Aratos too (he had translated the poem in his youth), so it is perhaps understandable that he responded to Lucretius' didactic poem as if it was a didactic poem like Aratos'.

Catullus also wrote a poem to welcome the arrival of Cinna's *Zmyrna* :

> The *Zmyrna* of my Cinna, at length nine harvests
> and nine winters after it was begun, is published!
> Hortensius, meanwhile, every single year
> has spawned fifty thousand verses.
> *Zmyrna* will travel far, to the deep-channelled waves of the Satrachus;
> long will the white-haired centuries read *Zmyrna*.
> But the *Annals* of Volusius will die before they cross the Padua
> and often make loose-fitting jackets for mackerel.
> Dear to my heart is the small-scale monument of my comrade . . .
> But let the mob enjoy long-winded Antimachus.
>
> (Poem 95)

The same 'allusive' approach to poetry is evident as we saw in Cinna's epigram about Aratos. Future generations are 'white-haired centuries'; the Satrachus is a river in Cyprus associated with Adonis (son of Zmyrna and Cinyras) which Cinna will have mentioned in his poem; Antimachus was the author of a poem criticized by Kallimachos for its excessive length. Cinna's poem—and by implication Catullus' poem—thus encapsulates the ideals of the New Poets: poems must be short, highly polished (Cinna spent no less than nine years over his), un-Roman (Volusius' *Annals* were probably a Roman epic in the tradition of Ennius), and erudite. We must never forget that even the most passionate, and apparently spontaneous, of Catullus' poems were composed with the same degree of effort and artistry.

A cultivated 'madness'

Catullus and the New Poets claimed that their poetry was for a small and sophisticated audience of friends: everybody else ('the mob') will have to be satisfied with 'long-winded Antimachus'. There will have been some truth in this, but it isn't the whole story. On the one hand, the knowledge required to appreciate this style of poetry was such that only a relatively few readers would be up to it: Kallimachos' poetic ideals had been developed in the context of the highly educated audience of the court of the Ptolemaic kings of Egypt. But in Catullus' mouth this is also a stance. By claiming that his poetry is only suitable for a select few he is implying how *special* his poetry is, and at the same time forging a bond with his readers: read Catullus and you too become one of his special friends. This is Catullus' way of doing what every writer must—gaining the loyalty and interest (and readiness to read on . . .) of his audience.

Although the Roman reading audience was never very large, Catullus' audience was certainly larger than he suggests. For example, Catullus waged an extended campaign of abuse against Julius Caesar, partly through direct attacks on the general and partly through attacks on Caesar's lieutenant Mamurra, to whom Catullus often refers simply as 'Prick'. According to the biographer Suetonius, Caesar believed that this series of attacks did lasting damage to his reputation. This would hardly have been the case if Catullus' poetry was only being read by his friends. Nevertheless, whether Catullus is addressing one of his close friends or some of the most powerful figures in the state, his poetry always maintains an air of intimacy and informality. Affectionate or abusive, the poems sound like first-hand exchanges between close associates, exchanges to which the reader is given privileged access. This makes a twentieth-century reader's experience of Catullus particularly exciting: we often feel as if we have been admitted into the charmed circle of the Roman aristocracy. Of course, a lot of work has gone into producing this impression of spontaneity and immediacy.

But what response did he expect to receive from this audience to his poetry? A difficult question. The reaction to the poetry in the young Roman 'smart set' of which Catullus was a part is liable to have been very different from that of the wider ruling class. Catullus' poetry offers an oblique insight into this area of contemporary Roman life: oblique, because even at his most passionate Catullus is first and foremost a consummate artist, who does not so much pour his soul into his poetry as re-create his experiences in art. Poem 41, an attack on Mamurra's girlfriend, is a case in point, blunt and obscene, but skilfully crafted, with a succinct but vivid portrait of the girl and a perfectly timed punchline:

> Ameana, a well-fucked girl,
> has asked me for a cool ten thousand sesterces,
> that girl with the rather ugly nose,
> girlfriend of the bankrupt from Formiae.

You relatives who are responsible for the girl,
summon friends and doctors.
The girl's unwell, and is not in the habit of asking
the image-filled bronze what she looks like.

Even obliquely, though, Catullus' poetry presents a fascinating picture of his social world, profoundly influenced by Greek culture, and also strikingly feminine. In contrast to Lucretius' almost exclusively male world, Catullus' poetry is populated by comparatively powerful and assertive women like Lesbia and Ameana. Ameana is defamed, but she is not ignored, which was the more traditional fate of Roman women. One of the unconventional aspects of Cinna's *Zmyrna* and Catullus' poem 64 was the prominence they gave to female characters, a departure from the generally military and male preoccupations of traditional epic. It is risky to infer from this that women also formed a significant part of Catullus' readership, but poem 35 humorously describes the effect on a girl of reading a similar short epic by another New Poet, Caecilius.

Furthermore, Catullus had a particular attachment to the work of the female poet Sappho (cf. Ch. 2, pp. 75–7), an important model for the passion, eroticism, and intensely personal quality of his shorter poems. Poem 51 is a version of one of Sappho's poems, an example (incidentally) of Catullus' great metrical proficiency: Catullus makes Sappho's rhythmical scheme a natural vehicle for the Latin language, a harder task than he makes it look. But there is a further implication to the rhythm. This poem describes the beginning of Catullus' affair with 'Lesbia', and poem 11 the devastating end of it, and both are in Sappho's characterisic metre. The affair thus began,

That man is seen by me as a God's equal
Or (if it may be said) the Gods' superior,
Who sitting opposite again and again
Watches and hears *you*
Sweetly laughing—which dispossesses poor me
Of all my senses, for no sooner, Lesbia,
Do I look at you than there's no power left me . . .
(51. 1–7, trans. Guy Lee)

and ended ,

Simply deliver to my girl a brief dis-
courteous message:
Farewell and long life with her adulterers,
Three hundred together, whom hugging she holds,
Loving none truly but again and again
Rupturing all's groins;

> And let her not as before expect my love,
> Which by her fault has fallen like a flower
> On the meadow's margin after a passing
> Ploughshare has touched it.
>
> (11. 15–24, trans. Guy Lee)

The metre is appropriate, because the pseudonym Catullus chose for his girlfriend, 'Lesbia', 'woman of Lesbos', equates her with Sappho. The girl of poem 35, also, is complimented as 'more learned than the Muse of Sappho'. The Catullan ideal was apparently a woman as educated, sophisticated, and self-sufficient as himself; and for the time this was a very unorthodox attitude indeed.

In wider society, though, the typical response to Catullus must have been shock. In poems like the fragmentary 14b ('If by any chance there are any of you who will read my idiocies and not shudder to lay your hands on us . . .') Catullus seems to anticipate (with relish) this kind of reaction. For a reader possessed of more traditional moral values much of what Catullus wrote would have been highly provocative. The provocation consisted in the extremely unconventional lifestyle he documented in his poems. Catullus invested his aristocratic energy not in the pursuit of the conventional Roman targets of wealth and status, but in the pursuit of boys and women. In a famous poem addressed to Lesbia (poem 5) Catullus extols the life of love and rejects out of hand traditional modes of behaviour:

> Let us live, my Lesbia, and love,
> and as for the mutterings of over-critical old men
> let us value them at a single farthing!

'Old-fashioned' moral values are thus dismissed as emphatically as 'old-fashioned' literary values. From a conventional Roman point of view the kind of obsessive love-affairs Catullus involved himself in were, as Cicero puts it, 'no different, or not far different, from madness'.

The same can be said of Catullus' more overtly political poetry. Poem 93 is a devastatingly simple, two-line attack on Julius Caesar which dramatically asserts Catullus' distance from Roman convention:

> I am not overly keen, Caesar, to wish to be liked by you,
> nor to know whether you are a white or a black man.

Quintilian uses the same word of Catullus' feigned ignorance of Caesar—'madness': *everyone* had heard of Caesar, and it was precisely in pursuit of this recognition and status that Caesar (in this respect a typical Roman aristocrat) had embarked on his remarkable career. Roman aristocrats lived to achieve, and to be seen to have achieved by their peers. This is what makes Catullus' apparently innocuous statement so striking. For Catullus to tell Caesar, conqueror of Gaul, that he couldn't care two hoots about him strikes at the very essence of Roman aristocratic self-motivation.

Similar in implication are a couple of poems (10 and 28) where Catullus, with a characteristic frankness, abuses Gaius Memmius, the addressee of Lucretius' poem. In 57–56 BCE Catullus and Cinna served on Memmius' staff when he was governor of Bithynia (this may also have been the date of Cinna's poem about Aratos). In poem 28, addressed to two friends also on service abroad, Catullus brutally attacks the traditional system of public service abroad:

> O Memmius, well and truly did you get me on my back,
> and mouthfuck me at your leisure with the full length of your beam.
> You, my friends, as far as I can see, have fared the same—
> stuffed by no less a prick.
> Find influential friends, they say!
> May heaven send you [i.e. the two governors] plagues aplenty,
> you slurs on the name of Romulus and Remus.

Memmius, that representative of traditional Roman values, is under assault from all sides, the Epicurean on the one and the thoroughly disenchanted *enfant terrible* on the other. By calling the governors 'slurs on the name of Romulus and Remus', the founders of Rome, Catullus is actually suggesting that he and his friends have more right to be called Romans than traditional aristocrats like Memmius: Catullus is radically redefining aristocratic norms of behaviour. The extent to which Catullus' readers sympathized with this radical stance is as hard to assess as it is with Lucretius. Who did read this poetry? Just the radical youth of Rome, or the Ciceros too? If the latter—and poem 49 is addressed to Cicero—we may suspect that most found it as hard to accept as Epicureanism.

But for an audience with a taste for style over content like that of contemporary Rome, there was much to be enjoyed in the sheer creative virtuosity of Catullus. There is an astonishing variety to his poetry, which ranges from short personal poems to the mythological content of poem 64, and right across the spectrum of metres and genres. One poem in particular, 68, stands out even in Catullus' eclectic collection, a remarkable blend of the autobiographical—Catullus refers to his affair with Lesbia and the death of his brother at Troy—and the myth of Laodamia and her husband Protesilaus, who was the first Greek to be killed at the siege of Troy. Not all critics regard poem 68 as an unquestioned success, but there is no doubting the boldness of the piece; and the same can be said for poem 63, the exotic story of a devotee of the eastern goddess Kybele who castrates himself (and then regrets it), which is composed in an correspondingly outlandish metre, the fast and frenzied galliambic. This latter poem, in particular, seems to have a purely literary rationale, as if Catullus encountered the galliambic metre (probably in a poem by Kallimachos), recognized its potential, and only then found a theme adequate to it, rather than the other way around. It is a *tour de force* of literary and metrical technique, without any obvious further justification.

We have already seen that the readers of the New Poetry were themselves potentially poets, equipped with the capacity to interpret this allusive verse. Whereas Lucretius' poem sought to control his audience like a firm teacher, this type of poetry gives its readers much more autonomy: *we* are left to do much of the work of interpretation. But this can cause interesting problems of interpretation, both in the New Poets and in the generation of poets which followed, who were greatly influenced by them. This style of poetry is a very delicate mechanism. In the context of its immediate reception—the readership of the 50s BCE—it made for a complex, stimulating literary experience, ultimately quite as controlling and manipulative of the audience as Lucretius, but in a very different way: the readers of Catullus were drawn into the game the poet had set for them, and motivated by the intellectual pleasure of that game to pursue the poet's design. But once the original context of a poem has gone, the allusiveness of the poetry—the insistence that subtle, inexplicit allusions be followed up if a poem is to be understood—is liable to have the effect of suggesting readings which the author did not intend, and leaving us little grounds to judge one reading against another. Put another way, we today are often in the position of not knowing how far we should read inexplicit meaning into poems.

In the Renaissance it became a question of almost international significance whether the 'sparrow' referred to in poems 2 and 3, 'my girl's pet, with which she likes to play and which she likes to hold in her lap' (2. 1–2) was in fact an allegory for Catullus' penis. Politian, a scholar from Florence, forcibly promoted this interpretation of the poems; only to be violently contradicted by scholars from Verona, Catullus' home town, enraged at the aspersion on their national poet. The debate continues, but is, arguably, incapable of resolution: the Callimachean style of poetry leaves much of the creation of poetic meaning to its audience. In the next generation we find poets equally influenced by Kallimachos, but now under an obligation to write politically directed poetry, poetry where it becomes very important what a poem does or does not mean. The problem of containing and controlling the various interpretations to which the poetry is open will become acute.

Poem 49 poses similar problems of interpretation. Superficially it is a gushing poem of thanks to Cicero for some unspecified service. It could be translated

> Most eloquent of all the descendants of Romulus
> that are and have been, Marcus Tullius,
> and ever will be in other years,
> Catullus, the worst poet of all,
> gives you his greatest thanks,
> as much the worst poet of all
> as you are the best advocate of all.

But the entire poem *could* in fact be bitterly ironic. The Latin I have translated as 'the best advocate of all' may be translated quite differently. Catullus may be calling Cicero 'the best advocate-of-all', i.e. a man without principles prepared to defend absolutely anybody.

If the latter interpretation is more compelling, that is because it seems more in tune with the lack of respect for conventional notions of public achievement and success which Catullus generally evinces. The Lucretius that Cicero and his brother read and enjoyed (but were not in any way persuaded by), and the Catullus who either eulogized or traduced the orator (probably the latter), seem *prima facie* to share little more than the period and the language in which they both happened to be writing. But the time of writing is a significant common factor. Each of these poets, whether in the fleshpots frequented by Rome's gilded youth or in the limitless tracts of the Epicurean universe, offers a vision of escape from the catastrophe which the orthodox values men such as Cicero embodied had visited upon Rome.

12 Creativity out of chaos: Poetry between the death of Caesar and the death of Virgil

LLEWELYN MORGAN

Early Virgil: Pastoral and patronage

The last survivor of the New Poets, Cinna, died in the violent aftermath of Julius Caesar's funeral. His cries of 'I am Cinna the poet, I am Cinna the poet' (according to Shakespeare's version) were of no avail, and his death is emblematic. Julius Caesar's assassination in 44 ushered in the most murderous period of the Roman civil wars, and neither poets nor poetry were exempt. But despite the general chaos—or more accurately in direct response to it, and in an attempt to make sense of it—this period also witnessed a creative efflorescence in Roman literature such as had never been seen before. Some of the greatest poets in the Latin language began their careers in this, the darkest period of Roman history. In particular, the years immediately after the death of Caesar formed the context for the first major work by Publius Vergilius Maro (70–19 BCE: styled 'Virgil' by Christian commentators by association with the word 'virgin'), the greatest of all Roman poets. This was a collection of ten poems known as the *Eclogues* or *Bucolics*: *Bucolics* (originally *Bucolica*), meaning 'Herdsmen's songs', was apparently the original name, whilst *Eclogues* (*Eclogae*), meaning 'short poems' and referring to the ten independent poems which make up the collection, has become the name standardly used of the collection today. These poems gave powerful, albeit oblique, expression to a yearning for release from the ghastly circumstances under which its author and readers were labouring. They have justifiably won a reputation as one of the most mysterious and beautiful collections of poetry ever composed. And in more than one respect they exemplify the characteristics of Roman poetry after Caesar.

The *Eclogues* are an example of one of the strangest genres of literature, a genre which has become known as Pastoral (or Bucolic) Poetry. Pastoral depicts a utopian world of simple, carefree herdsmen relaxing in an idealized rural landscape (the so-called *locus amoenus*) and whiling away their time singing songs to the accompaniment of a rustic pipe. Virgil's main model for this style of poetry was Theokritos, a Sicilian poet who shared Kallimachos' literary ideals of brevity, polish, and allusiveness, and who (in a typically Hellenistic way) enjoyed the paradox of applying his sophisticated poetic style to 'low-life' material, including the interactions of herdsmen (see pp. 231–3). This is poetry of the countryside, then, and although the countryside of the *Eclogues*—as we would expect from a writer influenced by the Hellenistic poets—is a very artificial, literary construction, Virgil is careful to relate this pastoral world to the contemporary realities of the real Italian countryside.

There, the situation was very grim indeed. In the aftermath of Caesar's assassination the Roman Empire found itself divided between two competing factions. On one side stood Marcus Antonius ('Mark Antony') and C. Iulius Caesar Octavianus ('Octavian', later to become 'Augustus' cf. p. 438), the political heirs of Caesar. On the other were the assassins of Caesar, led by M. Iunius Brutus and C. Cassius Longinus (Brutus and Cassius). In 42 BCE Antony and Octavian crushed Brutus and Cassius at the Battle of Philippi in northern Greece, a massacre in which perhaps as many as 50,000 men fell. Antony and Octavian were victorious, and secure (until they starting fighting between themselves). But they found themselves with vast numbers of soldiers awaiting demobilization who had nowhere to go. Their solution was of a callousness typical of the times. Land across Italy was abruptly confiscated from its rightful owners and given to the ex-soldiers. The effect on rural life in Italy was predictably shattering, and finds recurrent echoes in the *Eclogues*.

The allusive, 'Hellenistic' tone of the collection is established from its very first lines. At 1. 1–2 Virgil sketches a *locus amoenus* in which the pastoral musician Tityrus blissfully reclines:

> You, Tityrus, reclining beneath the spreading beech tree's cover
> practise the woodland Muse on a slender reed.

A simple rustic scene, apparently: but the simplicity is only superficial. To concentrate on just one element of the scene: the word for beech-tree here, *fagus*, recurs frequently in the collection, and in fact comes to epitomize the idyllic landscape Virgil constructs in the poems: the *fagus* provides the shade under which his rustics sing and pipe. The precise variety of tree is carefully chosen, and fraught with significance. The *fagus* is a native Italian beech-tree, but will have reminded Virgil's more alert readers of a tree which featured in the pastoral *Idylls* of Theokritos, the *phagos*. By using an Italian tree which looks (on paper) so much like one of Theokritos' trees Virgil is advertising—with great subtlety—the kind of poetry of which the following collection will consist: pastoral in a tradition inaugurated by Theokritos. But there is a further implication. Theokritos' *phagos* is in fact a completely different tree from Virgil's beech-tree. It is a species of oak, and Virgil's replacement of the Greek *phagos* with the pointedly Italian *fagus* symbolizes that, whilst he is indebted to Theokritos, he is also in another respect being highly original, remaking the Greek genre of pastoral in the Latin language.

So it goes without saying that reading the *Eclogues* is very different from experiencing the real countryside. And yet, for all their artificiality, the *Eclogues* nevertheless managed to be powerfully relevant to the ugly realities of contemporary Italy. Pastoral is an intensely nostalgic genre. It speaks to the fantasy of a carefree existence in the country shared by every city-dweller, and it was this escapist quality that Virgil exploited to give a contemporary relevance to his poems. The poet represents himself in the collection as a pastoral singer like Tityrus, and invests the poems with a musicality in style and sound which corroborates the impression that they are themselves pastoral song, the products of the pastoral idyll. We can imagine what impact this beautiful poetry, redolent of the peaceful, carefree existence of Theokritos' herdsmen, will have had on an audience mired in the most brutal spell of the civil wars. Its evocation of this seductive rural paradise must have been, in the circumstances, impossibly nostalgic.

The perfection of the pastoral life contrasted implicitly with the far from idyllic conditions of contemporary Italy, ruined by war and dispossession. But repeatedly and explicitly Virgil allows the unhappy contemporary realities of the Italian countryside to intrude, jarringly, into the pastoral idyll, sharpening the sense of its desirability (and impossibility). For example, the first *Eclogue* is a dialogue between Tityrus, a conventional pastoral character enjoying the bucolic life reclining at ease beneath his beech-tree, and Meliboeus, a victim of the real-life land confiscations which followed the Battle of Philippi. The poem begins with Meliboeus:

> You, Tityrus, reclining beneath the spreading beech tree's cover,
> practise the woodland Muse on a slender reed.
> I am leaving the bounds of my fatherland and its sweet fields.
> I am fleeing my fatherland. You, Tityrus, easy in the shade,
> teach the woods to echo 'Amaryllis is beautiful'.

The pastoral experience offers the possibility of release from the grim reality of contemporary life, the utopian hope of transcending the troubles of the everyday world, and the desperate need for salvation from the prevailing troubles is a recurrent theme of this collection. Tityrus describes a visit to Rome and an audience with a divine young man, who will most likely have suggested Octavian to Virgil's contemporary readers (but Virgil's failure to name him explicitly is a sign of the insecurities of the times), who exempts his land from confiscation and thus allows him to continue his happy pastoral existence.

Eclogue 4 also offers the hope of salvation. Drawing on a complex web of mystical imagery, Virgil welcomes the birth of a divine child who will inaugurate a golden age of innocence and peace:

> The final age of the Cumaean song has now come:
> the great order of the ages is born anew.
> Now also returns the Virgin, now returns the kingdom of Saturn,
> now a new people is let down from the lofty sky.
> Bless the newborn boy who will first put an end
> to the iron race and give rise to the golden, throughout the world,
> chaste Lucina: your brother Apollo is now king.
> In your consulship, yours, this glorious age will begin,
> Pollio, and the great months start to move;
> under your leadership, whatever traces of crime remain,
> nullified, will free the earth of its endless fear.
> He will receive the life of the gods, and will see
> heroes mingled with gods, and will himself be seen by them,
> and will rule a world pacified by his father's virtues.
>
> (ll. 4–17)

Yet despite these intimations of redemption the dominant impression of the collection is of a yearning, inevitably unfulfilled, for an impossible dream. In *Eclogue* 9 two herdsmen attempt (unsuccessfully) to remember pastoral songs, once again in the context of the land confiscations. The *locus amoenus* which formed the backdrop for the monologue by the rustic Corydon in *Eclogue* 2, 'the shady tops of the dense beech-trees' (2. 4), has decayed into 'the now shattered tops of old beech-trees' (9. 9): trees which can provide no shade. One of the herdsmen pessimistically asserts that 'our songs have as much power, Lycidas, amid the weapons of war as they say Chaonian doves have before the onset of the eagle'. Pastoral song is powerless in the prevailing conditions, and song is the main component of the pastoral idyll. *Eclogue* 9 exposes the dream of escape into this dreamlike utopia as no more than a pious hope.

In broader terms, though, the 'young man' of *Eclogue* 1 is a significant departure. A characteristic element of Roman literary culture which starts to gain particular significance with this collection is *patronage*. In this respect the poetry which followed the death of Julius Caesar differs significantly from the poetry of the previous generation. Lucretius and Catullus had addressed poetry to specific, named individuals, and these figures—Memmius, Lesbia, Caesar, and so on—constitute, ostensibly at least, the primary audience of the poetry, the people to whom a poem was especially pertinent, although we may often suspect that the poet had a much larger audience in mind when he was writing. Crucially, though, both Lucretius and Catullus write as the social equals of their addressees: deference is a very rare commodity in either author.

With the following generation the situation is rather different, and much closer to the state of affairs earlier in the Republic (cf. pp. 307–8). A strong note of deference has made an entrance. The named individuals in this poetry are often *patrons* rather than simple addressees, the distinction being that these are men who are in a position to help a poet in return for the honour he pays them by making them, for all to see, the privileged readers of his poetry. The patronage system was an old Roman institution, which applied as much outside the artistic world as in it: a system of duties and obligations between the powerful and less powerful in society which provided protection for the weaker, and respect and status for the stronger. Nevertheless it is hard not to see its return to prominence in the literature of this period as a sign of the limitations being placed on freedom of speech, and the concomitant dangers attendant upon literary creativity. We cannot imagine Catullus saying, 'From you is my beginning, with you shall I end: receive poems undertaken at your bidding', as Virgil does at *Eclogue* 8. 10–11, *apparently* to C. Asinius Pollio. Only 'apparently', because the object of Virgil's praise at the start of *Eclogue* 8 is left intriguingly anonymous. Pollio was an important facilitator of literature at this time, and made a number of contributions to the literary scene, both in the form of his own writings and more generally (as we shall see), but his role as a patron of poetry was apparently short-lived, and for significant reasons. Although he seems originally to have fulfilled the role of Virgil's patron during his composition of the *Eclogues*, he seems by the time the collection reached its final form to have lost out somewhat to Octavian and his circle: the 'young man' of *Eclogue* 1, respectfully placed at the very centre of the poem, effectively dedicates the collection to Octavian, albeit obliquely. And the same, subtle movement away from Pollio may perhaps explain Virgil's failure to name him in *Eclogue* 8.

Literary patronage could take very blatant forms. The *Thyestes* of Varius Rufus, a play performed in 29 BCE at games celebrating Octavian's victory at Actium, was awarded one million sesterces (enough to make him instantly super-rich) by him. In general, though, patronage was more discreet. Precisely what benefits Virgil gained from Maecenas for the honour the poet paid him in the *Georgics* (see below), for example, is less clear. It is often easier to see how the system benefited the patron. Being a patron of poets could bring a Roman aristocrat some of the status that was so important in Roman culture. As Virgil says to Alfenus Varus, a man who apparently had designs to be seen as Virgil's patron, whoever reads *Eclogue* 6 will associate it with his name (6. 9–12). And a poem did not need actually to be *about* Varus, or in praise of him, to bring this kind of credit to the patron. It is important to appreciate, however, that patronage was a free association on both sides. The patron did not tell the poet what to write: what held the relation together was a sense of mutual obligation rather than any influence being brought to bear by the patron.

Patronage could confer prestige on aristocrats who in the new political circumstances had a shrinking number of contexts in which they could assert themselves. The free politics which had been the main source of aristocratic status in the past was now limited, and power centralized in the hands of Octavian and Antony. In time their power came to be felt in the literary arena as well. Aristocratic patrons like M. Valerius Messalla Corvinus (the patron of Tibullus) or Asinius Pollio were gradually overshadowed by these superpowers dominating the state. The most important literary impresario of the generation after Caesar was not Pollio or Messalla but C. Maecenas, one of Augustus' right-hand men. In fact, of the four poets we shall discuss in this section—Virgil, Horace, Propertius, and Tibullus—all but Tibullus had Maecenas as their patron at some stage or other. A 'drift towards the centre' is discernible in a number of these collections. Virgil, Horace, and Propertius all apparently only started to enjoy Maecenas' patronage when their literary careers were well under way. Power at Rome was gradually becoming concentrated in a single pair of hands, and the effects of this process were felt in literature as well as in the wider world.

Pollio, Virgil's one-time patron, is credited with other important contributions to Roman literary life at this time. Besides establishing the first public library at Rome, he was also the first to organize, on a formal basis, the recitation by an author of his work to an invited audience. In the first instance this was Pollio's own work, but the practice was picked up by others and became a central institution of Roman aristocratic life in the imperial period. It is likely that every author we shall meet here performed at some point in such select gatherings. These 'live' performances could be memorable. The poet Julius Montanus used to say that he would happily steal material from Virgil if only he could steal his voice and face and delivery as well, so compelling were Virgil's recitations: 'the same verses sounded beautiful when he recited them, but banal and inexpressive without him.' Recitation was also, as compared with private reading, an interestingly unstable medium of communication. An audience, unlike a reader, can get rowdy. We are told that once when Virgil was reciting his *Georgics*, and reached 1. 299, 'Strip to plough and strip to sow; winter is a farmer's free time' (a poetic way of saying 'only farm in warm weather'), a listener interposed after 'Strip to plough and strip to sow' the rhythmically perfect supplement, 'and you'll have a 'flu in winter'.

Anecdotes like this are interesting, and incidentally alert us to the high sophistication of the literary public to whom our poets addressed themselves. But we should not overestimate the role of the recitation at this juncture. It is true that the poetry of this period was written to be read aloud by the private reader, and true that occasionally the poet himself would do the reading, in (relatively) public contexts or more privately, to friends. It is also the case that certain texts, the *Eclogues* in particular, found an avid audience in the theatre. But the Rome upper classes who were the core audience of this poetry—it is impossible to put a number to the immediate readership of texts like the *Eclogues*, but it is unlikely to have exceeded a couple of thousand (when the population of Rome was one million)—still had an essentially bookish culture rather than a performative culture. We are told that Virgil was an unenthusiastic reciter who as a rule presented his work in public only when he wanted a second opinion about passages with which he was unhappy, and in this he may well have been typical. It will be clear again and again that the poetry we are going to encounter catered first and foremost to readers, not an audience.

Nevertheless, the musical quality of the *Eclogues* helps to explain the intriguing fact that soon after its publication parts of the collection were performed on stage. The theatre, by its very nature, caters for a much larger audience than we would expect for poetry as complex and allusive as this; and we know that it continued to be an important—and much more 'democratic'—context for the performance of literature, and in particular Virgil, for some time. In the late fourth or early fifth century CE St Augustine distinguished between the few members of his congregation who knew Virgil's poetry from books and the much greater number who knew it from performances in the theatre. The only permanent theatre in existence in Rome at the time of the publication of the *Eclogues*, the Theatre of Pompey, could hold as many as 11,000 people, a much larger number than the *readership* of poetry of this degree of sophistication.

But how much of the complex experience of the *Eclogues* was accessible to a theatre audience? Theatrical performance was bound to alter profoundly the way the poetry was interpreted. *Eclogue* 2 is a monologue by the herdsman Corydon bewailing his unrequited love for a boy from the city, Alexis; and Virgil manages to imply that Corydon is way out of his league. But the appearance of passages from *Eclogue* 2 on the walls of Pompeii, presumably inscribed at some date close to the eruption of Vesuvius in 79 CE, suggests that, as far as this wider audience was concerned, the poem had lost that original element of amused condescension of the rustic Corydon, and was now treated as straightforward, unironic love poetry. The authors of this graffiti presumably knew the

Eclogues from the theatre. This ironing out of the complexities of poetry as its audience expands is a pattern we will see repeated.

In the longer term, however, it was (paradoxically) precisely the difficulty and allusiveness of the collection, as well as the name that Virgil went on to gain with his epic *Aeneid*, which ensured the survival of the collection beyond antiquity. In the Renaissance, and later, the *Eclogues* inspired a flourishing tradition of pastoral poetry in Italian, French, and English, poetry which shared the *Eclogues'* studied simplicity and a tendency to comment on contemporary events: Milton's *Lycidas* is the best-known English example.

But by far the most influential poem in the collection is *Eclogue* 4, ironically the least 'pastoral' of them all. This poem is tied very specifically to a date and time: 40 BCE, the year of Asinius Pollio's consulship and date of the Pact of Brundisium which temporarily patched up the differences between Antony and Octavian. The miraculous child whose birth is celebrated in the poem is most likely to have suggested to contemporaries the son expected of the marriage of Antony and Octavia, Octavian's sister, the alliance which had cemented the agreement. But the poem is deliberately enigmatic and unspecific, and sensibly so: no son ever came of the marriage (Antony was too busy having children by Kleopatra, queen of Egypt), and the marriage itself rapidly disintegrated as relations between Antony and Octavian deteriorated. The golden child was mysterious enough for Pollio's son, Asinius Gallus, to be able to claim to be him a generation later. But the dominant interpretation of the poem throughout the Middle Ages and beyond was that it prophesied the birth of Christ, and the Kingdom of God that would ensue. One line of the poem in particular, *iam redit et Virgo, redeunt Saturnia regna*, 'Now also returns the Virgin, now returns the kingdom of Saturn' (line 6), became the most quoted line of classical literature. In its original context 'the Virgin' is Justice, who will return to dwell amongst men when the Golden Age, or Age of Saturn, is restored. But Christians found it easy to interpret her as the Virgin Mary, returning to earth in the company of her son. Virgil consequently gained the status of a prophet of the coming of Christ, which is how he appears (for example) in Dante's *Divine Comedy*.

The poem thus developed a wealth of meaning and associations unimaginable to its author. Perhaps nobody exploited it more fully than Elizabeth I. With the new-found classical knowledge of the Renaissance the Virgin could again be identified as Justice, and Elizabeth could combine the Christian associations of the poem, the classical motifs of Justice and the return of the Golden Age, and her own mystical image as the pure virgin married to the welfare of her subjects, into a potent political manifesto.

Agriculture as a metaphor for Rome

The *Eclogues* probably appeared as a collection in 39 or 38 BCE. Virgil's second collection, the four-book poem *Georgics* (originally *Georgica*), was apparently published in 29. In between these dates Virgil had joined the circle of Maecenas, whose name appears at the very outset of the poem;

> What makes the cornfields happy, under which constellation
> it is best to turn the earth, Maecenas, and train the vine on the elm;
> the care of cattle, the method for keeping
> a flock, the skill you need for frugal bees:
> this is where I shall begin to sing.
>
> (1. 1–5, trans. C. Day-Lewis)

Maecenas proceeds to reappear with an uncanny regularity at the beginning of the remaining three books: at line 41, precisely, in books 2 and 3, and back at line 2 in book 4. Octavian also features prominently: extravagant eulogies begin (1. 24–42) and end the poem (4. 559–66), and also mark its middle (3. 1–48). Virgil clearly indicates his proximity at this time to Octavian's party: he describes the poem as the *haud mollia iussa*, 'far from easy bidding' of Maecenas (3. 41). We are told in an ancient biography of Virgil that the poem was recited to Octavian after his return to Italy from the Actium campaign in 29, when he was recovering from a throat complaint in Atella, near Naples. Virgil read it to Octavian over a period of four days, Maecenas taking over the task whenever Virgil's voice gave out.

The strict truth of this anecdote is less important than the light it sheds on Virgil's relation to his patrons. As we have seen, great works of literature bring status not only to the author but also to the author's patrons. It was put about in anecdotes like this that the *Georgics* was written, in the first instance, for Octavian. The poem itself is a farming manual (*Georgica* means 'Farming Matters'), or rather the highly literary and artificial version of a farming manual we would expect of the author of the *Eclogues*. Anyone seeking advice on agriculture would be far better advised to consult Varro's prose *On Rural Matters* (cf. p. 321), published in 37 BCE and a clear inspiration for Virgil's work, though Varro's work was itself more of a pleasant diversion for the landed gentry than a scientific treatise. One of the major sources of enjoyment for a contemporary reader was Virgil's achievement in making poetry out of something as intrinsically unpromising as the mud and ordure of farming. Seneca wrote of the poem that Virgil 'saw not what it was most truthful to say, but what would be most agreeable, and wanted not to teach farmers, but please readers'. To prove his point Seneca quotes from Virgil's instructions as to when different crops should be sown:

> It is our task, again, to observe the star of Arcturus,
> The days of the Kid, and the shining Serpent, as carefully
> As sailors who homeward bound on windy waters are daring
> The Black Sea and the straits by the oyster-beds of Abydos.
> When the Scales make the hours for daytime and sleeptime balance,
> Dividing the globe into equal hemispheres—light and darkness,
> Then set your bulls to work, farmers, and sow your barley
> Up to the last showers on the frost-bound limits of winter:
> The flax-plant and corn-poppy
> You should cover now in earth, and keep on hard at the ploughing
> While a bone-dry soil allows it and the weather has not yet broken.
> In spring you sow your beans: then too the softening furrows
> Will take lucerne, and millet requires its annual care;
> When the milk-white Bull with gilded horn begins the year
> And the Dog Star drops away.
>
> (1. 204–18, trans. C. Day-Lewis)

Seneca helpfully points out that millet is actually sown in June, not spring. But we do not need information like that to see that Virgil's emphasis is more on poetic expression than textbook accuracy.

The landscape of the *Georgics* is thus a very literary landscape, owing no less to Hesiod and Aratos than to contemporary agricultural reality. The kind of detailed advice about farming practice that Virgil offers in the poem can have been of no interest *per se* for the privileged élite who read his poem: they had slaves to deal with that kind of thing. And conversely, the demands made of the reader by this extremely complex poem required vastly better education than the average farmer would have enjoyed. One fairly extreme example: sharp-eyed scholars have noticed that whenever the river Euphrates is mentioned in Virgil's works its name is placed six lines from the end of the book: *Georgics* 1. 509, *Georgics* 4. 561, and *Aeneid* 8. 726. The explanation for this strange coincidence lies in Kallimachos' *Hymn to Apollo*, one of the most important statements of Kallimachos' literary principles, which contains a reference to the Euphrates—six lines from the end. Virgil is subtly communicating to his readership (and this device says astonishing things *about* that readership) his allegiance to Kallimachos' poetics. It goes without saying that the device also presupposes *written* texts which can be numbered, and compared.

Like Lucretius' poem, to which Virgil owes a lot, the *Georgics* is a didactic poem, a poem which teaches a lesson. But in the case of the *Georgics* this function is more apparent than real. A comparison of the roles of the addressees of each poem, Memmius and Maecenas, will clarify the differences. We saw in the previous chapter how Lucretius sought to guide his readers' response to his poem by means of an 'internal audience', Memmius, who 'stood for' the broader aristocratic audience at which Lucretius was aiming, and Lucretius' choice of him as the target of his argument *personalizes* the argument of the poem. In other words, Memmius is a teaching tool, an integral element of Lucretius' strategy for persuading and converting his readership. Can we say the same about Maecenas in the *Georgics*? No. Lucretius' poem is explicitly a course of tuition, with a pupil: Maecenas never fulfils any such role. After 1. 2 he is not mentioned again until the beginning of the next book, and the advice about farming which Virgil proceeds to give is directed at a very vaguely defined farmer figure. There are none of the teaching techniques here which Lucretius so brilliantly employed, and if the *Georgics* were really aiming to teach it would be supremely ineffective. But if Maecenas is not in the poem to be taught, his presence is nonetheless significant. First, his name at the beginning of every book informs the reader that the author of the most admired poem of recent years, the *Eclogues*, has deep respect for Maecenas, and the status that would accrue to Maecenas (and Octavian) from such a gesture should not be underestimated. Secondly, it would have been well known to Virgil's readers that Maecenas had minimal interest in farming, but did have an enthusiasm for the higher things in life. He had carefully fostered an image of decadent sophistication which concealed the political power he actually wielded. Amongst other things, then, the mention of Maecenas at the start of the *Georgics* would have alerted a contemporary reader that the *Georgics* was closer in function to Aratos' didactic than to Lucretius'.

Finally, however, it is hard not to think that the repetition of Maecenas' name, alongside the generous compliments paid to Octavian, encourages us to seek in the work some favourable commentary on Octavian's activities in the 30s. The Battle of Philippi in 42 had been followed by the Treaty of Brundisium in 40 between Antony and Octavian, the terms of which divided the Empire between Octavian and Antony. Antony went east to Alexandria (and to Kleopatra), and Octavian took control in Italy and the West. The 30s saw continued violent upheaval, in particular an extended and bloody sea war between Octavian and Sextus Pompeius, the son of Pompey the Great. The arrangement between Antony and Octavian, meanwhile, was fragile. After many false alarms it broke down decisively, and they came to blows. At Actium in 31 Octavian's forces defeated Antony and Kleopatra. Octavian now found himself with absolute control of Rome, but it was in a devastated and demoralized state. The period when the poem was composed (36–29) corresponds to the latter period of these upheavals, a time which also saw sustained propagandistic self-promotion on the part of Octavian as he sought to bolster his precarious position.

But whilst contemporary events certainly do impinge upon the poem, Virgil's attitude to them in the *Georgics* remains a source of enormous controversy. This poem is perhaps of all Roman poems the most fiercely debated by scholars. What we *can* say is that the agricultural world described in the poem is often not to be taken literally, but as a metaphor for the contemporary Roman world. In the *Georgics* Virgil exploits a powerful symbolism which the agricultural life exerted on the Roman upper classes, who for all their high urban sophistication liked to consider themselves at root farmers made good (hence the success of books like Varro's *On rural matters*). It was from their rustic origins, Romans felt, that all that was best about their culture—discipline, levelheadedness, a capacity for hard work—derived; and this myth of the rustic origins of Rome appears more than once in the poem. In the so-called 'Praise of Italy' (2. 136–76), for example, the success of Rome is attributed to the genius of the Italian countryside:

> Active her breed of men—the Marsians and Sabellians,
> Ligurians used to hardship, Volscian javelin-throwers;
> Mother she is of the Decii, Marii, great Camilli,
> The Scipios relentless in war; and of you, most royal Caesar,
> Who now triumphant along the furthest Asian frontiers
> Keep the war-worthless Indians away from the towers of Rome.
> Hail, great mother of harvests! O land of Saturn, hail!
> Mother of men!
>
> (ll. 167–74, trans. C. Day-Lewis)

But if as a consequence Virgil's countryside is always likely to symbolize contemporary Rome, it is an uncompromising picture of Rome that the poet offers. Repeatedly the advice offered to the farmer by the poet is shown to be quite unequal to the elemental forces with which the farmer has to contend. The world of the *Georgics*, whether that be the agricultural world or the world of Rome it represents, is frequently out of control:

> So, when racing chariots have rushed from the starting-gate,
> They gather speed on the course, and the driver tugs at the curb-reign
> —His horses runaway, car out of control, quite helpless.
>
> (1. 512–14, trans. C. Day-Lewis)

These are the last words of book 1. Book 3, concerned with the raising of flocks, punctuates its advice with two disturbing accounts of natural processes which are quite beyond the farmer's control, sex and disease. The book ends with a harrowing account of a plague among farm animals:

And now they died by whole companies, and the corpses
Rotting with vile decay lay piled in the very sheep-folds,
Till men had learnt to put them in pits, covered with earth.
The hide was no good, and no man
Could cleanse the carcass in water or burn it up with fire:
You could not even shear the fleece, it was so corroded
With the foul pus, or work the rotten wool in the loom:
But if you were so foolhardy as to wear the hideous garment,
Inflamed pustules and a noxious-swelling sweat appeared
All over your limbs: not long then
Before the fiery curse ate up your tettered frame.

(ll. 556–66, trans. C. Day-Lewis)

In book 4, which is devoted to apiculture (bee-keeping), the establishment of a bee colony and the needs and habits of bees are carefully described—but the account ends, as in the previous book, with a plague, which wipes out the hive. Again, certain elements of Virgil's account of bee civilization serve to establish parallels between the beehive and Rome; it is not hard to see in these destructive plagues a reflection of the civil wars which had had such a devastating effect on the Roman state.

Yet the poem does seem to promise some kind of solution to this catastrophe. It concludes with an extended mythological account of the hero Aristaeus, the loss of his beehive to disease, but then his recovery of his bee swarm under the direction of his mother Cyrene. The figure of Aristaeus cannot but have reminded contemporary readers of Octavian, who at the time was claiming to have restored the Roman state to life in a manner analogous to Aristaeus' regeneration of his bees. But few readers of the end of the *Georgics* have found the resolution very satisfactory. The cost of Aristaeus' success is the death of Orpheus, whose failed attempt to lead his dead wife back from the underworld is described at some length:

And now he's avoided every pitfall of the homeward path,
And Eurydice, regained, is nearing the upper air
Close behind him (for this condition has Proserpine made),
When a moment's madness catches her lover off his guard—
Pardonable, you'd say, but Death can never pardon.
He halts. Eurydice, his own, is now on the lip of
Daylight. Alas! he forgot. His purpose broke. He looked back.
His labour was lost, the pact he had made with the merciless king
Annulled. Three times did thunder peal over the pools of Avernus.
'Who,' she cried, 'has doomed me to misery, who has doomed us?
What madness beyond measure? Once more a cruel fate
Drags me away, and my swimming eyes are drowned in darkness.

> Goodbye. I am borne away. A limitless night is about me
> And over the strengthless hands I stretch to you, yours no longer.'
> Thus she spoke: and at once from his sight, like a wisp of smoke,
> Thinned into air, was gone.
>
> (4. 485–500, trans. C. Day-Lewis)

This is the passage which has captured the imagination of most readers, and it was Virgil's Orpheus, not his Aristaeus, who became a favourite theme of all artistic media—not least in *L'Orfeo* of Claudio Monteverdi, the first great achievement of the operatic tradition.

As Seneca's remarks in the mid-first century testify, the poem continued to be read by the upper classes—though judging by the absence of any graffiti of the *Georgics* at Pompeii it never developed the broader popularity of the *Eclogues* (and later the *Aeneid*). It is noticeable that Seneca omits any reference to the contemporary, political content of the poem. By his time the *Georgics* was apparently just a charming poetic evocation of the country life, and it was as such that it enjoyed a revival among those eighteenth-century English gentlemen who liked to consider themselves farmers but were happier with books than billhooks. It was, of course, an extremely good thing for the Agricultural Revolution that these readers did not attempt to apply any of Virgil's 'teachings'.

Early Horace: Us blaming them

The 'triumviral period' between the death of Julius Caesar and Octavian's final victory also saw the first works of Quintus Horatius Flaccus, or Horace (65 BCE–8 BCE). One was the two books of verse *Sermones* (a term which covers the ground from 'chats' to 'sermons' or 'homilies') or *Satires* (a name which captures their mildly critical nature), following in the tradition of the second-century BCE Roman poet and social critic Gaius Lucilius (cf. pp. 309–10). The other book, modelled on the abusive 'iambic' poetry of the Archaic Greek poets Archilochos and Hipponax (cf. Ch. 2), was probably originally named *Iambi*, but is now known as the *Epodes*, a technical term derived from their metrical scheme.

As with the *Georgics*, the very first words of the *Satires* immediately betray Horace's allegiances:

> How is it, Maecenas, that no one lives content with the lot
> which either choice has given him or chance thrown in his way,
> but praises those who follow different paths?
>
> (1. 1–3)

Both books of *Satires*, the first probably published in 35 BCE and the second in 30, were written under the patronage of Maecenas; in fact the first book describes Horace's admission into Maecenas' circle in some detail. But the situation with the *Epodes* is rather different. Although the beginning of the *Epodes* advertises Horace's proximity to Maecenas (his name appears in the fourth line of the first *Epode* and the whole poem is about him), many of the poems which make up the collection give the impression that they pre-date his adoption by Maecenas in about 38.

Poems like *Epodes* 1 and 9 glorify Maecenas' participation in the Battle of Actium in 31. This is the beginning of *Epode* 9:

> When shall I celebrate great Caesar's victory and drink
> the Caecuban laid down for sacred feasts
> with you, heaven-blest Maecenas, in the lofty home
> the gods have given you,
> to mingled music of the lyre and pipe,
> Dorian the one, the other barbarous?
> Just so not long ago we drank when Neptune's admiral
> was routed and his galleys fired,
> although he once had threatened Rome with chains
> struck off his friends, our treacherous slaves.
> Now Romans are a woman's slaves—O hear you this
> you generations yet to come—
> carrying arms and stakes for her, and at the beck and call
> of wrinkled eunuchs,
> and there the sun among our eagles sees
> —the shame of it—mosquito nets!
>
> (trans. David West)

What particularly appalled Romans about the civil wars was that they involved not the conquest of foreigners, which Romans bore with an easy conscience, but of other Romans. This is why in this poem Horace celebrates some of Octavian's activities in the civil wars—both Actium and earlier actions against Sextus Pompeius—as the conquest of Romans, yes, but treacherous Romans, Romans who have abandoned Roman values. Pompeius has thrown his lot in with slaves, and Antony himself is a love slave to Kleopatra. They are as good as foreigners, deserving defeat and death in return for their eastern effeminacy (mosquito nets, indeed!). There was a strong vein of racism and sexual and class prejudice in the Roman upper classes for poems like this to exploit.

But other poems in the *Epodes* collection sit awkwardly with such propaganda. In poems 7 and 16, in particular, civil war is a far less glorious business. Poem 16 despairs of an end to it all. Rome will destroy itself, and all the Romans can do is sail off to the Elysian Fields beyond the Ocean. Poem 7 presents the poet demanding of the Roman people an explanation of their compulsion for civil war:

> Why this mad rush to join a wicked war? Your swords
> were sheathed. Why do you draw them now?
> Perhaps too little Latin blood has poured upon the plains
> and into Neptune's sea,
> not so that Rome could burn the lofty citadels
> of Carthage, her great enemy,
> or that the Briton, still beyond our reach, should walk
> the Sacred Way in chains,
> but so that Rome might fall by Roman hands
> and answer all the prayers of Parthia.
>
> (trans. David West)

Receiving no reply he supplies his own explanation:

> It is harsh fate that drives
> the Romans, and the crime of fratricide
> since Remus' blameless lifeblood poured upon the ground—
> a curse to generations yet unborn.
>
> (ll. 17–20)

Romulus killed his own twin brother in the course of founding the city, and Rome, according to Horace, is cursed to repeat the crime unendingly. *Epode* 1, it could be argued, aims to 'neutralize' the *Epodes*, frame the collection as a whole as loyal to Maecenas, despite the disconcerting sentiments of poems like 7. But where readers place the emphasis of the collection is (arguably) ultimately up to them, in the privacy of their own reading.

Horace wrote the *Epodes* and the *Satires* simultaneously, and this was a natural choice. Though very different styles of poetry they have a lot in common. Archilochos and Hipponax wrote 'blame poetry', poetry which chastised the moral failings which the poets perceived in the people around them. Similarly, Roman satire, although different from modern satire in being a literary genre, shares with its modern counterpart the basic function of criticism. Lucilius' satires had already substantially conflated the two genres (cf. pp. 309–10). Horace's choice of two very different genres with the shared element of *blame* has an obvious contemporary rationale: Rome was not an exemplary society at this juncture.

But Horace had certain more subtle aspects of the genres in mind as well. Blame poetry, by its very nature, distances the poet and the reader from the vices it attacks. But by the same token it unites poet and audience in their moral outrage, and it reminds them of their shared moral values. Paradoxically, then, blame poetry makes *friends* of its audience, as it makes enemies of its targets. Friendship is a preoccupation of both the *Epodes* and the *Satires*, and it was one shared by Horace's contemporaries. *Amicitia*, friendship, was the value that bound Roman society together. But civil war had ripped it apart, pitting close associates and even family members against each other (hence the equation with fratricide). To Romans this felt like the breakdown of *amicitia*.

In poems like *Epode* 7 Horace addresses his target, here the Roman people, and attempts to 'blame' them into changing their terrible behaviour. But more subtly, whilst a contemporary Roman reader shared the blame being meted out to the Roman people he is also constructed by the poem as a counterpart of the outraged, blaming authorial voice: we also ask, in the process of reading, 'Why this mad rush to join a wicked war?' We read, and become part of Horace's group of right-thinking friends, berating the fratricidal madness of the Romans. So the *Epodes* restore friendship.

The *Satires* or *Sermones* offer a milder form of criticism, but in this respect their effect is somewhat similar. The poems have a very informal style, and aim to give the impression of immediacy, as if Horace is conducting a conversation with us. They thus dramatize an act of friendship, a conversation between friends, and like the *Epodes* offer an alternative to the social breakdown of civil war. But what makes Horace's strategy more pointed is that the friendships which Horace idealistically depicts in the *Satires* are largely those between the members of Maecenas' 'set'. In other words, the group being set up by Horace as the representative of decent values, which Rome needs in order to escape from civil war, just happens to be one of the parties vying (violently) for control of Rome. The reader witnesses an exemplary group of Romans, and is drawn into that group himself by the process of reading: Horace's friendly immediacy makes us feel we too are part of the group.

The underlying political rationale is exemplified by 1. 5. This poem describes a journey undertaken by Maecenas and his literary 'friends' from Rome to Brundisium, during which the group experiences various amusing misfortunes: stomach upsets, travel delays, wet dreams, fire, mud, and so on. It is an attractive picture of an ordinary group of male friends. In passing the poem also mentions the purpose of the journey:

> To Anxur excellent Maecenas was to come, with
> Cocceius, both despatched on important business,
> as ambassadors, well used to reconciling estranged friends.
> Here I smear black ointment on my eyes

for my conjunctivitis. Meanwhile Maecenas arrived with
Cocceius and Fonteius Capito, an exemplary
individual, Antony's closest friend.

(ll. 27–33)

The friends are going to attend a meeting, probably in 37 BCE, to patch up differences (again!) between Octavian and Antony. It is a mission of great seriousness, the failure of which would mean renewed civil war. But there is no hint of this in Horace's poem. Normality reigns. Even the split between Antony and Octavian is depicted as a temporary, and easily remedied, difference between friends. The reader witnesses, and enjoys, a scene far removed from the trauma of civil war—and we associate its harmony and good sense with Maecenas.

Horace, no less than Virgil, was profoundly influenced by the Callimachean ideals of the New Poets. Part of the reason Horace chose to wrote iambic poetry modelled after Archilochos and Hipponax was that Kallimachos had done so (see p. 238). The very first word of the *Epodes*, *ibis*, 'you will go', probably alludes to the title of a piece of invective by Kallimachos, the *Ibis*, and this degree of Callimachean complexity and allusiveness is maintained throughout the collection. The same, more surprisingly, goes for the *Satires*. Surprisingly, because the intricacy and polish demanded by Kallimachos was profoundly alien to the genre invented by Lucilius, which took pride in breaking the literary rules. Its concerns were humble and un-poetic, everyday life and (bad) behaviour, and the language of satire was the colloquial speech of the ordinary Roman. Yet the metre of satirical poetry was the dactylic hexameter, the rhythmical scheme associated with epic verse. Horace's readers would have felt about the colloquial language of the opening hexameter line in Horace's *Satires*, 'How is it, Maecenas, that . . .', the same as we would about a Shakespearian actor reciting a newspaper: the sublime perfection of the hexameter is being abused.

Horace's claim that his satire obeyed the tenets of Kallimachos pushes the Lucilian paradox of poetic satire a step further. Callimachean satire was a contradiction in terms. Horace's audience knew it, and enjoyed the literary joke. *Satire* 1. 10 is a statement of Horace's literary ideals in which he criticizes Lucilius for his verbosity and lack of polish:

If his life had been postponed by fate until our present age,
he would file off a lot from his work, and cut back everything which
trailed beyond what was ideal, and in composing his verse
he would often scratch his head and gnaw his nails to the quick.

(ll. 68–71)

But the end of the poem amusingly undermines Horace's claim to be a follower of Kallimachos. He concludes his literary criticism, and adds (line 92),

> Away, boy, and quickly append this to my book

as if his poetry is not the product of laborious care at all, but something dictated off the top of his head.

So the *Satires* were, as we would expect, sophisticated poetry for a sophisticated audience, in which play with the conventions of literature provides much of the diversion. But the wit and artistry concealed a deadly serious political intent. The Rome of the *Satires* is one of absolute normality: friends act like friends, civil upheaval is scarcely to be seen, and Horace chats in a homely style which it is hard to square with the grim reality of the 30s BCE. The unanswerable question, however, is whether the collection had the effect Horace intended. Were readers of Horace's *Satires* lulled into a contented acceptance of Octavian's leadership, or did the strenuous efforts which Horace put into *not mentioning the war* simply draw attention to the anxieties which were motivating him, and the grim realities he was trying to disguise? We cannot say, but we can recognize the various interpretative possibilities, and we know that Horace was dealing with an audience quite capable of second-guessing him. But whatever their immediate reception, the *Satires* join the list of Maecenas' success stories, reinventing the genre in a form which would be imitated and developed by Persius in the first century CE, Juvenal in the second (see pp. 501–2, 504–6), and the English satirists, especially the master of 'Horatian Satire', Alexander Pope, in the eighteenth—none of them, apparently, suspecting the disguise of genial social critic which Horace had assumed.

The elegists: All for love?

In comparison to Virgil and Horace our next poet, Sextus Propertius (*c.*50–*c.*5 BCE), has seemed to some readers a breath of fresh air, a writer determined to assert his independence from the regime of Octavian or Augustus. This is the Propertius of Ezra Pound, for example, whose paraphrase of Propertius' love elegies, *Homage to Sextus Propertius* (1917), makes of the poet a passionate, independent-minded lover of poetry for its own sake rather too obviously reminiscent of Ezra Pound. His version of Propertius' anticipation of Virgil's epic *Aeneid* is typical, importing as it does an explicit tone of condemnation quite absent from the original:

> Upon the Actian marshes Virgil is Phoebus' chief of police,
> He can tabulate Caesar's great ships.

He thrills to Ilian arms,
He shakes the Trojan weapons of Aeneas,
And casts stores on Lavinian beaches.
Make way, ye Roman authors,
clear the street O ye Greeks,
For a much larger Iliad is in the course of construction
(and to Imperial order)
Clear the streets O ye Greeks!

(2. 34. 61–6)

Pound saw in Propertius' poems a reaction against 'the infinite and ineffable imbecility of the Roman Empire', and a vehicle he could use at the height of the First World War to express his disgust at 'the infinite and ineffable imbecility of the British Empire'.

A contemporary assessment of the poet would have been more qualified. Propertius was an exponent of one of the most characteristically Roman genres, Love Elegy, so called because it was love poetry composed in the metre known as the elegiac couplet. Love Elegy had originated with Cornelius Gallus (cf. pp. 336–7), whose poetry (despite the influence it exerted on Virgil as well as the elegists) has almost completely disappeared. But we know enough about it to see that, young as the genre was, Propertius was already working within a set of rules and conventions. Gallus was a man of action who wrote poetry in which he represented himself as a very different kind of person, a man in thrall to a dominating mistress called Lycoris. We can assume that the persona he adopted in his poetry had little to do with real life, and that his readers did not expect it to. In other words, the poetry of the love elegists did not come 'straight from the heart', by any means.

The first book of Propertius' elegies was published in 30 or 29 BCE. There were probably five books in all, produced between 30 and about 16 BCE, although modern texts are divided into four (the text of Propertius rivals Catullus for the corrupt state in which it emerged from the Middle Ages). Most of his poetry is devoted to an account of an unequal relationship with a girlfriend, Cynthia, who dominates the poet's life. The first verses of book 1 set the scene:

Cynthia first, with her eyes, caught wretched me
Smitten before by no desires;
Then, lowering my stare of steady arrogance,
With feet imposed Love pressed my head,
Until he taught me hatred of chaste girls—
The villain—and living aimlessly.
And now for a whole year this mania has not left me,
Though I am forced to suffer adverse Gods.

Milanion by facing every hardship, Tullus,
  Conquered the cruelty of Atalanta.
Sometimes, distraught, he roamed the glens of Parthenius
  And was gone to watch the long-haired beasts.
Stunned by that blow from Hylaeus' club he even
  Groaned in anguish to Arcadian crags.
So he was able to master his fleet-footed girl;
  Such power in love have prayers and kindnesses.
For me, though, Love is slow, can think of no devices,
  And forgets to go his legendary way.

(1. 1. 1–18, trans. Guy Lee)

An author has to catch the reader's attention, preferably at the beginning of a collection. The strategy of the love elegist is to be outrageous. The lifestyle described here breaks every rule of Roman aristocratic morality. By allowing himself to be dominated by a woman Propertius is abrogating his position as a dominant Roman male; and by a woman, what is more, of dubious social status, in a society where status was everything. And whilst the Roman male was trained to aspire to success and honour in the public arenas of politics and war, Propertius describes his pursuit of Cynthia, an unworthy aspiration in itself, as his sole occupation. The slave-like devotion to a low-status woman which Propertius describes is thus an outrageous reversal of conventional ethics. And Propertius knows how to rub it in:

Had I not better be the slave of some harsh tyrant
  And moan in cruel Perillus' bull?
Not better be turned to stone by the Gorgon's glare
  Or even devoured by Prometheus' vultures?
No, I'll stand firm. Steel blades are worn away
  By rust, and flint by dripping water,
But love's not worn away by an accusing mistress;
  Love stays and puts up with her unjust threats.
When scorned he asks again. Though wronged he takes the blame,
  And back he comes, if on reluctant feet.

(2. 25. 11–20, trans. Guy Lee)

But this poetry is very aware how shocking it is. Notice how at the opening to book 1 Propertius condemns his own behaviour, guiding his readers to do the same (if they are not so minded already). Propertius is *self-consciously* immoral, and this helps to suggest to us the nature of his relationship with his audience: it is an audience which, as with all the poetry of this period, enjoys a literary game, and which recognizes (and takes pleasure in the fact) that what poets say about themselves need only bear a very oblique relation to reality. Propertius recounts his feckless, out-of-control lifestyle in elegant and witty verse and carefully constructed poems and collections, and illustrates his humiliating condition with erudite allusions to myth. For example the myth of Milanion he cites in his first poem has more significance than meets the eye. Milanion finally managed to endear himself to the unwilling object of his affection, the huntress Atalanta, by sharing her outdoor lifestyle; but he was also a figure with whom Gallus had identified himself in his efforts to gain the goodwill of *his* beloved, Lycoris. A contemporary reader would appreciate that Propertius' use of the myth says as much about his place in the history of the elegiac genre as his actual love life: in an allusive way Propertius informs his readership that he is working in the same tradition as Cornelius Gallus, but that his poetry is a new departure in the genre. The stratagems of Milanion, i.e. Gallus, do not work for Propertius. He will have to try others, which will be recounted in this (brand new) collection of love elegies . . .

We have already seen plenty of evidence that the sophisticated readership of Roman poetry could tell the difference (and enjoy the difference) between art and life. We don't know much about the historical figure Propertius, but what we do know suggests—not very surprisingly—that he was a respectable married man: at the turn of the first and second centuries CE there is an elegist who claims to be his descendant. Similarly, Cynthia, his girlfriend, is moulded as much by literary convention as by whatever real woman underlay her (*if* any in fact did). Her name gestures at a cult title of Apollo, god of poetry, 'Cynthius', and she operates in the collection as the source and inspiration of Propertius' poetry as much as the object of Propertius' love. As he says at the beginning of book 2:

> You ask me how it is I write so often of love
> And how my verses come soft on the tongue.
> These no Apollo, no Calliope sings to me;
> My only inspiration is a girl.
> (1. 1–4, trans. Guy Lee)

It is the poetry that shapes the love-affair, not the love-affair that shapes the poetry.

The audience Propertius pretends to write for is the ardent lover. In poem 3. 3 Apollo berates him for attempting to write epic poetry when his talent lies elsewhere:

> Idiot, what right have you to such a stream? And who
> Told you to turn your hand to epic?
> There's not a hope of fame, Propertius, for you here;
> Your little wheels must groove soft meadows.

Let your slim volume be displayed on bedside table
And read by lonely girls waiting for their lovers.
(ll. 15–20, trans. Guy Lee)

But Propertius' verse is more than simple love poetry, and his audience correspondingly wider, potentially as wide as for any poetic text at this time. In this particular instance we should be suspicious of the suggestion that Propertius' audience might be female. There may well have been women amongst his readership, but men predominated, and there is a strong voyeuristic element, aimed at his male readers, in this image of a girl reading love poetry in bed in preparation for her male lover's arrival.

There were, though, as with other writers, certain privileged readers. Propertius' first book is dedicated to Tullus, a young man from an eminent aristocratic family. The publication of book 1 clearly brought Propertius to the attention of important men, since in the first poem of book 2 it is Maecenas' name which appears. Propertius has followed Virgil and Horace into Maecenas' circle of patronage, and his poetic success would henceforth bring credit, by association, to the ruling regime.

Love elegy is in some respects an unusual style of poetry for Maecenas to associate himself with. But with a sophisticated readership alive to the highly artificial nature of love elegy, Propertius could represent his poetic persona as hopelessly immoral without necessarily implicating his real self. It is nevertheless a delicate balance. In a remarkable poem (3. 11) the poet exploits his immoral persona for propaganda, comparing his own condition as a slave to a woman with Kleopatra's domination of Antony—and condemning both. The effect of this poem depends on the capacity of the audience to distinguish the poet who condemns this lifestyle from the poet's lover persona, who lives it. But this is asking a lot, particularly since love elegy is a very 'realistic' genre. The relentlessly autobiographical nature of the poetry strongly encourages the reader to believe in, and identify with, the lover figure. The bruised lover who scribbled a couplet from Propertius on a wall in Pompeii was probably not alive to the irony:

Now anger is fresh, now is the time to part:
once the pain has gone, believe me, love will return.
(2. 5. 9–10)

Here it may be a question of education. Once Propertius' poetry had penetrated beyond the circle of sophisticates its author originally had in mind its reception was, as we have seen, liable to change. Ezra Pound was much more sensitive to the irony and playfulness of Propertius than his Edwardian and Victorian predecessors, but even he underestimated the remarkable artifice of the poetry.

If the same fate has not befallen another love elegist, Albius Tibullus (*c.*50–*c.*19 BCE), it is mainly because he has been too seriously neglected, despite having had a generally higher reputation than Propertius amongst ancient critics. His first book of poetry came out in 27 or 26 BCE, and in broad terms his love elegy resembles that of Propertius. Tibullus too is subservient to a mistress, Delia in his first book (another 'literary' name, based on 'Delius', a cult title of Apollo), and the ominously named Nemesis in the second:

> So, I see, slavery and a mistress await me:
> farewell, freedom that was my birthright.
> And a harsh slavery is my lot—I am held in chains,
> and never, alas, does Love loosen my fetters.
> Whether I have deserved it or am guiltless, he burns me.
> I am burning: ow! cruel girl, remove the torch.
>
> (2. 4. 1–6)

The slave motif, so offensive to Roman sensibilities, is shared with Propertius. But Tibullus gives his own twist to the elegiac rejection of traditional Roman values. His aspiration is the simple life of a small farmer in the company of his loved one:

> Not for me the riches of my fathers, and profits
> which the gathered harvest brought my grandfather of old:
> A small crop is enough, it is enough if I may sleep on my bed
> and ease my limbs on my accustomed couch.
> How pleasant to hear the harsh winds as I lie
> and hold my mistress in my gentle embrace!
> Or when the wintry South Wind pours down freezing showers
> to pursue sleep in safety, helped by a fire.
> Let this be my lot: let him by right be rich
> who can endure the rage of the sea and grim rain.
> O sooner let all the gold and all the emeralds in the world perish
> than any girl weep because of my travels.
> It is right for you, Messalla, to campaign by land and sea
> to adorn your house with the enemy's spoils:
> but I am held fast by the chains of a beautiful girl,
> and I sit as a gatekeeper before her cruel doors.
>
> (1. 1. 41–56)

Messalla is M. Valerius Messalla Corvinus, Tibullus' patron, a successful politician and general. It is noticeable how Tibullus distances Messalla from the elegiac lifestyle; Propertius had similarly been careful not to implicate Tullus or Maecenas in his immorality. But with Tibullus even more clearly than with Propertius we are dealing with a literary fantasy. The little information we have about Tibullus' real life shows us a conventional Roman aristocrat who, despite the anti-war sentiments in his poetry, was decorated for bravery on campaign with Messalla.

Messalla is regularly mentioned, and honoured, in Tibullus' poetry. His 1. 7 is a poem in honour of his birthday which praises his military achievements in Gaul and the Eastern Empire, as well as the repairs he had carried out on a stretch of the Via Latina, an important road, using some of the wealth he had won in his campaigns in Gaul. These are classic instances of Roman patronage, a poet giving his patron the benefit of honour in his poetry in return for the more tangible benefits the more powerful man could provide to him. Messalla in fact surrounded himself with quite an extended literary circle. Ovid was given his start in the literary world by Messalla (he calls him 'the encourager, cause and guiding light' of his poetry).

In 'Tibullus'' 'third book', which is in fact a collection of poems not by Tibullus at all but by poets associated with Messalla, we find a *Panegyric of Messalla* by an unknown poet and a short sequence of love poems by that rare phenomenon in the ancient world, a female poet, Sulpicia, who also addresses herself to Messalla and was probably his niece. This 'salon' is as close as any Roman aristocrat came in the Augustan period to the prominence in the literary world of Maecenas and his circle.

The benefits for Messalla were the status which association with good literature could bestow. It follows that although Messalla is given the role in this poetry of the 'first reader', and one of the charms of the poetry of his circle is the impression it gives of a small and intimate group (they have a particular fondness for birthday poems, for example), it clearly sought a much wider readership. Messalla would only gain the credit due him if people outside his circle read the poetry he had patronized and facilitated, and the occasional poems which directly praise him. Ovid in fact repaid him after his death with a poem in his honour which was recited in the Forum.

The case of Sulpicia is intriguing, though. She was another love elegist, and wrote (like Propertius and Tibullus) in the first person. If male love elegy already trod a thin line, it is hard to imagine the first-person account of respectable woman's extra-marital liaison finding a Roman readership outside her immediate circle:

> Venus has kept her promise. My joys can be the talk
>   of all who are said to have none of their own.
> I would not wish to send a message under seal
>   so no one could read it before my man.
> But I'm glad to sin, and bored of wearing reputation's
>   mask. The world will know I am matched with an equal.

We can readily imagine the kind of voyeuristic male audience these superficially artless sexual confessions by Sulpicia might have appealed to. But if her poetry had anything like a wide circulation it cannot have helped but be extremely controversial.

Tibullus' poetry makes an interesting test case for the degree of influence that the patron exerted over a writer. As compared with Propertius, Tibullus' style is plain, almost austere. There is much less in his poetry of the learned allusion and self-conscious literary play which we associate with Propertius and the other Callimachean poets, and it has been suggested that Tibullus' style betrays the influence of Messalla, since he had the reputation of being a literary purist. But this is a mistake. The Roman literary patron gave his writers great autonomy, and did not impose his tastes upon them, a fact for which we can be heartily grateful if we read the surviving fragments of the poetry that Maecenas produced, which was notoriously bizarre: Maecenas' words, according to Seneca, 'constructed so faultily, thrown out so carelessly, arranged so eccentrically, show that the man's character was equally strange, depraved and outlandish': it could hardly be more different from the poetry of Maecenas' circle. Tibullus' simplicity of style is quite adequately explained as the perfect vehicle for expressing his simple ideal of life: the countryside, an absence of unnecessary luxury, and the company of an appropriately unadorned girlfriend (1. 3. 91–2): 'Then, just as you are, your long hair tousled, | run to meet me, Delia, in your bare feet.' This is poetry *au naturel*, which of course betrays itself as the creation of a highly educated author. Tibullus' 'refined and elegant' love elegy, as the later critic Quintilian described it, was appreciated by an audience who enjoyed the fantasy of escape to an innocent rural life (cf. Virgil's *Eclogues*), but were alive to the artificiality of the message (they knew that Tibullus had no real intention of decamping to the country . . .) and the artificiality of the vehicle (. . . and that it takes a lot of effort to write so effortlessly).

Horace's *Odes*: The full range of lyric poetry

Horace's three books of *Odes* or *Carmina* (both words mean 'songs') came out as a collection in 23 BCE. A fourth book would be added later, in about 13 BCE. They were a fairly natural step on from the *Epodes*. Whereas the *Epodes* had been modelled on the Greek iambic poets, the *Odes* imitated the 'lyric' poets of the same period, and in particular Alkaios (cf. Ch. 2). The term 'lyric' is derived from 'lyre', and Greek lyric poetry such as Alkaios composed was *sung*, to the accompaniment of this lyre, and only subsequently written down. Quite how the audience of Horace's lyric 'songs' compares to these archaic audiences is a complicated issue we can best approach through Ovid's recollection of the poetic scene of his youth:

> Macer, much older, read to me his poem
> On birds and snakes and herbs that bring relief.
> Propertius would recite his fiery lyrics,
> So close a comradeship linked him and me,
> And epic Ponticus, iambic Bassus,
> Were pleasant members of my coterie.
> Horace too, master-metrist, charmed me, singing
> His polished stanzas to the Latin lyre.
> Virgil I only saw . . .
>
> (*Tristia* 4. 10. 43–51, trans. A. D. Melville)

Ovid describes the members of his poetic circle: Aemilius Macer (a writer of didactic poetry), Propertius, Ponticus (epic), and Bassus (a writer of *iambi* like Horace in the *Epodes*). At first sight it seems that Horace was a member of the same circle; what Ovid appears to be describing is a *performance* by Horace, singing his poems to a lyre. But Horace's poems were not designed to be performed at all. Unlike the lyric poetry he was imitating, the *Odes* were the product of an essentially *literary* culture, a culture where poetry was written down and read, not performed. Everything about the poetry we have been considering—its complexity, its allusiveness—tell us that it was designed to be appreciated by a reader rather than an audience member. And the *Odes* are no different.

But authors of works designed to be read rather than heard always aspire to create a richer experience than the mere process of reading—good literature 'leaps off the page', as the saying goes. Furthermore, in accordance with the ancient rules of literary imitation Horace was obliged to mimic the originators of the lyric genre closely enough to be able to claim membership of the same genre. How could he, when the conditions of performance in sixth-century Lesbos and first-century Rome were so different? Horace's solution was to *build* everything that a live performance had contributed to Alkaios' poetry—a lyre, an audience, spontaneity, and immediacy—into his unperformed poems.

The first thing Horace added into his poetry was personality. The 'monodic' (solo) lyric of Alkaios (see p. 75) was an essentially autobiographical genre, a genre in which poets (ostensibly, at any rate) talked in the first person from the standpoint of their own life and circumstances (cf. pp. 59–62). The first person is the dominant mode of speech in the *Odes* too, but this 'I' should not simply be equated with Quintus Horatius Flaccus. It is an artificial persona, lifelike and credible, but largely moulded by the traditions of the genre rather than by the reality of the author. The canon of lyric poets allowed Horace a lot of scope here. From Alkaios Horace constructed the persona of a mature individual who had seen some life and learnt from it, but knew how to enjoy his leisure time. The more elevated stance of the priest-poet which he occasionally adopts, particularly at the beginning of book 3, is reminiscent of choral lyric, as associated particularly with the name of Pindar, performed by choruses and in general of much higher aspirations than the monodic variety (cf. Ch 2). Clearly the very flexibility of Horace's lyric persona reveals the *Odes* for what they are: a highly artificial lyric which is even less close than archaic lyric to being the expression of an individual's subjectivity.

If the 'I' of the performer had to be invented, so did the 'live' audience to which the Archaic lyric 'I' had addressed himself. Archaic monodic lyric began as a performance before an audience of friends, typically in the context of a drinking party or 'symposium'. Again, Horace's written text has no such delimited audience: its readership is potentially as wide as the educated public of Rome. But the impression of intimacy was an essential component of the lyric experience. Horace's problem was to create it *on the page*. He overcomes the problem by addressing most of the poems to a single named 'friend', and thereby creating the illusion that the audience of the poem is smaller and more intimate—but also more vividly *present*—than it really is. Horace has thus created for himself an 'I' which was reasonably credible whilst not departing from the traditions of the genre, an audience—even a lyre, even though he doesn't really have one:

> We pray, if ever we have relaxed with you in the shade
> and played a melody that may live a year
> or more, come, my Greek lyre,
> and sound a Latin song.
>
> (1. 32. 1–4, trans. David West)

In short, Horace has constructed a lyric performance on the written page. The *Odes* achieve the remarkable effect of giving the impression of performance in reading. So, to return to Ovid, in 'Horace too, master-metrist, charmed me, singing | His polished stanzas to the Latin lyre' he is not describing a performance at all, but evoking Horace's allusions to the way lyric was originally performed.

Nothing in Latin poetry, as we are now aware, is that straightforward. The fact that Horace addresses his poems to named individuals does not, of course, preclude a wider audience, or limit the poetry's relevance. *Odes* 1. 7 ends with an admonition to L. Munatius Plancus to put his troubles behind him:

> The bright south wind will often wipe the clouds from the dark sky.
> It is not always pregnant with rain.

So you too, Plancus, would be wise to remember to put a stop
to sadness and the labours of life
with mellow, undiluted wine, whether you are in camp among
the gleaming standards or whether you will be
in the deep shade of your beloved Tibur. When Teucer was on the run
from Salamis and his father, they say that nevertheless,
awash with wine, he bound his brow with a crown of poplar leaves
and spoke these words to his grieving friends:
'Allies and comrades, Fortune is kinder than a father.
Wherever she takes us, there shall we go. Do not despair
while Teucer takes the auspices and Teucer is your leader.
Apollo does not err and he has promised
that in a new land we shall find a second Salamis.
You are brave men and have often suffered worse
with me. Drive away your cares with wine. Tomorrow
we shall set out again upon the broad sea.'

(ll. 15–32, trans. David West)

The sentiment is conventional enough, but gains both piquancy and a wider application from the person to whom Horace has chosen to address it. Plancus was a native of Tibur who had benefited from the upheavals which followed the assassination of Julius Caesar, becoming consul in 42 BCE. But his brother had been killed in the proscriptions of 43, and Plancus apparently suffered much ill will on the grounds that he had acquiesced in the killing of his brother. The myth of Teucer subtly alludes to Plancus' circumstances. Teucer had to flee Salamis because of his father's (unjust) anger at Teucer's failure to prevent the death of his brother Ajax. Teucer's circumstances match Plancus' closely, but the uplifting optimism and hope for the future of Teucer's speech—'Tomorrow we shall set out again upon the broad sea'—will have had force for all of Horace's readership, still less than a decade after the end of the civil wars, when many wounds remained unhealed. The imperative to *move on* from the civil wars is a recurrent theme in the *Odes*.

The *Odes* were dedicated to Maecenas again, and in both narrower and broader terms they collaborate in the reorganization of Rome which Augustus undertook after his victory at Actium. Poems like 3. 6, one of a series of poems at the start of book 3 on moral themes, known as the 'Roman Odes', delivered in the loftier priestly persona of choral lyric, give expression to the highly reactionary social policies with which Augustus concealed the revolutionary political changes through which he was putting the Roman state:

Though innocent, Roman, you will pay for the sins
of your fathers until you restore

> the crumbling temples and shrines of the gods
> and their smoke-blackened images.
> You rule because you hold yourself inferior to the gods.
> Make this the beginning and the end of all things.
> Neglect of the gods has brought many ills
> to the sorrowing land of Hesperia.
>
> (3. 6. 1–8, trans. David West)

Horace's encouragement to his readership to restore the religious buildings of Rome corresponds to an Augustan policy. Besides the building undertaken by himself and his family, Augustus encouraged other senior aristocrats to construct, restore, or embellish public buildings—Plancus, for example, restored the temple of Saturn. In Augustus' building policy we have a good illustration of his strategy as ruler. In order not to alienate the aristocrats on whom his administration depended Augustus needed to give them as much freedom as possible to lead the traditional status-seeking life aristocratic culture demanded, whilst not threatening the unity of the state. The *Odes* project an analogous image of aristocratic Rome. Horace's equivalent to Alkaios' circle of aristocratic friends is a cross-section of contemporary Rome—Pollio, Messalla, Plancus, Tibullus, Maecenas—each given that much-desired prestige by his appearance in a collection of such brilliance, but a collection unified under the overarching carapace of Augustus.

But in broader terms, if Augustus' cultural policies were about restoring confidence to Rome, the very fact of the writing of the *Odes* conveyed to its readers the sense of a new and confident age. Here was a Roman author equalling the achievement of the Greek lyricists, in fact encapsulating in his collection the achievement of all nine canonical lyricists, a remarkably ambitious undertaking. With the *Odes* and Virgil's *Aeneid*, in particular, Rome developed a literature which they could claim was the equal of the literature of Greece, a culture to which Rome had traditionally felt an oppressive inferiority.

But whatever the broader implications conveyed by the three books of *Odes*, it is poetry which works in intricate detail. Ovid called Horace *numerosus*, 'master-metrist'. It was an astonishing achievement on Horace's part to match the complex, strict, and highly diverse metres of Greek lyric with the Latin language, and so skilfully that the match seems easy. Some of the metres which Horace employs in the *Odes* had already been introduced to Latin—the characteristic metre of Sappho had been used by Catullus, for example (cf. pp. 354–5)—but the astonishing range of lyric metres was unprecedented, and when Horace begins the first book of *Odes* with nine poems all in different metres, he is impressing on the reader his absolute control of the lyric tradition.

IMPERIAL PIETY. The Altar of Piety in Rome dedicated by the Emperor Claudius in 43 CE shows a sacrifice in front of a precise rendering of the architecture of the Temple of the Great Mother.

An even more astonishing achievement was that, as well as mastering the metres, Horace created a Latin lyric style, concise and meticulous, of great expressive power. His greatest talent is in using his metres to place and arrange the words of his poetry to optimum effect: a later author talks of his *curiosa felicitas*, 'painstaking felicity'. Many of his *mots justes* are still familiar to us: *carpe diem* ('pluck the day'), 'golden mean' (*aurea mediocritas*), *dulce et decorum est pro patria mori* ('sweet it is and honourable to die for one's native land'), *exegi monumentum aere perennius* ('I have wrought a monument more lasting than bronze'). Thought is as intricate as word placement, and the expertise and pleasure in the game we have come to expect of contemporary readers was fully exercised. The relevance of the Teucer myth to Plancus in 1. 7 is never explicitly stated by the poet, but left to us to decipher for ourselves. The reader of the *Odes* begins from this aesthetic delight; the sense of belonging to the new Augustan dispensation comes later.

Horace sets out to transfer the essence of the whole (enormous) extent of Greek lyric poetry to the Latin language, and to this end he covers the full range of Greek lyrical themes, from wine and women to hymns to the gods and moral statements of high seriousness. The richness of metres is paralleled by a wealth of lyrical models: all nine canonical Greek lyricists have their place at some point or other in this Latin lyric. At all stages, though, the Archaic ethos of his models is filtered through the Hellenistic sensibility common to all Roman poets of this period. *Odes* 1. 33, addressed to Tibullus, will give a final sense of the richness and complexity of the collection:

> Do not grieve, Albius, remembering too well
> your bitter-sweet Glycera and do not keep chanting
> piteous elegies wondering why she has broken faith
>   and a younger man now outshines you.
> Love for Cyrus scorches the beautiful,
> narrow-browed Lycoris; Cyrus leans lovingly
> over hard-hearted Pholoe, but sooner will roe-deer
>   mate with Apulian wolves
> than Pholoe soil herself with a foul adulterer.
> Such is the decree of Venus, who decides in cruel jest
> to join unequal minds and bodies
>   under her yoke of bronze.
> I myself once, when a better love was offered me,
> was shackled in the delicious fetters of Myrtale,
> a freedwoman wilder than the Adriatic sea
>   scooping out the bays of Calabria.
>
> (trans. David West)

Superficially this is an intimate tête-à-tête between the older Horace, with his mature, hard-earned worldly wisdom, and the young (though not so young as he was) Tibullus. Tibullus, Horace suggests, should gain perspective on the nature of love, and plump for comfort (Myrtale) over passion (Glycera). The poem manages vividly to characterize both the younger and the maturer man in just four short stanzas. But a contemporary reader would recognize another level to the poem again. What they would appreciate is that behind the naturalism of the encounter between the two men lies a statement of literary affiliations. Horace here expresses the characteristic world-view of Alkaios' lyric (love is a trivial diversion, nothing more), and Tibullus embodies the contrasting elegiac view of love as an all-consuming passion. Horace's readers, besides anything else, would enjoy the literary game of the lyric persona and the elegiac persona being thrown together. In other words, Horace has grafted on to the archaic atmosphere of lyric a Callimachean compulsion to play with his readers' knowledge and expectations of literary genre.

In the final poem of book 3 Horace predicts the eternal fame of his poetry:

> I shall not wholly die. A great part of me
> will escape Libitina. My fame will grow,
> ever-renewed in time to come, as long as
> the priest climbs the Capitol with the silent Virgin.
> I shall be spoken of where fierce Aufidus thunders
> and where Daunus, poor in water,
> rules the country people. From humble beginnings
> I was able to be the first to bring the Aeolian song
> to Italian measures.
>
> (3. 30. 6–14, trans. David West)

There is some evidence that the *Odes* were initially not quite the success Horace had hoped, but in the long term their success has been astonishing, far outlasting the collapse of the Roman Empire. Horace's persona in the *Odes* has shown a remarkable capacity to appeal to readers of all periods and nationalities as one of their own. In Victorian Britain this combination of archaic Greek and first-century Roman was felt to be a prototype English gentleman. As a consequence the most famous modern reader of Horace was a hostile one. We have already seen Latin poetry informing and enriching responses to the First World War in Pound's *Homage to Sextus Propertius*. When Wilfred Owen attacked the romantic imperialism fed to schoolboys it was the English gentleman Horace he had read at school (and learnt so much from poetically) who came to mind. He is describing the victim of a gas attack:

> If you could hear, at every jolt, the blood
> Come gargling from the froth-corrupted lungs,
> Obscene as cancer, bitter as the cud
> of vile, incurable sores on innocent tongues,—
> My friend, you would not tell with such high zest
> To children ardent for some desperate glory,
> The old Lie: Dulce et decorum est
> Pro patria mori.

The Roman classic

With Virgil's twelve-book epic, the *Aeneid*, the literary efflorescence which coincided with the establishment of the Augustan regime, and both shaped and was shaped by these new political circumstances, reached its climax. It is a staggeringly ambitious work. Its first words are so familiar that it is hard to appreciate how audacious they would have seemed to a contemporary reader. *Arma virumque cano*, 'Arms and the man I sing', encapsulates in three words the two poems which were simultaneously Virgil's models and rivals in his writing of the *Aeneid*: the martial *Iliad* ('Arms') and the *Odyssey*, which began, 'Tell me of the *man*, Muse . . .' (cf. Ch. 1). The brevity of Virgil's evocation of his great epic predecessor dramatizes his absolute, confident control of the highest genre it was possible to aspire to, and implies an astonishing lack of anxiety about the task of rivalling Homer which he had set himself. Homer was much more than a poet. Greek culture rated him as the greatest poet there had ever been and could ever be, but, more, Homer was where all the wealth of Greek culture started, the source of all subsequent literary and intellectual culture—as a Hellenistic poet calls him, 'the ageless mouthpiece of the entire universe'.

Virgil never completed the *Aeneid*. He died in 19 BCE, before he had carried out the final revision: tradition relates that on his death-bed he demanded to be given the manuscript so that he could burn it, but no one would give it to him. Even before its release this was a work which generated a palpable excitement in the public. Propertius' remark that 'something greater than the *Iliad* is coming to birth' (2. 34. 66) has been interpreted by some as not entirely unequivocal. But there is no doubting Augustus' excitement, recorded in an ancient biography of Virgil: 'When Augustus was away on his Spanish campaign, he used to write insisting with pleas and even jocular threats that he be sent—to use his own words—"just the preliminary sketch or just a chunk of the *Aeneid*".' The enormity of the task was such that Virgil despaired of being able to achieve it; but the same impulse which prompted Virgil to burn it made Augustus desperate to see it, and the whole of Rome agog to read it. The *Aeneid* turned heads.

The *Aeneid* is the story of Aeneas (in Greek, Aineias), the son of the goddess Venus and ancestor of the Roman race who fled from Troy at its sacking by the Greeks and travelled with his followers to Italy, encountering great hardship on the way, and fighting a brutal war once they had arrived to secure their settlement. It is both a national epic and a poem honouring Augustus. Augustus is not directly referred to in the *Aeneid* particularly often, but he is a constant presence in it. Contemporary events are addressed *obliquely*, and this approach brings some advantages for Virgil. On the one hand tackling contemporary events through ancient myth softens the impact of the contemporary message: for all its political content, the *Aeneid* is always a compelling story, a 'self-sufficient' narrative which tells a coherent story. In addition the figure of Aeneas introduces a useful ambiguity as to the focus of the poem. Aeneas was the national ancestor of Rome: Lucretius' opening invocation of Venus, 'Mother of the sons of Aeneas' (cf. pp. 345–6), refers to the citizens of Rome in their entirety. But he was also, more specifically, the ancestor of the family of the Julii to which, through his adoption by Julius Caesar, Augustus had been

VIRGILIAN VIRTUE. *This mid-first-century wall-painting from Pompeii is closely inspired by a passage towards the end of the* Aeneid *(12. 383–416). While the doctor attempts to heal Aeneas' wound his mother Venus descends with a healing herb.*

admitted. We are never quite clear in this poem whether Aeneas is a proto-Roman or a proto-Augustus, and this tends to blur the distinction between 'Roman' and 'Augustan'. Augustus of course wanted the two categories to be indistinguishable, and wanted his personal success to be identified with the interests of Rome.

But if the *Aeneid* is a nationalistic poem, it is never a simple national anthem. Though it certainly did aim to celebrate the city of Rome and, more narrowly, to bolster the political position of its patron, Augustus—an aim it shares with more straightforwardly eulogistic works such as the *Panegyric of Messalla* (cf. pp. 382–4)—the *Aeneid* is in every respect a more subtle piece of work. Virgil recognized as well as Horace the devastating effect recent history had had upon the educated upper classes of Rome, his core audience. This was a section of society demoralized by decades of civil war. The twenty years between 49, when Julius Caesar crossed the Rubicon, and 29, when Augustus returned to Rome after his defeat of Mark Antony, seemed to represent to the Roman aristocracy the breakdown of their entire moral and cultural order. The later historian Tacitus talks of 'twenty years of unrelenting discord, no morality, no law'. Instances like Plancus' 'murder' of his brother became emblematic of a conflict which tore the tight Roman ruling class apart and set it against itself, friend against friend, father against son, brother against brother. No one was free of responsibility, but Augustus was particularly guilty, at the forefront of some of the most callous actions of the period.

The remarkable thing about this poem, a product of the patronage of the Augustan regime, is that it engages without embarrassment with the intense anxieties its audience felt about the civil wars and the regime which had emerged from it. Repeatedly the reader is confronted with, and emotionally drawn into, conflicts deeply reminiscent of the Roman civil wars. To a contemporary reader it will have been a deeply gruelling experience.

This *controversial* quality is evident right from the start. In an eleven-line introduction Virgil summarizes the plot of the poem and, in a conventional epic device, asks the Muse to explain the sufferings which the gods had inflicted upon Aeneas:

> I sing of arms and the man who first from the land of Troy,
> an exile by destiny, came to Italy and the Lavinian
> shores, a man much tossed on land and deep
> by the powers above, because of the unforgetting anger of fierce Juno.
> Great too was his suffering in war until he could found a city
> and carry his gods into Latium, whence rose the Latin race,
> the Alban fathers and the high walls of Rome.
> Tell me, Muse, the reasons, how he abused her divinity,

from what resentment the queen of heaven drove
a man renowned for piety to suffer so much calamity
and experience such toils. Are the gods capable of such anger?

The Muse replies to this question:

There was an ancient city . . .

In the light of the first eleven lines there will have been little doubt in the minds of Virgil's readers as to the city to which the Muse is referring. The *Aeneid* is about the destruction of one city, Troy, and Aeneas' escape from it to found another city which will replace it, Rome. The *only* place this 'ancient city' can be is Troy. But the Muse continues:

. . . occupied by colonists from Tyre,
Carthage, opposite Italy and the Tiber's distant
mouths

Carthage. If only we could be the first readers of this text, in 19 BCE, the intrusion of this name, of all names, into a poem which has just advertised itself as the national poem of Rome would have astonished us. Carthage was 'opposite Italy' in more than just the geographical sense. It was Rome's great enemy in the fight to dominate the Mediterranean basin, a fight quite literally to the death (cf. pp. 290–1). Neither city had felt secure whilst the other stood. The moment in 211 BCE when the great Carthaginian general Hannibal rode right up to the walls of Rome and, according to tradition, cast a spear into the city itself loomed large in Roman folklore. A striking moment in book 9 of the *Aeneid* has Turnus, Aeneas' great enemy in the second half of the poem, mimic that action of Hannibal, riding up to the camp which the Trojans have established and hurling a spear over its walls. To Roman thinking the conflict with Carthage had been a matter of 'kill or be killed'. In 146 BCE Carthage was utterly destroyed by Scipio Aemilianus, and a curse laid on anybody who should attempt to rebuild it.

The rest of book 1 is set in Carthage, and it is not until the end of book 4 that we leave it. Aeneas is shipwrecked on the coast near Carthage, and takes refuge with the queen of the city, Dido, an exemplary ruler engaged in founding a city, exactly as Aeneas wanted to do (and exactly as Augustus was claiming to have done, by bringing the civil wars to an end, an achievement he styled as the refoundation of Rome). Naturally they fall in love. The first view of Carthage which Aeneas sees, a bustle of constructive activity, will have reminded Virgil's first readers of nothing more than Rome in the grip of the building programme instituted by Augustus, which 'found Rome brick and left it marble', in Augustus' own words. This Carthage *looks like* Rome:

Aeneas marvels at great buildings, where once were shanties,
Marvels at city gates and the din of the paved streets.
The Tyrians are busy at work there, some extending the walls,
Manhandling blocks of stone and building the citadel,
Others choosing a site for a house and trenching foundations:
Laws are being made, magistrates and a parliament elected:
Here they dig out a harbour basin; here they are laying
Foundations deep for a theatre, and hewing from stone immense
Columns to grace one day a tall proscenium.

(ll. 421–9, trans. C. Day-Lewis)

Yet ultimately Dido will die. Book 4 recounts the love-affair between Dido and Aeneas, which is abruptly terminated when Aeneas is ordered by the gods to stop neglecting his destiny—which is to found Rome—and leave. His departure provokes Dido's suicide, which she carries out with Aeneas' own sword.

What is most striking in all this is the *sympathy* which Virgil elicits for Dido and the city she represents, despite the status of Carthage as Rome's ultimate *bête noire*. Carthage in the *Aeneid* is not the demonized 'other' of Roman folklore, but a fully humanized and attractive community. There will be many more victims of Aeneas' mission after Dido, right up to the brutal slaying of Turnus which concludes the poem. But the same always applies: we are never allowed to disregard these victims.

In fact Virgil insists that we identify with them. In books 2 and 3 Virgil constructs an 'internal audience' within the poem. Dido and her court listen to Aeneas' account of the fall of Troy and his travels as far as Carthage. Virgil repeatedly plays on the fact that in the course of two long books we are bound to forget who is narrating: Aeneas' narrative to the Carthaginians inevitably becomes confused with Virgil's narrative (the overarching 'voice' of the whole poem) to us. It is with some shock that at the end of book 3 we are reminded that we have been reading Aeneas' account to Dido, not Virgil's account to us, and have, in a sense, been occupying Dido's space, listening along with her and her courtiers to Aeneas' narration. An anecdote about the pre-performance of the *Aeneid* can focus this idea. Shortly before his death Virgil is said to have recited three books to Augustus and his close family, 2, 4, and 6. (The story goes that Augustus' sister Octavia was so moved by the lament for her son Marcellus towards the end of book 6 that 'she fainted and was revived with difficulty'.) Augustus, emperor of Rome, seated, listening to book 2 (recited by Virgil) corresponds to Dido, queen of Carthage, seated, listening to book 2 (recited by Aeneas).

But, for all this, Aeneas' mission to found Rome will bring about Dido's death. And when Virgil compares the aftermath of her suicide to the sacking of a city it is clear that Dido's death prefigures the historical destruction of Carthage by Rome in 146:

> She had spoken; and with these words, her attendants saw her falling
> Upon the sword, they could see the blood spouting up over
> The blade, and her hands spattered. Their screams rang to the roofs of
> The palace; then rumour ran amok through the shocked city.
> All was weeping and wailing, the streets were filled with a keening
> Of women, the air resounded with terrible lamentations.
> It was as if Carthage or ancient Tyre should be falling,
> With enemy troops breaking into the town and a conflagration
> Furiously sweeping over the abodes of men and of gods.
>
> (4. 663–71, trans. C. Day-Lewis)

Now as we have seen, the defeat of Carthaginians, and the destruction of their city, was in general to Roman thinking an unquestionably good thing, a prerequisite of their own survival: *delenda est Carthago*, 'Carthage must be destroyed', was the mantra of one of the most respected figures of the Roman past, Cato the Censor (cf. pp. 328–30). When Virgil makes us *sympathize* with the arch enemy, recognize her humanity, he is making of the Rome/Carthage conflict something in which his readers would recognize the experience of the recent civil wars, wars where demonization of the enemy was impossible because the enemy was known to you, even *related* to you. The destruction of Carthage was *callous*, Virgil is suggesting, but it was also *necessary* if Rome was to survive and prosper, and *the same goes for the civil war*. Virgil is thus not shy of confronting the civil wars. On the contrary, his poignant portrayal of Dido *replicates* the traumatic emotions of civil war. The contemporary Roman reader of the *Aeneid* was being trained, emotionally as well as intellectually, to accept the brutality and loss of civil war as a prerequisite of future success.

Or at any rate that is one way of reading the poem, one likely (I think) to have been a dominant reading in Virgil's core audience. But the *Aeneid* is a controversial text. What makes it so, above all, is the intricacy of its poetry. In undertaking the *Aeneid* Virgil had abandoned the imperative not to write Grand Epic (which was how Roman poets interpreted the precepts of Kallimachos, whether or not this was actually what he meant), but in his stylistics he remains loyal to the allusiveness and refinement of his New Poet mentors. Octavia's swoon, for example, is more explicable when we appreciate that the lament for Marcellus spoken by Aeneas' father Anchises in the underworld impersonates, with great subtlety, the address delivered by Augustus at Marcellus' real funeral in 23 BCE:

> Fate shall allow the earth one glimpse of this young man—
> One glimpse, no more. Too puissant had been Rome's stock, ye gods,
> In your sight, had such gifts been granted it to keep.
> (6. 869–71, trans. C. Day-Lewis)

The *Aeneid* is meticulous in detail, but huge in scope. Epic is the grandest of all genres, both in style and theme. This epic manages to encompass the whole of Roman history, from the fall of Troy to the rise of Augustus—not only the life of Aeneas, but all that followed. In book 8, for example, we visit the site of Rome before Rome was built, a village of simple cottages, but then at the end of the book enjoy a vision of contemporary Rome, engraved on a great shield made for Aeneas by the god Vulcan. Similarly, the war between Trojans and Italians which occupies the second half of the poem in a sense prefigures every war the Romans ever fought, but in particular the Punic Wars against Carthage and the recent civil wars—the war, between two peoples who will subsequently make up the population of Rome, is a civil war *avant la lettre*. The poem is also 'huge' in spatial terms. In its course we travel from the east of the Empire all the way to the vicinity of Rome (via Carthage), and are witness at all times to the responses of the great powers of Virgil's world, the gods, to the events going on on earth. In book 6 we even follow Aeneas down to the underworld to visit his father and hear, with Aeneas, about Rome's great future. The whole world, Virgil implies, is implicated in the struggle to found the Roman Empire, an event which (in turn) will shape the whole of history.

At the same time Virgil sets out to fulfil the expectation that epic, the first genre of them all, should encompass all other forms of literature. In Dido alone we hear echoes of Apollonios' Medea (cf. Ch. 7), the heroes and heroines of tragedy, Berenike, the queen of Egypt complimented by Kallimachos (and later Catullus), the Kleopatra of Augustan propaganda, and Carthaginians from Roman folklore and historiography. This impression of literary scope and ambition matches and reinforces the geographical and historical nationalisms which the poem communicates. Virgil's 'conquest' of the universal epic voice of Homer—the origin and essence of Greek literary culture—is closely analogous to Roman military dominion over the world. The Roman readers of the *Aeneid* experienced, besides everything else, an entire world of literary possibilities in Roman dress. It is with the *Aeneid* that Latin literature seemed to Romans once and for all to have come into its own.

Like Lucretius' *De rerum natura*, then, the *Aeneid* provides its readers with a vision of a totality, not the Epicurean universe of atoms and void but a world dominated now and forever by Rome. Emblematic of the Romanness of this text is the scene which unfolds at the poem's conclusion. All the conflict of the poem comes down to a duel to the death between Aeneas and Turnus for the hand of the princess Lavinia and the sovereignty of Latium. As the two mighty warriors battle it out, no longer mere mortals but massive heroes who seem to embody the powers of the universe, Romans would have recognized a cosmic struggle for global control, but one being fought out in a characteristically Roman context. The struggle between the two champions would have reminded contemporaries strongly of the gladiatorial combats which Romans held to celebrate ceremonial occasions. The Roman readership was at this point the audience in a Roman amphitheatre watching Roman destiny unfold (12. 919–29). (Note once again that the 'internal' audience whose viewpoint the reader is asked to share are the Italian supporters of Turnus . . .)

> So Turnus faltered: the other brandished his fateful spear,
> And watching out for an opening, hurled it with all his might
> From a distance. The noise it made was louder than that of any
> Great stone projected by siege artillery, louder than
> A meteorite's explosion. The spear flew on its sinister
> Mission of death like a black tornado, and piercing the edge of
> The seven-fold shield, laid open the corselet of Turnus, low down.
> Right through his thigh it ripped, with a hideous sound. The impact
> Brought giant Turnus down on bent knee to the earth.
> The Italians sprang to their feet, crying out: the hills all round
> Bayed back their howl of dismay, far and wide the deep woods echoed it.
> (12. 919–29, trans. C. Day-Lewis)

Virgil himself compared his laborious and painstaking technique of composition to a mother-bear slowly licking her cubs into shape. Every one of the 10,000 lines is crafted with meticulous care. But we have seen before that the Callimachean style *emancipates* the readership, gives it the freedom to pursue an allusion as far as they choose. A generation later Ovid was able to exploit meanings of *arma virumque* which Virgil certainly did not have in mind in order to make a subversive joke at Virgil's (and Augustus') expense. At *Tristia* 2. 533–6, addressing Augustus and ostensibly attempting to justify the erotic content of his poetry, Ovid points to its presence even in Virgil's poem:

> Yet the blessed author of your great *Aeneid*
> Landed 'Arms and the man' in Dido's bed,
> Love linked in bonds illicit; in the whole long
> Poem there's really nothing that's more read.
> (trans. A. D. Melville)

The joke is that both the word for 'arms', *arma*, and 'man', *vir*, could carry a sexual meaning. A contemporary would be liable to translate the second line as 'brought his tackle and his manhood to Dido's bed'. Could anybody who had read the *Tristia* subsequently read the opening of the *Aeneid* without a snigger? The paradox of the *Aeneid* is that it is a text which appears to have a very specific message to convey, but a style that militates against unequivocal communication.

The history of the reception of the *Aeneid* by its readers after its *post-mortem* publication is the history of Western artistic culture, which, along with Ovid's *Metamorphoses*, it dominates. But the text which aspired to survive as long as 'the house of Aeneas dwells by the immovable rock of the Capitol and the father of the Romans keeps his Empire' (9. 448–9), and yet was also so closely tied to its contemporary context, had to cope with dramatic changes in the ways its readers interpreted it in the subsequent two thousand years. Ovid informs us, for example, that at the end of Augustus' reign 'in the whole long | Poem there's really nothing that's more read' than the story of Dido and Aeneas. Book 4 has continued to be far the most popular portion of the poem, often read, and imitated (in all artistic media) in isolation from the rest of the whole. But such segmentation undermines the carefully constructed argument of the poem. Taken on its own, without the explanatory framework of the rest of the *Aeneid*, book 4 can be treated as a simple love story, and a love story, what's more, in which Aeneas can be dismissed as a cad for abandoning Dido, as in Henry Purcell's opera *Dido and Aeneas* (1689).

The *Aeneid* was an instant classic, and from its publication onwards suffered the classic's fate of an audience largely consisting of students at school, for many centuries and throughout the Empire (and for many centuries after the fall of that Empire). This expanded its audience beyond the relatively narrow circle of sophisticates for whom it was primarily designed, but it also radically altered its reception. In school the poem was studied for the exercise it could provide in grammar rather than its literary qualities: at Pompeii disaffected youth often proceeded to scribble what they had learnt on the walls.

As an example of how its role in education affected its reception we need only to consider the fate of Ennius (cf. pp. 294–7). Virgil's *Aeneid* replaced Ennius' *Annals* as the national epic of Rome—*and* as the dominant school text. The adoption of the *Aeneid* by schools largely explains the failure of Ennius' epic to survive antiquity intact. But of course Virgil's original audience *did* have Ennius. For them, after all, it was still the national epic. Naturally enough, Virgil regularly alludes to the *Annals*. Some allusions we can still recognize. At 2. 268–97, for example, the dead Hector appears to Aeneas and urges him to leave Troy and found a new city elsewhere. We are still able to see that Virgil is alluding to a passage near the beginning of the *Annals* where Ennius described how Homer had appeared to him in a dream and told him that he, Homer, had been reincarnated in Ennius. Hector is a Homeric character. When Hector

THE AENEID *IN SOMERSET. Virgil's* Aeneid *is the one work of Latin literature which is found reflected in art throughout the Roman Empire. This is even evidenced by several mosaics from remote Britain. This one, found at Low Ham in Somerset, shows scenes from the story of Dido and Aeneas in book 4.*

hands the future of the Trojans to Aeneas we can recognize, with the help of Virgil's allusion to Ennius, a further suggestion of Virgil's relationship with his epic predecessors: Hector handing the future to Aeneas is Homer handing on the epic tradition to Virgil. We can recognize it *because* we happen to have some knowledge about this point of Ennius' poem. But most allusions to Ennius we are just missing, and the paradox of this is that it is a direct consequence of Virgil's unparalleled success in finding an audience.

But if the *Aeneid* inevitably suffered 'dumbing down' as its audience expanded, this was a circumstance which the poet had arguably catered for.

The poem can be read on a number of levels. *Paradise Lost* is one of the greatest poems in the English language largely because John Milton was one of the most acute readers of the *Aeneid* there has ever been. But just a few years after the publication of Milton's epic it was the sheer visual exuberance of Virgil's narrative which inspired Claude Lorrain to paint *Aeneas Hunting in Libya*. He had been reading an Italian translation of the *Aeneid*. We know this because a preliminary drawing of the scene is marked 'Libro di Virgilio folio 10', 'Virgil's book page 10'.

13 Coming to terms with the Empire: Poetry of the later Augustan and Tiberian period

PHILIP HARDIE

Authorities poetical and political

'Virgil I only saw' (Ovid, *Tristia* 4. 10. 51, quoted on p. 385). Ovid's rueful comment in his verse autobiography, largely an account of his own place in the literary circles of Augustan Rome, is emblematic of a wider rupture between the works of what might be called the heroic age of Augustan literature and the poetry produced from the second decade onwards of Augustus' rule. We are not of course dealing with any absolute divide: many of the poets active in the 40s to 20s BCE continued to produce after the death of Virgil in 19 BCE, chief among them Propertius and Horace; and Ovid himself was very probably reciting his earliest love elegies in the mid-20s. Nevertheless both poets and public were quick to recognize that after the output of the 30s and 20s Rome could now boast of a canon of poetry, in the fields above all of epic, didactic, lyric, pastoral, and elegy, that need not fear comparison with the classics of Greek literature; and in the case of satire, Horace had brought to classical perfection a genre that Quintilian, the academic rhetorician of the late first century CE, could claim was all Roman. Already by the mid-20s Propertius proclaimed, perhaps not entirely respectfully, that with the slow gestation of the *Aeneid* 'something greater than the *Iliad* is coming to birth' (2. 34. 66). After 19 BCE the Roman public felt confident that they could point to a native work that was the equal of Homer, and to have equalled Homer was to have equalled the best and greatest that Greece had produced.

The consequence is a shift in the relationship of later Augustan poetic texts to their models. Latin poets continue to engage at all levels with Greek models, but they now come to measure themselves in the first instance against the Latin classics, and above all the *Aeneid*—and in so doing start a habit that will last for the rest of ancient Latin poetry, and indeed for much of post-antique poetry in the classical tradition (see pp. 399–400). Virgil in the *Aeneid* is deeply

HORACE AS POET LAUREATE. Augustus set up an inscription recording all the activities at the great games he organized in 17 BCE to mark the end of an alleged cycle of 110 years. In the third line of this passage can be seen CARMEN.COMPOSVIT.Q.HOR[AT]IVS.FLACCVS 'Q. Horatius Flaccus composed the hymn' (now known as the Carmen Saeculare*—see p. 410).*

concerned, it is true, to define his relationship to his *Latin* epic predecessor, Ennius, but the chief object of his imitative emulation is always Homer. Ovid, by contrast, for all that he is in many respects a continuator of the graecizing, neoteric, 'Alexandrian' school of poets (see pp. 349–52), is obsessed above all with the presence of Virgil. Not surprisingly his *Metamorphoses*, a long hexameter narrative poem, is a sustained challenge to Virgil's epic; but the first word of Ovid's first and least epic work, the *Amores*, is the same as the first word of the *Aeneid*, *arma* ('arms', 'warfare'); this is elegy that sets out by serving notice to the reader that it is love poetry *after Virgil*. The 'anxiety of influence' is displaced from the great Greek models to the Latin poems that imitate and successfully rival those models. The poetry of this period is marked by a sense of coming later than, of being a supplement to, the works of the early Augustan period (in the cases of some poets, notably Horace, of supplementing their *own* earlier poetry); the poets address themselves to a public that they know will measure them against these earlier achievements.

The poetry of this time is characterized also by its relationship to that other kind of authority, the political authority of the emperor. The poetry of the triumviral and early Augustan periods rarely loses sight of the momentous political and military developments of the 40s, 30s, and 20s, and is itself a vital part of the turbulent and experimental process out of which emerged the fully fledged principate. By the late 20s, when the dust had settled and the clear outlines of the new system had emerged, poets and their publics turn from an interest in the processes of constructing and defining a post-civil war order to the issues of how to live with the finished product. This period sees the emergence of a 'court poetry', particularly in the fourth book of Horace's *Odes* and in various of Ovid's works, that merges Roman ways of praising great men with

Alexandrian models for addressing the Hellenistic king. Horace's *Epistles* explore the etiquette of approaching and talking to the ruler; Ovid in his later works forges ways of coping with the less pleasurable consequences of an absolute autocracy and with a growing censorship, and in so doing helps to create the language used by later first-century CE analysts and critics of the imperial regime.

The poet confronts his audiences: Horace *Epistles* 1

> My Muse's first and final theme, Maecenas,
> I've been on show enough, obtained my discharge,
> yet you try to squeeze me back into those old games.
> I'm not the same age or the same man. The fighter [Veianius]
> has hung up his arms and is lying low in the country:
> no more begging the public for his life.
> A voice keeps ringing now in my unclogged ears:
> 'Be sensible: quick, loose the ageing horse,
> or they'll laugh when his flanks heave and he falls at the finish.'
> So now I lay down verse and all those games;
> my whole concern is to ask what is right and fitting.
> (*Epistles* 1. 1. 1–11, trans. Colin Macleod)

Horace's first book of *Epistles* was probably presented to the public in 20 or 19 BCE, and self-consciously defines itself by reference to the publication in 23 BCE of *Odes* 1–3, in terms both of Horace's previous role as author of lyric poetry, and of the public's reception of the *Odes*. Claiming at the age of 44 that his youth is now behind him, the poet now turns to the serious business of philosophical self-improvement, and claims (in hexameters, ironically) that he is no longer even writing poetry.

In the penultimate epistle (1. 19), also addressed to Maecenas, Horace lets slip that the reason for turning from lyric to philosophical verse may be not so much a self-generated desire for wisdom as disgust at the response to the publication of the *Odes*:

> If you want to know why ungrateful readers love
> my things at home, but disparage them elsewhere:
> I do not chase the fickle public's votes
> with costly dinners and presents of old clothing.
> I do not care to hear 'distinguished writers'
> (and get my own back) at the critics' hustings.
> There's the rub. I say, 'Light verse recited
> in close-packed theatres would gain too much weight,'

> and one replies, 'Joker! You keep your stuff
> for the highest ears; you dote on your image,
> sure you're the sole source of poetic honey.'
> (*Epistles* 1. 19. 35–45, trans. Colin Macleod)

The public's hostility is presented as the hypocritical expression of envy, conventionally the enemy of the poet's fame, and the poet's reaction is framed as yet another instance of the Callimachean scornful rejection of the undiscriminating crowd. But some readers have sensed here a genuine disappointment on Horace's part to a less than enthusiastic welcome to the *Odes*, poems that may genuinely have proved too difficult, too new, for the Roman reading public at large—an ancient example of the unrecognized genius, perhaps (in tension with pp. 3–4)?

Be that as it may, in *Epistles* 1 the solipsistic Horace, who in the allusion at 1. 1. 7–9 (quoted above) to the inner voice of Socrates envisages the extreme case of a philosophical dialogue with *himself*, betrays a sustained concern with audiences and with the reception of his writings. In particular he screws up to breaking point a tension, long present in ancient literature, between poetry addressed to a select individual or group of individuals personally known to the author, and poetry intended for a generalized readership both during and after the poet's lifetime (cf. pp. 352–4, 386). Horace achieves this by choosing for his new book the form of the verse epistle. For this he had precedent in isolated letters in verse by Lucilius and Catullus, but Horace seems first to have put together a whole collection of verse epistles, to be followed by Ovid in the *Heroides* (see pp. 423–4 below). Each epistle presents itself as a written communication typically addressed to a more or less close friend, to whom Horace can bare his inmost concerns; and the *Epistles* are an important document in the history of autobiographical writing as well as of epistolary fictions. Some of the poems purport to have an immediate and ephemeral purpose, for example to invite a noble friend to dinner, or to recommend a younger acquaintance to Tiberius; but whether or not these texts ever really had this immediate communicative function at discrete moments in the poet's life, the reader who picks up this scroll of twenty carefully arranged epistles is never in doubt that they aim at a readership beyond the named addressees.

In the first instance they are all intended for the eyes of Maecenas, who is effectively established as dedicatee of the whole book by the addresses to him in the first and penultimate epistles, significantly those with least pretence to epistolary form. That pretence is completely unmasked in the last poem, an address by the author not to a human friend, but to the book of epistles itself, personified as a vain slave-boy eager to run away from his master and prostitute himself to the world at large:

I see, book, you're eager for change, for openings
in town—to sell your charms, all smooth and glossy.
You loathe a chaste reserve; 'I'm not displayed
enough!,' you moan, and clamour for publicity.
With *your* upbringing!—but follow your urge to a come-down.
Once out, you can never return. 'What made me do it?'
you'll say when you're rejected; yet you know
you're put on the shelf when your sated lover flags.
Well, if disgust does not impair my forecast,
you will be prized at Rome till your freshness leaves you;
but when everyone has pawed at you and soiled you,
you'll end up dumbly feeding mindless vermin,
or packed off to an exile in the colonies.
And there's worse to come: your old age lisping sentences
with a classful of beginners at street-corners.

(*Epistles* 1. 20. 1–18, trans. Colin Macleod)

A heavy dose of Horatian irony barely conceals the poet's own desire for an international and posthumous audience, for a return in fact to the amphitheatre from which the retired gladiator Veianius escapes in the opening lines of the book (quoted above). The reference to booksellers in the second line of the passage acknowledges the importance for the poet of circulation through a by now well-established book trade, a form of textual distribution diametrically opposed to the delivery of a letter to a friend by personal courier. The transient occasionality of the letter is superseded by the canonization of the book in the syllabus of the grammar-school teacher, fulfilling the basic educational function of literary texts in antiquity, but one far removed from the more advanced philosophical pedagogy that Horace proposes as the purpose of the book in the first epistle.

No doubt part of the attraction of *Epistles* 1 for a Roman audience was its poise between a social and intellectual exclusivity and a wider accessibility: eavesdropping, particularly on those close to the centre of power, is irresistible. This balancing act is manifested in other ways. Despite the opening rejection of poetry, *Epistles* 1 mounts a sustained exploration of the philosophical uses of poetry, and is itself an example of the poetic popularization of ethical-philosophical themes. Philosophical didactic, with its individualized addressee, is one of the models, but the second epistle draws on the prevalent ancient belief that other poetry, in particular the great Homer, could yield philosophical lessons through moralizing or allegorizing readings. These connections between poetry and philosophy are largely alien for a modern audience, but were still very much alive in the eighteenth century, for example in the poetry of Alexander Pope, whose adaptations of selected Horatian epistles are among his most complex poetry.

Philosophical ethics in antiquity extended to the discussion of friendship and of social intercourse, topics also of ancient poetry, which in many of its manifestations was a medium for personal relationships. *Epistles* 1 may be read almost as a handbook of social etiquette, a verse parallel to Cicero's *On Duties*, another favourite text of the eighteenth-century gentleman (cf. Ch. 10), in which Horace displays his tact and discrimination in adapting his manner to the different statuses and ages of his addressees. Two of the epistles give advice to younger men on how to behave towards great men within the client-patron system at Rome. The greatest man at Rome of course was Augustus, whose presence radically transformed the whole nature of the power structures that determined social interaction among the upper classes. None of *Epistles* 1 are in fact addressed directly to the emperor; the closest that Horace comes to the imperial presence is in a 'letter' (1. 13) addressed to the doltish courier entrusted with the task of bearing to Augustus some poems of Horace (usually supposed to be *Odes* 1–3), and advising him on how best to make an entrance. This is typical of the displacements and evasions that only serve to reveal Horace's interest in establishing viable relationships with the great, and his corresponding desire to preserve a space of personal freedom, one of the book's obsessive themes, all with Augustus as their invisible or partly visible centre. Although the book is dedicated to Maecenas, that great patron of the triumviral and early Augustan period was in fact in eclipse by the time that Horace wrote *Epistles* 1 (and is not the dedicatee of any later Augustan poetry book). In *Epistles* 1. 19 Horace says that his opponents sneer at him that 'you keep your writings for the ears of Jupiter', i.e. of Augustus. By telling a story against himself Horace deflects envy from what he no doubt hoped for, that Augustus would be one of his readers, his ideal reader perhaps.

The attention of the emperor might not be an unmixed blessing. In the *Satires* Horace snobbishly describes the nuisance of being buttonholed by outsiders curious about life in the circle of Maecenas and Augustus. But Augustus might also be perceived as an inquisitive busybody, a Big Brother, by poets with their own lives to lead and their own poetic axes to grind. The presence of the emperor as at least a potential reader of every text written in Rome, the all-seeing eavesdropper, changed the way in which writers thought about their audiences. For understandable reasons this concern will come to be an obsession with Ovid.

Horace's second book of *Epistles* consists of just two very long poems, primarily on literary matters, thus extending what had emerged as a major theme in book one, despite its opening gesture of rejecting poetry. The first, now addressed to Augustus himself, is a complex account of the cultural and literary history of Rome, and of the poet's relationship to his community and to the ruler; beneath the courtly surface we catch Horace measuring his own authority with that of the emperor. The conversational tone and indirection of these works are continued in the *Ars poetica*, in form another letter in hexameters, to the Pisones. As the one surviving Latin treatise on poetics, it has had an immense influence on the later European tradition, and is the source of some well-known tags, such as *ut pictura poesis* ('as a painting, so is a poem'), on which great critical edifices have been built, despite the fact that as a didactic poem it consciously strives against systematic clarity of the kind that Lucretius had set as his goal.

Public and private audiences: Horace *Odes* 4 and *Carmen Saeculare*, Propertius 4, Tibullus 2

> Offspring of the good gods and best guardian
> of the race of Romulus, too long have you been absent.
> You promised the sacred council of the Fathers
> a swift return, so return.
>
> Give back your radiance, good leader, to your homeland.
> When your face shines like springtime
> on your people, the day passes more joyfully
> and the sun is brighter.
>
> As a mother calls with vows and prayers and the taking
> of omens, upon her young son detained across
> the Carpathian sea by the jealous blasts of the South wind,
> as he waits till the sailing year is over,
>
> far from the home he loves, and she never
> takes her eyes from the curve of the shore,
> so does your faithful homeland, stricken with longing,
> look for its Caesar.
>
> (*Odes* 4. 5. 1–16, trans. David West)

According to the ancient biographical tradition Augustus himself commanded Horace to write the fourth book of *Odes*. At best this will be an over-simplification of the more subtle relationship between the imperial patron and the poet, who after the death of Virgil had no rival, but it is true that the last book of odes contains a high proportion of poems praising the emperor and his stepsons, Tiberius and Drusus, the princes who represented the future of the imperial house. These poems are anything but crude and perfunctory command performances, but, in comparison with the more experimental essays in imperial panegyric in *Odes* 1–3, they conform more straightforwardly to the rhetorical schemata for praising a king or emperor as we know them from what remains of Hellenistic ruler panegyric and from the rhetorical handbooks of later antiquity (and would no doubt find them in the now lost prose panegyrics of the Augustan period). Poet and public have now become familiar with the vocabulary of praising the emperor.

If Horace had been disappointed by the reception of *Odes* 1–3, the fourth book both commemorates and may in part have been prompted by the glory that he had won as composer and impresario of a unique lyric performance, the *Secular Hymn* (*Carmen Saeculare*) that was sung by twin choruses of boys and girls at the Secular Games of 17 BCE, a long-planned ceremony by which Augustus sought to mark the beginning of a new age (in Latin *saeculum*; according to religious tradition such an age was supposed to begin every hundred, or hundred and ten, years), and in so doing to incorporate his own new regime within a divine historical rhythm. The *Secular Hymn* is unique in Horace's *œuvre* not least because here at last the Roman *uates*, 'bard', was able to actualize a direct link between written composition in the poet's study and ritual public performance in a way that seems to restore the original conditions of Greek choral lyric as written by an Alkman or a Pindar for ceremonial performance (cf. pp. 81–5). Generically the *Secular Hymn* is a 'paean', a hymn to Apollo and Artemis, a Greek form used in the context of a Roman ritual. The Secular Games as a whole were an exercise on Augustus' part in the invention of tradition, in which Roman and Greek religious elements were inextricably intertwined. From this point of view the gap between Roman social and political 'reality' and the artifice of the Hellenizing poetry of Horace (and other Augustan poets) becomes insignificant: Augustus' combination of Greek and Roman in the ritual of the Secular Games is analogous to Horace's use of Pindaric, Greek, panegyrical forms to celebrate the victories of the Roman general in poems such as *Odes* 3. 4 or 4. 4.

As composer of the *Secular Hymn* Horace becomes a part of public Roman religion; in that role his name may still be read in the public inscription of the Acts of the Games, discovered in 1890 and now in the Museo Nazionale in Rome (*carmen composuit Q. Horatius Flaccus* 'the hymn was composed by Quintus Horatius Flaccus'—see illus. on p. 404). Horace 'inscribes' his own name (the only time that he declares his name in the odes) in his proud assertion of the future commemoration of the occasion of the *Secular Hymn* on the lips of a member of the choir of girls, a very direct example of the impact on an audience (in this case also a performer) of the poet as teacher:

> In time to come when you are a Roman wife, you will say,
> 'When the Secular Festival brought back its lights,
> I performed the hymn which so pleased the gods,
> and was taught the music of the poet Horatius'.
> (*Odes* 4. 6. 41–4, trans. David West)

By its nature (composed for passing occasions, originally to be sung to the measures of the lyre) lyric is a genre bound up with time and an awareness of the passage of time, an awareness given added urgency in *Odes* 4 by Horace's complaints about his own ageing. In order to immobilize the effects of time he adopts two, contradictory, strategies that nevertheless both seek to ground the poet and his works in a context guaranteed durability by the Roman community at large under the leadership of Augustus. By the first strategy, continued from *Odes* 3. 30 ('I have completed a work more long-lasting than bronze . . . '), Horace attempts to convert his fleeting words into a fixed inscription or public monument, but of a kind superior to the perishable materials of real inscriptions or monuments. In *Odes* 4. 3 he hints at his transformation into a kind of living statue, pointed at by the fingers of passers-by. Poetry becomes a part of the new monumental landscape of Rome that Augustus was creating at the time. Virgil had already made brilliant use of the favourite Hellenistic device of ecphrasis (the verbal evocation of a visual work of art (cf. pp. 392–4)) in order to develop analogies between poetry and the visual iconography of Augustan Rome; the task of constructing a 'virtual Rome' in words was to be continued by Propertius and Ovid.

By the second strategy Horace ensures the survival of his poetry in its repeated oral performance and commemoration by successive generations of Romans, whose future continuity is guaranteed by the peace and prosperity brought by Augustus. In *Odes* 4. 6 the girl in the choir will speak of her role in the *Secular Hymn* when she is grown up and married, telling stories about her childhood to her own children, one imagines. At the very end of the book Horace goes so far as to merge his individual lyric voice in the recurrent communal celebration by nuclear Roman families of Roman history and of the Julian family, in a romantic fantasy of the recovery, through the benefits of Augustan rule, of a primitive *Gemeinschaft*:

> and on ordinary days as on holy day,
> among the gifts of cheerful Bacchus, let us first
> with our children and our wives
> offer due prayers to the gods
>
> and sing a song to the Lydian pipe in praise
> of leaders who have shown the virtues

of their fathers, in praise of Troy, Anchises,
and the offspring of life-giving Venus.
(*Odes* 4. 15. 25–32, trans. David West)

Horace alludes to the tradition that in early Rome the great deeds of the ancestors were sung at banquets (a kind of original folk-poetry that Macaulay tried to reconstruct in *The Lays of Ancient Rome*). In this kind of community the learned individual poet, always anxious about his relationship to society at large, becomes superfluous, withering away like political hierarchies in the perfected communist society.

In answer to the question of what prompted Horace to return to lyric poetry in *Odes* 4, the poet himself gives quite a different answer: not a nod from the emperor, not pride at becoming the poet laureate, but the renewed onslaught of the goddess of love:

Back to war, Venus, after all
these years? Spare, spare me, I beg you.
I'm not the man I was
in good Cinara's reign. Cruel mother

of the sweet Cupids, stop
driving a long-since hardened fifty-year-old
with your soft commands. Away with you!
Go and answer the charming prayers of young men.
(*Odes* 4. 1. 1–8, trans. David West)

Like the earlier books, *Odes* 4 contains a mixture of personal (erotic and sympotic) and public (political and panegyrical) poems, a combination that may puzzle modern audiences. One may appeal to generic considerations: Horace is merely being faithful to his archaic Greek lyric models, which include the same range of personal and public subject-matters. But generic origin should not unthinkingly be identified with the meaning of poetic forms in a different historical context; for one thing the nature of political power and the relationship between the public and private spheres hardly remained constant between the sixth-century Greek world and Augustan Rome. Furthermore, while *Odes* 4 introduces itself as a continuation, after an intermission, of Horace's previous lyric output, it is not simply business as usual. One difference from the earlier books is indeed a heightening of the contrast between the personal and the public components. The first ode focuses on the poet's slavery to desire for the boy Ligurinus, while the second explores different poetic and non-poetic ways of praising the triumphant Augustus. In the first ode the treatment of Horace's homosexual obsession frames an instruction to Venus to divert her attack to the young nobleman Paullus Maximus who will offer her some kind of semi-public worship, possibly an allusion to the forthcoming marriage of Paullus to Augustus' cousin Marcia. This may suggest a possibility of containing the irresponsible force of personal desire within the institutional structures of imperial Roman society, but we are not bound to find in it a way to an integrated reading of the several poems that make up book four of the *Odes*.

How to read the juxtaposition of self-centred erotic poems with poems about Rome and Augustus has become one of the most contentious issues in the criticism of Augustan poetry. Any answer must include some attempt to reconstruct the horizons of the Augustan reader. The problem seems to become particularly acute in later Augustan poetry. The fourth book of Propertius' *Elegies*, whose composition overlapped with that of Horace *Odes* 4, also stages the drama of a return to erotic subjects after the decisive and formal renunciation of Cynthia with which the third book ends. In the first poem of book four Propertius addresses an unnamed visitor to Rome and contrasts the present-day splendours of the city with the simple buildings and customs that would have been visible in Rome's primitive past; the poet then turns to a statement of his own poetic ambitions and a syllabus for the book on which he is embarking:

> Be gracious, Rome. For you the work proceeds. Grant happy
> Omens, citizens. Sing, bird, favouring the attempt.
> I'll say 'Troy, you shall fall and rise again as Rome';
> I'll sing of distant graves on land and sea.
> I'll sing of rites and days and the ancient names of places.
> This is the goal towards which my steed must sweat.
> (Propertius, 4. 1. 67–8, 87–8, 69–70, trans. Guy Lee)

Propertius is then rudely interrupted by the astrologer and fortune-teller Horus, of Greek and Oriental extraction, who warns him away from his historical and antiquarian Roman project and orders him instead to stick to his erotic elegiac matter:

> 'Unstable Propertius, why this ignorant rush to turn prophet?
> Your thread was not spun from a dexterous distaff.
> Your cantillations will end in tears. Apollo's against them
> You'll rue the words you force from a reluctant lyre.
> . . . .
> Well, make up elegies. Tricky work! This is your field.
> Let crowds of others write with you as model.
> You'll face campaigning under Venus' deceptive arms
> And make a useful target for her Cupids.
> Whatever palms of victory your hardships gain
> One girl will mock them and your grasp.

> Though you shake off the hook imbedded in your chin
> It's no good—the gaff's prong will spike you.
> At her dictation you will see darkness and light
> And shed a tear but when she orders it.
> To seal her door and post a thousand guards won't help you;
> A chink's enough if she's resolved to cheat.
> (Propertius, 4. 1. 71–4, 135–46, trans. Guy Lee)

Propertius here gives a new spin to the conventional elegiac *recusatio* (the 'refusal' to write a grander kind of poetry than humble love elegy): the rest of book four turns out to be neither one thing nor the other, but a mixture, as aetiological poems on Roman institutions alternate with erotic elegies. Further, this juxtaposition of the antiquarian and the erotic is instantiated within single poems, as in the account (4. 4) of the origin of the name of the Tarpeian Rock, in which Tarpeia's motive for betraying the Capitol to the enemy general is, unusually, love rather than greed. At the centre of the book (4. 6) is a kind of hymn celebrating Augustus' Palatine Temple of Apollo and including an extended and mannered narrative of the battle of Actium, turned in Octavian's favour by Apollo. The book concludes (4. 11) with a speech to the judges of the dead in the mouth of the deceased Cornelia, stepdaughter of Augustus, in which she gives an account of herself as the very type of the old-fashioned matronly virtues actively encouraged by Augustus' moral and legislative programme (in particular the marriage laws of 18 BCE and 9 CE), and the polar opposite of the irregular lifestyle of the elegiac girlfriend.

Formal literary considerations may take us so far. The Alexandrian privileging of novelty took on new urgency after the first wave of Augustan literary production; one way to tickle the public's jaded palates was to present old material in new combinations. Propertius reinvents himself as an elegist by forcing together elements familiar from earlier elegy with historical and nationalist matter hitherto considered alien to love elegy. This craving for the new is one (but only one) of the roots of the love of paradox that is so striking a feature of later Augustan and first-century CE literature. In the case of Propertius' fourth book a further twist is given by this new kind of self-legitimation by elegy as a faithful reproduction of a Greek model. Propertius boasts that he is a 'Roman Callimachus' (4. 1. 64). The Callimachean rejection of poetry on heroes and kings had been used by Roman poets writing in the 'Alexandrian' manner as a way of declining grand Roman themes since at least the time of Virgil's sixth *Eclogue*. But to be truly faithful to Callimachean elegy (the *Aitia*) a Roman elegist should write aetiological elegy, and to write Roman aetiology is inevitably to peddle national legend and history, particularly as elaborated in Virgil's *Aeneid*. The piquancy of Propertius' fourth book would be keenly savoured by a Roman public fresh from a reading of the new national epic. The versatility of this new Propertian poetics is embodied in the speaking statue of Vertumnus in the second elegy of book four, the god who can turn (*uertere*) himself to any number of disguises. Like Propertius, Vertumnus is of Etruscan origin, but he now stands in the Roman Forum in full view of the Roman crowd as it passes about its business.

But at what point does generic 'contamination' cease to be a purely formal play with literary kinds and turn into ideological challenge? Many modern critics read subversive intent into the incongruous combination of the erotic and the Roman in a work such as Propertius' fourth book. Fewer would make the same claim for Tibullus, whose second book of elegies, probably written shortly before his death in 19 BCE, juxtaposes poems on his love for the girl Nemesis with a hymnic account of the religious festival of the Ambarvalia (2. 1), largely drawing on Virgil's *Georgics*, and with a poem celebrating the inauguration of Messalla's son as one of the priests in charge of the Sibylline Oracles (2. 5), including accounts of early Rome and of the mission of Aeneas that substantially overlap with material in Propertius 4. 1. In Tibullus' case this does not mark a decisive break with the practice of his first book, which includes a full-blown celebration of the triumph of Messalla in 27 BCE (1. 7) in the midst of poems about his loves for Delia and the boy Marathus.

Tibullus frames panegyric of one of the leading Roman noble families within his love elegy, but Propertius deals with the ruler of Rome himself and his family. The compartmentalization of personal and public interests within a poetry book becomes problematic in an age when state supervision and regulation extend further into the private sphere than they had ever done under the Republic. It is difficult to feel that Ovid, for example, is not being at least provocative when near the beginning of his how-to-do-it manual for would-be lovers, the *Art of Love* (*Ars Amatoria*), in a list of good places to pick up a girl he includes the prospective triumph of the adopted sons of Augustus, Gaius and Lucius, where it will be easy to impress one of the girls in the crowd of spectators:

> Then one great day our darling we'll behold,
> Drawn by four snowy steeds and clad in gold.
> In front shall walk the chieftains fettered tight,
> Lest they take refuge in their wonted flight;
> While youths and maids look on in blithe array,
> And every heart is gladdened by the day.
> And if a damsel ask what chiefs are those,
> What towns or hills or streams the pageant shows,
> Tell everything she asks and more than that,
> And though you know not, give your answers pat.

That's the Euphrates with his crown of reeds,
And that the Tigris with the long grey weeds;
Yonder are generals; add a name or two,
Names that are fitting, though they mayn't be true.
(*Art of Love* 1. 213–28, trans. A. D. Melville)

Suetonius' *Life of Augustus* shows us an emperor not without his lighter side, a keen gambler, with a well-developed sense of humour, but also with strong ideas about the right place and time. On one occasion when he saw Romans wearing informal dress in a public assembly he indignantly quoted a Virgilian line (*Aeneid* 1. 282), 'Romans, masters of the world, the people of the toga', and thereafter forbade anybody to appear in or near the Forum except in a toga (the Roman formal dress) (Suetonius, *Life of Augustus* 40). It is legitimate at least to ask what he would have thought of using a triumph to cruise for pick-ups.

Ovid and the cultured reader

Ovid (Publius Ovidius Naso, 43 BCE–17 CE) is the dominating literary presence of the later years of Augustus' reign, and (from exile) forms a bridge into the first few years of Tiberius' reign. The influence of Ovid on the Western tradition over the last two millennia has arguably been greater than that of any other Greek or Latin writer (including Virgil). To take an example from English literature, there is much to reflect on in Francis Meres's judgement of 1598 that 'the sweete wittie soule of Ovid lives in mellifluous and hony-tongued Shakespeare'. It is only in the last century or so that, as a result of particular views about the seriousness and sincerity expected of 'great' literature, the mellifluous wit of Ovid has turned to his disadvantage, his sophistication denigrated as the mark of a superficial fluency. On the other hand, part of the appeal of Ovid for both ancient and later audiences has been the effortless fluency of his language and metre, cloaking a content that is also, at least on some levels, immediately accessible. After over a century and a half of refinement of the Greek models, Latin dactylic poetry finally attains with Ovid a seemingly natural ease and regularity. All of Ovid's extant poetry is in elegiac couplets or hexameters (had his tragedy *Medea* survived we would probably see a similar confidence in the handling of tragic metres, foreshadowing the pointed facility of Seneca's tragedies, cf. pp. 448–50). A leading authority on Ovid, referring to a tradition of classical education only recently defunct, remarks that 'The Ovidian manner, as generations of clever English schoolboys have discovered, is imitable; Virgil's is not.' One might compare the difference between Virgil and Ovid in this respect to that between the blank verse of Milton, sovereign in its control but heroically laboured, and the ready versatility of Dryden, himself an important translator and adaptor of Ovid.

Over the past couple of decades Ovid has undergone a remarkable rehabilitation, both inside and outside the academic world. Professional classicists have responded to the more 'difficult' aspects of Ovidian sophistication, exploring his self-reflexive and narratological games and that constant engagement with fictionality and textuality that makes of Ovid an ideal subject for the concerns of post-modernism. Modern poets and novelists have returned to what has always been one of Ovid's main attractions, the seductiveness of his storytelling, and also found a specifically late twentieth-century interest in Ovidian anticipations of the mode of magical realism. Ovid's later career has come to hold a fascination for an artistic intelligentsia attracted by the figurative image of exile for its own condition.

Like Cicero, that other great Roman exile, whose own complaints from exile, together with the legendary sufferings of the exile who founded the Roman race, Aeneas, are an important model for Ovid's construction of his own exilic image, Ovid found exile particularly hard to cope with because he identified himself so thoroughly with the city of Rome itself. For Cicero Rome meant above all the city of the ancestors, the site of the traditional constitution and values that as consul he had preserved against the threat of Catiline. Ovid's urban values are rather different, as may be seen from a well-known passage in the third book of the *Art of Love*:

> I start with care of body [*cultus*]: glebe and vine
> Well-cared for yield rich crops and bounteous wine.
> Beauty's a gift of God. How few can boast
> Of beauty? It's a gift denied to most.
> Looks come by art: looks vanish with neglect,
> Yes, though the charms of Venus they reflect.
> Women of old ne'er groomed themselves, it's true,
> But in those days the men were ungroomed too.
>
> . . . .
>
> Once life was rude and plain; now golden-paved,
> Rome holds the treasures of a world enslaved.
> The old and modern Capitols compare;
> Built for two different Jupiters, you'd swear.
> The Senate-house, fit home of high debate,
> Was wattle-built when Tatius ruled the state,
> And ploughmen's oxen grazed on Palatine
> Where glitter now the palace and the shrine.

The good old days indeed! I am, thanks be,
This age's child: it's just the age for me;
Not because pliant gold from earth is wrought,
Not because pearls from distant coasts are brought,
Not that from hills their marble hearts we hew,
While piles encroach upon the ocean's blue:
It's that we've learnt refinement [*cultus*], and our days
Inherit not our grandsires' boorish ways.

(*Ars* 3. 101–8, 113–28, trans. A. D. Melville)

Ovid the urban poet is Ovid the urbane poet. In Latin the terms denoting city-dweller (*urbanus*) and country-dweller (*rusticus*) had long been used in an evaluative sense to distinguish the civilized, urbane, and stylish in both life and literature from the boorish, rustic, and gauche (cf. pp. 326–7). The key-word in this passage is *cultus*, immediately the 'adornment' or *toilette* that the female addressee of the didactic poet must cultivate in order to attract a lover. But it is widened to embrace the senses of 'elegance', 'refinement', 'sophistication', that is to say, a particular aspect of our still wider term 'culture'. This is the value that the neoteric poets had established as the distinguishing mark of members of their exclusive smart set; Ovid extends membership of the cultivated circle to all modern Romans, who by implication will (all) be the ideal readers of Ovid's cultivated poetry on female adornment and other cultivated subjects. This redefinition of the audience for cultured poetry may mark a watershed in the Roman poet's awareness of his reading public, and of that public's awareness of itself. Mario Citroni claims that 'Ovid's work marks a crucial moment, a true turning-point in the development of the relationship between author and public in European literature. In Ovid for the first time on the poetic page there is an open dialogue between the author and the general reader.'

Another point of difference from the neoteric poets' definition of their 'fit audience, though few' is that Ovid makes no attempt to cordon off the interests of a cultured readership as something apart from the more practical pursuits of traditional-minded Romans. Instead Augustan city-building and empire-building themselves are the material precondition and manifestation of Roman culture. The wealth of Rome's world-empire, achieved by Roman armies, creates this new 'golden age' of civilization, whose products include the Temple of Apollo, built on the Palatine by Augustus to celebrate the Battle of Actium, as well as an advanced technology of cosmetics. Ovid sees Rome as the successor to the Greek world-city, Alexandria, whose immense wealth and cosmopolitanism fostered the artistic and intellectual sophistication of the Museum and of poets like Callimachus (cf. pp. 236 ff.). The sole exclusion—and an important one given the Romans' habit of defining themselves in terms of their past—is the rustic audience of ancestors, who would certainly not understand or appreciate Ovid's poetry. Ovid sees himself as perfectly in tune with his age; but this 'Ovidian age' is at best a partial definition of the 'Augustan age', which for Augustus himself would include the strong continuing presence of the values of the ancestors, as embodied for example in the emperor's marriage legislation or, in physical form, in the statue galleries of Roman ancestors in the Forum of Augustus (dedicated in 2 BCE). In this passage from the *Art of Love* Ovid in fact acutely identifies an irresolvable tension at the heart of Augustan ideology: Augustus is both the representative of modernity, the emperor who boasted that he found Rome a city of brick and left it a city of marble, and the increasingly austere upholder of what were held to be traditional values.

Ovid's games of love: Women reading and writing

Ovid's first work, the *Amores*, is pitched at the general reader, and is already a consummate display of literary *cultus*. In an opening epigram in which the three books present themselves as a slimmed-down version of an original five-book edition, Ovid's love poetry announces itself not as an instrument to win a girl's favours but as a text that may (or may not) afford pleasure to the reader at large. Corinna herself is not addressed until the third poem in the first book, and then in a manner that teasingly suggests that Ovid's real-life lover may have as much or as little reality as famous literary heroines such as Io and Europa.

In the first elegy the personification of love, Cupid, steals a 'foot' from a poet who pretends to be embarking on a grandiose military epic in hexameters, and thus condemns him to the limping metre of elegiac couplets (alternating the six feet of the hexameter with the five feet of the pentameter). This reveals its full significance only to a reader familiar with the texts, Propertius' elegies above all, to which it alludes (although, as usual, the Ovidian text makes a perfectly lucid sense even to a reader who does not come armed with literary learning). Latin love elegy had always been written to conventions, but Ovid foregrounds the conventionality of the genre in order to comment and ring the changes on it to a still greater degree than his predecessors. The term 'parody' is often used, but this is to suppose a seriousness of personal commitment to their elegiac life and art by Gallus, Propertius, and Tibullus that may be the result of wishful thinking on the part of the modern reader. It has been argued that the Latin elegist *always* invites the reader to laugh at the pitiful figure cut by himself as the slave of love (cf. pp. 379–80).

But the disempowerment of the elegiac poet debarred from writing hexameter epic may be more apparent than real. The first word of Ovid's first elegy is *arma* 'weapons', not coincidentally the first word of the *Aeneid*. Warfare turns out, in fact, to be an integral part of the elegist's world. It is not just that the god of love and virtual personification of love elegy, Cupid, uses his bow to shoot his victim, but the enamoured poet himself boasts of the military-style endurance and violence that carry him through to success in his campaign against a resistant girl, a theme explored at length in *Amores* 1. 9, beginning 'Every lover is a soldier'. Ancient works were often referred to by the first word or words of the text: 'weapons' is not a totally misleading title for the *Amores*.

A reading of the *Amores* is not exhausted at the level of literary playfulness. The cultured Augustan reader will have enjoyed the sensation of intermittently abandoning him- or herself to the 'reality effect', of following the sequence of elegies almost as a soap-opera serialization of the ups and downs of the poet's love-life. Ovid already shows a mastery, abundantly displayed in the *Metamorphoses*, of the manipulation of the reader's suspension of disbelief. In an exquisite moment he projects this equivocation between pretence and reality onto an unnamed female reader of the *Amores*:

> There's one I know who broadcasts she's Corinna;
> What would she not have given to really be!
> (*Amores* 2. 17. 29–30, trans. A. D. Melville)

Realism is a literary mode, but the realist *Amores* are also anchored in the personal and social realities of the author and his readership. An example of the fine balance between the real and the literary is the elegy on the death of Ovid's fellow elegist Tibullus (*Amores* 3. 9), which was undoubtedly written on the real occasion of his friend's death and, almost as undoubtedly, expresses the real grief of Ovid. Yet at the same time it uses sustained allusion to Tibullus' own love elegy to give a fictionalized picture of the death and the grief. Now for two examples of how the eternal experience of love is set within the political and historical context of Augustan Rome. First, at the end of *Amores* 1. 2 a highly artificial description of the Triumph of Cupid is directly related to the triumphs celebrated by the emperor when the god of love is asked to show as much clemency as his 'relative' Augustus, a cousin many times removed of Cupid through their shared descent from Venus. Beyond the immediate joke this passage reminds us that the Roman audience for Augustan ideology routinely exercised a sophisticated suspension of disbelief in responding to imperial fictions such as the legend of Aeneas. Secondly, in *Amores* 2. 14 the poet reproaches Corinna for having endangered her life through procuring an abortion; and he mimics the moralizing arguments attested for Augustus' own oratory in support of his marriage legislation, partly designed to bolster a falling birthrate among the upper classes:

> If in times past that practice had found favour,
> The crime would have destroyed the race of men,
> The empty world would need someone for throwing
> The stones of our creation once again.
> (*Amores* 2. 14. 9–12, trans. A. D. Melville)

The elegist's appropriation of the conservative and imperial rhetoric of 'the customs of our ancestors' is breathtaking.

In the *Art of Love* Ovid takes to its logical conclusion the relevance for the audience's own experience of the elegiac poet's lifestyle, by writing a didactic poem on how to succeed in love (followed later by the shorter *Remedies for Love*, giving instruction in how to fall out of love).

> Who in this town knows not the lover's art
> Should read this book, and play an expert's part.
> It's art that speeds the boat with oars and sails,
> Art drives the chariot, art in love prevails.
> Automedon was skilled with car and rein,
> And Tiphys steered the Argo o'er the main:
> For young Love's guide has Venus chosen me.
> Love's pilot and Love's charioteer I'll be.
> (*Art of Love* 1. 1–8, trans. A. D. Melville)

This is a deliberately paradoxical project in a number of ways. Traditionally the elegiac lover is at the mercy of an overwhelming force that sweeps away the conventions of society and civilization, but Ovid proudly presents himself as the Master of Love (a role in which he became very influential in the Middle Ages), with a body of rational precepts to convey, an art or science. Furthermore, while the traditional elegist portrays himself as an outcast from society, excluded from the normal pursuits of the male Roman citizen by his enslavement to his girl, in the *Art of Love* the second-person singular addressee conventional in the genre of didactic becomes the Roman everyman: this is written for you, any and every one of this people who is not an expert in the art of love. There is another paradox in the idea that love and sex should be a science like astronomy, philosophical ethics, farming, or hunting (the subjects of other surviving Latin didactic poems). By choosing this particular topic it might be thought that Ovid finally debunks any lingering idea that in this late age the real function of didactic poetry is still that of instruction. On the other hand, the *Art of Love* was perhaps the one Latin didactic poem that *was* eagerly unrolled by young, and not so young, sweaty palms looking for tips on how to make a catch, and what to do in bed once you had made the catch.

The readership for the *Art of Love* is not envisaged as exclusively male; at the beginning of the poem Ovid is careful to warn off (and thereby of course also to tempt) just one class of potential female reader, the *matrona*, the married woman viewed as the bearer of the Augustan family values to which the elegiac lifestyle is constructed as a self-conscious alternative. Already in *Amores* 2. 1. 5–6 Ovid had defined his ideal readers as *both* the passionate girl *and* the inexperienced boy. The *Art of Love* methodically addresses both sexes: the first two books instruct the male lover, and the third is addressed to women:

> Greeks have I armed 'gainst Amazons to stand,
> Remains to arm Penthesilea's band.
> Fair be the field, and to the cause success
> That Venus and her world-wide flyer bless.
> For men-at-arms are unarmed maids no match,
> A sorry triumph that for men to snatch.
> (*Art of Love* 3. 1–6, trans. A. D. Melville)

The image of the Amazons is an uneasy one: Ovid extends the elegiac cliché of the warfare of love (on which see p. 420 above) and puts his male and female readers on an equal footing by casting the latter in a mythological role that in Greco-Roman culture both symbolized the diametrical opposite of the sexual and social roles expected of women, and expressed male anxieties about maintaining their dominance within home and city. The image of the bare-breasted female warrior had also by this time become a highly eroticized one.

This passage raises difficult questions about the role of women in Ovid's poetry and as readers of Ovid's poetry. There is no doubt that at this time in Rome there was a significant readership of educated upper-class women; of all (male) Latin writers Ovid appears to invest most heavily in writing for a female audience and from a woman's point of view (on Catullus' female readers, cf. p. 354 above). But it would be too simple to claim him as a proto-feminist. At every point we must ask how far Ovid caters to a male voyeurism, whether he is more interested in woman as subject or as object. In the case of the third book of the *Art of Love* the illusion of an equality on the battlefield of love is quickly broken when we come to the instruction proper addressed to the would-be female lover. Ovid begins from *cultus*, female adornment, which places the woman in the passive role of a lure for the actively questing male. By contrast in the first book the male reader is told to go about his business like a hunter marking out the ground for his nets and traps, and is thus figuratively cast in the role of the reader of the established species of didactic poems on hunting (of which an example in Latin, the *Cynegetica*, survives by a contemporary of Ovid, one Grattius). Ovid elsewhere establishes his credentials within the didactic tradition by a heavy use of georgic (farming) imagery, in obvious allusion to the most important Latin didactic text, Virgil's *Georgics*. The use of both cynegetic and georgic imagery establishes an asymmetrical relationship between the male as the agent of culture, the hunter or farmer, operating on the female as a natural object, an animal wild or domestic, or a piece of land to be cultivated. In defence of the poet one might point to the endings of the second and third books where Ovid recommends simultaneous orgasm as the climax of the art of love, although even this advocacy of an equality of sexual enjoyment is qualified by the appended advice to the girl to fake it if she cannot manage the real thing.

The *Amores* are 'autobiographical' elegies written from a male point of view but about an experience that inverts the expected dominance in antiquity of male over female. Ovid next turned to a work that places elegiac complaints on the lips, or rather flowing from the pens, of powerless women, famous mythological heroines who have been abandoned or betrayed by their husbands or lovers. The *Heroides* ('Heroines') consist of fifteen letters written by separate characters; it may have been the popular success of this collection that prompted Ovid to follow it up with three pairs of double *Heroides* in each of which a letter from a male character is followed by the reply from the woman. Like the *Amores*, the *Heroides* combine psychological with more literary kinds of interest: these epistolary effusions forced out of women by acute emotional stress are cunningly inserted in undocumented 'gaps' in their histories as recorded in earlier literary texts, to which the writers of the epistles are made anachronistically, and in some sense unknowingly, to allude.

A major strategy of the love elegist had been to lend a romantic glamour to his affair by viewing it in the light of the great passions of the mythological past; this is reversed in the *Heroides* where mythological characters behave in the manner of a first-century BCE Roman lover. In the first poem, for example, Penelope, the great epic example of wifely fidelity, unburdens herself of the self-pitying complaints of the elegist. These arch games with anachronism and the modernization of myth have precedents in Hellenistic poetry, and the formula presumably worked for a Roman audience, as Ovid was repeatedly to use it for effect in the *Metamorphoses*. The verse epistle itself was a new form (see p. 406 above), and Ovid makes the written letter into a bearer of modernity: not only are the main models for the heroines' written complaints the predominantly oral performances of characters in Greek epic and tragedy, but Ovid's writers display a self-consciousness about the act of writing itself, that mirrors at another level the author Ovid's own self-consciousness about his interventions in a textual tradition. Dido ends her letter to Aeneas (*Heroides* 7) by appealing to him to visualize the image of herself as she writes:

> If only you could see the picture of me as I write!
>   I write, with the Trojan sword in my lap,
> the tears glide down my cheeks on to the drawn sword,
>   which will soon be stained with blood, not tears.
> How well your gift-offering matches my fate! —
>   your funeral arrangement for me comes cheap.
> Not for the first time is my breast now struck with a weapon;
>   that place already bears the wound of cruel love.
> Anna my sister, sister Anna, all too much party to my guilt,
>   soon you will make the last offerings to my ashes.
> After the pyre my inscription will not be 'Elissa, wife of Sychaeus';
>   this will be the only epitaph on my marble tomb:
> AENEAS PROVIDED THE CAUSE OF DEATH AND SWORD;
>   DIDO'S OWN HAND IT WAS BY WHICH SHE FELL.
>
> (*Heroides* 7. 183–96)

Of course the sword of Aeneas, and the use to which Dido will shortly put it, are well known to the reader from another written text, the *Aeneid*.

Ovid's Dido concludes with reference to another form of writing, the inscription of her name and of a brief outline of her story on her tomb. This is at once a more permanent kind of writing than the flimsy and (as we all know) totally ineffectual letter that she is writing at this moment. It is also a written monument that challenges the version of the story of Dido and Aeneas inscribed in the great written monument that is the *Aeneid*, placing the blame for what happened fairly and squarely on the shoulders of Aeneas. *Heroides* 7 is the first of a long line of rewritings of the Virgilian story from Dido's point of view, of which Chaucer's *House of Fame* and Purcell's *Dido and Aeneas* are examples. Here perhaps a feminist critic might find an Ovid ventriloquizing a female voice in true sympathy with the victim of the male hero of the Roman epic, that most masculine of genres. Or is the male reader of the *Heroides* in the position of a voyeur, enjoying the spectacle of a defenceless female victim? As in the case of Horace's very personal *Epistles*, there is the added *frisson* of eavesdropping on a private communication: the Medea of the tragic stage addresses her impassioned monologues to the world at large, whereas the Medea of *Heroides* 12 writes a letter not intended for our eyes.

Similar questions about how to read Ovidian women are prompted by the mythological narratives of the *Metamorphoses*, which include a number of examples of the Euripidean type of tragic monologue delivered by a woman in an impossible erotic dilemma. One of the most typical narrative motifs in the *Metamorphoses* is that of the female rape victim 'saved' from her pursuer's attentions through transformation out of her human shape. Ovid certainly does often explore the point of view of the rape victim, but there is also an undoubted pleasure for the male viewer/reader of the female victim's plight. Metamorphosis itself can function not just as an escape route from sexual penetration, but as the narrative realization of the transformation of the female body into an object under the male gaze.

In the archetypal example of this motif Daphne eludes Apollo's embrace in her flesh-and-blood existence, but hardens into a beautiful tree, the laurel, an object which will for ever be 'possessed' by Apollo as one of his attributes. The *Metamorphoses* also provides the classic image of the female body eroticized and objectified under the male gaze in the figure of Andromeda chained to the rock and waiting to be devoured by the sea-monster, viewed through the eyes of her rescuer and lover Perseus, who is almost induced by her petrified motionlessness to think that what he sees is a statue, a work of art.

> Andromeda was pinioned to a rock.
> When Perseus saw her, had a wafting breeze
> Not stirred her hair, her eyes not overflowed
> With trembling tears, he had imagined her
> A marble statue. Love, before he knew,
> Kindled; he gazed entranced; and overcome
> By loveliness so exquisite, so rare,
> Almost forgot to hover in the air.
> He glided down. 'Shame on those chains!' he cried;
> 'The chains that you deserve link lovers' hearts.
> Reveal, I beg, your name and this land's name
> And why you wear these shackles.' She at first
> Was silent, too abashed to face a man,
> So shy she would have held her hands to hide
> Her blushing cheeks had not her hands been chained.
> But weep she might and filled her eyes with tears.
> (*Metamorphoses* 4. 672–84, trans. A. D. Melville)

This 'image of beauty' was to be replicated many times in later art and literature, from Ariosto's Angelica to sadomasochistic bondage magazines.

The *Metamorphoses*: Ovid's Roman poem

The *Metamorphoses*, Ovid's hexameter narrative poem in fifteen books, is a kaleidoscopic and constantly shifting text that has appealed to many different kinds of audience, who have read it at different times through the centuries as an encyclopaedia of Greco-Roman myth, a Scheherezade-like treasury of

ANDROMEDA EXPOSED. *A large villa at Boscoreale near Pompeii was lavishly painted in about 40 BCE and then buried in the eruption of Vesuvius. This painting shows the myth of Andromeda exposed to be consumed by a sea monster before being rescued by Perseus.*

seductive story-telling, a store of philosophical and ethical profundity (often accessed through allegorical modes of interpretation), the subversive expression of a counter-culture in defiance of the Augustan norm, or a celebration of the cultural and political achievement of the principate.

The sheer reach and variety of the poem will have appealed to a contemporary audience's awareness of the power and riches of Augustan Rome. The temporal scope of the *Metamorphoses* extends from the creation of the universe down to the poet's own day, and the last major narrative episode is the transformation of the murdered Julius Caesar into a god (and the prospective apotheosis of Augustus). The work is thus a version of the popular prose genre of universal history (cf. p. 328), which by leading up to the narrative of Roman success flattered the Romans' sense that their empire was the natural culmination of the history of the world. The poem also traces a trajectory from the world of Greek myth and literature to Italy and the stories that fashion the

Roman identity. Taken as a whole the *Metamorphoses* is the supreme monument to the Roman appropriation of Greek culture, which from another point of view is the story of the Hellenization of Rome.

The *Metamorphoses* embodies another kind of literary 'imperialism' in its inclusion within its hexameter narrative (the form of epic) of a multiplicity of other genres, hymn, tragedy, pastoral, elegy, and so on. This inclusiveness makes it very difficult to define the poem, and twentieth-century critics have argued endlessly whether it should be described as an epic or as a loose concatenation of recherché mythical narratives in the manner of the Alexandrian 'epyllion' (short, mannered, narrative poem). The recent trend has been to see the question of definition as a theme of the poem itself, the answer to which is always teasingly deferred. But this too had an extra-literary resonance for the contemporary audience, confronted with the need to define the new order at Rome, for example with reference to ancestral traditions on the one hand and Greek monarchical structures on the other. Modern historians' accounts of the nature of Augustus and his power are as various as attempts to circumscribe the essence of the *Metamorphoses*.

The pluralism of the poem is also paralleled in the diversity and eclecticism of Augustan art and architecture, in which the formal and solemn classicism sometimes associated with the period is in fact but one register among many. Here we touch on the thorny issue of the ideological 'correctness' or otherwise of the *Metamorphoses*: some would claim that piquant juxtapositions such as the two appearances of Jupiter in book one, firstly as the king of the gods presiding over a celestial Senate and punishing mortal sinfulness, and secondly as the philandering rapist of the defenceless girl Io, whom he transforms into a cow in an attempt to deceive his shrewish wife Juno, would have caused no more offence than the co-presence in Augustan art of archaizing images of the gods alongside rococo decorative fantasies. Against this one might point to the importance in Roman culture of a hierarchy of decorum. What Augustus might think of as appropriate for the decoration of his recently excavated private study on the Palatine is very different from what was required in the major iconographical features of the Forum of Augustus. Ovid is as aware of the constraints of decorum as is any ancient poet, and a sustained testing of those constraints is characteristic of all of his works; ultimately it is for the reader to decide whether he oversteps the limits or not.

These features—the universal pretensions of the *Metamorphoses*, its 'literary imperialism', its investment in issues of national and literary definition—can all be predicated of Virgil's *Aeneid*. Ovid's fifteen-book hexameter poem demands to be read as a continuous engagement with and overbidding of Virgil's twelve-book epic. Ovid's relationship to Virgil is that of a respectful but unabashed epigone; as in the case of his reworking of earlier love elegy, 'parody' may be a misleading term. As he works through universal time, Ovid naturally catches up with the timespan of the *Aeneid;* and books 13 and 14 contain an elliptical and oblique retelling of the story of Aeneas (sometimes referrred to as Ovid's 'Little Aeneid'). But the structures, themes, and detailed verbal matter of the *Aeneid* are spread over the whole poem in displacements and recombinations—metamorphoses, if you will.

For example book nine opens with the river-god Achelous' narration, at a banquet, of his own defeat by Hercules in a fight for a woman:

> Why the god groaned and how his brow was maimed
> Theseus enquired, and Calydon's great river,
> His tangled tresses bound with reeds, began:
> 'Sad is the task you set. For who would wish
> To chronicle the battles that he lost?
> Yet the whole tale I'll tell. It was less shame
> To lose than glory to have fought the fight:
> Much comfort comes from such a conqueror.
> You may perhaps have heard of Deianira,
> Once a most lovely girl, the envied hope
> Of many a suitor. I was one of them.'
>
> (*Metamorphoses* 9. 1–10, trans. A. D. Melville)

This combines elements from the beginning and end of the story of Aeneas in the *Aeneid*: the agreement to narrate a personal sorrow despite the grief it causes echoes Aeneas' introduction of his narration of the Sack of Troy to Dido at the beginning of the second book of the *Aeneid*, also at a banquet; but Achelous' misadventure is modelled on the final duel in *Aeneid* 12 between Aeneas and Turnus, and in this perspective it is Hercules, rather than Achelous, who takes the part of the victorious Aeneas. This is only to begin an exploration of the intertextual links: for example Ovid's allusive identification of Hercules and Aeneas is true to Virgil's own use of Hercules as a model for the character and exploits of Aeneas. Also the occasion for the fight between Achelous and Hercules reminds the reader that the climactic duel between Aeneas and Turnus, a foundational moment in Roman history, also concludes a quarrel over a woman, the Latin princess Lavinia. Ovid never tires of drawing attention to the fact that all the great epic plots can be reduced to contests or quests for a woman.

The *Metamorphoses* also shows itself to be a text of the moment in its address to a sophisticated audience accustomed to kinds of performance and spectacle both old and new. One of the big gaps in our knowledge of Augustan literature is the history of stage performance. We have lost the two tragedies of the period that won a lasting reputation, Varius' *Thyestes* of 29 BCE, and Ovid's own *Medea*. Under Augustus the performance of tragedies became marginalized, although there is evidence of an intense interest in the condition and possible revival of Roman theatre. Horace's two major exercises in literary history and criticism, the *Art of Poetry* and the *Letter to Augustus*, are both largely concerned with the theatre (rather than with the kinds of poetry that Horace himself wrote, to the frustration of some modern students). As regards tragedy, there may already have been a move towards performance in the recitation hall rather than on the public stage. In the *Metamorphoses* Ovid follows Virgil's lead (above all in the Dido story) in the wholesale importation into a narrative poem of tragic material, with long dramatic monologues that would lend themselves well to recitation, for example in the episodes of Medea and Althea, the mother of Meleager; the Hecuba episode in book thirteen is modelled closely on an extant play of Euripides, and was particularly appreciated in the Renaissance for its horror and pathos (and correspondingly deprecated by more recent taste).

The stage performance of tragedy, however, was edged out after 22 BCE by the 'pantomime', in which a solo dancer performed scenes often taken from tragic subjects, with instrumental music and a chorus. The emphasis on individual episodes, often of a sensational kind, and the versatility and skill required of the dancer, catered to a taste that might also be satisfied by certain aspects of the *Metamorphoses*. The earlier literary mime also flourished under Augustus, and its popular subject-matter of escaping tricksters, the concealment of adulterous lovers, and the like, influenced more elevated forms. Elements of mime may be detected in some of Ovid's *Amores* and in some episodes of the *Fasti*. More generally one might point to an Ovidian interest in widening the scope of literary imitation to include more popular forms within traditionally 'high' literature. There are intriguing similarities between some episodes in the *Metamorphoses* and the surviving prose novels from later antiquity that suggest that Ovid was drawing on the prose fiction of his own time. Such a combination of high literary forms with popular and (real or supposed) 'folk' forms has precedents in Alexandrian literary practice; and within the narrative fiction of the poem Ovid likes to include a number of low-class or naïve narrators.

The links between the *Metamorphoses* and stage performances and dramatic texts are part of a wider tendency to evoke the spectacular and the visual, that makes of the poem an important stage in the development of what in first-century CE literature becomes a dominant aesthetic of theatricality and spectacularity. Once again the aesthetic is closely linked to the political: the emperor expresses his power and communicates with the audience of the Roman people through elaborate displays of pageantry, triumphal and otherwise, through performances in the theatre and amphitheatre, and through great works of architecture, sculpture, and painting. Roman readers cannot have kept their response to literary scenes of physical violence separate from their experience of the real violence staged in the arena. The fascinated gaze directed at the grotesque deaths and wounds suffered in the Battle of Lapiths and Centaurs in book twelve—an episode substituted by Ovid for the narrative of the Trojan War that is expected at this point in the poem—has a strong feel of the amphitheatrical; the half-man, half-beast Centaurs may be read as a phantasmagoric image of the confusion of man and beast in the arena.

The poem works hard to evoke the visual through the verbal, both in descriptions of works of art (ecphrases), such as the Palace of the Sun at the beginning of the second book, or the tapestries of Arachne and Minerva at the beginning of the sixth book, in descriptions of landscape; and, in the ultimate test of the poet's ecphrastic power, in a series of major personifications, detailed visualizations of an abstract idea such as Hunger:

> She found Hunger in a stubborn stony field,
> Grubbing with nails and teeth the scanty weeds,
> Her hair was coarse, her face sallow, her eyes
> Sunken; her lips crusted and white; her throat
> Scaly with scurf. Her parchment skin revealed
> The bowels within; beneath her hollow loins
> Jutted her withered hips; her sagging breasts
> Seemed hardly fastened to her ribs; her stomach
> Only a void; her joints wasted and huge,
> Her knees like balls, her ankles grossly swollen.
> (*Metamorphoses* 8. 799–808, trans. A. D. Melville)

The poem's opening account of cosmogony is modelled in part on Homer's famous description of the Shield of Achilles, depicting the several divisions of the universe. Ovid's demiurge is a figure for the poet himself, the creator of a poetic world of words that is offered to us programmatically as a version of the oldest and most famous ecphrasis of a visual artefact in the Greco-Roman literary tradition.

Ecphrasis more often than not describes something that does not exist; the trick is to create the persuasive illusion of a visual presence. Ovidian narratives of metamorphosis function in the same way. In many instances the process is strongly visualized, often through the eyes of an internal spectator whose surprised experience of the reality of the supernatural event is the model for the effect that the narrator aims at on the external reader. One of the pleasures of the text is its power to convince us of the actuality of events that we know to be impossible. Ovid writes for a sophisticated reader well able to savour the paradoxes involved in the suspension of disbelief on the part of both viewers and readers. Ancient art and literature had long explored the problems of visual illusion and verbal fictionality, but Ovid's extended thematization of these issues is distinctive.

The theme of the illusion of reality in the visual arts comes to a climax in the story of Pygmalion (and it should not be forgotten that the tale is narrated by Orpheus, the archetypal wonder-working poet whose words have a magically direct effect on the world outside):

> Pygmalion, his offering given, prayed
> Before the altar, half afraid, 'Vouchsafe,
> O Gods, if all things you can grant, my bride
> Shall be'—he dared not say my ivory girl –
> 'The living likeness of my ivory girl.'
> And golden Venus (for her presence graced
> Her feast) knew well the purpose of his prayer;
> And, as an omen of her favouring power,
> Thrice did the flame burn bright and leap up high.
> And he went home, home to his heart's delight,
> And kissed her as she lay, and she seemed warm;
> Again he kissed her and with marvelling touch
> Caressed her breast; beneath his touch the flesh
> Grew soft, its ivory hardness vanishing
> And yielded to his hands . . .
>
> . . . .
>
> His heart was torn with wonder and misgiving,
> Delight and terror that it was not true!
> Again and yet again he tried his hopes —
> She was alive! The pulse beat in her veins!
>
> (*Metamorphoses* 10. 273–89, trans. A. D. Melville)

The lifelikeness that the ancients valued so highly in their art is narrativized and transformed into life itself. The challenge taken up by the poet in turn is to persuade the reader of the plausibility of this miracle, to rival the power of a painter like Zeuxis whose painted grapes were said to be so realistic that the birds flew down to peck at them.

In a similar way Ovid's ongoing fascination with the nature and power of textual fictions is inscribed into the fictional narrative of the poem itself. There are many occasions when the reader is delightfully brought to an awareness of the paradoxical simultaneity of assent and disbelief that is involved in reading a text like the *Metamorphoses*. But few are as intense as the moment, significantly at the very heart of the poem, when two internal mythological narrators argue about the truth-value of the stories that they themselves narrate. The river-god Achelous has just told (a *river* telling a story?) a tale of metamorphosis in which he was personally involved:

> The river finished and fell silent. All
> Were moved and marvelled at the miracle.
> Ixion's son, a daredevil who scorned
> The gods, laughed at their gullibility.
> 'Fables!' he said, 'You make the gods too great,
> Good Achelous, if they chop and change
> The shapes of things.' All were aghast; such talk
> They all condemned, Lelex especially,
> Mature in years and mind, and he spoke up.
> 'The power of heaven is great and has no bounds;
> Whatever the gods determine is fulfilled.
> I give you proof. Among the Phrygian hills
> An oak tree and a lime grow side by side. [trees into which the pious
> Baucis and Philemon have been transformed]
>
> (*Metamorphoses* 8. 611–23, trans. A. D. Melville)

The implications even of this passage cannot be confined to an autonomous world of art, for the question of what the gods can or cannot do, and whether indeed they exist, is one that bears on the contemporary reader's experience of the state religion of Rome. As we have seen, the poem's final tale of divinely engineered change is the transformation of the real Roman ruler himself into one of those same gods. Just a poetic fiction? Or is it we moderns who misread Ovid if we assume that ancient religion can be discussed in terms of a simple belief or disbelief in the gods?

The delights of antiquarianism

The murder and apotheosis of Julius Caesar are also briefly narrated in the *Fasti* ('calendar'), a poem in elegiac couplets on the Roman religious calendar, planned in twelve books to cover the twelve months, but of which only the first six survive (or were ever written). The *Fasti* and the *Metamorphoses* were composed during the same period, and are best read as being in constant dialogue with each other, in some sense two parts of the same project, one way of understanding which is as a two-pronged response to the *Aeneid*. But the history of the reception of the *Fasti* has been very different from that of the *Metamorphoses*. The latter has become an almost timeless centrepiece of the Western literary canon, while the *Fasti*, which is indeed a poem about Roman ways of thinking about time, came to seem irrelevant as a work of literature, useful only as a quarry for the historian of Roman religion. Just recently the work's critical fortune has undergone a revolution and the *Fasti* has been restored to a central place in Ovid's poetic output. But this has been achieved only through the careful location of the poem within its contemporary historical and cultural contexts, and it may be true that its readership will be largely confined to a circle of classical scholars or those prepared to acquire a certain baggage of historical background.

Scholarship of a kind is in fact what the Roman reader would have looked for in the *Fasti*. One of the main features shared by the *Fasti* with the *Metamorphoses* is an interest in origins, in aetiology. The *Metamorphoses* narrates the origins of the world itself, of Rome, of Augustus. Metamorphosis is an aetiological device, offering a fantastic account of the origin of a species of animal, a plant, a geographical feature. The *Fasti* deals in antiquarian origins, the historical causes of the various rituals and festivals in the Roman religious calendar. Given the centrality of religion in the Roman view of its past, the poem comes to be a fragmented and partial history of Rome, arranged not according to an annalistic chronology but in the accidental order within the calendar year of the days that commemorate historical events. The appeal of such a poem for an educated Augustan readership is twofold. First, it caters for connoisseurs of Alexandrian poetry; specifically, the *Fasti* is the Roman version of Callimachus' *Aitia*. Secondly, the late Republic had developed a keen antiquarian interest in the recovery of the remote Roman past, both the history of the Roman state and of individual Roman families (obsession with genealogies is not a modern phenomenon), an interest that Augustus had diverted to the legitimization of the new principate through the claim to be restoring the institutions and the values of the Roman past. Ovid draws heavily on the learning of scholars such as Varro and Verrius Flaccus; as in Hellenistic Alexandria there was no sense that scholarship and poetry were quite separate pursuits.

The *Fasti* develop aspects of the *Aeneid*, which might be defined as an aetiological epic, and had been anticipated more closely still in the fourth book of Propertius, whose claim to be the Roman Callimachus, as we have seen, rests on his project of writing a Roman *Aitia*, proclaimed in the first poem and in part realized in the rest of the book. Aetiological poetry is closely related to didactic poetry. A poem on the calendar inevitably deals with the heavenly bodies whose movements define the course of the year, and Ovid at various points signals his dependence on the Hellenistic astronomical didactic poem by Aratos, the *Phainomena* (cf. pp. 247–8). For reasons that are not entirely easy to explain, Aratos' poem enjoyed a long-lasting popularity in Rome, and was frequently translated and adapted in Latin, by among others the young Cicero,

Ovid himself in a lost *Aratea*, and by an imperial prince, the nephew and adoptive son of Tiberius, Germanicus. Ovid naturally hoped to find in him a most receptive audience when, after the death of Augustus, the exiled poet rededicated the *Fasti* to Germanicus in the proem to the first book.

This taste is also exemplified in the astronomical and astrological didactic poem, the *Astronomica*, of Marcus Manilius, written in the last years of Augustus and the early years of Tiberius, and today perhaps the least read of all the major surviving Latin poems of antiquity. Like Aratos, Manilius propounds a Stoic view of the divine order of the universe, and polemicizes against the Epicureanism of Lucretius. The *Astronomica* will have appealed to those educated Romans who found in Stoic physics and theology an outlet for a religious sense, and also to the many Romans (including Augustus and Tiberius) who took astrology seriously.

Like Ovid's other poems, the *Fasti* has become a battleground between those who claim that a Roman audience would have read it as straightforwardly supportive of Augustus' religious and antiquarian programme, and those for whom it would have provoked subversive thoughts, above all through the constant irruption of themes and attitudes associated with Ovid's earlier elegiac works, all of them erotic.

> 'Kindly mother of love, requited or slighted, indulge me.
> She turned her face in this poet's direction.
> 'What do you want with me? Surely you were singing a grander song.
> Have you got that old wound in your sensitive heart?'
> 'You know, goddess,' I replied, 'about the wound.' She smiled,
> and at once that region of the sky was cloudless.
> 'In sickness or in health, have I ever deserted your service?
> You were my only subject, my only work.
> In my early years, as was proper, I dallied innocently;
> now my horses are running on a bigger track.
> The dates—and their origins—dug up in ancient chronicles,
> stars rising and setting—of that I sing.
> I have come to the fourth month, full of honour for you;
> Venus, you know both the poet and the month are yours.'
> Stirred by this, she gently touched my temples with her myrtle
> from Cythera, and said, 'Complete the work you've begun.'
> I felt it, and suddenly the origin of the days was revealed.
>
> (*Fasti* 4. 1–17, trans. B. R. Nagle)

The generic play between different kinds of subject, public and personal, weighty antiquarianism and light eroticism, is clear (complicated here by allusion to the Venus of the proem to Lucretius' didactic poem, on which see pp. 45–6). Once again the reader has to judge whether the elegiac Venus is safely contained within the religious project, or whether love's empire swallows up the world of state religion.

Exile poetry—in search of an audience

'I've come, an exile's book, sent to this city,
   Frightened and tired; kind reader offer me
A calming hand. Don't fear that I may shame you:
   In these sheets no line teaching love you'll see.
My master's fate's not such that he could rightly
   Cloak it, poor soul, in any levity.
That work too, once his green youth's wrong amusement,
   He's learnt too late to censure and to hate.
See what I bring: there's nothing here but sadness,
   Poems that suit their sorry time and state.
If in alternate lines the couplets hobble,
   Blame the long journey or the limping metre.
If I'm not pumice-smooth or cedar-yellow,
   My master's drab; I'd blush if I were neater.
If there are any letters blurred and blotted,
   The *poet's* tears have done the harm you've scanned;
And if some phrase seem perhaps not Latin,
   The place he wrote in was a barbarous land.
Readers, if it's no trouble, tell me where I,
   A book strange to the city, ought to stay
And where to go.'

(*Tristia* 3. 1. 1–20, trans. A. D. Melville)

In 8 CE Ovid was exiled by Augustus to Tomis on the Black Sea coast; he tells us that the charges were a poem, the *Art of Love*, and an 'error'. What the precise nature of the latter was he never says, prompting endless speculation ever since, but it was probably connected with a scandal in the palace, open discussion of which would only have compounded the offence. It is dangerous to use the exile as evidence that Ovid's poetry had been widely perceived as subversive at an earlier date. The *Art of Love*, the work which purports most directly to urge the reader to an elegiac life of 'naughtiness', may have been a convenient pretext to divert attention from an offence which the emperor himself did not wish to air too publicly. Furthermore in his later years Augustus became more suspicious and censorious, so creating a very different climate for the reception of Ovid's way of writing about public and private matters.

In his elegiac epistles from Tomis, the five books of *Tristia* ('sad, gloomy poems') followed by the four books of *Ex Ponto* ('from the Black Sea'), Ovid presents his exile as a complete break with his previous life and literary career. Exile is felt as a kind of death; the post-exilic writings are a communication from the tomb. He complains repeatedly of a loss of poetic power; among the barbarians of the frozen north he is in danger even of forgetting Latin. All too often Ovid has been taken at his word, and the exile poetry written off as the pathetic and tedious whining of a poet starved of the metropolitan oxygen that fuelled his wit. But this is to commit the fallacy of taking too simply at its word the poet's account of his own experience, a mistake that no reader today would make in the case of the supposedly confessional works of the Latin love elegists—and that no skilled reader in the early first century CE is likely to have made in the case of Ovid's exile poetry either. The continuities with the earlier works are as carefully cultivated as the protest at discontinuity, to the point where the reader might be forgiven for feeling that had Ovid never suffered exile it would have been necessary for him to invent it.

The genre of elegy had long been associated with complaint: the complaints of the lover are now replaced by the more urgent complaints of the exile, for whom Rome and Augustus become the objects of desire for the excluded lover. In exile Ovid is condemned to become a further instalment in his own catalogue of tales of metamorphosis, his fortune so utterly transformed that he experiences the loss of identity and even of humanity that is a recurrent focus of psychological interest in the *Metamorphoses*. As always Ovid confuses the boundary between life and literature: the picture of his (real-life) location on the Black Sea is processed through ethnographical conventions for describing barbarian peoples at the end of the world. In the exile poetry the not intolerable climate of the region is turned into the extreme cold of the Scythian north.

Ovid is as powerless as the heroines for whom he had written the *Heroides*, desperate letters doomed to fail in their attempt to persuade their addressees. In the exile poetry Ovid develops to the limit the potential of the epistolary form for exploring both the spatial and temporal gap between writer and addressee, and the uncertainty as to whether the written words will have their intended effect on the reader. As with Horace's *Epistles*, one of Ovid's models, Ovid exploits the tension involved in penning letters to individual addressees that are at the same time intended to be 'public songs' (*Ex Ponto* 5. 1. 23). It is indeed only in these last works Ovid returns to the older practice of addressing poems to individual addressees, and the personalized system of literary patronage takes on an immediacy of purpose for the client-poet that it can rarely ever have had. For there can be little doubt that Ovid did hope that his circle of well-connected friends at Rome might intervene with Augustus, and later Tiberius, to secure his recall.

Under an authoritarian emperor, however, the smooth working of the patron-client system is impaired. The addressees of the *Tristia* (unlike those of the later *Ex Ponto*) are left pointedly unnamed, lest an approach from the disgraced Ovid may involve them too in danger. For the general reader this is of course an additional titillation, for not only is he or she privy to a private correspondence, but has to guess who the addressee is. For the ultimate reader, the emperor himself, there is an implied rebuke: what kind of a society is it where friends dare not address each other by name?

Anonymity is also a potent device in another Ovidian exile poem, the bizarre *Ibis*, a stream of violent but extremely learned abuse, modelled on a lost curse poem by Callimachus, directed at an unnamed enemy of the poet, whose identity inevitably provokes the same kind of curiosity as the unnamed error which led to exile. The *Ibis* is at once Ovid's most outspoken and his least forthcoming poem.

In *Tristia* 3. 1 (quoted above) and in other poems Ovid dramatizes the hesitant approach of his books of exile letters to the general reader in Rome: will his books find any audience, will they be turned away from the public libraries in Rome? Even more anxious is his approach to the emperor himself, the 'god' who has struck him down with a thunderbolt and who alone has the power to restore him to life. Horace's humorous treatment in *Epistles* 1. 13 of how to gain an audience with the emperor has now become a far more serious business altogether. Ovid's exile poems are a suitable point at which to end this chapter; their self-conscious rhetoric of obsession, dissimulation, and suspicion will become a dominant strain in certain types of literature of the first century CE.

14 The path between truculence and servility: Prose literature from Augustus to Hadrian

CHRISTINA S. KRAUS

The power—and danger—of books

The Augustan period is variously dated from 44 BCE—the year of Julius Caesar's assassination and the appearance on the scene of his heir, the 19-year-old Gaius Julius Caesar Octavianus (Octavian), later Augustus—or from 31 BCE, the year in which Octavian defeated Mark Antony and the Egyptian Queen Kleopatra at the Battle of Actium, and after which his rule received no serious challenge (see pp. 359–60). A third possible date is 27 BCE, when Octavian 'restored the Republic' and took the title 'Augustus', with its connotations of *aug*ury and *au*thority. The flexible starting-point appropriately indicates the uncertain, shifting perceptions of the times. It was not clear then, or indeed later, what role Augustus would play: he called himself *princeps*, 'first man', an *ad hoc* title with republican precedent (as in the 'first man of the Senate', the senator with dominant authority) which would, ultimately, become a proper imperial title: 'Prince'. His dominance in Rome lasted until 14 CE, when he died at the age of 76; in that half-century he gradually encroached on many of the powers of the Senate, and devised some new powers of his own. Through a process today often characterized as 'trial and error', or experimentation, Augustus invented a kind of sole rule that was, by and large, acceptable to the majority of Roman citizens, despite their traditional hatred of kings. It preserved the names and forms of most Republican offices and privileges, though replacing their content by revolutionary measures; and, most important, it ended the protracted and bloody struggles that marked the decades of civil war between the late-republican 'strong men'. By the time he died, Augustus' rule was definitively established as a hereditary monarchy (though the emperors were never called *Rex*, 'King'), passed on to his adopted son Tiberius without debate—though not without private objection on the part of those aristocrats who wished a return, however unrealistic, to their republican power. On his deathbed, the former Octavian is said to have asked if he had played his part in the 'mime of life' well, an apt metaphor for one whose life was spent creating and coping with paradox, making radical change look like the preservation of sanctified tradition.

The Empire would survive, in various forms, until the fall of Constantinople in the fifteenth century—though Augustus' own dynasty lasted only until 68 CE, ending with the suicide of his great-great-grandson Nero. This chapter will chart some of the developments in Latin prose literature between (roughly) Actium and the end of the reign of Hadrian (138 CE). Some of the same issues that we saw in republican prose will reappear here, together with some new ones, and some new kinds of literature. Throughout, we can trace a consciousness of decline, a model that until recently was used by literary scholars and historians alike to describe the imperial period: it is silver, not golden, debased, not classical. The trouble with all such schemata, however, be they chemical or biological, is that they oversimplify; in this case, moreover, the schema locates the 'golden' apogee of Latin literature in the principate of Augustus—the very place where ancient literary theorists also located the beginnings of decline. For this is an ancient model as well as a modern one, applied particularly to oratory, as the genre that most fully represented the intersection between literary and public life, between theory and practice. It is also a model that reflects the essential conservatism of Roman audiences: in a culture in which the phrase 'new things' (*res novae*) denoted 'revolution', the past always exerted a powerful pull. In imperial Latin prose, much as in Hellenistic literature, the two poles of tradition and originality vibrate in constant tension. Imperial literature is some of the most inventive, experimental, exciting literature in the ancient Mediterranean world—and yet it is permeated with the sense of its own belatedness (see also pp. 403–4).

Between September 44 and April 43 BCE Cicero delivered a series of fourteen orations against Mark Antony, whom he accused of trying to seize despotic power after Caesar's murder; he called them the *Philippics*, a deliberate reference to the orations with which Demosthenes tried to rally the Athenians against their future conqueror, Philip of Macedon. The speeches were landmarks, in more ways than one. First, they led directly to Cicero's execution on Antony's orders, on 7 December 43:

> Marcus Cicero had left the city at the approach of the triumvirs [Antony, Octavian, and Lepidus], rightly regarding it as certain that he could no more be rescued from Antony than Cassius and Brutus from Caesar. . . . He put out to sea several times, but sometimes the winds were against him and forced him back, sometimes he himself could not endure the tossing of the vessel. . . . Finally he grew weary of flight and of life, and returning to the inland villa . . . said, 'I shall die in the country I so often saved.' There is no

> doubt that his slaves bravely and loyally showed readiness to make a fight of it; and that it was Cicero himself who ordered them to put down the litter and suffer calmly the compulsions of a harsh fate. He leaned from where he sat and offered his neck without a tremor; his head was struck off. . . . The soldiers . . . cut off the hands, too, cursing them for having written attacks on Antony. The head was taken back to Antony, and, on his orders, placed between the two hands on the rostra [the speakers' platform in the Forum] where as consul, and often as ex-consul, and in that very year attacking Antony he had been heard amid such admiration for his eloquence as had rewarded no other human voice. The Romans could scarcely bear to lift eyes wet with tears to look on his mutilated body. (Livy, fragment from book 120 = Seneca the Elder, *Suasoria* 6. 17, trans. M. Winterbottom)

There is a layering of audiences in this extraordinary account: an unspecified one—posterity?—to whom Cicero directs his (alleged) last words; the slaves; the soldiers; the Roman audience in the Forum, whose opinion of Cicero is quoted as defining his importance; and the reader, both contemporary (who might well remember Cicero) and modern. Most importantly, however, there is Mark Antony. This is an early example of something that would soon become more common, that is, a political execution resulting from the publication (in Latin, *editio*, 'giving forth', either orally or in writing) of a work of literature. No more direct connection between author and audience can be imagined; no more eloquent testimony to the power, and danger, of books.

From this point on, even if authors remained unmolested, their books could be burned, a punishment that was particularly Roman. Cicero, at least, lived on through his books. Not so everyone, even under the comparatively tolerant Augustus:

> It was for Labienus that there was first devised a new punishment: his enemies saw to it that all his books were burnt. It was an unheard of novelty that punishment should be exacted from literature. Certainly it was to everyone's advantage that this cruelty that turns on genius was devised later than the time of Cicero: for what would have happened if the triumvirs had been pleased to proscribe Cicero's talent as well as Cicero? . . . How great is the savagery that puts a match to literature, and wreaks its vengeance on monuments of learning; how unsatisfied with its other victims! Thank god that these punishments for genius began in an age when genius had come to an end! (Seneca the Elder, *Controversies* 10 Preface 5–7, trans. M. Winterbottom)

(Paradoxically, it was the mad tyrant Caligula who saw to it that copies of Labienus' works were returned to the libraries.) This excerpt from Seneca's memoirs of the Augustan practitioners of declamation shows many typical features of the Latin of imperial Rome: a desire to shock the audience; the use of emotive devices like rhetorical questions and exclamations to draw readers in. Then there is the striving for novelty of expression and content, both pernicious and perniciously attractive; and above all, a love of paradox: genius is punished only after genius has perished. In that is summed up the feeling of the post-Augustan age: 'after the Battle of Actium,' Tacitus would write (of historians) some eighty years later, 'that literary genius fell idle.' Lucius Annaeus Seneca, known as Seneca the Elder, an orator and scholar of oratory, is here writing under the Emperor Tiberius, Augustus' immediate successor. For him, Cicero marked the end of oratorical genius. What is it about the Augustan period that so definitively spoke to Seneca of immediate and irretrievable decline?

The answer lies in the second respect in which Cicero's *Philippics* represent a landmark in the history of ancient oratory. They were the last time a political orator spoke so publicly, and so freely, on a matter of state importance: they are, in short, the last example of truly outspoken republican oratory. As the emperors arrogated more and more power and responsibility to themselves, so the Senate's sphere of influence contracted; increasingly, political matters and even trials were decided in the emperor's private council, with advocates and prosecutors speaking directly to him, not to an audience of their peers or to a large jury. Though senatorial debates continued, their content, according to Tacitus, was a sham: speakers would try to anticipate the emperor's wishes, even if he were not present, and all argument took on an extra dimension of self-consciousness. How would the emperor react? What motives would he attribute to the speaker? Should the senators indulge in flattery or freedom of speech—a specious demonstration, says Tacitus, since it was never really free:

> I would hardly mention this year's adjournment if it were not worth noting the differing opinions of Gaius Asinius Gallus and Gnaeus Calpurnius Piso regarding it. Although the emperor had said he would be away, Piso opined that this was an additional reason for business to continue, as it was in the public interest that the Senate and knights could undertake their proper duties in the *princeps'* absence. Gallus, since Piso had anticipated him in the display of freedom, said that nothing had enough distinction or was compatible with the national dignity unless it happened in the presence and under the eye of the emperor. . . . Tiberius listened in silence as the matter was hotly debated—but the adjournment was carried. (Tacitus, *Annals* 2. 35)

> So tainted were these times, so meanly obsequious, that not only did the leading men of the state have to protect their positions by subservience . . .

> but all ex-consuls, most ex-praetors, even many ordinary senators vied to propose the most repulsive and excessive motions. There is a story that whenever he left the Senate House Tiberius used to exclaim in Greek, 'Men fit for slavery!' Even he, who opposed public freedom, clearly was tired of such grovelling endurance in his slaves. (*Annals* 3. 65)

There was still room for free senatorial action on matters less close to home, especially concerning embassies from the provinces bringing petitions for citizenship, or asking to be allowed to dedicate temples to members of the imperial family, or claiming possession of ancient religious sites. Tacitus in his *Annals* devotes what may seem an inordinate amount of space to these debates, partly because some of the emperors were themselves interested in such matters, but partly because in them at least the Senate had relatively free rein.

Some civil and criminal cases were still held in public, though no longer outside in the Forum. Pliny (see pp. 457–8 below) describes a particularly lurid one:

> Attia Viriola was a woman of high birth, the wife of a praetorian senator, disinherited by her eighty-year-old father ten days after he had fallen in love and brought home a stepmother for his daughter, and now suing for her patrimony. . . . One hundred and eighty judges were sitting . . . both parties were fully represented and had a large number of seats filled with their supporters, and a close-packed ring [*corona*] of onlookers, several rows deep, lined the walls of the courtroom. The bench was also crowded, and even the galleries were full of men and women leaning over in their eagerness to see and also to hear, though hearing was rather more difficult. Fathers, daughters and stepmothers all anxiously awaited the verdict. (Pliny, *Letters* 6. 33. 2–4, trans. B. Radice)

The audience's engagement here is personal: the outcome of this trial may have an impact on their own families. Often, however, the crowd of spectators consisted of hired claques, brought in to distract the speakers and cause a disturbance:

> Audiences follow who are no better than the speakers, being hired and bought for the occasion. They parley with the contractor, take the gifts offered on the floor of the court as openly as they would at a dinner-party, and move on from case to case for the same sort of pay. The Greek name for them means 'bravo-callers' and the Latin 'dinner-clappers'; wittily enough, but both names expose a scandal which increases daily. Yesterday two of my attendants . . . were induced to add their applause for three *denarii* each. That is all it costs you to have your eloquence acclaimed. (Pliny, *Letters* 2. 14. 4–6, trans. B. Radice)

A similar technique was occasionally used towards the end of the Republic, and simple intimidation—or so the story goes—worked effectively to silence Cicero in the trial of Milo. Also under the Republic, orators had to contend with interruptions from unexpected sources, such as the noise from a passing funeral procession. Under the Empire, however, there is a pervasive sense that affairs are being stage-managed. Oratory becomes a spectacle, indeed a spectator sport, choreographed long in advance, even to the point of providing cue cards for the audience: 'for this sum seats can be filled, any number of them, a huge crowd assembled, and endless cheering raised whenever the chorus-master gives the signal. (A signal there must be for people who neither understand nor even hear; most of them do not listen but cheer as loud as anyone.)' (Pliny, *Letters* 2. 14. 6–8, trans. Radice.)

Another way in which formal oratory diverged from republican forms was through its increasing transformation into panegyric (praise oratory). This certainly existed under the Republic (Cicero's speech of 66 BCE, *For the Manilian Law*, is a thinly disguised panegyric of Pompey the Great), but the genre became formalized under the Empire. Pliny the Younger delivered our only completely extant example from the early Empire, the *Panegyric to Trajan* of 100 CE; more examples exist from the fourth century onward (see pp. 539–41). The written text that Pliny published is an expanded version which he first delivered to a circle of friends in three sessions of about two hours each. The expansion may have been due to Pliny's desire to speak at greater length than the Senate session allowed; but the resulting double audience also reflects the same kind of self-consciousness that we have seen above in Tacitus' accounts of the Senate. Though Pliny retains the second-person singular address, Trajan will not have heard the longer piece; nevertheless, it shows the loyal Pliny to best advantage, as well as demonstrating his rhetorical skills:

> As for the lives and characters of the young—how you are forming them in true princely fashion! And the teachers of rhetoric and professors of philosophy—how you hold them in honour! Under you the liberal arts are restored, to breathe and live in their own country—the learning which the barbarity of the past punished with exile, when an emperor acquainted with all the vices sought to banish everything hostile to vice, motivated less by hatred of learning than by fear of its authority. But you embrace these very arts, opening arms, eyes and ears to them, a living example of their precepts, as much their lover as the subject of their regard. Every lover of culture must applaud all your actions, while reserving his highest praise for your readiness to give audiences. Your father had shown his magnanimity by giving the title of 'open house' to what . . . had been a stronghold of tyranny—yet this would have been an empty formula had he not

adopted a son capable of living in the public eye. (*Panegyric* 47. 1–5, trans. B. Radice)

A little of this does go a long way! It is worth noticing, however, the intimate connection that Pliny draws between the moral character of the young, the liberal arts, and the emperor's willingness to open his palace, indeed his own character, to inspection. Learning has authority, and particularly authority both to expose vice (hence the tyrant's fear of it) and to guide human actions. Underlying Trajan's openness is the same accord that Cicero perceived between Cato the Elder's words and his actions: a perfect match, fostered by a love of the precepts found in literature, between a man's inner thoughts and outer actions. Such a vision of the Empire contrasts sharply with the (contemporary) Tacitean picture of the flattering servility shown by the Senate to their emperor; instead, it offers a positive formulation made by a senator trying to live in a system that could turn randomly violent. Words *are* dangerous, and the emperor as audience is especially so. In praising Trajan, Pliny chooses to highlight an ideal situation, in which author and audience live in reciprocal harmony.

Pliny delivered the original, shorter version of this speech in the Senate during the two months that he was consul. Similarly, during his consular months in 97 CE Tacitus famously delivered an eloquent eulogy of a distinguished ex-consul, Verginius Rufus. For comparison, reckon that during his consular year Cicero delivered four orations against the revolutionary Catiline; a speech in defence of the consul-elect on a charge of electoral corruption; three speeches against an agrarian law designed to distribute land to the plebs; and several others, a collection of orations of which he claims to have published twelve and of which we still have nine. Though Cicero maintained that oratory truly flourishes under a peaceful state, it would seem that the diagnosis in the *Dialogue on Orators*—whether serious or not about the 'one wisest man'—comes closer to the truth:

> Great and famous oratory is the protégé of licence, which fools call freedom, an associate of revolution, a spur for an unbridled populace. It has no obedience, no self-restraint; it is defiant, thoughtless, overbearing; it does not arise in well-regulated communities. . . . So long as the state was unsettled, so long as it destroyed itself with factions and dissensions and discord, so long as there was no peace in the Forum, no concord in the Senate, no control in the courts, no respect for great men, no restraint in the magistrates, Rome certainly grew sturdier eloquence, just as untilled fields produce more luxuriant vegetation. . . . [But] what need is there for long arguments in the Senate when the best men agree so quickly? What is the use of many public harangues [*contiones*], when the ignorant multitude

does not decide political issues, but one man, and he the wisest? (Tacitus, *Dialogue on Orators* 40. 2–41)

Declamation and the layering of meaning

Where, then, did all the Roman oratorical/rhetorical energy go? One phenomenon of the Augustan period, due partly to an increased interest in all types of scholarship (see below), partly to the diminished use for practical oratory, was a development of rhetorical theory. As with many trends, this began earlier: the *Rhetoric to Herennius*, once ascribed to Cicero, is a treatise on speaking written in the 80s BCE; and Cicero himself wrote rhetorical handbooks, some very technical (e.g. *On Invention* or *The Divisions of a Speech*), some more wide-ranging (*Brutus*, a history of Roman oratory, or the *Orator* on the best kind of public speaker and oratorical style). Still, with the beginning of the Empire came a flowering of such theoretical studies, culminating around 96 CE in the great *Education of an Orator* by Quintilian (Marcus Fabius Quintilianus), which contains not only practical and theoretical precepts but also hundreds of anecdotes about and quotations from earlier oratory. One of the methods by which a young man could learn to be a good speaker was by imitating established orators, using them as living examples; another way was by practising himself, learning to speak on any side of any topic—in short, to do exercises like those delivered by Karneades to the shocked Senate over a century earlier (see p. 311). The technique derived from Greek education, and dates back at least to the Sophists in the fifth century BCE (see pp. 145–7, 192–4). In the Augustan period and for centuries after, well into the Byzantine Empire, it became a means not so much of training as of display, a literary amusement for the educated classes, and a way of thinking that permeated literature at all levels, prose and poetry, from tragedy to epic, history to letters.

There were two basic kinds of specimen speeches or declamations: the *controversia* and the *suasoria*. In the former, an orator spoke for one or the other side of an imaginary court case. The topics, which are preserved for us in the Elder Seneca's memoirs of the Augustan declaimers and in two later collections of declamations attributed to Quintilian, range from the melodramatic to the downright fabulous:

> A woman condemned for unchastity appealed to the goddess Vesta before being thrown from the Tarpeian rock. She was thrown down, and survived. She is sought to pay the penalty again.

> A man killed one of his brothers, a tyrant. The other brother he caught in adultery and killed despite the pleas of his father. Captured by pirates, he

PAYING FOR CONCORD. The great temple to 'Harmony' (Concordia) was dedicated by the future Emperor Tiberius in 10 CE. It is quite accurately reflected on this coin issued by Tiberius in 36 CE.

> wrote to his father about a ransom. The father wrote to the pirates, saying that he would give double if they cut off his hands. The pirates let him go. The father is in need; the son is not supporting him.
>
> While a certain city was at war, a hero lost his weapons in battle, and removed the arms from the tomb of a dead hero. He fought heroically, then put the weapons back. He got his reward, and is accused of violating the tomb. (Seneca the Elder, *Controversiae* 1. 3, 1. 7, 4. 4, trans. M. Winterbottom)

The *suasoriae*, or 'persuasions', are designed to develop skills at extended argument, typically inviting an orator to deliberate on a course of action. The topics, again, are somewhat removed from reality. Should Alexander the Great sail the Ocean? Imagine that Antony promised to spare Cicero's life if he agreed to burn his books—what should he do? Even mythical characters speak, as in this extract in which Agamemnon deliberates whether to sacrifice his daughter in order to calm the storm that is holding back the Trojan expedition:

> God poured forth the waters of the sea on the express understanding that not every day should go as we hope. And it is not only the sea that is thus limited: look at the sky—are not the stars subject to this same condition? Sometimes they deny their rain and burn up the soil, and when the wretched farmers collect up the seed, it is burnt. . . . Sometimes the clear skies are hidden, every day weighs down the firmament with cloud. . . . Perhaps this is the law of nature; perhaps, as the story goes, the regulating factor is the course of the moon. . . . Whatever the case, it was not on the orders of a god that the sea held no perils for the adulterer [Paris, who carried off Helen of Troy]. . . . I was pursuing him so as not to have to fear

> for the virginity of my daughter [i.e. and now I have to fear for her life instead]. When Troy is conquered, I shall spare the daughters of the enemy. —*Priam's* maiden daughter as yet has nothing to fear. (Seneca the Elder, *Suasoria* 3. 1, trans. M. Winterbottom)

Seneca's excerpts stress the epigrammatic and the *outré*; moreover, he gives no complete text, only pieces of the argument. Still, it is possible to see the fundamental lack of emotion in this rhetoric, even when, as here, the speaker takes on the role of the anguished protagonist. And emotion, especially emotion projected by the orator's own (often simulated) feelings, was what Cicero had chiefly relied on as a persuasive force. If you can rouse the audience's indignation, anger, fear, or pity, you can make them believe what you want them to. Here, in the hands of the famous declaimer Arellius Fuscus (one of Ovid's teachers), Agamemnon makes a laboured point about the fact that the gods are not immediately responsible for the storm that failed to impede Paris and Helen, nor (presumably) for the one that is keeping the Greek ships from giving chase. He then moves to a paradox involving his own and the enemy's virgin daughters: his (Iphigenia) is due to be sacrificed to the angry gods, but he will spare (or so he claims) Priam's. Like the other declaimers, Fuscus speaks at one remove from 'genuine' emotion, and in so doing shows what one might call a postmodern approach to oratory, an exploration of form at the expense of content, or, in one critic's words, of 'the primacy of language over spectacle'.

Declamation was a phenomenally popular activity among poets, prose writers, senators, and the leisured class in general. Even the emperors declaimed, and listened to declamation. And it happened not only in Latin: glamorous Greek sophists and rhetors declaimed throughout the first and second centuries CE to packed audiences (see pp. 265–70). It was a competitive genre, each speaker trying to outdo the next in novelty, paradox, and compression of language and argument. Despite its popularity, however, it is still essentially literature for the inner circle, for those educated men whose energies would, under the Republic, have been directed elsewhere. And as such, it could sometimes be used, albeit obliquely, for very relevant political purposes. Like other scholarship it could even be, the imperial scholar Suetonius tells us, a vehicle for topical debate, with its continued popularity guaranteed by its prestige and by the nobility of those who practised it:

> Gradually, rhetoric itself also came to be regarded as useful and honourable, and many people cultivated it for the sake of both protection and prestige: Cicero continued the practice of Greek declamation all the way down to his praetorship, whereas in Latin he declaimed when already elderly . . . certain historians report that on the very eve of the civil war Gnaeus Pompeius resumed the habit of declamation, the better to rebut

> the very articulate young Gaius Curio, who was supporting Caesar's claims, and that even during the war at Mutina both Marcus Antonius and Augustus maintained the habit; Nero Caesar gave a declamation in public during his first year as emperor, and had done so twice before. Furthermore, a large number of orators also published declamations. Accordingly, when people had been filled with a great enthusiasm for the discipline, there also arose a great flood of professors and teachers, who enjoyed such favour that some were able to rise from the meanest circumstances to reach the senatorial order and the highest offices of state. (Suetonius, *On Teachers of Grammar and Rhetoric* 25. 3, trans. R. Kaster)

Later, when the freedom of debate enjoyed by Pompey and Curio was no more, declaimers might use topics such as the popular *controversiae* about tyrannicide covertly to advocate the elimination of the emperors and a return to the Republic (see p. 469). Such criticism could be risky, not least because its effect depended entirely on the sensitivity of the audience. Cicero's *Philippics* were directly and undeniably hostile to Antony, and the orator paid the penalty for his freedom. Speaking in figurative language against an emperor, however, was an especially dangerous game, in which one had to bet either that the emperor was a worse 'reader' than the rest of the audience or that he would be unwilling to show himself insulted by a piece of rhetorical display. Seneca has an early example of a risky declamatory argument, from a case which involved adopting the son of a prostitute:

> Latro was declaiming . . . in the presence of Augustus and Marcus Agrippa, whose sons—the emperor's grandsons [by his daughter Julia, later exiled for adultery]—the emperor seemed to be proposing to adopt at that time. Agrippa was one of those who were made noble, not born noble. Taking the part of the prostitute's son . . . Latro said, 'Now he is by adoption being raised from the depths and grafted on to the nobility'—and more to this effect. Maecenas signed to Latro that the emperor was in a hurry and he should finish the declamation off now. . . . The blessed Augustus, I feel, deserves admiration if such licence was permitted in his reign; but I cannot feel any sympathy for those who think it worth losing their head rather than lose a jest. (Seneca the Elder, *Controversia* 2. 4. 12–13, trans. M. Winterbottom)

Roman audiences were used to reading one character 'through' another—seeing Hektor and Achilles in Virgil's Aeneas, for example—so such layered effects would not be lost on them. Drama was traditionally the place for such covert criticism (see pp. 299–301); during the late Republic, for instance, a line from a tragedy had to be repeatedly encored, as the crowd cheered the playwright's 'judgement' against Pompey: 'To our misery are you great [or 'the

Great']!' Such play continued under the Empire, as when an Augustan audience turned a line about a eunuch priest into a slur on the emperor by clapping loudly and pointedly: 'Do you see how that pervert controls the globe with a finger?' (Suetonius, *Life of the Deified Augustus* 68).

Such large-scale public misreading would be difficult to punish, given that the Roman people did not (much to Caligula's regret) have a single neck. But more pervasively pointed drama may have gone underground. Heavily rhetorical, owing both shape and content to the influence of declamation, are a series of tragedies on Greek mythological themes by Lucius Annaeus Seneca, called Seneca the Younger, son of the orator and declaimer. He was not only one of the richest men of his day, but a prominent Stoic philosopher and tutor to the young Emperor Nero. His plays, which date from the 40s and 50s CE, are meditations on anger, lust, greed, and other typically monarchical characteristics. Seneca's work shows the same fascination with shock value, epigrammatic paradox, and novelty as his father's collection of declamatory titbits. And like some declamations, Senecan tragedy often cut close to the bone, its legendary characters revelling in the same sort of bloody megalomania as the all-too-real Roman emperors. Here is the Greek tyrant Atreus, after murdering his brother's children and feeding them to their unhappy parent:

> I walk equal to the stars and above all men,
> Touching with my proud head heaven's height.
> Now I hold the glory of the kingdom,
> Now my father's throne. I release the gods:
> I have reached the utmost of my desires.
> Well done, and more than well—now it is enough even for me.
> But why should it be enough? I will go on,
> And fill this father with his dead children.
> Lest shame deter me, daylight has departed.
> Would that I could hold back the fleeing gods, drag them back by force
> So that they all might see my vengeful feast!
> But the father shall see it—that is enough.
> . . . .
> Crowds of slaves, open the doors, let the festal hall lie open.
> It pleases me to see his face change colour
> When he looks on his children's heads—
> To hear the words his pain first pours out,
> To see his body stiffening, stupefied,
> His breath gone. This is to be the reward
> For all my trouble—to see him not only miserable,
> But to watch the misery as it comes upon him.
>
> [Seneca, *Thyestes* 885–95, 901–7]

We do not know if these Senecan plays were ever performed, even as recitations. But in the *Dialogue on Orators* Tacitus' fictional character Maternus is imagined as having just recited his own *Cato*—based on the life of Cato the Younger, Julius Caesar's most heroized opponent. Maternus' friends fear that his writing might be too easily 'misunderstood'—but the playwright knows exactly what he is risking, and plans to go on to a *Thyestes* which will say whatever the *Cato* left unsaid (see pp. 468–70).

The dramatic date of the *Dialogue* is 75 CE, during the reign of Vespasian, the only emperor who, according to Tacitus, changed for the better. But it was written by a man who had lived through the tyranny of Vespasian's son Domitian, whose reign—like Nero's—quickly degenerated into a terror of executions, paranoia, and covert opposition. That experience, generalized to all emperors, resonates in the apprehension felt by Maternus' friends. Despite the danger, however, both the fictional Maternus and the real Seneca show a certain glee in their work, a delight in manipulating declamatory themes, in using their audience's familiarity with the rules of literary genres to push the boundaries out a little further each time—in short, to use all their imagination and energy in the continued creation of a literature that in spite of its apparent aridity could be an exciting, intellectually challenging game.

The glamour of libraries and recital halls

One of the major changes from the Republic to the Empire was the increased visibility and prestige accorded to scholarship. Our impression of this is partly due to our concentration on the person of the emperors, who possessed not only power but star quality, and who, like the Sicilian and Hellenistic monarchs before them, well understood the importance of creating a climate in which literature and intellectual study could be seen to flourish, demonstrating the nurturing, sophisticated, and enriching atmosphere of the regime. Literature could also, not incidentally, directly celebrate the achievements of the ruler, while the study of and commentary on earlier poetry, together with research into historical or cultural topics, had potential political use as well: the way literature is interpreted, after all, can provide a powerful key to manipulating opinion. Many of the Roman emperors in the period under discussion had serious literary or scholarly interests of their own: Augustus wrote at least one tragedy (though not, according to him, a very good one) and was fond of culling literature for exemplary stories to send to his friends; Tiberius studied philosophy and rhetoric on Rhodes and maintained a lifelong passion for legal and grammatical study; Claudius wrote histories of Rome, Etruria, and Carthage, plus an autobiography, and added three letters to the Latin alphabet; Nero composed all kinds of poetry, sang, and patronized many different arts before turning tyrant; Hadrian was a practising architect, wrote poetry, and debated. And though the Flavians, Nerva, and Trajan were not themselves as artistically inclined, they recognized the importance of intellectual endeavour to the emperor's image. Though scholarship at Rome began long before Augustus, it is under his rule that the prestige of teachers and grammarians began to increase, and a whole imperial industry in antiquarian research grew up around his projects to restore the dilapidated temples and revive the traditional laws and festivals of republican Rome (see pp. 324–7).

The emperor tended to look out towards the larger populace, avoiding the close, inner focus of the aristocratic republican Senate. Hence, perhaps, the move, also beginning with Augustus, from private to public libraries, as emperors took more and more control over the public dissemination of literature (see pp. 258–9). Books had always travelled, whether as booty or by special request (so Cicero, for instance, would order books from Athens from his friend Atticus). Private citizens certainly still owned books, and some of them had impressive collections; to house such collections the Augustan architect Vitruvius advises on the ideal orientation for a private library. But books could also be a symbol of prestige, as for the 'many ignorant men' who, according to Seneca the Younger, buy books 'not as instruments of learning but as decorations for their dining rooms'; or for the freedmen parodied by the Neronian novelist Petronius (see pp. 502–4), whose Trimalchio piques himself on his learning:

> Tell me, Agamemnon my dearest friend; have you any recollection of the twelve labours of Hercules, or the story of how Ulysses had his thumb twisted off by the Cyclops with his pincers? I used to read these stories in Homer when I was a boy. . . . But in case you think I am an ignoramus, I'm perfectly aware how Corinthian bronze originated. At the capture of Troy, that rascally slimy lizard Hannibal piled all the statues of bronze, gold, and silver on a pyre, and set fire to them; all the various elements merged into an alloy of bronze. . . . I have something like a hundred three-gallon bumpers . . . with the motif of Cassandra killing her sons . . . and a bowl which King Minos bequeathed to my patron; on it Daedalus is enclosing Niobe in the Trojan horse. (Petronius, *Satyricon* 48, 50, 52, trans. P. G. Walsh)

The imperial libraries, in particular, will have fostered this association of books and prestige, together with a rivalry between Greek and Latin that was itself fuelled by the literary critics' comparisons of authors in the two languages, the most famous being found in book 10 of Quintilian's *Education of an Orator*. So Cicero is the Roman Demosthenes, Sallust the Roman Thoukydides, Livy the Roman Herodotos. The first public library in Rome, sponsored by Julius Caesar, was to be assembled by the great scholar Varro, though he never completed the task. Gaius Asinius Pollio, the anti-Caesarian historian and tragedian, founded one in the 30s, pointedly located in the 'Hall of Liberty'. This was quickly overshadowed by Augustus' two libraries, one adjoining the temple of Palatine Apollo and presided over by the learned freedman Hyginus, the other near the Theatre of Marcellus; they were later joined by buildings by Tiberius, Vespasian, Trajan, Caracalla, and Diocletian. The aim of these collections was not only cultural equality with the Greeks, but also literary immortality: even as genres such as history and epic could ensure the immortality of their subjects (not least the Roman people), so any work of literature made its author live on. All you needed was a place in a library niche—though not all papyrus rolls were so lucky, as one of Ovid's banned books of exile poetry tells us:

> Here were the works of learned men, both ancient
> And new, open to every reader's eye.
> I sought my brother books . . .
> I searched in vain; the library's custodian
> Commanded me to leave his holy shrine.
> I sought another temple, near the Theatre;
> This too might not be trod by feet of mine.
> And Liberty's halls, too, the first thrown open
> To learned books, refused me access there.
> My author's fate redounds upon his offspring:
> The exile he has borne, from birth we bear.
> Perhaps, one day, to us and him great Caesar,
> By long years vanquished, will be less severe. . . .
> Meanwhile since I'm debarred a shelf in public,
> Let me lie hidden in a private place.
> You too, the people, if you may, receive my
> Rejected verse, dismayed by its disgrace.
> (Ovid, *Tristia* 3. 1. 65–82, trans. A. D. Melville)

The picture of Apollo as stern librarian is a comic one, but the situation is far from humorous; it shows, moreover, how much control an emperor might be thought to have even over (theoretically) public collections. Ovid's poetry has to hope for private circulation among 'the people'—presumably his friends. The emperor's control could be absolute: when Caligula allowed Labienus'

READING MATERIALS. This wall-painting from Pompeii shows an ink-pot and pen, a half-unwound papyrus roll (with title-tag), and an open set of wax tablets with stylus for inscribing temporary contents on them

vitriolic prose to circulate again, he did so for political point, despising as he did the classics of Greek and Latin literature:

> He allowed the writings of Titus Labienus, Cremutius Cordus, and Cassius Severus [Labienus' prosecutor] to be chased down, circulated, and read, though they had been suppressed by senatorial decrees, it being entirely in his own interest that all events be handed down to posterity. . . . He even considered suppressing the Homeric epics, asking why he should not have the same power as Plato, who expelled Homer from his ideal state. And he came close to removing the writings and the portraits of Virgil and Livy from all the libraries, railing at the one as having no talent and very little learning, and at the other as a wordy and careless historian. . . . He regarded smooth, well-groomed style with such disdain that he used to say that Seneca, who was very popular at the time, composed 'mere school exercises' and that he was 'sand without lime'. (Suetonius, *Life of Caligula*, 16, 34, 53)

Labienus, Cremutius, and Cassius had the merit of sophisticated rarity (and, of course, of having been banned by Caligula's imperial predecessors); the judgements on Virgil and Livy show Caligula exploiting the public library system to thumb his nose at the conservative reading public and the snobbish, literary élite.

With the decline of political oratory, when not declaiming (above), that élite had to find something else to do. Throughout the period under discussion, but especially in the second half of it, from the Emperor Claudius (reigned 41–54 CE) through to Hadrian (117–38), they practised scholarship and literary dalliance in almost equal parts. Some, like Julius Caesar before them—who could keep four secretaries busy at once and who is said to have written his *On Grammatical Analogy* 'while the javelins were flying about him'—lost no chance to pursue scholarship, reading, and taking notes at table, while riding, even at the baths.

Gaius Plinius Secundus, known as Pliny the Elder, who died in the eruption of Mount Vesuvius in 79 CE, is the most famous example of this type. He wrote many works, including a treatise on using a throwing-spear, a biography of his patron G. Pomponius Secundus, a history of the German wars, a collection of pointed remarks for use in declamation, a history of the Roman Empire under the Julio-Claudians, and—the only one to survive—a *Natural History* in thirty-seven books, containing (according to its preface) 20,000 facts from 2,000 written sources. It was, among other things, an 'inventory of the world', an attempt to preserve the wonders of nature and of human achievement: along with his readers, Pliny himself is an astonished spectator of this collection of marvels, biological facts, historical information, architectural details, recipes, charms, measurements, etc. He is conscious of the potential aridity of his subject; yet he advertises it to the future Emperor Titus, its dedicatee, as a service to mankind:

> My subject is a barren one: the nature of things, that is, life; and life in its least elevated aspect. . . . Moreover, my way lies not along a road well trodden by scholars, nor one in which the mind seeks eagerly to travel; no one among us has made the same attempt. . . . It is hard to give novelty to what is old, authority to what is new, shine to the dingy, light to the obscure, attraction to what is scorned, credibility to the dubious. . . . Even if I have not succeeded, it is fully honourable and glorious to have tried. And indeed I feel that there is a special place in scholarship for those who, having overcome their difficulties, prefer the useful service of helping others to the popularity of pleasing them. (Pliny the Elder, *Natural History*, Preface 13–16)

By showing his awareness of the desirability of novelty and polish in a work of literature Pliny uses the conventional ploy of authorial modesty, one familiar from oratory, as for instance from the beginning of the *Milo* (above, p. 318), in which Cicero plays down his own courage. Obviously, the reader is to understand that this book *will* be novel, polished, interesting—and on top of that, *useful*, a quintessential old-fashioned Roman virtue. For Pliny the Elder was nothing if not old-fashioned, at least in the persona he chose to present in the

Natural History. Like the Elder Cato, Sallust, and other moralists, he attacks luxury and conspicuous consumption, arguing for the force of traditional Roman values even in the face of the astounding diversity and threatening bulk of the Empire, which now encompassed the known world. As we saw of prose under the late Republic, such conservatism can be a weapon designed to bolster social and cultural structures that are perceived to be at risk. Unfortunately, Pliny's opening bluff has not succeeded in distracting modern readers from the ponderousness of his book, which since the Renaissance was little read or even consulted, until recently, when it is receiving some attention. Older audiences were less critical: until the fifteenth century the encyclopaedia was an extremely influential work.

Fifty years after Pliny, Gaius Suetonius Tranquillus, one of Hadrian's senior secretaries, exploited his access to the imperial archives to write biographies of a dozen Caesars and brief lives of literary figures, as well as treatises on Greek and Roman games and festivals, weather signs, the names of winds, the Roman calendar, and many others. The breadth of his learning and interests recalls that of Varro (see pp. 321, 322–5), though in some ways he was even more of a professional scholar than his republican precursor, probably gaining his imperial post as director of libraries (*a bibliothecis*) at least partly as a recognition for his literary achievements.

Other imperial officials who wrote technical treatises in the first century include Sextus Julius Frontinus, the Flavian overseer of the water supply who produced a treatise on how to do his job, perhaps directed at future curators of aqueducts. Some compiled manuals both in Greek and in Latin on military strategy and generalship, continuing the process of which Cicero had complained a century earlier, of teaching young men how to fight out of books. One of these, also by Frontinus, is a collection of famous stratagems employed by famous generals, culled from ancient histories and presented in list form as a source of examples to imitate. Similar is the collection of moral examples by Valerius Maximus, written during the reign of Tiberius and perhaps designed as a source book for declaimers, perhaps as a sort of reference book for would-be gentlemen, a rising class of entrepreneurs and *arrivistes* who needed quick exemplary history to provide a sort of 'instant ancestry'. Finally, Pliny's near-contemporaries Aulus Cornelius Celsus and the wealthy landowner Lucius Junius Moderatus Columella—authors respectively of an encyclopaedia of knowledge (of which only the book on medicine survives) and a twelve-book treatise on agriculture—wrote a stylish, up-to-date Latin. Columella even incorporated a book of verse on gardens in explicit imitation of Virgil's *Georgics* (see pp. 471–5).

Like the Elder Pliny, the Neronian philosopher and politician Seneca the Younger had an active public career, though interrupted by a period of exile and ended by one of voluntary retirement; unlike Pliny, however, he was anything but old-fashioned. He, too, wrote an encyclopaedia, three books of *Natural Questions*, a sort of Stoic philosophy of nature which in style was fully modern. He also wrote a bitingly funny satire of the Emperor Claudius—well after his death!—called the *Pumpkinification* (the Latin title, *Apocolocyntosis*, parodies the Greek *apotheosis*, or 'divinification'). Apart from his tragedies (discussed above), he is best known for his ethical philosophy, a collection of ten dialogues on themes such as *Anger*, *The Tranquil Spirit*, and *Providence*. Seneca has a fine sense of humour, a cutting wit, and a good eye for a self-deflating anecdote. Here is the scholar on the vanity of scholarship:

> This was particularly a Greek disease, to ask how many rowers Ulysses had and whether the *Iliad* or the *Odyssey* was written first, and besides, if they are by the same author, and other things of the same sort. If you keep them secret, they do your private knowledge no good; if you tell people about them, you appear not a scholar but a bore. And lo, now this empty enthusiasm for learning useless things has invaded the Romans as well. Recently I heard someone reporting which Roman leader did what first: Duilius was the first to win a naval battle, Curius Dentatus was the first to lead elephants in a triumph. (Seneca the Younger, *On the Shortness of Life* 13)

Seneca's 124 philosophical letters, addressed to his friend Gaius Lucilius, show a remarkable combination of modesty, humour, and gentle advice—the optimum combination, carefully learned in the schools of rhetoric, for delivering potentially unpalatable lessons. Here too he can be biting on the habits of contemporary scholarship and on what this learned audience misses in literature, being too caught up in matters of linguistic detail and literary history:

> A future grammarian [that is, an explicator of poetry], on looking at Virgil, does not read that famous line, 'time flies beyond catching,' in this spirit: 'we must pay attention; unless we hurry we will be left behind; swift time drives us and is driven; we are carried along, unknowing . . . ' but he reads it to observe that when Virgil speaks of the swiftness of time he uses this word 'flees'. . . . And the grammarian reading Cicero's *Republic* first notes that Cicero says 'the thingself' [*reapse*], that is, 'the thing itself' [*re ipsa*]. . . . Then he moves on to usages which have changed over time, such as the finishing line in the Circus which we now call '*creta*', the ancients used to call '*calx*'. Then he compares some Ennian verses . . . (Seneca, *Moral Letters* 108. 24, 32–3)

Seneca's technique is close to that of the didactic poet Lucretius (see pp. 339–49), whose famous simile of the honey on the cup of medicine would equally fit Seneca's approach to teaching Lucilius the rudiments of Stoic philosophy. And, through Lucilius, he teaches the wider world: for Seneca's ethical philosophy, like Cicero's, is designed to reach the literate reading public of Rome, not simply its private addressees.

Since Augustus, literature maintained at least the façade of reaching a wider audience. Asinius Pollio, in addition to founding his library, instituted the habit of fairly formal recitation, either in a private home or in a hired recital hall. These literary performances, which became increasingly fashionable, are most memorably parodied by the Neronian poet Persius (see the passage quoted on p. 506).

Recitations of prose works, though not targeted by the satirist, are well attested throughout the period, being best documented in the letters of Gaius Plinius Caecilius Secundus, called Pliny the Younger. These, modelled on the letters of Cicero, are carefully written for future publication by a man constructing his own image with one eye on the past and one on the opinion of posterity. They give us a remarkable picture of imperial society, with a special concentration on literary circles. The biographies of the emperors by Suetonius provide another rich source of information about recitation and its audiences.

As usual, the most prestigious auditor was the emperor himself (see p. 486, on Domitian as 'super-reader'). So, for example, besides listening to declamation, Augustus heard recitations of history, oratory, and philosophical dialogues; Claudius recited his own history and listened to that of Servilius Nonianus. The Younger Pliny recited speeches, including his *Panegyric*, and listened to history, invective, and eulogies of famous men; the Younger Seneca speaks of crowds of philosophers reciting their works. On a less elevated level, fabulous tales such as the ghost stories in one of Pliny's better-known letters, or the animal fables of Phaedrus, might be told for entertainment at dinner parties (see pp. 492–518). This flurry of recitation did more than simply fill the aristocrat's increasingly vacant leisure time, though there was certainly something of that about it. Except for those in business, public service no longer occupied as much senatorial attention when the emperor and his bureaucratic staff were in control, and so they put their talents to work elsewhere. But, just as during the Republic, competition and display were at the heart of this new public activity.

A select audience's reaction was particularly important as a form of critical feedback, as the younger Pliny explains (see pp. 495–6):

I am too diffident to feel confident that I have done everything I can to what has only my own approval. I have therefore two reasons for reading in public; the reader is made more keenly critical of his own work if he stands in some awe of his audience, and he has a kind of panel of experts to confirm his decision on any doubtful point. He receives suggestions from different members and, failing this, he can infer their various opinions from their expressions, glances, nods, applause, murmurs and silence, signs which make clear the distinction between their critical judgement and polite assent. . . . But now I am arguing this point as if I invited the general public to a lecture hall instead of having my friends in my own room—though if I have many friends to invite this has been a source of pride to many people and a reproach to none. (Pliny, *Letters* 5. 3. 8–10, trans. B. Radice)

Pliny's modest persona, which pervades his letters, is a deliberately assumed mask: diffident he may have been, but he was also intensely proud of his talent. And the process he describes here on a small scale may operate on a large one: audience tastes and expectations could determine the style of a whole generation, as happened with declamation. But the process could become a vicious circle, with audiences going on to imitate the bad habits they have themselves encouraged in their taste for novelty. Quintilian, in his discussion of Latin authors, has strong views on Senecan style (which the nineteenth-century English historian Macaulay memorably compared to a diet of anchovy sauce):

Seneca had many great virtues: a quick and abundant talent, with much learning and wide knowledge (in which, however, he was sometimes deceived by those to whom he entrusted his research). For he handled almost every area of scholarship: speeches and poems and letters and dialogues circulate under his name. He was not very critical in philosophy, though he was a remarkable denouncer of vice. His works contain many notable epigrammatic formulations and much that is worth reading to improve one's character—yet his style contains many corrupt things which are exceedingly dangerous because they abound in attractive faults. One could wish that he had spoken with his own intelligence, but with someone else's judgement. . . . If he had not been so enamoured of all his ideas, and if he had not fractured the dignity of his subject with epigrammatic brevity, he would be approved by a consensus of learned men rather than by infatuated boys. (Quintilian, *The Education of an Orator* 10. 1. 128–30)

We saw the same worries surfacing under the Republic; now, however, in a literary society in which a small coterie of experts engaged in an intimate process of improvising, competing, imitating, and striving always to outdo each other, the dangers of solipsism and unregulated display are much to the fore. Quintilian is worried about Seneca's style at least partly because he sees how popular it has become, and wants to warn the young against it. It is, in fact, from Seneca himself that we have the most explicit discussion of the dangerous effects of imitation, in his letters to Lucilius. Though acknowledging that imitation is not in itself the sign of a corrupt mind or of decadence, he nevertheless points out that a charismatic figure's faults can be those of an entire age:

> Maecenas [one of Augustus' friends] was clearly effeminate, not gentle. . . . His misleading word order, expressions that get in the way, and extraordinary thoughts—often great, yes, but emasculated in their expression—make it clear that his head was turned by excessive success. This fault is due sometimes to a man and sometimes to his times. When prosperity has poured out luxury far and wide, bodily culture starts to get too much attention. . . . When the mind has become used to scorning ordinary things and regarding customary things as shabby, it begins to look for novelties in speech also, sometimes recalling and displaying obsolete, old fashioned words, sometimes coining new words . . . sometimes bold and frequent metaphors are considered sophisticated. Some amputate their sentences hoping to make a good impression if the meaning is left in doubt and the listener suspects his own lack of wit; some dwell on their sentences and stretch them out; others, too, not only fall into stylistic fault (for someone aiming high must do this) but actually love the fault for its own sake. (Seneca, *Moral Letters* 114. 8–11)

Seneca's criticism of Maecenas modulates into a discussion of the interconnection between literary style and culture, and finally centres on the relationship between speaker and audience, for it is there that a literary character can most clearly be perceived and (more importantly) judged.

Styles change; literary fashions come and go. Just after our period, there was a revival of archaic Latin, with the orator Marcus Cornelius Fronto (tutor to the Emperor Marcus Aurelius) imitating Cato the Elder in preference to Cicero. The modernity of Senecan prose must have looked very dated indeed. And lastly there is Aulus Gellius, a scholar living in the second half of the second century CE, both in Athens and in Rome. He compiled a miscellany in twenty books, the *Attic Nights*, a collection of quotations, facts, and trivia concerning philosophy, law, and grammar, including literary and textual criticism. Though intended as a source of entertaining information for his children, it enjoyed a wide influence in late antiquity and beyond. Like much of imperial scholarship, especially the books of Frontinus, Valerius Maximus, and Pliny the

Elder, it was produced both for use and out of a delight in collection for its own sake. It gives us an interesting picture of one ancient scholar's reading—and an invaluable trove of fragments of Latin literature that would otherwise be lost to us.

The power of memory

History continued to be as popular as ever under the Empire, although, as the future Emperor Claudius' experience showed, choice of topic was as important as sturdy furniture in the recital hall:

> As a young man he began to write history with Livy's encouragement and the help of Sulpicius Flavus. But when he first recited to a large audience he barely got through it, since he more than once gave himself a 'chill'. For at the beginning of the reading a laugh arose when several benches broke under the weight of a fat man, and not even after the disturbance was quieted could Claudius help recalling the incident and chuckling all over again. . . . He started his history with the death of the dictator Caesar, but moved on to a later period, beginning at the 'civil peace' since he understood that he was not allowed to speak frankly or truly about the earlier time, having often been taken to task both by his mother and by his grandmother. (Suetonius, *Life of the Deified Claudius* 41)

Even a member of the imperial household could not afford to be too critical of the regime, or to reveal what the emperor's family preferred not to reveal. People outside the royal family who did risk complimenting the 'Liberators' Brutus and Cassius, for example, could pay with their lives, as did Cremutius Cordus, one of the historians whose works had been restored by Caligula after he was disgraced and his books burnt, under Tiberius. Curtius Rufus, who (probably) lived under Claudius, took an indirect way around this problem, choosing instead to write a history of Alexander the Great. His Alexander bears a remarkable resemblance to a Roman emperor, but he is a foreign, exotic figure, distant enough from the potentially dangerous present. Another route was ethnography, the history of distant peoples; our only complete ethnography from antiquity is Tacitus' monograph on Germany, the *Germania*. It, too, reflects obliquely on the Empire, especially in its portrait of a nation of noble savages untouched by the corrupting effects of civilization.

Finally, one could write an epitome, or short history, touching on only the high points of the Roman past. The conventional epitome-writer's excuse of being in a hurry could enable one to pass by a number of uncomfortable incidents—even if, like the Tiberian writer Velleius Paterculus, you were in fact loyal to the regime (Velleius had served in the army under Tiberius and so had first-hand knowledge of his considerable military abilities and virtues). Another epitome, by Lucius Annaeus Florus, may date from the second century CE: it is far more florid and panegyrical than Velleius' text, employing exclamation and exaggeration to enhance the author's enthusiasm for his often lurid subject:

> First luxury, then lack of money pushed Catiline into his unspeakable plan. . . . With what allies—oh, horrible!—did he undertake to run the senators through, butcher the consuls, rip the city apart with fire, ransack the treasury—in a word, to uproot the whole state from its foundations and do things that not even Hannibal seems to have desired! (Florus, *Epitome of Roman History* 2. 12)

Florus preserves the minimum of Sallust's social critique, but seeks more to thrill his reader with the horror of Catiline's plans than to offer any historical analysis; this really is history as entertainment, a far cry from Pliny the Elder's call for difficult but useful topics.

Florus is, however, an exception in imperial historiography. The genre begins 150 years earlier with Titus Livius (Livy), a private citizen from Padua in northern Italy, who spent most of his life in Rome, writing what would become itself a monument: 142 papyrus rolls of Roman history from the beginning through to Livy's own time, probably ending in 9 BCE. Three-quarters of it, including everything after 167 BCE, is lost, making it impossible to tell how Livy would have treated the problematic years of the early Empire. The earliest books, which cover the legendary and regal periods, are restrained by comparison with Livy's contemporary, the Greek-speaking historian Dionysios of Halikarnassos, who took eleven books to cover what Livy does in three (see pp. 262–4). They show the scepticism, sometimes bordering on cynicism, that pervades the whole of the work as we have it:

> One day during a meeting to review his troops on the Campus Martius . . . a sudden storm with mighty thunder claps enveloped the king in such a dense cloud that the crowd lost sight of him. Nor was Romulus seen again on earth. . . . Although the soldiers readily believed the senators who had been standing closest that he had been snatched up in the air by a whirlwind, still . . . they were stricken with the fear of having been orphaned, so to speak, and for quite a time stood in mournful silence. Then, after a few proclaimed Romulus' divinity, the rest joined in, hailing him with one accord as a god, born to a god, king and parent of the city of Rome. . . . I

> believe that even then there were some people who maintained privately that the king had been torn apart by the hands of the senators—for this version, though little known, has also been handed down. Still, admiration for the man and the alarm felt at the time gave the other version wider currency, and it was further strengthened by the testimony of a single individual. This man was Proculus Iulius, a highly respected citizen according to tradition ... who stepped forth in a public assembly to affirm the truth of a most extraordinary event.... It is astonishing how absolute was the conviction that Proculus Iulius' words carried and how, once belief in Romulus' immortality had been confirmed, the grief felt by the army and people was mitigated. (Livy, *From the Founding of the City* 1. 16, trans. T. J. Luce)

Livy is particularly fond, as in this episode, of using internal audiences (as we saw also above, in his description of Cicero's death). Here, he plays with layers of audiences: the crowd at the time, later tradition—split in two by the distinctly anti-tyrannical story of Romulus' murder—and the contemporary reader, joined by Livy himself in trying to sort out some kind of truth about this legendary past. It is possible to read it either completely straight or with tongue-in-cheek. Proculus Julius, for instance, has a remarkably significant name in this story of the divination of a Roman emperor, and was probably invented by the Julian family in order to heighten their clan's importance. Livy could not possibly comment: 'it is astonishing,' he says simply, a comment which can be taken two ways, in Latin as in English.

Livy's construction of early Rome and the first centuries of the Republic is both sentimental and postmodern. He accepts that it is impossible to tell what really happened, about such matters ranging from the number of battles fought in third century BCE wars to the real story behind Scipio Africanus' charismatic appeal. It *is* possible to use good historical methods, including arguments from analogy and from probability, and he painstakingly teaches his reader how to deploy those sifting tools to reach a likely version of the past. But what he is most interested in is not what actually happened, but how the past is remembered, and how that memory functions in and can help change the present and the future.

Through a process of careful analysis, vivid reconstruction, rhetorical technique, and allusion to the topographical and literary monuments of Rome, he enlists his reader in a process of recovering what the Roman people saw as their past, and in using that past critically as an exemplary guide for the future. While his own persona is patient, diffident, and often misleadingly uncertain, his history is dynamic and demanding:

> Whether in writing the history of the Roman people from the foundation of the city the result will be worth the effort invested, I do not really know

(nor, if I did, would I presume to say so).... My wish is that each reader will pay the closest attention to the following: how men lived, what their moral principles were, under what leaders and by what measures at home and abroad our empire was won and extended: then let him follow in his mind how, as discipline broke down bit by bit, morality at first foundered; how it next subsided in ever greater collapse and then began to topple headlong in ruin—until the advent of our own age, in which we can endure neither our vices nor the remedies needed to cure them. The special and salutary benefit of the study of history is to behold evidence of every sort of behaviour set forth as on a splendid memorial; from it you may select for yourself and for your country what to emulate, from it what to avoid, whether basely begun or basely concluded. (Livy, *From the Founding of the City*, Preface 1, 9–10, trans. T. J. Luce)

Livy takes his Sallustian awareness of Rome's current debasement and turns it into a programme for socio-political improvement. His approach is almost clinical (and indeed in this passage uses medical language), and has much in common with Augustus' own plan to use ancient monuments and tradition to rebuild a radically new Rome. Owing to the loss of the later books, it is impossible to tell how radically new Livy's Rome would have been. We can tell, however, that his work is particularly important in being open-access history, written not by a senator but by a historian uninvolved in the government or the military, directed neither exclusively at the élite nor the non-élite, a mix of scholarship and popularizing, avoiding the polemics of the late-republican memoir and insider histories such as Sallust's or Asinius Pollio's.

Sallust and Livy together were formative influences on the greatest historian of the imperial period, Cornelius Tacitus. Like Livy, he came from the north (probably from southern France); unlike him, however, he was a senator, with a successful career even under the tyrant Domitian, ending up under Trajan as governor of the province of Asia (112–13 CE). His two works of narrative history, the *Histories* and the *Annals*, borrow the annalistic or year-by-year form from Livy's history, structuring the narrative around the annual rotation of consuls, the chief magistrates of the old republican government. Deliberately anachronistic, and jarring with the reality of imperial rule, this structure sets the tone for his bleak, overpoweringly cynical view of the first sixty-five years of the Empire, from the death of Augustus through to the accession of Vespasian in 70 (later books of the *Histories*, which continued through Domitian's rule, together with the reign of Caligula and parts of Claudius and Nero from the *Annals*, are lost).

Tacitus' world is populated with duplicitous, violent emperors, craven senators, unexpectedly brave freedwomen, charismatic but useless military

SETTING EXAMPLES. The background to trials in the Forum of Augustus was a curving portico with the statue of one of the great men of the past and an inscription recording his deeds in each niche.

leaders, gluttonous aristocrats, exaggeratedly stubborn philosophers, poisoners, spies, and innocent doomed youths. His style combines Sallustian unpredictability with consummate Livian structure and variety to produce a dazzling, challenging Latin that demands repeated readings. It is a Latin whose deceptive surface conceals a hidden meaning, like the world about which Tacitus is writing, in which only those survive who manage to steer a middle course between 'precipitous obstinacy and a wasteland of servility'. The only successful readers in Tacitus' text are those who can read the all-powerful emperor who, as the focus of aristocratic and plebeian attention alike, has himself become a dangerous new text which demands, yet frustrates, correct reading. Tiberian opacity we have seen above, in discussing oratory and the Senate. Nero, who delights in exploiting the range of theatrical effect, is even worse: misinterpreting such an emperor can easily be punished by death.

There is a dense concentration of such theatrical scenes in *Annals* 15, culminating in the great fire of Rome. First, the emperor himself takes to the stage, not at Rome but in a town of Greek foundation, the better to foster the illusion of performance in the country which invented literary festivals:

> Hitherto Nero had sung in private houses or gardens . . . but these he now scorned, as too little attended and too restricted for such a fine voice. Not daring, however, to start at Rome, he chose Neapolis [Naples] because it was a Greek city. From this starting-point he could cross to Achaia. . . . Accordingly, a crowd of townspeople was collected . . . and filled the theatre at Naples. There an incident took place which many thought unlucky, though Nero believed it due to the providence of the auspicious gods. For after the audience had left, the empty building collapsed without harm to anyone. (Tacitus, *Annals* 15. 33–4)

Lucky for the spectators—though perhaps not so, considering the lengths to which, it is alleged, Nero later went to keep his audiences captive: it is said that since he allowed no one to leave his performances, pregnant women gave birth in the theatres, while some men tried to leap from the walls, others even going so far as to feign death so that they could be carried out of the building.

Instead of continuing to Greece, however, and though wanting badly to go to the exotic province of Egypt, Nero stays in Rome, making himself popular with the people—though not, it goes without saying, with the conservative senators:

> To assure people that no place pleased him as much as Rome, Nero gave banquets in the public places, treating the whole city as his private house. Of these feasts the most famous . . . were those given by Tigellinus, which I will describe as an example. . . . He constructed a raft on Agrippa's lake, put the banquet on board and had it towed by other boats. These vessels were decorated with gold and ivory; the degenerate crews were arranged according to age and experience of vice. . . . On the quays stood brothels filled with noble women, and on the opposite bank were seen naked prostitutes. As darkness approached, nearby groves and surrounding buildings resounded with song and shone with lights. Nero, polluted by every lawful and lawless act, had omitted no abomination by which he could be further corrupted—except that a few days later, in a solemn wedding ceremony, he became the wife of one of that filthy herd, a slave named Pythagoras. The bridal veil was put on the emperor; witnesses, dowry, couch and nuptial torches were there—everything, in a word, was visible. (*Annals* 15. 37)

Constructing what is essentially a stage set covering a large portion of Rome (and one which, it has been argued, is deliberately intended to reproduce the

Egypt which Nero longed to see), Nero takes over public entertainment for his own obscene pantomime, even going so far as to play the part of a bride in a homosexual wedding. Tacitus singles out the most lurid elements, emphasizing that this was done to be seen—and, of course, is here laid out for you, the reader, to see. Both the emperor and his historian play to their respective audiences. But it is Nero who will have the best part:

> A disaster followed, one . . . more serious and dreadful than any which has ever happened to this city by the violence of fire. . . . The flames first swept through the level portions of the city, then rising to the hills . . . outstripped all preventive measures by their speed, and by the fact that the city was vulnerable owing to its narrow alleys winding here and there and its irregular blocks. . . . In addition the wailing of terror-stricken women, the feebleness of age and the inexperience of childhood, people looking after themselves and looking after others, dragging the weak along or waiting for them, some delaying, some fleeing, all got in the way. . . . Nero at this time was staying at Antium and did not return to Rome until the fire was nearing his house. . . . A rumour spread that at the very moment when the city was aflame, the emperor had gone on to his private stage and sung the destruction of Troy, comparing modern evils with ancient disasters. (*Annals* 15. 38–9)

The fire becomes a backdrop to the mad emperor's private performance, an opportunity for bringing life to ancient history: on Nero's stage, Rome becomes Troy, and the emperor is author, actor, and audience rolled into one.

It is Tacitus, however, who has the last word. Though his history is neither sentimental nor hopeful, it does share with Livy's an intense desire to be useful, to turn the past, however horrifying, into something from which one can learn. One of the new genres that sprang up under the Empire was the martyrology, or eulogy of political victims. Though none of these survives from before the Christian period (where they commemorate victims of religious persecution), we know the subjects of some of them. They are mainly Stoic philosophers, men whom Tacitus characterizes as uselessly indulging their opposition to the Empire, going to an ostentatious but ultimately pointless death. Yet he borrows from the genre in his first monograph, the *Agricola*, a historical biography of his father-in-law, a man who Tacitus says managed to follow that path between truculence and servility. It is a testament not only to the man, but to the power of the written word to reach out beyond its immediate circumstances to audiences unimaginably far away:

> If there is any place for the spirits of the just, if, as philosophers believe, great souls do not perish with the body, may you rest in peace. May you

call us . . . to contemplate your noble character, for which it is a sin either to mourn or to shed tears. May we rather honour you by our admiration and our undying praise and, if our powers permit, by following your example. . . . Images of the human face, like that face itself, are weak and perishable. The beauty of the soul lives for ever, and you can preserve and express that beauty, not by the material and artistry of another, but only in your own character. All that we have loved in Agricola, all that we have admired in him, abides and is destined to abide in human hearts through the endless procession of the ages, by the fame of his deeds. Many of the men of old will be buried in oblivion, inglorious and unknown. Agricola's story has been told for posterity and he will survive. (Tacitus, *Agricola* 46, trans. A. R. Birley)

15 Oblique politics: Epic of the imperial period

MATTHEW LEIGH

Cultures of recitation

In his *Dialogue on Orators*, Tacitus depicts a small gathering of writers and orators at the house of one Curiatius Maternus (cf. p. 450). The dramatic date is 74 CE, the actual date of publication around a quarter of a century later. The initial context is intriguing. For this is the day after the recitation by Curiatius of his new tragedy *Cato* and all the town is buzzing with talk of the offence given to the powerful by the energy with which Curiatius threw himself into the part of the eponymous hero of his work. Now the tradition attaching to Cato the Younger (cf. p. 517) is of immense significance for the political and philosophical thought of this period and the impassioned impersonation of this figure must give out messages which are hard to misunderstand. To a Seneca, Cato's inflexible devotion to virtue and resolute dedication to the position he has once adopted make him the great Roman example of the Stoic wise man. To Cato's Neronian biographer, Thrasea Paetus, his Stoicism must be inseparable from his republicanism. For Cato had led the forces of the Senate in the civil wars of the early 40s BCE against Julius Caesar and the convictions to which he so rigorously adhered were those of the traditional political order. Finally defeated at the Battle of Utica, he committed suicide rather than accept the principle of autocracy, and in doing so set down a standard for other critics of imperial rule to emulate. To put words into the mouth of the dying Cato could be an indirect way of commenting on whichever tyrant currently held sway in Rome.

That politics is the most prominent concern of Curiatius' play is apparent from Tacitus' description of his initial exchanges with the first of his guests, Julius Secundus:

> Well, on entering Maternus' room we found him sitting with a book in front of him—the very same from which he had given his reading on the

> previous day; whereupon Secundus said, 'Has the talk of your detractors no terrors for you, Maternus? Does it not make you feel less enamoured of that exasperating Cato of yours? Or is it with the idea of going carefully over it that you have taken your drama in hand, intending to cut out any passages that may have given a handle for misrepresentation, and then to publish your *Cato*, if not better than it was at least not so dangerous?'
>
> To this he rejoined, 'The reading of it will show you what Maternus considered his duty to himself: you will find it just as you heard it read. Yes, and if *Cato* has left anything unsaid, at my next reading it shall be supplied in my *Thyestes*; for so I call the tragedy which I have already planned and of which I have the outline in my head. It is just because I want to get the first play off my hands and to throw myself whole-heartedly into my new theme that I am hurrying to get this work ready for publication.' (Tacitus, *Dialogue on Orators* 3. 1–3)

Those passages which risk misrepresentation and which may be considered dangerous acquire this status through their political content. Curiatius has retired from forensic rhetoric and later—however disingenuously—proclaims the blessings of the current peace; but he can put into the mouth of his Cato a commentary on tyranny and liberty which the audience will interpret as transcending the specific historical context of the play. That this mediated expression of dissent is what is at issue is apparent from the reference to the forthcoming *Thyestes*: how a play on the woes of ancient Mycenae can elucidate a previous work on the Roman civil wars is unclear until one notes the recurrent tendency of a succession of Roman writers from Ennius and Accius onwards to use this theme, and in particular the psychopathic rule of Atreus, to evoke the perils of autocracy.

It is unclear where exactly Curiatius has given his recitation, but he seems almost to have courted the attention of those at the imperial palace who might wish to denounce him. The same recklessness shows through in his attitude to the eventual published version of his work, which Secundus expects him to make more anodyne but which Maternus promises to deliver unchanged. Maybe these are hints at what has been inferred from other evidence: that the dialogue is set immediately before the death of the tragedian. Contrast Thrasea Paetus and his *Cato*. The Neronian books of the *Annals* close with Tacitus' description of the suicide of Thrasea. He has been denounced by the loathsome Cossutianus Capito and the principal accusation is that, for all his unrelenting withdrawal from the Senate, Thrasea has not abandoned political life but rather is engaged in a form of politics by other means. Central to this claim is the literary circle surrounding Thrasea, and it is no accident that Tacitus has him receive the news of his condemnation when gathered in his gardens with a number of prominent friends in order to listen to the Cynic philosopher Demetrios. It is as if the Roman politician's house is a miniature state in which he can rule virtuously over those who elect to follow him. In public the followers of Thrasea are damned and mocked in equal measure for their high-minded, contumacious air; in that small space apart formed by his house and gardens, Thrasea must give readings from his *Cato* and affirm his political tradition.

We have so far encountered Cato the Younger in tragedy, history, and philosophical dialogue. He is also prominent in at least one epic poem of the period: the *Pharsalia* or *Civil War* of Lucan. Yet there are other epics to be considered as well, poems on anything from the Second Punic War to the expedition of Jason and the Argonauts, the war between the sons of Oedipus for rule over Thebes, and the life of Achilles. What did it mean to recite and then to publish works on these themes? Does all literature fall into the pattern of mediated comment suggested above? A very different picture is supplied by the opening of the first satire of Juvenal (cf. pp. 501–2):

Must I always be a listener only, never hit back,
although so often assailed by the hoarse *Theseid* of Cordus?
Never obtain revenge when X has read me his comedies,
Y his elegies? No revenge when my day has been wasted
by mighty Telephus or by Orestes who, having covered
the final margin, extends to the back, and still isn't finished?
No citizen's private house is more familiar to *him*
than the grove of Mars and Vulcan's cave near Aeolus' rocks
are to *me*; what the winds are up to, what ghosts are being tormented
on Aeacus' rack, from what far land another has stolen
a bit of gold pelt, how huge are the ash-trunks Monychus hurls —
the unending cry goes up from Fronto's plane-trees, his marble
statues and columns, shaken and shattered by non-stop readings.
One gets the same from every poet, great and small.
I too have snatched my hand from under the cane; I too
have tendered advice to Sulla to retire from public life
and sleep the sleep of the just. No point, when you meet so many bards, in sparing paper (it's already doomed to destruction).
But why, you may ask, should I decide to cover the ground
o'er which the mighty son of Aurunca [Lucilius] drove his team?
If you have time and are feeling receptive, here's my answer.

(Juvenal, *Satires* 1. 1–21)

Juvenal unleashes his scorn against epic, tragedy, comedy, and elegy alike but it is epic which is most prominent in this passage. The very title *Theseid* proclaims the poem of Cordus an epic; the standard motifs of the grove of Mars, the cave of the winds, the golden fleece, and the arms of the Centaurs are the stock-in-trade of mythological epic. All these epicists, to whose voices the villa of Fronto resounds, share with Juvenal the same training: anyone who has advised Sulla to retire from political life and sleep securely has studied the stock speech of persuasion known as the *suasoria* so central to the curriculum of the declamation schools (cf. pp. 445–8). In this educational system, no scene from history is too controversial to be trivialized by eager schoolboys in search of point and paradox, not even, as Persius shows, the death of Cato the Younger himself. What Juvenal therefore affects to damn are windy, empty poems on hackneyed themes, all pullulating with the same rhetorical figures and tricks. Satire, the path of Lucilius, must somehow be different. Wherein that difference lies is made explicit in the final lines of the poem:

> So take this man who administered poison to three of his uncles –
> is he to go by, looking down on us all from his aery cushions?
> 'Yes, when he comes to *you*, seal your lips with your finger.
> Simply to utter the words 'That's him!' will count as informing.
> Without a qualm you can pit Aeneas against the ferocious
> Rutulian; no one is placed at risk by the wounded Achilles,
> or Hylas, so long sought when he'd gone the way of his bucket.
> Whenever, as though with sword in hand, the hot Lucilius
> roars in wrath, the listener flushes; his mind is affrighted
> with a sense of sin, and his conscience sweats with secret guilt.
> *That's* what causes anger and tears. So turn it over
> in your mind before the bugle. Too late when you've donned your helmet,
> for second thoughts about combat.'
> 'I'll try what I may against those
> whose ashes are buried beneath the Flaminia and the Latina.'
>
> (Juvenal, *Satires* 1. 158–71, trans. N. Rudd)

The image of Lucilius in his chariot sums up the impression of the early satirist's remorseless aggression; now he brandishes his sword and rages while his imitator dons his helmet and waits for the trumpet to sound. In other words, to denounce one's contemporaries after the manner of Lucilius would be to act like the great warriors celebrated in epic verse. Those, meanwhile, who compose such verse can sleep easy at night because their poetry is so vacuous that it has no chance whatsoever of causing offence: the duel of Turnus and Aeneas, the death of Achilles and the loss of the Argonaut Hylas are shorthand for epic. That Juvenal actually closes by choosing the safer course of speaking ill only of the dead is scant comfort to the epicists whom he pillories. Do they really, he asks, have anything to say at all?

Recitation is central to the literary culture of the imperial period. The passages chosen from Tacitus and Juvenal illustrate the range of experience which can be accommodated under the heading. In what follows, we shall see poets who write for an audience as determined to interpret and find meaning as that of Curiatius Maternus, poets who write for an audience whose benevolence is acquired in the market-place of literary patronage, poets even whom we may secretly suspect were rather too like those whose inanity Juvenal lampoons.

It is no accident that Tacitus sets his *Dialogue on Orators* in 74 CE. No more than six years have passed since the fall of the Emperor Nero, the last representative of the Julio-Claudian dynasty, and only five since the civil wars which engulfed Rome in 69 CE, the famous Year of the Four Emperors. The reign of Vespasian is still new and scores are still being settled from the years of Nero. Malicious prosecutors have been targeted for retribution by the families of their victims; fresh efforts have been made to reassert the authority of the Senate. Yet Vespasian will give way to his son Titus and he to his brother Domitian. Nero is dead but the autocratic spirit lives on. The impact of these years is palpable in all the epic poets of the age.

The *Pharsalia* or *Civil War* is Lucan's account of the conflict between Caesar and Pompey and their climactic struggle in 48 BCE on the fields of Pharsalos in Thessaly. It is perhaps the most overtly political and, indeed, rebellious work of its age and is unsparing in its condemnation of the corruption of Rome in the age of the emperors. Its youthful author did not live to see the overthrow of Nero. Lucan's fall from grace with the emperor and eventual enforced suicide at the age of only 26 is testament to the potential hazards of composing verse on the same controversial themes as Curiatius employs for his tragedies.

M. Annaeus Lucanus was the nephew of the philosopher and tragedian L. Annaeus Seneca (cf. pp. 449–51). Born in Spain in 39 CE but educated in Rome and Athens, Lucan declaimed with distinction in both Greek and Latin, held the quaestorship at a prematurely early age, performed verse in honour of Nero and became a member of the emperor's cohort of friends. His swift advance must have owed as much to his uncle's role as tutor to the young emperor as it did to his prodigious abilities. All this before one most unfortunate event.

The worst misfortune which a reciter could endure was known as a *frigus* or a 'chill'. Where an enthusiastic audience would call out its approval through various familiar terms, those who were hostile to the poet could subject him to the silent disdain of the *frigus*. Suetonius records in his life of Lucan that the poet suffered just such a rebuff and from none other than the Emperor Nero himself. The motivation for Nero's behaviour is not stated by the biographer but we may perhaps infer from his decision to end the performance by calling a meeting of the Senate that this was the best way to break up an audience of some of the leading men of the day.

The exiguous remains of Nero's poetry bear witness to his artistic ambitions. The emperor was also enamoured of the tragic stage and is said to have acted the roles of Orestes the matricide or Canace in labour. Tacitus records the distaste at these transgressions which helped drive the loyal centurion Subrius Flavus to conspire against his ruler. Yet the man whom he sought to place on the throne in his stead, C. Calpurnius Piso, had himself performed in Greek at the theatre in Naples while that notorious sober-sides Thrasea Paetus had sung in tragic dress at the games of Antenor in his native Patavium. Among Lucan's own works are counted an unfinished tragedy entitled *Medea* and fourteen plays with dancing. There is no evidence of his having actually appeared on the stage.

The course of Lucan's early career in public life was meteoric but the feud with Nero soon put a stop to this. The displeasure which the emperor showed at Lucan's verses had far-reaching consequences. The 'chill' was extended to a ban on performance and on work as a lawyer—the public voice of Lucan was silenced. The poet responded by assaulting Nero and his friends in defamatory verses and never held back from abusing him. The image suggested by his biographers up to this point smacks less of steely republican conviction than of petulance and backbiting in a small and competitive group. Suetonius even describes Lucan in the latrines of the imperial palace: the poet lets rip a magnificent fart and caps his achievement with a snatch of Nero's own verse 'You might think that it had thundered beneath the earth'—all those sitting around him flee as fast as they can rather than associate themselves with this levity. When finally Lucan becomes involved in the conspiracy to replace Nero with C. Calpurnius Piso, Suetonius has him declaiming against tyrants and offering Caesar's head to his associates, while Tacitus and Vacca report his attempt to shift accusations of participation onto his mother Acilia. Is this the Lucan whom the auditoria heard recite his *Pharsalia*?

Immature, egotistical, treacherous—Lucan is not flattered by his biographers. Yet this is not the only story. When Tacitus in the *Annals* tells of the death of Annaeus Mela, he states that it is a great aid to his distinction that he was the father of the poet; in the *Dialogue on Orators*, M. Aper urges speakers to draw quotations from the sacred shrine of a Horace, a Virgil, or a Lucan. Both Statius in his birthday poem for Lucan and Martial in a series of epigrams testify to the efforts of Lucan's widow to celebrate his memory and both pay tribute to his work. Statius becomes the first writer to treat Lucan as a heroic enemy of tyranny and his *Pharsalia* as an underground work surviving the best efforts of Nero to suppress it. One might compare the story in Seneca the Elder of the incorrigible Pompeian Labienus who broke off a recitation of some of his histories, skipped some passages, and announced that they would be read after his death. Tacitus, similarly, tells of Cremutius Cordus, the historian driven to his death by Tiberius but whose works lived after him and only grew in reputation as a result (cf. pp. 452–4).

The ancient evidence for the life of Lucan is of huge significance for any account of his *Pharsalia*. It is difficult, however, to know how to handle it. To refuse to imagine a Lucan who is any better than the worst of what we are told about him is to risk trivializing the political voice of the poem: however eloquent his words, they are undermined by our sense of the bad faith of their author. Yet entirely to discard the implications of the evidence for the poet's character and milieu may be the first step to inventing Lucan as the romantic republican dissident and herald of freedom which it would be most stirring to believe him to be.

The ancient life of Lucan attributed to Vacca places the ban on recitation after the publication of the first three books of the *Pharsalia*. By the end of the third book, Lucan's account of the civil wars between Caesar and Pompey has advanced as far as Caesar's invasion of Italy, the flight of Pompey and the senatorial forces, the gathering of auxiliaries from the East and Caesar's siege of Massilia *en route* to the Spanish campaign. It is common to claim that these sections of the narrative are free from the hostility to imperial rule which comes to dominate the latter books. This is, however, very largely a fiction. So heavy-handed an interpretation of the poem's content is a good instance of the pernicious impact of biographical evidence. An alternative response to this evidence might be to assume that the 'chill' administered to Lucan by the emperor was in response to some aspect of the first three books and to wonder what it might be.

The proem to the *Pharsalia* is a thirty-two-line lament for the civil wars, their corrosive impact on Roman ethics, and their destruction of a once-great imperial power. At this point, however, Lucan adopts a very different perspective. He turns to the emperor and finds in him a grand consolation for all the sorrows of Rome:

> But if the Fates could find no other way
> for Nero's coming, if eternal kingdoms are purchased
> by the gods at great cost, if heaven could serve its Thunderer
> only after wars with the ferocious Giants,
> then we have no complaints, O gods; for this reward we accept
> even these crimes and guilt; though Pharsalia fill its dreadful
> plains, though the Carthaginian's shade with blood be sated;
> though the final battle be joined at fatal Munda;

> though added to these horrors, Caesar, be the famine of Perusia
> and the struggles of Mutina, the fleets overwhelmed
> near rugged Leucas, and the slave wars under burning Etna,
> yet Rome owes much to citizens' weapons, because it was
> for you that all was done.
>
> (Lucan, *Pharsalia* 1. 33–45)

Lucan goes on to anticipate the apotheosis of Nero, urges him to occupy the centre of heaven, lest he should overbalance the cosmos or look askance on Rome, begs him to look serenely on the city and finally dismisses Dionysus and Apollo in proclaiming the emperor his muse. The interpretation of all of this is troubled. To many, this is the standard language of imperial panegyric and is evidence, if not of Lucan's sincere admiration for Nero, then at least of his sincere desire to flatter him. Other voices, however, continue to resist this approach. The late-antique commentators on Lucan were the first, claiming that the section urging Nero to occupy the centre of the universe played on his obesity and his squint. I would prefer to emphasize the extreme pressure on Nero to justify the calculation of profit and loss in the passage quoted, the absence of any other reference to this theme in the remorseless pessimism of the rest of the poem, and the scorn heaped on the deification of dead emperors elsewhere in the text. To this approach, any investigation of whether Lucan meant what he said in the dedication must take account of the repeated tendency of the later stages of the poem to comment on and dismiss the consolatory motifs which here he so zealously proclaims.

One might now consider this issue in terms of the audience for the *Pharsalia*. Vacca states that Lucan was banned from recitation in response to the first three books of the poem; Suetonius that he suffered a 'chill' from Nero himself. Let us therefore imagine a situation in which the young poet has completed the first three books of his work and decides that it is time to publicize them by means of recitation. The poet-emperor, his senior by only two years, is certain to be in the audience. Can Lucan possibly have failed to recite his dedication to Nero? Could it not be that it was something in this very dedication which so offended Nero that he responded by freezing out the reciter? Horace in his *Satires* is well aware of the dangers of flattering the young Octavian and fears that his response may be to kick out like a horse. Does Nero administer just such a kick? The poet-emperor was, I suggest, the first reader to see through the posturing of Lucan's dedication.

If the opening of the *Pharsalia* and its encomium of the emperor were enough to provoke displeasure, one can only imagine how Nero might have responded to the content of the rest of the poem. Lucan implicitly invites his reader to engage in this imaginative exercise; and Statius will explore the possibility even further in his dedications to Domitian. Meanwhile, the further development of the *Pharsalia* establishes an alternative ideal audience, and one which refuses to view the civil wars and the subsequent development of Roman history in the same consoling light as the passage quoted above. This pattern emerges most clearly in the seventh book and its account of the crucial conflict of the civil wars: the Battle of Pharsalus. Here, Lucan adopts the strategy of describing what 'we' see or do, and there is the clear sense of his audience thus being drawn into a common political sympathy with the narrator. When, for instance, the Pompeian party foolishly drive their general into an unnecessary and calamitous engagement with the enemy, Lucan asks the gods whether it pleases them 'to add this guilt to our mistakes'. Responding to the same event, he complains that 'We charge to disaster, demanding warfare which will injure us; | in Pompey's camp, Pharsalia is their prayer.' Even when erring, therefore, *we* are clearly Pompeians.

Compare the following passage in which Lucan laments the impact of the battle on his generation:

> From this battle the peoples receive a mightier wound
> than their own time could bear; more was lost than life
> and safety: for all the world's eternity we are prostrated.
> Every age which will suffer slavery is conquered by these swords.
> How did the next generation and the next deserve
> to be born into tyranny? Did we wield weapons or shield
> our throats in fear and trembling? The punishment of others' fear
> sits heavy on our necks. If, Fortune, you intended to give a master
> to those born after battle, you should also have given us a chance
> to fight.
>
> (Lucan, *Pharsalia* 7. 638–46)

Where the dedication to Nero had represented the new Rome of his reign as the happy recompense for all past suffering, now there is just an unbroken continuum of woe. Moreover, the issue is not just the destruction of the nation but the political enslavement of the people. The group which Lucan represents in the first-person plural straddles the time of Pharsalus, in which it is laid low, and the time of Nero, in which its servitude endures. The complaint which Lucan expresses therefore is that *we* did not betray ourselves through cowardice, and that *we* did not have the chance to continue the fight against the monarchy into which *we* were born.

Lucan speaks here for a partisan community. That that community consists of the poet and his audience is further suggested by some further famous lines from the same seventh book. Lucan here is rounding off a lengthy catalogue of the omens which foretold the disaster of the day ahead:

> O mightiest of men—your Fortune gave displays
> throughout the world, on your destiny the entire sky was intent!
> Even amongst later races and the peoples of posterity, these events—
> whether they come down to future ages by their own fame alone
> or whether my devotion also and my toil can do anything
> for mighty names—will stir both hopes and fears together
> and useless prayers when the battle is read;
> all will be stunned as they read the destinies as if
> to come, not past and, Magnus, still they will side with you.
>
> (Lucan, *Pharsalia* 7. 205–13)

To read the *Pharsalia* will be to be immersed in the immediacy of the battle, to become a partisan of Pompey and to endure an eternity of frustrated hope. There is a massive sting to the final two claims. The suggestion that a narrative could be so vivid as to make the events recorded seem present and not yet past was a commonplace in ancient historiography. Yet what Lucan offers his audience is not just a vivid narrative. Rather, his achievement as a writer will be to create the temporal space in which they can disavow the consequences of the events he describes, consequences which shape every aspect of their lived political experience. Inseparable from this, however, is the terrible force of the disappointment which he must inflict on them. To discover that Pompey did not win is to remember that Caesar did, and that Caesar begat Augustus and with him the whole Julio-Claudian house right down to Nero himself.

What is the ideal reading audience, then, to which Lucan serves up his terrible cocktail of illusion and disillusion? It is an audience who perceive themselves as defeated, who reject the system which emerged from Pharsalus, but whose defeat enjoys no prospect of reversal as the generations roll on. It is an audience which will learn from the hopelessly compromised figure of Lucan's Pompey its first lesson in the perils of allowing a leader to overtake his cause. It may hear in Cato the Younger the true voice of republican principle, but may also be alienated by his grotesque self-regard and futile shows of virtue.

Lucan grew up and first performed in an ugly and treacherous world. To be the prodigiously talented nephew of the emperor's tutor was a short cut to celebrity but also to misfortune. Many reciters were surely given a 'chill' by their audience, but few can have suffered thus at the hands of Nero himself. Tales of poetic jealousy, of defamatory verses and lavatorial mockery of the ruler's verse are properly colourful but it must be remembered that the consequence of that 'chill' was the denial to Lucan of the right either to perform his verse or to act as an orator. Perhaps it is in this experience of exclusion that the seeds of the *Pharsalia*'s account of the true Rome lost are to be found.

Silius and the poetry of retirement

The longest extant Roman epic of them all is the *Punica* of Silius Italicus (25–100 CE). The theme of the poem is the Second Punic War, Hannibal's invasion of Italy, the disasters of Trasimene and Cannae, then the turning of the tide through the generalship of Q. Fabius Maximus and Scipio Africanus. The great Ennius had already covered the same ground in his *Annales* (cf. Ch. 9, pp. 293–7) and Silius is duly deferential. Seventeen is an unusual number of books for an ancient epic but the figure suggests that Silius aspires to something comparable to the eighteen books of the *Annales* and Ennius himself is pictured fighting in Sardinia. The patron deity of verse, Apollo, is even on hand to protect the poet destined to sing of Roman wars and equal the Greek Hesiod in glory and honour. Another author who had covered these events and whom Silius will have revered was the great historian Livy, like Silius a native of Patavium (cf. pp. 461–3). As we shall see, such affinities mattered to the poet.

An orator, politician, and imperial administrator before he was a poet, Silius enjoyed the rare privilege amongst his contemporaries of a public career free, if not from rebuke, at least from retaliation. Pliny the Younger marks the poet's death with the following summation of his two careers as statesman and as poet:

> The news has just come that Silius Italicus has starved himself to death in his house near Naples. Ill-health was the reason, for he had developed an incurable tumour which wore him down until he formed the fixed resolve to escape by dying; though he had been fortunate in life and enjoyed happiness up to the end of his days, apart from the loss of the younger of his two sons. The elder and more gifted he left well established in his career and already of consular rank. Italicus had damaged his reputation under Nero—it was believed that he had offered his services as an informer—but he had maintained his friendship with Vitellius with tact and wisdom, won fame for his conduct as governor of Asia, and removed the stigma of his former activities by his honourable retirement. He ranked as one of our leading citizens without exercising influence or incurring ill-will; he was waited on and sought after, and spent many hours on his couch in a room thronged with callers who had come with no thought of his rank; and so passed his days in cultured conversation whenever he could spare time from his writing. He took great pains over his verses, though they cannot be called inspired, and frequently submitted them to public criticism by the readings he gave. Latterly his increasing age led to his retirement from Rome; he made his home in Campania and never left it again, not even on the arrival of the new Emperor: an incident which reflects great credit on the Emperor for permitting this liberty, and on Italicus for venturing to

> avail himself of it. He was a great connoisseur; indeed he was criticised for buying too much. He owned several houses in the same district, but lost interest in the older ones in his enthusiasm for the later. In each of them he had quantities of books, statues and portrait busts, and these were more to him than possessions—they became objects of his devotion, particularly in the case of Virgil, whose birthday he celebrated with more solemnity than his own, and at Naples especially, where he would visit Virgil's tomb as if it were a temple. In this peaceful atmosphere he completed his seventy-fifth year, surrounded by attentions though not really an invalid. He was the last consul to be appointed by Nero, and the last to die of all the consuls Nero appointed; and also remarkable is the fact that not only did the last of Nero's consuls die in him but it was during his consulship that Nero perished. (Pliny, *Epistle* 3. 7. 1–10, trans. Radice)

The implications of this passage merit consideration; for they offer an intriguing glimpse of the literary world in which the *Punica* was produced.

The public career of Silius is of some significance. Pliny notes that he reached the consulship in 68 CE, the final year of Nero's reign, and that the troubled times of 69 CE saw him side with the third of the four emperors to rule in that year, Vitellius. Tacitus also refers to negotiations carried out on behalf of Vitellius by Silius; and the opening of the fourth book of his *Histories* reveals the unhappy fate which awaited many of those who had taken the same side when the troops of Vespasian entered Rome. Silius came through all of this and his poem exhibits an unusual absence of rancour towards any of the fallen monarchs under whom he had lived. His Jupiter prophesies a glorious Roman future marked out by the achievements of Vespasian, Titus, and Domitian; the narrative of Cannae even depicts a Galba of glorious name, and has him present the same peculiar claim to be descended from Pasiphaë as his namesake who overthrew Nero. Only when the same account introduces an audacious young horseman Claudius Nero descended from the blood of the Spartan Clausus, do things become more complicated. For here it is hard not to think of the Emperor Nero, the adopted son of Claudius. When last seen, this mid-republican Nero is savagely brandishing the head of the noble Carthaginian general Hasdrubal, an event fully attested by Livy and yet oddly appropriate to the reputation of the fallen ruler. Silius will use no more direct means to disavow the memory of a monarch on whom his peers are happy to heap scorn.

Pliny is evidently less than in love with what he regards as the careful but uninspired poetry of Silius. Martial's epigrams (cf. pp. 496–8) repeatedly flatter the poet as the darling of the Muses and the equal of Virgil but there is some suggestion that he too has his tongue buried pretty firmly in his cheek. Twice the epigrammatist speaks of 'deathless Silius' but the adjective used to express the immortality of the poet (*perpetuus*) is also that used by Ovid in the proem to his *Metamorphoses* to describe the continuous single narrative of a long epic poem. To those faced with the ever-expanding masterpiece of the venerable ex-consul, he may truly have seemed 'perpetual'. Would they ever, could they ever get to the end of his poem? Classical scholars still preen themselves on occasion for having read the whole of the *Punica*.

The disingenuous zeal with which Martial celebrates the rhetorical and poetic achievements of Silius may suggest that the public criticism to which he subjected himself at recitations was not the most exacting. Young writers had every reason to flatter Silius because he was one of the great purchasers and consumers of poetry of his day. In one epigram, Martial sends a copy of his poetic trifles to Silius and likens himself to Catullus presenting Virgil with a collection of his poems. In another, Martial celebrates the same poems 'which the bookshelves of deathless Silius deign to hold'. This is consonant with Pliny's description of the villas of the poet which teem with books, statues, and busts: the purchase of literature as much as its study and its composition is the passion of Silius' indulgent old age.

For Silius, life and literature rather blend into each other. That of which he is proud or towards which he feels affection is almost certain to find itself celebrated at some point in his poem. Pliny refers to the honourable manner in which Silius governed the province of Asia, an undertaking which will have followed his consulship and which is normally dated to around 77 CE and the reign of Vespasian. Silius narrates the allegedly clement and restrained sack of Syracuse by the great M. Claudius Marcellus in book 14 of the *Punica*, and closes his account with the following commentary on the abuses which Domitian has had to correct:

> Happy the peoples, if, as was once the way in war,
> now too our peace left cities undespoiled!
> Yet, had not the care of that man who has now given the
> world ease held back the unreined rage to plunder all,
> greedy rapine would have stripped bare land and sea.
> (Silius Italicus, *Punica* 14. 684–8)

Silius is happy to trumpet the example of Marcellus because the verdict of his contemporaries is that he himself is a living model of the right sort of rule. Of this he was evidently rather proud.

Sermons of this sort are rare in the *Punica*. Silius expresses his own nostalgia for the moral greatness of Rome in the Second Punic War, and laments the paradox of a victory in arms which brought only complacency and the corruption of prosperity. But he is no Lucan. There is no condemnation of imperial power or representation of modern Italy as a land in ruin. Rather, the world of Silius, which penetrates the world of the *Punica* manifests itself in allusions to friends and fellow townsmen and in celebrations of those whom he loved most dearly: the authors who sat upon his shelf. An important example of the former category may be related felicitously to one from the latter. The full name of Silius Italicus is revealed by an inscription found in his province of Asia: Titus Catius Asconius Silius Italicus. This should be compared to that of the famous literary scholar and contemporary of the poet, Q. Asconius Pedianus: note that the *cognomen* of Silius is also the *nomen* of the critic, i.e. Asconius. Now the critic Asconius is known to have been of Paduan descent and a number of historians have inferred that this must also be true of Silius. A touching hint at the writers' shared origins is offered by book 12 of the *Punica* and the sudden entry into the fray of a dashing Paduan hero whose only given name just happens to be the *cognomen* of the critic:

> Young Pedianus dressed in Polydamantean arms
> waged war ferociously and proclaimed himself
> of Trojan seed and origin and of Antenor's stock,
> as famous for his family and the holy Timavus
> and a name blessed for his glory on Euganean shores.
> To him father Eridanus and the peoples of the Veneto in turn
> and the race rejoicing in the Aponus—whether he roused wars
> or in calm preferred the Muses and the silence of the learned life—
> proclaimed no peer, nor was any other youth
> more famed in war, or any youth more famed in verse.
> (Silius Italicus, *Punica* 12. 212–22)

Silius strings together a number of place-names of significance to the people of ancient Padua and the myth of their origins. The claim that they are Trojans and descended from Antenor is familiar from Virgil and Livy; the association of Polydamas with Antenor is far more recherché, and perhaps appeals not just to a learned reader but in particular to a learned Paduan reader. Moreover, there can be no doubt that the ideal reader to whom this passage is directed above anyone else is none other than Q. Asconius Pedianus, flattered to discover a heroic ancestor and recognizing in the youth's literary pursuits an amiable reflection of his own special gifts.

Asconius was a good twenty years older than Silius. By the time that Silius was of an age to receive his training in poetry and rhetoric, Asconius must already have established himself as one of the leading critics of the day. It is tempting to see in this passage the pupil's tribute to his teacher. The young Silius, eager to establish himself in Roman life and letters, must have found in his famous fellow townsman a model and an important supporter on his arrival in the capital. Asconius is read now for his commentary on the speeches of Cicero, but he was also known in antiquity for his work *Against the Critics of Virgil*. His influence can surely be detected in the signal dedication to both these writers which distinguishes so much of the life and work of Silius. When Martial flatters the oratorical and poetic compositions of Silius, he represents him as the equal of Cicero and of Virgil; in his wealthy later life, Silius famously bought one of the Campanian villas of Cicero, and he worshipped at the tomb of Virgil, celebrating the poet's birthday with more reverence than his own. In the *Punica*, meanwhile, the literary heroes whose works clutter the bookshelves of Silius and whose busts adorn his mantelpiece find ancestors very similar to Pedianus the Paduan. When Silius catalogues the Roman and Italian forces at the Battle of Cannae, Mantua, home of Virgil, is given a signal place amongst the list of troops from the Po valley:

> You too, peoples of the Eridanus, shorn and stripped
> of men, for no god then paid heed to your
> prayers, rushed to a fight doomed to fail.
> Rocked by war Placentia vied with Mutina,
> Mantua with Cremona in sending youths,
> Mantua, home of the Muses, lifted to the stars
> on Aonian song and a rival to Smyrna's lyre.
> (Silius Italicus, *Punica* 8. 588–94)

Smyrna is here to Homer what Mantua is to Virgil. And what of Cicero? Happily, his native town of Arpinum is also represented at the battle and the leader of the contingent is none other than a distant ancestor of M. Tullius Cicero himself:

> But they who live by the Liris as with Fibrenus it joins
> its sulphurous stream and flows over silent shallows to the shore,
> the shaggy men of Arpinum, the youth stirred from
> Venafrum and the right hands of the Lirenates, shake
> their allied arms and drain huge Aquinum of men.
> Tullius snatched the bronze-clad regiments to war,
> descendant of kings and blood of lofty Tullus.
> O youth of such qualities and fated to give so great
> a fellow-citizen to the peoples of Ausonia in time to come!
> He, heard beyond the Ganges and the Indians,
> will fill the lands with his voice and with the
> thunder of his tongue will quell mad wars and then will
> leave to none of his descendants the hope of equal glory in words.
> (Silius Italicus, *Punica* 8. 399–411)

One might think it more plausible for the forces of Arpinum to be led by the ancestor of its other famous son, the great general C. Marius, but that would be to misconstrue the character of the man and of his work. Silius lived amidst possessions, amidst markers of his devotion to writers and to books. His poem collects poets and orators as he himself did in life.

Statius—in and out of the market-place

Publius Papinius Statius (*c*.61–95 CE) represents the other face of the artistic milieu in which Silius Italicus moved. Born into the artistic culture of Campania which Silius adopted, Statius was a professional poet and the recipient, not the distributor, of artistic patronage. He was from a part-Greek, part-Samnite background and inherited his *métier* from his father, who had combined the life of the writer with that of a teacher of language and literature to the young. The father of Statius began his professional life in the still intensely Greek city of Naples and competed in the Neapolitan games, which were instituted as late as 2 CE but soon became a natural part of the circuit which took in the four great festivals of mainland Greece—the Nemean, Olympian, Isthmian, and Pythian games—as well as the Actian games founded by Augustus. In each of these, artists competed for substantial financial rewards. When the father established himself as a teacher at Rome he had the good fortune to acquire as a pupil the future Emperor Domitian. He very likely also made money from various poetic commissions. The artistic life of the son seems to have followed a very similar path. While Statius is perhaps most famous for his epics, the *Thebaid* and the *Achilleid*, he is also the author of a five-book collection of occasional poems, the *Silvae* (cf. Ch. 16, pp. 409–501, 511–13).

Silius is indulged by his critics because he has the money and the instinct to indulge them in return. For those less financially secure the situation can be very different. The seventh satire of Juvenal urges writers to look to the emperor for support at a time when all other forms of patronage have now failed them. This poem evokes all the shady compromises and starveling indignities of his own Grub Street, and depicts the impact of economic circumstances on two of the authors under discussion in this chapter:

> Lucan may well be content with fame, as he lies at ease
> in his marble gardens. What use, however, to the haggard Saleius
> and Serranus is glory, no matter how great, if it's *only* glory?
> When Statius has made the city happy by fixing a day,
> there's a rush to hear his attractive voice and the strains of his darling

> *Thebaid*. He duly holds their hearts enthralled by his sweetness;
> and the people listen in total rapture. But when with his verses,
> he has caused them all to break the benches in their wild excitement,
> he starves—unless he can sell his virgin *Agave* to Paris.
> Paris also confers positions of military power,
> and puts the gold of six months' service on a poet's finger.
>
> (Juvenal, *Satires* 7. 79–89)

Of the poets named in this passage, only Lucan is unconcerned. He is not just dead but dead and rich. His family can afford to bury him in gardens decorated with marble; his widow Polla Argentaria can commission from Statius himself a poem to honour the dead poet (*Silvae* 2. 7). The works of Serranus and Saleius Bassus have not survived, but Quintilian lists them among the great epicists of Rome. The financial circumstances of the latter are also described in the *Dialogue on Orators* of Tacitus, when M. Aper talks of Bassus working all year on his new book of verse, then forced to hire a recitation hall at his own expense and rush round urging friends to attend—and all for the reward of insincere compliments and a little desultory applause. Yet once, as Aper himself goes on to confess, this same Bassus so impressed the Emperor Vespasian that he was presented with the substantial sum of 500,000 sesterces. There was therefore money to be made from poetry, but no security and always the pressure to bow to the market. Hence Juvenal's description of Statius. The image which runs throughout this passage is that of the poet as pimp: the reaction of the crowd to the feminized *Thebaid* that of the lover panting with lust. Yet there is no reward in this. If he wants cash and with it status, Statius must write a new libretto for a performance of the *Agave* by the noted pantomime artist Paris, and concoct some suitable words as an accompaniment for the gestures and gyrations of the dancer. And they had better be new words—Paris is figured as the pernickety client, refusing to sleep with a prostitute without proof of her virginity.

For a poet acting on Juvenal's advice to seek patronage from the new emperor, an obvious opportunity presented itself in the form of the new literary contests which Domitian instituted in the course of his reign. These were surely based on the Greek festivals in which the father of Statius had competed, but their focus seems to be specifically on poetry and not on gymnastics, athletics, or charioteering. The Alban games were held annually at the villa of Domitian in Alba Longa, and Statius is full of pride for his victorious entry on the theme of the emperor's campaigns against the Germans and the Dacians. The Capitoline games were held only every four years from 86 CE onwards and were apparently rather more prestigious. Statius does not disguise his disappointment at his failure to win the contest of 90 or 94 CE.

Two poems from the *Silvae* are particularly valuable for their commentary on the different levels of Statius' artistic career. In 3. 5, Statius describes his wife who was at his side as he won the Alban games, and was a partner in his grief at his defeat in Domitian's Capitoline games, who heard with vigilant ear the lines he murmured all night long, who shared in the great toil of the *Thebaid* and counted the years of its composition. In 5. 3, Statius laments the fact that his father lived only to see him victorious in the Neapolitan games, but was not there to share in the joy of the Alban games or to console him in his later defeat. Here too Statius closes by describing his father's role in urging him to compose the *Thebaid* and giving him his first lessons in heroic narrative and epic topography. In both these cases, therefore, the *Thebaid* constitutes the true summit of the poet's career, and holds a place above all the verse he wrote even for the greatest competitions. The poem on which he claims at its close to have worked through twelve long years is his artistic monument, a world apart from the more ephemeral efforts with which he competed for the prizes which were his income. This too is the implication of Juvenal's passage. Statius treats the people of Rome to snatches of his masterpiece, but in the market-place they have the value of a loss-leader, generating good publicity and bringing in the short-term remuneration of a libretto here, a praise-poem there.

The *Thebaid* is a monstrously dark epic on the rivalry for the throne of Thebes between the sons of Oedipus, Eteocles, and Polynices. It twice makes pious references to the insuperable majesty of the *Aeneid* but its subject-matter and its aesthetic owe far more to Lucan. Quite different is the *Achilleid,* the attempt to tell the entire story of the life of Achilles. Statius devoted much of his later years to this, but never reached beyond the middle of the second book and the departure of Achilles with Ulysses and Diomedes from the island of Scyros where he has been hidden by his mother Thetis. This poem takes a positively Ovidian pleasure in exploring the sexual ambiguities of the young hero still beautiful enough to be disguised as a daughter of King Lycomedes, whose femininity is sufficiently masculine to prompt schoolgirl crushes on the part of his fellow members of the chorus, and whose determination to show himself a man both in battle and in his yearning for the lovely Deidamia finally forces him to reveal his true identity. Yet, for all the features that make the *Thebaid* and *Achilleid* such very distinct works, they do have one fundamental characteristic in common: the adoption of a theme from Greek mythology and therefore the frustration of the ambitions of the very figure to whom they are both dedicated. The *Achilleid*, for instance, opens with a statement of the poem's theme and then turns to the Emperor Domitian with the following words:

> But you at whom the glory of Italy and Greece wonders from
> afar, for whom the twin laurels of general and poet flower
> rivalrously (the one already regrets its defeat), excuse me
> and permit me in my nervousness briefly to sweat in
> this dust. Long in training and still insecure, I shape to
> write of you and great Achilles plays the prelude for you.
> (Statius, *Achilleid* 1. 14–19)

Compare the proem to the *Thebaid* which first asks where the narrative should begin and considers the different cycles of destruction overwhelming the royal family of Thebes. As Statius fixes on his proper theme, he simultaneously defers the composition of another:

> Rather at present I'll permit the joys
> and agonies of Cadmus to have passed.
> The troubled house of Oedipus shall set
> the limit to my lay, since I'll not dare
> as yet to hymn the standards of Italy,
> the triumphs in the North, the Rhine reduced
> twice to our yoke, the Danube twice beneath
> our jurisdiction, Dacians hurled down
> from rebel peaks, Jove saved from war's assault
> when boy had scarce reached man, and thee, the grace
> and glory given to the Latin name,
> youthful successor to thy father's fresh
> achievements, prince whom Rome would fain possess
> for ever.
> (Statius, *Thebaid* 1. 15–24)

The proem goes on to anticipate the deification of Domitian after the manner of Virgil's dedication of the *Georgics* to Octavian or Lucan's dedication of the *Pharsalia* to Nero, and to promise that some day Statius truly will compose a historical epic on the emperor's exploits. For now, however, he will have to make do with Thebes.

Domitian thus emerges as a form of super-reader for Statian epic. Any other Roman reading the *Thebaid* or the *Achilleid* is invited simultaneously to imagine the experience of the emperor as he reads, and to judge his reaction to the poems as they unfold. The same conceit recurs in the poet's farewell to the *Thebaid* at the close of the final book. Statius prepares to send forth into the world the work of twelve years of toil and wishes it immortality. Already, however, it seems that parts of the poem are in the public domain, for he describes how Caesar deigns to know it and the youth of Italy learn and recite it in their lessons.

One fundamental point about this construction of an audience for the epic must be established from the beginning. The strategy whereby a poet deflects pressure to compose a work on an evidently uncongenial theme—by promising to do so at a later point in his career and then offering something different instead—is familiar from the poetry of the Augustan age. It is the habitual stance of the elegists towards their patron Maecenas with his plans for an epic celebration of the deeds of the emperor. The difference is that Statius actually makes good his promise. For he himself states that his winning entry for the Alban games was on the German and Dacian campaigns of Domitian; and a brief four-line scrap of an epic entitled *On the German War* is preserved for us by an ancient commentator on Juvenal. These two works may not be identical—the Alban games might well have been won with a lyric celebration of victory—but Statius is clearly not shirking the task. Domitian seems finally to have obtained the laudatory account of his military exploits which the poet elsewhere defers. Statius is a poet in the market-place and it would scarcely be wise to frustrate the ambitions of the poet-emperor and greatest patron of them all.

More important still is the impact on interpretations of the *Thebaid* of the poem's construction of Domitian as super-reader of the text. The poem's theme, for all that the action is firmly located in the distant past of Greek mythology, for all that it is one of the great *literary* themes of epic and tragedy, may have something to say to the Rome of the Flavians. Statius' father had composed a notable poem on the Year of the Four Emperors in 69 CE; his son side-steps this contemporary civil war, but one wonders how much of the father's work found its way into that of the son through allusion and imitation.

Statius sets out to describe the conflict of two brothers for the throne. How resonant was this for a Rome which had seen Britannicus dislodged by Nero or heard rumours of tension between Titus and Domitian themselves? In the sixth book of the *Thebaid*, funeral games are held for the dead child Archemorus. Polynices participates in the chariot-race, is the recipient of much wise counsel from his father-in-law Adrastus, but still falls out of his chariot and is led away all in a daze. Nero too had suffered just such a fall when attempting to drive a ten-horse chariot at the Olympic games. Might the reader who is invited to imagine the reaction of the super-reader Domitian pause and form a picture of the emperor stumbling on this allusion to his hapless predecessor? Does a smile pass across his lips? Or does he grimace as he realizes that these Theban tyrants are not so distant from his world as Statius might pretend? The example is trivial, but the underlying principle is not.

The audience of the *Thebaid*, whether Domitian the dedicatee or the chanting pupils in the schoolroom, or the public at a recitation, are not required to find in every episode of the poem a correspondence to recent Roman life as direct as that between Nero and Polynices in their chariots. It is clear from the evidence of the Roman theatre in this period, as well as in the late Republic, that gesture and intonation on the part of the actor could suggest a particular identification to the audience, but texts such as the *Thebaid* are sold short by an approach which sees behind every mythological mask a specific Roman figure of recent history. The eloquence of the poem lies in its ability to depict in grotesque and hyperbolic form the systematic frailties undermining all monarchical power: the jealous paranoia of the ruler, the fear of the counsellor to give advice which will be unwelcome even if just, the violence done to religious observation and the perversion of martial courage in a struggle for the throne. If Lucan had provided Statius with the vocabulary to describe the corrosive impact on religious and martial values in time of civil war, the terrible events of 69 CE had reminded Rome of the relevance of his vision. The Thebes of the *Thebaid* is a cipher. Statius never follows Lucan's example to mourn the grandeur of the city overwhelmed by civil war, and has no room for a Cato who identifies his cause with that of Rome. Rather, the walls of Thebes must be shattered or defended only inasmuch as they encircle and defend the one goal which drives Eteocles' and Polynices' every action: the throne. There is in the raw nakedness of this pursuit more than a little of the Otho and Vitellius whom Tacitus will present in his *Histories*.

An *Argonautica* for imperial conquerors

Of all the writers of epic in the Neronian and Flavian periods, least is known of Gaius Valerius Flaccus (d. *c*.90 CE). Manuscripts of the remaining eight books of his *Argonautica* also call him Balbus Setinus but this only indicates that he came originally from the hilly, vine-clad town of Setia in Latium or from its Spanish namesake. Quintilian's review of Roman epic poets probably refers to him when it states that 'We have recently lost something big in Valerius' but there is no mention of him in Pliny or Martial. Statius seems to rework Valerius' account of the Hypsipyle story in the *Thebaid*, but never names him in the *Silvae*. Valerius does not seem to have been one of the great characters of the Flavian literary world. Though it is not possible to describe his relationship with his Roman audience, something may be said about the significance of the *Argonautica* for the Rome of the period.

Valerius was not the first Roman to tell of the voyage of the Argo to Colchis, the struggle with Aeetes for the golden fleece and the beginnings of the affair between Jason and Medea. Varro of Atax had already achieved great distinction for his *Argonautica*, apparently composed some time in the mid- to late 40s BCE and in the wake of the successful Pontic campaigns of Pompey in the 60s and Caesar in the early 40s BCE. Ethnography is the foster-child of empire and the poetry of Varro pandered to the hunger for information about new worlds and peoples. It is some indication of Varro's concerns that he also composed a poetic geography called the *Chorographia* and an epic on part of Caesar's Gallic Wars entitled the *War with the Sequani*. Valerius too expatiates on the peoples of the Black Sea region and introduces in book 6 a lengthy description of fighting between Aeetes and his brother Perses which leaves him with no choice but to provide a catalogue of all those who came to fight.

The time of Valerius did not quite see the same succession of Pontic campaigns as had that of Varro, but there had been some significant fighting and it has been shown that he is the first Roman writer to give a convincing description of certain native tribes, in particular the Sarmatians. Moreover, there is some evidence that epics of navigation grew in appeal every time the Roman Empire spread across the seas. Varro of Atax wrote soon after Julius Caesar's invasion of Britain; but Valerius could legitimately claim that his dedicatee Vespasian had more truly earned comparison with the Argonauts by his participation in Claudius' permanent subjugation of that island country. Note how the opening lines of the epic emphasize this exploit, and then twist the commonplace of the emperor's future as a god by making him a star surer to guide by than even the pole star:

> I sing of the first seas through which the sons of the gods passed
> and of the prophetic ship, which dared to aim for the shores
> of Scythian Phasis and burst straight through the clashing
> rocks, finally to reach port on flaming Olympus.
> Apollo, counsel me, if there stands in my chaste home a tripod
> which knows the Cumaean priestess, if the laurel's green
> covers a worthy brow. You too, who have the greater glory
> of opening the seas, ever since the Caledonian Ocean
> bore your sails, previously indignant at the Phrygian Julii,
> snatch me from the crowd and the cloudy earth,
> O holy father, and show me favour as I sing of
> the venerable deeds of old-time men. Your offspring tells of Idume
> overthrown—for so he can—and of his brother black with the dust of Solymus,
> brandishing torches and raging at every tower.
> For you he will institute divine honours and for your family
> a shrine, when already, O father, you shall shine from every
> part of heaven, nor shall the pole star be for Tyrian ships

> a surer guide or Helice a more trusted marker for the helmsmen of Greece, whether you give the signs or whether Greece and Sidon and the Nile send out ships with you to show the way. Now may you serenely aid my enterprise, that this voice may fill the Latin cities.
>
> (Valerius Flaccus, *Argonautica* 1. 1–21)

For Vespasian the navigator, for his imperialist people, the time is right for a new *Argonautica*.

The problem with any work on the theme of the Argonauts is that there is no escaping the encounter with Medea, her agency in the winning of the fleece, and the catastrophic consequences of her marriage to Jason. Valerius, like Apollonios before him (cf. pp. 241–4), peppers his narrative with allusions to what must occur once Jason is back in Greece. Medea then must represent the dark side of advancing into unknown lands. Yet Valerius has a consolation and is sure to give it a specifically Roman coloration. In the first book, Jupiter reveals his long-term plan after the fashion of his speech to Venus in *Aeneid* 1: the Argonauts will open the seas and will bring Asia to blows with Greece. This will lead to the fall of Asia but the supremacy of Greece will finally fail and pass to what must be assumed to be Rome: 'This then is my resolution concerning the end of the Greeks; soon I shall cherish other nations.' The Virgilian trope is almost forced into the narrative and contributes very little to what follows: Jason has no idea of Rome, he undergoes no gradual revelation of his Roman destiny, his fate is not bound up in any meaningful way with that of Rome. Yet the manner in which Valerius ensures that Rome finds a place in his epic of ancient Colchis is as revealing in its own way as the care with which Statius keeps up the pretence that it is nowhere to be seen in his Thebes.

The other difficulty for the historical plan which Jupiter propounds is that it has no obvious end. As with Pythagoras in book 15 of Ovid's *Metamorphoses*, we are left wondering whether other nations in turn will not be cherished in place of Rome. There is nothing here to suggest that Rome is endless or immutable. Moreover, if the one explicit reference to Rome in the main body of the *Argonautica* is anything to go by, then Valerius is no optimist. No contemporary reader will have forgotten how Vespasian the new Jason came to the throne. When the scythe-bearing chariots of Ariasmenus are turned back on his own men by the aegis of Athena, a striking simile reminds us that by now civil war is a specially Roman activity:

> Just as when most savage Tisiphone stirs
> Roman legions and kings, their columns glittering on
> both sides with spears and eagles, their fathers tillers
> of the same lands, sent as recruits by the same sorry

> Tiber from all the fields to wars not these,
> so men recently united and seeking to slay a foreign foe
> panicked to see Pallas, so did chariots turn and rush to
> their destruction, though their drivers called them back.
>
> (Valerius Flaccus, *Argonautica* 6. 402–9)

The Flavian audience of the *Argonautica* will not have missed the importance of these lines.

16 Imperial space and time: The literature of leisure

CATHERINE CONNORS

Leisure time as hard work

Alongside the more formal modes of literary production—epic, tragedy, history, philosophy, and oratory—Roman imperial audiences also enjoyed less formal literary modes. Examples produced during the post-Augustan period include satire, epigram, mixed collections, the versified fables in the style of Aesop composed by the freedman Phaedrus, and Petronius' satirical and inventive novel, the *Satyricon*. These works are generally presented as ones to enjoy in leisure time, *otium*, and their informal qualities can include smallness of scale, a low or everyday subject-matter and style (as opposed to lofty national or mythological themes), or signs of spontaneous (as opposed to laborious) composition.

But leisure is a cultural artefact: how people describe, spend, and pay for their leisure time reveals processes of self-definition and cultural formation. Literary works which describe themselves as light or insubstantial can thus play a significant cultural role in their capacity to define their élite audiences as élite enough to indulge in a literature of leisure. The category 'élite enough' is a broad one, ranging from emperors and their courtiers, to wealthy families possessing substantial libraries and highly educated slaves, on to those who possess only a few books and scarcely enough time to enjoy them. Authors can be born into the élite, or they can use the practice of literature to blur the line between working for a living and sharing in élite literary leisure. Women can be part of the élite audience for literature to the extent that they have access to education and leisure: this seems likely in wealthy families and possible in the upper echelons of the courtesan trade. Above all, membership in Rome's upper social and economic classes enables a man to have time free of what he would call work and to fill that time with literature among other pursuits—filling that time with literature is one element of what enables a man to be numbered among the élite. In its capacity to communicate the social message that 'this man has time and money enough to read for pleasure', the literature of leisure is like the toga, the expensive draped garment for citizen men to wear which with its cumbersome folds proclaims the wearer free from the demands of physical labour.

Only those who have the luxuries of time and books and education have access to literature's lessons and pleasures: there are good reasons why the meanings of the Latin word *ludus* include both 'game' and 'school'—both fall into the category of things one does instead of working. So in one sense all literature is a product of leisure. Yet for ancient authors and audiences there are clear differences between the serious works of epic, history, tragedy, rhetoric, and philosophy on the one hand and the frivolity of epigram, satire, or otherwise light poetry and fictional prose on the other. Roman epic poetry offers its audiences all-encompassing and eternal views of the imperial world order originating in myth and embodied in the physical city of Rome. Historical works record the men and events that brought the Empire into being. Philosophy and rhetoric offer disciplines of the soul and body and voice, training men to take their appropriate places within Rome's web of social relations. And all of this happens with the full knowledge of authors and audiences: epic poets, historians, philosophers, and rhetoricians are all overtly instructive, passing on Rome's traditions to form the next generation of imperial citizens and subjects. By contrast, the light works to be considered here leave aside the instructive project of the formal, serious genres to present themselves as amusing diversions for their audience's leisure time.

We can explore Roman thinking about the social and cultural meanings of leisure by considering the term *otium*. This word can be translated as 'peace' or 'leisure' but its meaning is best revealed by exploring the other terms against which Romans could define it. *Otium* is space and time from which the obligations of an élite man have been emptied out: *otium* is time free from work (*labor*), from business dealings (*negotium*), from the performance of duties (*officia*), or from political, administrative, or military service. But it is also defined by the élite in relation to how the non-élite are thought to spend (or indeed waste) their free time: a wise man's *otium* is empty of work and other obligations but full of purposeful and productive contemplation, rest, or literary activity. So Cicero can record in his *On Duties* that according to Cato, Scipio Africanus was never so busy as when he was at leisure (3. 1–4). Seneca too emphasizes the purposeful and productive use of *otium* in his *On Leisure*, arguing that the contemplation and investigation of the nature of the world made possible during *otium* can contribute to the greater good of humanity. By contrast, the *otium* of the unwise is taken up with meaningless frivolities such as games, races, jokes, gossip, extravagant meals, and long afternoons at the baths. These definitions of productive as opposed to wasteful leisure form just one part of a larger élite practice of denigrating the work of those whose labour made Rome function: the privileged élite who live off the labour of others prove that they deserve their freedom from work because of the good use they make of their leisure. Poets producing the literature of leisure take their bearings from this opposition between productive élite *otium* and wasteful popular *otium*.

The elder Cato (cf. pp. 292, 313–14) is introduced to begin many a version of Roman literary history. Here, though, we start with his dramatic exit. At a celebration of the Floralia, games in honour of Venus, the female performers hesitated to perform their usual strip-tease. Cato realized that he was the reason for their hesitation and departed so that the show could go on. Authors use the anecdote of Cato's famous departure to characterize their works as frivolous entertainment, not worthy of a Cato's productive *otium*. Martial (see p. 496 below) uses it in the preface to book 1 of his epigrams:

> Epigrams are written for people who go to the Floralia. Let Cato not come into my theatre, or, if he does come in, let him stay to watch. I think I am within my rights if I end this preface with a poem.
>
> Since you knew about bawdy Flora's charming festival,
> the holiday shows and the crowd's outrageous behaviour,
> why, stern Cato, did you enter the theatre?
> Or had you come just so you could make an exit?

The narrator of Petronius' (see p. 502 below) racy *Satyricon* programmatically rejects serious Catonian readers in the same way:

> You Catos, why do you wear that frosty look?
> Why slate my new and unpretentious book?
> The language is refined, the smile not grave,
> My honest tongue reports how men behave.
> For mating and love's pleasures all will vouch;
> Who vetoes love's hot passion on warm couch?
> Hear Epicurus, father of truth, proclaim:
> Wise men must love, for love is life's true aim'.
>
> (132. 15, trans Walsh)

These dismissals of Cato dissociate literary works from serious literature and from productive leisure and align them with popular entertainments. When Martial describes his epigram book as 'my theatre' the outdoor, popular mime-attending audience is imaginatively identified with the private, indoor, book-buying audience. But this identification can go only so far: simply by being written works Martial's and Petronius' books reach only a fraction of the popular audiences. This simultaneous sense of identification with and distance from popular entertainment seen in dismissals of Cato from a text's audience is one strategy available to producers and consumers of Rome's literature of imperial leisure.

Others embrace the idea of productive leisure, where literary entertainment prepares a man to return to his administrative or political work with renewed vigour. We see this productive vision of literature and *otium* in Phaedrus' collection of verse fables.

Gaius Iulius Phaedrus, born a slave sometime around 15 BCE and freed by the Emperor Augustus, wrote during the reigns of Tiberius, Caligula, and Claudius and died around 50 CE; under Tiberius he offended the emperor's associate Sejanus somehow and received an unspecified punishment. Following the model of Aesop, he uses short episodes (often animal tales) with funny punchlines to provide gentle moral instruction: 'I don't mean to single out individuals but to represent life itself' (3. prologue 49–50). He locates the origin of this discourse in the language of slavery:

> the slave, subject to punishment
> expressed his true feelings in stories
> because he did not dare to say what he wished
> and so by using invented jokes he escaped punishment for his speech.
> (3. prologue 34–7)

Though Phaedrus situates the origins of fable discourse in the slave experience, he frames his own verse fables as requiring leisure from their élite audiences, and indeed providing an opportunity for relaxation that is necessary for the resumption of productive work. Phaedrus traces such relaxation back to his model Aesop with this story. Upon noticing Aesop playing with nuts in a group of boys, an Athenian laughs at him. Aesop shows him an unstrung bow and eventually explains:

> 'You will quickly break your bow if you always keep it strung;
> but if you loosen it, it will be ready for use when you want it.
> In the same way the mind should be allowed some relaxation
> so that it may be better at thinking when it returns to work.'
> (3. 14. 10–13)

Even Martial can embrace the notion of productive *otium* when it suits him. Though, as we have seen, Martial excludes 'Catos' at the outset of book 1, in a poem designed to flatter the younger Pliny (cf. pp. 442–4, 457–8 above) he includes 'Catos' among his potential audience. Here is Pliny's painstakingly defensive account of his own practice of sometimes writing and performing light verse, an activity which might seem insufficiently constructive to be worthy of a man's leisure (see also p. 458 above):

> you say that there were some who did not find fault with the poems themselves but still blamed me in a friendly and candid way for writing and performing them. . . . I grant that I sometimes compose verse that is not serious; and I listen to comedies, I watch mimes, I read lyric poetry, and I make sense of Sotadic verse; moreover sometimes I laugh, make jokes and enjoy myself; to deal with all these kinds of harmless relaxations in brief, I am a man. (*Epistles* 5. 3. 1–2)

Martial in his turn flatters Pliny's seriousness and his productive *otium* when he directs his book of epigrams ('not very polished and not very serious, but still not boorish') to go to Pliny's house not during the day, when he is hard at work writing speeches comparable to Cicero's, but 'you'll go more safely late when lamps are lit: this is your hour, when Bacchus goes wild, when the rose rules, when hair is damp: then may even unbending Catos read me' (*Epigrams* 10. 20. 18–21).

This flattering strategy worked to Martial's advantage. Born in Bilbilis in Spain sometime within the years 38–41 CE, Marcus Valerius Martialis arrived in Rome in 64 CE and enjoyed some contact with his fellow countrymen Seneca and Lucan before they were forced to commit suicide by Nero in the aftermath of the failed conspiracy to assassinate Nero in 65 CE. Martial's first widely circulated work was his book of epigrams on the games celebrating the dedication of the Colosseum in 80; in the years 84–5 he published *Xenia* ('guest gifts', now book 13) and *Apophoreta* ('presents for guests to take home', now book 14). Twelve books of epigrams followed at intervals from 86. He retired to his birthplace in Spain in 98 and died in approximately 104. A letter of Pliny's (3. 21. 2) informs us that Pliny made a gift towards Martial's travelling expenses to return the favour Martial had done him by mentioning him in verse, as we have seen above.

But this vision of Martial's epigrams as part of a productive 'Catonian' *otium* is a one-off. More often, he flaunts the frivolity of his epigrams. At the opening of his eleventh book, he flatters his addressee Parthenius by saying that as he is too busy to read Martial, his book must settle for 'lesser' hands, the hands of those who use *otium* wastefully and idly in betting and gossiping about chariot-racing as they loiter in various places in Rome:

> Book with no work to do [*otiose*], dressed in holiday purple,
> where, where are you going?

You aren't going to see Parthenius are you? But of course.
You'd come and go unopened.
He reads petitions to the emperor, not books;
and he is too busy for the Muses, or else he would have time for his own literary pursuits.
Or do you think you are fortunate enough
if you fall into less important hands?
Go to the Portico of Quirinus nearby.
Neither the Portico of Pompey, nor the Portico of Europa
nor the Portico of the Argonauts
has a crowd with more time on its hands.
There will there be two or three to
unroll the bookworms in my frivolous works,
but only after they have tired of betting and gossip
about the chariot racers Scorpus and Incitatus.

(*Epigrams* 11. 1)

The best spot for this anti-Catonian *otium* is the portico associated with the temple of Quirinus, near Martial's own house on the Quirinal. In the next poem, an implicit contrast then emerges between the easy walk to these haunts of leisure and more rigorous journeys when Martial says, 'Harsh readers, study rugged (*salebrosum*) Santra [a grammarian of the late Republic]; I have nothing to do with you. This book is mine' (*Epigrams* 11. 2. 7–8); the word for 'rugged' is a metaphor drawn from descriptions of paths which are rough and hard to travel (cf. *Epigrams* 11. 90. 2). Still, Martial boasts in the next epigram that his poems *do* find audiences among soldiers at arduous distances from Rome—but only to frame his complaint that his books' capacity to amuse on the chilly and hardworking fringes of Empire does not actually make him any money:

My poetry doesn't divert just Rome's free time
nor do I give it only to ears that aren't busy.
Amid Getic frosts by the standards of Mars
a hardened centurion wastes his time on my book
and Britain is said to recite my verses.
What good is that? My wallet knows none of it.
What enduring pages could I pen,
What great battles I could sound on a Pierian horn,
if, when the holy gods restored Augustus to earth [in the person of the emperor Nerva],
they had also given a Maecenas to you, Rome.

(*Epigrams* 11. 3)

Martial here blames his failure to write lofty verse on the absence of a generous patron who could provide him with necessary funds. Instead he is practically forced to write a multitude of epigrams which can be exchanged for gifts from lesser patrons, and which can be collected to be sold to the general public, though apparently such sales do not yield a direct financial benefit for the author. Elsewhere he admits that even with a Maecenas as his patron he would not be a Virgil (8. 55). That he was not as needy as he sometimes makes himself sound is clear from his possession of a villa at Nomentum, about thirteen miles north of Rome, where he can relax and sleep peacefully, away from the noise of the city, for as he says self-deprecatingly, 'in Rome a poor man's got no place to think or rest' (12. 57. 3–4). Paradoxically, the poet whose works are to be enjoyed at leisure constructs his career as constant hard work analogous to the duties performed by clients for their patrons. He makes the point that he sends poems to his friends instead of getting up early to perform the early morning greeting, the *salutatio* (1. 70, 108). And from retirement in Spain, Martial looks back on the constant busyness of a poet's life at Rome, contrasting the pleasant 'work' of his leisure with his friend Juvenal's hectic schedule:

> Juvenal, while you perhaps go here and there restlessly
> in the noisy Subura,
> or waste time on mistress Diana's Aventine hill
> while your sweaty toga flaps around you
> on powerful men's thresholds
> and the Greater Caelian hill and the Lesser wear you out as you wander,
> [my hometown] Bilbilis, proud of its gold and iron,
> which I've sought after many Decembers
> has welcomed me back and made me a country fellow.
>
> . . . .
>
> I enjoy disgracefully long sleep
> which often not even the third hour [9 a.m.] marks the end of,
> and I pay myself back in full for thirty years of vigils . . .
>
> (*Epigrams* 12. 18. 1–9, 13–16)

Martial flaunts the frivolous, time-wasting side of his poetry in rejecting the Catos as readers, but when it suits him, he stresses the ways in which his poems are like work. In general, the relations between *otium*, literature, work, and social and economic class are not fixed and definite but shifting, flexible, and available for opportunistic use by authors and audiences. A man can disdain frivolous literature and claim the moral high ground with Cato, or can be furtive or flamboyant in the pursuit of literary pleasure. An author can flirt with the possibility that his poems have the wide appeal of mime and other shows, but his verbal craftsmanship and technical expertise allow his audience to distinguish their educated leisure from the pleasures of the masses.

Otium and the bay of Naples

The space most closely associated with élite Roman leisure is not at Rome at all, but in luxurious villas dotted along the bay of Naples, especially in the vicinity of the resort town of Baiae. For those who could afford such getaways, Rome was for work while Baiae was for pleasure. Martial entertainingly reverses this conceit when he contrasts a friend's non-productive Roman estate with a paradoxically productive farm near Baiae, one not given over to 'leisured myrtles':

> But you Bassus have a property near Rome, lovely but totally unproductive.
> Your view from a high tower takes in only laurels,
> and you are carefree, for your Priapus fears no thief.
> You feed your vineyard workers with city flour
> and when you go to your painted villa on vacation you bring
> vegetables, eggs, chickens, apples, cheese, new wine.
> Should this be called a country place or a city home out of town?
> (*Epigrams* 3. 58. 45–51)

Statius, Juvenal, and Petronius each describe the pleasures available on the bay of Naples in ways which suggest different understandings of relations between work and pleasure and literature.

Statius, like Phaedrus, aligns his informal verse with an understanding of *otium* as a productive and purposeful relaxation which can restore an imperial official for the rigours of his duties, or ready a poet for the demands of the higher literary forms. Born Publius Papinius Statius around 45 CE at Naples and educated at first by his father, who was both teacher and poet, Statius won favour with Domitian upon making his way to Rome. A lost poem *On the German War* praised Domitian's triumphal celebrations in 89. His epic *Thebaid* was published around 91 CE; and the five books of his *Silvae* began to appear in 92 (the title designates a 'miscellaneous collection' from the word *silva*, whose meaning ranges from 'uncultivated woodland' to 'raw material'). He died in Naples in 96, leaving another epic, the *Achilleid*, unfinished (see also pp. 483–8). Although Statius is a professional poet, he often contrives to represent his poetic work as *otium*. He stresses the informality of the *Silvae* and the rapidity of their composition in prefaces attached to the individual books. One effect of this is to blur the boundary between the work he does as a poet and the leisure of his aristocratic audience. The *Silvae* depict a world of imperial *otium*: by praising men for achieving a peaceful refuge from their obligations, Statius celebrates the magnitude of those obligations. In a verse epistle to Vitorius Marcellus, for example, Statius urges him to stop working over the summer at

Rome and take a holiday: his excellent qualities will be greater after relaxation (*maior post otia virtus, Silvae* 4. 4. 34). The poem combines various manifestations of *otium*. Statius writes to Vitorius at Rome from his own leisured retirement on the bay of Naples, and sends his letter by way of the Via Domitiana. This recently constructed road makes access to the pleasures of the area more convenient from Rome; Vitorius is charged with overseeing the road, so his work facilitates Roman pleasures. Statius meanwhile is pausing to relax from his own labours between finishing his long epic poem the *Thebaid* and starting work on the *Achilleid* (he describes the *Thebaid* as a 'long labour' at 3. 5. 35). He had already made the relation between epic and lighter poetry clear in the preface of his first collection of *Silvae*, asserting that all great poets write works of a lighter sort:

> I have long hesitated a great deal about whether I should gather together these pieces which welled up in me with a sudden burst of feeling mixed with some pleasure in their quick composition and issued from me one by one. Why indeed should I take trouble over producing an edition at a time when I am still worried about my *Thebaid*, though it has already left me? Why, we read the 'Gnat' [a mock epic attributed to the youthful Virgil] and we acknowledge the 'Battle of Frogs and Mice' [a mock-epic attributed to Homer], and there is no great poet who has not produced preliminary work in a lighter style.

Like Cato, Hercules is a figure so associated with labour that it is exceptional when he does relax and embrace *otium*. The god appears as a paradigm of the renunciation of labour and the embrace of *otium* in *Silvae* 3. 1, which celebrates the restoration of a temple of Hercules on the bay of Naples near Surrentum by Pollius Felix:

> Come here and bring your presence to the newly-founded shrine.
> Dangerous Lerna does not require you, nor the plains of poor Molorchus,
> nor the dreaded land of Nemea nor the Thracian caves,
> nor the Pharian ruler's desecrated altars,
> but a blessed and straightforward household, unskilled in evil deceit
> a spot worthy of even divine guests.
> Put aside your fierce bow and your quiver's savage horde,
> and your club, stained with much royal blood,
> take off the enemy stretched across your unyielding shoulders.
>
> (3. 1. 28–36)

In withdrawing to a refuge on the bay of Naples, Hercules follows the example of Pollius himself, whose pursuit of undisturbed peace is described in *Silvae* 2. 2, a celebration of his villa near Surrentum:

> Live, richer than Midas' treasure or Lydian gold,
> fortunate beyond the crowns of Troy and the Euphrates,
> whom neither changeable political power nor the fickle mob
> nor laws nor military camps trouble, who with a magnificent heart
> overcomes hope and fear, transcending every desire,
> freed from the limits of Fate, proving resentful Fortuna wrong;
> the last day will overtake you not beset by a storm of unresolved business
> but having had your fill of life and ready to depart.
>
> (2. 2. 121–9)

Hercules' withdrawal to the bay of Naples follows the example of many wealthy Romans, whose luxurious villas dotted the shores of the bay, making it the place most associated with the Roman experience of *otium*. In *Silvae* 3. 5, Statius writes of his own plans to retire to Naples; the poem is addressed to his wife, who apparently was reluctant to go on the grounds that she was preoccupied with the marriage prospects of her daughter from a previous marriage. Statius describes the area as an escape from all that keeps men busy at Rome:

> There is undisturbed peace there, and the leisure of an idle life
> undisturbed rest and uninterrupted sleep.
> There is no madness in the forum, or laws drawn in disputes . . .
>
> (3. 5. 85–7)

On the bay of Naples by contrast there are plenty of amusements for his wife to enjoy: theatres, baths, temples, and so forth, 'the pleasures of a varied life are all around' (3. 5. 95).

The poet Juvenal (born Decimus Iunius Iuvenalis in approximately 67 CE; his first poem was written after 100 and his fifteenth after 127) makes the Roman desire for peace and quiet on the bay of Naples the framework of his third satire. Satire, the only Roman literary form thought to be wholly Roman in origin, prides itself on representing Rome's seamier side without flinching. Like his predecessor Horace (above pp. 375 ff.), Juvenal mocks excess, hypocrisy, and bad taste, though he tends to be boisterously extreme where Horace is subtle and rather moderate. Here, in the third satire, the poet-narrator goes to Rome's Capena gate to meet a friend named Umbricius who has decided to withdraw to the peaceful isolation of Cumae, 'gateway to Baiae' (Juvenal, *Satires* 3. 4). According to Umbricius it is impossible for a man who does not know how to lie to make his way at Rome. Instead, Umbricius—whose name plays on the associations of *umbra*, 'shadow' or 'ghost'—turns away from the struggle of living at Rome towards quiet Cumae, which is more famously a gateway not to Baiae but to the underworld presided over by the Sibyl. So the poet describes the ghostly Umbricius as 'thus providing the Sibyl with a solitary fellow townsman' (Juvenal, *Satires* 3. 3, trans. Rudd). Direct mention of the Sibyl invites readers to recall her role as Aeneas' guide in the underworld in the sixth book of the *Aeneid*. Indeed, Juvenal has evoked the parade of heroes before Aeneas in Virgil's underworld at the very end of the immediately preceding poem when he imagines what the shades of Rome's republican heroes would feel about the arrival in the underworld of the ghost of an imperial degenerate:

> What does Curius feel,
> or the Scipios twain? What do Fabricius and the shade of Camillus,
> and Cremera's legion and the valiant lads who fell at Cannae
> and the dead of all those wars—when a ghost like this descends
> from the world above? They'd insist on purification . . .
> (Juvenal, *Satires* 2. 153–7, trans. Rudd)

Umbricius' move from Rome to Cumae reverses Aeneas' foundational journey from Cumae to Rome. Juvenal has to stay behind if he is to continue to produce satire: Satire would die if the satirist too abandoned Rome for the restful pleasures of the bay of Naples.

Another satirical treatment of the pleasures available on the bay of Naples forms the framework of the best-preserved sections of the fragmentary *Satyricon* (by Petronius—see below). The surviving sections of the *Satyricon* (mostly from books 14–16, apparently) recount the adventures of a hapless hero Encolpius and his friends as they wander on the bay of Naples, and in the aftermath of shipwreck near Croton in southern Italy. Encolpius is convinced that his difficulties in general, and with sex in particular, result from being pursued by the wrath of the phallic guardian god Priapus. The novel combines parody of epic and of Greek idealizing romantic fiction (perhaps via a tradition of racy Greek fiction which had already mocked the chaste and noble heroes and heroines of Greek romance). It also enthusiastically exploits motifs familiar from verse satire such as extravagant parties, dissolute women, and legacy hunting, and expands farcical situations which seem to have been popular in mime. The prose narrative is interrupted at various points by outbursts of verse. A literary form known as Menippean satire had combined verse with prose in short satirical pieces on various subjects; the satirical account of the aborted deification of the Emperor Claudius attributed to Seneca and known as the *Apocolocyntosis* (*Pumpkinification*) is the only surviving Classical Latin example (see p. 456 below). Petronius' use of verse is more complex and sophisticated than what survives in the Menippean tradition. The surviving fragments of the *Satyricon* include some thirty short poems and two longer poems performed by a character who is a professional poet: sixty-five verses in tragic style on the Fall of Troy, and 295 epic verses on the civil war between Caesar and Pompey.

MOMENTO MORI. A silver beaker, made about the turn of BCE/CE and found at Boscoreale near Pompeii, shows a Hamlet-like fascination with the great figures of the past reduced to skeletons. Trimalchio in Petronius shows a similarly macabre imagination.

On the bay of Naples, as they alternately cadge hospitality and try to escape those they have antagonized, Petronius' main characters Encolpius, Ascyltos, and Giton live alienated from the world of work and from the secure pleasures of *otium*. When they wangle a dinner invitation to the home of the fabulously wealthy freedman Trimalchio, his extravagant entertainment takes Roman amusements to outrageous extremes. Trimalchio is obsessed with death in all its forms, from the cooking and eating of meats to ghost stories to the orders for the carving on his own tomb. His house is described in terms which recall the labyrinthine paths to and from the underworld. Add to this his memories of seeing the Sibyl at Cumae shrivelled up in a bottle, and the whole dinner with Trimalchio parodically recalls Aeneas' heroic encounter with the Sibyl at Cumae and his harrowing journey to the underworld.

So, Statius and Petronius all shuffle the same pack of cards and deal different hands. Petronius' bay of Naples is a land of excess and unmaking the heroic past; Statius' is peaceful and restorative, free from the troubles of Rome; Juvenal's, centred on Umbricius in lonely Cumae, is a sterile place where satire cannot thrive.

Otium and a good nose

It is harder to speak about the life of Petronius than about the other authors we have seen so far. He is probably to be identified with the Petronius described by Tacitus as Nero's 'arbiter of elegance' at *Annals* 16. 17–19, in which case he served as consul in 62 and was forced by Nero to commit suicide in 66. In Tacitus' account, which mentions nothing about the *Satyricon*, Petronius is represented as a master of the amusements of *otium* as well as the business of Empire:

> He spent his days sleeping, his nights in work and life's amusements. Where others earned fame through hard work, he earned it through idleness, and, unlike others who waste their resources, he was not considered a wastrel or spendthrift, but regarded as a man of extravagantly refined tastes. His unconstrained and apparently unselfconscious words and actions were welcomed for their appearance of candour. Nevertheless as proconsul of Bithynia and then as consul, he showed himself to be active and suited for business. (Tacitus, *Annals* 16. 18)

This same theme of finding the middle ground between excessive luxury—as evidenced by sleeping late—and too much hard work is taken up by the satirist Persius. Born into a wealthy Etruscan equestrian family in 34 CE, Aulus Persius Flaccus was educated at Rome and knew the poet Lucan (on whom see above, pp. 472–7 and who, we are told in an ancient biographical notice, admired his works) as well as Thrasea Paetus, a Stoic who took the stern morality of Cato the Younger as his model. Persius' surviving works are six satires and a short prefatory poem; after his death from natural causes in 62, the collection was published by the Stoic Cornutus, who had been Persius' teacher, and another literary friend, Caesius Bassus. In his fifth satire, Persius praises his friend and teacher Cornutus for helping him to understand that true freedom comes from the wisdom not to pursue money or luxury to excess. With a physical concreteness that is typical of his compressed and arresting style, Persius constructs a dialogue to describe a man being roused from sleep by Greed only to be rebuked for his pursuit of profit by Luxury:

In the morning you sleep in and snore. 'Get up,' says Greed, 'hey,
get up!' You refuse. She insists, 'Get up,' she says. 'I can't.' 'Get up.'
'To do what?' 'He asks! Look, import salt fish from Pontus,
beaver-musk, oakum, ebony, frankincense, slippery Coan silk.'

Greed succeeds in persuading the narrator to prepare to embark on a commercial trip, when Luxury interrupts to discourage him:

You dash aboard! Nothing prevents you from
hurrying across the Aegean on a huge ship unless Luxury shrewdly first
gives you a private warning: 'Madman, where oh where are you rushing off to?
...What do you want? Is it that the money that you've cultivated here at a modest five per cent should
end up sweating out a greedy eleven per cent?
Do yourself a favour. Let's snatch our pleasures while we can. That you live well is in my purview;
you will become ashes, a ghost, a story.
Live with death in mind: time flies, even these words spend it.'

(Persius, *Satires* 5. 132–54)

The poet considers two extremes: sleeping late and doing nothing on the one hand, and working tirelessly for money on the other. The implication is that only some activity such as writing poetry or contemplating philosophy will serve to use *otium* productively. But even writing can pose difficulties. In the third satire a stern friend awakens the poet, rebuking him for sleeping late and telling him to get to work: the poet reaches for parchment and reed pen but complains that the pen doesn't work (Persius, *Satires* 3. 1–14)!

How Persius describes *otium* may have to do with the fact that (according to an ancient biography) he was a member of a wealthy family. He thus has access to the leisure required for writing and has little financial need for a literary patron. He makes an implicit contrast between what will emerge as his private, secretive poetic stance ('Who will read that?' 'Are you asking me? No one at all.' Persius, *Satires* 1. 2) and the derivative productions of poets who depend on winning an audience's approval and financial support, described contemptuously in the poem which serves as a preface to the collection:

Who trained the parrot to say 'hello'?
and who taught the magpie to imitate our speech?
The belly, master of arts and generous source of talent,
ingenious at mimicking words nature denies.
And if the hope of tricky cash should gleam
you'd believe that crow poets and magpie poetesses
were singing Pegasus' sweet song.

(Persius, *prologue* 8–14)

Persius' first satire explodes with outrage as it depicts outlandish literary performances which pander to decadent tastes:

> we write in private, one in metre, one without,
> something big for lungs full of breath to huff and puff over.
> Of course you'll finally read this to a crowd from a raised platform
> all combed, shining in a fresh toga, wearing your birthday sardonyx,
> when you've rinsed out your nimble throat with a luscious trill,
> looking like you're overcome by sexual ecstasy.
> Then you'll see huge Tituses shudder disgracefully with shrill sounds
> when the songs penetrate their loins and
> the trembling verse tickles their most private parts.
>
> (Persius, *Satires* 1. 13–21)

Here Persius positions his private satire which he claims to expect no one to read against the works of those who stir the passions of larger crowds through excessive performances.

Elsewhere, Statius is the target of Juvenal's denunciation of the kind of poetry that is excessively and dramatically appealing to the general public (Juvenal, *Satires* 7. 82–7, see also pp. 483–4 above). The audience loves Statius' epic *Thebaid*, but because they are only a crowd, not a wealthy patron, no financial support is forthcoming unless he sells a text for a pantomime *Agave* to a famous and wildly popular performer Paris (for pantomimes, see p. 494 above). Here too a distinction is being asserted between the 'serious' literature that should be produced under the umbrella of patronage and read reverently, and the literature of popular entertainment. Statius' epic *Thebaid* has a certain popular appeal, but—at least according to Juvenal—only the truly mass-market appeal of a pantomime will keep dinner on Statius' table.

Martial distances his work from the tastes of the general public when he warns his book that in venturing out to booksellers it will expose itself to harsh criticism:

> Would you prefer to inhabit the shops of Argiletum,
> little book, though my boxes have space for you?
> Ah, you don't know Mistress Rome's disdain:
> believe me, Mars' crowd has much too much taste
> Nowhere are there bigger snorts of disdain: young and old,
> even boys have a rhinoceros' nose.
>
> (*Epigrams* 1. 3. 1–6)

Because it plays off of the standard image of the nose as an organ of literary sensibility—Horace for example admiringly calls his satiric predecessor Lucilius a man 'with a clean nose'—Martial's comparison to a rhinoceros mocks the coarse tastes of the sneering public. Elsewhere he self-deprecatingly acknowledges that his own poems are vulnerable to critical sniffs, but again the noses in question are extra-large:

> You may be as big-nosed as you like, you may be completely nose,
> so big that Atlas if asked would not want to carry it,
> you could mock Latinus himself,
> but you can't say more against my trivial poems
> than I myself have said.
>
> (*Epigrams* 13. 2. 1–5)

The notion of the nose as an organ of élite good taste is also central to Martial's mockery of one Caecilius. Caecilius claims to be an urbane wit (like, say, Catullus) but he is instead like a mere vendor who sells his goods indiscriminately to the crowd :

> You think you are a sophisticated wit, Caecilius.
> You aren't, trust me. What then? You are a buffoon.
> You are what the peddler from across the Tiber is,
> one who trades pale yellow sulphur for broken bits of glass,
> you're what the one who sells hot porridge
> to the leisured crowd is,
> what the keeper and master of snakes is,
> what the worthless boys of the salt-fish sellers are,
> what the loudmouthed cook
> who sells smoking sausages in stuffy cook-shops is,
> what the inferior street poet is,
> what the disgraceful show producer from Cadiz is,
> what the sharp tongue of an old catamite is,
> so stop thinking you are
> what only you think you are,
> one who can outdo Gabba with jokes and Tettius Caballus himself.
> Not every one can have a nose;
> someone who jokes with unsophisticated impudence
> is not a Tettius, he's a mere old nag [*caballus*].
>
> (*Epigrams* 1. 41)

In imperial Rome, the practice of producing and consuming literary works can play an important role in defining the self. In other words, as Martial says, 'It is not given to everyone to have a nose,' not everyone has taste enough to sneer at the right things. In fact, most people (the *turba*) sneer ignorantly through a rhino's nose. *Producers* position their works anywhere along a spectrum from the disgracefully and obscenely frivolous to the pleasantly refreshing to the purposefully contemplative. *Consumers* could encounter the literature of leisure at a relatively open public performance, or at a more private invitation-only gathering. One could purchase a book from a bookseller, or receive a poem or a book of poems as a gift, from a friend, or from the author himself, with the reciprocal obligations that would entail. Each literary transaction marks the consumer as the sort of person who partakes of literature in that particular way: as part of an exclusive and discerning circle of friends, or as one of an indiscriminate crowd, or as something in between.

Those who read Statius can congratulate themselves that his praises of escape from the demands of Empire will refresh them too; they can imagine that they share the wealth that makes leisure possible and the skill that makes literature successful. Those who read Persius and Juvenal can share the satirists' indignant and mocking detachment from everyday Rome. Enjoying what we could call the anti-Catonian literature of leisure of Martial and Petronius allows audiences to partake imaginatively of several experiences at once: to laugh at mime with the masses, to smile alone in the study, or to exchange jokes with friends at a dinner party. Ostensibly those who read Martial and Petronius abandon—at least while they are reading—the obligation to use *otium* in a productive, Catonian way. But these literate and well-crafted works allow the audience to have it both ways—to go slumming in the world of popular amusements while keeping a firm grip on the education and culture that mark them as élite.

Surely a number of Roman readers did relax at readings by these authors, or with texts of their works. The social and cultural importance of these texts extends beyond a narrowly recreational understanding of *otium*. In acquiring and consuming the literature of leisure, as in acquiring and consuming other luxury goods, individuals define themselves. They define not just the dimensions of their own critical noses but the cultural norms which structure society as a whole.

Orbis and *urbs*: Maps in marble

Martial addresses an epigram to one Sextus, apparently Domitian's librarian of the Palatine library:

> may there be a spot somewhere for my books,
> where Pedo, Marsus, and Catullus are.
> Put the great work of buskin-shod Virgil
> beside the divine poem on the Capitoline War
> (*Epigrams* 5. 5. 5–8)

In other words, the books on lighter subjects are kept separate from those on national themes, in this case from Virgil's *Aeneid* and what was apparently a poem by Domitian on the siege of the Capitol in 69. Yet however far apart Romans might keep the literature of *otium* from the hefty tomes of national epic, what Roman men did at leisure was never wholly separate from what they did while carrying out the business of Empire. Even informal works 'in a lighter vein' participate in the discourses which create imperial culture, reflecting and extending their authors' and audiences' experiences of Empire. In informal works, audiences find not the universalizing perspectives of epic nor the carefully marshalled details of history, but fleeting glances at Empire, snatched amid the complicated business of finding one's way through Rome's crowds. The background of myth that authenticates epic's visions of Empire is not absent, but glimpsed from unfamiliar oblique angles. Imperial power is manifest not so much in accounts of campaigns and conquests as in representations of the people and objects streaming into Rome from all over the world (cf. also pp. 325–6, 488–9 above).

Satire and epigram perpetrate, then, mainly through negative example, their own versions of the disciplines of the soul, body, and voice which define the appropriately male and Roman citizen of Empire. Informal works enjoyed at leisure reinforce their audience's status as educated men and contribute to their sense that Rome is the centre of Empire. Into the city money, imported goods, and newcomers pour in torrents, and from it administrators and orders are sent out. Informal literary works help constitute and illuminate the imperial dimensions of the experiences of *otium* along two axes: the spatial experience of Empire extending from its centre at Rome to its distant frontiers, and the temporal experience of Empire, from its legendary Trojan origins through the Republic to the institution of the principate under Augustus and his successors.

A long-standing punning juxtaposition of *orbis* (world) and *urbs* (city) enacts a Roman fascination with measuring the city of Rome against the world. The *orbis* is conceived of as a space which is mastered through military, administrative, and commercial work. This active hard-won imperial mastery gets talked about in the literature of leisure in various ways: work in the world feeds *otium* in the city; the city serves as an archive or epitome of the world. Inhabitants of the city (at least some of them—and the emperor most of all) need go nowhere besides Rome to consume the spoils of all the world. Imperial Rome was a cosmopolis of consumption, and the spoils of Empire adorning its houses, temples, and tables are reproduced in its literature from the elder Pliny's encyclopaedia to Martial's epigrammatic gift labels (books 13 and 14). The imported luxuries are often 'tagged' with their origins. The geographical 'footnoting' of these spoils implicates texts in the physical, objectively real, world.

Yet, though geographical terms of reference have this objective quality (the places referred to really do exist), at Rome, as elsewhere, geographical information is at the same time an imperial product constructed by the mechanisms of travel, trade, and military campaigns, and authenticated by myth. As such, it is never only an objective report of the world. It is always an utterance in the discourses that animate and uphold Empire: geographical stories communicate imperial aspirations. Transgressive geographical communication can be fatal: the historian Dio records that during the reign of Domitian a certain Mettius Pompusianus was put to death for habitually reading the speeches of kings and other leaders in Livy (presumably in a pointed way) and for having a map of the world painted on his bedroom walls (Dio, 67.12.2–4). A man so interested in figures who once wielded power in Rome and in the far reaches of Rome's Empire evidently made Domitian uneasy.

Mastery of the unimaginably vast spaces of Empire is asserted in written, spoken, or implicit narratives of acquiring and transporting luxury goods to Rome. Luxurious imported food and its trappings—whether actually served or described in literature—become part of narratives of imperial ascendancy. Juvenal's account of the huge turbot offered to Domitian overtly maps Empire onto the dinner table:

> In the days when the last of the Flavian line was tearing to pieces
> the half-dead world [*orbem*], and Rome was slave to a bald-headed Nero [i.e. to Domitian],
> off the temple of Venus, which stands above Doric Ancona,
> an Adriatic turbot of wonderful size was caught.
>
> (Juvenal, *Satires* 4. 1–4, trans. Rudd)

The fish is so huge that no dish is big enough to serve it; a council of advisers is summoned. A later commentator's note tells us that this episode parodies a council scene in Statius' poem (now lost) on Domitian's campaigns on the German frontiers. Satire transforms the business of conquest into the culinary amusements of *otium*, while the fish takes on the configurations of the Empire and its border defences :

> 'So what do you recommend? Cut him in pieces?'
> 'Ah, spare him that indignity!' pleaded Montanus, 'Make him a platter
> fit to encircle his massive bulk [*spatiosum . . . orbem*] with its thin defences—'
>
> (Juvenal, *Satires* 4. 130–2, trans. Rudd)

But the emperor is not the only one who consumes the world (*orbis*): a wealthy man dines unsociably alone in Satire 1, 'chewing his way through the finest produce of sea and woodland. Yes off all those antique tables [*orbibus*], so wide and stylish . . . ' (Juvenal, *Satires* 1. 135–8). The wide circles of the tables

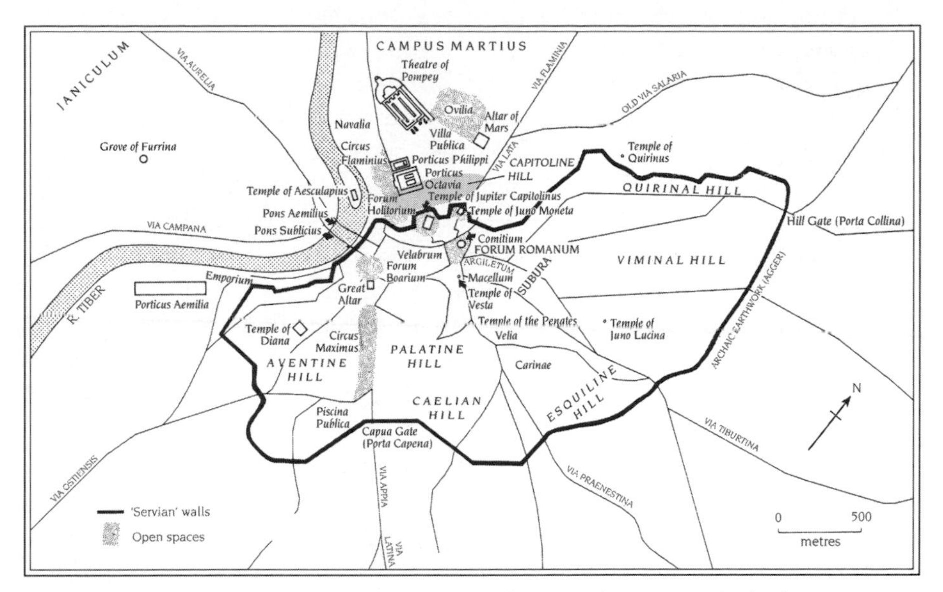

THE URBS THAT RULED THE ORBIS. *Many works of Roman literature, including poetry, are informed by an awareness of the urban topography and layout of the great city of Rome.*

replicate in miniature the wide spaces of the imperial world. In a similar fashion, Petronius' Trimalchio has himself served a tray of hors-d'oeuvres that replicates the zodiac (*Satyricon* 35). According to Statius (*Silvae* 1. 6) Domitian's celebration of games in honour of Saturnus on the first of December gathers tasty foods, lovely women, and birds from the world over into the Roman amphitheatre in a demonstration of Domitian's cosmos-ordering position as emperor. Statius' poetic account of this spectacle renders the popular experience of the amphitheatre 'safe' for the élite man's *otium*.

In the literature of leisure too we can find the same strategies of measuring the city of Rome against the world at large. To take one arresting example, Martial's epigram (2. 14) on Selius' frantic circuit of the Campus Martius in an attempt to obtain a dinner invitation maps a journey of leisure through the Campus Martius against a series of world-mastering journeys represented by monuments there. Selius begins and ends his trip at what Martial calls 'Europa'; this refers to a painting of Europa's abduction by Jove in the form of a bull. The painting seems to have been near or even within the Porticus Vipsania. This building housed a monumental map of the world produced using a geographical commentary by Marcus Vipsanius Agrippa, the close associate of Augustus. The map served as a memorial to Agrippa's mastery of the sea under the sponsorship of Augustus. The myth of Europa would have been an obvious candidate for a decorative counterpart to the Agrippan map: Jove's abduction of Europa in a sense brings the Western world into being because she becomes the mother of Minos, king of Crete, the first dominant sea power in the Aegean. And the voyage of the Argonauts depicted in the nearby Portico of the Argonauts likewise could offer a mythical foil to the story of sea mastery told by the Agrippan map. Now while there is no reason to doubt that these porticoes really were the scene of much leisured relaxation and trawling for dinner invitations, Martial's account of Selius' movements through the Campus Martius is not solely representational. In a move comparable to Juvenal's equation of Domitian's fish with the Empire, Martial implicitly juxtaposes Silius' search for dinner throughout the Campus Martius with the mythical map of Europa's abduction and Agrippa's imperial map of the world. The hard work of urban leisure is mapped against the hard work of winning—and representing—the world.

There were numerous 'maps' of the world at Rome. Even great buildings lavishly decorated with coloured marble served the knowledgeable élite as imperial maps, because the colour of the various marbles signalled their geographical origins. A certain greenish marble came from near Sparta, a greyish-blue from Carystos, a reddish one from Phrygia and so forth. When poets describe such buildings, the audience no doubt expected them to catalogue the marbles on display. In his *Silvae*, Statius tests his audience's connoisseurship of stone and poetry by combining standard information about the colour and source of the stone with vocabulary that is specially chosen to suit the particular building he is describing. In *Silvae* 4. 2, on Domitian's palace, as Kathleen Coleman has shown, the imported stones are described in words which emphasize rivalry and striving for pre-eminence: the Libyan and Phrygian marbles are modified with the adjective 'emulous' (*aemulus*, 26), and the blue marble of Carystos is described by saying that the stones are 'contesting with' (*certantia*, 28) the blue sea nymph Doris.

In a description of one particularly beautiful sea-view room in Pollius' villa at Surrentum Statius (*Silvae* 2. 2) uses terms which reflect the construction of the villa itself: some imported stones are said to come from Greek mines, some to have been dug up by Phrygian axes, and marble 'which is green and imitates the soft grass with its crags' was 'cut from' (*caesum*, 90) a mountain in Sparta. All of this is designed to reflect the construction of the villa which has already been described as a vast mountain-moving project. In the account of Violentilla's house in 1. 2, the terms in which the stone is described are chosen to allow comparisons with Violentilla's emotional shift in the course of the poem: at Venus' persuasion she has softened her resistance and yields to the overtures of her suitor, a man named Stella. The hard stone silex, and the 'hard stones' of Spartan marble correspond to Violentilla's rejections of Stella. The 'winding pattern' (*flexus*) of onyx prefigures Violentilla's change of heart: 'And now she begins gladly to bend [*flectere*] her stubborn heart and now to account herself hard' (1. 2. 199–201). And the sea-blue stone of Carystos shows the trace of Violentilla's reconciliation to Stella: instead of the terms of rivalry associated with it elsewhere there is a notion of agreement when Statius describes it as 'the vein that matches the deep sea's blue' (lines 149–50). Precisely because the shared geographic lore of stone connoisseurship was so detailed and conventional—everyone was no doubt already expecting reddish Phrygian, bluish Carystian, and greenish Laconian stone to be mentioned—Statius can flatter his audience with the craftsmanship of his 'installations'.

The literature of leisure encourages its audience to imagine the world as storehouse for treasures to be transported to and consumed by Romans. These works thereby contribute to the geographical knowledge that is part of the experience of imperial subjects who even in their amusements can enjoy or reflect on their position as global citizens and rulers. Unlike the dangerous map of Empire on Pompusianus' bedroom wall, the private 'maps' which unfold in the literature of leisure make the pleasures of imperial mastery safe for ordinary mortals to enjoy.

Memories of republican Rome

Though the literature of leisure does not aim primarily to tell historical stories, it taps into veins of memory which run through Roman culture at large: memories of the Republic, memories of Troy, and memories of earlier emperors. Think again of Pompusianus reading the speeches of kings in Livy and mapping the Empire on his bedroom walls: if the literature of leisure makes the scope of Empire safe to enjoy, it also makes the past safe to remember.

The literature of leisure incorporates memories of Rome's rise to Empire when it contrasts imperial luxury with republican simplicity and hard work. In his second satire, Persius decries the influx of luxuries into Rome, saying that it is pointless to waste money on lavish offerings to the gods when simple grain will do just as well; he complains that gold vessels have replaced traditional votive objects:

> Gold has pushed out Numa's vessels and Saturn's bronzes,
> and has changed the Vestals' urns and Tuscan earthenware.
> (Persius, *Satires* 2. 59–61)

For Juvenal too, imperial luxury has displaced republican simplicity when he promises his friend Persicus a simple dinner of kid, asparagus, eggs, chicken, and fruit:

> That was the kind of dinner, quite lavish by then, which the senate
> would eat in days gone by. Curius picked his greens
> in his plot and cooked them himself on his tiny hearth. Such a menu
> is now despised by a filthy labourer digging a ditch
> in chains (he remembers the taste of tripe in a stuffy tavern).
>
> (Juvenal, *Satires* 11. 77–81, trans. Rudd)

The idealized self-sufficiency in the vignette of Curius is parodied by Petronius in an account of Trimalchio's vast estates. One of Encolpius' fellow guests says that 'You shouldn't think that he purchases anything. Everything originates at home: mastich, cedar resin, pepper'—a list of trees believed to grow only in their native lands, not throughout the world (Petronius, *Satyricon* 38.1).

In his own way, Juvenal has as much fun with the idealization of republican simplicity as Petronius does:

> When people trembled before the Fabii and stern old Cato,
> and before such men as Scaurus and Fabricius, when even a censor
> feared the harshness that might result from his colleague's austerity,
> nobody thought it a matter for grave and serious attention
> what kind of turtle, swimming then in the ocean's waves,
> might make a splendid and noble prop for our Trojan élite.
> Couches were small, their sides were plain, and only the headrest
> was bronze; it showed the garlanded head of a common donkey;
> beside it the lively country children would romp and play.
> The soldier was rough, and untrained to admire the art of Greece.
> When, after the sack of a city, he found in his share of the spoil
> cups produced by famous artists, he would break them up
> to give his horse the pleasure of trappings, and to set designs
> on his helmet, so that the foe might see at the moment of death
> Romulus' beast grown tame, as imperial destiny ordered,
> the Quirinal twins within the cave, and the naked image
> of Mars, as, grasping his shield and sword, he swooped from above.
> And so they would serve their porridge on plates of Tuscan ware.
> What silver they had would shine on their weapons and nowhere else.
>
> (Juvenal, *Satires* 11. 90–108, trans. Rudd).

In this vision of republican Rome, people eat off of earthenware not simply because they have yet to be corrupted by the spoils of conquest, but because they are capable of resisting such corruption, and elaborate metalware is broken up to decorate helmets and to give a war horse 'the pleasure of trappings'. Juvenal is pointedly reversing accounts of Corinthian bronze: when the city of Corinth was sacked by Rome in 146, metal statues of Corinth were allegedly melted down for tableware and luxurious statuettes (Pliny, *Natural History* 34. 6). Petronius for his part parodies the connoisseurship of Corinthian bronze in Trimalchio's garbled account of his bronzes, genuine 'Corinthian' because they were made by a slave named Corinthus (*Satyricon* 50). The theme that increasing luxury marks a rupture between the republican past and the imperial present also appears in the *Satyricon*: the poet Eumolpus launches into an epic treatment of the civil war between Caesar and Pompey and begins (using a strategy modelled on the opening of Lucan's epic on the civil war) with the assertion that Rome turned to civil war as desires for luxuries became insatiable (119. 1–38).

Statius' *Silvae* 4. 6 also distils republican history into luxurious dining accessories. Statius reports being invited to dinner by one Novius Vindex, who eschews all imported gourmet luxuries but shows off his collection of Greek art-works, including a statue of Hercules 'epitrapezios' ('at table'). The statue, we are told, once belonged to Alexander the Great, who took it with him on campaign. Then Hannibal owned it; he too took it on campaign, but this only inflamed Hercules' anger, especially on behalf of the citizens of Saguntum (founded under his patronage) when Hannibal laid siege to the city. Subsequently it came into the possession of Sulla. Unlike the warrior owners who boasted to Hercules of their own campaigns, Novius Vindex inhabits a world of *otium*, undertakes no military campaigns, and sings to the statue only of the legendary labours of Hercules himself. The opening scene of the poem, in which Statius receives the dinner invitation while spending his leisure time (*otia*) in the Saepta Julia, implicitly goes over the same historical ground. This enclosure (*c.*300 × 95 metres) in the Campus Martius, planned by Julius Caesar and eventually completed by Agrippa, had once been used for electoral assemblies. As its electoral purpose became obsolete under the emperors, it was used as the site of gladiatorial displays before the opening of the Colosseum in 80. After a fire the site was rebuilt and used as a market known for its luxurious goods. In the Saepta, Romans once gathered for elections, then gladiatorial spectacles, then finally up-market shopping: it is the perfect space from which to enter upon the tale of the Hercules statue.

Again and again in the literature of leisure the public story of historical transformation from republican to imperial Rome is scaled down to a private story of dining. Another set of memories of the Republic centres on conceptions of freedom (*libertas*) and language: here too what was public becomes private as republican civic practices give way in the face of imperial realities. As was the

HERCULES IN MINIATURE. This Roman miniature sculpture is a copy of a famous Greek sculpture Herakles Epitrapezios (i.e. at the table).

case for Roman literature of the Republic and Augustan periods, the production of literary works during the first and second centuries CE continued to be by and for men who had acquired a rhetorical education. Rhetoric continued to be a focus for defining Romanness around ideals of masculinity, mastery of language, and placing oneself in the right spot along the spectrum which led from rustic native Italianness on the one hand, through a cosmopolitan Romanness at the centre, on towards a corrupt and effeminate otherness variously categorized as Greek, Eastern, or Egyptian. But between the end of the Republic and the Neronian period, since most power now rested overtly or covertly in the hands of the emperor, the social role of oratory had moved away from a direct connection to governance and had become a site for virtuosic display.

Persius inserts himself as a young and resisting participant into this story of republican excellence subsiding into imperial mimicry:

> I remember that as a young boy I often smeared my eyes with olive oil
> if I didn't want to recite Cato's last words,
> words much praised by my mad teacher
> as my father listened, sweating, with friends he'd invited.
>
> (Persius, *Satires* 3. 44–7)

The younger Cato, who struggled to defend the institutions of the Republic against the dangers of the civil strife between Caesar and Pompey, is the exemplary exponent of republican *libertas*. Lucan represents him as a spirited defender of freedom (cf. p. 470) and Seneca pictures Cato in ringing terms: 'He speaks with the voice of freedom [*vocem liberam*] and urges the Republic not to fail in the defence of liberty but to try everything possible, saying that it is more honourable to fall into servitude by chance than to proceed toward it of their own will' (Seneca, *Epistles* 95. 70). Persius takes up the topic of freedom explicitly in his fifth satire, in praise of his teacher the Stoic Cornutus, and rejecting civic and political definitions of freedom, he defines it in solely philosophical terms. A student asserts:

> Is anyone free, except the man
> who can spend his life as he pleases?
> I can live as I like, am I not
> freer than Brutus?
>
> (Persius, *Satires* 5. 83–5)

Cornutus corrects the student on 'able' and 'choose', asserting that to be truly free one must have insight into what are the truly useful and worthy things in life:

> When you can truly say 'These are mine, I own them',
> then you are free and wise, with the blessing of Jove and the praetors.
>
> (Persius, *Satires* 5. 113–14)

In this exchange, republican freedom of political speech, as exemplified in the public speeches of the first Brutus, the man who brought the Republic into being by expelling the tyrant Tarquinius Superbus, is reconfigured as a private freedom, independent of political and social structures. The other Brutus, the assassin of Julius Caesar, is reduced from national figure to private diversion, when in Statius' witty verses to his friend Plotius Grypus he rebukes Plotius for giving him Brutus' tedious works (probably speeches) as a gift instead of something more enjoyable (*Silvae* 4. 9.20–2). In each case, public republican discourse exemplifying *libertas* is reduced and reconfigured to be the stuff of private diversion in an imperial framework.

The notion of an assertive republican freedom of speech dissolving into the stuff of private imperial entertainment also operates in accounts of the history of satire itself, as we can see in Persius' comparison of his satires with those of his predecessors Lucilius (see pp. 308–9 above) and of Horace (see above pp. 375 ff.):

Lucilius tore up Rome
and you Lupus and Mucius, and broke his molar on them.
Sly Horace mentions every fault while his friend laughs;
once welcomed in he plays on the feelings,
clever at dangling the public from his well-blown nose.
Is it forbidden to me to whisper? not even in secret? in a ditch? nowhere?
Nevertheless I'll dig a hole for it here: I have seen it, seen it myself, little book.
Who does not have ass's ears? That is my secret,
my joke. Though it's small, I wouldn't sell it for any
Iliad.

(Persius, *Satires* 1. 114–23)

Juvenal too voices a paradoxically outspoken discretion. Although he writes during the time of Trajan (98–117) and Hadrian (117–38), he writes mainly about the time of Domitian (81–96). His first satire describes Lucilius' outspoken attacks on his contemporaries:

> Whenever, as though with sword in hand, the hot Lucilius
> roars in wrath, the listener flushes; his mind is affrighted
> with a sense of sin, and his conscience sweats with secret guilt.
> That's what causes anger and tears.
>
> Juvenal, *Satires* 1. 165–8, trans. Rudd)

Juvenal adds that by contrast he will write only about the dead: 'I'll try what I may against those whose ashes are buried beneath the Flaminia and the Latina' (*Satires* 1. 171–2). According to Persius and Juvenal, Lucilius and Horace gave readers front-row seats for satire's relatively public attacks on its targets: Persius and Juvenal themselves frame satire as private, marginal, and secretive. So here too, as in its stories of dining, the literature of leisure keeps telling the same imperial story. What had been public (military conquest, freely uttered mockery) has become private (lavish dining, wary and secretive mockery).

Although the works I have been describing as Rome's literature of imperial leisure make few claims to be consequential, they offer us important points of access to the world of ancient Rome. They showcase strategies for defining oneself as an inhabitant of Rome and of Rome's Empire. The trajectories from public to private traced in these works may reflect a questioning of Empire's institutions or an endorsement of them. Either way, we should listen carefully to Rome's literature of leisure to hear the stories it tells of imperial space and time while claiming to leave Empire's work aside.

17 Culture wars: Latin literature from the second century to the end of the classical era

MICHAEL DEWAR

Small town boys (made good)

Sex sells, as any publisher knows. That much was true in the second century too, though it seems a little magic and a lot of learning could be usefully added to the mix. The proof of this contention may be found in *The Golden Ass*, the celebrated novel of (?Lucius) Apuleius (*c*.125–70 CE) who came from Madaura in the province of Africa. Known formally as *The Metamorphoses*, this is the only Latin novel to survive complete from antiquity, and a remarkable piece of work it is (cf. pp. 274–7, 502–4). Our hero, a young man by the name of Lucius, is travelling in Thessaly, in northern Greece, a part of the world famous for its witches. Lucius' character is distinguished by a rampant curiosity about, on the one hand, the illicit knowledge of magic and, on the other, a young maidservant who is privy to many of the secrets of her mistress, a sorceress with a nice line in corporeal transformation. The maidservant's skills are corporeal too, but not quite in the same way. Eager to experiment, Lucius attempts to reproduce the witch's spells, but instead of becoming, as he hoped, a bird, he is transformed into a shaggy old ass. Luckily, there is an antidote: all he has to do is munch on a few rose petals, and all will be as good as new. But of course, if he were to do that straight off, there would be no novel, so poor Lucius in his grotesque inhuman form is subjected to a series of misadventures that take him from one end of Greece to the other, and see him repeatedly stolen, sold, beaten, humiliated, owned by all kinds of unpleasant characters, and threatened by all kinds of even more unpleasant deaths, before eventually being scheduled for a performance in the arena at Corinth. His role is intended to be a central one, fitting to his, as it were, assets: he is to copulate with a woman condemned to death, and thus provide the instrument of her execution.

What was the literary purpose of such a scandalous composition? Apuleius himself explains in the prologue (1. 1):

> Now, in this Milesian style, I shall string various tales together for you, and caress your kindly ears with pleasurable murmurings, if only you are not too proud to take a look at Egyptian paper inscribed with the sharpness of a Nile reed-pen—to make you marvel at the shapes and fortunes of men changed into other forms and then turned back once more in due sequence into their own. Time to begin. 'But who is this fellow?', I hear you ask. I can tell you in a few words. Attic Hymettos and the Isthmus of Corinth, and Spartan Taenarus, blessed lands made famous for ever in books more blessed still, are my ancient ancestry. There I did my boyhood service in the tongue of Athens. After that, I came to the city of the Latins as a stranger, and with pain-filled labour, but with no teacher to coach me, I tackled and mastered the native tongue of Roman scholarship. And so I ask first for your indulgence, if, as an unpolished speaker of the strange language of the courts, I give any offence. But as a matter of fact, this very change of speech is appropriate to the kind of writing I am taking on—an art like that of an acrobat, leaping from one horse's back to another. It is a Greek tale that I begin. Reader [*lector*], pay attention: you will enjoy some fun [*laetaberis*].

Having fun, then, would appear to be the dominant motive, and readers who had casually picked up this particular papyrus scroll might think that what they had in their hands was just a literary romp of no great moral pretensions. Indeed, quite the reverse, since Apuleius also makes it clear that his 'novel' is, as much as anything, a compendium of tales in the 'Milesian style'. Such tales got their name from Aristeides of Miletos, who, in about 100 BCE, wrote a collection of saucy stories translated into Latin soon after by Sisenna. These originals have long since vanished, but their disreputable nature is commemorated in Plutarch's story that copies were found in the baggage of Roman officers who shared the defeat of the legions commanded by Crassus at the disastrous Battle of Carrhae in 53 BCE. When they found them, the victorious Parthians were duly scandalized, and passed censorious (though gleeful) comments on the moral character of their humiliated opponents. A fine lot they were to talk, observes Plutarch in his *Life of Crassus*, given that their own royal family was descended in part from Milesian prostitutes; but we get the picture.

Apuleius' prologue encourages us, however, to make a few more deductions about the kind of readership he expected to attract. And 'readership' is here the key word. True, he promises to caress 'kindly ears', but that is because, in accordance with ancient practice, the reader was not expected to read silently, with lips tight shut. Indeed, those who failed to voice the words would be denying themselves most of the marvellous pleasures of Apuleius' sonorous and incantatory narrative. At any rate, as the prologue continues, it is made clear to us that Apuleius expects that we will be encountering his works through the medium of Egyptian papyrus and Nile-reed pen, and if the last word is 'fun', it shares its sentence with a direct address to the 'reader'. This addressee is the ancestor of the 'gentle reader' of eighteenth-century novels, just as Apuleius' characters are the spiritual and cultural ancestors of many of the eccentric figures who litter the pages of Boccaccio, Fielding, and Voltaire. But do the links between Apuleius' implied readers and those undisciplined Roman soldiers show that nothing much had changed in the last two centuries since Carrhae?

The scrolls at Carrhae were Aristeides' Greek originals. Like Virgil and Cicero before him, Apuleius has played a part in the great process of adapting Greek literature into Latin: now the Latin West had its own high-grade pornography, just as it had its own epic poetry and rhetoric. But note that this is the product of the provinces, not of Rome herself. Indeed, it is the product of that very part of the world which, as Livy was at pains to stress, almost won out over Rome for mastery of the world. Apuleius completed his literary studies at Carthage, and it seems to have been there that he spent most of his adult life, and there that he wrote *The Metamorphoses*. Latin literature no longer belonged solely to Rome and Italy; careers in Latin letters now lay open to educated men throughout the Western world. As the Roman Peace encouraged the spread of the Roman tongue, there developed a larger middle class to administer the economy and bureaucracy of the empire, a class with the money to buy such scrolls, the leisure to read them, and the education to appreciate their literary and stylistic values, and their hidden meanings. This was the Empire's glorious high summer, from the accession of Nerva in 98 CE to the death of Marcus Aurelius in 180 CE, the age that Gibbon famously called 'the period in the history of the world during which the condition of the human race was most happy and prosperous'. The borders were secure, the economy flourishing, and the emperors just and mild. For once, the Roman world seemed less concerned with wars than with building and beautifying, with buying and selling, and even with a little reading and writing.

The question of the level of education that Apuleius expected in his readers is almost as important as the fun he provided them. *The Metamorphoses* is a work of Roman literature that, as so often, is more than it pretends to be. It takes the form of a pseudo-biography, and in the last book Lucius, having finally found some roses while on his way to perform his terrible duties in the arena at Corinth, has resumed his human shape. What follows is an account, less racy but no less remarkable, of the hero's spiritual salvation through initiation into the mysteries of the goddess Isis. Those of his contemporaries who knew about Apuleius' other interests might not have been all that surprised after all: he was also the author of a number of treatises on philosophy, such as *On Plato and his Teaching* and *On Socrates' God*. And at the very heart of the novel is a long tale that can hardly be called 'Milesian' at all, though it does share all kinds of elements with folk-tales from many cultures. It is told by an old crone to cheer up a pretty girl (obligatory in ancient novels, as in most modern ones) who has been kidnapped by a group of wicked bandits (obligatory in ancient novels, though optional in modern ones). In this tale, a princess with the by no means insignificant name of Psyche ('Soul') is offered up in sacrificial marriage to a mysterious monster whose identity she is sworn not to try to discover. Promises in fairy stories are made to be broken, and this one is no exception. Driven by a mixture of fear and curiosity for illicit knowledge, she sneaks a look one night, only to wake her mysterious lover up by accidentally dripping candle wax on him as she gazes in awe at his astounding beauty. For her 'monster' husband turns out to be a beautiful young god, albeit one with wings and a bit of a temper—none other, in fact, than Cupid, whose name in Latin ('Cupido') means 'Love'. Love is accordingly what she immediately feels, and she tries to make amends for her misdeeds. She is eventually purified by a number of terrible trials imposed on her by Venus. These prove her love, but once again her curiosity gets the better of her. Venus commands her to bring back from the world of the dead a mysterious jar, and on no account to look into it. Although she therefore has to endure a kind of death in order to enter the underworld, Psyche succeeds in completing her quest, only to make the terrible error of violating the goddess's prohibition once she has safely returned to the world of the living. The jar, in keeping with its provenance, contains a death-like trance, to which Psyche immediately succumbs. Only the love of divine Love himself is able to revive her, and, when he has done so, she is raised to heaven, in the story's last scene, as a goddess. There she is accepted as Cupid's bride and granted the true happy-ever-after ending we already knew to expect. The tale is plainly a Platonic allegory of sorts, and, although scholars argue about its exact meaning, the experiences of Psyche surely mirror and predict those of Lucius. Like Psyche, he is made to undergo a number of thoroughly dehumanizing trials to punish him for his impious curiosity, and like Psyche, too, he is eventually saved, not by his own merits, but by the intervention of a divine being whose power is matched only by her benevolence. We are not told if the pretty girl kidnapped by the bandits got the message, but it is clear that Apuleius was counting on the likelihood that his readers would, if only—as instructed in that prologue—they remembered to 'pay attention'.

Some two centuries or more later, around 400 CE, another African small-town boy who had made big in Carthage and abroad, and who, indeed, had been to school in Apuleius' home town of Madaura, wrote another long, novel-like story of a young man's misdeeds and unmerited salvation. He began, though, with an appeal to a reader who could be guaranteed to pay attention, and he made no promises of fun of any kind:

> Great are you, Lord, and much to be praised; great is your power, and of your wisdom there can be no reckoning . . . Grant me to know and understand, Lord, whether I should first call on you, or praise you, and whether I should first know you or call upon you . . . My faith, Lord, calls upon you, which you have given to me, which you have inspired in me by the humanity of your Son, and by the ministry of your preacher. (Augustine, *Confessions* 1. 1)

The third century had been a dark time of economic, political, and military crisis, of plague and depopulation, of usurpers and emperors who were assassinated almost before the news of their elevation to the purple had been announced in the more distant corners of the Empire: a grim end indeed to Gibbon's vaunted time of happiness and prosperity. The Empire came close to collapse, and reached a terrifying new low in 260 CE, when King Shapur I of Persia captured the Emperor Valerian alive in battle. According to the gloomier accounts preserved for us, poor Valerian spend the rest of his natural lifetime serving Shapur as a footstool whenever the victorious king wanted to mount his horse, and, when he had finally gone to his rest, he was stuffed and put on display as a trophy. By the end of the century, however, the situation had been turned around by such stern and uncompromising rulers as Aurelian (reigned 270–5 CE), who restored the frontiers and was known to everyone by the nickname 'Manus ad Ferrum' ('hand on steel'), and Diocletian (284–305 CE), a visionary bureaucrat with a good sense of military strategy and an even better sense of civil administration. By this time, Africa and many other parts of the West were more than ever a part of the Roman cultural world, with knowledge of the Latin language and respect for education firmly established. Those with social and literary ambitions could study in peace in smaller provincial centres, then go on to the grander schools in the provincial capital. The most gifted could even hope to emulate Augustine (Aurelius Augustinus, 354–430 CE), and make for the bright lights and smart social circles of old Rome. Or better still, if they had an eye to real success, they would go to the new imperial capitals closer to the frontiers which it was now more important than ever to defend.

Augustine headed for Milan, where the Christian emperors of the late fourth century held court, and there won himself enough admirers to be appointed Public Orator. His duties included the official celebration of the emperor's virtues as well as the instruction, in the hallowed style, of young aspirants in search of a proper grounding in traditional élite culture and the elegant rhetoric that was its hallmark. But though the Empire itself must have seemed as much a part of the natural order as the sun that shone down upon it and the taxes it collected, those opening words (quoted above) from his *Confessions* show that the world had changed for ever. The official faith of the court and state was now an Eastern salvation-cult, and not the one that Apuleius had trumpeted in the last book of *The Metamorphoses*. In Milan, Augustine came within the orbit of one of the most forceful and influential characters in the history of the Latin West, the city's irascible bishop, Ambrose (Ambrosius, 339/40–397 CE). A hard man to argue with, Ambrose had given his life to combatting heretics and, when he had the time to spare, those recalcitrant pagans who stubbornly clung to the old ways. He had even once forced the Emperor Theodosius to do public penance in his cathedral for ordering a massacre in the Greek city of Thessalonike.

Augustine never stood a chance. He looked around him, he looked inside him, and he did not much like what he saw. What on earth was the point, he wondered, of this traditional public display literature he was paid to profess? One day, when he was due to recite yet another elegant panegyric to the emperor, he saw something that led him to ruminate on the state of his soul, and came to the conclusion that all his aspirations to worldly happiness were utterly insubstantial and ephemeral:

> That same day, the one when I was preparing to recite to the emperor praises in which I would tell many a lie, and would, as I lied, win favour from people who knew I was lying . . . I saw a poor beggar, already, I think, drunk and happy. And I groaned and spoke to the friends who were with me about all the sorrows that come from our own madness . . . we wanted nothing but to achieve the carefree happiness which that beggar had achieved before us, and at which we might perhaps never arrive. (*Confessions* 6. 6)

What the beggar had achieved with a few pennies, Augustine had been seeking to achieve with much labour and much roundabout effort: 'the joy of a *temporary* felicity.'

It might be felt that it tells us a lot about Augustine that the sight of someone having a good time made him miserable. But that is, in a way, the whole point about the *Confessions*. They are one of the most astoundingly original creations of ancient literature—not a pseudo-biography, like that of Lucius, but the authentic record of a soul in search of peace. They are part autobiography, part theological treatise, part prayer—or perhaps mainly prayer. Although Lucius' salvation seems assured, Augustine feels that his is not only unmerited, but almost as precarious as it is inexplicable, a mystery of God and God's mercy. His

BREAD AND CIRCUSES. This ivory relief probably made in Rome in the early fifth century CE shows an aristocrat of the family of the Lampadii presiding over chariot-races in the Circus Maximus. The old Roman world took a long time to die.

is a mind that cannot relax, and just as Apuleius' work might be said to reflect the settled serenity of his age, so Augustine's belongs to a more unsettled time, when the old world was crumbling away, when Rome itself would not be safe from the barbarians, but when, even so, the battles for civilization were as nothing compared to the war that raged in each man's soul between darkness and light.

Who were the *Confessions* written for? Not, it seems, other mortals, whom Augustine assumes to be hostile, mocking, and worldly:

> And yet allow me to speak before your mercy, me that am but dust and ashes, allow me yet to speak, since behold, it is your mercy, not man, my mocker, to whom I speak (1. 6)

But later this initial impression is modified. We discover that in part, at least, they were written with an eye to the faithful, for whom Augustine, in his role as bishop of Hippo in his home province of Africa, was obliged to provide such guidance as he could from his own spiritual journey and self-examination:

> Upon my return from Madaura . . . the expenses for a further journey to Carthage were being got ready for me, in keeping rather with my father's high spirit than with his resources, since he was only a citizen of middling standing at Thagaste. But to whom am I telling all this? Not to you, at any rate, my God, but in your presence I tell it to my own race, the human race, to whatever small part of it chances upon my writings. And to what end do I do this? Plainly so that I and anyone who reads this may reflect, how deep are the depths from which we must cry to you. (2. 3)

With that readership in mind, a readership that probably knew the psalms better than they knew their Virgil, Augustine writes in a loose but hymnic Latin that is new and fresh, and full of the resonances of a cultural and literary tradition that would have been inexplicably alien to the world of Cicero or Augustus. They are sometimes, with justice, thought of as the first work of medieval literature. But above all, to call them by a title that more accurately reflects the sense of the Latin word *Confessiones*, they are 'Acknowledgements', acknowledgements of the truth of Christian salvation and of the unworthiness of any human individual to earn that salvation, which came of God's mercy, and not of man's deserving. Augustine writes for himself, as a kind of therapy, to adopt the modern view, or as a kind of prayer and examination of conscience, if we try to see things as he himself must have done. His audience includes that greater public to which classical authors traditionally directed their words, but first and foremost he speaks to his own soul and, through his own soul, to the God who made it. It is hardly a purely 'classical' work: but the world of late antiquity was no longer a classical world. It was one of extremes and accommodation, and perhaps Augustine exemplifies both. The *Confessions* could not have been written without the Bible. But neither, one imagines, could they have been written without that rhetorical education Augustine received, and passed on to his pupils, before his conversion under the influence of Ambrose. At any rate, a degree of continuity is discernible amidst the strangeness. And Augustine's addressee might even be said to be the ideal Roman audience, despite His regrettable foreign origins. After all, He was learned to the point of omniscience, and so select that not even the most generous arithmetic could make Him number more than three.

Fighting the good fight

From the late second to the late fourth centuries, traditional pagan Latin literature, especially poetry, was in decline. But so, over the same lengthy period, was paganism itself. Our view of things is no doubt skewed by the relative dearth of traditional literature surviving from, above all, the troubled third century. There is little worth recording, apart from a learned didactic treatise on hunting and some graceful bucolic poems by one Nemesianus, a few poems in light genres from the *Latin Anthology*, a learned hotch-potch of geographical and ethnographical data by Solinus, some handbooks of medicine and traditional moralizing, and a whimsical parody of legal language called *The Piglet's Last Will and Testament*.

Instead, the real innovation and creativity seem to be found overwhelmingly in the pages of Christian authors, both those whose purpose was to attack pagans or attract them to the new faith, and those whose aim was literally to preach to the converted. The readership and audience these Christian writers had before them included many who were excluded from traditional élite culture, and conscientious efforts were made to respond to their needs. A symbolic break here was the preference Christian authors had for the new codex, the direct ancestor of the modern book. Made of sheets of papyrus, and later parchment, bound together, the codex was far easier to read than the cumbersome conventional papyrus roll, which had to be rewound again on its rods when the reader had finished. Duly uplifted by the Word of God, or the writings of His servants, the Christian simply had to slam the codex shut. In addition, the codex was far easier to consult for a particular passage, and this was of the greatest utility when it came to looking up the correct scriptural text needed to quote against heretics and heathens. It was also cheaper, and held much more. Christian authors and Christian readers were creating an entire alternative literary culture, just as they were creating an alternative society.

Similarly, great ingenuity was shown in adapting traditional modes of writing, and whole new genres were in effect being created. The taste for narrative that could not be met among the faithful by such racy works as Apuleius' *Metamorphoses* was satisfied instead by exuberant prose lives of the martyrs, where sex was replaced by titillating accounts of sexual advances repulsed by girls who, though desirable, were pure. These were not tempted into curiosity about illicit knowledge at all, but they were just as attractive, and, if any lack of excitement was still to be felt, then the increase in the component of violence might perhaps serve as adequate compensation. Violence of another kind was visible in the more aggressive works of such Christian apologists as Tertullian of Carthage (*c*.160–*c*.240 CE). Tertullian, who was almost as suspicious of pretty girls as he was of pagans, wrote, for example, treatises *On Veiling Virgins* (he was in favour), *On Chastity* (in favour), *On The Games* (against), and *On The Worship of Idols* (very much against). Not to put too fine a point on it, Tertullian was an intransigent fanatic, obsessed with purity and opposed to the whole structure and outlook of the society that surrounded him. But he helped create a whole new literature that had to be taken seriously on its own terms, one made up of rhetorically magnificent and logically persuasive diatribes against pagan folly and hypocrisy, while his passionate exhortations to those facing persecution also served to hearten the faithful.

A different line was taken by Minucius Felix (*fl.* 200–40 CE), who wrote a Ciceronian-style philosophical dialogue entitled *Octavius*, in which a Christian of that name debates with a pagan apologist called Caecilius. This gentlemanly respondent obligingly excuses the judge—Minucius himself—from having to make a formal adjudication when, with old-fashioned aristocratic courtesy, he confesses himself beaten by Octavius' transparently superior arguments. Minucius, no doubt, was writing for pagans of traditional education whom he thought more inclined to listen to reason than invective. Not all Christian authors, however, were likely to be taken so seriously by their sophisticated pagan opponents in the religious debate. Probably in the third century—though the date is by no means certain—an obscure but sharp-tongued poet from Palestine by the name of Commodian wrote a poem with the title *Against the Jews and Greeks*, which offers more in the way of blistering denunciation of its unhappy targets than it does of doctrinal or literary subtlety. It does, though, give us a clear indication of the extent to which some Christian authors were prepared to adapt—one might say, travesty—the old literary forms in their quest to reach out to their audience. Nominally written in hexameters, the prestigious six-foot quantitative metre of Homer and Virgil, Commodian's poem effectively ignores the rules of classical metrics, with their careful variation of long and short syllables. In their place, he substitutes metrical lines of roughly equal length, where the rhythm is carried instead by the beat of the natural stress of the words in speech, much as in modern English poetry. It is not certain whether Commodian even knew the traditional rules of metre: what is reasonably clear is that he assumed his audience would not. There was a war on, and Commodian was rallying the troops.

The century or so that followed the death of Tertullian saw first the Great Persecutions of Decius and Diocletian, then Constantine's Edict of Milan of 313 granting religious toleration to the Christians, and finally the establishment, through Constantine himself and his quarrelsome sons, of a Christian imperial establishment. In short, Christianity came to be considered acceptable, and even became the preferred faith for those seeking a career in the state bureaucracy. Accordingly, the social rank of converts was now often higher than before. This brought into the faith men—and women too—well educated in the traditional classics. Since the faith was no longer under the same kind of threat, and since there was consequently a less compelling need to keep the faithful uncontaminated by contact with pagan ideas, many of these new converts were less inclined to anathematize the authors and genres they had been brought up to revere. True, the battle was far from over. The real and present danger that the temptations of pagan literature could offer to an insecure soul concerned for its eternal welfare is famously summed up in the dream that afflicted the aristocratic scholar and translator of the Bible Jerome (Eusebius Hieronymus, *c.*347–420 CE) one night on his first visit to the Holy Land. He had gone there to live the life of a monk and learn Hebrew so that he could understand the Bible better. But he was still in some ways a scholarly Roman gentleman of the old school, and had taken along to his desert retreat some light reading, both classical works and religious texts. These he read in alternation, until he fell asleep and was visited by God in His aspect as Divine Judge. Asked to identify himself, the saint replied, 'I am a Christian.' 'You mean a Ciceronian [*Ciceronianus*], not a Christian [*Christianus*],' God thundered back.

But the trend, even so, was towards compromise. Jerome himself, in his seventieth letter, continued to maintain that pagan literature could serve a useful purpose if only its power and its rhetorical beauty could be harnessed to the faith's purpose of saving souls and glorifying God. What he recommended, some upper-class Christians were already doing, and sometimes in quite remarkable ways. A noble lady called Proba composed, some time in the middle of the fourth century, a *cento* from scraps of Virgil (the word *cento* means, in Latin, 'patchwork cloak'). What Proba did was to take innumerable phrases and part-lines from the poems of the most prestigious author of classical Latin literature, and ingeniously stitch them together again in such a way as to create a completely new poem on the Old and New Testaments. Classical literature was thus literally being recycled into a new Christian form so as to provide a devotional text for an audience that wanted to combine the prestige of the old learning with the new faith. Proba's success was so great that Pope Gelasius, in 494 CE, was apparently obliged to give a formal warning to the faithful that it ought not to be treated as a canonical work inspired directly by the Holy Spirit.

POWER OF THE POET. This late mosaic of Orpheus found in Palestine is now in Istanbul. It seems to reflect the figure of the pagan poet still singing and surviving in an uncultured and barbarous world.

The restoration of peace and economic prosperity after the chaotic decades of the third century also permitted the building of many new schools throughout the Roman world, not least in Gaul, to train up the men needed to administer and run the renewed Empire. Perhaps the most spectacular and most successful of its polished products was Decimus Magnus Ausonius of Bordeaux (*c.*310–*c.*394 CE), who made such a hit as a teacher of rhetoric in his native city that he was summoned by the Emperor Valentinian to his capital at Trier on the Moselle, a city conveniently placed to keep guard over the Rhine frontier. There he acted as tutor to Valentinian's son Gratian, an office he filled so well that he was eventually promoted to the position of Governor of Gaul in 378 CE, and given the supreme honour of the consulship the following year. Emperor, prince, and professor were all three Christians, but the atmosphere of the court was not the atmosphere of the discreet and secluded world inhabited by well-born pious ladies like Proba. Valentinian himself was a soldier through and through, and has been well described as the last Western emperor who systematically patrolled the borders of his Empire. But he was also a man well grounded in the traditional *paideia* ('education') that was still the hallmark of the social élite. His respect for that *paideia* is seen not only in his determination to ensure that his son acquired it from the best teacher available, but in his readiness to engage in competition with that self-same teacher in composing showpiece poems, and in particular a Virgilian *cento* on a theme that might have made Proba blush: the celebration and consummation of a marriage.

In a cover letter to his friend Paulus, Ausonius explains what happened:

> For I am sorry to have disfigured the dignity of Virgil's verse with so frivolous a theme. But what was I do? It was written to order, and the order was of the most powerful kind, for it was requested by one who could impose the request, namely the blessed Emperor Valentinian—a man of great learning, in my opinion. He had once described a wedding in a playful composition of the same kind, with appropriate lines and amusing juxtapositions. Then, since he wanted to see how much it surpassed my own efforts in composition, he ordered me to fashion something similar on the same subject. Just how delicate a task this was for me, you will understand; I wanted neither to beat him nor to be beaten myself, since, if I let him win, my clumsy flattery must be obvious to the judgement of others, and, if I rivalled and surpassed him, my discourtesy would be equally obvious. So I took on the job as if I was reluctant, but met with success, and, since I was deferential in my manner, I kept his favour and managed to give no offence when I won. (*Nuptial Cento*, preface)

Ausonius is concerned to explain to Paulus the difficulty that he was put in by the emperor's challenge: courtesy required that he lose, professional pride that he win. He therefore did his best, but showed as much modesty as he could in earning the palm of victory. But he is also embarrassed—or rather, affects to be—by the subject-matter. And so he might. Virgil, for example, had described the Cyclops Polyphemus with the line

> a terrifying monster, shapeless, huge . . .

Ausonius uses the phrase to describe the bridegroom's penis. Virgil had spoken of the Italian hero Turnus on the battlefield as

> the young man borne hither along the path he knew so well.

Ausonius applies the same line to the new husband as he prepares to insert the aforementioned monster into a place described with words applied by Virgil to the entrance to the underworld. And the exertions that follow, up to and including the moment of climax, are vividly brought before the reader's eyes by a concatenation of lines and phrases used by Virgil in his lofty epic to describe various battles and athletic competitions. The end result is quite a *tour de force*.

Ausonius is at pains to stress that there is a great difference between a dissolute poem and a dissolute author. 'Be satisfied, my friend Paulus | With my page's being naughty: | All I want is to raise a laugh', he says in a postscript, before justifying himself for his actions by learnedly referring Paulus to the precedents set by the likes of Apuleius and Cicero, Plato and Virgil—pagans all. Ausonius, in other words, seems to have achieved a compromise that suited him between the faith he professed and the raunchier but also more urbane culture he had inherited. And it must be noted that his attitude is shared by the emperor himself, and presumed to be equally acceptable to Paulus and the other Gallo-Roman nobles Ausonius addresses through him, by publishing this *cento* and its cover letter. The 'culture wars' are not quite over, but they are no longer being fought to the death as Tertullian thought they should.

Ausonius wrote for the court, for his fellow bureaucrats, for those who, like him, continued to value the poetry, rhetoric, and learning of the world they had inherited as well as the new world that Christianity was promising them. His poems include some that, to modern taste, seem arid and dusty in their academic preoccupations: versifications, for example, of elaborate lists, such as the names of the Muses, the Seven Sages, or the chief cities of Gaul; or ingenious verse disquisitions, not without humour, on the kind of problem of grammar and metre than furrowed the brows of those who earned their bread as Ausonius did. His other works have specialized readerships in mind. *The Daily Round* describes the activities of a high-ranking imperial bureaucrat from morning to sunset: it was written for other bureaucrats, and for those who wanted to know how they spent their time, with a view to advertising the usefulness of a dedicated public servant. *The Professors of Bordeaux* was a work of local civic patriotism, no doubt written principally for the circles in which the great man moved before he was summoned to Trier and glory, though it gives us a rare and welcome look into the high level of sophistication to be found in provincial centres of literary activity. A few others seem to reach out to a wider audience, above all the beautiful *Moselle*, a hexameter description of the poet's journey down that river, through an idyllic world of settled, peaceful cultivation, of lavish villas on the river's banks, of trees drooping over waters full of half-exotic fish, of vines mirrored in the river's calm surface so that land and water can hardly be told apart:

> That is a sight a man may freely enjoy, when the grey-green river
> reflects the shady hill, the waters of the stream
> seem to be in leaf, and the flood thick-planted with vines.

What a colour the shallows have when the Evening Star
has driven forwards his late-coming shadows and drenched
the Moselle—with green mountains!
Whole hillsides float upon the ruffling eddies, and the vine
that is not there ripples, and in the glassy waves the budding vintage swells!
The boatman, fooled by nature, counts up the green shoots,
the boatman who floats in his little barge out over the watery plain,
out in midstream where the image of the hill is blended
with the river and the river joins the edges of the shadows.

(*Moselle* 189–99)

Such passages are relatively rare in Ausonius. But pedantic though it must often seem to us, his poetry is primarily designed to preserve and celebrate the learning and achievements of the pagan world that was passing, or being transformed for ever, before the professor-consul's very eyes.

'Where your treasure is, there will your heart be also'

Not everyone regretted the passing of this old world. Another local celebrity, and a former pupil of Ausonius', seemed set for a career even more glittering. Paulinus of Nola (Meropius Pontius Paulinus, 353/4–431 CE) was originally Paulinus of Bordeaux. He was a well-connected young man, who beat his tutor to the consulship by one year, and was then sent off to govern the rich and peaceful province of Campania, around the bay of Naples. But this was the age of Ambrose as well as Ausonius, and of those like Augustine who were sickened by the emptiness of the world's glory. Paulinus married a rich Spanish lady whose influence seems to have encouraged his own ascetic inclinations. He abandoned his career, became a priest, and settled in the Campanian city of Nola, where he eventually became bishop. There he wrote poems in epic language for the yearly festivals of the local saint, Felix, and adapted the subject-matter and style of classical poetry to Christian thought. A 'consolation' poem in the old style, for example, turns into a half-logical, half-passionate demonstration of the foolishness of men who insist on lamenting one who has been taken out of the miseries of a fallen world and carried to glory by the intercession of Christ. Indeed, many of Paulinus' poems were primarily designed to lift up the spirits of his congregation, and to confirm them in their faith. They tend, more or less, to turn into sermons, but are distinguished by vivid descriptions of the town and its festival, the saint and his basilica, the priest and his people. More interesting to us, perhaps, because more personal in nature, are the verse letters Paulinus exchanged with other luminaries of the age, Jerome and Augustine among them.

He received letter after letter from his respected old tutor too, but a great gap had opened up between the wordly author of the *cento* and the secluded ascetic and future devotee of St Felix. Ausonius begged Paulinus to come and visit him, and when his repeated requests were met with silence, he burst out in invective against Therasia, Paulinus' wife, that was at best only half-joking:

You stand firm by the law of silence.
Are you ashamed to have a friend still living who claims the right of a father? . . .
Or is it that an informer is treading on your heels,
and what you fear is an inquisitor's over-stern rebuke? . . .
Write your letters in milk, then, and as it dries the paper will keep them
permanently invisible, until the writing is brought forth to view by a scattering of ashes! . . .
I can show you countless kinds of concealment
and unbar the ancients' ways of writing secret messages.
If, Paulinus, you fear betrayal and live in dread of being
charged with friendship with me, your harridan of a wife need know nothing of it.
Scorn others if you must, but do not disdain to address a few words to one
who is a father to you. I am your old foster-father and your tutor,
the first to lavish on you the honours of the ancients,
the first to introduce you into the Muses' guild!'

(Ausonius, *Epistle* 28)

It was the wrong tack to take. More silence followed, and then finally a letter full of affection as well as hurt, but not one that can have given much comfort to Ausonius. Paulinus would not, could not join in the kind of game that Ausonius had enjoyed with Valentinian, not even if the subject-matter were less salacious. The break, the definitive repudiation of that classical learning which had raised Ausonius to glory and to which he had given the whole of his life finally came:

Why do you bid the Muses, whom I have rejected,
to return once more into my affections, father?
Hearts dedicated to Christ refuse the Camenae (Muses)
and are closed to Apollo.
Once I had with you this shared purpose—though we were not equals
in skill, we were equals in our zeal—
to summon deaf Apollo from his Delphic cave,
and call the Muses goddesses . . .
But now another power inspires my mind, a greater God,
who demands of us another way of life, claiming back for himself from man the gift he gave us,

> that we may live for the Father of Life.
> To spend our time on idle things, whether for leisure or for work,
> and on a literature made of myths, he does forbid.
>
> (Paulinus to Ausonius: *Epistle* 31)

'Idle things', 'a literature made of myths': these were not, to Paulinus' puritanical way of thinking, a proper occupation for a servant of Christ. And with these lines he condemned not only the traditional pursuit of classical literature and all those who read it, but the whole career and being of the old tutor who regarded himself as a kind of father to him. But though the tide was strong, it was not all one way. Or at least, not yet.

Rearguard action

The most important sign of an incipient pagan backlash in the fourth century was the accession to the imperial throne of Julian, whose sobriquet 'the Apostate' trumpets his challenge to the new Christian establishment just as much as it records the scandalized hostility of those who gave it to him. Julian's reign (361–3 CE) was too short to undo the work of Constantine and his successors, but his aggressive stance towards his enemies gave comfort and inspiration to the traditionalists who clung both to the old gods and to the old ways in literature. Particularly significant in this regard was the ban he promulgated against Christians' holding official positions as teachers of classical literature and rhetoric. Had that held in place, it would have prevented the rise of Ausonius and men like him, since, now that access to traditional literary culture seemed in danger of being cut off, it became clear to everyone that mastery of these skills remained essential for those who aspired to positions of authority in the imperial bureaucracy, in law, and in administration.

Moderate Christians at least were thus growing more willing to come to an accommodation between pagan culture and the demands of life in a Christian empire. That, needless to say, was not the same thing as tolerating pagan worship, or pagans in person. The reign of Theodosius the Great (379–95 CE) was distinguished for such acts of cultural warfare as the prohibition of all pagan sacrifice, the banning of the Olympic games, and the closing or even outright destruction of pagan temples in many parts of the Eastern Empire. The most spectacular casualty was the temple of Serapis, the main centre of pagan culture in Alexandria, still the Roman world's major literary centre. But in the Latin-speaking West, the senatorial aristocracy, which was still largely pagan, retained enormous wealth and social influence. Its last-ditch political resistance ended with the defeat of the usurper Eugenius, yet another teacher of rhetoric, at the Battle of the river Frigidus (394 CE). But even after this victory Theodosius and his son Honorius sought to conciliate rather than browbeat these old 'Romans of Rome'. One major result of this toing and froing on the political level was a certain renaissance in pagan literature over the half-century or so from the time of Julian to that of Honorius, especially under the ascendancy of Honorius' chief general and father-in-law, Stilicho. That renaissance, too, was sometimes aggressive, but more usually conciliatory. And not the least of its fruits was the impetus it gave in its turn to magnificent new works by Christians who sought to complete the work of purifying the old canons.

To an admirer of Julian's, albeit one with his eyes open as well as his mind, we owe the last great work of classicizing Latin historiography. Ammianus Marcellinus (*c.*330–*c.*400 CE), a Greek-speaking soldier from Antioch, took upon himself the task of completing the *Annals* and *Histories* of Tacitus by recounting the *Deeds* of the Roman emperors from the accession of Nerva in 98 CE to the death of Valens at the hands of the Goths in the catastrophic Battle of Adrianople in 378 CE. Like Tacitus, Ammianus took as his themes decline and its close link with immorality and corruption among the ruling class. He offers us a famous description of the idle rich of the old capital, with their extravagant banquets and odious affectations, their arrogant cruelty towards their slaves and their utter 'provinciality' and ignorance of the affairs of the wider empire. There might thus seem to have been little hope of a cultural renewal spearheaded by these senatorial lightweights, some of whom

> loathing learning like poison, read with care and enthusiasm Juvenal and Marius Maximus, but in the depths of their idleness never touch any volumes at all save these; though why that should be so lies beyond our poor power to judge. (28. 4. 14)

The satires of Juvenal contained plenty to amuse those avid for salacious reading, and the biographies of the Caesars from Nerva to Elagabalus by Marius Maximus were infamous for their uncritical reporting of court gossip. If Ammianus is telling us the truth, their choice of reading material hardly redounds to the credit of these noble heirs of the energetic and cultured senators of the republic and high empire. But then, who was Ammianus writing for? That last bit about his 'poor power to judge' may possibly conceal his pique at the failure of the senators to show much interest in public readings from his own lofty but dour work, to the early parts of which, indeed, Marius Maximus could be thought of as a rival. The very fact that we still have them shows that Ammianus' *Deeds* must have reached a contemporary audience of some kind. But at times, obsessed with his tale of decline, he seems more concerned to write for himself, to help make sense of the deplorable changes he saw in the world around him, with Rome fallen victim to barbarian invaders on the one hand and to unscrupulous courtiers and military thugs on the other. But occasionally he almost seems to be writing for the approval less of his contemporaries or posterity than of the revered past he is trying in some way to save: the approval of those ancient ghosts who light his way, Thucydides and, above all, Tacitus himself.

Honest and literate, patriotic and independent-minded, Ammianus may be said to be himself a good advertisement for the renewed bureaucracy and education system of the fourth century and for the chance of cultural renewal it presented. He is even fair-minded enough to admit that only 'some' of the Romans of Rome were failing their ancestors and their dependants in this shameful way. And he would, one imagines, have felt more kindly towards some of those who come to prominence in the last two decades of the century. Girding their loins for battles both physical and ideological, such men as Nicomachus Flavianus, consul in 394 CE and praetorian prefect under the usurper Eugenius, ostentatiously celebrated pagan rites once more in the old capital. Flavianus indeed set out from Milan for the Frigidus after boasting that, when he returned in victory, he would turn Ambrose's cathedral into stables and conscript his clergy into the army. Ambrose, as usual, had the last laugh, and for Flavianus, defeat could be followed only by honourable suicide. But there was a more peaceful side to Flavianus' activities. He wrote *Annales*, no doubt another historical work designed to complete the labours of Tacitus—and he is one of the stars of Macrobius' *Saturnalia*. This work, which may be more or less contemporary with the events it describes (but which, according to some scholars, may have been composed in the fifth century) is a fictional dialogue set in the holiday season of December 384 CE. It narrates how three leaders of the pagan revival movement, Vettius Agorius Praetextatus, Flavianus himself, and the orator Quintus Aurelius Symmachus act as host on successive days to gatherings of pagan intellectuals who discuss such matters as Roman priestly law and the oratory and philosophy of Virgil. The families of Symmachus and Flavianus in particular also made great efforts to gather and emend the texts of the authors who featured so prominently in the pagan canon. It is largely to their scholarship that we owe the preservation of the works of such authors as Martial, Apuleius, and above all Livy. Also Juvenal, but not, however, Marius Maximus—though whether that was a deliberate response to the censures of Ammianus lies beyond our poor power to judge.

Among these public-spirited men, the best known is Symmachus (Quintus Aurelius Symmachus Eusebius, *c*.340–402 CE). Although they have been castigated as nothing more than elegant if verbose visiting-cards, his *Letters* serve much the same purpose as those of Pliny the Younger (cf. Ch. 14, pp. 457–8) almost three centuries before, putting before our admiring eyes the busy and bustling life of an aristocrat devoted to the service of the state. To that extent, they are also similar to the poems his Christian friend Ausonius wrote under the title *The Daily Round*. Symmachus kept out of trouble during the revolt of Eugenius that claimed the life of his other friend Flavianus, and he even kept up a correspondence with Ambrose, though he was much too polite to allude directly to their religious differences, or even to acknowledge familiarity with Ambrose's episcopal dignity, treating him instead as just another leisured Roman aristocrat.

Though equally courteous, his most celebrated exchange with the feisty bishop of Milan, however, was indirect. The Emperor Gratian, Valentinian's son and Ausonius' pupil, refused to accept the Senate's traditional offer of the robes of the Pontifex Maximus, the head of the ancient priestly colleges of the city. And by an edict of 382 CE he formally disestablished the ancient cults, such as those of the Vestal Virgins, and deprived them of their state endowments. A concomitant result was the removal from the Senate House of the altar to the goddess of Victory which had kept a benevolent eye on the deliberations of that august assembly since time immemorial. Symmachus, as Prefect of the City, made a graceful but powerful plea to Gratian for their restoration, appealing in his *Third Referral* to tradition, to the services the old gods had performed in preserving Rome and in raising her to her state of glory, and to the spirit of religious toleration. In what may well be the most famous phrase of the century he observed of religious truth that 'it is not by one path alone that man can arrive at so great a secret'. But his rival for Gratian's ear was Ambrose, who was as victorious then as he would later prove against Flavianus.

It should be noted that, on both sides of the religio-political fence, the purpose of 'literature' was still more often pragmatic than purely aesthetic. Symmachus' elegance was deployed for a definite aim that had implications for the use of public money as well as for symbolic ideology. Editing Livy was intended to preserve for the education and inspiration of contemporaries the great story of Roman republican *pietas* and the reward it had earned from the gods. On the other side, Jerome was commissioned to replace a wide range of sometimes inaccurate, if much-loved, current translations of the Bible, and he conscientiously applied himself to the study of Hebrew before presenting the world with the Vulgate version that became the standard sacred text of the Catholic Church down to modern times. Pope Damasus (reigned 366–84 CE) wrote short poems to accompany and explain his work in renovating and beautifying the churches and shrines of the martyrs in a city now thought to belong as much to the Apostles Peter and Paul as to Jupiter and the Olympians. Prudentius (Aurelius Prudentius Clemens, 348–*c*.405 CE), a retired Spanish civil servant, was inspired by some of these, and by the cult of the martyrs of his native land, to compose longer hymns celebrating the victories of these champions of the faith. He seems to have consciously set out to replace the patriotic odes of Horace with Christian ones, celebrating martyrs whose virtues outstrip those of Regulus and the other pagan heroes of antiquity.

In this he was to some extent emulating the activity of Ambrose, who hated heretics even more than he hated pagans. The biggest bugbear of the early years of his time as bishop was the Arian heresy, whose followers obstinately refused to accept that the Son was the equal of the Father. They had until quite recently made up almost half the population of the city of Milan, but their protectress, the Empress Justina, outraged him by seeking to secure for their use a single church in the capital, the Basilica Portiana. 'Jezebel', as Ambrose called her with his customary restraint, obviously had to be made to back down. So the bishop shut himself up inside the disputed church with a large army of his supporters until, fearing a massacre and massive civil unrest, she did. Ambrose's Catholic shock-troops—among them, it seems, Augustine's mother Monica—may well have felt some hesitation in the face of the empress's soldiers. To strengthen their resolve Augustine wrote some of the earliest known Latin hymns 'in the manner of the East, so that the people would not grow faint through the weariness of their sorrow' (Augustine, *Confessions* 9. 7).

Pragmatic compositions aimed at defying imperial authority were, however, far less common than those whose purpose was to celebrate and justify it. Prose orations delivered for such occasions as the arrival of an emperor in a particular city or on the anniversary of his accession were composed in vast numbers. Inevitably ephemeral, they have almost all disappeared, but a few were preserved by accident, or thanks to the fame of their author or the admiration won for their style. A collection of a dozen such speeches, known as the *Latin Panegyrics*, appears to have been assembled in the late fourth or early fifth century in Gaul. It comprises the model *par excellence* of the genre, Pliny the Younger's thanksgiving speech to Trajan for his consulship (cf. pp. 443 ff.), and a mixture of others by authors named or anonymous, delivered to emperors from Constantine to Theodosius—and, in one case, to a governor of Gaul. Useful for the information they preserve on contemporary history, albeit often obliquely, they also reveal much about the ceremonial nature of such public literature and about the audiences who dutifully attended to hear them recited. Invariably elegant and invariably laudatory, their function is primarily to celebrate the virtues of those they honour and to display the loyalty of those on whose behalf they were delivered. Nonetheless, they often do a careful job of presenting to the all-important governing classes the emperor's policies, while also—though more rarely—serving on occasion to give the emperor a discreet reminder of his subjects' needs and an indication of their concerns. In short,

CHRISTIAN CONQUEST. *These ivory portraits of the young Emperor Honorius were made in 406* CE. *In the left-hand panel he holds an inscription which says 'In the name of Christ may you always be victorious'. The abbreviation for 'Christ' uses Greek letters (as in our modern 'Xmas').*

though they may seem to modern eyes the emptiest and most distastefully adulatory compositions to survive from classical antiquity, their social function, to help cement the bond between ruler and ruled in the interests of social harmony, was of enormous importance.

Since so much of what the panegyrists say is obscured by the conventions of praise, and since so much of the historical circumstances that provided the backdrop to individual speeches can no longer be recovered, a detailed understanding of the circumstances of their recitation, and therefore of their effect on a given audience, is often impossible. A partial exception to this rule is provided by the panegyrics delivered by Claudian of Alexandria (Claudius Claudianus, *c.*370–*c.*404 CE) over a period of some ten years in the early part of the reign of Honorius (394–404 CE). Claudian is an exception in other ways too: his panegyrics are in verse, and he, like Ammianus, was a Greek-speaking easterner (compare Nonnos, pp. 282–4). He belongs to a distinct class of poets who cannot be thought of in quite the same terms as men like Ausonius, men of high birth and high position. Claudian is a highly succesful example of the 'wandering poets', professional authors who moved from city to city and earned their keep by putting their talents at the service of the city government or of individual wealthy patrons. He is sometimes called 'the last of the classical poets', not just because of his strictly pagan themes and idiom, but also because of the superb technical accomplishment of his verse and his thorough familiarity with the classical authors of the canon. He also had a glorious style that, were it not for his contemporary subject-matter, might trick one into thinking his poems had been composed under Nero or Domitian rather than under Honorius and the power behind his throne, Stilicho. Most of Claudian's poetry was explicitly designed to serve Stilicho's purposes. The career of Stilicho offers a spectacular example of the cultural changes Rome was currently undergoing. His mother was a Roman, but his father belonged to a German tribe called the Vandals. In time the Vandals would give the Romans a great deal of trouble; indeed, they later conquered Africa and even sacked Rome itself in 455 CE with such horrifying violence that their name has come into English as a word for any barbarous thug who wilfully destroys property of any kind. In the late fourth century, however, some of them, including Stilicho's father, were serving as mercenaries in the Roman army against other barbarians and were becoming assimilated. Stilicho himself rose to such prominence that Honorius' father, the Emperor Theodosius, chose him as a husband for his niece and adopted daughter Serena, and after Theodosius' death he exercised a kind of semi-official regency over the young Honorius.

It would be simplifying matters too far to speak of Claudian merely as a vehicle for broadcasting Stilicho's propaganda, but his poetry, for all its sophistication, clearly serves practical political purposes. He not only celebrates, for example, the young emperor's consulships and his marriage to Stilicho's daughter Maria, but also denounces Stilicho's political opponents in satirical invective worthy of Juvenal. Pity Eutropius, chief minister of Honorius' brother, the Eastern Emperor Arcadius. Eutropius had dared, though a eunuch, to accept a consulship and, worse still, had had the audacity to have a real man, the brave and noble Stilicho, declared an 'enemy of the people' by the Senate at Constantinople:

What a fine sight he made, as he strained to move his feeble limbs
beneath the weight of the toga, borne down by the consular garb,
an old man made to look more repulsive still by the gold he had donned!
Like an ape that imitates human form, decked out
by some mocking lad in precious Chinese silks,
his back and buttocks left uncovered,
something for the supper-guests to howl at . . .

(*Against Eutropius* 1. 300–6)

That no doubt answered to all the prejudices of the Milanese courtiers against effeminate Easterners in general, let alone the ones who aspired to lead armies and govern the state when they lacked the full complement of manly assets. On other occasions, Claudian's brief was to smooth down ruffled feathers closer to home. In 401 CE Alaric the Visigoth led his people on to Italian soil, and threw the whole country into a panic. It took months to get him out again, and though Stilicho finally achieved a comprehensive victory at Pollentia in the Po valley on Easter Day 402 CE, resentment was felt against the general by the senators, who had seen their estates burned, their slaves conscripted, and the very walls of Rome threatened. Worst of all, Stilicho had struck some kind of bargain with an enemy who surely ought simply to have been dealt with in the Roman way, not by treaty but by brute military force. Nothing to worry about, Claudian assured them some eighteen months later, when Honorius made a rare, conciliatory visit to the old capital to inaugurate his sixth consulship. In Claudian's epic-style account Alaric himself is made to explain how Stilicho had it all worked out in advance:

With what cunning, with what skill,
did Stilicho, always my doom, entrap me! While pretending to spare me,
he blunted the edge of my warlike spirit and found the power to carry the war
back over the Po I had crossed once before! A curse on that treaty,
worse than the yoke of slavery! Then it was that the power of the Goths was extinguished,
then for my own self, then did I bargain death!'

(*On The Sixth Consulship of Honorius* 300–5)

It is not recorded whether the senators found this explanation acceptable, though one imagines that they quite liked hearing themselves called 'a host worthy of worship, gods!' in the preface to the poem with which Claudian began his recitation on the Palatine Hill on that first day of January, 404.

Whistling in the wind

Within seven years, Claudian was dead, Stilicho had fallen from grace and been beheaded, and Alaric was back. Rome fell to a foreign army for the first time since the Gauls had taken the city after the Battle of the Allia eight centuries before (390 BCE.). From far Palestine, Jerome let out a cry of anguish: true to both his Christian and his Ciceronian selves, he compared the dreadful calamity to the destruction of Moab and to the fall of Troy, quoting from the second book of Virgil's *Aeneid* (*Letter* 127). Augustine, more thoughtful and more methodical, applied his vast erudition and his powerfully original mind to propounding a new understanding of the very nature of history and of civilization in his *City of God*, demonstrating that all cities fall, save only the holy Jerusalem carried by the faithful in their hearts, exiled as they are in this fallen world from that heavenly state.

Pagan authors had no such consolation, their very existence being bound up with the fate of the earthly city that Christians and barbarian spies like Stilicho had destroyed. That, at least, was the view of Rutilius Claudius Namatianus, who has left us an elegiac poem recording his journey home to his estates in Gaul through an Italian countryside shattered by war. Namatianus vented his spleen against Christians in general, and especially monks, a tribe that hid themselves in dark monasteries instead of doing their duty and fighting. He also inveighed passionately against Jews and corrupt officials, but most of all Stilicho. It is a diatribe against what could not be changed, written, it seems, for a dwindling band of marginalized pagan aristocrats whose powerlessness was now painfully visible.

The Western Empire limped on for most of the next century, but, though there were hopes of renewal under Honorius' energetic general Constantius and, later, the Emperor Valentinian III's able first minister Aetius, who defeated Attila the Hun in 451 CE, all such hopes proved transitory. Imperial control contracted, as first Britain was given up, and then Gaul and Spain partitioned among the Visigoths, the Burgundians, and the Vandals. Paganism lingered among the peasants of the more remote country areas, but it was no longer a force worth considering among the embattled Gallo-Roman élite.

Men like Gaius Sollius Modestus Appollinaris Sidonius of Clermont-Ferrand in Gaul (*c.*431–*c.*486 CE) still aspired to both literary and political success, but they were too busy dealing with the urgent matters of the present to refight the battles of the past. Sidonius was a local aristocrat, who rose, like Ausonius before him, to be Prefect of the City of Rome and who, like Claudian, wrote verse panegyrics of reigning, if short-lived, emperors; and, again like Claudian, won a reward in the form of an honorary statue in the Forum of Trajan. In

Sidonius' hands poetry remained pragmatic in aim as well as ceremonial. So, for example, in his laudation of the brutal Majorian, we see Sidonius pleading with the new emperor to pardon the city of Lyons its sin in rising in revolt after the murder of his predecessor Avitus, and to relax the harsh conditions imposed upon it. The task cannot have been to Sidonius' taste: Avitus was his father-in-law. But he was carrying on the ancient tradition of *noblesse oblige*, putting his learning and his oratorical skills at the service of his countrymen. His other poems comprise marriage-songs and descriptions, in the manner of Statius, of the villas of rich men like himself. It is hard to see who else would have read them. Sidonius' world was shutting down around him. His poetry served to preserve *Romanitas*, Roman culture, in a country that had passed under the authority of its barbarian invaders.

The main cultural divide was now between, not pagan and Christian, but Catholic Roman and Arian German. The Church now represented the only effective arm of Roman power in Gaul, and men like Sidonius came under pressure to protect their countrymen with such means as it afforded them. So, though stronger on classical mythology than on the Scriptures, he accepted the role of bishop, and largely gave up the luxury of poetry. Diplomacy and administration now took up much of his time, but when not tactfully losing at backgammon to the king of the Burgundians, he wrote letters to other embattled Gallo-Roman nobles and bishops, letters that still attempted to do what Pliny's had done (cf. pp. 457–8), and show for the world—or for that small part of it that could understand their self-consciously elaborate Latin—a good man whose varied and dutiful life was spent in the service of his country.

However classicizing their motivation, the extraordinary style and diction of Sidonius' letters reveal very clearly that the pursuit of Latin literature in the classical mode was swiftly turning into an elevated kind of whistling in the wind. The rhetoric schools were closing, since the new rulers had less need of their products, and the cities they served were shrinking. And the very language was rapidly undergoing that massive shift in its pronunciation that made the old metrical rules of classical verse more and more alien to the spoken word. To attempt to pin down the precise moment and the cause of the death of classical Latin literature would result only in an arid debate—more arid than anything in the works of Ausonius. There is a good case for saying that it lingered for some time longer in quieter parts of the West still under the control of the Empire or of barbarian kings with aspirations to be accepted. Dracontius recited part of his mythological *Romulea* in the presence of the proconsul Pacideius around the year 480 CE, apparently in a concert-hall attached to the Baths of Gargilius in Carthage. As late as 544 CE, Arator read his two-book adaptation, in the hexameters traditionally associated with heroic poetry, of *The Acts of the*

Apostles to an appreciative audience, including Pope Vigilius, in the Church of S. Pietro in Vincoli in Rome. And twenty years later at the Eastern court of Constantinople, the African poet Corippus celebrated in dazzling hexameters, modelled on those of Claudian, the accession of the Emperor Justin II. But by the end of the fifth century, Latin, as Cicero or Virgil would have understood it, was for practical purposes no longer a living language in most of the West. The schools had retreated from the forum to the cloister; and the audience was gone. The literature that had come to maturity amidst the clamour of the law-courts and the rough-and-tumble of the wooden theatres of the Republic (cf. p. 306 above) was shivering to its death in the chilly silence of Sidonius' study.

But it would be neither fair nor sensible—indeed, one might say hardly Christian—to blame Sidonius, who, after all, had a lot on his plate. These were complex times, and the combination of aloof protestations of cultural superiority with outrageous xenophobic simplification seemed, no doubt, the best means for preserving sanity in a world that was ceasing to be Roman and was gradually edging its way into the Middle Ages. At any rate, it was in a spirit of humorous self-knowledge as much as of cultural arrogance that Sidonius responded when he was asked by the senator Catullinus for a wedding-song in the traditional mode. He could not write cheerful songs in hexameters (six-foot verse), he said, obliged as he was to listen instead to the songs of the great clumping brutes who were his new masters (*Poems* 12. 1–11):

Why, even supposing I had the power, do you bid me compose a poem
of Venus, who loves the wedding-songs of old?
I find myself placed in the midst of long-haired hordes,
enduring the sound of German words,
and, time and time again, praising with a straight face
the compositions of some Burgundian glutton who gels his hair with rancid butter.
Shall I tell you what breaks the power of song?
My Muse has been driven away by barbarian strummings,
and has spurned six-foot verse ever since she saw
that her only patrons were seven feet tall.'

Further Reading

1. HOMER AND RELATED POETRY

W. Burkert, 'The Making of Homer in the 6th Century BC: Rhapsodes versus Stesichorus', in *Papers on the Amasis Painter and his World* (J. Paul Getty Museum, Malibu, 1987), 43–62.
D. Cairns (ed.), *Oxford Readings in Homer's Iliad* (Oxford, forthcoming).
A. Dalby, 'The "Iliad", the "Odyssey" and their Audiences', in *Classical Quarterly*, 45 (1995), 268–79.
M. W. Edwards, *Homer: Poet of the Iliad* (Baltimore, 1987).
R. Janko, 'The Homeric Poems and Oral Dictated Texts', in *Classical Quarterly*, 48 (1998), 1–13.
J. Latacz, *Homer, His Art and His World* (1985, English trans., Ann Arbor, 1996).
C. W. Macleod, *Homer Iliad Book XXIV* (Cambridge, 1992).
I. Morris, 'The Use and Abuse of Homer', in *Classical Antiquity*, 5 (1986), 81–138.
G. Nagy, *Homeric Questions* (Texas, 1996).
R. Osborne, *Greece in the Making 1200–479 BC* (London, 1996).
R. B. Rutherford, *Homer*, Greece and Rome new surveys in the Classics, 26 (Oxford, 1996).
S. Schein (ed.), *Reading the Odyssey* (Princeton, 1996).
E. Stehle, *Performance and Gender in Ancient Greece* (Princeton, 1997).
W. M. Thalmann, *Conventions of Form and Thought in early Greek Epic Poetry* (Baltimore, 1984).

Translations

Homer

Homer: Iliad, trans. R. Lattimore (Chicago, 1951).
Homer: Iliad, trans. R. Fitzgerald (New York, 1974; Oxford World's Classics: Oxford, 1984).
Homer: Iliad, trans. R. Fagles (New York, 1990).

Homer: Iliad, trans. M. Hammond (in prose, Penguin: London, 1987).
Homer: Odyssey, trans. R. Lattimore (New York, 1965).
Homer: Odyssey, trans. R. Fitzgerald (New York, 1961).
Homer: Odyssey, trans. R. Fagles (Penguin: London, 1996).
Homer: Odyssey, trans. W. Shewring (in prose, Oxford World's Classics: Oxford, 1980).
Homer in English, ed. G. Steiner (Penguin: London, 1996).

Hesiod
Hesiod, trans. M. L. West (Oxford World's Classics: Oxford, 1988).

Homeric hymns
Homeric Hymns, trans. T. Sargent (New York, 1973).
Hymn to Demeter, trans. H. Foley (Princeton, 1993).

2. ARCHAIC GREEK POETRY

Important general discussions

E. L. Bowie, 'Early Greek Elegy, Symposium and Public Festival', *Journal of Hellenic Studies*, 106 (1986), 13–35.
C. Calame, *Choruses of Young Women in Ancient Greece* (London, 1997).
A. Carson, *Eros the Bittersweet* (Princeton, 1986).
K. J. Dover, 'The Poetry of Archilochos', in *Archiloque*. Fondation Hardt pour l'étude de l'antiquité classique. Entretiens 10 (Geneva, 1964), 183–212; repr. in K. J. Dover, *Greek and the Greeks: Collected Papers I* (Oxford, 1987), 97–121.
T. Figueira and G. Nagy (eds.), *Theognis of Megara: Poetry and the Polis* (Baltimore, 1985).
B. Gentili, *Poetry and its Public in Ancient Greece from Homer to the Fifth Century* (Baltimore, 1988).
M. Griffith, 'Personality in Hesiod', *Classical Antiquity*, 2 (1983), 37–65.
C. J. Herington, *Poetry into Drama: Early Tragedy and the Greek Poetic Tradition* (Berkeley and Los Angeles, 1985).
L. Kurke, *The Traffic in Praise: Pindar and the Poetics of Social Economy* (Ithaca, NY, 1991).
I. Morris, 'The Strong Principle of Equality and the Archaic Origins of Greek Democracy', in J. Ober and C. Hedrick (eds.), *Dêmokratia: A Conversation on Democracies, Ancient and Modern* (Princeton, 1996), 19–48.
G. Nagy, *The Best of the Achaeans* (Baltimore, 1979).
—— *Pindar's Homer* (Baltimore, 1990).
E. Stehle, *Performance and Gender in Ancient Greece* (Princeton,1997).
M. L. West, *Studies in Greek Elegy and Iambus* (Berlin, 1974).

J. J. Winkler, 'Double Consciousness in Sappho's Lyrics', in *The Constraints of Desire: The Anthropology of Sex and Gender in Ancient Greece* (New York, 1990), 162–87.

Studies of the symposium

F. Lissarrague, *The Aesthetics of the Greek Banquet: Images of Wine and Ritual*, trans. A. Szegedy-Maszak (Princeton, 1990).
O. Murray (ed.), *Sympotica: A Symposium on the Symposion* (Oxford, 1990).
R. Neer, *Communicating Vessels: Style and Politics in Athenian Vase Painting, ca. 520–470 B.C.E.* (Cambridge, 2000).
W. J. Slater (ed.), *Dining in a Classical Context* (Ann Arbor, 1991).

Translations

Greek Lyric Poetry, trans. M. L. West (Oxford, 1993), provides verse translations of all archaic poetry down to 450 BCE, excluding Pindar and Bakchylides.
Greek Lyric, ed. D. A. Campbell, 5 vols. (Loeb Classical Library: Cambridge, Mass., 1982–93) offers prose translations and includes Bakchylides.
For Pindar, the most readable translation is F. J. Nisetich, *Pindar's Victory Songs* (Baltimore, 1980).

3. THE GREAT AGE OF DRAMA

P. Cartledge, *Aristophanes and his Theatre of the Absurd* (Bristol, 1990).
E. Csapo and W. Slater, *The Context of Ancient Drama* (Ann Arbor, 1995), an accessible and comprehensive collection of the ancient evidence (with all texts in translation) for the theatre in its social and historical context.
P. Easterling (ed.), *The Cambridge Companion to Greek Tragedy* (Cambridge, 1997).
S. Goldhill, *Reading Greek Tragedy* (Cambridge, 1986).
E. Hall, *Inventing the Barbarian: Greek Self-Definition through Tragedy* (Oxford, 1989).
J. Herington, *Poetry Into Drama: Early Tragedy and the Greek Poetic Tradition* (Berkeley and London, 1985).
J.-P. Vernant and P. Vidal-Naquet, *Myth and Tragedy in Ancient Greece* (New York, 1988).
J. Winkler and F. Zeitlin (eds.), *Nothing to do with Dionysos?: Athenian Drama in its Social Context*, (Princeton, 1990).

For contrasting views on the specific issue of women in the audience:

S. Goldhill, 'Representing Democracy: Women at the Great Dionysia', in R. Osborne and S. Hornblower (eds.), *Ritual, Finance, Politics: Athenian Democratic Accounts Presented to David Lewis* (Oxford, 1994), 347–69.

J. Henderson, 'Women and the Athenian Dramatic Festivals', *Transactions and Proceedings of the American Philological Association*, 121 (1991), 133–47.
R. Seaford, *Reciprocity and Ritual: Homer and Tragedy in the Developing City-State* (Oxford, 1994).

Translations

The Complete Greek Tragedies, ed. D. Grene and R. Lattimore (Chicago), various translators: this is a generally reliable and sometimes excellent edition, though some of the translations date from the mid-century.

Other recommendations

Aeschylus, 'The Oresteia', ed. and trans. M. Ewans (Everyman: London, 1995).
Sophocles: Antigone, Oedipus the King, Electra, trans. H. Kitto, ed. with introduction and notes by E. Hall (Oxford World's Classics: Oxford, 1994).

Two new translations of Aristophanes

Aristophanes: Birds, Lysistrata, Assembly-Women, Wealth, trans. with introduction and notes by S. Halliwell (Oxford World's Classics: Oxford, 1998);
Loeb Classical Library edition and translation by J. Henderson, in production.

4. HERODOTOS AND THOUKYDIDES

On Herodotos, his contemporaries, and his oral background

C. Dewald, 'Narrative Surface and Authorial Voice in Herodotus' *Histories*', *Arethusa*, 20 (1987), 141–70 (plus other essays in this special issue on *Herodotus and the Invention of History*).
J. A. S. Evans, *Herodotus, Explorer of the Past: Three Essays* (Princeton, 1991).
R. L. Fowler, 'Herodotos and his Contemporaries', *Journal of Hellenic Studies*, 116 (1996), 62–87.
J. Gould, *Herodotus* (London, 1989).
F. Hartog, *The Mirror of Herodotus: The Representation of the Other in the Writing of History*, trans. J. Lloyd (Berkeley and Los Angeles, 1988).
J. M. Redfield, 'Herodotus the Tourist', *Classical Philology*, 80 (1985), 97–118.
R. Thomas, *Oral Tradition and Written Record in Classical Athens* (Cambridge, 1989).

On Thoukydides

W. R. Connor, *Thucydides* (Princeton, 1984).
G. Crane, *The Blinded Eye: Thucydides and the New Written Word* (London, 1996).
S. Hornblower, 'Narratology and Narrative Techniques in Thucydides', in S. Hornblower (ed.), *Greek Historiography* (Oxford, 1994), 131–66 (as well as the other essays in this volume).
J. Ober, *Political Dissent in Democratic Athens* (Princeton, 1998).

On Xenophon

J. K. Anderson, *Xenophon* (London, 1974).

S. Johnstone, 'Virtuous Toil, Vicious Work: Xenophon on Aristocratic Style', *Classical Philology*, 89 (1994), 221–52.

S. Murnaghan, 'How a Woman Can be More Like a Man: The Dialogue Between Ischomachus and his Wife in Xenophon's *Oeconomicus*', *Helios*, 15 (1988), 9–22.

J. Tatum, *Xenophon's Imperial Fiction* (Princeton, 1989).

On Aesop

For English Translations of the 'Life of Aesop' and Aesop's fables, see L. W. Daly, *Aesop without Morals* (New York and London, 1961).

W. Hansen (ed.), *Anthology of Ancient Greek Popular Literature* (Indianapolis, 1998).

Translations

Herodotus, trans. R. Waterfield, with Introduction and Notes by C. Dewald (World's Classics Series: Oxford, 1998).

Thucydides: History of the Peloponnesian War, trans. R. Warner, with Introduction and Notes by M. I. Finley (Penguin: London and New York, 1972).

Xenophon: A History of my Times, trans. R. Warner, Introduction and Notes by G. Cawkwell (Penguin: London and New York, 1979).

5. GREEK WISDOM LITERATURE

J. Barnes, *Aristotle* (Oxford, 1982).

M. Detienne, *The Masters of Truth in Archaic Greece*, trans. J. Lloyd (New York, 1996).

P. Friedländer, *Plato*, trans. Hans Meyerhoff, 3 vols. (Princeton, 1958–65).

W. K. C. Guthrie, *A History of Greek Philosophy*, 6 vols. (Cambridge, 1962–81).

E. A. Havelock, *A Preface to Plato* (Cambridge, Mass., 1963).

G. A. Kennedy, *The Art of Persuasion in Greece* (Princeton, 1963).

G. B. Kerferd, *The Sophistic Movement* (repr. Cambridge 1984).

G. E. R. Lloyd, *The Revolutions of Wisdom. Studies in the Claims and Practice of Ancient Greek Science* (Berkeley, 1987).

A. A. Long, *Hellenistic Philosophy: Stoics, Epicureans, Sceptics* (2nd edn., Berkeley, 1986).

A. A. Long (ed.), *The Cambridge Companion to Early Greek Philosophy* (Cambridge, 1999).

R. Martin, 'The Seven Sages as Performers of Wisdom', in C. Dougherty and L. Kurke (eds.), *Cultural Poetics in Archaic Greece* (Cambridge, 1993).

A. Nehamas, *The Art of Living. Socratic Reflections from Plato to Foucault* (Berkeley, 1998).

M. C. Nussbaum, *The Fragility of Goodness: Luck and Ethics in Greek Tragedy and Philosophy* (Princeton, 1998).
K. Robb (ed.), *Language and Thought in Early Greek Philosophy* (La Salle, Ill., 1983).
G. Vlastos, *Sokrates, Ironist and Moral Philosopher* (Ithaca, NY, 1981).

Translations

Presocratics

The Presocratic Philosophers, trans. G. S. Kirk, J. E. Raven, and M. Schofield (2nd edn., Cambridge, 1983).

Sophists

The Older Sophists: A Complete Translation, R. K. Sprague (Columbia, SC, 1972).

Socrates and Plato

The Dialogues of Plato, vol. i: *Apology, Euthyphro, Crito, Meno, Gorgias, and Menexenus*, trans. R. E. Allen (New Haven, 1984).
Plato: Complete Works, ed. with introduction and notes J. M. Cooper, associate ed. D. S. Hutchinson (Indianapolis, 1997).
The Collected Dialogues of Plato, trans. E. Hamilton and H. Cairns (Princeton, 1961).
Xenophon: Conversations of Socrates, trans. H. Tredennick and R. Waterfield (London, 1990).

Aristotle

The Complete Works of Aristotle, 2 vols., trans. J. Barnes (Princeton, 1984).
The Poetics of Aristotle, trans. and commentary S. Halliwell (Chapel Hill, NC, 1987).
Aristotle: On Rhetoric, trans. G. A. Kennedy (Oxford, 1991).

Isocrates

Isocrates, vols. i and ii, trans. G. Norlin (Loeb Classical Library: Cambridge, Mass., 1928–9).
Isocrates, vol. iii, trans. L. Van Hook (Loeb Classical Library: Cambridge, Mass., 1945).

Hellenistic Philosophy

Hellenistic Philosophy: Introductory Readings, trans. with introduction and notes B. Inwood, L. P. Gerson (Oxford, 1991).
The Hellenistic Philosophers, vol. i: translations of the principal sources with philosophical commentary by A. A. Long and D. N. Sedley (Cambridge, 1987).

6. THE ATHENIAN ORATORS

R. G. A. Buxton, *Persuasion in Greek Tragedy: A Study of Peitho* (Cambridge, 1982).
T. Cole, *The Origin of Rhetoric in Classical Greece* (Baltimore, 1991).
M. Edwards, *The Attic Orators* (Bristol, 1994).
E. M. Hall, 'Lawcourt Dramas: The Power of Performance in Greek Forensic Oratory', *Bulletin of the Institute of Classical Studies*, 40 (1995), 39–58.
G. Kennedy, *The Art of Persuasion in Greece* (Princeton, 1963).
D. M. MacDowell, *The Law in Classical Athens* (London, 1978).
I. Worthington (ed.), *Persuasion: Greek Rhetoric in Action* (London and New York, 1994).

Translations

C. Carey, *Trials from Classical Athens* (London and New York, 1997), contains a selection of translations of speeches from the classical orators, with brief interpretations.
The Loeb Classical Library contains a full set of translations of the orators, with separate volumes on the major writers and a two-volume collection of *Minor Attic Orators*, trans. K. J. Maidment.
A complete collection of translations is in preparation by the University of Texas Press. The following are available to date:
Antiphon and Andokides, trans. D. MacDowell and M. Gagarin (Austin, 1997).
Lysias, trans. S. C. Todd (Austin, 2000).
Aischines, trans. C. Carey (Austin, 2000).

7. GREEK LITERATURE AFTER THE CLASSICAL PERIOD

A. Cameron *Callimachus and his Critics* (Princeton, 1995) (for wider social and intellectual context).
—— *The Greek Anthology: From Meleager to Planudes* (Oxford, 1993).
L. Canfora, *The Vanished Library* (London, 1989).
P. M. Fraser, *Ptolemaic Alexandria*, 3 vols. (Oxford, 1972) (on Alexandria itself).
A. S. F. Gow and D. L. Page, *Hellenistic Epigram* (Cambridge, 1965).
—— *The Garland of Philip* (Cambridge, 1968).
—— *Theokritos*, 2 vols. (Cambridge, 1950).
W. V. Harris, *Ancient Literacy* (London, 1989), see esp. pp. 116–46.
A. S. Hollis, *Callimachus' Hecale* (Oxford, 1990).
R. L. Hunter, *The New Comedy of Greece and Rome* (Cambridge, 1983).
—— *The* Argonautica *of Apollonius: Literary Studies* (Cambridge, 1993).
—— *Theocritus and the Archaeology of Greek Poetry* (Cambridge, 1996).
R. Pfeiffer, *Kallimachos*, 2 vols. (Oxford, 1949–53, repr. 1998).
G. Sifakis, *Studies in the History of Hellenistic Drama* (London, 1967).

Translations

Jason and the Golden Fleece (the Argonautika), trans. R. Hunter (Oxford World's Classics: Oxford, 1998).

Callimachus: Hymns, Epigrams, Select Fragments, trans. with introduction and notes S. Lombardo and D. Rayor (Baltimore, 1988).

Theocritus: The Idylls, trans. R. Wells (Penguin Books: London, 1989).

Where no other translation is specified, the reader is referred to that given in the Loeb Classical Library. W. G. Arnott's translations of the plays of Menander in this series are particularly highly recommended.

8. LATER GREEK LITERATURE

G. Bowersock, *Greek Sophists in the Roman Empire* (Oxford, 1969).

K. J. Clarke, *Between Geography and History: Hellenistic Constructions of the Roman World* (Oxford, 1999).

E. Gabba, *Dionysius and the History of Archaic Rome* (Bari, 1996).

M. Gleason, *Making Men: Sophists and Self-Presentation in Ancient Rome* (Princeton, 1995).

W. V. Harris, *Ancient Literacy* (Cambridge, Mass., 1989), see esp. pp.175–284.

F. Millar, *A Study of Cassius Dio* (Oxford, 1964).

J. R. Morgan and R. Stoneman (edd.), *Greek Fiction: The Greek Novel in Context* (London, 1994).

G. L. Schmeling (ed.), *The Novel in the Ancient World* (Leiden, 1996).

S. Swain, *Hellenism and Empire: Language, Classicism, and Power in the Greek World AD 50–250* (Oxford, 1996).

—— 'Biography and Biographic', in M. J. Edwards and S. Swain (eds.), *Portraits: Biographical Representation in the Greek and Latin Literature of the Roman Empire* (Oxford, 1997), 1–37.

J. Tatum (ed.), *The Search for the Ancient Novel* (Baltimore, 1994).

Translations

Menander Rhetor, ed. with trans. and commentary by D. A. Russell and N. G. Wilson (Oxford, 1981).

Galen: Selected Works, trans. P. I. Singer (Oxford World's Classics: Oxford, 1997).

Plutarch: Greek Lives, trans. R. Waterfield (Oxford World's Classics: Oxford, 1998).

Plutarch: Selected Essays and Dialogues, trans. D. A. Russell (Oxford World's Classics: Oxford, 1993).

Appian's 'Civil Wars', trans. C. J. Mackenzie (Penguin: London, 1996).

Collected Ancient Greek Novels, trans. B. P. Reardon (Berkeley, 1989).

Where no other translation of a cited work is specified, the reader is again referred to the translation in the Loeb Classical Library.

9. THE BEGINNINGS OF LATIN LITERATURE

W. S. Anderson, *Barbarian Play* (Toronto and London, 1993).
E. Fraenkel, *Elementi plautini in Plauto* (Florence, 1960).
S. Goldberg, *Epic in Republican Rome* (New York and Oxford, 1995).
—— 'Plautus on the Palatine', *Journal of Roman Studies*, 88 (1998), 1–21.
A. S. Gratwick, 'Drama', in *The Cambridge History of Classical Literature*, vol. ii: *Latin Literature*, ed. E. J. Kenney and W. V. Clausen (Cambridge, 1982), 77–132.
E. S. Gruen, *Culture and National Identity in Republican Rome* (London 1993).
—— *Studies in Greek Culture and Roman Policy* (Berkeley and London, 1996).
R. L. Hunter, *The New Comedy of Greece and Rome* (Cambridge, 1985).
D. Konstan, *Roman Comedy* (Ithaca, NY, 1983).
E. Segal, *Roman Laughter* (Oxford, 1987).
O. S. Skutsch (ed.), *The Annals of Ennius* (Oxford, 1985).
L. R. Taylor, 'The Opportunities for Dramatic Performances in the Time of Plautus and Terence', *Transactions and Proceedings of the American Philological Association*, 68 (1937), 284–304.

Translations

Plautus, trans. P. Nixon, 5 vols. (Loeb Classical Library: Cambridge, Mass., 1916–38).
Terence, trans. J. Sargeaunt, 2 vols. (Loeb Classical Library: Cambridge, Mass., 1912).
Naevius, Ennius, Pacuvius, Accius, Lucilius, trans. E. H. Warmington, *'Remains of Old Latin'*, 4 vols. (Loeb Classical Library: Cambridge, Mass., 1935–40).

10. PROSE LITERATURE DOWN TO THE TIME OF AUGUSTUS

E. Badian, 'The Early Historians', in T. A. Dorey (ed.), *Latin Historians* (London, 1966).
M. Beard and M. H. Crawford, *Rome in the Late Republic* (London, 1985).
E. Fantham, *Roman Literary Culture: From Cicero to Apuleius* (Baltimore and London, 1996).
E. J. Kenney, 'Books and Readers', in *The Cambridge History of Classical Literature*, vol. ii: *Latin Literature* (Cambridge 1982), 3–32.
M. Winterbottom, 'Literary Criticism', in *The Cambridge History of Classical Literature*, vol. ii: *Latin Literature* (Cambridge 1982), 33–50.

Translations

Caesar: Civil War, trans. J. Carter (Oxford World's Classics: Oxford, 1997).
Caesar: Gallic War, trans. C. Hammond (Oxford World's Classics: Oxford, 1996).

Cato and Varro: De re rustica, trans. W. D. Hooper and H. B. Ash (Loeb: Cambridge, Mass., 1935).
Cicero: Defence Speeches, trans. D. H. Berry (Oxford World's Classics: Oxford, 2000).
Cicero: Republic, trans. N. Rudd (Oxford World's Classics: Oxford, 1998).
Cicero: Letters to Atticus and to his Friends, trans. D. R. Shackleton-Bailey (Penguin: London, 1999).
Cicero: on the Nature of the Gods, trans. P. G. Walsh (Oxford World's Classics: Oxford, 1998).
Sallust, trans. J. C. Rolfe (Loeb: Cambridge, Mass., 1931).

11. POETRY OF THE LATE REPUBLIC

J. H. Gaisser, *Catullus and his Renaissance Readers* (Oxford, 1993).
Monica Gale, *Myth and Poetry in Lucretius* (Cambridge, 1994).
David West, *The Imagery and Poetry of Lucretius* (Edinburgh, 1969).
T. P. Wiseman, *Catullus and his World* (Cambridge, 1985).

Translations

Catullus: The complete poems, trans. G. Lee (Oxford World's Classics: Oxford, 1990).
Lucretius: On the nature of the Universe, trans. R. Melville (introduction and notes by D. and P. Fowler) (Oxford, 1997).

12. POETRY BETWEEN THE DEATH OF CAESAR AND THE DEATH OF VIRGIL

S. H. Braund, *Roman Verse Satire* (Oxford, 1992).
Francis Cairns, *Virgil's Augustan Epic* (Cambridge, 1989).
Emily Gowers, *The Loaded Table* (Oxford, 1993).
P. R. Hardie, *Virgil* (Oxford, 1998).
Duncan Kennedy, *The Arts of Love* (Cambridge, 1993).
R. O. A. M. Lyne, *Further Voices in Virgil's Aeneid* (Oxford, 1987).
—— *The Latin Love Poets* (Oxford, 1980).
P. White, *Promised Verse: Poets in the Society of Augustan Rome* (Cambridge, Mass., 1993).
G. Williams, *Horace* (Oxford, 1972).

Translations

Virgil: the Eclogues, the Georgics, trans. C. Day-Lewis (Oxford World's Classics: Oxford, 1983).

Virgil: the Aeneid, trans. C. Day-Lewis (Oxford World's Classics: Oxford, 1986).
Virgil: the Aeneid, trans. R. Fitzgerald (Oxford World's Classics: Oxford, 1983).
Virgil: the Eclogues, trans. Guy Lee (Penguin: London, 1984).
Propertius: the poems, trans. Guy Lee (Oxford World's Classics: Oxford, 1994).
Tibullus: Elegies, trans. Guy Lee (Leeds, 1990).
The Satires of Horace and Persius, trans. Niall Rudd (Penguin: London, 1979).
Horace: the complete Odes and Epodes, trans. David West (Oxford World's Classics: Oxford, 2000).
Virgil's Aeneid: A New Prose Translation, trans. David West (Penguin: London, 1991).
Virgil's Georgics, trans. L. P. Wilkinson (Penguin: London, 1982).

13. POETRY OF THE LATER AUGUSTAN AND TIBERIAN PERIOD

On individual authors and works

Horace Epistles

E. Fraenkel, *Horace* (Oxford, 1957).
R. S. Kilpatrick, *The Poetry of Friendship* (Edmonton, Alberta, 1986).

Horace Odes 4

M. C. J. Putnam, *Artifices of Eternity. Horace's Fourth Book of Odes* (Ithaca, NY, and London, 1986).

Ovid. General

A. Barchiesi, *The Poet and the Prince. Ovid and Augustan Discourse* (Berkeley and Los Angeles, 1997).
G. K. Galinsky, *Ovid's Metamorphoses: An Introduction to the Basic Aspects* (Oxford, 1975).
N. Holzberg, *Ovid. Dichter und Werk* (Munich, 1997) (Eng. trans. to be published by Cornell U.P. in 2001).
H. Jacobson, *Ovid's Heroides* (Princeton, 1974).
R. Nagle, *The Poetics of Exile: Program and Polemic in the Tristia and Epistulae ex Ponto of Ovid* (Brussels, 1980).
C. Newlands, *Playing with Time: Ovid and the Fasti* (Ithaca, NY, 1995).
J. B. Solodow, *The World of Ovid's Metamorphoses* (Chapel Hill, NC, and London, 1988).
F. Verducci, *Ovid's Toyshop of the Heart: Epistulae Heroidum* (Princeton, 1985).
L. P. Wilkinson, *Ovid Recalled* (Cambridge, 1955).
G. D. Williams, *Banished Voices. Readings in Ovid's Exile Poetry* (Cambridge, 1994).

Translations

There are translations of all the works discussed in this chapter, of varying readability, in the Loeb Classical Library.

In the Oxford World's Classics series there are translations of the following:

Horace: The Complete Odes and Epodes, trans. David West (1997)

Propertius: The Poems, trans. Guy Lee (1994).

Ovid: The Love Poems, trans. A. D. Melville (1989).

Metamorphoses, trans. A. D. Melville (1986).

Sorrows of an Exile (*Tristia*), trans. A. D. Melville (1995).

Ovid's Fasti: Roman Holidays, trans. B. R. Nagle (Bloomington, Ind., 1995).

14. PROSE LITERATURE FROM AUGUSTUS TO HADRIAN

E. Fantham, *Roman Literary Culture: From Cicero to Apuleius* (Baltimore and London, 1996).

D. C. Feeney, '*Si licet et fas est*: Ovid's Fasti and the Problem of Free Speech under the Principate', in A. Powell (ed.), *Roman Poetry and Propaganda in the Age of Augustus* (London 1992), 1–25.

K. Galinsky, *Augustan Culture* (Princeton, 1996).

N. Horsfall, 'Empty Shelves on the Palatine', *Greece and Rome*, 40 (1993), 58–67.

Translations

Livy: The Rise of Rome: Books 1–5, trans. T. J. Luce (Oxford World's Classics: Oxford, 1998); the rest of his history—various translators, in Penguin or Loeb.

Pliny, Letters, and Panegyricus, trans. B. Radice (Loeb: Cambridge, Mass., 1969).

Seneca the Elder: Declamations, trans. M. Winterbottom (Loeb: Cambridge, Mass., 1974).

Seneca the Younger: Tragedies, trans. D. R. Slavitt (Baltimore, 1992–5).

Tacitus: Agricola and Germania, trans. A. R. Birley (Oxford World's Classics: Oxford, 1999).

Tacitus: The Histories, trans. W. H. Fyfe, rev. D. S. Levene (Oxford World's Classics: Oxford, 1997).

Tacitus: The Annals of Imperial Rome, trans. M. Grant (Penguin: London, 1989).

15. EPIC OF THE IMPERIAL PERIOD

F. M. Ahl, *Lucan: An Introduction* (Ithaca, NY, 1976).

—— 'Statius' Thebaid: A Reconsideration', *ANRW*, 2. 32. 5 (1986), 2803–912.

—— M. A. Davis and A. Pomeroy, '*Silius Italicus*', *ANRW*, 2. 32. 4 (1986), 2492–561.

W. J. Dominik, *The Mythic Voice of Statius. Power and Politics in the Thebaid* (Leiden, 1994).

D. C. Feeney, *The Gods in Epic* (Oxford, 1991).

P. Hardie, *The Epic Successors of Virgil* (Cambridge, 1993).

D. Hershkowitz, *The Madness of Epic* (Oxford, 1998).
—— *Valerius Flaccus' Argonautica* (Oxford, 1998).
G. O. Hutchinson, *Latin Literature from Seneca to Juvenal* (Oxford, 1993).
M. G. L. Leigh, *Lucan: Spectacle and Engagement* (Oxford, 1997).
J. H. W. G. Liebeschuetz, *Continuity and Change in Roman Religion* (Oxford, 1989).
J. Masters, *Poetry and Civil War in Lucan's 'Bellum Civile'* (Cambridge, 1992).
W. C. Summers, *A Study of the Argonautica of Valerius Flaccus* (Cambridge, 1894).
D. W. T. C. Vessey, *Statius and the Thebaid* (Cambridge, 1973).
—— 'Flavian Epic', in *Cambridge History of Classical Literature*, ii. 558–96 (Cambridge, 1992).
M. Wilson, 'Flavian Variant: History, Silius' Punica', in A. J. Boyle (ed.), *Roman Epic* (London 1993), 218–36.

Translations

Lucan, trans. J. D. Duff (Loeb Classical Library, 1928); S. Braund (Oxford World's Classics, 1999).
Silius Italicus, trans. J. D. Duff (Loeb Classical Library, 1934).
Statius, trans. J. H. Mozley, 2 vols. (Loeb Classical Library, 1928).
Statius: Thebaid, trans A. D. Melville (Oxford World's Classics: Oxford, 1995).
Valerius Flaccus, trans. J. H. Mozley (Loeb Classical Library, 1934).

16. THE LITERATURE OF LEISURE

J. C. Bramble, *Persius and the Programmatic Satire: A Study in Form and Imagery* (Cambridge, 1974).
S. Braund, *Beyond Anger: A Study in Juvenal's Third Book of Satire* (Cambridge, 1988).
—— (ed.), *Satire and Society in Ancient Rome* (Exeter, 1989).
M. Coffey, *Roman Satire* (2nd edn., Bristol, 1989).
K. M. Coleman, *Statius Silvae IV, edited with an English Translation and Commentary* (Oxford, 1988).
C. Connors, *Petronius the Poet: Verse and Literary Tradition in the Satyricon* (Cambridge, 1998).
D. P. Fowler, 'Martial and the Book', *Ramus*, 24 (1995), 31–58.
E. Gowers, *The Loaded Table: Representations of Food in Roman Literature* (Oxford 1993).
A. Hardie, *Statius and the Silvae* (Liverpool, 1983).
J. Henderson, *Figuring out Roman Nobility: Juvenal's Eighth Satire* (Exeter, 1998).
—— *A Roman Life: Rutilius Gallicus on Paper and in Stone* (Exeter, 1998).
H. Hofmann, *Latin Fiction: The Latin Novel in Context* (London, 1999).

D. M. Hooley, *The Knotted Thong: Structures of Mimesis in Persius* (Ann Arbor, 1997).
G. L. Schmeling, *The Novel in the Ancient World* (Leiden, 1996).
N. W. Slater, *Reading Petronius* (Baltimore, 1990).
J. P. Sullivan, *Martial the Unexpected Classic* (Cambridge, 1991).
J. Tatum, *The Search for the Ancient Novel* (Baltimore, 1994).
J. P. Toner, *Leisure and Ancient Rome* (Oxford, 1995).
P. White, 'The Presentation and Dedication of the Silvae and Epigrams', *Journal of Roman Studies*, 64 (1974), 40–61.
—— 'The Friends of Martial, Statius, Pliny and the Dispersal of Patronage', *Harvard Studies in Classical Philology*, 79 (1975), 265–300.
—— 'Amicitia and the Profession of Poetry in Early Imperial Rome', *Journal of Roman Studies*, 68 (1978), 74–92.

Translations

Petronius: Satyricon, trans. P. G. Walsh (Oxford, 1997).
Juvenal: The Satires, trans. N. Rudd, ed. W. Barr (Oxford, 1992).
Persius: The Satires, trans. G. Lee, introduction and commentary W. Barr (Liverpool 1987).
For translations of Phaedrus, Statius' *Silvae*, and Martial's *Epigrams*, see the editions of the Loeb Classical Library.

17. LATIN LITERATURE FROM THE SECOND CENTURY TO THE END OF THE CLASSICAL ERA

General

P. Brown, *Augustine of Hippo* (London, 1967).
—— *The Cult of the Saints* (Chicago, 1981).
—— *Religion and Society in the Age of St Augustine* (London, 1972).
—— *The World of Late Antiquity: From Marcus Aurelius to Muhammad* (London, 1971).
A. Cameron, *Claudian: Poetry and Propaganda at the Court of Honorius* (Oxford, 1970).
T. Hägg, *The Novel in Antiquity* (Oxford, 1983).
Robin Lane Fox, *Pagans and Christians* (London, 1986).
F. J. E. Raby, *A History of Christian Poetry* (Oxford, 1953).
P. G. Walsh, *The Roman Novel* (Cambridge, 1970).

Translations

Ammianus Marcellinus: The Later Roman Empire (A.D. 354–378), selected and trans. Walter Hamilton (Penguin, 1986).

Apuleius: The Golden Ass, trans. and ed. P. G. Walsh (Oxford World's Classics, 1999).
Augustine: The Confessions, trans. Henry Chadwick (Oxford World's Classics, 1991).
Ausonius, with an English trans. by Hugh G. Eveleyn-White, 2 vols. (Loeb Classical Library) (repr. Cambridge, Mass., and London, 1988).
Claudian, with an English trans. by Maurice Platnauer, 2 vols. (Loeb Classical Library) (repr. Cambridge, Mass., and London, 1972).
Sidonius: Poems and Letters, with an English trans., introduction, and notes by W. B. Anderson, 2 vols (Loeb Classical Library) (repr. Cambridge, Mass., and London. 1980).

Chronology

Date	Historical Events	Literary and Related Developments
BCE	Traditional date of first Olympic Games (776) Traditional date of foundation of Rome (753) Age of Greek settlement in Italy, Sicily, and East	Development and dissemination of Greek alphabet on Phoenician model (800–750)
750	Development of heavy 'hoplite' armour and emergence of polis society	
700	Spartan expansion (from *c.*730)	Homer and Hesiod active about now Archilochos active as poet (675–640)
650	Greeks begin to penetrate Egypt	Terpander, Kallinos, Semonides, Tyrtaios, Mimnermos, Alkman active as poets
600	Earliest Greek coins minted (*c.*595) Solon archon at Athens: social and political reforms (594) Greek mercenaries carve their names on the Abu Simbel inscription (591)	Sappho and Alkaios active as poets (610–575) Solon active as poet (600–560)
575	Age of 'Tyrants' in major Greek states other than Sparta	Thales predicts eclipse of the sun (585) Rise of panhellenic festivals (Pythia 582, Isthmia 581, Nemea 573) Anaximander active as philosopher (570–550) (570–475) lifetime of Xenophanes (philosopher-poet)
550	Croesus king of Lydia (560–546) Cyrus the Great founds Persian empire (559–530) Cyrus' conquest of Lydia and Ionian Greeks— *'The year the Mede arrived'* (546) Carthaginians and Etruscans check Greek expansion in western Mediterranean	Stesichoros, Theognis, Hipponax, and Ibykos active as poets Anaximenes active as philosopher

Date	Historical Events	Literary and Related Developments
525	Darius seizes the Persian throne (521)	Anakreon active as poet (535–490) City Dionysia festival established at Athens (by 534) Pythagoras active as philosopher Simonides active as poet
500	Foundation of Roman Republic (traditional date) (509) 'Democratic' reforms of Kleisthenes at Athens (508) Ionian Revolt against Persian rule (499, defeated with Battle of Lade and sack of Miletos 494) First Persian expedition to mainland Greece: Battle of Marathon (490) Persian and Carthaginian invasions of Greece and Sicily: Battles of Artemision, Thermopylai, Salamis (480); Plataia, Mykale (479); Himera (480)	Alkmaion (doctor), Hekataios (historian), Herakleitos, Parmenides (philosophers) active Earliest surviving poem of Pindar (498) Phrynichos prosecuted for his play *The sack of Miletos* (494) First comedy performed at the City Dionysia at Athens (480s) Bakchylides active as poet First victory of Aischylos (active 499–456)
475	Foundation of Delian league against Persia under leadership of Athens (478) Battle of Eurymedon effectively ends Persian threat (467) Radical reforms and murder of Ephialtes at Athens Perikles' supremacy begins (461–429)	First victory of Sophokles (active 468–406) Anaxagoras (philosopher) arrives in Athens
450	Athenian expedition to Egypt ends in disaster Treasury of Delian League moved from Delos to Athens—regarded as beginning of 'Athenian empire' (454) 'Peace of Kallias' ends hostilities between Athens and Persia (449)	First production by Euripides (active 455–406) Zeno and Empedokles active as philosophers Work begins on Parthenon in Athens Herodotos active as historian (445–426) Publication of the Laws of the Twelve Tables at Rome
425	Peloponnesian War between Athenian and Spartan alliances (431–404) First Athenian expedition to Sicily 427 'Peace of Nikias' between Athens and Sparta and their allies (421) Disastrous Athenian expedition to Sicily (415–413)	Thoukydides begins his *History* (431–404) Demokritos (atomist philosopher), Hippokrates (doctor), Sokrates and Protagoras (philosophers), Hellanikos (historian) active

Date	Historical Events	Literary and Related Developments
425 *cont.*		Embassy of Gorgias to Athens also begins the formal art of rhetoric *Acharnians* of Aristophanes (active 420s–380s) Hippias (antiquarian and polymath) active
400	Oligarchic coup of 'the 400' at Athens (411) Democracy restored at Athens (410) Spartans destroy Athenian fleet at Battle of Aigospotamoi; Siege of Athens (405) Capitulation of Athens; installation of regime of 'the Thirty' (404) Fall of 'the Thirty'; democracy restored at Athens (403) Sack of Rome by the Gauls	Andokides and Lysias active as speech-writers (410–387) Antisthenes (cynic), Aristippos (hedonist), and Euklides, pupils of Sokrates, active (400–360) Trial and execution of Sokrates (399) Isokrates (writer and educator) active (397–338) Plato (philosopher) active (396–347); founds the Academy (387) Antimachos, epic poet, active Xenophon (historian and essayist) active (390–354)
375	Following Corinthian War (395–386), Peace of Antalkidas ('King's Peace') imposes Persian-backed control by Sparta on Greece (386) Thebes destroys Spartan power at Battle of Leuktra (371) Domination of Greek world by Thebes under Pelopidas and Epaminondas (371–362)	Diogenes (cynic philosopher) active (360–323)
350	Philip II becomes king of Macedon (359) Phokians seize Delphi and provoke Sacred War, bringing Philip into central Greece against them (356–352) Philip defeats Athens and Thebes at Chaironeia: end of Greek independence (338)	Theatre at Epidauros built Literary and political careers of Demosthenes (d. 322) and Aischines (left Athens 330) begin Theopompos (historian) active (350–320) End of *History* of Ephoros (340)
325	Death of Philip: accession of Alexander (336) Alexander crosses into Asia: Battle of Granikos and conquest of Asia Minor (334) Foundation of Alexandria in Egypt (331) Conquest as far as Punjab (327) Death of Alexander, aged 32; regency of Perdiccas (323) and period of 'the successors'	Aristotle begins teaching at Athens and founds the Lykeion (Peripatetic school) (335) Pyrrho (sceptic) active as philosopher Career of Menander (321–289); *Dyskolos* performed 317

Date	Historical Events	Literary and Related Developments
300	Peace between the successors recognizes in effect the division Antigonos (Asia), Cassandros (Macedon/Greece), Lysimachos (Thrace), Ptolemy (Egypt), and by omission Seleukos (the Eastern domains) (311) Battle of Ipsos: destruction of power of Antigonos and Demetrios; Antigonos killed (301)	Klearchos (Peripatetic philosopher) visits Ai Khanum in Afghanistan (310) Zeno of Kition establishes Stoic school in *Stoa Poikile* at Athens (310) Philitas of Kos (scholar and founder of Alexandrian poetry) appointed tutor to future Ptolemy II Epikouros establishes his philosophical school at Athens (307) Ptolemy I founds Mouseion of Alexandria Zenodotos royal tutor and first head of the Library Euclid (mathematician) active
275	Pyrrhos of Epeiros crosses into south Italy to aid the Greek cities: is defeated by the Romans (280–275) Earliest Roman coinage Antigonos Gonatas, son of Demetrios, defeats Gauls; becomes king of Macedon, founding Macedonian dynasty (276) Ptolemy unsuccessfully supports Greek independence from Macedon (267–262)	Douris of Samos (leading exponent of 'tragic history') active
250	First Punic War between Rome and Carthage, ending in Roman victory (264–241) Eumenes I founds independent power at Pergamon (263–241) Diodotos establishes independent Greek kingdom in Bactria (239–130)	Kallimachos, Theokritos, Lykophron, Aratos, Poseidippos active as poets Manetho (historian and Egyptian priest) lays foundations of Egyptian history Hieronymos of Kardia (historian of the Successors) dies aged 104; Timaios of Tauromenion (historian of the West) dies aged 96 (260) Apollonios of Rhodes writes the *Argonautika* Herodas (author of Mimes) active
225		Livius Andronikos (earliest Roman poet and playwright) active (240–207) First play of Naevius produced (236) Chrysippos succeeds Kleanthos as head of Stoic school (232)

Date	Historical Events	Literary and Related Developments
200	Second Punic ('Hannibalic') War—Hannibal invades Italy (218–201) First war between Rome and Macedon (214–205) Scipio Africanus defeats Hasdrubal in Spain: Spain divided into two provinces (211–206) Scipio defeats Hannibal at Battle of Zama; Carthage becomes a dependent of Rome Roman conquest of Cisalpine Gaul (202–191) Second Macedonian (200–197)	Career of Plautus (204–184); *Miles Gloriosus* performed (204) Ennius active at Rome as poet and teacher (204–169) Q. Fabius Pictor writes first prose history of Rome, in Greek (202)
175	Battle of Pydna: end of Antigonid kingdom of Macedon; Rome divides territory into 4 republics (167)	Polybios the historian arrives in Rome (167) Plays of Terence produced (166–159)
150	Macedonia becomes a Roman province (149–148) Carthage destroyed by Romans; Africa becomes Roman province (149–146) Achaian War: sack of Corinth (146)	Karneades (head of the Academy) comes to Rome on an embassy (155) Publication of Cato's *Origines* or history of Rome Panaitios (Stoic philosopher, *c.*185–109) arrives in Rome (144)
125	Attalos of Pergamon bequeaths his kingdom to Rome (133) War against Jugurtha in Numidia (122–106)	Calpurnius Piso (Roman historian) consul Lucilius (Roman satirist) active
100	Gaius Marius consul for first of six times; he reforms the army (107) Social War in Italy over citizenship (91–88)	Meleagros of Gadara (poet and collector of earliest epigrams in *The Greek Anthology*) active Aristeides of Miletos' 'Milesian Tales' translated into Latin by Sisenna
75	Sulla appointed dictator of Rome: Sullan reforms (87) Slave Revolt of Spartacus (73–71) Pompey's reorganization of East: end of Seleucid monarchy, and of independent kingdom of Judaea; Bithynia, Cilicia, Syria, Crete, organized into provinces; client kingdoms established elsewhere (66–64)	Poseidonios (philosopher, historian, polymath) active at Rhodes (87–51) Cicero's earliest extant speech (81) Philodemos (poet, Epicurean philosopher) active at Rome (75–35)

Date	Historical Events	Literary and Related Developments
50	Caesar campaigns in Gaul (58–49) Civil War between Caesar and Pompey (49) Dictatorship of Caesar (47–44; murdered 15 March 44) Octavian seizes consulate (43) Defeat of Republicans at Philippi by Octavian and Mark Antony	Diodoros of Sicily, Dionysios of Halikarnassos (historical writers) active Sallust (historian and moralist) active Catullus active as poet (59–54) Caesar writes his account of the *Gallic Wars* (58–52) Death of Lucretius: posthumous publication of his poem *On the Nature of the Universe* (55) M. Terentius Varro (antiquarian) active (49–27) Virgil's *Eclogues* published (38) Horace's *Satires* written (37–30)
25	Octavian defeats Antony and Kleopatra at Actium: annexation of Egypt by Rome (31–30) 'The Republic Restored'—first constitutional settlement; Octavian takes name 'Augustus' (27)	Strabon (geographer and historian) active (44–21 CE) Propertius' *Elegies I* published (29) Vitruvius' *On Architecture* (28–23) Ovid begins his *Amores* Death of Tibullus and of Virgil (19)
1CE	Final dynastic settlement: Tiberius given tribunician power (2–4)	End of Livy's history of Rome (9 BCE) Death of Horace and of Maecenas (8 BCE) Ovid banished to the Black Sea (8 CE)
25	**The Julio-Claudians**: reign of Tiberius (14–37) Reign of Gaius Caligula (37–41)	Philo (Jewish writer) active Death of Elder Seneca (writer on oratory) (37)
50	Reign of Claudius (41–54) Reign of Nero (54–68) Pisonian conspiracy against Nero (65) Jewish Revolt (66–73)	St Paul's *Letter to the Corinthians* (58) Younger Seneca's *Letters* (62) Lucan (epic poet) and Persius (satirist) active Suicides of Seneca and Lucan (65) Josephus, rebel leader in Judaea and future author, deserts to the Romans (67) Chariton, Heliodoros, Achilles Tatius, Longus (Greek novelists) active (precise dates uncertain)

Date	Historical Events	Literary and Related Developments
75	'The Year of the Four Emperors': Galba, Otho, Vitellius, Vespasian struggle for power (69) **The Flavians**: reign of Vespasian (69–79) Reign of Titus (79–81) Eruption of Vesuvius: destruction of Pompeii and Herculaneum (79) Reign of Domitian (81–96) Campaigns of Agricola in Britain	Frontinus (administrator and technical writer) active Death of Elder Pliny (administrator, naturalist, and encyclopedist) investigating eruption (79) Statius, Silius Italicus, Martial (poets), and Quintilian (writer on rhetoric) active
100	**The Antonines**: reign of Nerva (96–8) Reign of Trajan (98–117): under him, Roman Empire reaches its greatest geographical extent Trajan conquers Dacia; annexes Armenia and Mesopotamia (101–17) Jewish Revolt (115–17)	Dio Chysostom (Greek orator), Epiktetos (moralist), and Plutarch (essayist and biographer) active in Greek literature Pliny the Younger (orator and letter-writer) consul and governor of Bithynia (100–11) Tacitus writes *Histories* and *Annals*
125	Reign of Hadrian (117–38) Hadrian's visit to Britain; Hadrian's Wall from Tyne to Solway (122–7) Final dispersal of Jews following Bar Kochba's revolt (132–5)	Appian (historian), Arrian (philosopher and historian), Lucian (satirist), and Ptolemy (astronomer) active in Greek literature; Suetonius (biographer) and Juvenal (poet) in Latin
150	Reign of Antonius Pius (138–61)	Pausanias writes his description of Greece Herodes Atticus (Greek orator) and Fronto (Latin orator) active Aelius Aristides, Dion (orators) active Apuleius (poet) and Galen (doctor and polymath) active
175	Reign of Marcus Aurelius (161–80) Reign of Commodus (180–92)	*Meditations* of Marcus Aurelius (174–80) Athenaios writes *Deipnosophistai*
200	**The Severans**: reign of Septimius Severus (193–211) Severus campaigns in Britain and dies at York (208–11) Reign of Caracalla (212–17) *Constitutio Antoniniana* grants citizenship to all inhabitants of the Empire (212) Reign of Elagabalus (218–22)	Philostratos (literary biographer), Herodian (historian), Marius Maximus (biographer), Sextus Empiricus (Sceptic philosopher), Alexander of Aphrodisias (commentator on Aristotle), Tertullian, Clement, and Origen (Christian writers) active

Date	Historical Events	Literary and Related Developments
225	Reign of Alexander Severus (222–35)	Cassius Dio (historian), Plotinos (Neoplatonist philosopher), Nemesianus (Latin poet), Minucius Felix (philosophical writer) active
250	Period of military anarchy, with almost twenty emperors, problems on frontiers and with bureaucracy and economy (235–84)	
275	**The Late Empire**: Diocletian re-establishes central power and founds the Tetrarchy (284–306) Roman Empire partitioned into Eastern and Western portions	
300	Career of Constantine the Great (306–37) Christianity declared official state religion at Rome (312) Constantine reunites Empire Last persecution of Christians in Rome (303–11) Edict of Milan: Constantine establishes toleration of Christianity (313)	
325	Foundation of Constantinople (324) Seat of Empire moved to Constantinople	
350	Rome splits into two Empires again under sons of Constantine (340) Reign of Julian the Apostate (360–3)	Gregory of Nazianzus (Bishop and letter-writer) active Ausonius (teacher of rhetoric, poet) active (*c.*310–94)
375	Reign of Theodosius the Great (378–95) Roman legions begin to evacuate Britain Visigoths cause trouble on eastern frontiers Theodosius reunites the Empire for the last time (392–5)	Ambrose (bishop) active Ammianus Marcellinus (Latin historian) active Symmachus (letter-writer) active Prudentius (composer of hymns) active
400	Division of Empire between sons of Theodosius Sack of Rome by Alaric the Visigoth (410)	Saint Augustine's *City of God*, following sack of Rome (411) Jerome (Christian writer) active (*c.*347–420) Paulinus (bishop, poet) active (*c.*353–431) Claudian (poet and panegyrist) active

Date	Historical Events	Literary and Related Developments
425	Barbarians settle in Roman provinces – Vandals in southern Spain, Huns in Pannonia, Ostrogoths in Dalmatia, Visigoths and Suevi in Portugal and northern Spain	*Digest* of Roman law is compiled (439) (?)Macrobios (Intellectual writer) active
450	Vandals sack Rome (455)	Proklos (neoplatonist philosopher), Nonnos (Greek poet), Sidonius Apollinaris (Gallic prelate and Latin writer) active
475	End of Roman Empire in the West: German Odovacar deposes the derisively titled Emperor Romulus Augustulus and is proclaimed king of Italy (476)	
500	Clovis, king of the Franks, founds Merovingian power; is converted to Christianity Conquest of Italy by Theodoric the Goth: he founds the Ostrogoth kingdom of Italy (493)	Boethius (scholar, philosopher, theologian) active Stobaios' *Anthology of Greek literature*
525	Justinian, Eastern emperor, seeks to reconquer Italy and Africa (527–65)	Justinian orders the closure of the Academy at Athens (529)

Acknowledgements

National Archaeological Museum, Athens p. 43
National Archaeological Museum, Athens. Photo: Hirmer Fotoarchiv, Munich p. 47
Museo Nazionale di Villa Giulia, Rome. Photo: Soprintendenza Archeologica per l'Etruria Meridionale p. 48
© British Museum p. 52
The J. Paul Getty Museum, Malibu, California p. 65
© British Museum p. 67
Staatliche Antikensammlungen und Glyptothek, Munich p. 76
Piraeus Archaeological Museum, Port of Athens p. 91
Based on a drawing by Peter Connolly p. 98
The J. Paul Getty Museum, Malibu, California p. 103
National Museum, Naples. Photo: Archivi Alinari p. 174
The Bodleian Library, University of Oxford, Shelfmark MS. Gr. Class. c. 54(P)V p. 183
Alison Frantz Collection, American School of Classsical Studies at Athens p. 198
Kunsthistorisches Museum, Vienna p. 199
National Museum, Naples. Photo: Archivi Alinari p. 225
The J. Paul Getty Museum, Malibu, California p. 227
Photo: Henry Stierlin, Geneva p. 259
Abegg-Stiftung, Riggisberg, Berne p. 283
Museum of the Aquila. Photo: Soprintendenza per I Beni Ambientali Architettonici Artistici e Storici p. 298
The Louvre, Paris. Photo: © RMN – Chuzeville p. 320
Soprintendenza Archeologica di Roma, Rome p. 326
Photo: German Archaeological Institute, Rome p. 333

© Egyptian Museum of Antiquities. Photo: Egypt Exploration Society p. 337
The Metropolitan Museum of Art, New York, Rogers Fund, 1911. (11.90) p. 340
Museum of Roman Civilization, Rome. Photo: Fototeca Unione p. 389
National Museum, Naples. Photo: Archivi Alinari p. 393
Somerset County Museum, Taunton. Photo: © University of London, Warburg Institute p. 401
The Metropolitan Museum of Art, New York, Rogers Fund, 1920. (20.192.16) p. 426
American Academy in Rome. Photo: Fototeca Unione p. 446
National Museum, Naples p. 453
Drawing by Richard H. Abramson p. 464
The Louvre, Paris. Photo: © RMN p. 503
© British Museum p. 516
Civici Musei d'Arte e Storia di Brescia. Photo: Fotostudio Rapuzzi p. 525
Archaeological Museum, Istanbul p. 530
Collezione dell' Accademia di Sant' Anselmo. Photo: Archivi Alinari p. 540

Index

NOTE: Figures in italics denote illustrations.